SERPENT RISING:
THE KUNDALINI COMPENDIUM

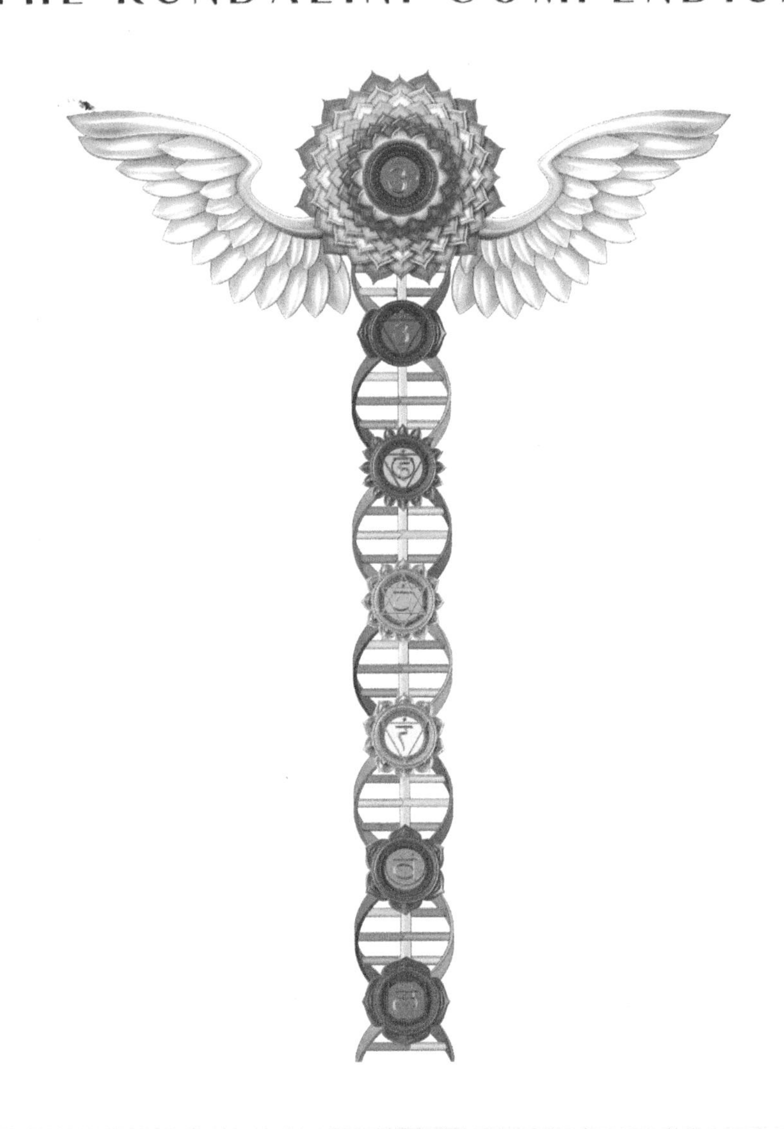

THE WORLD'S MOST COMPREHENSIVE BODY OF WORK
ON HUMAN ENERGY POTENTIAL

NEVEN PAAR

Serpent Rising: The Kundalini Compendium

Cover design by Neven and Emily Paar
Illustrations by Neven Paar

Printed in Canada
First Printing: October 2022
By Winged Shoes Publishing

ISBN—978-1-7770608-5-5

I dedicate this work to the Kundalini Initiate. May this book guide you on your path of awakening and I hope that my seventeen-year journey of Self-discovery with the Kundalini energy has been of service to you, as intended.

—Neven Paar

Other books by Neven Paar

The Magus: Kundalini and the Golden Dawn

www.nevenpaar.com

Winged Shoes Publishing
Toronto, Ontario

List of Figures:

List of Tables:

SERPENT RISING: THE KUNDALINI COMPENDIUM
By Neven Paar

Contents

AUTHOR'S JOURNEY TO WRITING THIS BOOK

THE DIVINE VOICE

My whole life, I've been haunted by a voice I've never heard. But my mother heard it. And somehow, I owe my life to it. She only heard it once. And because she listened, I'm still here. But even before that voice made itself known to her, I was plagued by different Demons.

You see, from the moment I was born, I was deadly ill. I had an ongoing high fever, couldn't keep food down, and couldn't sleep. It was as if some invisible, external force did not want me to survive. So every time I got better, I would end right back where I started, the hospital.

Whatever was trying to kill me soon found out I was a stubborn baby who didn't want to give up. Nobody knew what was wrong with me, and nothing the doctors were doing was helping. Finally, they were so puzzled by my mysterious illness that they invited medical students to see me and hopefully find answers.

My mother, Gordana, stood by my side and prayed daily for my recovery. She wasn't a religious woman, but she believed that her pain allowed her to contact some higher Divine force and request its help. After all, she was my guardian, my protector. Then, after three years of being in and out of the hospital almost daily and putting my family through Hell, I miraculously recovered. Whatever my mother prayed to must have answered.

If it was some otherworldly force that wanted me gone from this world, it failed. Instead, there was an opposite power that wanted me to survive. And so, I grew up with a boon that protected me from rough times. I felt like maybe I had a purpose in this world, even though it took me many years to find it truly. But before I found it, there would be another trial I would have to overcome.

It was the spring of 1992 in a country on the brink of war, Yugoslavia. We had just come out of the building's bomb shelter after a night of listening to gunshots in the background, exhausted. Although tensions grew between opposing factions, most people believed that things would blow over soon and life would go back to normal. There weren't many people willing to leave everything behind without certainty that a full-blown war would erupt.

It was five in the morning, and my sister Nikol and I went straight to bed, as did my father, Zoran. My mother lay down beside him and put her head on the pillow, emotionally and mentally worn out. She looked at the clock beside her, watching the needle move around its centre, contemplating the predicament we were in and what the future held for our family.

What happened next was going to change everything and create a new branch in the timeline of our lives. This unique event would not only take us from one continent to the next, but it was a precursor to a monumental Spiritual journey for me—one that would shape me into a messenger of God-the Creator.

Suddenly, an authoritative male voice began to speak to her in her right ear. It wasn't my father since he was sound asleep on her left side, lightly snoring as he usually does. The voice spoke in a calm yet commanding tone, heralding the things to come for the people in Bosnia and Herzegovina. It said that a war would indeed break out in my hometown. Garbage would fill the streets, food and water would be scarce, and there would be no heat and electricity. This Divine Voice said that she needed to leave the city with my sister and me immediately. That was her mission.

She regained consciousness, but something had changed in her. Her mind was going a mile a minute as if she was still in some trance. What just happened? Her experience left her both shocked and mystified. Most of all, she was scared. And she knew that this feeling of fear wasn't going to leave until she did something about it.

She didn't wake my father yet. Instead, she tried to collect her thoughts. As she was doing that, she began preparing our passports and other travel documents. Then, against all logic, she left the bedroom and began to pack a suitcase for all of us. She knew in her heart what she had to do, and nothing anyone would say could stop her.

After one suitcase was loosely packed, she made a coffee and sipped it beside the living room window, shaking. Then, heavy with emotion, she looked outwards onto the adjacent playground to our building, contemplating the strength she would have to exhibit the next few days to fulfil her mission and save her children.

Suddenly, two hands were on her shoulders, shaking her. "Gordana, Gordana, can you hear me? Say something! My mother must have looked like a woman possessed. Then, finally, she turned to my father and came back to reality. "We have to leave the city," she yelled. "Now!"

The rest of that day wasn't easy for my mother since nobody believed her story. Being a very logical man, my father tried to rationalize her experience and thought it was a trick of the imagination. After all, it was such an extraordinary story to believe happened to an ordinary family like ours. She knew what she heard, though, and steadfast as she was, there was no stopping her. She had to secure the safety of her children and take us out of the city immediately.

And so, she packed our bags and bought us plane tickets so we could fly out the next day. Unfortunately, my father didn't feel the same sense of urgency as my mother, plus he was still waiting for some essential documents before a major travelling expedition, so he planned to stay behind and meet with us in a few weeks.

The next day, we got to the airport around noon. Right before boarding started, the unthinkable happened. Shooting began at the airport from all sides. If the country was on the brink of war, this was the precipice. The shots usually occurred during the night, so this was different. People at the airport began to scramble in panic, kneeling every time they heard a shot while others were lying on their stomachs. It was chaos. This went on for the next four hours. It seemed like we weren't going to be able to leave the city anymore.

Finally, the shooting briefly stopped long enough for us to board the plane. Our medium-sized passenger aircraft became so packed with people that there weren't enough seats for everyone, so many were left standing, including us. It seemed that all the people at the airport rebooked their tickets to get on our plane.

Once the plane took off, I looked outwards through the window at my hometown as it got smaller and smaller, not knowing this would be the last time I saw it for many years. During the plane ride, I remember my mother holding both my sister and me with tears in her eyes. She completed her mission, but this was just the beginning of our arduous journey, and she knew it. Once we landed in the neighbouring country of Serbia, we got word that our plane was the last plane that left the city. After escaping in the nick of time, the airport was officially shut down.

The war began in Bosnia that day and lasted for three long years. Sarajevo, my hometown, was under siege. When we said goodbye to my father at the airport, we had no idea it would be the last time we would see each other for a long time. Oh, how I wished that he came with us, but fate played its hand for all of us that day.

The war was religious, with political connotations, the reasons for which I will not get into at the present moment. As pertains to the story I am about to tell you, everything that the Divine Voice said would happen did indeed happen. A Divine Intervention saved our lives—the reason for which was unknown to me at the time.

As the days passed, my mother wished the Divine Voice returned to guide her. It accomplished the job of securing her children's safety from immediate danger, but as the war began to widen, it was hard to know where we should go next to avoid the chaos that became unleashed in my country. And so, we bounced around from one city and country to the next, orbiting Bosnia and Herzegovina, waiting patiently for my father to get a chance to leave and join us.

The front lines of the war were in my neighbourhood. Many people died in my hometown, especially around where I lived. It was horrific to hear about the atrocities that happened to the people living in Sarajevo. Neighbour fought against neighbour; one could not leave their home for fear of being gunned down by snipers. When people ran out of food and water and had to leave their homes to resupply, they said goodbye to their loved ones, not knowing if they would return. We received this information firsthand from my father, who sadly had to endure it all.

By the end of the war, my mother lost both of her parents and brother. Yet, she did what the Divine Voice said, so why weren't her people spared? When I found out about my family and friends perishing in the war, I was sad and confused. Why were we saved, and others were not? I began to question my mother when she told me about the Divine Voice. For some reason, I was the only one that believed her. Most people thought we got lucky to leave last second, but I knew there was more to it than that. It is as if the information she gave me activated something inside me, but it would take many years for the next piece of the puzzle to unravel itself.

It was not until I had a Kundalini awakening in 2004 that I thought maybe it had something to do with this Divine Intervention, considering it was such a rare and monumental Spiritual experience. Perhaps we were saved so that I would experience everything I did after the Kundalini awakening, and seventeen years later would be writing these very words to you, the reader. Perhaps my message is vital to the people in the world in today's day and age.

SPIRITUAL EVOLUTION AND PERSONAL POWER

After two long years of living in Hell, my father came to join us in Croatia. Soon after, the four of us came to Toronto, Canada, as war refugees and started our lives here in North America. My parents promised me that Canada would be a fresh start and that I could be anything I wanted and be free to pursue any dreams I had. I soon realised that the highest calling or pursuit that I cared about most of all was to be happy. The best way to honour all the people who didn't make it in my country was to be happy and lead a good life since they couldn't.

As my teenage years passed, I noticed I was different. For one, none of my friends felt emotions as strongly as I felt them. Where they had crushes, I had crushing obsessions. I was an extremist by nature. It wasn't just enough to allow life to throw things my way; I would actively chase down the things that made me happy and bring them home to me.

Other people were looking for a quick high, but I wanted to stay there forever. There was no sense of coming back down to Earth after you had a taste of what else was out there. Once I embraced the transcendence of true love, how could I ever return?

Part of me knew it couldn't be this easy, that I could take a pill, smoke a herb and suddenly be in Heaven. And yet it was; you're feeling normal one second, and the next, you are entirely in a different state. But it wasn't enough to get high on the weekends; I wanted to live in that state forever. I wanted to achieve a permanent state of happiness.

My first quest to find that was through love. The problem with it is that you don't have complete control since it's a partnership. So, even if I felt pure love energy and devotion to that person, if they didn't feel it the same way, then it wasn't real. It was like a magic trick without an audience. And so, I knew that there was more out there for me, but I didn't quite understand what that could be.

It was not until my high school years that I started to connect to the Spirit and learn about God-the Creator, during my first long-term relationship. This feeling of being in love opened me up Spiritually for the first time, and I became a seeker of the Light. Learning about the invisible reality of the Spirit is something I was predisposed to from an early age, as many of my philosophies on life just came naturally.

I was always focused on pleasure and the pursuit of happiness, so I got engaged to my first love thinking I could bypass all the trials and tribulations in life. However, the Universe had other plans for me. Once my relationship catastrophically ended, I was at a crossroads in my life. Instead of dwelling on my loss and being depressed, I decided to use the momentum I gained from learning about the Spirit and continue my journey.

I collected everything that reminded me of her and put it into a black garbage bag. Then, in a nearby forest, I burned everything in the blazing fire to symbolise a new beginning in my life. As I watched the smoke rise and the artefacts turn to ashes, I felt the Gods looking down on me and finally saying, "The boy is ready now."

I had gone to University for Architecture during the day as my parents desired of me. When my classes ended and the night set it, I continued my studies in other ways. Through the books I was reading and putting those lessons into practise, I began rebuilding and refining myself. I realised I could still have women in my life and experience that love reciprocation, but without the same type of attachment as before. In the same fashion, I was detached from the person I was becoming to constantly remake myself into something better. And so, daily, I shed my skin like a snake. Like a phoenix who rises out of the ashes renewed. The more knowledge and wisdom I internalised prevented me from being a slave to my overwhelming emotions.

After experiencing love, the next step was to develop my personal power, so I learned about attraction between men and women. I began learning how to manifest whatever reality I desired and realised it was possible once the proper knowledge is integrated. I was a scientist of the mind as I tested the limits of human potential in many areas. I sought to master my mind once I learned of its power to shape what we call "reality." I realised that I can tap into the mind's full potential when I can access the "Now," the present moment. I became obsessed with mastering this skill since it brought on the genuine excitement and joy of being alive.

Certain areas of my life became chaos. It's not that I wanted everything, but I pursued everything. I turned the same intensity I had for seeking love into the pursuit of Spiritual knowledge. I imbued each book with the same passion and devotion as I did my ex-fiance, so I filled myself with knowledge and wisdom daily. There seemed no limit to how much I could learn. And I realised that a man could spend an entire life reading every book without putting into practice what he has learned.

It was then that *The Kybalion* came into my hands. The manual to life itself. It was the first time that I truly fell in love again. I knew that I needed to devote myself to this book and integrate every sentence into my mind and heart to extract its Eternal wisdom. This was the second Divine intervention in my life and the precursor and catalyst to a Kundalini awakening I was to have that same year.

The Kybalion is a Hermetic occult book discussing the Universal Laws, referred to as the Principles of Creation. (Note that italicized terms are further defined in the Glossary at the back of the book.) *The Kybalion* focuses most of its teachings on the power of the mind and states that the "All is Mind, the Universe is Mental." It says that we live in the "Dream of God" and that everything is "thought" energy, including the Physical World. This thought energy is the very Spirit that religious and Spiritual texts speak of. The difference between the thought of God and one of man is just a matter of a degree or frequency of vibration. Our power of the mind and ability to think is what shapes our reality.

I worked with the Laws and Principles of *The Kybalion* daily, and it was compellingly transforming me from the inside. I had the utmost faith in *The Kybalion* Principles and was so fascinated by this book that I carried it with me everywhere I went. I was being remodelled daily by everything I was learning and experiencing. Along with growing in wisdom, I focused on transforming myself into an attractive and powerful man. I enhanced my dating life to an unimaginable degree using the Principles in *The Kybalion*.

The summer of 2004 was the culmination of everything I was experiencing and learning, and I obtained a level of personal power in my life that I had only dreamed of before. My life was a movie, and I was the main star. I had developed myself into a Mystic, a "Wizard of the Mind." My Spiritual journey was on an upward trajectory, and I felt it was just a matter of time before something extraordinary happened.

KUNDALINI AWAKENING

In October of 2004, after reading *The Kybalion* over twenty times, I had a few new epiphanies about the Principles of Creation. Firstly, we have a Spiritual double, a replica within us made of pure Spirit, which occupies the same space and time, but our consciousness is not attuned to it. Secondly, our power of imagination and ability to think things into existence is far more potent than we give it credit. As God-the Creator imagined us, we can imagine and experience our images as real if we only choose to believe what we see. Testing these two new understandings that evening during a meditation, which unknowingly was a form of Tantric sex practice, resulted in a very intense Kundalini awakening.

A powerful stream of energy rose up my spinal column, blowing open the Chakras simultaneously on the way up. It entered my head and brain and enveloped my whole Being with Light. It pierced my Mind's Eye, expanding it exponentially before rising to the Crown and resulting in a liquid fire pouring over my body, awakening what I later learned are the Seventy-Two Thousand Nadis or energetic channels. This experience was coupled by a powerful vibratory sound I heard on the inside, which at its peak sounded like a jet plane engine upon takeoff.

The climax was me opening my eyes as I was being "electrocuted" by this energy from the inside and seeing the room I was in as a Hologram, and my hands made of pure golden Light. This sight changed how I view reality forever. My first Out-of-Body Experience (OBE) followed this, where I saw the onset of the White Light as my consciousness was being sucked out of my body.

The entire experience left me mystified and confused. What just happened to me? It took me two months of obsessive research to figure out what that was, and since then, my life has never been the same again. After my

Kundalini awakening, I was awakened to a reality which I never knew existed—the Fourth Dimension of Vibration or Energy. It was the stuff of a Hollywood movie on Mysticism and Spirituality. I felt like I had just won the lottery—one which was unknown to people even to exist.

Transcendental experiences became a standard way of living as I was being transformed in mind, body and Soul daily. It soon became apparent that my consciousness had expanded as I began to perceive the reality around me from a much higher source. I started to view the world around me from God's perspective as if standing in the clouds and looking down on everything like I am looking at an architectural model. I now perceived Light in all things, which gave everything I looked at a digital makeover. Over time, I developed the ability to see people's energy fields (Auras) and intuitively feel their energy inside of me. This experience gave me telepathic and empathic abilities that were a gift and a curse at the same time.

My dream world opened up to a whole new reality as well. I started having Out-of-Body Experiences nightly, where I flew in strange yet beautiful lands and exhibited powers reminiscent of super-heroes in movies. I felt like I had become a super-hero myself since no one I knew or heard of, other than Gopi Krishna (whom I read about at the time), described this new world I was projected into. It was the same world that I lived in before but enhanced inside me by Light energy brought on by the Kundalini. This Light remodelled my old Self and transformed me into something new, better, more advanced.

I accepted the call from the Divine to learn anything and everything about Spirituality, religion, philosophy, psychology, and other topics about God-the Creator and the destiny of humanity. I became obsessed with developing myself into a Messianic presence, as I felt it was my calling. As some other people do in my position, I never sought to be the "One" since I knew from the onset that we are all the "One". We all are Beings of Light and have the potential to awaken the Kundalini and transcend this material world.

I knew that my calling was to be a messenger of God-the Creator—and my message was the Kundalini. I became a believer that the purpose of the Divine Intervention, which saved my sister and me in 1992, was for this exact reason. As such, I aligned myself completely with *Hermes Trismegistus*, considering that so much of my Spiritual journey was related to his teachings.

Hermes is also the messenger God in the Greek and Roman pantheons, the intermediary between the Gods and humans. The unique wand that he carries in all of his pictorial depictions, the Caduceus, symbolises the Kundalini energy itself.

Even though I began living an otherworldly existence, I was undergoing intense episodes of fear and anxiety very often, considering that all of my Chakras were activated fully after the Kundalini awakening. I felt blessed to have had the awakening, but since I often had to deal with incredible fear and anxiety, it felt like a bane also. Furthermore, I learned that other people who also underwent a full Kundalini awakening, such as my own, were also experiencing this. Sadly, this double-edged sword was something we all had to learn to live with and endure. However, I did not want to accept that. If there is a will, there is a way, I thought. Every problem has a solution. *The Kybalion* taught me that. So I became determined to help myself at all costs and began to seek various ways of doing so.

I tried many different Spiritual practices within a year of awakening the Kundalini, from Yoga to transcendental meditation to Gemstones (Crystals) and beyond. To show you how desperate I was, I even joined Scientology for a month and practised their method of becoming a "clear." But, sadly, nothing seemed to work for me. I still had fear and anxiety present in my heart that was debilitating me daily and a loud vibration in my ears that was very uncomfortable, keeping me up all night. I had almost given up hope until my Higher Self led me to the doorstep of an ancient mystery school—the *Golden Dawn*. Consequently enough, *Ceremonial Magick*, which they practised, sounded like the possible solution to my problem.

MAGICK OF THE GOLDEN DAWN

I joined the Esoteric Order of the Golden Dawn in the summer of 2005 to help with the emotional and mental issues that plagued me. Ceremonial Magick involves using ritual exercises to invoke energy into the Aura. I delved deep into the Hermetic Golden Dawn system right from the start. As I progressed through the different grades or levels, I worked with Elemental energies, which correspond with the Chakras.

There are Five Elements of Earth, Water, Air, Fire, and Spirit related to the Seven Chakras. The first four Chakras correspond with Earth, Water, Fire and Air Elements, while the last three higher Chakras belong to the Spirit Element. The Elemental energies correspond with different parts of the psyche, such as emotions, thoughts, reason, willpower, imagination, memory, intuition, etc. Working with the Elements enabled me to fine-tune those parts of myself, which was necessary to integrate the newly expanded consciousness.

The energies I was invoking through Ceremonial Magick became the very "tool" I sought after awakening Kundalini. They allowed me to cleanse my Aura and Chakras of the negativity plaguing me. Furthermore, invoking the Elements through Ceremonial Magick allowed me to shed my Karmic energy quicker as it removed all fear and anxiety from inside of me. Not only that, but it also allowed me to develop different parts of the Self and realize my full potential.

Ceremonial Magick is a powerful tool to combat one's Karmic energy and purify the old Self, the Ego whose use allows the higher Will of the Spirit to take precedence over the consciousness. What stood in the way of experiencing the newly awakened Spiritual energy was my memory of who I was, whose foundation is my perception of past events. The Ego processes reality in dualistic terms, some events accepted as good and some bad, leaving us chained to a perpetual Karmic wheel, which is continuously in motion.

The bad memories are locked within the Self and generate attachment to the Ego through emotional pain and fear. We can access the emotional charge of memories by invoking the Elements through Ceremonial Magick, bringing them to the surface from the subconscious to "shed" them through integration and evolution. As a result, the potential energy stored in the Chakras in the form of Karma releases back into the Universe, restoring one's initial state of purity.

After seeing the positive effects it had on me in a short while, I fell in love with the Golden Dawn system. I had even built a personal Temple in my home, where I practised Magick daily. Along with the *Spiritual Alchemy* process I was undergoing with the Elements, I also learned about many esoteric topics in the Golden Dawn, including the Qabalah, Tree of Life, *Tarot*, Astrology, *Hermeticism*, and much more.

I developed myself into a ritual master as I practised the art of Ceremonial Magick daily for just over five years. During this time, I was initiated into all the Outer Order Grades of the Golden Dawn, which correspond with the Four Elements. Afterwards, I continued my Magickal journey on my own as I worked with Adept-level ritual exercises corresponding with the Spirit Element and beyond.

As I moved around in my house, my first Temple was transformed into a shared living space, enabling me to build a second, more elaborate Temple to commemorate my solitary path as a Magi. Consequently, this change occurred when the communal Toronto Temple fell apart, leaving many fellow Golden Dawn members without a home. The Divine petitioned me to open my home to them and use my advanced knowledge and ritual experience to mentor them. And so, for the first time, the student became the teacher.

I mentored a group of up to a dozen ex-Golden Dawn members who came to visit me weekly for teachings and group rituals that I led in. I also met new friends on the street who were Light seekers, who sought my Golden Dawn teachings. A few of them were Kundalini awakened individuals who needed help as I did some years back when I was groping in the dark for answers.

As my Golden Dawn journey came to a pinnacle, I practised other Spiritual disciplines that involved the invocation/evocation of Gods and Goddesses, namely from the Hindu and Voodoo pantheons. I aimed to experience their energies through the performance of their ritual exercises and compare them back to what I had learned through Ceremonial Magick.

I also joined *Freemasonry* because of its Hermetic roots, and within two years, I attained the highest degree of Master Mason in the Blue Lodge. I was a scientist of the art of ritual Magick whose laboratory is the invisible world of energy and sought to find commonalities in the different Spiritual traditions and religions.

Through my work and the similarities in our paths, I aligned my vibration with a previous member of the Golden Dawn Order, the infamous *Aleister Crowley*. He would contact me often in dreams to impart on me cryptic teachings in his Shakesperean style of speaking.

I practised *Sex Magick* with Crowley's guidance for over a year and used *Enochian Magick* and the *Thirty Aethyrs* to "cross the Abyss". Crossing the Abyss is a process that implies raising your consciousness past the Mental Plane of duality, where the fear and pain manifest, into the Spiritual plane of Unity. Once I did this, I fully integrated with unconditional love energy in the Spiritual Plane and my consciousness permanently aligned with my Spiritual Body.

This Spiritual achievement allowed me to completely transcend fear and anxiety, which plagued me since awakening the Kundalini. My thoughts no longer had any emotional power over me, and I overcame my negative Karma. And so, my journey with ritual Magick came to an end, allowing me to focus only on my Kundalini energy from that moment forward.

SECOND KUNDALINI RISING

In early 2010, six years after my initial Kundalini awakening, I had another intense Kundalini rising. It was nowhere as powerful as the first rising since that was a once-in-a-lifetime activation. However, to my surprise, the Kundalini energy rose through my spine into my Crown and expanded my consciousness further.

I believe that the hard work I had put in with Magick and the fact that I was no longer invoking outside energy into my Aura stimulated my Kundalini to reactivate and remove any blockages I had after the initial awakening. Perhaps I did not awaken all the petals of Sahasrara Chakra during the initial Kundalini awakening and this second rising served to open the Crown Lotus fully. Doing so completed the circuit of the Kundalini energy and opened up a new, essential Chakra at the top back of the head called the Bindu.

At first, I was undergoing a very intense fire inside me, which was more unbearable than ever. Ingesting food became an issue since it made the fire stronger, so I lost twenty pounds the first month after the second rising. However, I did perceive an even higher sense of consciousness, and my psychic abilities were heightened. What's most important is that I now started to function on intuition alone and was in a constant state of inspiration that is impossible to describe. The word "epic" tossed around haphazardly nowadays is one I use to describe best how I felt and feel to this day.

Along with this constant inspiration, I started to feel out of my body in my waking life, and strange things began to occur. I felt a numbness in my whole physical body, which has become a permanent part of my life. When I apply an ice pack on my skin, I cannot feel the cold, but it feels entirely numb. The same goes for any other part of my physical body. It is as if the Kundalini gave my body a permanent shot of novocaine, a numbing agent.

A transcendent feeling permeated my heart, and the fire, which was raging at first, cooled down to become soothing, love energy. I started to have mystical experiences every time I put on a song I liked, as my consciousness would lose itself in a few seconds of giving it attention. I fell in love with epic movie music and felt like it was playing just for me as every action I performed now felt glorious.

I reached the apex of this Kundalini awakening experience, and as I brought Prana into my system through food, my consciousness would continue to expand. The more I ate, the better I felt. I did get some help from naturopathic medicine, especially Vitamin B Complex, Zinc, Selenium, Gabba, 5-HTP, and even Saw Palmetto, which worked well to transform the fire energy. The fear and anxiety present immediately after the second rising, when my nerves were in overdrive, was gone. It was washed away by the Prana I was building up through food and the supplements I took. I gained back the weight I lost as I now lived in this state of perpetual inspiration 24/7, which is impossible to describe in a way that will give it the credit it deserves.

My new state of Being became a permanent Out-of-Body Experience within a short period. I began to perceive myself from outside of myself as a "Silent Witness" of whatever action my physical body was performing. My mind became clear and still, and it is when I listen to the thoughts inside my head, I go inwards and can no longer see myself from the outside. Otherwise, I can see my facial expressions as if my essence is hovering right above and in front of me, enabling me to have complete control as to what energy I put out into the outside world through animating my physical body.

As I am outside myself, I feel complete rapture and unity with all things in existence. I perceive the whole world now as an immaculate, digital simulation; a Hologram, Maya-Illusion. I can hear a constant vibration within my head as if I am plugged into an electrical outlet, and my energy system is generating a substantial amount of bio-electricity.

This new state I was in started a memory shedding process, where I lost touch with the Ego completely and would perceive old memories in my Mind's Eye, which just came randomly to me throughout the day. This process seemed endless, and it was occurring all the time. I was in an inspired state of Being, functioning fully on intuition and being present in the "Now". I could perceive my thoughts as wave patterns in my Mind's Eye as I became very attuned to sound. I soon realised that sound is the most metaphysical of the five senses. I could see the thought images behind the sound in most things I heard which was and still is very transcendental.

Although I do not associate myself with any religion, I believe that every Holy scripture holds some kernel of truth. As such, I found many references between the Kundalini awakening process and Jesus Christ's teachings. Therefore, I believe that my new state of Being is the *Kingdom of Heaven* and the "Glory of the Whole World" he spoke of. I realised that, like many other Sages and Adepts of history, Jesus had a Kundalini awakening which enabled him to reach this lofty state of higher consciousness and then share his experiences and teachings with others to become awakened as well.

CREATIVE EXPRESSIONS

With this newfound state of Being, my creativity has expanded a thousandfold, and I felt the calling to express myself creatively through different arts. So, I began to paint, considering that painting has been a big part of my life since childhood. For the first time, I felt a calling to start painting in the abstract form and allow my newfound creativity to guide my hand.

I painted many works over the next two years. I never bothered to plan the subject matter of my painting but just let it come naturally. My goal was always to be in a state of expression, and my process consisted of automatically applying different colours until I saw faint images on the canvas. Then I would focus on them and bring them out further.

I often found myself painting diverse landscapes, which I believe were real places on Earth. My consciousness would project into these landscapes and experience them as real as I was immersed in the painting process. After I ended my session, this painting process would continue in my Mind's Eye when I closed my eyes. It would go on for about an hour on automatic, making me believe that I was channelling some images and forms from outside of myself.

I felt drawn to music, so I began singing in a band about a year after the second rising. I also started writing Kundalini inspired lyrics/poetry that flowed out of me effortlessly. I found it came naturally to express myself through music and words, and since I was so attuned to sound now, time would fly when I was "jamming" with friends.

I also gave comedy and voice acting a shot since I found myself able to imitate cultural accents by mimicking their vibration of consciousness. However, it soon became apparent that these creative expressions were my Soul's attempt to find the ultimate way to communicate my new state of Being. As such, I put away visual arts, music, and comedy to pursue writing. I knew that my destiny was to become not only an embodiment of the Light but also its emissary.

I began writing articles for Spiritual newsletters and online blogs on Kundalini and human energy potential. In addition, I gave talks on online radio shows on the power of Ceremonial Magick as the key to the daily purification of the Chakras and elevating the consciousness past the fear and anxiety experienced by Kundalini awakened individuals. I was getting myself out there now as an Adept in the Western Mysteries and the Kundalini. My role as a teacher on these subjects solidified more and more as time went on.

However, before I could fully take the reigns with my Spiritual direction, I had another test to overcome, which presented as an enticing once-in-a-lifetime opportunity. Having left the daily practice of Magick for a few years by this time, the Chief Adept of the Golden Dawn pulled me back in by offering me to lead my own official Temple here in Toronto. He was aware of the hard work I put in within the Order, mainly having organised and mentored a group of Golden Dawn students without a Spiritual home once the Toronto Temple fell apart. The carrot dangled before me was the title of Grand Imperator of Canada within the Order, which meant that I was to oversee all the existing Esoteric Golden Dawn Temples or sanctuaries in Canada.

At first, I salivated over the idea and welcomed the opportunity with open arms. Can you blame me? Every aspiring Ceremonial Magi dreams of leading their own Temple one day and overseeing the affairs of all the Temples in the entire country. Think of the power and fame of that position. Thousands of people would revere me. The men would want to be me while the women would want to be with me. So my Ego thought of the possibilities and relished in them. This is everything I always wanted, isn't it?

And so, I pursued this venture for a little while. I organised the few people in Toronto and began to mentor them. New potential members started calling me, and I met with some to petition them to join the group. I did this for about six months, slowly building the sanctuary, which would eventually become a full-fledged Temple. However, the more I became engaged in this venture, I noticed my heart was not in it. And day after day, this became more and more of a problem for me.

You see, when it comes to the Spiritual journey, it was never about power, fame, women, or any of that stuff for me. It was about finding my purpose and pursuing it all the way. After all, I never chose to have the Kundalini awakening; it was determined for me by some higher power. From the start of my Ceremonial Magick journey, I knew that the Golden Dawn was always a means to an end and not the end in and of itself.

My final goal, purpose, and ultimate calling was to be a leader within the field of Kundalini science, not the Golden Dawn Order. And in my heart, I knew that. Now that I had the second rising and reached the pinnacle of the transformation process, I knew I had to keep going unhampered by external influences. I had to focus solely on the Kundalini energy and let it speak to me and guide me towards my ultimate purpose. So, I chose to keep going. Keep discovering. Keep writing in my spare time and let my true purpose solidify over time.

FINDING MY PURPOSE

Three years passed, during which I went through many changes and developments in my personal life. I got engaged for the second time, which may have been my biggest challenge to date since it forced me to draw out all of my temporal desires and sacrifice them on the altar of righteousness to integrate this higher level of consciousness. My ethical and moral nature became enhanced, and, over time, I learned to function by upholding higher virtues instead of personal desires. My perseverance to overcome these challenges and assume dominance over my Ego took me to a higher level where I talked the talk and walked the walk as well.

After my second engagement ended, I Soul-searched for a year until I moved to a house—Exbury St. A fitting name since this is where I was to bury my old Self for good, enabling me to find my purpose finally. During this time, I quit smoking marijuana—my long-time mistress but a massive distraction. Following marijuana, drinking and cigarettes came to a complete halt, as did my desire for partying. These sacrifices set the stage for something extraordinary, but all I needed was a catalyst to push me through the doorway—my father.

It was October of 2016, precisely twelve years after awakening the Kundalini. A fitting number, twelve, represented the completion of a grand cycle in my life. I wrote about a dozen articles for Spiritual newsletters and online blogs by that time, but it was merely a hobby, something I did in my spare time. However, I printed out my latest article for the first time and brought it to my father to get his opinion, not knowing that his reaction to it was about to change my life. You see, my father is a very hard guy to impress if you are just an average person, but if you are me, his troublemaker son, it is nearly impossible. Until that moment.

He looked it over and put it down, chuckling, telling me not to toy with him. At first, I was confused with his reaction but then realized he thought I copied it from somewhere and put my name on it. I had to convince him for five minutes straight that I had written the article. When I finally convinced him, his composure changed; he got serious and told me I have a special gift. He inquired why I am wasting my time with friends and romantic relationships that never seem to work out and why I am not entirely devoted to writing. His words impacted me on a deep level. It is as if something clicked inside of me; some wheel turned and activated a power within me that was never to turn off again.

Excited that I finally impressed him, I woke up at six in the morning the following day and started writing. As with my painting and poetry creative process, I didn't plan what to write; I just wrote. I let the Spirit guide my hands as I typed away on the computer for hours. And the next day, I did the same thing. And the next, and the next. Months passed with me writing almost every day. Some days I would take off since I juggled my day job that started at ten, but then I wrote the entire weekend to make up for what I lost that week. Was this it? Did I finally find my purpose? Is this the reason my family was saved from being stuck in a mindless war some thirty years ago? Is this why I had the Kundalini awakening, something I never asked for but that I embraced all these years?

I have worked with my parents in their Architectural design company since 2004; consequently, the same year I had the awakening. However, after the first year of my obsessive writing, my parents recognized my passion and allowed me to start work in the afternoon, enabling me never again to miss a morning of writing. My original intention was to write one book. But as the information grew over the next three years, the one book turned into four bodies of work, each with concise but interrelated subjects, all centred around the subject of the Kundalini.

The foundation for the book you are reading right now was channelled to me by my Higher Self during those first three years of writing, as was most of *The Magus: Kundalini and the Golden Dawn* and *Man of Light*, my autobiography. The fourth body of work deals with my world travels, which synchronously also began when I started this writing process. This book, titled *Cosmic Star-Child,* talks about Ancient civilizations and their connection not only to the Kundalini energy but to Extraterrestrials.

Writing books became the most optimal way to channel pertinent information from Divine realms and leave a permanent record. And so, I accepted my role as the Scribe of the Gods. Consequently, this is the title of the Egyptian God Thoth, who is Hermes' equivalent. Everything made perfect sense now. As I discovered my purpose and pursued it every day, I also found a way to integrate my passion for art into my books. And so, I broke up my free time to write in the morning and draw pictures at night. Thus, I found a way to use art to convey the Spiritual messages in my books and enhance them, which became part and parcel of my daily work.

A MAN ON A MISSION

Although it took many years of Spiritual cleansing and curbing my lower desires, I discarded my old Self. My newly discovered purpose, which I pursue every day, gave me a foundation to build a new life around. After witnessing many years of trials and tribulations, God-the Creator saw that I was a changed man, a new man that can be trusted to fulfil this most Holy of tasks and inform the world of the Kundalini energy's existence and potential.

It was then, in early 2019, that the Universe sent a life partner my way, Emily. After an epic engagement in Teotihuacan, Mexico, "The City of the Gods," we married the following year. The third time is the charm, as they say, but in my case, I needed to find myself and my purpose before I could finally settle down. And Emily complements my Spiritual journey in a way that no previous woman in my life has before. Having her in my life inspires me and gives me the necessary drive to maintain my mission of finishing my books at all cost.

You see, I could've continued living the life of a playboy, a rockstar, and even led an occult order. But all of these options were limited, and I wanted to be limitless. So instead, I chose the unsure, unforged, humble path of being an author. I decided to go down the road unpaved and pave the road myself. In truth, I did this for you. So that I may help awaken you the same way I was awakened and give you the keys to life and death. The Kingdom of Heaven is for all of us, not just the select few.

Having been born a religious mutt, I know why I was saved from that war. I wasn't born to thrive in division, the World of Duality we live in; I was born to teach others about unity. The concept of reconciling opposites was embedded in me from birth and my name, Neven Paar, is a testament to it. While I recognize my first name representing the Five Elements, the two masculine, active Elements reconciled by the Spirit (the symbolic V) with the two feminine, passive Elements, my last name means "pair" in German, concerning duality.

You see, I am a descendant of the Von Paar family line who were Counts in the Austro-Hungarian Empire hundreds of years back. However, my kingdom now is of a Spiritual nature, the Kingdom of Heaven, and one that every human being is privy to, not just the select few. Having experienced a Kundalini awakening and knowing that every human has this mechanism inside them, I see us all as Children of the Light, the Kings and Queens of the Spiritual domain. Some, like myself, are realized, while others are still in a state of potential. Regardless, all can unleash this power within themselves and enflame their Being with the inner Light, thereby establishing their Spiritual Kingdom on Earth.

This, I believe, is my purpose on this Planet. To unite the people through my experiences and teachings and make them see beyond their religion and race; to enable others to know that we are all the same. We are all built the same, with the same framework and features, and our physical differences do not change our constitution in any way. We have the same Father and Mother and are united through love energy as brothers and sisters.

For this reason, I work as hard as I do daily with relentless intensity. I don't know why I feel compelled to fulfil this mission, nor do I see the end-goal, but I know I live my purpose. I am honouring the Divine Voice that saved my family's lives almost thirty years ago and all those people who died in my country due to the ignorance and darkness that can overtake people's hearts and minds.

Although I laid the groundwork for this book earlier, I continued working on it during the Covid pandemic, which started in December 2019, right when my first book came out. About 30% of this book is knowledge I acquired on my seventeen-year journey with the Kundalini, while the other 70% is based on rigorous, daily research and contemplation. Therefore, some parts of the invisible science of the human energy system I am presenting here are a work in progress that I will surely update for many years to come.

During this two-year project, I added at least 100 new books to my already massive home library to ensure the most comprehensive exposition of every subject, with no shortcuts taken. So, saying that I poured my heart and Soul into this book is an understatement. And, as much as it will be a journey of learning for you, the reader, it was quite the ride for me as well.

I want to thank the love of my life, my wife and muse Emily, for not only doing the cover art for *Serpent Rising* but for being my model and putting up with my tireless requests for impromptu photoshoots. I also want to thank Daniel Bakov, my creative consultant and editor of *Man of Light*, who helped me find the right words to introduce myself in a worthy and epic fashion. Also, a thank you to my fellow Kundalions, Michael "Omdevaji" Perring and Joel Chico. Michael gave me plenty of insights into the vast and intricate subject of Tantra and Yoga, while Joel and I compared notes on the role cannabis can play in the Kundalini awakening process. And lastly, a most gracious thank you to my sister and parents for giving me the greatest gift of all, that of a loving and supportive family that never left me wanting or needing more.

In closing, thank you, dear reader, for deciding to join me for this journey as I examine the Kundalini energy, its evolving science, and the philosophical framework behind how it operates. I am confident that you will benefit greatly from my knowledge and experience and that this book will answer many of the questions you may have. As such, your Spiritual Evolution will be furthered, which is the goal of all my work. For more information about me and the work I have been undertaking since awakening the Kundalini seventeen years ago, please visit my website at www.nevenpaar.com.

Fiat Lux,
Neven Paar

"A man will be charged with destroying the temple and
religions altered by fantasy. He will harm the rocks
rather than the living. Ears filled with ornate speeches."

"...He will fly through the sky, the rains and the snows,
And strike everyone with his rod."
He will appear in Asia, at home in Europe.
One who is issued from great Hermes..."

"...At the eve of another desolation when the perverted
church is atop her most high and sublime dignity...
there will proceed one born from a branch long barren,
who will deliver the people of the world from a meek and
voluntary slavery and place them under the protection of Mars."
"...The flame of a sect shall spread the world over..."

—Nostradamus

PART I: KUNDALINI AWAKENING

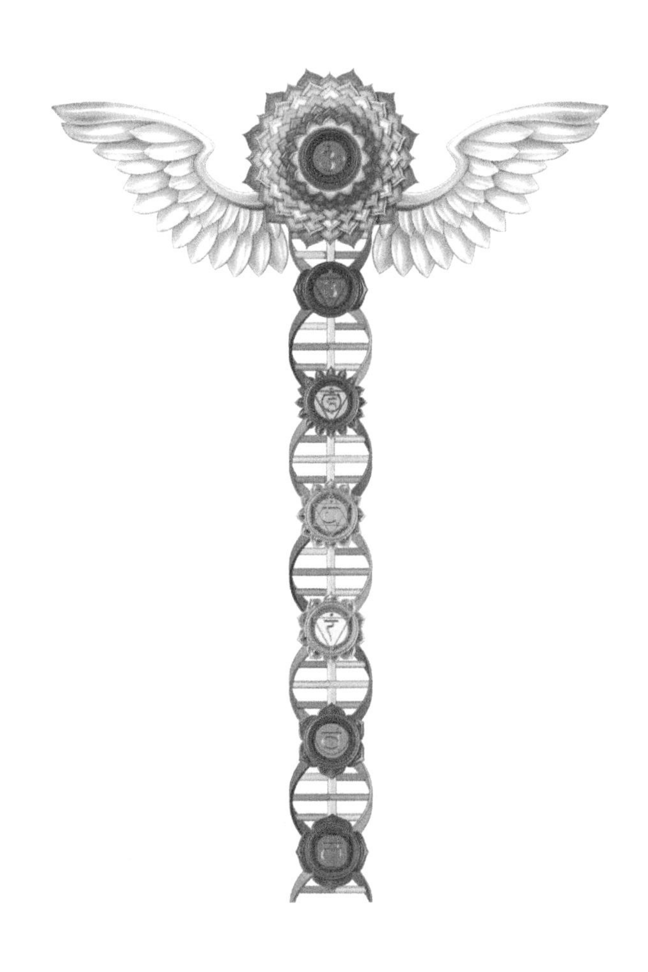

INTRODUCTION TO THE KUNDALINI

Kundalini is the greatest secret known to man, yet few people understand what it really is. Most people think it is a type of Yoga instead of the aim of all Yoga. Some people even dare say it is a type of pasta. Regardless, from my experience of talking to random folks on the subject, strangers, even ones who claim they read many books on the Kundalini and know what it's all about, they only know about 30% of the story. And I am being generous with that number. This book, however, will change all that.

I stated inside the front cover that *Serpent Rising* is the "The World's Most Comprehensive Body of Work on Human Energy Potential," and I meant it. It wasn't the Ego talking. I believe this statement is a fact. And I think that by the time you are finished reading this book, you will agree. Keep in mind that *Serpent Rising: The Kundalini Compendium* is Part I of the series. I am already well underway on Part II, which examines Ancient civilizations and traditions and the role that the Kundalini played in their systems of Spiritual Evolution. Also, my previous book, *The Magus: Kundalini and the Golden Dawn*, although not a direct part of the series, contains a plethora of information on the Kundalini from a Western Mysteries perspective, including the Qabalah and the Tree of Life, whose knowledge is essential to understanding the wisdom teachings.

Knowledge of the Kundalini has existed since time immemorial. I am talking about the deep understanding of Kundalini's ultimate potential from people that have gone all the way on their journey of Spiritual awakening. The Ancients hid the secrets of the Kundalini in the symbolism of their mystery traditions, usually conveyed through art and sculpture. This knowledge mainly was kept hidden, reserved for the chosen few and veiled from the profane, as was the Ancient method of passing on the esoteric mysteries. The teacher taught the student from mouth to ear. This information was not written down until recently, and even then, you had to have been initiated into a mystery school to get the real secrets.

Over time, individuals came along with claims that something extraordinary happened to them—God touched them, they said. These unique people awakened the Kundalini, usually by accident, so they used the most familiar language to explain this metaphysical event. They would often be regarded as mystics, or prophets even, displaying supernatural powers that astonished the masses. In their attempts to describe their experience, they referred to the Kundalini by many names—the "Dragon Force," the "Serpent Power," the "Holy Fire," and other variations of these *Archetypes*.

But as time went on and more people became awakened, it created more confusion than clarity regarding this subject. And the answer to this is simple. There has never been a powerful enough work of reference that unified all the Ancient traditions, philosophies, and religions regarding the Kundalini. The schools of Yoga and Tantra, which hold the most comprehensive keys on the Kundalini and the process of its awakening, are only one piece of the puzzle, albeit the largest one since the Kundalini science originated from them.

This brings me to why I wrote this book. I wrote it partly out of necessity and partly out of personal desire. I wanted to give humanity the keys to understanding this most cryptic and elusive of subjects. *Serpent Rising: The Kundalini Compendium* features a scientific approach to the Kundalini that includes the study of its energetic framework and so much more, using simplified language that is understandable to the everyday person—a language that unites the Eastern and Western schools of thought regarding Spirituality.

While writing this book, my Higher Self led me to research one subject to another, avoiding all shortcuts as I connected the dots and created the work you are holding in your hands. In the end, although my name is on *Serpent Rising*, this work transcends me as a person. I was merely a conduit for my Spiritual Self to channel this knowledge to me. By the time you finish reading it, you will understand everything you need regarding the subject of the Kundalini. And that was the point—that's why it took me so long to do this. To equip you with the necessary knowledge to inform others about the Kundalini so that the whole world may know its power and ultimate potential, and we can collectively evolve Spiritually.

You see, Kundalini is the most critical esoteric topic in the world. When it comes to Spiritual evolution, its exploration is of utmost importance. A Kundalini awakening allows one to realize their full Spiritual potential. There are many components to one's energy system, which I will discuss in great detail in this book, including how the Kundalini impacts each part. The Kundalini awakening process unfolds systematically over time, involving a necessary and often challenging period of intense purification that can be rather meticulous. Beyond the awakening and purification process itself, a more significant challenge consists in learning to live and operate with the Kundalini energy daily and controlling it instead of being controlled by it since it can be very volatile.

I will discuss the many different aspects of how the Kundalini transformation unfolds and affects one's life in the aftermath and clear up many of the common misunderstandings about the Kundalini and the awakening process itself. My seventeen years of experience of living with an awakened Kundalini is invaluable to someone in the midst of their journey and is seeking guidance.

Next, I will share valuable information on the different types of Kundalini awakenings and the transfiguration process, and its general timeline. There are common challenges along the way that I will discuss, as well as tips and insight into troubleshooting the Kundalini circuit when things seem to "break down." This last section includes effective practices and meditations in or around the head area to "kick-start" or re-align Ida and Pingala channels necessary for the engine to run smoothly. You won't find this crucial information anywhere else. Since my awakening, I have been the scientist and laboratory in one. As such, my creativity, courage, and persistence have led me to find unconventional solutions to the many challenges I have been faced with along the way. And there were many.

There is a myriad of other topics on the Kundalini that I will get into to further your knowledge of the subject and to enlighten and reconcile the many differing viewpoints you may have. From how human anatomy is involved in the Kundalini awakening process to various Spiritual healing practices and an in-depth study of the science and practice of Yoga with components of Ayurveda. I tried to cover every subject I believed was relevant for you to know about that gives insight into the Kundalini and how to heal your Chakras once you've had the awakening. My desire to be the best at what I do, the Michael Jordan of the Kundalini science, if you will, pushes me every day to expand my knowledge as I continue developing myself into the foremost authority on this subject. Consider it my life's mission, one that I devote all of my time to.

As a final note, since this is a rather large book, I don't want you to feel intimidated by its size, thinking you need to read through everything sequentially. The Yoga and Spiritual healing practices sections, for example, can be saved for last if you wish to read specifically about the Kundalini and the awakening and transformation process.

Then, when you're ready to delve into working with the exercises to heal your Chakras and balance your inner energies, you will have all the tools to do so.

The path of the Kundalini initiate is the path of the Spiritual warrior. A warrior needs the proper equipment, training, and insight to succeed. With these teachings, I intend to equip you, the initiate, with the necessary understanding of the human energy potential so that you may attain success on your Soul's evolution journey. Though the Kundalini awakening and transformation path is difficult, it is also rewarding beyond measure. Let us begin.

KUNDALINI AWAKENING PROCESS

The Kundalini is evolutionary energy at the base of the spine (in the coccyx region) that is said to be coiled three and a half times in its state of potential in unawakened humans. The word "Kundalini" is of Eastern origin, namely Yoga and Tantra. In Sanskrit, Kundalini means "coiled snake."

Once awakened, the Kundalini rises up the spinal column through the three main Nadis, all the way to the top of the head. The term "Nadi" is a Sanskrit word that translates as "tube," "channel," or "flow." Simply put, Nadis are channels that carry energy in the body.

In Chinese medicine, the Nadis are known as Meridians. The main difference between the two systems is that the Nadis are not defined in the limbs, only the head and central trunk, unlike the Meridians. In *Serpent Rising*, we will stick to the Yogic science and philosophy of the Nadis and Chakras, coupled with the Transpersonal Chakras model and many of my discoveries regarding the Body of Light's energy centres and energy flow.

The central Nadi is called Sushumna. It is essentially the hollow tube of the spinal column. Intertwining around Sushumna are two ancillary, or supplementary Nadis, Ida and Pingala. Ida is the feminine, Moon Nadi, which regulates cold in the body, while Pingala is the masculine, Sun Nadi, which controls heat in the body. These two Nadis represent the masculine and feminine principles contained within all things in the Universe. In Sanskrit, the Ida and Pingala channels are often referred to as the Chandra (Moon) and Surya (Sun) Nadis.

During a Kundalini awakening, as the energy rises simultaneously through the three main Nadis, it systematically blows open the Chakras from the root of the spine upward to the brain centre (Figure 1). Ida and Pingala meet at these Chakric points and terminate in Ajna Chakra. The Kundalini will continue rising upwards to the centre, top of the head, breaking the "Cosmic Egg," which fully activates the Body of Light—the Holographic Body. In Tantric philosophy, the Cosmic Egg relates to the Brahmarandhra. (More on this subject in a later chapter.)

The Cosmic Egg is a container that holds the Ambrosia nectar. Once the Kundalini energy pierces through it on its upwards rise, this Ambrosia is released, infusing the Seventy-Two Thousand Nadis, which refers to the Body of Light activation. This part of the process feels like someone cracked an egg over your head and the yolk (Ambrosia) pours all the way down to your feet, covering and enveloping your entire body.

Although the Body of Light activation feels as if the physical body is being electrically charged, the released Ambrosia is only working on a subtle level. However, the person experiencing this event feels like a human battery being charged and infinitely expanded by a current of bioelectricity. For example, every Kundalini awakened individual I have spoken to that has had this experience describes feeling intensely "electrocuted" by the Kundalini energy.

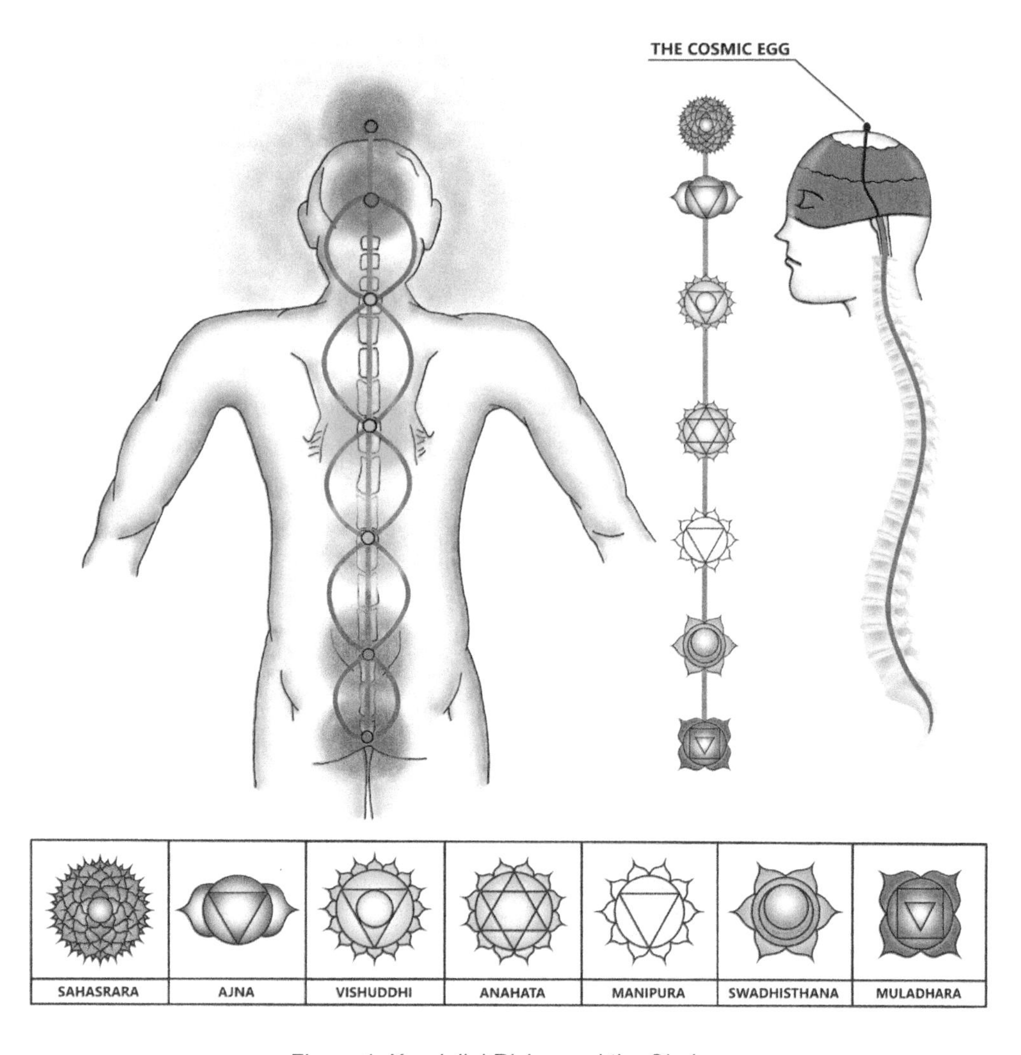

Figure 1: Kundalini Rising and the Chakras

By activating the Body of Light, all the Subtle Bodies become activated, including the Spiritual Body and Divine Body. There are, in fact, numerous Subtle Bodies within the Body of Light. However, after a full Kundalini awakening, it is essential to align the individual consciousness solely with the Spiritual Body since it transcends the duality of the mind.

In my Kundalini awakening experience, once the Seventy-Two Thousand Nadis were in the process of being charged and activated, I jolted out of bed and opened my eyes. What I saw next changed my life forever. Firstly, I witnessed firsthand that the Body of Light is not an idea or a concept but a real, tangible thing. When I looked at my hands, I saw them made of pure golden Light, beautiful to behold and perfect in every way. Then, as I looked around my room, I saw the Holographic blueprint of the world we live in. The room had what I describe as a digital makeover with transparent, vapour-like walls and objects that appeared like they were suspended in mid-air. The colours were sharper, deeper, and more reflective. To clarify, what I saw was not a Mind's Eye vision inside my head, but I saw this with my own two physical eyes.

You see, there is a component of the world that is transparent and made of pure energy, occupying the same Time and Space as the Physical World, just at a different degree of vibration—one closer to Spirit. The awakening of the Kundalini and activation of the Body of Light is a process whereby the consciousness becomes able to perceive and experience this reality. Another name for this reality is the Fourth Dimension—the Dimension of Vibration or energy. Since all things in existence are held in vibratory motion, this dimension is the realm where each object, thought, or emotion has a quantifiable essence. It can be perceived by the Mind's Eye and the intuitive faculty of a human being.

Once the Light Body activation is complete, the experience does not end there. Instead, the Kundalini energy continues to rise upwards. The next step in the awakening process is the energy leaving the body altogether, through the Crown, taking the individual consciousness with it. This experience results in the momentary unification of the individual consciousness with the Cosmic Consciousness, the Fifth Dimensional White Light principle —the source of Divinity. Once this transcendental experience occurs, the individual consciousness re-enters the physical body, having seen the vision of the true nature of reality. Thus, the human becomes One with God for a brief moment, only to come back down and tell their story.

Alternatively, if the awakened individual becomes fearful of uniting their Being with the White Light, the Kundalini energy subsides and drops back down to the Root Chakra, Muladhara. After all, it is common for people who experience a spontaneous Kundalini awakening to become fearful during the activation process. It makes them feel like they are undergoing a physical death due to the intensity of the energy felt in the body and consciousness being liberated from it.

ACTIVATING THE BODY OF LIGHT

The Kundalini energy's goal is to activate the Body of Light and the corresponding Subtle Bodies. Once this occurs, the entire Tree of Life is awakened within the individual, and all the Cosmic Planes become available as states of consciousness. Since the Body of Light is the vehicle of the Soul, once it is fully activated, the Soul is permanently freed from the physical body. Thus, over time, the Soul must align with the Spiritual Body of the Spiritual Plane, where the Soul and Spirit become one.

Of all the Subtle Bodies, the Spiritual Body is most important since, once your consciousness aligns with it, your Soul elevates past pain and suffering. A person who can achieve such a feat permanently rises above their Wheel of Karma. Karma is still operational since one can never escape its effects. Still, they are no longer emotionally affected by the energy of fear that the mind experiences due to living in a world of Duality.

The Body of Light is the next vehicle of consciousness in the process of human evolution as it allows one to perceive and fully experience the inner Cosmic Planes. However, the Spiritual Body is the transcendental sheath or layer we are trying to align with to be our vehicle of consciousness while living in the waking reality of the material world. It is the Causal Body of the Eastern System—Anandamaya Kosha. It is inextricably connected to the Body of Light as its highest expression our consciousness can embody while living in the flesh. However, there is still one sheath higher, the Divine Body, although we cannot sustain its experience for an extended period during our waking life unless we are in deep meditation.

The Body of Light is the vehicle of consciousness for the Soul when it enters the Inner Planes during meditation and sleep. The Inner Planes are experienced through the Mind's Eye (Ajna Chakra), one of the three Spiritual Chakras concerned with intuition and clairvoyance. The most prominent Inner Plane experiences occur during Lucid Dreams, enabling you to be conscious when you dream and control your dreams' content. It also allows you to explore the inner Cosmic Planes during dream states and have incredible Soul experiences you can't duplicate in real life. Lucid Dreaming basically lets you experience anything you ever desired, without the consequences. It is one of the more significant Spiritual gifts received on the Kundalini awakening journey and one that I will discuss in more detail later on in the book.

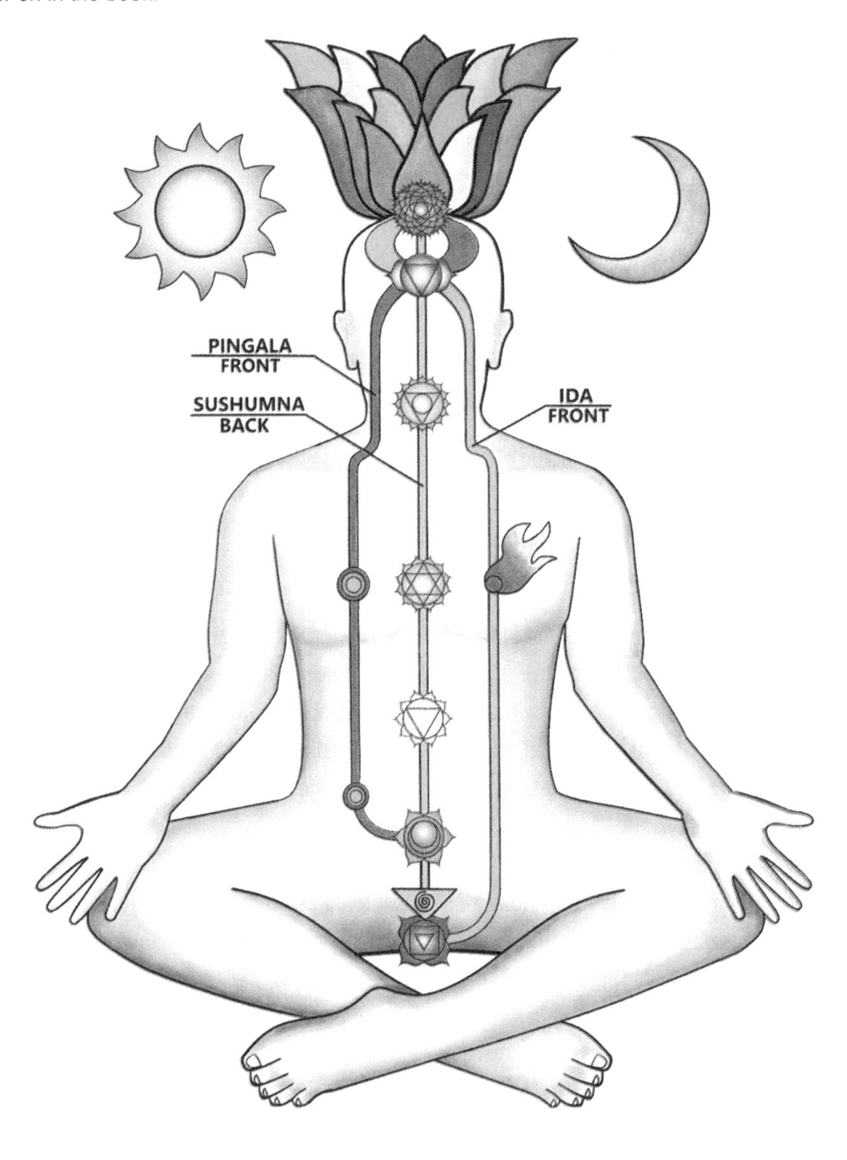

Figure 2: The Three Nadis Post-Kundalini Awakening

Once the activation is complete, the Kundalini energy becomes a permanent part of the awakened individual's existence, signalling a new way of functioning and experiencing the world. The Kundalini, over time, becomes a self-sustaining energy circuit (Figure 2) fueled by food and water that grows and gets stronger, expanding the individual consciousness daily. And as the normal waking consciousness slowly aligns to the Spiritual Body, which is a process that may take many years, the awakened individual will be living in the same reality as everyone else but experiencing it entirely differently. This experience of life is a true gift from the Divine.

SPIRITUAL GIFTS AND SENSE UPGRADES

After the awakening, every morsel of food transforms into Pranic (Life Force) energy which powers the Kundalini circuit and expands the consciousness, giving rise to many types of transcendental experiences and the dawning of new psychic abilities. Thus, the awakened individual now begins to function at a new level of life experience, within the Dimension of Vibration or energy. In this new dimension, they develop an ability to feel the world around them as a quantifiable essence.

Over time, this newly developed ability to feel the world through energy becomes the dominant way of navigating through life, causing a disregard for the rational, thinking mind. Finally, the awakened individual starts to experience the world entirely through intuition as a primary mode of functioning since they are in direct contact with the Inner Light and the Truth. Illusion goes away as their consciousness aligns with the Spiritual Body over time.

As illusion (Maya) vanishes, the Ego dissipates as well, since it belongs to the realm of the rational, thinking mind. Its impulse becomes less and less active until the awakened individual can fully function on intuition through the Fourth Dimension of Vibration, or energy. By doing so, they become attuned to the most precious gift that the Divine has given humanity, which is the present moment, the "Now", a "present" from God. In the "Now," they are tapped into a field of all possibility, enabling them to reshape their own lives to maximize their highest potential. Truly successful and happy people all have one thing in common—they all live in the "Now".

The perceptive abilities of the awakened individual, the five senses of sight, smell, sound, taste, and touch, are upgraded through the Kundalini energy. Smelling and hearing things at a distance become an everyday part of their lives. They can taste something and feel it by merely observing that thing with their eyes. Through the power of their minds, they can feel the energy of objects before them and use all of their inner senses. This is because Ajna Chakra is now open permanently through which these transcendental experiences occur. Reality is perceived now at a much higher level than ever before.

I saved the sense of sight for last because the upgrade received is the most amazing in my experience. Once the inner Light is awakened through the Kundalini energy, it reshapes everything one sees and perceives visually, giving it a complete makeover. Moreover, the outside world appears like it is inside your head, being projected onto a movie screen before your eyes (Figure 3). I like to use the analogy of the progression of video game technology to explain this visual phenomenon since it is the only reference point that I can come up with that people can relate to.

If you have ever played the early generation of video games (like I did since I grew up in the 90s), remember how the game world was drastically upgraded as we went from the PlayStation 2 to the PlayStation 3 console? The graphics became sharper, crisper, more refined. Now imagine what would happen if you went straight from the

Playstation 2 to the Playstation 5 console while playing the same game. The characters and environments of your game are the same, but the radical digital makeover brings the game to life in a whole new way.

Figure 3: The Universe Inside the Head

To specify, however, this visual perception upgrade is least common in Kundalini awakened individuals, but it is the most significant "wow" factor that I have experienced in my awakening process. As such, my account serves as a testament to its reality. In fact, it is so rare that out of dozens of Kundalini awakened individuals I have spoken to about their "upgrades," only one or two had this particular one.

But then again, I haven't come across anyone who witnessed the Holographic nature of reality with their own two eyes either. I believe that my upgraded sense of sight is a sustained version of this same reality. Interestingly, the Holographic Universe theory is not a new concept but is supported by prominent Astrophysicists in modern times. Some have taken this idea further, stating that we may even live in a computer simulation. Elon Musk, the 21 century's real-life Tony Stark (Iron Man), a genius of our modern age, once said that how technology is progressing, there is a one in a billion chance that we are NOT living in a computer simulation right now.

Although I cannot say for sure whether we are living in a computer simulation, the world does have a Holographic blueprint that is imperceptible to most people that I would best describe as pure consciousness. Whether this pure consciousness is a projected Hologram is uncertain, but the possibility is very much there.

However, what I do know for a fact is that the world I experience now appears as a digitized version of the world I lived in before but with more enhanced graphics. Witnessing the downtown of a big city like Toronto at night, for example, with its LED signage, bright lights, and flashing colours, is like stepping into a futuristic video game wonderland—a breathtaking experience to this day.

The two words that best describe how I see the external world now are "Interstellar" and "Intergalactic," since these words inspire the idea that our Planet is just one of many with life in the vastness of space. There are countless other worlds that we will explore in due time and make contact with Beings unimaginable to us. However, we must first strip away our material sheath via the Kundalini mechanism that our Creator put inside us to see reality's hidden, Holographic nature and experience our true essence as Beings of Light.

THE TREE OF LIFE AND THE CHAKRAS

In my first book, *The Magus: Kundalini and the Golden Dawn*, I discuss at great length the Western Mystery Tradition and their relation to the Eastern Spiritual system. In this book, however, since our main subject is the Kundalini (an Eastern term), I will take the converse approach, primarily holding to the Yogic and Tantric systems while referencing the Qabalah and the Tree of life in some instances.

The Tree of Life, the main component of the Qabalah, is the blueprint of existence. It is the map of our Solar System and the human psyche. The Tree of Life consists of ten Sephiroth (Spheres), representing states of consciousness that humans partake of daily that give rise to inner faculties such as intuition, memory, willpower, imagination, emotion, desire, logic and reason, and thought. Qabalists say that everything in nature can be categorized on the Tree of Life since all things relate in some way to our Solar System and its energies.

The Qabalistic system relies on the energy of numbers, symbols, and letters (Hebrew). The ten Sephiroth are connected by twenty-two paths, corresponding with the twenty-two *Major Arcana* of the Tarot and the twenty-two *Hebrew Letters*. These, in turn, correspond with the Five Elements, Twelve Zodiac, and Seven Ancient Planets. As such, the Tree of Life encompasses the totality of the Universal energies, including Constellations, that impact life on Earth.

The Qabalah that I have extensive experience with is Hermetic, which is why it is spelt with a "Q." Hermeticism is the study of our Solar System and the Universal energies that comprise who we are. In addition, there is a Jewish Kabbalah (with a K) and a Christian Cabala (with a C)—all three systems have the same foundation, however, since they use the Tree of Life as their central glyph. Consult the "Glossary of Selected Terms" in the Appendix for a detailed description of each of the Sephiroth of the Tree of Life and other relevant Western Mysteries terms undefined in the main body of text.

The Chakras originated in Ancient India. They were first mentioned in the Hindu Vedas (1500-1200 BC), a large body of sacred texts containing Spiritual knowledge. The Chakras are part of a complex energy system that describes different aspects or parts of the human Aura (energy field). Knowledge of Chakras has only recently been brought to the Western world, with the growth in popularity of Yoga and as part of New Age philosophies in general.

Human beings have Major Chakras as well as Minor Chakras. However, the Seven Major Chakras are the primary ones that essentially power the Aura. The Minor Chakras are connected to the Major ones and do not function independently but instead work to carry out their duties further. In this book, I will cover both the Major and Minor Chakras and the Transpersonal Chakras.

Chakra is a Sanskrit word for "spinning wheel" or "vortex." The term "Chakra" is used to describe the invisible energy centres along the spinal column and within the head. These energy centres are comprised of multi-coloured flowing energy that we find in the Aura. The Chakras power the Aura and regulate the nervous system, endocrine glands, and major organs. They are central energy stations that govern the entire human being; mind, body, and Soul.

The Chakras manage and distribute Life energy throughout our various Subtle Bodies, which are vehicles of consciousness for the multiple Cosmic Planes of existence that we partake in. Chakras are conductors of energy, and each Chakra has different properties, which powers and expresses our inner Self. They are responsible for the work of our thoughts, emotions, willpower, intuition, memory, and other components which make up who we are.

Figure 4: The Tree of Life/Seven Chakras/Kundalini

It is essential to understand that Chakras are not physical; instead, they are located in the Body of Light. They represent forces coming from the Subtle Bodies that manifest in a circulating pattern in seven major areas of the Body of Light. Chakras are often described as being shaped like flowers in full blossom. Each Chakric flower has a specific number of petals that create wheel-like vortexes of energy that radiate outwards, in right horizontal angles, while the top and bottom Chakra (Sahasrara and Muladhara) project vertically. To further add to their flower-like appearance, each Chakra also has a stem-like channel that projects within and connects to the spinal cord and brainstem.

The Chakras can spin clockwise or counter-clockwise, depending on the Gender of the Chakra and whether it is giving out or receiving energy. The rate of a Chakra's spin determines the quality of its function. If the spin is fast, they are well-tuned, channelling more Light energy. If their spin is slow and stagnant, they are out of tune, meaning they channel less Light energy. In general, people whose Chakras are out of tune are aligned more with their Ego than their Soul. To align with the Soul and express its properties, one needs to have well-tuned Chakras since Soul expression depends entirely on how much Light is channelled through the Chakras.

Once the Kundalini has risen to the top of the head to be permanently localized in the brain, the entire Tree of Life becomes fully activated. The highest Sephira is called *Kether*, the Crown, at the top of the Tree of Life. Kether corresponds with the seventh Chakra, Sahasrara. Both are called the "Crown," concerning their placement on top of the head. Kether relates to the Spiritual White Light that underlies all of physical existence.

Conversely, the lowest Sephira is called *Malkuth*, the Planet Earth, as the tenth Sephira on the Tree of Life—directly opposite to Kether. On the Chakric system, Malkuth relates to the first Chakra, Muladhara, and the Earth Element. These two sets of Sephiroth and Chakras have direct correspondence and relations, although Malkuth is placed at the feet while Muladhara is placed in the groin region. The rest of the Tree of Life Sephiroth and Chakras correspond as well, although one must have direct experience with both systems to see how they relate. Thus, it is not as simple as unifying the opposite Spheres on the Tree of Life to get the seven Chakras, although this method works mathematically.

After a full Kundalini awakening, the Chakras (and Tree of Life Sephiroth) become permanently infused with Light energy, activating their states of consciousness within the individual (Figure 4). The Chakras become like light bulbs, which emit Light respective to how clean, pure, and in-tune they are. For example, if there is a lot of Karma in a particular Chakra, it emits a dim Light rather than a bright one. It is the solemn duty you owe to your Creator to cleanse your Chakras and remove negativity from each so that they can shine brightly, allowing you to align your consciousness with your Soul.

PURIFYING THE CHAKRAS

Karma is a Sanskrit word for "action," "work," or "deed" that forms part of the Universal Law. It implies that every action is the effect of one or more previous actions and will cause one or more future actions. Thus, Karma is cyclic, and it affects us all. Since reality moves in cycles like a revolving wheel, the Wheel of Karma represents good or bad Karmic energy in our life that will manifest in the future either as blessings or issues that need to be resolved. Our behaviour in life determines whether we have good or bad Karma and that behaviour is expressed through the Chakras.

Each Chakra is a power source for how your character and personality express themselves in the inner and outer worlds. Character is inherent in you as it is the essence of who you are, while personality changes over time. Character is your higher, ethical beliefs and expressions of your Soul, while personality deals more with Ego expressions and its likes and dislikes. Each Chakra is a power reservoir for different parts of your character and personality, from how you think to what you feel to what drives you and beyond.

When you have Karmic energy in a Chakra, part of the Self carries negative energy, which will need to be worked through. Therefore, all the Chakras need to be cleansed and optimised so that your thoughts, emotions, and actions can come from a place of love. If they are imbued with love energy, you are enlightening the Chakra of that expression of Self. Therefore, if you are selfish, fearful, lustful, angry, arrogant, greedy, self-righteous, and so on, then that means that you need to work on those parts of Self and turn them into their loving, positive opposites. It means that you need to overcome the Karma of those Chakras that express this behaviour.

Karmic energy present in a Chakra can be a very challenging experience. It makes life very uncomfortable, preventing you from functioning as well as you should, or want to. For the Kundalini awakened individuals, those unprepared for the experience as I was, Karmic energy in the Chakras can bring on debilitating fear and anxiety.

A full awakening localises the Kundalini energy in the brain permanently, uniting the conscious and subconscious minds. If there is dormant negative energy present in the Chakras, it will flood the consciousness in the form of unpleasant thoughts and emotions. One can't hide from their Demons (negative thought-senders) anymore after the Kundalini enters the brain resulting in a resurgence of harmful viewpoints, beliefs, and attitudes toward life that will have to be overcome. Therefore, you must purge fear energy from your system, which starts with cleansing the Chakras.

Through Chakric purification, you alter your beliefs about yourself and the world. After all, if you are to experience the Divine Light within you, a complete transformation of your character and personality is necessary. You must become a Spiritual Being whose consciousness is higher in vibration than before. There is no way around this. And to accomplish this, your Ego must die and be reborn. This is the ultimate Rebirth concept alluded to by many religions, new and old. However, it is more than an idea for the Kundalini awakened people—it is the only reality they need to concern themselves with until the process is complete.

Kundalini awakened individuals have to learn who they are deep inside, the good and the bad, and accept and love themselves. And once they go within, they can bypass the Ego and get in touch with their real Self, the Higher Self of the Spirit. But to do so, they must build virtues, remove vices, and adapt moral and ethical behaviours into their lives if they are to overcome the fear and anxiety that is hampering their very existence.

So you see, the gift of the Kundalini can be seen as a curse at first if you had a spontaneous awakening and were Karmically unprepared. However, there is no shortcut to Enlightenment, and once the genie is out of the bottle, there is no putting it back in again. The Kundalini rapidly accelerates your Spiritual Evolution journey, but to raise the vibration of your consciousness, you must overcome the negative energy stored within each Chakra. It is a systematic process, starting from the lowest Chakra, Muladhara, and finishing with Sahasrara at the Crown. Since the Ego is present within the physical body, which is the densest part of you, you need to start there and begin peeling away layers of your consciousness, each of which is less dense than the one that came before. When you get to the final layer, you have found your *Philosopher's Stone*, the Quintessence, and have reached the Higher Self of the Spiritual Plane.

The process towards Enlightenment is alluded to by the story of the crucifixion of Jesus Christ. Once he died on the cross, instead of being Resurrected (Enlightened) right away, he had to spend three days in the Underworld, the

Demonic realm, to become the King of Hell before becoming the King of Heaven. So here is a metaphor for Jesus having to master his Demons since they barred the path towards Enlightenment. And he did so by facing them without fear in his heart, which allowed him to assume mastery over them.

So you see, when you approach your inner Demons with courage instead of fear, you automatically take away their fuel since they feed on fear energy; it is their sustenance. Then you can master them and give them back their wings, metaphorically speaking. Thus, all Demons are essentially unmastered *Angels*. They can all be used for good if the mind is strong and the individual learns how to wield their powers. For to maximise our willpower, we must master our dark side. In fact, before reaching Heaven, the Spiritual Realm, this is a prerequisite. Let those with ears of understanding hear this great mystery of Life, Death, and Resurrection. It has been hinted at in many Ancient Spiritual traditions before the advent of Christianity.

SPIRITUAL HEALING PRACTICES

The journey towards Spiritual Rebirth is filled with mental and emotional trials and tribulations that can often be gruelling. Regardless, to rise in consciousness, one must overcome the negative energies stored in the Chakras and "enlighten" them before experiencing the ineffable beauty of the Crown Chakra, Sahasrara. Cleansing the Chakras is inevitable and whether you have chosen to work with them through a Spiritual healing practice or allow the Kundalini to purify each Chakra systematically over time is totally up to you.

Spiritual healing practices include, but are not limited to, Ceremonial Magick, Gemstones (Crystals), Tuning Forks, Aromatherapy, Tattvas, and Yogic and Tantric practices such as Asana, Pranayama, Mudra, Mantra, and meditation (Dhyana). As someone who has tried most Spiritual healing practices, I have found that Ceremonial Magick isolates each Chakra best and allows you to overcome the Karmic energy in each and tune the Chakra. My first book, *The Magus: Kundalini and the Golden Dawn*, is an entire course of study for the aspiring Magi, and it gives you all the ritual exercises you need to work with your Chakras.

While Ceremonial Magick is a Western Spiritual practice, Yoga and Tantra are Eastern practices. However, people in both the East and the West practise Crystal Healing, Sound Healing with Tuning Forks, and Aromatherapy. Although initially an Eastern Spiritual technique used in the Yogic system, Tattvas have found their way into the Western Mystery Schools because of their potency to connect with the Five Elements, the unifying factor between the Eastern Chakric System and Western Qabalistic system.

Since the purpose of this book is not only to give answers pertaining to the Kundalini but also to offer alternate methods of healing the Aura and the Chakras with the aim of Spiritual Evolution, I have devoted the entirety of Part V and Part VI to the practices mentioned above. I will briefly go through some of them to give you an overall impression. Of course, there are other methods of working with the Chakras, and I am only mentioning the major ones that I have extensive experience with. In the end, what you choose to work with is up to you.

Gemstones (Crystals)

The use of Gemstones, otherwise called Natural Stones, or Crystals, is a powerful Spiritual practice that has existed for thousands of years and is widely used by energy healers today. We find evidence of the use of Gemstones for Spiritual healing, energy manipulation, and protection in virtually all Ancient cultures and traditions. For example, the Ancients incorporated Gemstones into jewellery, cosmetics, decorative statues, and talismans as a testament to their powerful ability to heal mental, emotional, and physical issues while protecting them from adverse forces.

Each of the hundreds of Gemstones in existence has a broad spectrum of healing properties. We can use Gemstones to target the corresponding energy centres in the Body of Light to remove blockages and increase energy flow in these zones. By tuning and optimising the Chakras through Crystal Healing, the corresponding Subtle Bodies, including the physical body, become rejuvenated as well—As Above, So Below.

To truly understand how a Gemstone affects one on the physical, emotional, mental, and Spiritual levels, it is necessary to get some personal experience with each stone. After all, each Gemstone relates to a Chakra or Chakras but also different Elements, Planets, and Zodiacal energies. Therefore, the use of Gemstones is a viable practice to work on your Microcosm, your Aura, and one that can balance your energies and heal you on all levels if you devote yourself to it. I have included a list of Gemstone correspondences in this work, including techniques you can use to work with them.

Tuning Forks

Using Tuning Forks in Sound Healing is a relatively new field, although it has grown in popularity because of its therapeutic effectiveness. It is based on the principle that everything in the Universe is in a state of vibration, including our thoughts, emotions, and physical body.

When the practitioner strikes a Tuning Fork in a healing session, they create a sound wave whose vibration travels deeply into the patient's Aura, accessing their Body of Light's energy pathways (Nadis) and affecting the consciousness. There are many uses for Tuning Forks, including healing the subtle energy system, adjusting the body's natural cycles, balancing the nervous system, relaxing the muscles, and promoting good sleep.

The most popular Tuning Forks on the market are the ones that correspond with the Major Chakras. Since each Chakra vibrates at a specific frequency when healthy, a Tuning Fork can be calibrated to resonate at that same frequency. When placed on or near the Chakra, the Tuning Fork's vibration sends a sound wave that tunes the corresponding Chakra, returning it to its optimal vibratory state. The process of allowing two oscillating bodies to synchronize with each other when they are near one another is called "entrainment."

Aromatherapy

Aromatherapy is a holistic medicine that has also been around for thousands of years, dating back to the time of Ancient Sumer. It uses compounds extracted from plants that capture the plant's fragrance or scent—its essence. The most commonly used plant extracts in Aromatherapy's "essential" oils are generally inhaled through various means and methods, although we can also use them topically.

When inhaled through the nose, essential oils impact the Limbic System, the part of the brain that plays a role in emotions, behaviours, and memories. In addition, the Limbic System produces hormones that help regulate breathing, heart rate, respiration, and blood pressure. For this reason, many essential oils have a calming effect on the nervous system, making them beneficial as a precursor to meditation, Tuning Fork Therapy, Tantric and Yogic practices, and other Spiritual healing modalities that require relaxation. Conversely, some essential oils have an energizing, uplifting effect and are great energy boosters when feeling sluggish and depleted.

Each essential oil fragrance has specific vibrations with healing properties that positively impact our consciousness. Their use can remove energy blockages in the Aura while realigning the Subtle Bodies and recalibrating the Chakras. In addition, essential oils make excellent companions to Gemstones and other energy invoking tools. They are generally safe and easy to use and provide a different yet potent method to heal the mind, body, and Soul.

Tattvas

Working with Tattvas is an Eastern practice that has been around for over two-and-a-half thousand years. The very word "Tattva" is a Sanskrit word meaning "essence," "principle," or "element." Tattvas represent the Four Elements of Earth, Water, Air, Fire, and the fifth Element of Spirit. There are five primary Tattvas, each of which has five Sub-Tattvas, making a total of thirty.

Tattvas are best looked upon as "windows" into the Cosmic Planes, corresponding to the Chakric energies. As such, they can assist us in working with the Chakras and the Karmic energy contained therein. They do not generate any energy in and of themselves, like Gemstones and Tuning Forks, but they are helpful to zero in on the inner Cosmic Planes and work on the corresponding Chakras. In my experience, working with the Tattvas goes hand-in-hand with using Ceremonial Magick rituals of the Elements since the type of energy each deals with are virtually the same.

Tattva work is similar to Ceremonial Magick as it does isolate each Chakra, but the energy invoked is less potent. Some may prefer the Tattvas method, though, since it allows one to work with the Sub-Elements safely and efficiently. In addition, Tattvas can be used in tandem with other Spiritual practices presented in this work, especially Aromatherapy.

Yoga and Tantra

The Eastern Spiritual systems of Yoga and Tantra contain many exercises that can be practised individually or in unison with other components of the two systems. Although Yoga and Tantra share the same practices, their philosophies differ. While Yoga applies Spiritual techniques to striving after particular goals and attainments (such as Self-Realisation or Enlightenment), Tantra focuses on using the same methods to liberate oneself from all desires, inevitably bringing about the same outcome as Yoga. Thus, Tantra can be seen as an approach to Yoga. It originated as a householder tradition that focused on embracing the material, mundane world instead of transcending it, as is the aim of Yoga.

Asana is the practice of standing or sitting Yoga postures. There are many benefits to performing Asanas, including toning the physical body, developing flexibility and strength, balancing and harmonising our inner energies, opening the Chakras, removing blockages in the Nadis, and grounding us with the Earth. Asana practice also has a calming effect on the mind, making it an excellent tool for combating anxiety and depression while boosting the brain's "happy" chemicals. Asanas are practised in tandem with breathing exercises (Pranayama) and meditation (Dhyana). Meditation Asanas, however, are a prerequisite for mostly all Yogic practices, including Mudras and Mantras.

Pranayama is the Yogic practice of controlled breathing—bringing Pranic energy into the body. We can practise it independently or as a precursor to meditation and all energy invoking exercises. For example, the "Four-Fold Breath" exercise from *The Magus* is an adapted Pranayama technique that works well with the ritual exercises from the Western Mystery Tradition. Similarly, Pranayama plays a crucial role in the performance of Asanas, Mudras, and Mantras since breathing is the key to controlling the mind and body. Pranayama exercises in this book are used for various purposes, including balancing the feminine and masculine energies, calming down the nervous system, neutralising negative energy, and preparing the mind for raising and manipulating energy.

Mudras are symbolic, ritualistic gestures or poses that generally involve only the hands and fingers, although they can also engage the entire body. They enable us to manipulate energies in our bodies (Microcosm) and invoke higher powers in the Universe (Macrocosm). Mudras connect us with Archetypal forces and raise the vibration of our consciousness. This book presents Mudras for awakening and fine-tuning the Chakras, balancing the Elements, invoking peace of mind, and even harnessing Pranic energy to awaken the Kundalini (Bandhas-Lock Mudras). You can use Mudras with meditation exercises, Mantras, Pranayamas, and Asanas, especially meditation Asanas.

Sanskrit Mantras invoke/evoke energy by attuning us to certain powers in ourselves and our Solar System. They often involve the invocation of Hindu or Buddhist Gods and Goddesses in some form or aspect of their powers. This powerful method of inducing energy into the Aura has been used for thousands of years by devotees of the Eastern Spiritual systems. Mantras generally carry the Karmic energy of the systems respective to the specific traditions or religions they originated from. They go hand-in-hand with Pranayama techniques, meditation exercises, and other Yogic practices. For example, since the energy invoked through Mantras usually encompasses more than one Chakra, we can combine their use (especially Bija Mantras) with Hand Mudras to efficiently isolate and heal individual Chakras.

And finally, meditation, or Dhyana, is one of the most widely practised disciplines for focusing the mind that we find in both the Eastern and Western Spiritual systems. For example, in *The Magus*, the "Mind's Eye Meditation" is a precursor to energy invocations because it effectively calms us down, facilitating an *Alpha State* of brain-wave activity, and preparing the mind for ritual invocations/evocations. Meditation techniques involve visualising an object within, concentrating on an object without, or employing Mantras to help focus the mind. Meditation is meant to silence the Ego and empty the mind, bringing healing to all the Chakras. It raises our power of awareness, making us present here and now and allowing us to tap into the field of pure potential. Meditation is used side-by-side with breath control (Pranayama).

***

I have found that Kundalini awakened individuals who choose to allow the Kundalini to work with individual Chakras naturally are often left at the mercy of this energy which can be very harsh at times. The pain and anxiety can be so high that some have lost complete control over their lives and have contemplated suicide. Finding a Spiritual practice to heal the Chakras allows you a significant level of control over this process, which can be very uplifting and give you the confidence and strength to move ahead on your journey. The Kundalini awakening process is a lifetime endeavour. Therefore, it is essential to remain inspired as it is happening to get the most from it and have the most comfortable time as you evolve Spiritually.

THE KUNDALINI TRANSFORMATION

It is imperative to discuss how the functioning of the Chakras ties in with the brain, considering that the expansion of consciousness, which is the primary purpose of the Kundalini awakening, occurs inside the head. You see, by awakening the Seven Chakras and raising the Kundalini to the Crown, new energy pathways open up within the brain, which feels like your head becomes hollow on the inside. The brain undergoes a remodelling process, expanding its capacity from 10%, which the average human uses, to the complete 100%. Dormant areas of the brain become unlocked, enabling us to take in a tremendous amount of outside information all at once and process it. Think of this as a process of brain-power expansion.

Once the Cosmic Egg has blown open, activating the Body of Light, it takes some time for Pranic/Light energy to infuse the Nadis and power up the new energy system. This process is achieved through the process of food transformation into Light energy via the digestive system. Since there is no defined word for this process, I will use "sublimate" since it implies a thing changing its form but not its essence. And since all things are made of Spirit and Light, including the food we eat, sublimation refers to its transformation from a solid state to a subtle one that infuses and powers up the energy pathways in the Body of Light. This phenomenon is responsible for not only the expansion of consciousness but for inducing transcendental states.

However, you will not be able to fully attune to the Spiritual Body (one of the Subtle Bodies of the Light Body) before you have completely worked through the lower four Chakras and have integrated and mastered the Elements of Earth, Water, Fire, and Air within your psyche. Since, to do so, you must go beyond the Abyss, into the realm of Non-Duality. Thus, during the lengthy Kundalini transformation process, your consciousness begins slowly attuning to *Chokmah* and *Binah*, the second and third highest Spheres (Sephiroth) on the Tree of Life that correspond with the inner functions of wisdom and understanding.

In this book, I will be introducing you to certain Qabalistic Archetypes and relating them to the Tree of Life. Although this work stands on its own, many of the ideas presented here continue and expand the knowledge presented in *The Magus*. After all, its description of the Kundalini energy relates to the Western Mystery Tradition while *Serpent Rising* holds to the Eastern system. By continually introducing new ideas and concepts to you, I aim to build up your memory and learning ability so that your Higher Self can take over and continue teaching you through Gnosis—the direct communication with higher energies. Before this occurs, however, you must have a thorough understanding of the Kundalini process and reconcile any divergent viewpoints about this subject.

BINDU ACTIVATION

Once the Light in the body has been built up with food intake, which may take three to four months after a full Kundalini awakening event, you will feel a release valve being formed at the top back of the head, which is the Bindu Chakra (Figure 5). Its location is exactly where Brahmins grow their tuft of hair. Bindu is a Sanskrit term meaning "point" or "dot," and it is the liberation access-point for the individual consciousness—the gateway to "Shoonya," the state of Void or nothingness. However, for Bindu to unlock, you must fully have awakened the Thousand-Petalled Lotus of Sahasrara, and the Kundalini must reside in the brain now permanently. Also, a sufficient amount of Chakric cleansing must be complete if the awakening was spontaneous and you were Karmically unprepared.

The Bindu's more common name is Bindu Visarga which means "the falling of the drop" in Sanskrit, in reference to the Amrita nectar that Tantra Yoga says discharges from the Bindu. The Amrita nectar, often called the "Nectar of Immortality," secretes from Sahasrara, but it enters the body through the Bindu. The Amrita and Ambrosia are the same thing and refer to the "Food of the Gods," the "Elixir of Life" that you often hear about in different Spiritual traditions. This nectar nourishes the Body of Light and is said to prolong life, provide sustenance, and play a key role in experiencing transcendence after a full and sustained Kundalini awakening.

In Tantra, the Bindu symbolizes Lord Shiva, the Source of Creation. Because of its intrinsic property to reflect thoughts from the Cosmic Consciousness, this Chakra is often referred to as the Moon Chakra. The Bindu is considered one of the Transpersonal Chakras, so it is not mentioned in most books on Yoga. In the Transpersonal Chakra model, the Bindu is called the Causal Chakra. As I examined various Spiritual schools of thought, I have found that the location of both Chakras and their properties and characteristics are identical.

The Bindu Chakra plays a crucial function in the Kundalini transformation process. This Chakra is next to awaken after Sahasrara. It serves as a gateway or channel of energy for the two higher Transpersonal Chakras, the Soul Star and the Stellar Gateway. After a full Kundalini awakening, Prana/Light begins to channel through the newly activated Body of Light. Over time, consciousness naturally gets pulled towards the Bindu Chakra, unlocking it in the process. Simultaneously, the Seventh Eye opens, whose auxiliary channel is crucial in sustaining the Kundalini circuit and creating a transcendental mind state. (More on the Seventh Eye later on.) One of Bindu's functions is to regulate the Light energy and distribute it throughout the Body of Light. It acts as an energy transformer and conductor. As this Light energy increases, your consciousness expands.

Once Bindu is fully opened, your consciousness has direct access to the realm of Non-Duality, the Spiritual Realm. This experience is accompanied by a feeling of complete Spiritual rapture in your Heart Chakra. You begin to intuitively feel what Jesus Christ meant when he discussed the Glory of God or the Kingdom of Heaven and the beauty of this magical realm that is the birthright of all human beings. The Bindu is our doorway into Cosmic Consciousness. Once opened, a constant feeling of inspiration enters your life. You begin to feel like you are living on Planet Earth, but emotionally you are in Heaven.

Once Bindu becomes unlocked in the Body of Light, it encourages the Sushumna, Ida, and Pingala Nadis to maximize their capacity to channel energy. The Kundalini Light now flows through these channels unimpeded, with more velocity than ever before, powered by the Bindu. Light energy powers the Chakras in the Aura, enabling you to attune to any of the inner Cosmic Planes or Realms of existence. These include the Physical, Lower and Higher Astral, Lower and Higher Mental, Spiritual, and Divine Planes. The Planes below the Divine Planes correspond with the Seven Chakras.

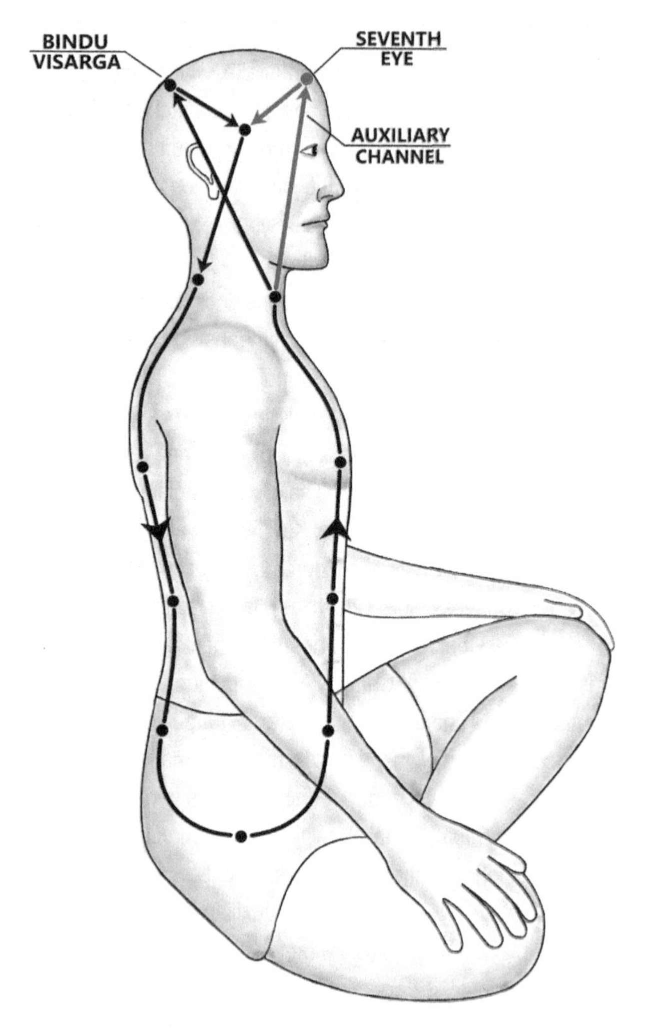

Figure 5: The Complete Kundalini Circuit

The Bindu is the release valve for the sublimated Light energy to channel into, which, when awakened, completes the Kundalini circuit. It unifies one's thoughts and emotions, allowing us to experience complete transcendence in consciousness. Its activation raises the vibration of our consciousness, aligning us with the Spiritual Body. The Bindu serves as a black hole for the individual consciousness. By entering it, we unite with Cosmic Consciousness and become One with the Universe.

Through the Bindu, your consciousness can easily leave your body when you become absorbed in any form of meditation. Once this occurs, you begin to channel thoughts from the Cosmic Consciousness. It is the realm of the Spiritual Plane since all thoughts and feelings are reconciled in the "Lake of Fire" which lies within it. This fire activates the "Glory of God" concept as a tangible emotion felt in the Heart Chakra and the physical heart. Figure 5 illustrates the movement of the Light, which is the Kundalini energy in its more sublimated state.

In the Hindu religion and Jainism, it is customary to wear a bindi, a coloured dot on the centre of the forehead. It implies the connection between the Mind's Eye (Ajna Chakra) and the Bindu Chakra. In essence, we reach the Bindu Chakra through Ajna, as is the case for Sahasrara Chakra. However, as mentioned, we cannot access the Bindu unless Sahasrara is fully opened since an alignment in one implies an alignment in the other. The Hindus call the Bindu a "point of creation," where all things are held together by Unity. They describe the bindi then as "the sacred symbol of the Cosmos in its unmanifested state."

ERADICATION OF MEMORY

After the awakened Bindu aligns your consciousness with the Spiritual Plane, the next phenomenon in the Kundalini transformation process is the streaming of random memories before your Mind's Eye. This occurrence results from the Bindu's intimate relation to Ajna Chakra and the Pineal Gland. Since the mind becomes silenced in the Spiritual Plane, it gives rise to old memories resurfacing for a brief moment, one after the other, like waves in an infinite ocean of consciousness. These memories can be recent, although they are usually from an older time, going as far back as your childhood.

The Self uses the Mind's Eye to experience these past memories that the Bindu produces. To be accurate, the Bindu "fishes" them out from the Causal Chakra, one of three Transpersonal Chakras above the head and one that has an intimate connection to the Bindu. The Fifth Dimensional energy of love influences the Bindu to release old memories, thereby removing the emotional charge that binds them to your Chakras. And as these memories stream across your consciousness, the psyche is being liberated, one memory at a time.

The visual component of seeing these random memories flash before you one by one is accompanied by an intuitional feeling of what the memories felt like as those events were happening. So, in a sense, you get to relive these experiences all over again. However, this time, your Self is in a neutral state, meaning that you are no longer psychologically affected or emotionally attached in any way to these occurrences. You are now operating from the realm of Non-Duality, meaning that the Ego and the mind are bypassed.

As you are discarding old thoughts and emotions through the Bindu, you may feel like you are losing your mind often because your Ego realizes its hold over the consciousness is weakening. However, this memory eradication process is normal and can often continue for a very long time. After all, it took the Ego many years to develop, and with each memory, it became stronger. Now the process is reversing, as you are reverting to your original, innocent state before the Ego started to develop.

Now, you can't abolish the Ego altogether while living in the physical body since it does serve the purpose of protecting your body from immediate harm. Jesus Christ, one of the most extraordinary Holy men to live on this Planet, lived with an Ego his entire life, guiding and commanding it. His second last sentence on the cross was, "My God, My God, why have you forsaken me?" (Matthew 27:46) This utterance came from his Ego, which came through in consciousness in the last moments of Jesus' life to petition God for help knowing that the physical body is about to perish. This statement was followed by, "It is finished." This is the last thing his Higher Self said before he died. Here is a perfect example of the dichotomy of Ego and Higher Self and how each can take over the consciousness at any point in time, depending on circumstances and irrespective of how Spiritually evolved we are.

So, you see, you can't destroy the Ego in this life. However, you can remove its clutches so that the Soul can take over the driver's seat and be your guiding force in life, including everyday decision-making. And since you are no longer plagued by fear by attuning to the Spiritual Plane, the Ego has nothing to bribe you with anymore. A big part of the Ego's functioning includes how it reacts to fear energy and the fictional yet scary scenarios that the mind creates, which the Ego seeks to prevent from happening. Another significant part of the Ego's modus operandi is enticing you with thoughts and desires of tending only to the pleasures of the body and your own needs and wants. However, since you are no longer bound to your body and recognize the oneness of all existence, the Ego has little power over you in this regard as well.

The Kundalini awakening experience will take you from Earth to Heaven in a single decade in most cases. As these subtle processes take place, trying to rationalize what is happening to you is futile. The same faculty you are using to rationalize things is being eradicated by the Kundalini Fire to enable you to start operating entirely on intuition. Memory seems to dissipate through this process, as does the impulse to rationalize and explain everything happening to you through logic and reason. Hence, the notions of "letting go" and "going with the flow" are part of the Kundalini transformation process. By questioning the process too much with your Ego, you will be impeding the flow of the Kundalini, in the long run, making your transformation take longer than it should.

Think of the analogy of what happens when you apply fire to water in the physical reality—you get steam or vapour. The Fire Element is the awakened Kundalini energy, while your memory belongs to the Water Element whose essence is pure consciousness. Expressing itself physically as your body's water content, the Water Element comprises over 60% of your Physical Self. The steam or vapour is the gunk, or harmful components of your Water Element, the memories of who you were or thought you were when these past events occurred. However, these memories are nothing more than illusions bound to your Karma, clouding your essence and preventing the inner Light from shining into the world. As time goes on, and the Kundalini Fire continues acting on the different Chakras, purifying them in the process, these old memories become extricated out of you. This Ego eradication is also a Soul cleansing process. After some time passes, you will begin to see waves and energy patterns in your Mind's Eye as visual images resulting from the impressions that your environment makes on you. To get there, though, many personal memories have to be purified. You may even see memories of past lives since this purification process is not bound to only this lifetime. Remember that the Soul, which we are trying to purify and exalt here, has existed for many lifetimes.

As consciousness withdraws more and more into the Bindu, you begin to lose awareness of your physical body to the point of becoming numb to sensations from the outside world. At a higher level of Spiritual Evolution, your consciousness leaves your body entirely, accompanied by a feeling of the physical body being injected with novocaine, a powerful painkiller and numbing agent. It reaches a point where, if you were to apply an ice pack onto the skin, you would not feel the cold but only a numbing sensation. High levels of histamine are released to accomplish this phenomenon. Once the major brain centres are opened up, higher dopamine and serotonin levels are released, contributing to an elated, blissful emotional state and super-human willpower.

This process of consciousness expansion is never-ending. You begin to live in this reality continuously as the Bindu gets increasingly fueled with Light energy brought in through food intake. As nutrients get absorbed by the body, the Kundalini Light being circulated inside your Nadis grows in size and speed of movement, perpetually expanding your consciousness unceasingly.

COMPLETE METAMORPHOSIS

You begin experiencing different physical sensations through the Kundalini transformation process. The first physical manifestation of these energetic changes is the feeling of ants crawling on the skin. Some people experience their body parts being zapped as the Seventy-Two Thousand Nadis, or energetic channels are being infused by the Pranic energy. A sensitivity to the air around you may develop, making you susceptible to getting a cold or flu. I have found that this phenomenon is dependant on whether the Air Element is dominant in your Natal Chart. Remember to keep warm to avoid getting sick if you begin to feel the cool air on your skin in a new way. You also might start to develop allergies as your sense of smell is heightened. You will begin to smell particular scents as if the object or person is in front of you, although, in reality, they might be miles away.

All of the processes I've outlined so far are interconnected. Together, they activate and develop the powers of the Body of Light so that the consciousness can gradually align to its vibration and experience Cosmic Consciousness. The Body of Light is like a tree whose branches (Nadis) reach out to the skin's surface from the inside. Its centre is in the Heart Chakra, Anahata, the central area of the body where multiple Nadis intersect. These branches serve as receptors that use the air around them as a medium or conduit for communication. They are antennae that connect with the invisible worlds, the Cosmic Planes I have mentioned previously.

Further growth of this energy tree occurs through feeding the physical body with the correct nutrients, vitamins and minerals. Protein is essential as it helps build up the Body of Light. Vitamin C is also critical as it helps regulate the Adrenal Glands, which get exhausted by the Kundalini awakening process. Fear puts a strain on the Adrenals, and as you are experiencing a catatonic crash, the *Dark Night of the Soul*, fear becomes greatly amplified. Therefore, it is vital to drink orange juice or other fruit juices which contain Vitamin C to avoid having the Adrenal Glands damaged permanently.

The Kundalini transformation process is such a shock to the Ego as it is dying off. As a result, there might be a tremendous amount of negativity that surfaces from your subconscious. If you had a complete and permanent Kundalini awakening, this process begins right away since it's the full activation of the Body of Light by the breaking of the Cosmic Egg that generates the beginning of a completely new life. At first, your new life is met with many unique challenges as you try to make sense of the process. Having the proper guidance is helpful as it allows you to "let go" from trying to control the process and allow things to happen to you naturally.

LIGHT AND VIBRATION INSIDE THE HEAD

After a full Kundalini awakening, in addition to Light energy now being present inside of your brain at all times (Figure 6), you will also experience a buzzing, vibratory sound. This sound is heard because the Kundalini energy is permanently localized in your head, meaning it doesn't move up and down your spinal column anymore, nor does it drop down to Muladhara. So what often sounds like the buzzing of a swarm of bees can also be described as the sound of an electrical current or radiation.

The vibratory sound can best be heard on the inside when the clamour of the outside world is quieted down. You will also notice that it becomes higher in pitch when you bring food into the body since your energy current increases.

The sound varies from its neutral state that sounds like the buzzing of a swarm of bees, to a more aggressive sound, like a jet engine, although not as pronounced. When it gets more dynamic or higher pitched, this indicates more vigorous Kundalini activity in the Body of Light.

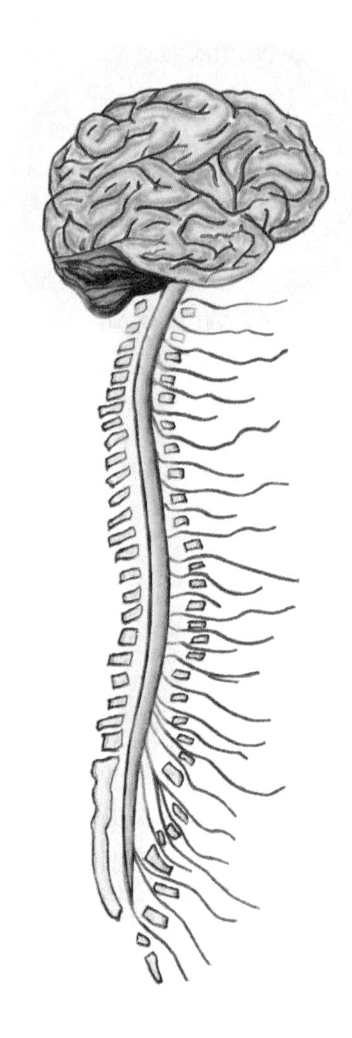

Figure 6: The Brain Filled with Light

Some awakened people have expressed concern about this permanent vibratory sound in their heads, saying it has made their lives rather uncomfortable. My advice is to learn to live with it instead of fighting it or hoping it goes away because it doesn't. It is a permanent part of your life now since it is the sound of the Kundalini energy inside of you. However, once you distance yourself from the Ego and align with your Soul more, you will accept the vibratory sound as part of the process and may even learn to enjoy its presence.

I have found that using earplugs when going to sleep allows me to use the sound to soothe and quiet my mind, enabling me to fall asleep quicker. It did take many years, though, to learn to let go and appreciate this sound but knowing that it is a natural part of the process and not some malicious foreign entity in your Aura is half the battle.

These two manifestations, the Light inside the head and the constant buzzing in the ears, mark a permanent awakening. Remember that the Cosmic Egg needs to have been blown open by the initial Kundalini rising and the Seventy-Two Thousand Nadis of the Light Body activated via its Ambrosia nectar. If this event has not occurred, then the full Kundalini activation did not happen. You may be dealing with a partial rising into individual Chakras, the most common of which is a rising into the Heart Chakra Anahata.

TYPES OF KUNDALINI RISINGS

A Kundalini awakening can occur in many different ways and for various reasons. The most common one is a spontaneous awakening through the use of recreational drugs or after having undergone severe trauma in your life. With trauma, a Kundalini awakening occurs as a defence mechanism once the Soul has had enough of the pain being caused in the body. The Soul hijacks the consciousness long enough to induce relaxation in the body. This total surrender, accompanied by a rush of positive emotions, can awaken the Kundalini energy, and it has for many people.

A less common method of awakening the Kundalini is through a transmission known as Shaktipat from a person who has had this experience themselves. The Kundalini can also be stimulated by studying religious and Spiritual books and understanding some profound truths about the nature of the Universe and God-the Creator. Put simply, for the Kundalini to be awakened, something has to trigger it. A trigger could be either a thought or an emotion, your own or somebody else's. Shaktipat occurs because of the power of an awakened master's thought and their ability to impart that thought into your subconscious.

Then there are Kundalini awakenings which occur as a result of direct Spiritual practice intended to awaken this energy. It can happen through Yogic practices, meditation, ritual exercises from various traditions, Tantric sex, and other Spiritual methods solely designed to awaken the Kundalini. These cases are less prominent in the world today, and most people that I have encountered have awakened the Kundalini spontaneously and not through direct practices with conscious intention. The performance of Spiritual healing practices, like the ones I will present later in this book, can raise the vibration of your consciousness long enough for the Kundalini to awaken. However, this again counts as an unplanned, spontaneous awakening.

Some people leave their modern, fast-paced societies and go to Temples and Ashrams and live in seclusion for many years in an attempt to awaken the Kundalini. Many spend a dozen years or more meditating and doing Spiritual practices to awaken this power, with no success. It is my personal belief that if you are meant to awaken the Kundalini in this lifetime, no matter how hard you try or don't try, it will happen to you. Essentially, this process will not require your effort, but life events will present themselves to you in such a way that will awaken this power. However, knowing the power and potential of the Kundalini energy, especially for those people reading about this subject for the first time, can develop the Soul desire that can be the catalyst to put this event into motion.

PARTIAL AND PERMANENT KUNDALINI AWAKENINGS

There are two types of Kundalini awakenings—permanent and partial ones. The difference between the two needs to be correctly understood to know where you are in your process of Spiritual Evolution so that you can know what to do to progress further.

In a permanent awakening, the Kundalini energy rises from the base of the spinal column (Muladhara Chakra), moving through Sushumna and into the brain until reaching the top of the head (Sahasrara). Along its path lie the Three Granthis, the psychic "knots" that obstruct the flow of the Kundalini. Each of them needs to be pierced systematically for a full awakening to occur. Since it forms part of the science and philosophy of Yoga and Tantra, I will discuss the Three Granthis in detail in the section dedicated to their practices.

If the awakened Kundalini rises with enough force, it will break the Cosmic Egg at the top of the head. Once the Cosmic Egg breaks, a nectar-like liquid substance, Ambrosia, pours over the body downwards from the top of the head, invigorating the Seventy-Two Thousand Nadis of the Body of Light (Figure 7). This constitutes a "permanent" awakening since the Kundalini never drops back down to Muladhara. Instead, it stays in the centre of the brain for the rest of your life.

In a partial awakening, however, the Kundalini never rises to the brain centre or at least doesn't generate enough power to untie the Three Granthis and rise to the top of the head to blow open the Cosmic Egg. Instead, the Kundalini energy drops back down to Muladhara only to repeat the process of rising in the future. The Kundalini wants to rise to the top of the head, and it will continue to attempt to do so until it unties all Three Granthis and achieves this goal.

Therefore, in a gradual or "partial" awakening, the Kundalini usually rises to a particular Chakra on its systematic upward movement. It does this to open that specific Chakra so that you can gradually work to purify the Karmic energy stored within it. In this case, there will not be a flood of negativity since the entire Tree of Life is not opened, only certain Spheres or Sephiroth of the Tree of Life. Therefore, this gradual or partial awakening is a more comfortable way to evolve Spiritually. However, there is no guarantee that the Kundalini will ever reach the top of the head in this lifetime.

Remember always that we cannot choose how we awaken the Kundalini. I wish I could tell you that a method works 100% of the time or even 10%, but I would be lying. So whoever tells you that they have discovered a technique that always works is fooling themselves and others, whether intentionally or not. My personal belief is that you cannot choose with your Ego to have this experience in this lifetime but that it must be a Soul decision.

It is even possible that we choose to have this experience before we incarnate on this Planet in this lifetime since it is such a radical shift from the average, everyday reality that unawakened individuals live in. As such, higher powers must be involved in the process of making a Kundalini awakening happen. However, the permanent Kundalini awakening is meant for everyone, whether in this lifetime or other lifetimes. As I said, knowing what to look for and preparing yourself for this experience is the first step—also, moving beyond the constrained social structures that keep our consciousness bound to the material reality.

If, after reading this book, you still prefer spending your time and energy on trying to get rich instead of working on furthering yourself Spiritually, then a Kundalini awakening may not be meant for you in this lifetime. There might still be necessary lessons to learn to see that nothing is as important as having this experience.

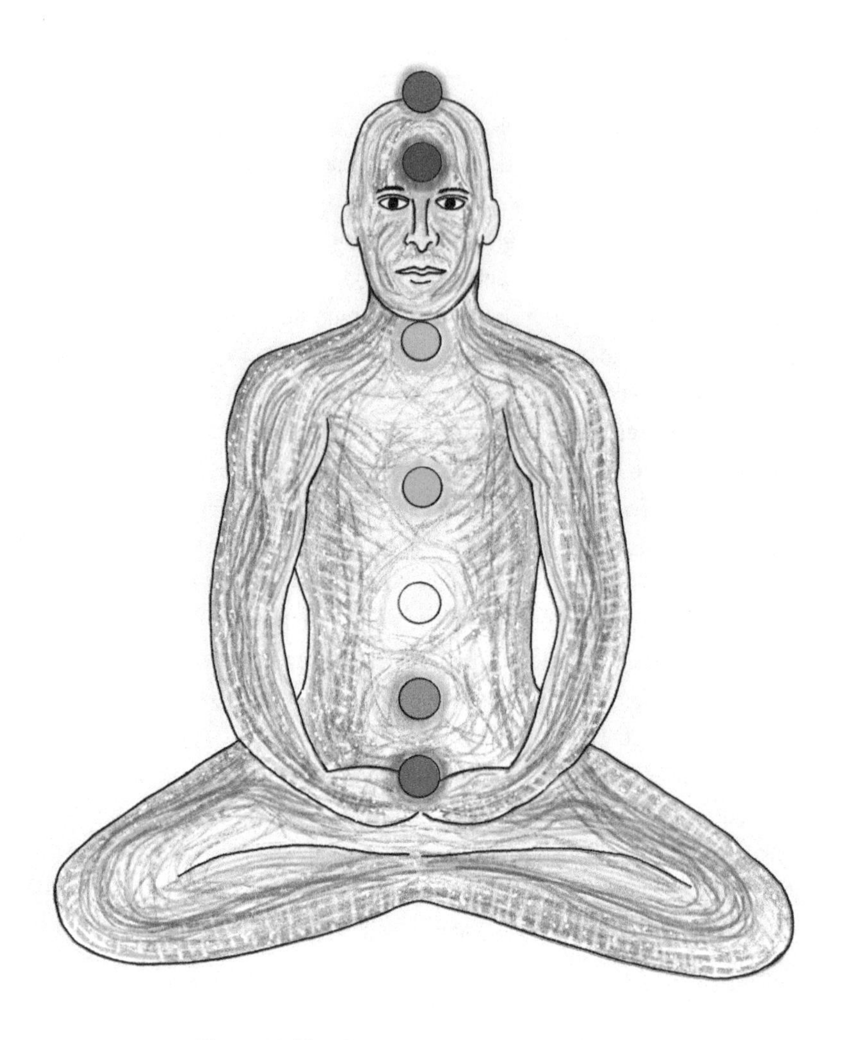

Figure 7: The Seventy-Two Thousand Nadis

The Hindus call this the process of Shakti (the Kundalini) rising upwards to meet Shiva (Cosmic Consciousness), where they consummate their Divine Marriage and become One. Once they unite in ecstasy, Shiva comes down into the Heart Chakra to produce the continual act of renewal within the consciousness of the Kundalini initiate. While in this perpetual, regenerative state, you become free from the burden of sin as you lose yourself within yourself. You become like an innocent child again, looking into the world with fresh, new eyes, from one moment to the next. This experience is what being in the "Now," the present moment, truly means. The Now is the field of pure, unlimited consciousness potential that can be experienced when you have released yourself from bondage to the material world.

SEEING THE LIGHT IN ALL THINGS

Once the energy finally reaches the top of the head and breaks open the Cosmic Egg, you will develop an extraordinary world experience. As the Light builds up inside of you, it transposes itself onto everything you see with your physical eyes, giving a shimmering, silvery glow or sheen to everything you perceive in the material world. When I unfocus my vision and stare at an object for ten seconds or so, this very Light will de-materialise that object right before my eyes.

In the same way someone might see the world on LSD or magic mushrooms, I see it without any drugs. It became a permanent part of my life after naturally developing the ability to perceive this Holographic reality, the Pure Energy blueprint or "double" of the material world. It exists right here and now, but because our bodies and brains are composed of Matter, we cannot perceive beyond it without completely transforming our consciousness.

Planet Earth is meant to be experienced with an awakened Kundalini because the fact is that the material world is alive and is Pure Energy. I remember how I saw things before this transformation, and I can safely say this is Planet Earth 2.0. It is almost as if I was given a permanent virtual reality headset to wear 24/7. This is what I was referring to when I said that the outer reality becomes "digital."

With a full Kundalini awakening, you also begin to feel the essence of everything you perceive in your Heart Chakra, Anahata. Once attained, this new experience of reality is a permanent transcendental change in how you experience the world around you. Once it happens, you can never turn it off again.

As I mentioned previously, however, not everyone sees Light in all things after a full Kundalini awakening. Most do not. The first person who corroborated this experience for me was not someone I spoke to personally but a renowned author on the topic of Kundalini, Gopi Krishna. Gopi talked about this phenomenon in his books, namely *Living with Kundalini*, which captured the essence of this gift. The book painted a solid portrait of the Kundalini awakening process and its manifestations and gifts, including this new visual lens that develops.

This phenomenon occurred in me five months after the initial Kundalini awakening in 2004 and is still with me today. This visual upgrade is not the only varied gift in Kundalini awakened individuals, though. However, it is the most crucial one, in my opinion, since it drastically changes your perception of reality and allows you to see the Holographic nature of the world, its digital blueprint, with your very own eyes.

I have even had moments in deep meditation when the outer world appeared like a 2D movie screen projection, whose surface was made of golden Light. The weirdness didn't end there, though. I was able to "scry" inside this vision and see parallel Universes that exist here and now but are imperceptible to normal human sight. (Scrying is a process of looking into physical objects using the Mind's Eye.)

I experienced this vision as a complete rapture that swooped up my consciousness. It came over me like a wave, and I became pure consciousness embracing it. These parallel world visions often transported me to medieval times for some reason, only to a much smaller scale than our present time world. It made me understand that parallel worlds exist here and now within the 2D beam of Light coming from the Sun. Once I could alter my inner vibration, I could see them with my very eyes.

Imagine having this ability and being reminded every waking moment that the world you live in is made of pure energy. It makes it very easy to disassociate with the Ego and prioritise the Spiritual life, which I did and never looked back.

Because of the intensity and force of the Kundalini energy as it surged through my spinal column during the awakening process, it blew open my Mind's Eye exponentially before rising to the top of the head. This event occurred because I was performing a mental visualisation exercise utilising the Mind's Eye during the awakening process. Gopi was doing the same as recounted in his books. By focusing attention on the Mind's Eye tunnel, our doorway into the inner Cosmic Planes, the Kundalini enters it upon rising, expanding its circumference before rising to Sahasrara. The Mind's Eye tunnel is doughnut-shaped, serving as a mental screen that visual images play on when experiencing visions.

It is possible that if you do not implement a visualisation exercise that brings attention to the flower head of Ajna Chakra (between the eyebrows), the Kundalini doesn't fully activate its power. In this case, the Kundalini does reach Sahasrara and may even blow open the Cosmic Egg, but the full potential of Ajna Chakra is not awakened. This is one option. The other option is that Ajna does open but not with enough intensity that it causes this radical shift in visual perception.

Of course, these are my theories, but ones based on logic and reason since many people who report having had the Cosmic Egg blow open and the feeling of being "electrocuted" don't see Light in all things afterwards. Whatever the case, let it be known there are varied Kundalini awakenings and experiences, and not all are the same.

KUNDALINI AWAKENING FACTORS

When attempting to awaken the Kundalini energy directly, many factors must be working together at the same time to be successful. For one, if you are trying to awaken it through mindfulness meditation, the vibration of your willpower must be substantially higher than your mind chatter for you to induce silence. Thus, it is unlikely you will awaken the Kundalini with this method unless you have been doing it for a long time and are proficient in it.

A simpler approach is to use a visualization meditation instead. You are to hold an image of a symbolic object (such as a lotus flower or a God or Goddess statue) in your Mind's Eye for an extended period. By holding a constant and steady image in your mind, your willpower begins to vibrate at a vigorous intensity, pulling your consciousness inwards. If you can hold this image while neglecting the random thoughts that come into your head, you will have some level of Spiritual experience and maybe even awaken the Kundalini energy at the base of your spine. At the least, you will enter the Mind's Eye portal to experience the Astral World, which can be an exhilarating experience if you have never done this before.

Now, if the image you are holding in your mind has a sexual component, it is possible to stir the Kundalini into activity at the base of the spine. Sexual energy is essential in this regard since any kind of sexual excitement, when projected inwards, can activate the Kundalini. I had heard of many cases of spontaneous awakenings that occurred after the individual experienced a higher-than-normal level of sexual excitement while maintaining a pure and silent mind.

A Kundalini activation can occur when sexual energy is sublimated and channelled into the brain upon climax instead of being released externally by ejaculating. A visualization meditation during sexual activity focuses energy inwards, towards the Mind's Eye in the brain. It can cause the Kundalini to awaken and rise up the spine, systematically blowing open all lower Chakras until it enters the brain. However, to ensure that it rises with enough force, it is crucial to be performing some kind of visualization exercise to pull the Kundalini into the brain, where it can rise to the top of the head and complete the process.

The key to this process is to generate raw sexual energy with a pure mind and heart, thus stimulating Muladhara and Swadhisthana Chakras into activity. When done correctly, you will feel sensations in your abdomen that are both euphoric and ecstatic. Your whole body will begin to tremble and shake, and you may even get goosebumps from how pleasant these sensations feel.

The sexual energy has to build on itself and get stronger with merely the power of your thoughts. Most people are unaware that sexual excitement can grow exponentially, and it doesn't always have to result in an external orgasm. When trying to awaken the Kundalini, the key is to channel the sexual energy inwards using your willpower and imagination instead of expelling it through your genitals.

During my Kundalini awakening, I was holding an image in my mind of a beautiful and erotic woman, which I focused on so intensely that I projected into the Mind's Eye portal and could experience her as real. However, what generated the intense force with which the Kundalini awakened was the buildup of sexual energy as I made love to her in my mind. This sexual energy amplified and grew in power until I experienced my first internal orgasm. However, the experience didn't end there. Another internal orgasm followed it, and multiple more, all in succession with increasing intensity and velocity. My genital area felt like a locomotive speeding up and building momentum with every turn of its wheels.

A feeling of sexual excitement in my abdomen grew exponentially in synchronicity with the internal orgasms. They came in continuous rushing waves for about fifteen to twenty seconds. Then, at their peak, when it felt like my brain and body couldn't take any more ecstasy, the Kundalini awakened at the base of the spine. It felt like a golf-ball-sized sphere of energy that just appeared out of nowhere.

COMPLETING THE KUNDALINI AWAKENING PROCESS

Once the Kundalini awakens, it naturally travels upwards through the spinal column. However, if you awaken the Kundalini spontaneously, without a meditative practice, it will likely not reach Ajna Chakra. As I mentioned, to rise with force, which is necessary to reach Ajna Chakra inside the brain, it is essential to consciously hold an image in your mind with willpower and imagination. Note that spontaneous Kundalini awakenings that occur from the use of hallucinogenic drugs can be powerful since they involve a change in perception that stimulates the Mind's Eye.

A complete awakening requires that the Kundalini rises into the brain through Sushumna, the middle channel, accompanied by Ida and Pingala, which fuse into one energy stream at Ajna Chakra. Once they have joined their masculine and feminine energies, they unite with Sushumna as One to rise to Sahasrara and blow open the Cosmic Egg (Figure 8) which holds the potential of your Body of Light, your Cosmic Self.

Sahasrara can potentially be opened with Sushumna alone. However, if Ida and Pingala don't join forces at Ajna, there could be debilitating problems in the energy system that can wreak havoc on your thoughts and emotions. Such is the example of Gopi Krishna's initial rising, where he awakened Pingala and Sushumna but not Ida. His nervous system was in complete disarray after the awakening since he didn't have the cooling energy of Ida present, which caused ongoing anxiety with no end. After almost losing all hope, he tried a visualization meditation in a desperate attempt to awaken Ida. Because Ida represents the feminine principle, the essence of the Water Element that is the source energy of all visual images, Gopi finally succeeded in awakening Ida, which rose to Ajna to complete the Kundalini awakening process.

It is essential to understand that Sushumna Nadi always accompanies Ida or Pingala or both simultaneously, which is the desired option. Ida, Pingala, or both can't rise into a Chakra without Sushumna being present since the Sushumna Nadi carries the Kundalini energy. Ida and Pingala channel the feminine and masculine energies, but the Kundalini rises up the spinal column, which is the Sushumna Nadi.

Before Kundalini can enter the brain, it must pierce Vishuddhi, the Throat Chakra. Vishuddhi is more advanced than the lower Chakras since it is the first Chakra of the Spirit Element. To pierce it, one must have evolved past major Karmic energy of the lower Elements, which correspond with the lower four Chakras. (More on the connection between the Elements and Chakras and Nadis in a later chapter.)

If you have awakened the Kundalini through meditative means, I advise you to continue performing your meditation instead of just letting go once you feel the Kundalini rising. Doing so is the key to gathering enough force for the Kundalini to pierce Vishuddhi Chakra on its upwards rise and then enter the brain to try and complete the process.

To awaken the Thousand Petalled Lotus of Sahasrara, the three Nadis of Sushumna, Ida, and Pingala have to unify into one energy stream in the middle of the brain in the Third Ventricle before rising to the top, centre of the head. Once the Lotus begins opening like a flower in bloom, the Cosmic Egg atop the head gets pierced by the Kundalini. However, the Lotus does not have to open fully for the Cosmic Egg to break. If the Kundalini rises with enough force, the Cosmic Egg will break right after Sahasrara begins opening. Then, the Ambrosia nectar from the Cosmic Egg is released, which pours over the body from the top-down, activating the Seventy-Two Thousand Nadis of the Body of Light.

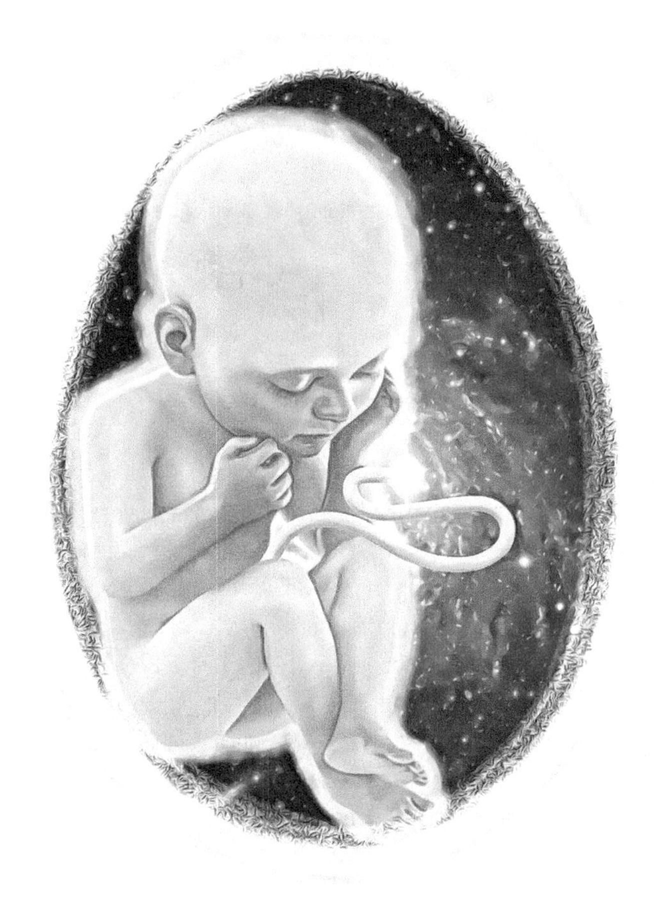

Figure 8: The Cosmic Egg

So you see, having a full Kundalini awakening requires some conscious effort on your part to complete the process. Most spontaneous awakenings are partial Kundalini risings. My case is one of those rare situations where the Kundalini awakened with incredible force, but only because I was unknowingly performing a Tantric sex meditation with a sexual visualization component. Because I had such an intense Kundalini awakening seemingly by accident, I always considered myself blessed and obligated to share everything I have learned and experienced with the world.

It is crucial to understand the Kundalini awakening process and memorize its mechanics. There are many differing viewpoints on this topic from people that experienced this event. However, I have found that a small percentage of those people completed the process and raised the Kundalini to Sahasrara. And even fewer still broke open the Cosmic Egg and activated the Body of Light. Then there are those who activated the Body of Light but don't report seeing Light in all things with their physical eyes, which tells me that they did not have a full Ajna Chakra activation. So you see, there are many varied experiences of this same Universal process.

I can generally ascertain what type of Kundalini awakening someone had from listening to their experiences and comparing reports. Generally, the ones that did not complete the Kundalini awakening lack the knowledge of the final part of the process. For example, most people know that the Kundalini awakens the Chakras and seeks to expand the consciousness. However, in my experience, most people are unaware of the existence of the Cosmic Egg, the Body of Light activation (which results in the feeling of being electrocuted), and especially the remodelling of the brain to perceive a higher level of reality through an expanded Ajna Chakra.

By memorizing the entire Kundalini awakening process, you are giving your mind a road map of how this event can occur for you. Sharing this information is one method to help you awaken the Kundalini yourself and complete the process.

ALIGNING WITH THE SPIRITUAL BODY

Although it feels as if the Kundalini activation is happening in the physical body, it is taking place in the Body of Light. As I discussed in *The Magus*, we are all born with the Body of Light, inextricably tied to our physical body. However, we need to fully activate its powers in this lifetime to optimize our energy system, which can only be achieved by awakening the Kundalini and raising it to the Crown.

When the Kundalini begins to rise upwards, awakening the Chakras, your consciousness recognizes the existence of the Body of Light, allowing it to embody the different Subtle Bodies that correspond with the Chakras that you awakened. The full activation of the Body of Light is one of the primary purposes of the Kundalini awakening. The Seventy-Two Thousand Nadis serve to make the Body of Light an antenna to the vibrations of the outside world. These vibrations are received through the highest of the Subtle Bodies, the Spiritual Body. Your consciousness gradually attunes to it after it has cleared the Karmic energy of the lower Four Chakras. To accomplish this, it must systematically embody the Subtle Bodies that correspond with those Chakras.

When your consciousness attunes to the Spiritual Chakras, the highest three, it will align itself entirely with the Spiritual Body, which becomes its new vehicle. When this occurs, you will discard old modes of functioning and function through intuition alone. Being in this state does not mean that you will not feel anything emotionally or won't be able to use logic. It only means that intuition will become your primary mode of functioning.

You will perceive the world around you through direct energy experience since your Being will be elevated to the First World of Atziluth, representing the Spiritual Plane in the Qabalah. (More on this in the next chapter.) Atziluth is where the thoughts of God exist, the Archetypes that give humanity a template to work with, uniting our reality. Since

Creation is a systematic process, your conscious experience of life's events filters downwards into the lower three Worlds (there are Four Qabalistic Worlds in total) that evolve out of the First World.

By aligning your consciousness with the Spiritual Body, thoughts and emotions will no longer have the same impact on your mind and body because they are expressions of the Lower Planes. And since you are now elevated to a Plane above them, you get to overcome their harmful effects. Of course, you will still have negative thoughts and emotions since your Ego is forever tied to the physical body, but you will bypass their energetic effects. Instead, your Soul will interpret negative emotions as learning lessons rather than allowing them to take over your consciousness and weigh it down. As a result, what you experience will be fleeting and in the moment. Also, you will be able to use logic and reason and think intellectually, without binding yourself to the Ego and associating with it like before.

The Cosmic Egg breaking after the Kundalini reaches the Crown signifies the complete, permanent awakening. Within this context, permanent means that the energy does not fall back down to Muladhara, the Root chakra. Instead, it stays in the brain. Symbolically, Kundalini Shakti and its consort Shiva, the Cosmic Consciousness, will have united in a Spiritual Marriage. This is the Eastern viewpoint of the Kundalini awakening completion.

From the Western Mystery Tradition's view, you will have received the wings of the Caduceus of Hermes by completing the Kundalini awakening process. You will become a prototype of the God Hermes, who is called Mercury by the Romans. It means that you will have inherited his winged helmet and winged shoes. Symbolically, this means that you will have your head in the sky (Heaven) and your feet on the ground (Earth). Your consciousness will always be in "flight" mode, and you will have a natural high, almost like you are gliding through Space and Time. These sensations are what it feels like to have expanded consciousness.

Once you have completed the Kundalini awakening process, over time, you will develop a connection with your Holy Guardian Angel (HGA), who will become your guide and teacher in life. Thus, you will have become a God-human whose transcendental consciousness will continue to live on past this life and into the next.

YOUR NEW LAMBORGHINI VENENO

The activation of Ajna is essential to have the complete Kundalini experience. I have already described some of the gifts associated with this phenomenon. Other gifts include the ability to view yourself from outside of yourself and live in a permanent Out-of-Body Experience. However, the latter is more so a manifestation of the awakened Sahasrara Chakra. As you see yourself and the world around you from a higher perspective, you will realize that Cosmic Consciousness is not just a concept or idea, but a real thing indeed.

I hope I have done a good job introducing the Kundalini, the awakening process, and some of the more incredible Spiritual gifts that unfold. Though, by using words to describe the transcendental experience of reality after a full Kundalini awakening, I feel I am limiting how extraordinary it really is. Like Morpheus says in The Matrix, "No one can be told what the Matrix is. You have to see it for yourself." In the same fashion, you need to experience this for yourself to understand the big picture. But for now, my words will have to suffice.

A Kundalini awakening transforms the mere human into a Demi-God, a modern-day superhero, in one lifetime. Only, your newly received powers are generally not something you can prove to others, but you live and embody the truth of what you become. Over time, through your expanded knowledge and your kind deeds towards humanity, you may be recognized as a Being of Light and its emissary. But to get there, many years will have to pass, and many challenges overcome.

The key takeaway from this introduction to the Kundalini is that although there are various ways to awaken this energy, the process will always be the same. However, without a proper understanding of the process, it's like being gifted a Lamborghini Veneno, a 4.5-million-dollar sports car, but not getting its instructions manual nor having any driving experience. My attempt in *Serpent Rising: The Kundalini Compendium* is to write the manual for this invisible Kundalini science of energy to the best of my ability. And once you have the instructions and blueprints, I want to give you insight into how to drive your new Lamborghini. To be precise, if your current vehicle of consciousness can be likened to an old Ford Focus, then this upgraded vehicle is an Intergalactic spaceship. So, again, I say Lamborghini so people can relate.

I am grateful to the Universe for having had the Kundalini awakening, as anyone in my position would. I also believe that luck had nothing to do with it, and my Soul chose this for me before I was even born. It is not a coincidence that I was given specific skills and abilities in this life that would serve me on this Spiritual journey. Due to my obsessive nature and the need to find the Spiritual tools to help myself early on, I have developed an exceptional understanding of the Kundalini over the years. My experience and research on this topic are unprecedented. My journey has led me to assume the role of messenger to the people about the existence of the Kundalini energy and the potential of Ceremonial Magick in aiding the Spiritual transformation process.

My work aims to serve my Creator and fulfil my mission to impart knowledge to others walking in the same shoes I was many years ago when I was groping in the dark for answers. We are all warriors in training on this path of Spiritual Evolution, and our purpose is to evolve and collectively raise the consciousness of the Earth. By sharing what I know, I aim to pass on the tools you will need if and when your new Lamborghini breaks down and you need guidance.

And for those times when others turn to you for guidance, you will know how to help them also because you were helped. And for those of you who haven't yet received your new Lamborghini, now you will learn about it, how it works and drives, and will know what to look for consciously. As the old saying goes, "Seek, and ye shall find. Knock, and the door will be opened unto you." But if you don't know what to seek or which door to knock on, the Universe will not know how to help you. Knowledge is the most significant power in the Universe.

***

This completes the introduction to the Kundalini and the awakening process in general. Now I want to segue into other pertinent subjects to give you an inside look at how your energy system operates; its components, mechanics, and how it interacts with the physical body. This next portion of the book is devoted to the Kundalini science of energy. It includes the critical chapter on human anatomy describing the changes that occur in the physical body during and after a Kundalini awakening.

PART II: THE MICROCOSM AND MACROCOSM

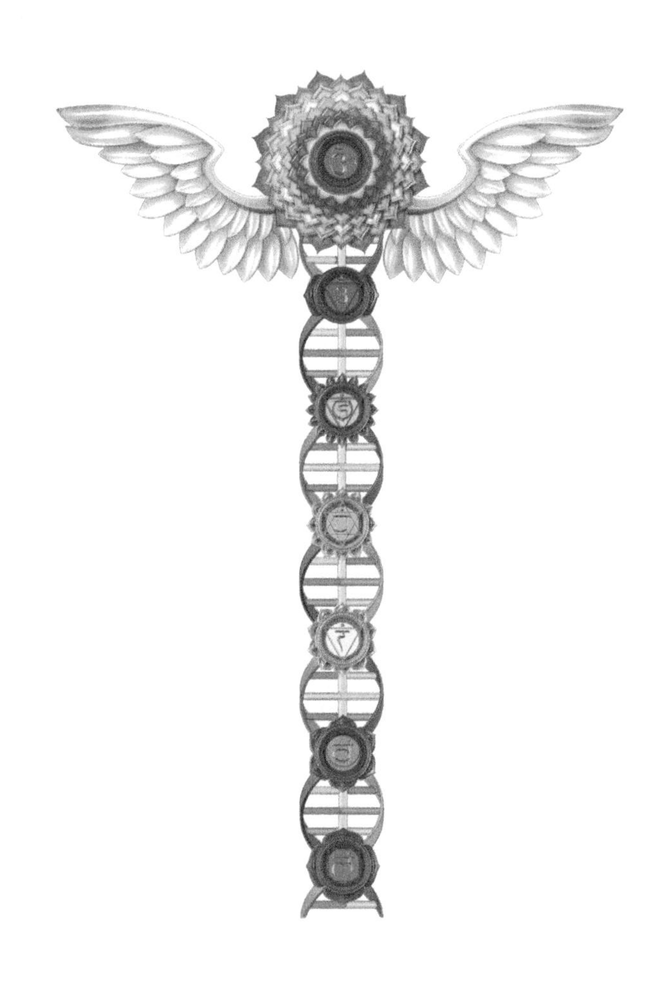

THE FIVE ELEMENTS

Classical Elements refer to Earth, Water, Air, Fire, and Spirit. Ancient cultures such as Greece, Egypt, Persia, Tibet, India, and Japan considered the Classical Elements as the building blocks of the Universe. They used the concept of Elements to explain manifested Creation's complexity and nature in simpler terms. Their lists of the Elements and sequence of manifestation varied slightly but held the same meanings. The Spirit Element was interchangeable with Aethyr, Ether, Void, Akasha, and Space, depending on the tradition. (Note that Aethyr or Aether is just the Latin spelling for Ether.)

The Chinese Wu Xing system is slightly different since it describes various types of energy in a state of constant flux and interaction with one another, referred to as the "Five Phases" of natural phenomena. The Five Phases of Wu Xing are Wood, Fire, Water, Metal, and Earth. The Chinese Elements are seen as ever-changing and moving, while the Classical Elements are separate from one another even though they are parts of a whole.

The Ancients postulated that the outside Universe (Macrocosm), including the energy composition of every human being (Microcosm), consists of the Five Elements. The Five Elements correspond with the Seven Chakras (Figure 9). They comprise our Aura and the Cosmic Planes and Subtle Bodies that our consciousness partakes of.

The first four Chakras correspond with Earth, Water, Fire, and Air, while the three higher Chakras correspond with Spirit. The Chakras, in turn, compare with the Sephiroth on the Tree of Life in the Western Mystery Tradition. Their correspondence is complex and not as apparent as many Spiritual teachers believe, but the relationship is there. For a thorough exposition on the Sephiroth and the Five Elements, consult *The Magus: Kundalini and the Golden Dawn*.

Understanding how the Elements operate is an essential pre-requisite for Advanced Yogic practices, many of which are presented in this book. In the Eastern Spiritual system, the Five Elements correspond with the Tattvas, which will also be explored in *Serpent Rising*.

The Five Elements are the basis of Yoga and Ayurveda (Sanskrit for "knowledge of life"), which is traditional Indian holistic medicine developed around the same time as Yoga (approximately 3000 BC). Ayurveda is based on the three constitutions, or Doshas—Vata, Pitta, and Kapha. Vata is the energy of movement (Air and Spirit), Pitta is the energy of digestion and metabolism (Fire and Water), and Kapha is the energy that forms the body's structure (Earth and Water). Every person has a unique balance of the Elements within them and, therefore, a unique Dosha. The Elemental dominance found in a person's Western Astrology Birth Chart, especially as per their Sun, Moon, and Rising (Ascendant) Signs, often determines their Dosha. However, one should analyze their Vedic Astrology Birth Chart to obtain a correct diagnosis, as is done traditionally in Ayurveda. (More on Ayurveda and the Three Doshas in the Yoga section.)

The Five Elements also relate to the five senses: Spirit, or Aethyr, is the medium through which sound is transmitted; thus, the Spirit Element corresponds with the ears and hearing. The Fire Element is related to the eyes and the sense of sight since fire manifests Light, heat, and colour. The Air Element relates to the nose and the sense of smell, while the Water Element is related to the tongue, the organ of taste. And finally, the Earth Element is associated with the skin and the sense of touch. This information is essential when exploring Spiritual Healing practices since the application of each one requires using one or more of the senses to impact the consciousness.

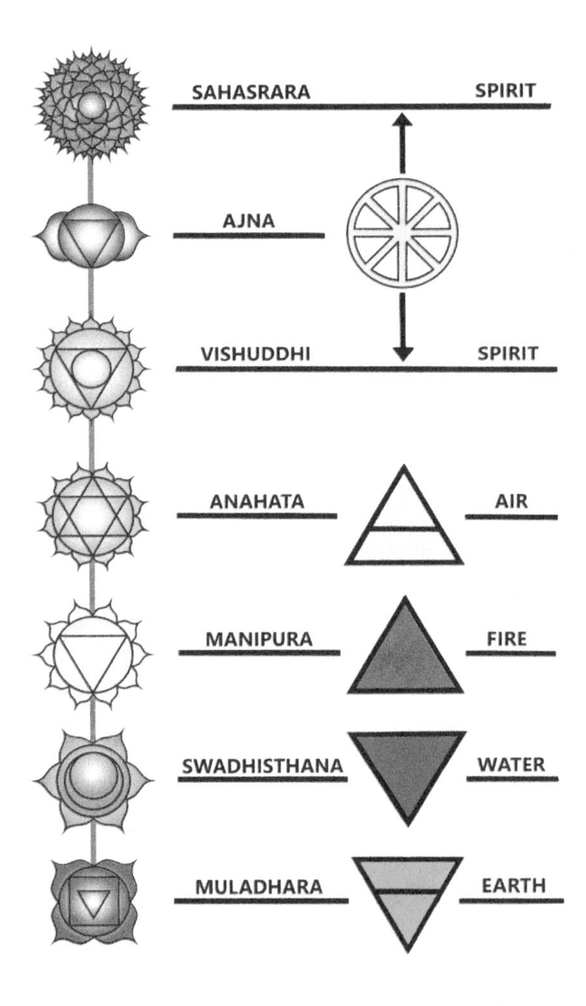

Figure 9: The Five Elements and the Seven Chakras

By purifying and balancing the Elements within ourselves, we attain and maintain good health and raise the vibration of our consciousness. All Spiritual practices essentially aim at this goal. Whether performing a Ceremonial Magick Spiritual Alchemy Program (as presented in *The Magus*) or performing Yogic practices regularly, the goal is always Spiritual Evolution.

Hermetic Qabalah and the science and philosophy of Yoga state that the Microcosm is the direct reflection of the Macrocosm, and vice versa—As Above, So Below. In *The Kybalion*, this concept is called the Principle of

Correspondence, a Universal Law or truth underlying all existence. All Spiritual traditions are built around this Law, and they all contain some Solar or Lunar element to them, representative of the Masculine and Feminine Principles of Creation.

On a basic level, the Principle of Correspondence implies that the Microcosm, the human Aura (our energetic composition), finds its reflection in the Macrocosm—the Universe and, more particularly, our Solar System. (This concept works the other way around as well.) We all carry Planetary and Zodiacal energies within ourselves. Balancing them and rising in consciousness is the "Great Work" of the Alchemist, referring to our undying quest to unite our consciousness with the Cosmic Consciousness of the Creator—it is our pursuit of Enlightenment.

THE PENTAGRAM

The symbol of the Pentagram, or "Five-Pointed Star," has been around since the time of Ancient Babylonia and Greece. In Western Esotericism, the upright Pentagram (Figure 10) is called the "Star of the Microcosm." When the Pentagram is inscribed in a circle, it is called a Pentacle, used mainly by Wiccans. According to Pythagoras, five is the number of the human being. Each of the five points of the Pentagram represents one of the Five Elements of Earth, Air, Water, Fire, and Spirit, as symbolized by the legs, arms, and the head.

Figure 10: The Pentagram

The Pentagram's magical associations make it a potent ritualistic symbol used to invoke the power of the Five Elements, notably in Ceremonial Magick and Witchcraft. It is also used as a religious symbol by Modern Neo-Pagan faiths and the Freemasons. When the Pentagram is oriented upright, it stands for the Spirit presiding over the Four Elements and is, therefore, a symbol of Light, love, and the Higher Self. The upright Pentagram attracts Angelic forces while serving to protect from Demonic ones. As such, it is used in White (Light) Magick.

Interestingly, the upright Pentagram was a Christian symbol long before modern Neo-Paganism adopted it. It represented the five wounds of Jesus Christ on the Cross of the Four Elements and the daily self-sacrifice necessary to achieve the upright Pentagram, symbolically, which causes the Spirit Element to descend into the Four Elements and completely transform the consciousness.

When the Pentagram is inverted, it has opposite magical associations. An inverted Pentagram represents the Four Elements commanding the Spirit, symbolizing darkness and Ego dominance. This symbol invites Demonic energies while repelling the Angelic ones, making it a fitting symbol for Black Magick practices (the Dark Arts), which uses supernatural powers for evil and selfish purposes.

Satanists use the inverted Pentagram as a symbol of their faith. They refer to this symbol as the "Sigil of Baphomet"—the goat-headed God associated with duality, materialism, and the Carnal Self. Many Satanists are Atheists who don't believe in the afterlife and only value this lifetime. Hence, they argue that the inverted Pentagram is not a symbol of evil but one that aligns them with the types of energies that will help them achieve their goals in life. However, if you believe that this life is just one in a continuous chain of lives that your immortal Soul experiences, aligning yourself with dark forces to satisfy your Ego's desires is catastrophic for your Spiritual Evolution.

THE FOUR WORLDS AND THE PENTAGRAMMATON

Although this is a condensed version of two significant lessons from *The Magus: Kundalini and the Golden Dawn*, it is worth mentioning again since it sums up the entire Kundalini awakening process and its purpose from an occult perspective. In *The Torah* (*The Old Testament*), the name of God is Jehovah, whose esoteric name is the Tetragrammaton (YHVH), which means "four letters" in Hebrew. (Keep in mind that the Hebrews read and write right to left.) The four Hebrew Letters stand for the Four Elements—Yod (Fire), Heh (Water), Vav (Air), Final Heh (Earth). The Four Elements are found in the four lowest Chakras, while the Fifth Element, Spirit, represents the higher three Chakras. As you can see, in the Tetragrammaton, the Spirit Element is absent. There is a reason for this.

The four letters of the Tetragrammaton also represent the Four Worlds of the Qabalah—the Qabalistic model of the Creation and manifestation of the Universe (Figure 11). The Qabalistic Four Worlds make up the entirety of the Tree of Life: Yod (Fire) represents Atziluth, the Archetypal World, Heh (Water) stands for Briah, the Creative World, Vav (Air) is Yetzirah, the World of Formation, and Final Heh (Earth) is Assiah, the Physical World. The Four Worlds directly relate to the Cosmic Planes. However, in the Qabalistic framework, the World of Primal Fire (Atziluth) represents the Spiritual Plane, while the other three Elements relate to the Mental, Astral, and Physical Planes, respectively.

You will notice that the Cosmic Planes correspondences omit the Spirit Element from the Four Worlds model; Qabalists believe that we lost connection with the Spirit Element after the Fall from the Garden of Eden. As such, it is something that we must obtain in this lifetime. However, the method of achieving this feat is given in the mystery of the Pentagrammaton.

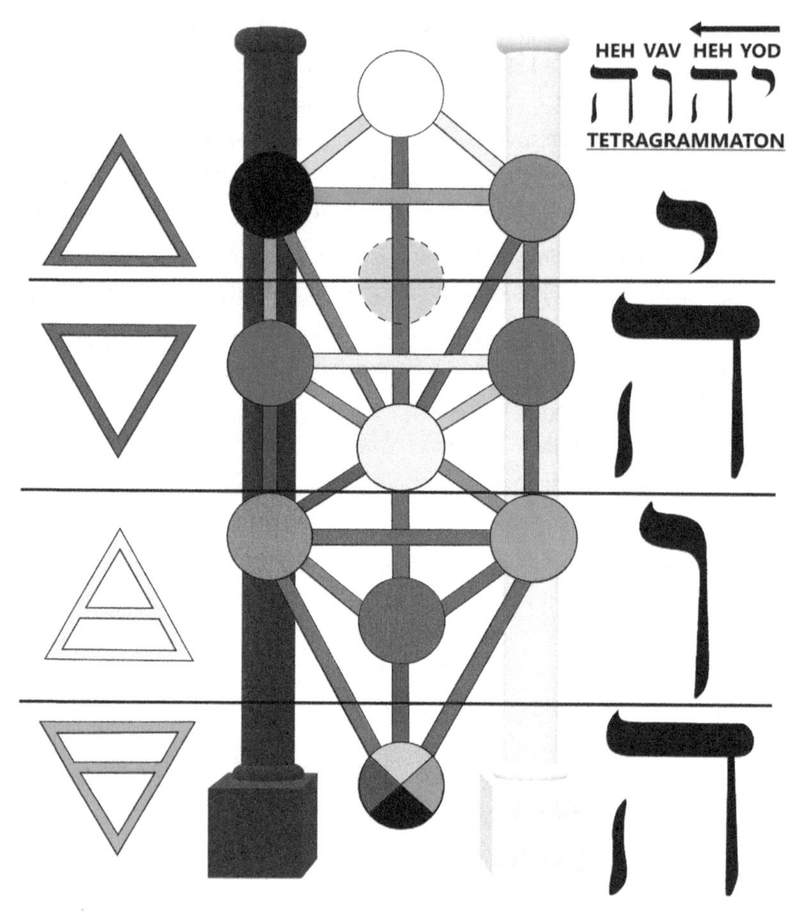

Figure 11: The Four Worlds and the Tetragrammaton (YHVH)

The Pentagrammaton (YHShinVH), meaning "five letters," implies the integration of the symbolic Hebrew Letter Shin (Figure 12), referred to as the "Three-Fold Flame of the Soul." Shin contains three strokes that visually resemble the three main Nadis of Ida, Pingala, and Sushumna that rise along the spine during a Kundalini awakening. The Nadis, in turn, correspond with the two intertwining snakes around the central staff of the Caduceus of Hermes.

When placed amid the Tetragrammaton, Shin reconciles the opposing masculine (Fire and Air) and feminine (Water and Earth) energies within the Self. It represents the Judgement Tarot Card whose Tree of Life path is called the "Spirit of the Primal Fire." This card alludes to the awakening of the Holy Spirit and its integration within the Self. Shin's Fire of consecration burns away impurities over time, an allusion to the Kundalini Fire's lengthy purification process once awakened.

The Pentagrammaton is also the occult key to the Christian mysteries since it represents the name of Jesus Christ, according to Renaissance occultists. Jesus's English name is derived from the Classical Latin "Iesus," based on the Greek form of the Hebrew name Yahshuah (Yeshua), usually translated as Joshua. Yahshuah, however, is spelt YHShinVH, which is the Pentagrammaton. The Pentagrammaton also connects us with the five wounds of Jesus and the Kingdom of Heaven we reach in consciousness when we have sacrificed ourselves, our Egos, and have integrated the Spirit Element.

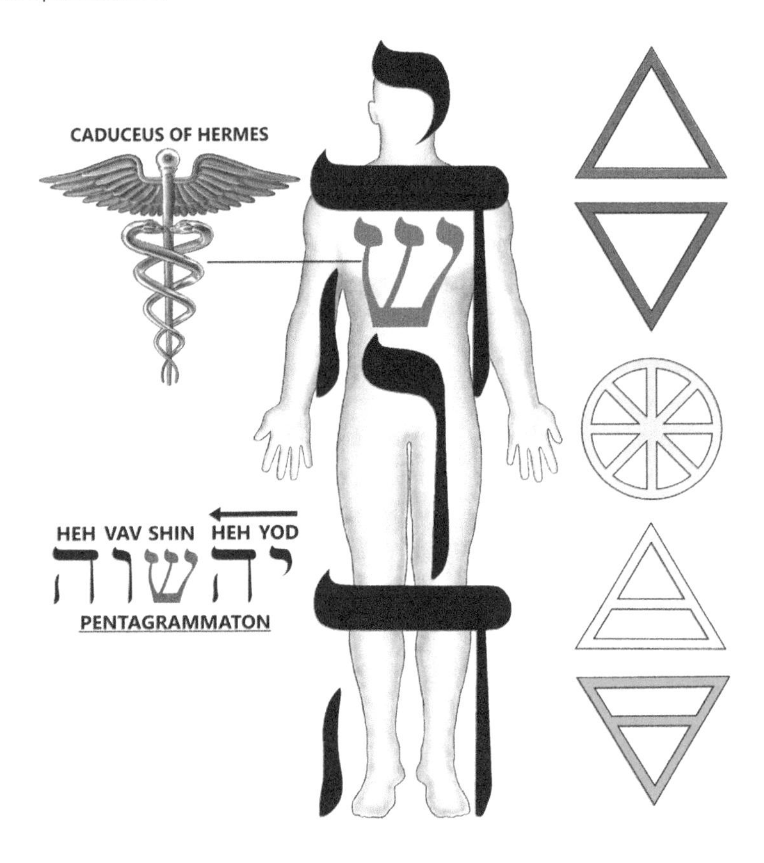

Figure 12: The Pentagrammaton (YHShinVH)

So you see, Jesus Christ was the prototype of the Kundalini awakening process; he represents God-the Creator's Divine Love and the expanded consciousness that enables us to partake of the Spiritual and Divine Realms. While in *The Old Testament*, humanity was in a fallen state Spiritually, in *The Holy Bible* (*The New Testament)*, Jesus brought the Holy Spirit into the world so that all who believe in him and follow his example can become Resurrected or Reborn Spiritually and attain Eternal life.

Spiritual Rebirth can only truly be attained when we embody Jesus' teachings, whose foundation is unconditional love being the guiding force in our lives. One doesn't have to be a Christian to appreciate the Spiritual value of such a mindset. We find historical examples cross-culturally of Yogis, Saints, Adepts, Sages, and others who became Enlightened through humility, piety, and ethical conduct towards their fellow humans. This includes people like Mahatma Gandhi, Mother Teresa, Martin Luther King Jr., the Dalai Lama, Swami Vivekananda, and others.

It is a fact that if you devote yourself to cultivating only loving thoughts and actions, fear will leave you entirely, allowing the impulse of your Ego to fall away, which will prepare you for a Kundalini awakening. Hateful, selfish, dishonest people can never awaken the Kundalini energy, no matter what method they use and how hard they try. The Soul must be readied for such an experience, which we can only achieve by becoming loving, honest, and just.

Whether you are Christian, Muslim, Jewish, or Buddhist, it does not matter; the process of salvation is Universal. Therefore, instead of waiting for some *Deity* to save you according to whatever religious scripture you believe in, you must be your own Messiah (Saviour) by assuming the role of Jesus, metaphorically speaking. You are all Gods and Goddesses by birthright, but you need to awaken and raise the Kundalini to the Crown, thereby infusing the Divine Light into your Chakras to optimise your energetic potential.

THE ELEMENTS IN NATURE

Everything you see before your eyes consists of Spirit energy. Hence, the Spirit Element is termed "Space" in the Eastern Yogic and Tantric tradition—the idea of physical space being all around us and extending out infinitely in all directions. Spirit vibrates at the highest frequency of vibration; hence, it is invisible to the senses. It interpenetrates all of physical Matter as the base energy that comprises all of it.

During the creation of the Universe, the high vibration of the Spirit Element began to slow down, manifesting sequentially as the four primary Elements of Fire, Water, Air, and Earth. All created things retained the Spirit energy in its state of potential—meaning that the Spirit is found within all things in existence, as are the other Four Elements. Other than the Physical Plane of Matter, which is visible to the senses and represents one aspect of the Earth Element, the other Elements are invisible but can be accessed through consciousness.

The four primary Elements are divisions of nature and the foundational energy of everything in the Universe. However, the Four Elements are not technically four, but three; since the fourth Element of Earth is the composition of the three foundational Elements in their densest form. Therefore, Earth and Spirit are alike in many ways but exist at opposite ends of the vibratory scale. The three fundamental Elements are Water, Air, and Fire.

The Planet Earth represents the gross aspect of the Earth Element. In the Qabalah, we refer to our physical existence on Planet Earth as Malkuth (the Kingdom), which includes the land we walk on. Through Malkuth and our corporeal senses, we can experience the physical manifestation of the other three Elements: the oceans, seas, rivers, and lakes (Water), oxygen-containing air (Air), and finally, the Sun (Fire) as our primary source of Light and heat.

Each of the Five Elements represents a state of Matter. For example, Earth constitutes all solids (including food), Water is all liquids, Air is all gaseous substances, and Fire relates to combustion or flame, which has the power to transform states of Matter. For example, water can change into a gas (steam) through fire application, which turns back into water, and then ice (solid) if fire/heat is withdrawn long enough.

We require all the Elements for survival. The Sun is our heat source; without it, we would freeze. Water and food give our bodies sustenance; without them, we would die in a matter of days (water) or weeks (food). Breath (air) is the evidence of life, and without oxygen, we could not survive for more than a few minutes. Finally, we have Spirit, or Space, the Void representing darkness, emptiness, and vastness, that serves as the basis for all Spiritual experiences.

Many Ancient systems regard the Four Elements as inner Realms and Kingdoms which we can access through Spiritual practices, some of which are explored in this book. Understand that you are working with the Five Elements whenever you work with the Seven Major Chakras. The Spirit Element is the only one that corresponds with more than one Chakra since its scope is greater than the other Four Elements. As such, we can only explore the Spirit Element through multiple Chakras.

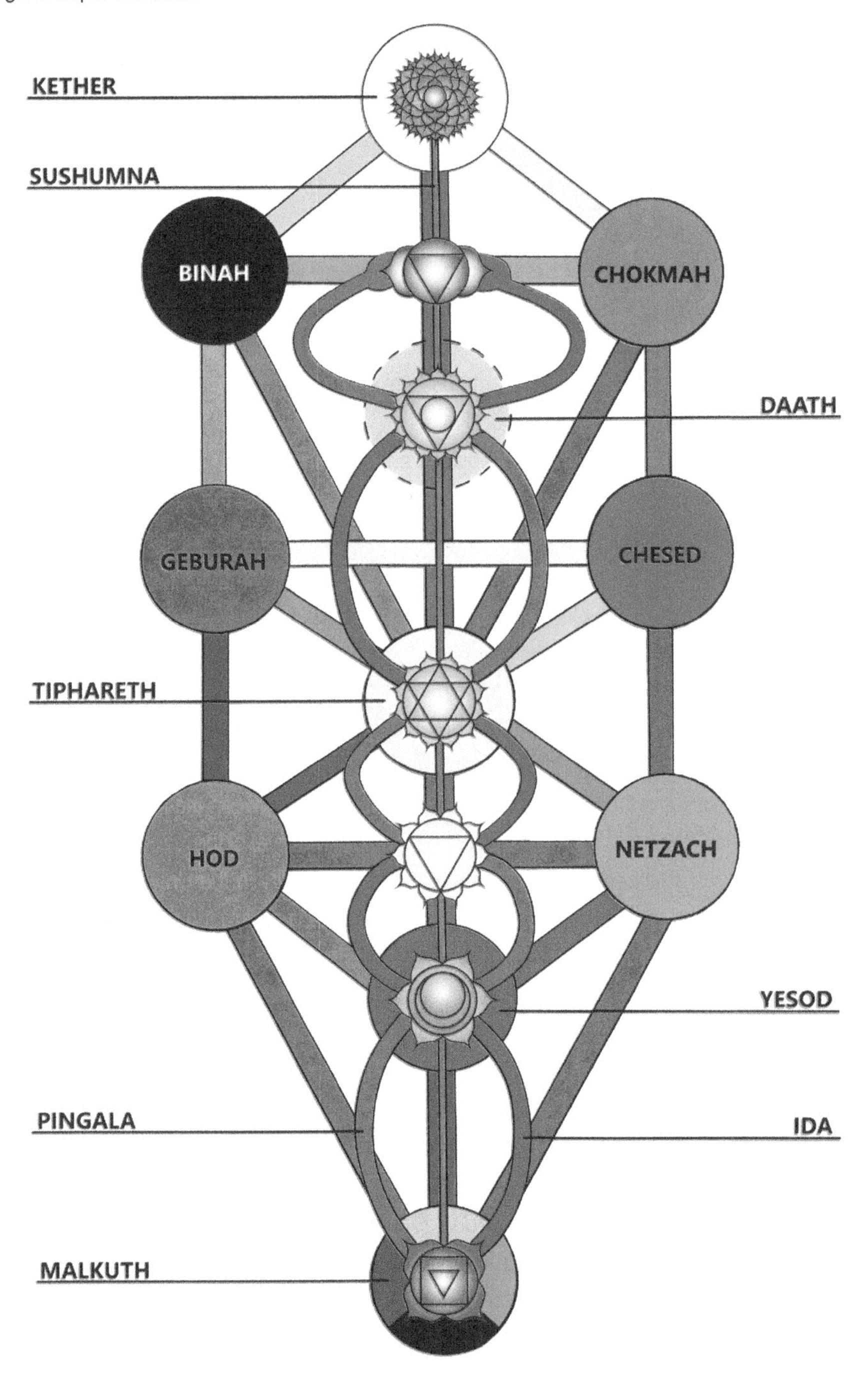

Figure 13: The Tree of Life Sephiroth and the Three Nadis

THE SPIRIT ELEMENT

Spirit is the *Prima Materia*, the First Substance and the Source of all things in existence. It is not technically an Element in and of itself but is the composition of the sum of the Four Elements—it is the building block, the medium, the glue which holds them all together. As mentioned, since all things in the Universe came from Spirit, all things will eventually re-absorb back into Spirit, in due time. For this reason, we seek to Spiritually evolve and reunite with our Creator's mind—it is an innate desire within us to do so.

The English word "Spirit" comes from the Latin word "spiritus," meaning "breath." This correlation between the two words tells us that there is a correspondence with the Spirit energy and the act of breathing the oxygen-containing air around us, a physical manifestation of the Air Element.

All living beings who breathe to sustain their lives require this continuous process of bringing Spirit into their bodies. Thus, breath is evidence of life. For this reason, breathing techniques (called Pranayama in Yoga) are essential in all Spiritual disciplines. In addition, controlled breathing facilitates meditation, which raises the vibration of our consciousness to experience higher Cosmic Planes.

Aethyr is another name for Spirit in Ancient traditions and modern physics. Aethyr represents the formless and invisible medium or substance that permeates the Cosmos. In *The Magus*, the Aethyrs are a succession of thirty Inner Worlds through which we can explore the Elements within ourselves.

The Spirit/Aethyr/Space Element is attributed to the Throat Chakra (Vishuddhi), the Mind's Eye Chakra (Ajna), and the Crown Chakra (Sahasrara). All three Spirit Chakras are expressive of the Spiritual Plane. In the Qabalah, the Spirit Element represents the Supernals—the Spheres of Kether, Chokmah and Binah, which sit atop the Tree of Life. The Spirit Element also includes the upper part of the Sphere of *Daath*, the invisible eleventh Sphere, corresponding directly with the Throat Chakra. (Consult Figure 13 as reference for the Tree of Life Sephiroth and their relation to the Chakras and three Kundalini Nadis.)

Daath is called the "Abyss" in the Qabalah as the separation point between the lower seven Sephiroth's duality and the Non-Duality of the Supernals. The only duality that exists at the level of the Supernals is Chokmah-the Father and Binah-the Mother. Chokmah and Binah are the sources of all duality in the Universe, as the Force and Form components, Soul (Fire) and Consciousness (Water). These two Sephiroth are the source of the Primal Elements of Fire and Water, although at the level of Spirit (Fire of Spirit and Water of Spirit). Kether is the White Light that contains these two dual aspects, which is also the Air Element source (Air of Spirit).

The three Spheres of Kether, Chokmah, and Binah work as a whole. Chokmah receives its Archetypal energy from Kether, and Binah transforms those Archetypal ideas into Form. The Christian equivalent of the Supernals is the Trinity—the Father, the Son, and the Holy Ghost (or Spirit). The concept of the Trinity is at the root of all Spiritual traditions, although under different names. For example, in Hinduism, the Trimurti (Sanskrit for "three forms of trinity") represents the triple Deity of Supreme Divinity—the Cosmic expression of Creation (Air), maintenance (Water), and destruction (Fire). Again, we see the three foundational Elements in action, although in a different sequence. Air is always at the top of the pyramid, although Water and Fire might be interchangeable.

Daath corresponds with the Throat Chakra, Vishuddhi. As Daath represents knowledge and the purpose of our voice box (larynx) is to generate the vibration (pitch and volume) in our vocal rods, verbal communication expressed through language links us to the Creator.

The *Book of Genesis* says, "In the beginning was the Word, and the Word was God, and the Word was with God" (John 1:1). Therefore, the Word is our connection to God. As such, the practice of Mantras involving the use of Words of Power and vibrating our voice box in a deep tone is one way to connect with our God-given powers and attune our consciousness to Higher Realms. Since Spirit is the unifying factor of the other Four Elements, the Throat Chakra, Vishuddhi, represents the synthesis of the Four Elements into Spirit, expressed through communication.

The sixth Chakra, Ajna, is concerned with psychic sight (clairvoyance)—the ability to see visual images Astrally, on an inner level. These messages are often projected from Divine and Spiritual Worlds and give us the gift of precognition, the ability to predict events before they happen. Since Ajna's psychic gift is inner visions, it is called the Third Eye, or Mind's Eye. (More on the importance of Ajna Chakra and its vision portal later on). Ajna is directly linked to Chokmah and Binah since, through this Chakra, we access both of these Spheres.

Ajna Chakra is the seat of the intuition, our highest inner faculty of perception. Intuition allows us to read the energy around us directly instead of using our intellect or emotions. It gives us a sense of knowingness, although it doesn't reveal precisely how we know what we know. Intuition also allows us to access inner guidance from Divine Worlds as it links us to our Holy Guardian Angel, who resides in the Chokmah Sphere. Ajna enables us to cut through illusion, access deeper truths, and see beyond the mind and words. It allows us to experience the Archetypal energy behind the images.

The seventh Chakra is the Crown Chakra, Sahasrara, at the top of the head. It is the highest of the Major Chakras and their culmination. Sahasrara is the source of the Spiritual energy and the Great White Light, which pours into the lower Chakras, thereby powering them. The beginning point of our Transpersonal Self expresses through our Transpersonal Chakras above the head and below the feet. Sahasrara is our connection to the Divine Source of all of Creation and the Spirit Element's highest expression—it represents unity and the reconciliation of opposites since it is the Chakra of Oneness.

Qabalistically, Sahasrara Chakra corresponds with Kether-the Crown as the beginning of the Three Veils of Negative Existence, also called *Ain Soph Aur*. Sahasrara is the meeting point between the Finite and the Infinite—it is beyond Time and Space as it is Eternal, meaning it always existed and will continue to exist until the end of time.

Although the top three Chakras are of the Spirit Element, only Sahasrara is Non-Dual. Ajna is our mind's vehicle to reach the Crown, while Vishuddhi connects to the Spirit energy through the spoken Word. Ego consciousness reaches as high as Vishuddhi, although it loses itself entirely in Ajna because of Ajna's connection with Sahasrara. Below Ajna, we experience fear and suffering, while above it, we transcend the Ego. Through transcendence, we access states of bliss that accompany the Spiritual experience, which is incomprehensible to the ordinary person who mainly occupies their mind with Ego desires.

THE FIRE ELEMENT

The Fire Element purifies and transforms all things that are no longer useful to our body, mind, and Soul. All new things come out of Fire, as old things are consumed by it—Fire is a powerful cleanser since it burns up impurities.

The Fire Element is the Masculine Principle and the Father (Chokmah) energy—the Soul. In Alchemy, the Soul and the Fire Element refer to *Sulfur*, one of the three Principles in nature. Fire represents Force and willpower, and it is the closest of the three foundational Elements to Spirit. The active part of the Self relies on the Fire Element—it represents the conscious mind and vitality, confidence, creativity, and courage.

The Fire Element is the third Chakra, Manipura, located in the Solar Plexus. Due to its location and type of energy, it is related to the digestive and metabolic processes in the body. The Fire Element represents combustion within the World of Matter, manifesting both heat and Light. It brings about transmutation, regeneration, and growth through the application of heat.

The Fire Element's Qabalistic correspondence is the *Geburah* Sephira, whose Planetary attribution is Mars. The Fire of Geburah is one of will-power and drive. The Fire Element is also expressed through *Netzach* as desire and passion, which are powered by the Fire Element. Desire is often instinctual and involuntary, such as sexual or sensual desire. On the other hand, passion usually involves creativity and is something that we have control over.

The Fire Element also stimulates and powers intelligence; hence, it expresses also through the *Hod* Sephira—as the strength of mind (fortitude) in the face of fluctuating emotions. Intellect and reason are the willpower's driving force at the lower levels, while the Soul is the driving force at the higher levels.

Manipura is expressive of the Higher Mental Plane, right below the Spiritual Plane. It has direct contact with the Spirit Element and the Supernals. When Spirit energy descends into Manipura, the willpower is exalted as it becomes motivated by unconditional love.

Fire is dynamism and motivation, the cause behind the effect. Fire is the focused willpower that powers the thought behind every consciously induced action—it requires its opposite (Water) as a barometer and an impetus for action. A person uses their willpower either out of Self-love or unconditional love for all of humanity. Therefore, Fire and Water Elements exist as a duality regarding one another, whether in the body or mind.

People whose Fire Element is inactive have low personal power and no real control over their lives. Other people do their thinking for them, and they lack the raw energy to manifest their life's desires. In contrast, people with an abundance of the Fire Element have the necessary power to manifest their dreams. They are confident and attract their Soul's desires, including choosing their romantic partners and not merely settling for whatever comes their way.

Manifestation requires the application of the Fire Element, which is filtered through the Earth Element. There are a back-and-forth action and reaction, continually occurring between the Fire and Earth Elements when your Soul is your guiding force. Conversely, when your Ego is the guiding force, the willpower becomes hijacked, and your Earth Element draws its primary energy from the Water Element's involuntary emotions instead.

The Air Element is needed to fuel both Fire and Water, and your thoughts can serve your Soul or your Ego. Your Free Will determines who you are choosing to serve since you cannot attend to both your Soul and Ego simultaneously.

Fire Element, much like the Spirit Element, expresses through the other three Elements. It is the highest of the Four Elements in scope and demands our utmost attention.

THE WATER ELEMENT

The Water Element is the Feminine, Mother Principle; the Yin to the Fire Element's Yang. Thus, the Water Element relates to Form and consciousness, as the Fire Element relates to Force and Soul. These two exist in a symbiotic relationship with one another. In Alchemy, the Water Element relates to the *Mercury* Principle.

As the fluid energy of consciousness, the Water Element also relates to the Sephira Binah, the Astral, or invisible blueprint of all solid bodies in the Universe. On an inner, human level, the Water Element comprises our feelings and emotions. It is the passive, receptive part of the Self—the subconscious. Water (H2O) consists of the hydrogen and oxygen molecules that sustain material life physically. All aquatic life also relies on oxygen in the water to breathe.

The Water Element is the second Chakra, Swadhisthana (Sacral), located between the navel and lower abdomen. Swadhisthana is expressive of the Higher Astral (Emotional) Plane. Emotions are primarily concerned with expressions of love in one's life, including the love of Self and love of others. The Water Element's Qabalistic correspondence is with *Chesed*, whose Planetary attribution is Jupiter. Chesed is the expression of unconditional love, mercy, and altruism, all of which are the Water Element's highest expressions.

Since it is related to emotions, the Water Element encompasses other Sephiroth on the Tree of Life, the same as the Air Element (thoughts). Since the Sphere of Netzach is the form of lower, more instinctual emotions, such as lust and romantic love, the Water Element expresses through this Sphere as well. Netzach corresponds to the Planet Venus and desire, which is felt as an emotion tempered by the Fire Element.

The Water Element also powers the logical, reasoning mind of Hod, as Hod and Netzach work to complement one another. Hod corresponds to Mercury, and therefore in this aspect of the Water Element, it works in combination with the Air Element and thoughts.

The Water Element is also related to sexual energy and instincts found in the Moon, corresponding with the Sphere of *Yesod*. As you can see, the Water Element encompasses multiple middle and lower Sephiroth of the Tree of Life, as do the Air and Fire Elements.

The Water Chakra's overall human lesson is learning to love without attachment, through the Soul. You must transform your lower love emotions into higher ones by allowing your Soul to lead the consciousness instead of the Ego.

THE AIR ELEMENT

The Air Element is the offspring of the Fire and Water Elements as the next stage of manifestation. As the offspring, the Air Element represents the Son energy. For humanity, Air is associated with the intellect and the logical mind. Thinking and thoughts, just like the air around us, are rapid, quick to change, and without Form.

As the Fire Element is related to action, Air is associated with communication. Like the Fire Element, Air is of a masculine quality, representing activity and energy, but on an inner, mind-level. Air supports all of life through the act of breathing the oxygen-containing air around us. Within the physical reality, the Air Element makes up the Earth's atmosphere as a mixture of gases.

The Air Element corresponds with the fourth Chakra, Anahata (Heart), located between the two breasts in the chest's centre. Anahata is also the central Chakra in the Seven Major Chakras model, separating the three Spirit Element Chakras above, with the three lower Elemental Chakras below. In the Cosmic Planes model, Anahata is expressive of the Lower Mental Plane, which separates the Water Element below and Fire Element above. As such, the Air Element interacts most with these two Elements psychically.

Qabalistically, the Air Element corresponds with the Sphere of *Tiphareth* (whose Planetary attribution is the Sun) and the Sphere of Yesod (which is attributed to the Moon). As part of the Supernals, the Air Element is attributed to Kether as the creative energy.

Tiphareth is our source of imagination, which requires one being in a constant act of creation, an expression of the Air Element. Tiphareth is the centre of the Tree of Life, as it receives all the other Sephiroth energies, except for Malkuth-the Earth. Malkuth is reached through Yesod-the Moon. The Air Element has a dual nature. It can be deceptive like the Moon, or expressive of the truth, like the Sun. Truth is received and perceived through intuition.

As the Earth Element Chakra (Muladhara) is about stability, the Air Element Chakra (Anahata) is about its opposite—thoughts. Since thoughts are comprised of an ethereal substance, they belong to the mind. All living beings use thoughts to navigate their reality since thinking breathes life into the Fire and Water Elements within the psyche. Fire represents willpower, while Water represents emotion and love. One can have neither though without Air, since thought powers them both. Before you can accomplish anything in this world, you must first have thought of doing that thing. Thus, thought is at the root of all of Creation, whether for humans or other animals.

Air also directly correlates with the Element of Spirit/Aethyr and the Supernals. The Air Element is the balancer of all things mental, emotional, and Spiritual. As such, it is directly linked to Kether, the source of the Spirit energy.

Hermeticists argued that although animals have feelings and imagination, only humans have logic and reason, which they referred to as "Nous." Nous is a faculty of the mind that is the building block of intelligence, powered by the Air Element. In the Qabalah, the Sphere of Hod is linked to the intellect directly. However, in the instance of Hod, Air is tempered by the Water Element.

Air is also connected to the Element of Fire and emotional thought or impulse. Thus, Air directly correlates to Netzach—emotions and desires. A well-functioning mind means that the individual is well balanced in the Element of Air.

THE EARTH ELEMENT

The Earth Element represents the Three-Dimensional World, the material expression of the Universal energy. During the Creation process, the Earth Element was manifested when the Spirit has reached the lowest point of density and frequency of vibration. As such, it represents all solids that have mass and take up space, a term we call "Matter." Earth is the synthesis of the Fire, Water, and Air Elements in their most dense form and the container of those Elements on the Physical Plane. In Alchemy, the Earth Element relates to the *Salt* Principle in nature.

Earth represents movement and action; we require Earth energy to perform any physical activity. On an energetic level, the Earth Element represents grounding and stability. An adequate dose of Earth energy is needed to manifest what is in our minds and hearts; otherwise, our mental and emotional energy remains in the inner Cosmic Planes.

Within the physical reality, Earth is the organic and inorganic compounds of our Planet. It represents growth, fertility, and regeneration concerning Gaia, Planet Earth, the Mother that nurtures our bodies. The terms "Mother" and "Matter" sound the same and share similar meanings. Similarly, the Water and Earth Elements have a close relationship as the only passive, receptive Elements. Earth is the material expression of the Astral World, represented by the Water Element.

The Earth Element is Muladhara, the Root Chakra, corresponding Qabalistically to the Sphere of Malkuth. Muladhara is expressive of the Lower Astral Plane, which is inextricably connected with the Physical Plane as the connecting link. Therefore, Muladhara is the first Chakra whose location (between the tailbone and perineum) is closest to the physical Earth.

The Earth Element's expression in our psyche is always related to our connection to the material world. Some of the more mundane aspects of the Earth Element include having a job and owning a home and a car. Anything and everything related to money and ownership of material goods is an expression of the Earth Element. Too much of the Earth Element results in being overly materialistic and greedy, which takes away from one's Spiritual energy.

Earth is the opposite of Spirit—as the Spirit uses the energy of Fire, Water, and Air on a higher level, Earth uses those three Elements on a lower, denser level. Earth energy seeks to provide us with the things we need to make our material, physical existence happy and content.

However, as the Hermetic axiom states, "As Above, So Below"—Kether is in Malkuth, and Malkuth is in Kether. God is in everything we see before us and within us—the Spirit energy interpenetrates all of existence. Therefore, Earth Element directly links to Spirit since Spirit embodies the Earth. Spirit requires the Earth Element to be enabled to manifest reality in the World of Matter. When the Spirit manifests through the Soul, the outcome is fruitful, while when it works through the Ego, the result yields negative Karma.

The Earth Element focuses on satisfying our basic physiological needs vital to our survival, such as shelter and the need for air, water, food, and sleep. Physical exercise is also essential, as is the quality of the food and water we bring into our bodies. The Earth Element also deals with procreation and our desire for sexual relations. The Earth Element's energy quiets our minds and offers us the fuel to tackle our daily physical activities whose purpose is to keep us moving forward in our Earthly existence.

THE COSMIC PLANES

The Kundalini transformation process begins as a blazing, volcanic fire, which burns away the dross and impure in the different Subtle Bodies of the Self. Each Chakra has a corresponding Subtle Body, which the newly activated Body of Light moulds into since Light is an elastic substance. Your consciousness then embodies these different Subtle Bodies to experience their corresponding Cosmic Planes of existence or manifestation. Your Soul experiences the Cosmic Planes through the mind since it is the mediator between Spirit and Matter. It acts like a receiver that can tune into these different Cosmic Planes.

It is essential to understand the concept of the Soul, what it is and how it is different from the Spirit. The Soul is the individual spark of Light that we all carry inside us. The Ancients say that the Soul comes from the Sun. For this reason, they call the Sun "Sol," which is the origin of the word "Soul." A Kundalini awakening liberates the Soul from the physical body to travel in these inner Cosmic Planes of existence. The Soul is the highest part of the expression of who you are as a Divine spark from the Sun. Whether the Soul is particular only to this Solar System is left for debate. In theory, since all the Stars channel Light energy, the Soul might be that which can travel from one Solar System to another and manifest in an organic body on a different Planet.

The Spirit is the highest essence of the Divine energy and is the blueprint of all things in existence. Spirit is the "thought stuff" of the Divine or Cosmic Mind, which projects the known Universe. Therefore, the Spirit is the animating substance of all things, and it is Universal, while the Soul is individual and particular for each human being. The Soul is a Fire while the Spirit is above the Four Elements of Fire, Water, Air, and Earth as their synthesis—consciousness. The medium of consciousness is the mind and brain, while the medium of the Soul is the heart. The Spirit is that in which both the Soul and the mind have their existence.

It may be somewhat complex to understand these distinctions truly, mainly because the word Spirit and Soul are tossed around in our society haphazardly without a clear definition of what each means and how they are different. Most people generally seem to think they are the same thing. The Ancients have done their best to define both Soul and Spirit, but since the average person of today's day and age is at a lower level of Spiritual evolution, the collective understanding is not there yet. Therefore, I hope this very basic definition of each will help you understand the difference better.

As you are progressing through the Kundalini transformation process, your Soul will gradually enter the different Cosmic Planes of existence systematically and integrate those experiences into your psyche. You can also induce particular mental states through Ceremonial Magick ritual techniques, which invoke one of the Five Elements of Earth, Air, Water, Fire, and Spirit, as well as the Sub-Elements of each. These ritual exercises will allow you to access the Cosmic Planes directly since the Five Elements correspond to the Chakras. Consult *The Magus: Kundalini and the Golden Dawn* for these ritual techniques.

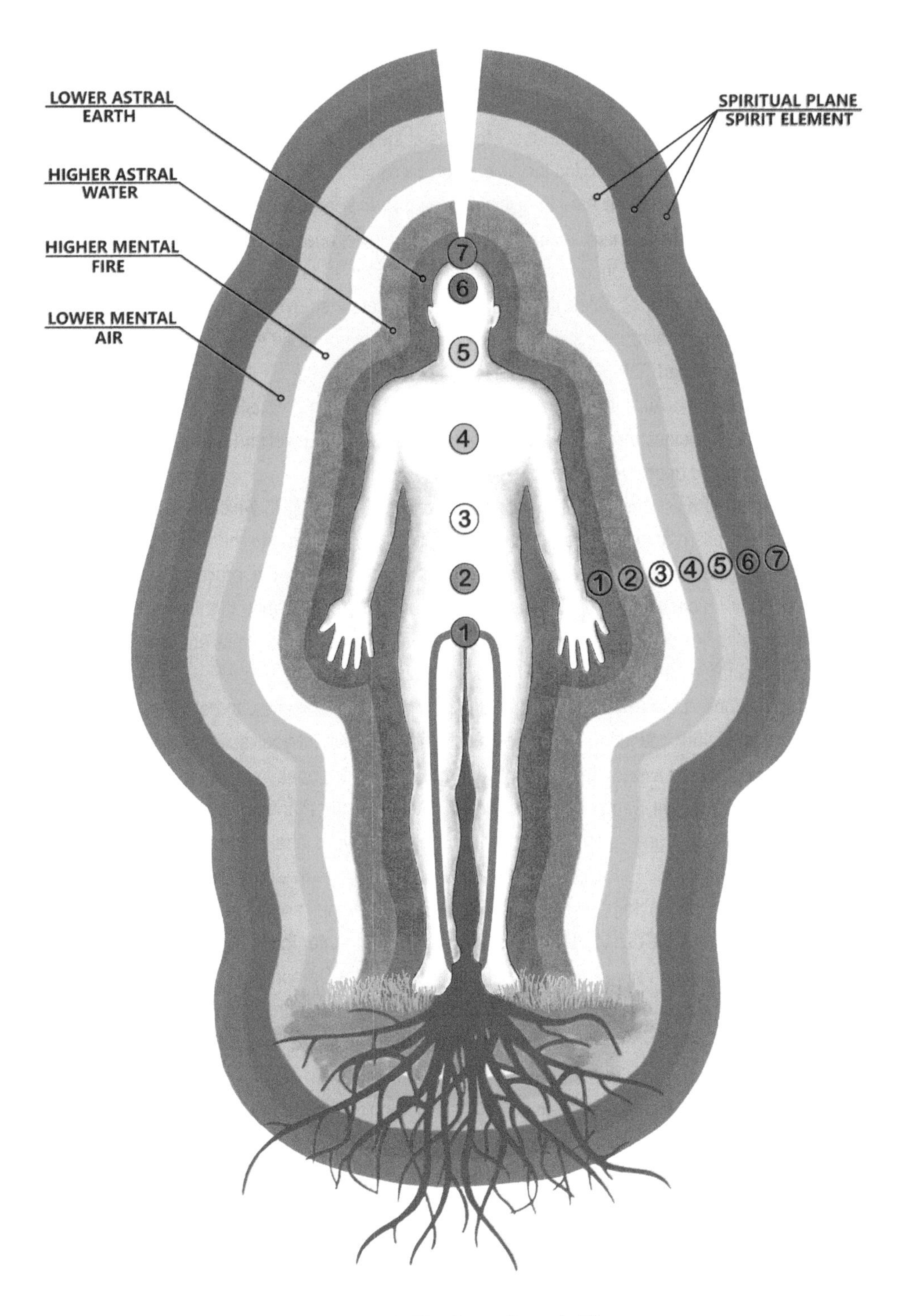

Figure 14: The Inner Cosmic Planes

The Cosmic Planes of existence occupy the same space and time but exist in varying degrees of vibration. The lowest and most dense vibration will be the Physical World of Matter that we live in our day-to-day life. Once you increase the vibration, you enter into the different Planes of existence, Astrally, through the mind. The higher the rate or frequency of vibration, the higher the Plane. Matter is at the lowest frequency, while Spirit vibrates at such a high frequency that it is practically at rest and invisible to the senses.

The Cosmic Planes exist within the Aura in layers (Figure 14), the same as the layers of an onion overlaid one on top of the other. The higher layers interpenetrate and impact the lower ones. The image in Figure 14 is a schematic showing the sequence of the layers concerning the Chakras. However, it is not an exact depiction of the Aura itself. In the human Aura, each of its Major Chakric layers is closer to one another, overlaid with four more extensive layers related to the Transpersonal Chakras. As such, eleven primary layers compose the Aura. (For more information on the Aura, see the discourse titled "The Aura-Toroidal Energy Field.")

Also, keep in mind that the Aura is dynamic in its expression and is in a constant state of flux and reflux as it expresses the individual consciousness. At every moment, different colours swirl and twirl within the Aura respective to what content the mind and heart focus on and experience.

The Cosmic Planes all exist sequentially, emanating from the White Light, which is found in Sahasrara, the Crown Chakra. The process of manifestation of the Divine filters downwards into these different Planes, and one Plane affects another—there is a symbiotic relationship between them. As the process of manifestation filters downwards, once it has reached the Physical Plane, it rises back up to the White Light, systematically impacting each Plane. The manifestation process then is the continuous back and forth flow of this entire process, infinite times in a finite moment, exemplified in the Hermetic axiom of "As Above, So Below."

As you perform actions in the Physical World, you impact these Inner Planes, thereby forming Karma. Karmic energy is the sum-total of your actions and the expression of their quality. If your actions are not performed in the name of God-the Divine, who works through the energy of unconditional love, then they will carry Karmic consequences. As such, negative Karma will get lodged inside one of the Planes of manifestation, for you to learn the lessons of that Plane and attune your actions correctly, optimising your Chakras in the process.

By experiencing these Cosmic Planes, you can learn about parts of yourself that need work. And you can work on those parts of Self by experiencing these Cosmic Planes. For example, sometimes Demonic entities will lodge themselves in one or more of the Cosmic Planes, and you need to encounter these Demons and "slay" them. Often, this action is visually perceived in a vision or a dream as you infuse a Demon with White Light, disarming them. However, facing them with courage is generally enough to transform them and remove fear energy from the Cosmic Plane they dwell in. In turn, the corresponding Chakra will become fine-tuned, allowing more Light energy to shine through it.

When working with Karmic energy, you are primarily working with fear, as fear is the fuel of all Demonic energies. The purpose and goal of all Demons are to scare you somehow. Since fear is quantifiable, by working with Karmic energy, you are removing fear out of your Aura, little by little, until it is all gone. However, this process takes many years and requires you to be strong in mind and heart. You must become resilient and stubborn to succeed if you want to overcome your Demons. Once all the fear is drawn out of you, the Demons can no longer scare you, and you will finally have ultimate command over them. This process is the essence of obtaining true personal power.

THE FIVE COSMIC PLANES

Physical Plane & Lower Astral Plane (Earth Element)

Your journey towards transcendence starts in the Physical Plane, corresponding with Muladhara, the Base Chakra and the Earth Element. Muladhara is the lowest of the Chakras, representing the densest Plane of existence, the World of Matter. This Chakra also affects the Lower Astral Plane, the energy blueprint of all things in existence. There is a correspondence with the Physical Plane and the Lower Astral since both partake of the Earth Element and Muladhara Chakra. The Subtle Body corresponding to this Inner Plane is the Lower Astral Body. The Physical Body is the body that we use to experience the world of Matter. This relation is obvious.

A human being is inextricably connected to the Earth through the force of gravity. On an energetic level, we are connected to the Earth via the Foot Chakras and energy channels in the legs that connect to Muladhara Chakra. This connection allows us to ground our Chakric system while the Sciatic Nerve grounds our nervous system and physical bodies to the Earth. The human energetic system is like a tree with roots deep into the Earth. The Earth nurtures us through this two-way communication, which supports and sustains our consciousness.

Higher Astral Plane (Water Element)

As you are rising upwards in the Planes, the next in the sequence is the Higher Astral Plane. It is often referred to as the Emotional Plane, related to the lower, more instinctual emotions—our actions in the Physical World illicit an emotional response involuntarily. The Higher Astral Plane is associated with sexuality, fear, and the Ego since it relates directly to the subconscious mind. It corresponds to the Water Element and Swadhisthana, the Sacral Chakra. The Subtle Body particular to this Plane is the Higher Astral Body.

After a full Kundalini awakening, once the conscious and subconscious minds are bridged, emotional chaos dominates the psyche for quite some time. Facing your Shadow Self can be a scary thing, especially if you are unprepared for such an experience. However challenging it may be, the Karmic energy of the Water Element needs to be overcome for you to move ahead on your journey of Spiritual Ascension. Fear energy may take a longer time to purge, depending on the level of your Spiritual Evolution. With courage and determination, however, it can be achieved, resulting in Swadhisthana Chakra becoming tuned, allowing the consciousness to rise above its level and enter the Plane above it.

Lower Mental Plane (Air Element)

Once you are done integrating the lessons of the Water Element, the following Inner Plane to deal with is the Lower Mental plane, corresponding with the Air Element and Anahata, the Heart Chakra. This Plane relates to your thoughts and rational thinking as well as imagination. Emotions affect thoughts and vice versa. Because of its connection with the Spirit Element, Anahata deals with higher emotions, such as compassion and unconditional love. As such, you may encounter tests of the Soul pertaining to those energies. The Subtle Body particular to this Inner Plane is the Lower Mental Body.

Once you have entered the Mental Plane and your consciousness is vibrating at its level, you will begin to Lucid Dream. Since Anahata is directly linked to the Spirit Element in Vishuddhi (the Chakra above it), your consciousness can vault out of your physical body through Sahasrara Chakra and embody your Body of Light if you have received a full activation through the Kundalini awakening. Because of its higher density, the Mental Plane is the contact point for the Body of Light to enter a Lucid Dream. Once you embody it, you will project into one of the higher Cosmic

Planes. Depending on the Lucid Dream experience you are having, it is either the Spiritual or Divine Planes. Lucid Dreams begin occurring once your consciousness is in Anahata, as the influx of the Air Element is what allows you to project out of Sahasrara.

In a Lucid Dream, you will be fully consciously aware. You will experience the dream as real since the Body of Light is a vehicle of consciousness, similar to the physical body, just at a lower density level. Lucid Dreams are generally characterized by absolute freedom to experience whatever you desire while in the dream state. Once your consciousness is projected out of Sahasrara Chakra, a Lucid Dream becomes a full Out-of-Body Experience. (I will discuss Lucid Dreaming in greater detail in the second half of the book since it is one of the more significant gifts received after awakening the Kundalini).

Higher Mental Plane (Fire Element)

The next Plane you will have to work through is the Higher Mental Plane, corresponding with the Fire Element, and the Third Chakra, Manipura (Solar Plexus Chakra). Manipura relates to your willpower, beliefs, motivation, and your drive in life. It is where your Soul lies, which filters through the conscious mind. Your beliefs are formed through habitual actions and thinking. This connection with the Soul in the Mental Plane gives rise to Lucid Dreaming as the Body of Light is the vehicle of the Soul. Keep in mind that both the Fire and Air Elements are connected with the Spirit Element, and so the Mental Plane is the contact point for reaching the higher Cosmic Realms.

Many of our ingrained beliefs prevent us from tapping into our highest potential as Spiritual human beings. Overcoming negative, limiting beliefs is paramount to living the kind of life you want to live. Beliefs also, in turn, affect your dreams and goals. The purpose of experiencing these Planes is to purify the negative Karma stored in each Chakra. Once cleansed, your consciousness naturally elevates above a Chakra to learn further Soul lessons in a Chakra above it. The Subtle Body corresponding to this Plane is the Higher Mental Body.

Spiritual Plane (Spirit Element)

Once you have graduated past the Lower Planes of existence related to the Four Elements, the Kundalini energy will sublimate and transform into a soothing, liquid fire, which is much more pleasant. Its quality is of the Spirit Element, and once this transformation occurs, it becomes your "modus operandi" for the rest of your life. This Spirit energy elevates your consciousness into the highest three Chakras of Vishuddhi (Throat Chakra), Ajna (Mind's Eye Chakra), and Sahasrara (Crown Chakra). It corresponds to the Spiritual Plane of existence experienced through Sahasrara Chakra and the Bindu Chakra. It has been referred to as the Philosophical Mercury of the Alchemists and the Philosopher's Stone.

The Subtle Body corresponding to the Spiritual Plane is the Spiritual Body. This Spiritual Body is the next vehicle of consciousness which the newly activated Body of Light works to align with permanently. While in dream states, the Body of Light moulds into the Spiritual Body to travel in the Spiritual Plane.

The Spiritual Plane is often referred to as the "Aethyr," and there are often references to the Aetheric or Etheric blueprint of all forms of Matter. It is synonymous with the Astral blueprint already mentioned. People often lack the language to explain this very particular invisible science, so reference to these terms implies the basic energy blueprint we all have. Do not be confused if you cannot readily grasp how everything works but be open to learning, and over time, as you expose yourself to this invisible reality more, your understanding will heighten.

It is essential to understand that the Kundalini energy is never static; it is ever-changing in its expression, function, and state. This constant transformation of the Kundalini energy allows you to enter these different Planes naturally unless you choose to do it intentionally through ritual invocation techniques.

Keep in mind that thus far, I am describing the process of rising on the Inner Planes through consciousness. As the vibration of your consciousness is increased, you experience higher and higher Planes until reaching the Spiritual Plane. Your consciousness can reach as high as the Divine Planes, although their experience usually occurs during Lucid Dreams. The actual manifestation process is a continuous cycle of Spirit filtering into Matter and back up again. This process is instantaneous, unceasing and constant, and all of the Planes in between the two are affected.

THE DIVINE PLANES

The Divine Planes of existence refer to the Transpersonal Chakras above Sahasrara; the lower ones generally relate to the Soul Star Chakra while the higher ones relate to the Stellar Gateway. Theoretically, there are limitless Divine Planes of consciousness. Any attempt to explain their actual number is futile since human consciousness can reach as high as the Mind of God, which is Multi-Dimensional. Those who attempt to define the Divine Planes err in their judgement of them since their experiences cannot be categorized with any degree of continuity.

I will not go into too much detail on the Divine Planes since the purpose of this work is to focus on the Seven Chakras primarily, as the initial challenges after awakening Kundalini lies in mastering and purifying those. Experiencing the high vibrational energy of the Divine Planes in dream states or waking visions is a transcendental experience that cannot be put into words since to do so is to limit the experience and bring it down to this realm of duality.

The Divine Planes are Non-Dual and ineffable, as they are the contact point between the Unknown and the Known. Information from the Divine Planes is filtered via the Causal/Bindu Chakra into Sahasrara, the Crown, allowing otherworldly Beings to make contact with your consciousness. Whenever you have an "out of this world" experience in your dreams and are visiting realms never seen or experienced before, you are working with the Chakras above Sahasrara and "surfing" one of the Divine Planes.

The experience of the Divine Planes is different for everyone. In *The Magus*, I have tried to explain some of my experiences with these energy sources, but I believe I limited those incredible experiences by doing so. If you have awakened the Kundalini and are experiencing incredible dreams, sometimes Lucid ones, you are invariably going to contact the Divine Planes of existence.

You will see landscapes never seen before, beautiful to behold. You will feel like you are on a different Planet in another Solar System, and in reality, you might be. Once your consciousness is freed from the physical body, you can raise it through an inspiring idea or thought. It is uncommon to experience the Divine Planes during the day unless you are in meditation, but once you open this door, you may visit it at night.

Once you have made contact with the Divine Planes in your consciousness, you may be able to feel their presence intuitively, but at night you can use your Body of Light to enter and experience them. A pull upwards occurs in your consciousness, and when you enter the Alpha State during sleep, you can officially vault into the Divine Planes with your Body of Light. If you feel like you are in this world physically, but your mind is on another Planet, or another higher Dimension, then chances are you are experiencing the Divine Planes.

VARIATION IN THE AURIC LAYERS SEQUENCE

You will notice that the sequence of Spiritually evolving through the Elements follows the succession of the Auric layers concerning the Chakras, except that instead of progressing into Fire after overcoming the Water Element, I have experienced that one reaches the Air Element instead. Thus, there's a gradual jump into a higher layer before going back into a lower one. That, or the sequence of the layers in the Aura does not follow the order of the Chakras.

Suppose we follow the Qabalistic Tree of Life system of Spiritual Evolution towards the Godhead (White Light of Kether). Once we rise above Earth's Physical Plane, the consciousness experiences the other three Elements in two separate sequences before reaching the Spiritual Plane. After leaving Malkuth, the Earth, the individual reaches Yesod (lower Air), followed by Hod (lower Water) and then Netzach (lower Fire). Then they rise into Tiphareth (higher Air), followed by Geburah (higher Fire) and finally Chesed (higher Water). Then they are at the doorstep of the Spirit and the Spiritual Plane, represented by Daath on the Tree of Life. And even within the Spiritual Plane, the first Sephira, Binah, is attributed to the Water Element, while the second Sephira, Chokmah, is related to Fire. Binah and Chokmah are considered the primary sources of the Water and Fire Elements, Qabalistically. Kether, the highest Sephira, corresponds with the Air Element and is also considered its highest source.

The Air Element on the Tree of Life is considered the reconciler between the Fire and Water Elements. For this reason, it is found strictly on the *Middle Pillar* on the Tree of Life, also called the Pillar of Balance. On the other hand, the two Elements of Water and Fire interchange on the opposing Tree of Life Pillars, the *Pillar of Severity* and *Pillar of Mercy*. Thus, in my experience of rising in consciousness and Spiritually Evolving, I did not experience the Chakras sequentially. I believe this process is Universal. Therefore, either the Qabalistic system is correct, or the Chakric system is, but not both since they are different. I will get more into this subject later on when I describe and discuss the Eastern concept of Koshas.

IDA, PINGALA, AND THE ELEMENTS

The correct flow of energy through Ida and Pingala is of paramount importance to the Kundalini circuit's proper functioning. Blockages in either of these Nadis will prevent the energy from working as it should. If there are blockages, you will undergo severe mental and emotional problems since Ida and Pingala regulate the Chakras and consciousness. Ida and Pingala are powered by thoughts and emotions, which are influenced by the four Chakras below Vishuddhi (Throat Chakra) and the Elements of Earth, Water, Air and Fire.

In this chapter, I will discuss how the Five Elements affect the flow of Ida and Pingala. Through the Spiritual practices presented in this book or the Ceremonial Magick ritual exercises presented in *The Magus*, you can attune your Chakras. Doing so allows the energy currents in Ida and Pingala to flow correctly, easing any mental and emotional difficulties you may be experiencing. As described in *The Magus*, the Thirty Enochian Aethyrs directly influence Ida and Pingala since they use the sexual energy combined with the Elemental energy to work on either or both channels at once. I have found this ritual operation to be the best in attuning both Kundalini channels and helping them reach their most optimal state.

The Earth Element represents stability and is signified by the Root Chakra, which is between the anus and genitals. This Chakra is vital as you have to have energy flowing through it correctly to power the Kundalini system. The Earth Element gives you the means to correct this Chakra and attune it properly. As mentioned, energy lines from the Foot Chakras run through the legs up to the Earth Chakra, Muladhara. These lines need to be fully activated and optimised after the Kundalini has awakened. Their proper flow allows the Earth Chakra to work at its maximum capacity. Their flow also powers the Ida and Pingala Nadis, which begin in Muladhara but receive their masculine and feminine energies from the primary energy channels in the legs.

Working with the Earth Element allows one to become grounded, maximising the flow of energy in the legs. The Water Element and the emotions influence the flow of Ida (feminine), while the Fire Element influences the flow of Pingala (masculine). The Air Element animates both the Ida and Pingala channels since it gives life to the Water and Fire Elements. Its placement is in the Heart Chakra, Anahata, which contains the largest confluence of minor Nadis in the body.

Anahata regulates all the Chakras as well as the Elements in the body. Furthermore, the Heart Chakra connects to the Hand Chakras, which channel healing love energy, and serve as receptors to read the energy around you. Once the correct flow is established between the Hand Chakras and the Heart Chakra in fully Kundalini awakened individuals; it results in the further weightless feeling in the physical body and the mental disassociation with it. The Spirit energy needs to permeate the entire physical body counterpart, the Body of Light, to completely liberate the consciousness from the physical realm.

When working with the Air Element, you are working with stimulating both the Ida and Pingala Nadis. As the two Nadis cross each other at each of the Chakric points during a Kundalini awakening, they terminate at Ajna Chakra (Figure 15) in the middle of the brain at the Thalamus centre. Ajna Chakra's portal is the Third Eye—between and above the eyebrows and one centimetre inside the head. If the two channels are not crossing correctly, or if there is a blockage in the movement of either of them at the Mind's Eye centre, the entire Kundalini system is thrown out of balance, affecting its function. Often, this results in obsessive thoughts or mental problems similar to those of schizophrenic or bipolar patients.

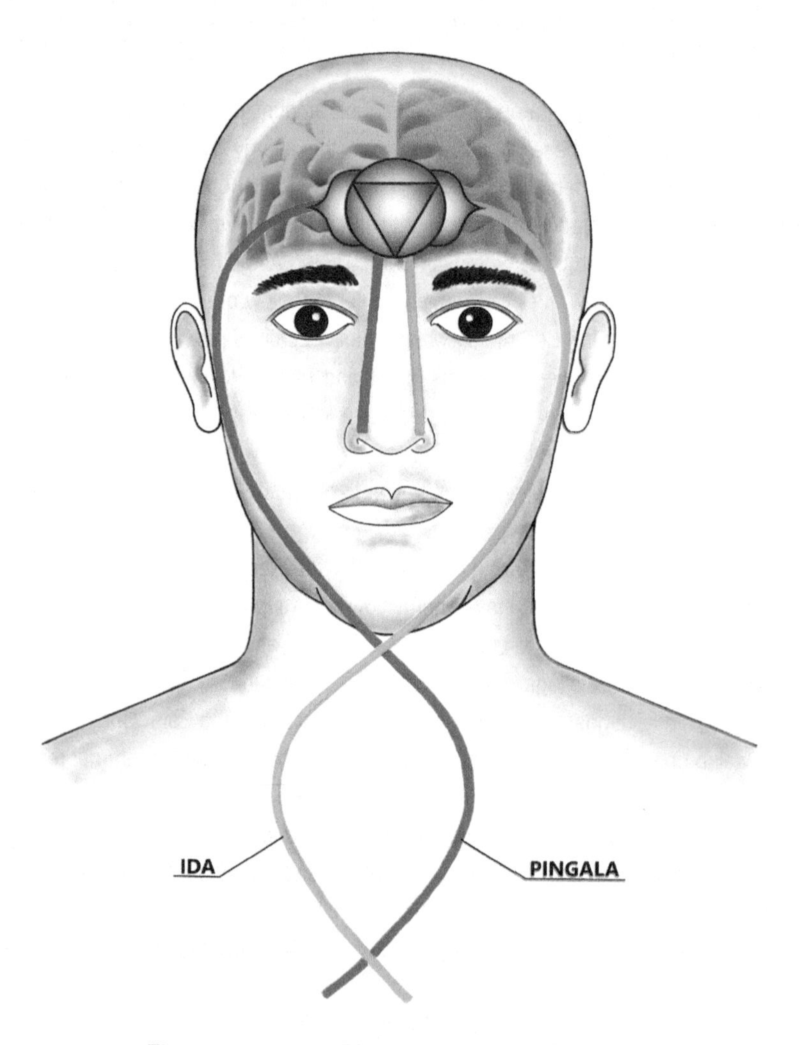

Figure 15: Ida and Pingala Nadis and Ajna Chakra

Mental health problems in individuals stem from an improper flow of Ida and Pingala and imbalances in the Chakras. However, we cannot prove this with modern-day scientific measuring tools. After seventeen years of observing my mental processes and the ups and downs in my thoughts and emotions, I have come to this conclusion. I believe these issues are Universal since Ida and Pingala are active in all people as they regulate consciousness.

However, in fully Kundalini awakened people, their flow is optimized since the Three Granthis are unlocked, allowing sublimated Pranic energy to continually feed the system, inducing the transcendental state.

LEFT AND RIGHT BRAIN HEMISPHERES

In the Qabalah, the two highest inner faculties of a human being are Wisdom and Understanding; both received through intuition. These two aspects of Self exist in duality with one another, as you cannot have one without the other. They are both related to the Spirit Element as they represent the Supernal part of the Self, which was never born and will never die. On the Tree of Life, they are the Chokmah (Wisdom) and Binah (Understanding) Spheres. They also relate to the ultimate expression of the masculine and feminine components of the Self, found within the brain as the left and right brain hemispheres.

The left-brain hemisphere is influenced by the Chiah (found in the Sphere of Chokmah). Qabalistically, the Chiah is our True Will. It is the masculine, projective part of the Self, belonging to the Fire Element. As our Holy Guardian Angel, this part of us continually fuels us to come closer to Divinity. The Chiah is powered by the Pingala Nadi, which is also associated with the left-brain hemisphere in Tantra Yoga. It relates to analytic thought, logic, reason, science and math, reasoning, and writing skills. The Chiah is fundamentally Archetypal, meaning it is to some degree outside of our ability to understand it fully. We can use the left side of our brain, but we cannot understand why we know what we know nor the source of that knowledge.

The Lesser Neschamah is found within the Sphere of Binah. It is feminine and receptive, belonging to the Water Element. The Lesser Neschamah serves as our psychic intuition. It is the Self's highest aspiration and our deepest longing or most elevated state of consciousness. After all, our intuitive power links us directly to the Divine. The Ida Nadi powers the Lesser Neschamah. It influences the functions of the right-brain hemisphere, such as understanding, emotions, creativity, imagination, insight, holistic thought, and awareness of music and art forms in general.

NADI SHORT-CIRCUITS

Throughout your Kundalini transformation journey, you may encounter a time when either Ida or Pingala are short-circuited, meaning that they cease their function for the time being. It is crucial to understand that once you have opened your Kundalini circuit, it will remain active for the rest of your life, and short circuits and blockages are temporary bumps in the road. With short-circuits, you have to rebuild the Ida or Pingala channels (whichever has collapsed) through food intake, which occurs naturally over time. At this time, you may be prompted by your Soul to eat more than regularly to accomplish this since your Soul will recognize what you need to do to fix the problem.

Short-circuits are Universal issues, and many Kundalini awakened people have reported this happening to them. If Ida has short-circuited, it is usually a result of a fearful event in your life that causes such a negative emotional charge that it over-charges the channel and zaps it with negative bio-electricity. Pingala short-circuits are less common and are usually a result of someone or something taking over your life and doing your thinking for you for an extended period. If this happens, the Pingala channel, whose purpose is to channel the willpower, will cease its function.

Both channels can be rebuilt over time with food intake and making changes in your life that may negatively affect their functioning. How you lead your life invariably affects the entire Kundalini system and how well the Chakras function, including the Ida, Pingala, and Sushumna channels.

Sushumna requires the brain centres to be open and the Bindu to be functioning correctly, but it also requires that the connection to the Crown is well established. If Ida or Pingala, or both, cease their function and are short-circuited, it can result in Sushumna also not functioning correctly, especially at the higher brain level. It is impossible to stop Sushumna's flow altogether since it is our medium for experiencing expanded consciousness, which, when awakened, can never be annihilated. The ancillary channels of Ida and Pingala, which regulate the consciousness, can be tempered with, but not the actual higher consciousness itself.

I will further discuss Kundalini short-circuits in greater detail in "Part X: Kundalini Damage-Control" and present meditations in the following section that you can use to rebuild and realign the channels in the head instead of waiting for it to happen naturally.

PART III: THE SUBTLE ENERGY SYSTEM

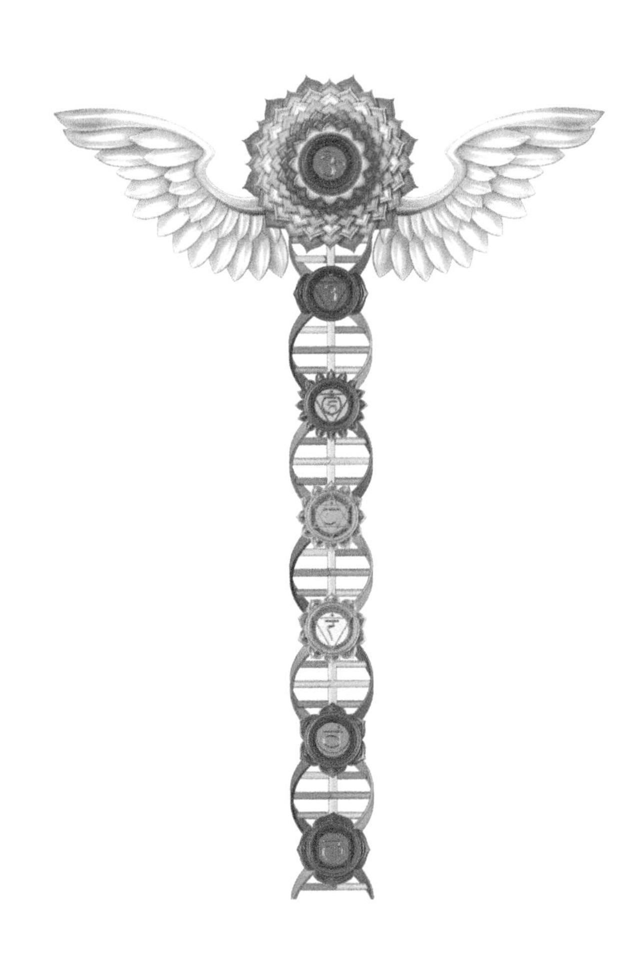

THE AURA-TOROIDAL ENERGY FIELD

An electromagnetic field is a combination of electrical and magnetic energies. Electromagnetic fields are primary fields that generate and sustain life. The Aura is an electromagnetic field of energy that exists around every living and non-living thing in the Universe. It is toroidal in shape since the torus is the preferred form that the Universe uses to create Matter from energy.

The torus consists of a central axis and vortices at each end that circulate energy. In a cross-section, the torus resembles a dynamic doughnut with a hole in the middle that is infinitely small. Most torus dynamics contain male and female aspects, where energy spirals upwards in one and downwards in the other.

The toroidal energy field is a self-sustaining system that continually circulates energy. The infinity symbol is an ancient 2D representation of the toroidal field since it carries similar properties of being continuous and self-balancing. It also represents the Source of all Creation. The Source created all the tori in existence and is connected to them inextricably.

Every human and animal living on Planet Earth, including the Planet itself (Figure 16), has its own Aura. The same applies to other Planets and even Galaxies. All of the Auras in the Universe are influenced by and feed off each other. After all, we are all interconnected. The many different ecosystems within the Earth's atmosphere, such as plant and animal life, oceans, and even amoebas and single-celled organisms, are linked together energetically. Through a dynamic exchange of energy, the Universal toroidal system connects every cell and atom through our physical bodies and consciousness.

The torus is affected by the continuous movement of Universal energy or Prana. Its activity is similar to how a wave fluctuates with the movement of water. Pranic energy is everywhere around us—it is continually flowing in and out of our Auras. So long as our Sun exists, so do Light and Prana, which give life to all living things in our Solar System.

One of the primary purposes of the Aura is to exchange and process communication signals. The Aura of living biological organisms continually fluctuates depending on what input it receives from the Self, the environment, or other living things. Although non-living, inanimate objects have an Aura, theirs doesn't change much through interaction with other living or non-living things. The Aura of non-living things is frequently referred to as the Etheric, or energy body. Essentially, the energy body of anything is its Aura, which is the product of the continuous movement of a torus.

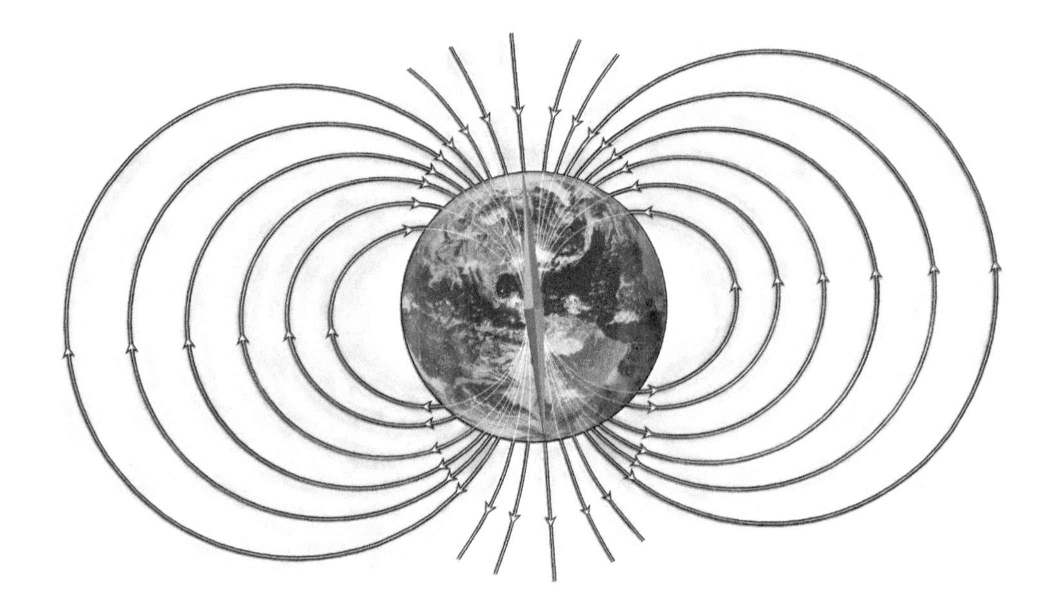

Figure 16: The Electromagnetic Field of the Earth

THE HUMAN AURA

The Aura helps us interact with the world around us and relay information into our physical bodies. It extends around the physical body but also flows through it. The physical body is the Holographic projection of the individual consciousness powered by the Aura.

I have already described the Aura layers in the human being, which correspond with the Seven Major Chakras and the Cosmic Planes of existence. Each of the layers in the Aura has its frequency of vibration and holds different forms of information. The following four Auric layers relate to the Transpersonal Chakras of the Earth Star, the Causal Chakra, the Soul Star, and the Stellar Gateway. They emanate sequentially past the first seven Auric layers.

The Earth Star Chakra's Auric layer projects out first after the Sahasrara Chakra layer, which serves to ground the whole Chakric system as it connects with the Etheric Body of the Lower Astral Plane. Next is the Causal Chakra's Auric layer, which connects the Spiritual and Divine Planes. Then we have the Auric layer of the Soul Star, which allows us to access the lower Divine Planes, followed by the Stellar Gateway layer, representing the higher ones. Finally, Hara Chakra, a part of the Transpersonal Chakras model, does not have its own Auric layer but instead interpenetrates various aspects of the Aura since it is our primary Pranic centre. Each of the eleven Auric layers has a toroidal flow that is nested together to create the shape of a giant energy egg (Figure 17).

With the inclusion of the layers mentioned above, the main body of the Aura is created. In addition, other subtle fields affect our bioenergy and connect us to one another, other living beings, the Earth, and the Universe as a whole. These include electrical and magnetic fields that are undetected in the electromagnetic spectrum, which affect us physically and psychically. Then there are sound and other electromagnetic forces that affect us, such as infrared light, microwaves, radio waves, ultraviolet light, X-rays, Gamma rays, to name a few.

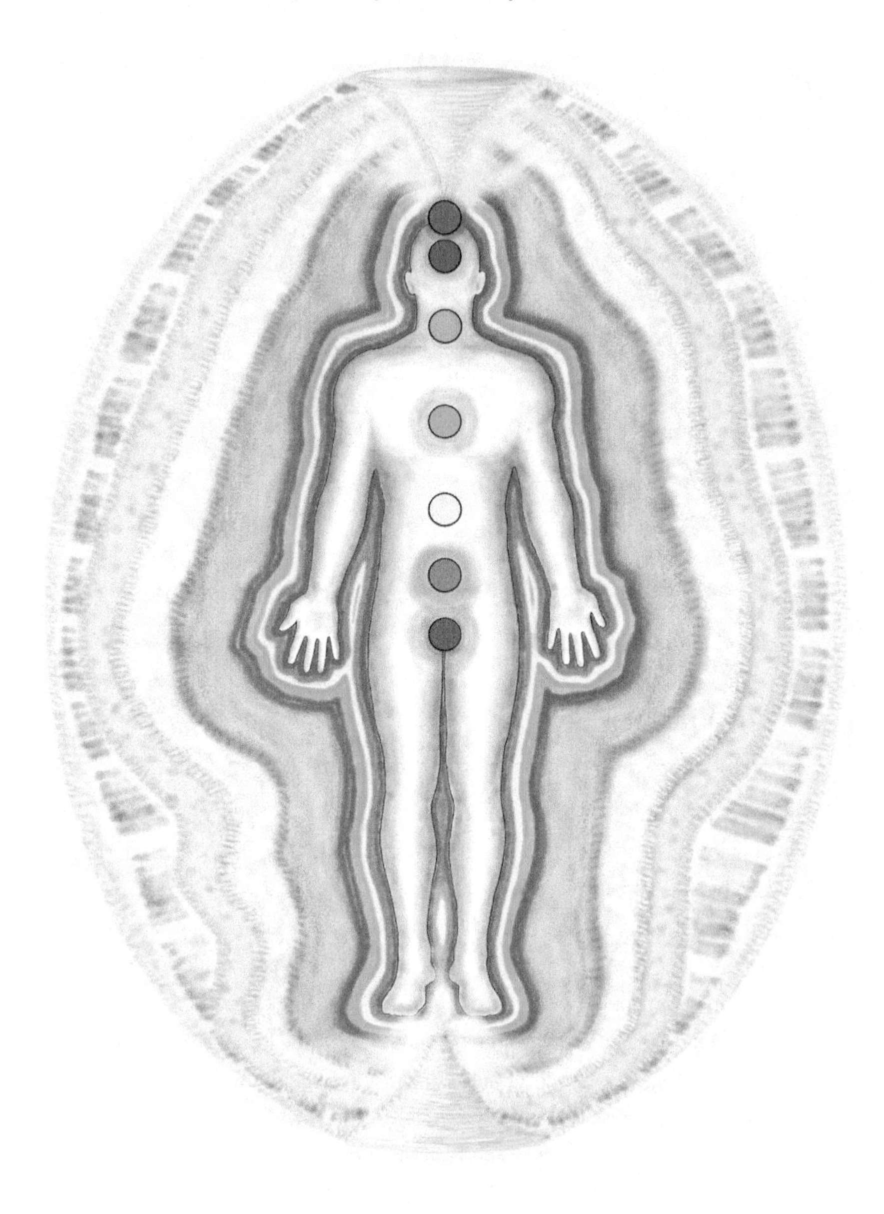

Figure 17: The Human Aura

Every cell in the body and every thought and emotion generates an energy field. As such, there are hundreds, if not thousands, of subtle energy fields in existence, some of which have not been discovered yet. Scientists are discovering new energy fields on a regular basis, which further adds to our understanding of the interconnectedness of all of existence.

In the human being, the axis of the torus runs from the crown of the head to the groin area, encompassing the Major and Transpersonal Chakras, and extending down to the feet. Energy flows through one vortex along the axis and out of the second vortex, where it wraps around its circumference and passes back again through the original vortex. As the torus spins around its vertical axis, the ring itself revolves around its circular axis as well. Incoming energy particles that enter our torus follow a spiral path.

The centre of the torus is the heart, which has its own electromagnetic field that extends further out from the body than the Auric field. When people are near one another, an exchange of electromagnetic energy is produced by the heart, which gets registered by the brainwaves. (See "Power of the Heart" chapter for more information on this subject.)

The heart houses the Soul. The torus is essentially the Soul's structure to express itself in the World of Matter. It allows the Soul to make contact with other Souls in existence. Since philosophically, the Soul expresses itself through the mind, the mind chose the torus as the most optimal shape in nature to manifest the physical body. Through the mind, the desires of the Soul are communicated into the physical body. The body cannot exist without the mind. When the physical body perishes, the mind does as well, which eradicates the torus. On the other hand, the Soul can never be extinguished, and it continues its life journey after physical death.

AURA CHARACTERISTICS

Aura photography is a relatively new technology (since the 1970s) that uses a biofeedback imaging system to record and display a person's electromagnetic energy. Aura reading machines usually take readings from the hand via a sensor, which records one's inner energies and delivers a colourful image of the Aura's current state.

The Aura reading biofeedback device I work with is AuraFit, created by Bettina Bernoth. It integrates cutting-edge technology to display the Aura in "real-time" using a "smart" bracelet instead of a hand sensor. I obtained the snapshots of my Aura as presented in this book with the AuraFit System. As a result of Aura reading technology like AuraFit and others, we can determine the Aura size, its dominant colours, and the health of the Chakras at any given moment.

When we look at an individual's energy field, we see the colourful energy flowing around within the Aura. The type and quality of energy within you depends on what your consciousness is focusing its attention on. It may change from one moment to the next since the Aura is continuously fluctuating regarding expressions of consciousness. The thoughts and emotions we think of and experience utilize their corresponding Chakras in those moments in time. When an individual Chakra is being expressed within the Aura, its respective layer will be dominant, including its corresponding colour.

Auric colours are continually changing and shifting concerning what the consciousness focuses on and which layers are involved. However, each person has a base colour in their Aura, reflecting their personality and disposition. The person's foundational colour gives us an idea of their general disposition and emotional state, influenced by their beliefs, values, and behaviours. The level of a person's Spiritual progression also affects the colour range within which a person vibrates.

Aura Size

Through Aura reading technology and validated by clairvoyants, we have determined that the circumference of a healthy Aura with well-functioning Chakras extends as far as six feet around a person, on average. If there are blockages or stagnation of Light energy in the Chakras, it will weaken the Aura, which will reduce its circumference size. Unhealthy Auras can shrink to as low as three feet and even to just outside the person's skin.

The size of the Aura varies and fluctuates in the same way as do its colours. For example, if a person is contemplative or desires solitude and rest, they will be inwards focused and keep their energies to themselves, which shrinks the Aura. Conversely, if the individual desires a connection with others and adventure, they will be extroverted, which will expand the Aura. Generally speaking, focusing outwards and sharing your love energy with others grows the Aura while being introverted and focusing on Self-love shrinks the Aura.

The Aura is like a living, breathing organism in the sense that it expands or contracts, depending on whether we are introverted or extroverted and the type of energies we are expressing. For example, if a person is tired and depleted of their Life energy, their Aura will shrink, while if they are energized and have a lot of vitality, they will have a more expansive Aura. Stress also impacts the size of the Aura as it makes it contract while the consciousness is experiencing tension.

Breathing also affects our Aura size; people who breathe from their abdomen continually nourish their Seven Chakras with Pranic energy, keeping the energy system balanced, thereby expanding the Aura. Those who only breathe through the chest keep their middle to higher Chakras activated while their lower Chakras remain relatively unused. These people will have smaller Auras and need to change their breathing patterns to balance their Chakras and optimize their Aura size.

The general size of the individual's Auric field is also dependant on where they are in the Spiritual Evolution process and how much Light energy they have integrated into their Aura. People with higher vibrations generally have larger Auras, while those with lower vibrations have smaller Auras. People with larger Auras have more powerful abilities to achieve their goals and dreams, while those with smaller Auras have a more challenging time manifesting the life they desire.

Kundalini awakened individuals who have integrated the Light energy into the Chakras have Auras whose circumference is well beyond six feet. It has been reported that fully Enlightened individuals, Adepts, Sages, and realized Yogis, have radiant Auras whose Light can fill an entire room and make an impression on everyone in their vicinity.

If someone is being extroverted, optimistic, and engaged in sharing love energy, yet their Aura circumference is still well below six feet, it is an indication that there might be illness in the physical body. According to the Hermetic Principle of Correspondence, the quality of energy in the Aura will manifest as that same quality physically, and vice versa.

If someone goes through significant psychological and even physical changes, it will show in their Aura. For example, people who are too spacey and need grounding will manifest an abundance of energy in their head area and minimal energy around their feet. For a balanced mind, body, and Soul connection, the energies should be evenly spread out in the head (mind), feet (body) and heart (Soul) areas.

Aura Shape and Colour Intensity

When looking at a person's Aura in real-time, various factors are at play that reflects the Aura's look, from its size and shape to colour intensity. Firstly, the Aura should be egg-shaped and symmetrical, reflecting the toroidal energy flow of the individual. The egg shape of the Aura should have a smooth surface on its outer shell when it is in a neutral state. A fuzzy outer shell indicates a lack of personal boundaries. If the Aura has holes, rips, or tears, it gives it a spiky look, indicating mild to severe energetic problems. Stagnant energy will show as some debris or dark colour spots in the outer shell.

Bright and radiant colours in the Aura reflect positive and harmonious aspects of the corresponding Chakras, while dark colours reflect negative, discordant aspects. For this reason, each colour in the Aura can be lighter or darker.

All areas of the Aura should radiate the same intensity and brightness. Areas of colour that aren't distributed equally on both sides of the Aura in terms of colour intensity indicate Chakric imbalance.

Balanced energy shows stationary, brighter colours, while imbalanced energies manifest as darker colours. Red, for example, represents the raw energy of action, which is a positive attribute of Muladhara Chakra, while dark red represents anxiety and stress.

When the individual is experiencing physical, mental, or emotional stress, a dark red colour will appear on the body's left side. If the stress persists, the dark red will come into the heart, throat and head areas, enveloping the first few layers of the Aura closest to the body.

When the individual shifts their focus away from whatever was giving them anxiety, of their own accord or through some external influence, tension will leave the psyche and body, followed by the dark red colour pouring out of the Aura. However, if stress persists further, it will continue to fill the rest of the Auric layers and permeate the entire Aura until it is resolved (Figure 18).

Figure 18: Stressful Energy Entering and Leaving the Aura

Whatever colour is replacing the dark red in the Aura is often seen in the left side of the body (right side of Aura picture) before it permeates the heart, throat, and head areas. It will then flow into the first few Auric layers, followed by the rest of the layers if whatever the consciousness is focusing on is powerful enough. The new energy will then stabilize within the Aura until a shift in consciousness occurs.

Suppose we are looking at this experience in real-time with an Aura reading device. In that case, it appears like a wave of new energy that sweeps into the heart area, projecting outwards until it fully replaces all the dark red spots within the Aura. The last remnants of the deep red are sometimes seen on the right side before they disappear altogether.

When a thought or emotion dominates one's energy field, it looks like the Aura takes an in-breath, while when an inner shift occurs, the Aura takes an out-breath, thereby expelling the corresponding colour out of the system.

The colours that come into the Aura are always a result of intention and attention concerning thoughts and emotions the consciousness focuses on. We can change them at any moment with the application of willpower. What you think about or give attention to determines your reality, and we can see its manifestation in the Aura.

Figure 19 shows a progression of Auric colours from a stressful state to a peaceful and balanced meditative state. The first pic shows a deep red that fills the entire Aura, which gets replaced by a calmer red in the next pic, followed by a complete clearing in the third pic from an applied mindfulness exercise.

The tranquil mind raises the vibration of consciousness progressively through the Chakras. After orange, it manifests the yellow colour in the Aura, followed by green, blue, indigo, violet, and lavender, in sequence.

The final white colour represents one's state of mind when they are clear of all thoughts, positive and negative, representing the most substantial connection with Sahasrara—the Divine White Light. A white Aura brings Divine bliss that we can feel in the Heart Chakra.

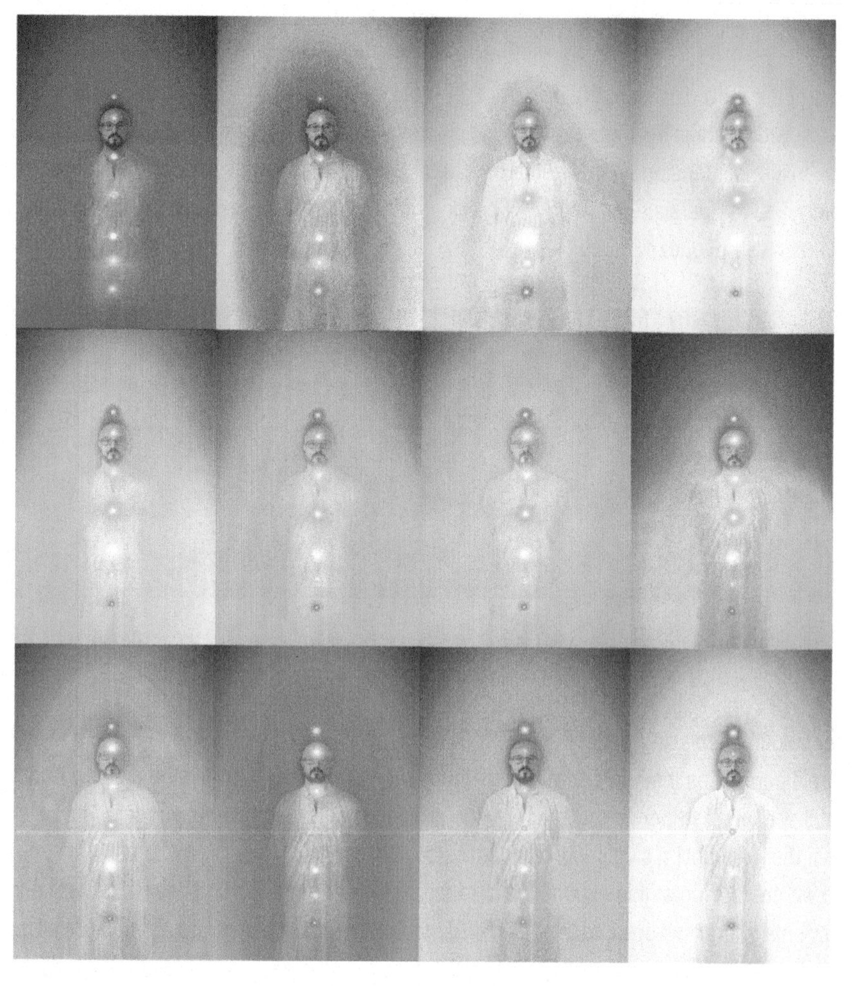

Figure 19: Progression of Auric Colours from Lowest to Highest Chakra

AURA ANATOMY (AREAS OF COLOUR)

Above the Head

The colour above Sahasrara Chakra represents your consciousness and the present moment. Therefore, it relates to your thoughts and what is currently on your mind. Your thoughts are projected from the Mental Plane and are more changeable than the emotions. As such, the colour above the head is the fastest to change.

If a band of colour stretches like an arch across the upper part of the Aura, it indicates one's hopes, goals, and aspirations (Figure 20). The band's colour tells us what type of aspirations or goals the individual has on their mind. For example, if the band is indigo or violet, it indicates that the person's current ambitions are Spiritual. A blue band shows one's aspirations to be concerned with creative expression. On the other hand, a red band indicates more monetary goals concerned with increasing the quality of one's earthly life.

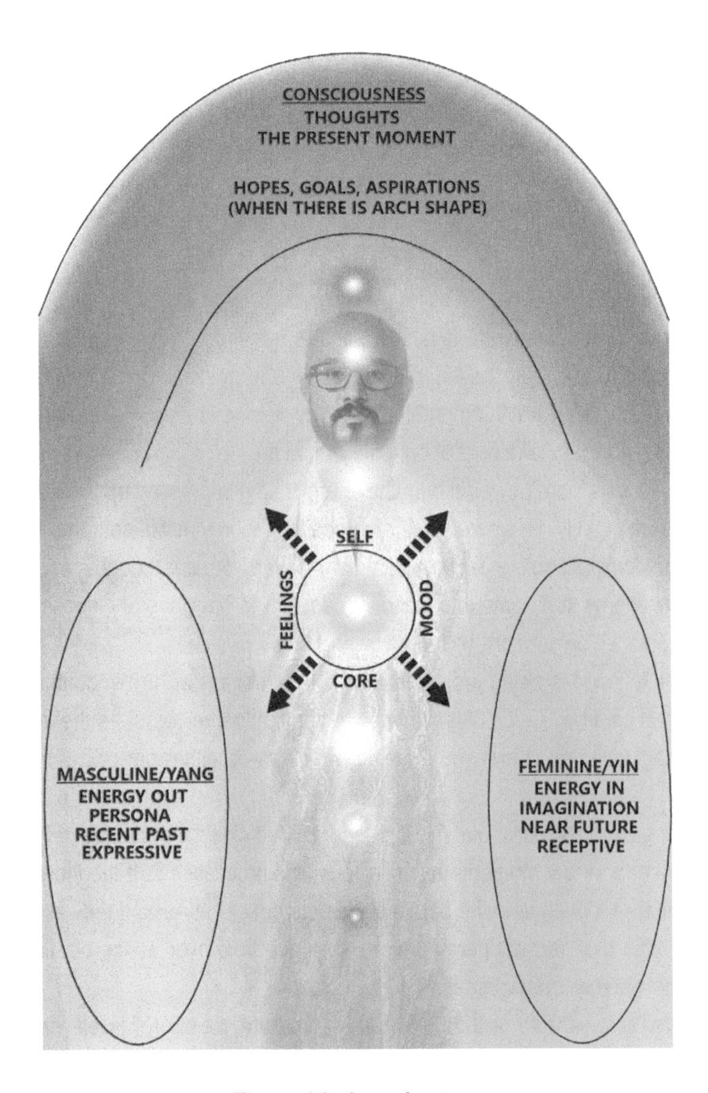

Figure 20: Aura Anatomy

Around the Heart

The colour around your heart area is expressive of your mood and general disposition. This colour relates to the Astral Plane, which includes the first two layers closest to the body. These two layers surround the physical body, stretching around the head and enveloping the feet.

Since how we feel is more substantial and less changeable than what we think about, the heart area is expressive of our core personality. It represents the Chakra that we utilise the most throughout the day. It is common to see the same colour above your head and around your heart and body since we often think about things that are in line with how we feel.

The heart area colour is your foundation; it is the dominant colour in your Aura representing the Self at this moment in time. As your general beliefs and views on life change, so does your core colour. If the individual undergoes a life-changing event, there is often a radical shift in their core colour.

Your core colour changes throughout the day to reflect changes in your emotions, but it generally goes right back to its neutral state. As such, the best way to obtain your core colour is to monitor the Aura for a shorter period. Taking a single snapshot of an Aura with an Aura reading device is insufficient to get the core colour.

Another factor impacting our core colour is how well we utilise our Throat Chakra, our centre of communication. When we intensely express ourselves verbally or through body language, the Throat Chakra tends to become illuminated, which lights up the throat area, brightening up our core colour. So speaking your truth and expressing yourself is crucial to having a healthy, unclogged Aura with free-flowing energy and bright colours.

Left Side of the Body

The left side of the body represents the feminine, passive, receptive, Yin energy that is being impressed upon the imagination. The colour present on the left side shows us energy coming in either Self-cultivated or projected into us by another person or even environmental stimuli. As such, this colour energy represents the future if we absorb and accept it and allow it to take hold of our consciousness.

If our present disposition is more powerful than the energy being impressed upon us, it will linger on the left side shortly and leave the Aura entirely. However, if we embrace this energy, it will pour into the heart area and spread outwards to become the dominant colour in our Aura that has overtaken our thoughts and emotions. As mentioned, though, unless the new energy that came into our centre is akin to our general disposition, it will vanish from the Aura soon after to be replaced by our core colour.

If the energy on the left side is being projected into us by a person we are in contact with, either in a healing session or through verbal communication, it is common to see that same colour as the dominant one in their Aura. Remember that our imagination must always be fueled by willpower, either our own (as it is optimal) or someone else's.

In many Aura readings, a dark red colour will come into the left side if a person is being triggered emotionally or mentally. It will stay there for a few moments as consciousness processes it. If the individual's nervous system is strong enough, they will overcome it, and the dark red will pour out of the Aura. If they allow it to take over mentally or emotionally, or both, the dark red will permeate the Aura and take over as the dominant colour, meaning that stress has fully taken hold of the consciousness.

If the colour on the left side is the same throughout the entire Aura, the energy is felt very strongly as the individual is congruent with their thoughts, emotions, and actions. If the colour on the left side is the same as the colour on the right side, the individual carries out what they are thinking, even though they may not be feeling it. For us to tangibly feel any energy, it has to take over as the base colour and permeate the heart area and the first few layers of the Aura.

Right Side of the Body

The right side of the body represents the masculine, active, projective, Yang energy. It portrays recent energy that has passed through us and is now being released and expressed. It is the energy of action that is a by-product of what we are thinking and feeling. Since it is the energy we are putting out into the world, it represents how other people perceive us—our persona.

When we express something, we are making an impression upon the Physical Plane and building memories. Every act we perform has meaning as it either liberates us or binds us further to our Wheel of Karma. We need to make sure that the energies we are projecting into the material world are not dark and muddy, as they are expressive of the negative qualities of the Chakras.

As the colour on the right side represents the conscious Self in the act of expression, the left side colour represents the subconscious. As such, the left and right sides of the Aura show our introverted and extroverted Selves. If we are naturally very social and extroverted, then the colour on the right side will shift and change often as we express ourselves in the world. However, if we are more introverted and spend a lot of time thinking and contemplating our emotions, then we will get more energy shifts on the left side, with very little to no movement on the right side.

For example, a writer who spends time thinking and contemplating ideas will have consistent colour and energy shifts on their left side. Conversely, a singer performing in a concert will be in a continual act of expression, and so the colours on their right side will be changing and shifting concerning the emotions they are expressing through their songs. They will have little to no time to go inwards and become introspective to consciously make an impression upon their imagination. However, the colours coming into their left side will correspond with the energies being projected at them by their fans in attendance.

ENERGETIC PROBLEMS IN THE AURA

Energetic problems within the Aura manifest as holes, rips, or stagnant energy (Figure 21). Holes in the Aura can be found on the outer shell and look like vacuums of draining energy; they represent severe energy loss and vulnerability to negative influences. Aura holes can quickly create an imbalance in the energetic system by leaking energy out and allowing unwanted energies to enter from the outside.

Aura holes manifest when individuals spend too much time daydreaming and not being present in their bodies. Any activity that promotes absent-mindedness and not dealing with your emotions as they happen can potentially make holes in the Aura. Substance and alcohol abuse are notorious for making Aura holes, as is everyday cigarette smoking.

A highly porous Aura is like an energy sponge. Being overly sensitive to environmental stimuli creates confusion about your own identity over time. Simply put, it becomes difficult to ascertain which thoughts and emotions are your own and which are other people's. Individuals with holes in their Aura often turn to people-pleasing to feel safe in an environment. When triggered or met with confrontation, instead of dealing with the situation, these fearful people tend to consciously leave their bodies to avoid experiencing the negative emotions.

We all need to face reality head-on to grow mentally, emotionally, and Spiritually. By avoiding dealing with reality as it happens, self-confidence and self-esteem are significantly impacted over time, creating further energetic problems.

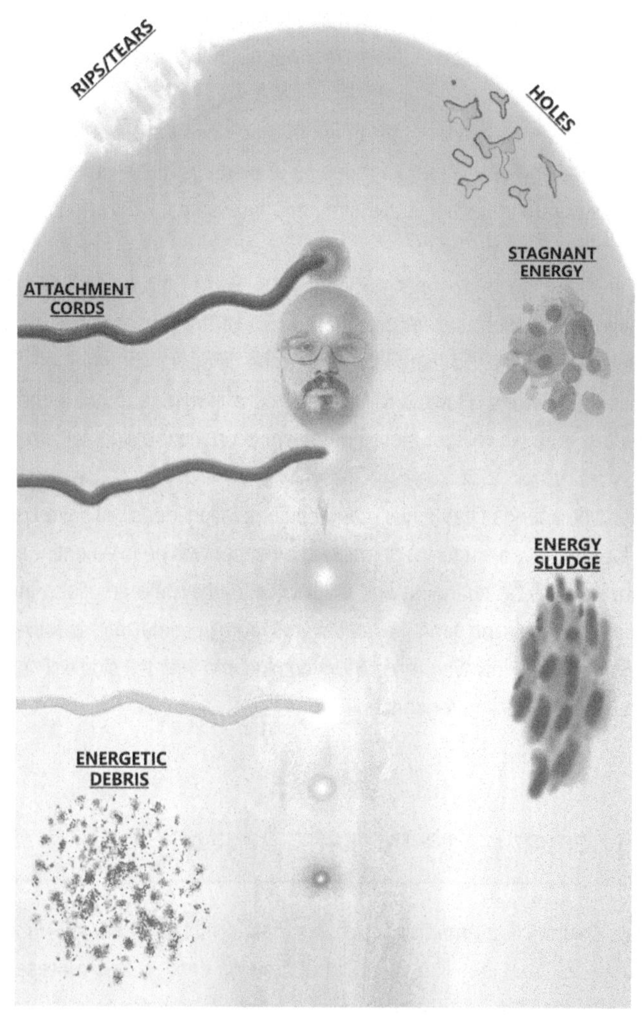

Figure 21: Energetic Problems in the Aura

Rips in the outer shell of the Aura are signs of past physical and psychological trauma that look like tears in a smooth piece of cloth. Rips allow for psychic vulnerability and energy loss, similar to holes in the Aura but less intense. Aura rips indicate a history of abuse, whether physical, sexual, mental, or emotional. On the other hand, a person's harmful habitual behaviour creates Aura holes, although avoiding dealing with reality indicates deep-seated subconscious issues.

A person who is deeply wounded constantly feels threatened by others. They are reactive and ready for conflict at all times. Often, they inadvertently hurt other people, even when they are just trying to help them. These individuals must diagnose the source of their pain and treat it through therapy or Spiritual healing practices. Doing so will help them regain their sense of identity, repairing the rips and holes in their Aura.

Stagnant energy in the Aura manifests in a variety of ways. Debris particles represent stagnant, ungrounded energy that manifests in the Aura or along the Body of Light. Energetic debris consists of dirty, static particles that are usually dispersed in one area and result in scattered thoughts and emotions.

Another example of stagnant energy is dark colour spots along the Aura's outer shell that look like thick, muddy puddles of water. When stagnant energy accumulates over a more extended period, it becomes denser and turns into energetic sludges—thick oil-like blots that are dark in appearance.

Stagnant energy is caused when the individual holds onto thoughts or emotions for too long without expressing them. Over time, it can turn into dense or heavy pockets of energy that back up in parts of the Aura, making the mind sluggish. Colour blots are usually found in the same area and involve one or more of the corresponding Chakras (depending on the colour). Energy clouds on the inside of the Aura are often felt as stress that lies hidden deep within the subconscious.

Dark spots in the Aura are like psychic residue that separates us from the present moment. By not allowing ourselves to express what we think and feel, we take away our ability to make strong connections with people. Instead of relying on truth and facts to guide our reality, we tend to live life through associations and assumptions since we lack the courage to be more expressive. Not loving oneself enough weakens the Throat Chakra, which is usually associated with stagnant energy in the Aura. People with many dark spots in the Aura tend to live in seclusion as they feel safer being isolated from others.

Finally, unhealthy attachments manifest as energy cords that connect two people through one or more of their Seven Chakras. Interactions that constantly contain intense fear, anger, or some other negative emotion imply the existence of an attachment cord (or cords). Attachment cords are often found in unhealthy relationships between family members. They are often the result of guilt or other unresolved emotions that bind two people psychically.

Attachment cords may also be created through a shared traumatic memory between friends or strangers. Two common examples where energetic cords may be present are co-dependent and sadomasochistic relationships.

Spiritual ties are the opposite version of negative attachment cords. They represent positive attachments between two people, which channel loving, healing energy from one to another. Spiritual ties are often shared between a person and their pet, especially with dogs who channel high vibrational energy to their owners and are tied to them in this lifetime.

THE AURA AND VIBRATIONS

The Hermetic Principle of Vibration states that all things in the Universe vibrate at a particular frequency. Since our bodies are mostly made up of water, sound vibrations in the environment are continually being inducted into us, directly affecting what we think and how we feel. In turn, these vibratory states affect our Auric toroidal field and either strengthen or weaken it. Keep in mind that a person's heart electromagnetic field works in concert with their Auric field, inducing it with emotional energy.

Sound is the most transcendental of the senses and one that attunes us most to the higher Cosmic Planes. Pleasant sounding music that has harmonic rhythm affects our Aura, eliciting a positive emotional state. It puts us in touch with our Souls, healing us. On the other hand, music with discordant tones creates sound waves that do the exact opposite. It can make us feel anxious and agitated, thereby inducing fear energy. In the case of the former, our Aura expands since pleasant-sounding music creates a loving emotional state that makes our hearts vibrate with joy. In the latter, our Aura contracts to shield and protect us from harmful vibrations. For example, modern-day hip-hop music uses the 808 drum machine whose low-frequency beats tune us into the Root Chakra, Muladhara. Its dense vibration keeps our consciousness bound to the material plane, often inducing irritation and aggressiveness.

We are strongly affected by electromagnetic energy released from technological devices in our homes, even though most of us are unaware of this fact. Computers, cellphones, tablets, and especially WiFi routers interfere with the natural flow of our toroidal field and can cause disturbances. For this reason, it is not uncommon for people who are sensitive energetically to turn off their cellphones or plug out their WiFi routers when going to sleep. Some go even as far as plugging out all technological devices out of the electrical sockets to neutralize the electromagnetic energy present around them.

The foundation of all higher vibratory energies is love. In contrast, all lower vibratory energies are based on fear. The general rule to keep in mind is that positive, loving energies make the Aura expand, while negative, fear-based energies make it contract. The contraction of the Aura occurs to safeguard the person's energies, while the expansion occurs to allow more of the positive outside energies to enter in.

We are naturally drawn to loving, peaceful, and calm people since they affect our Aura positively. How many times have you heard the saying, "This person has a nice Aura about them." Here is implied that the individual has an abundance of Light energy, which they share readily with others. Conversely, pessimistic, hostile, angry, and generally chaotic people are challenging to be around since they negatively affect our Aura. Therefore, we naturally try to stay away from these people unless they bring out something inside of us that we wish to heal in ourselves.

It is propitious to the health of our Auric field to spend time outside and ground with the Earth often. Whether you have been exposed to electromagnetic frequencies or need to clear your head after an encounter with a negative person, it helps to go for a walk, especially in nature. Most people who are drawn to going for a walk after being exposed to negative energy are consciously unaware that Earth energies aid in releasing negativity from the Aura by facilitating grounding. The Soul hijacks the consciousness long enough to motion you to go for a walk to expose yourself to nature's elements, allowing you to reset and neutralize your energies.

Walking barefoot in nature on a sunny day is the best and quickest way to ground yourself with the Earth. The Sun feeds our Auric energies, while the torus aligns itself with the Earth. Treating the physical body directly affects our Chakric energies, and vice versa—As Above, So Below. Through grounding and physical exercise, we clear out negative energy from the body and detox while relieving physical tension and optimizing the flow of our Nadis. In turn, our vitality increases, and our Aura strengthens.

Between *The Magus* and *Serpent Rising*, I have covered powerful Spiritual practices such as Ceremonial Magick, Crystal Healing, Tuning Fork Sound Healing, Aromatherapy, and others. All of these practices aim to heal and balance the Chakras, optimize the Aura, and Spiritually evolve. Of course, it helps to combine these practices with Yoga, physical exercise, or any other methods that work directly on the physical body and ground it. When the body is healthy, so is the mind, and vice versa.

Your toroidal field is an autonomous battery powered by Prana, which requires food and water for fuel. Once the Kundalini pierces Sahasrara Chakra and opens the Thousand-Petalled Lotus, consciousness unites with Cosmic Consciousness, expanding and optimizing your toroidal energy field.

As the Chakras become cleansed and purified over time by the Kundalini Fire, Light energy permeates the Aura further, powering and optimizing the Chakras. As such, the Auric field strengthens since the amount of Light energy a person channels directly influences how magnetized the Aura becomes. In turn, the physical body reaches its most optimal, healthy state, and the overall vitality increases.

During the Kundalini transformation, the Hand and Foot Chakras open, allowing the Spirit to descend and permeate the deepest corners of the Self. In addition, the flow of energy from the fingers and toes strengthens the torus and further amplifies the velocity of energy circulating within (Figure 22).

Other energy channels open as well that facilitate the optimization of the torus. The entire Kundalini awakening process and the transformation that follows is designed to enable the individual to reach their highest potential as a Spiritual human being, which is reflected in the expansion of their bio-energy that comprises the Auric field.

It is no coincidence that a Kundalini awakened person appears unique to others. Since we are all interconnected, when our energy fields interact, we can realize intuitionally when someone's energy field is more prominent than usual. Therefore, a person with an enhanced energy field is naturally attractive to everyone who comes into contact with them.

Since the centre of the torus is the heart, people who live from the heart, instead of the head, have naturally more powerful toroidal energy fields. They are more magnetized and electric, meaning that they naturally channel more Light energy than someone who lives through the intellect alone.

People who live from the heart love themselves and others since they are in touch with their Souls. Remember, the Soul lives through the heart, while the Ego lives through the mind. A person who lives through their heart is in touch with their intuitive ability. They feel the energies around them instead of interfacing with their environment through the intellect.

By bypassing the mind and the Ego, you gain touch with the present moment, the Now, which is the field of infinite possibility. Being in the Now and living through the heart and Soul expands your energy field, maximizing your Spiritual potential.

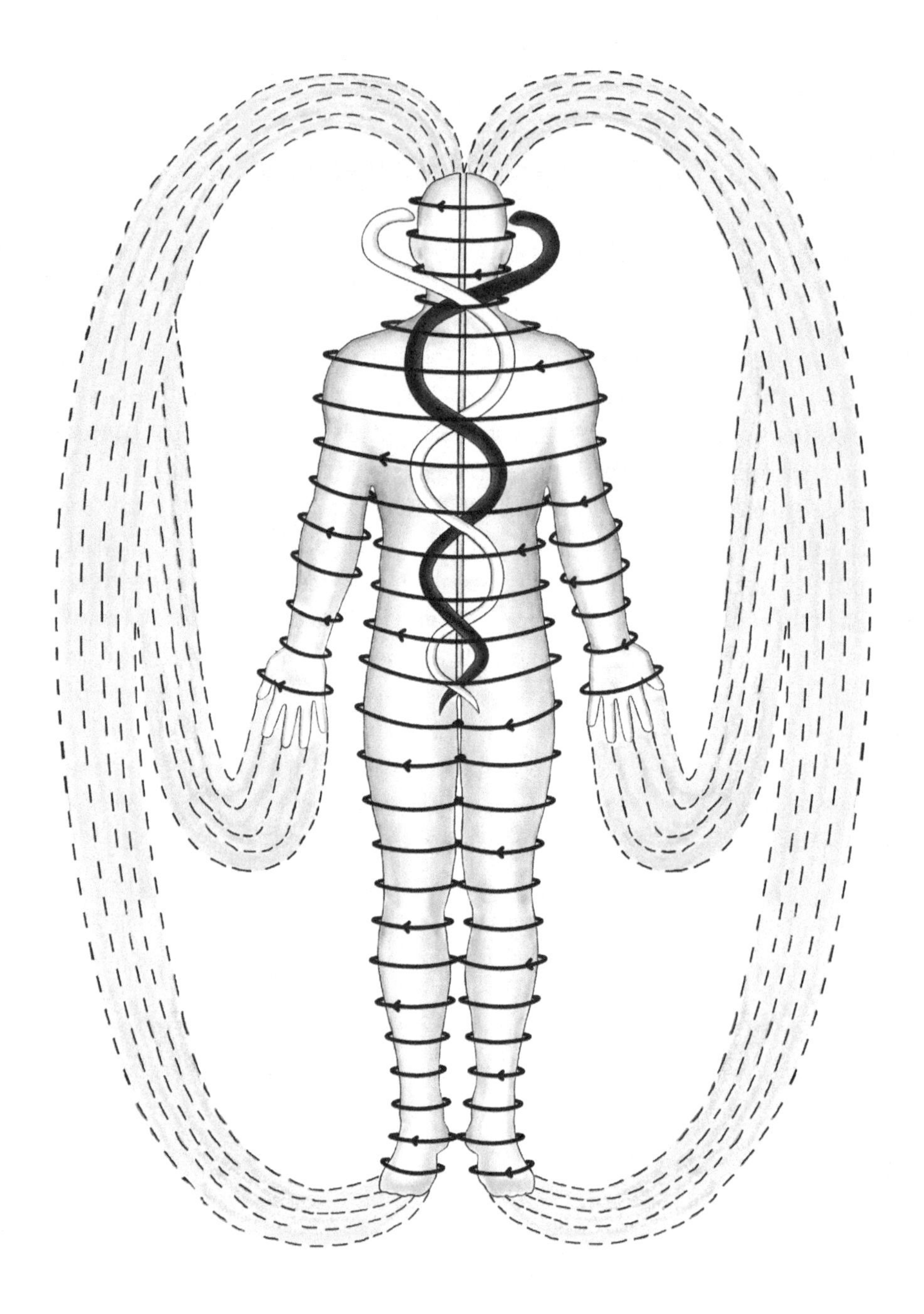

Figure 22: The Kundalini Toroidal Field

THE SEVEN MAJOR CHAKRAS

If you have awakened the Kundalini and risen it to Sahasrara, the Seven Chakras, corresponding with the complete Tree of Life, are now fully activated inside of you. Each Chakra is expressed through different parts of the psyche and affects bodily functions. We can further break down Chakric energies into the Five Elements since each one corresponds with either Earth, Water, Fire, Air or Spirit.

The Chakras within the Body of Light and the corresponding Elements and Cosmic Planes of existence occupy the same space and time as your physical body. They all exist inside your Aura and form layers of it, which are, in essence, interconnected and interpenetrating. The higher the Chakra or Element, the further out it projects.

Muladhara Chakra

The first Chakra, Muladhara, is located between the coccyx (tailbone) and the perineum. It is the lowest of the Seven Major Chakras and is related to the Element of Earth and Planet Saturn, the slowest-moving of the Seven Ancient Planets, relating to Karma and time-cycles. Muladhara is the centre of our physical energy and grounding. Its modus operandi is the security and survival of the physical body. Since Muladhara is related to the World of Matter, its energy is related to physical expression—all physical activities require Earth energy.

The Kundalini lies coiled at the base of the spine, and it is inextricably connected with the Planet Earth through the energy lines in our legs, which connect to our Foot Chakras. Muladhara is also called the Root, Base, or Earth Chakra because it is the foundation as the lowest of the Seven Major Chakras. This Chakra's energy is most dense, vibrating at the lowest frequency of all the Chakras. In the Hermetic axiom of "As Above, So Below, Muladhara deals with the aspect of manifestation—the Below.

Muladhara has four petals, or vortices, and is the colour red. Foods that correspond with Muladhara Chakra are root vegetables, red meat, red fruits, pepper, cayenne, and paprika. Challenges in this Chakra relate to the things we acquire in our material life and their quality. For example, do we have the right job, home, vehicle for transportation, life partner, friends, or lack stability and security in these areas?

An open and active Root Chakra makes one confident, stable, and grounded. They have an easy time manifesting the life they desire and are balanced emotionally and mentally. An overactive Root Chakra makes one materialistic and greedy. On the other hand, an underactive Root Chakra makes one overly fearful and anxious. By lacking emotional and mental stability, it is seemingly impossible to manifest anything of value in your life.

Swadhisthana Chakra

The second Chakra, Swadhisthana, is located in the lower abdomen and is related to the Element of Water and the Planet Jupiter, the benevolent Planet of mercy and justice. Swadhisthana deals with emotions, feelings, and instincts projected through the subconscious mind. Being related to the subconscious, Swadhisthana is the source of fear energy that significantly influences who we become in life.

Swadhisthana is called the Sacral or Spleen Chakra. On a basic human level, the Sacral Chakra affects our sexual expression, social interactions, and how comfortable we are with ourselves and others. The Sacral Chakra is the personality aspect of the Self—Ego consciousness that is formed over time. The Ego is tempered by fear, as it avoids all activities that make the body and mind feel bad while embracing everything that makes it feel good. The Ego is primarily concerned with seeking pleasure, irrespective of how its actions will affect other people.

Swadhisthana has six petals and is the colour orange. Foods that correspond with Swadhisthana Chakra are orange coloured fruits and vegetables, eggs, tofu, soy products, peanut butter, nuts, seeds, honey, and vanilla. Challenges in Swadhisthana are found in what kind of emotions we carry inside ourselves. Do we feel a lot of fear, and is the fear preventing us from manifesting our Soul's desires? Do we have joy in our lives, or is life bland and boring? Do we have issues with intimacy, and are we sexually expressive? Are we comfortable with who we are, or do we hide from the world?

When Swadhisthana is open and active, one is in touch with their emotions and is candid with others, allowing them to form healthy relationships. They are comfortable with intimacy and are expressive of their inner desires. A balanced Sacral Chakra enhances creativity and allows you to go with the flow of life without being too attached. It enables you to feel happiness and joy in small, everyday activities.

If your Sacral Chakra is blocked or underactive, you become closed off emotionally from others, naturally withdrawing and going within. In this state, a person becomes introverted and in overly in-touch with their Ego and insecurities. In contrast, an overactive Sacral Chakra makes you excessively emotional, attached to other people, and too sexual, resulting in promiscuity.

Manipura Chakra

The third Chakra, Manipura, is located at the Solar Plexus, above the navel. Its other name is the Solar Plexus Chakra. Manipura corresponds with the Fire Element, and the Planet Mars, hence why it is the source of our willpower. Our motivation, drive, vitality, and level of creativity are all governed by Manipura. In addition, this Chakra is in charge of our confidence, self-esteem and the ability to be assertive in life.

Manipura governs digestion which allows us to transform nourishment into valuable energy for the body and mind. Manipura works with the Chakras above and below it since it is the "Seat of the Soul." The Soul governs our character, while the Ego governs our personality. The Soul requires intelligence, mental clarity, and the harmonizing of the will with logic, reason, and imagination. As such, Manipura draws energy from the Air Chakra above it, Anahata. The Fire of Manipura also activates the creative impulse, which requires Swadhisthana's emotions for expression.

Manipura has ten petals and is the colour yellow. Foods that correspond with Manipura Chakra are yellow and gold fruits and vegetables, dairy products, complex carbohydrates and grains, mustard, turmeric, cumin, and ginger. The challenges found in this Chakra relate to how we use our willpower. Are we in charge of our own lives, or are other people? Are we motivated and driven to accomplish our goals, or do we lack in this area? Do we express our innermost desires, or are we locked in our emotions too much? Do we know how to exact severity when others wrong us, or are we a doormat for others to use?

When Manipura is open and active, we exert dominance in our lives and feel in control. We have enhanced personal power and are manifesting our life's goals. Manipura works with the Earth Chakra, Muladhara, to accomplish these tasks.

If Manipura is underactive, we tend to be passive, indecisive, and timid. If it is overactive, we become domineering and overly severe. Too much Fire energy can result in tyranny and oppression over other people. Willpower needs emotions for balance, which are supplied by Swadhisthana. If the Water Chakra does not balance our Fire Chakra, we can become overly aggressive to get what we want and hostile. Willpower needs love to guide it; otherwise, one's action contains Karmic consequences. As such, Manipura relies on Anahata for guidance.

Anahata Chakra

The fourth Chakra, Anahata, is located between the two breasts in the centre of the chest. Otherwise known as the Heart Chakra, Anahata corresponds with the Air Element and the Planet Venus. Anahata is our love centre which deals with compassion, affection, altruism, kindness, and inspiration. It stimulates our imagination, thoughts, as well as fantasies. The challenge of Anahata is to overcome the Karmas from the lower three Chakras so that you can attune to the energy of unconditional love.

Anahata is our Spiritual centre since it receives the energy of the higher three Chakras. It is the centre where we feel unity with all things through the binding power of love. As such, Anahata is the centre of group consciousness.

Anahata is connected to our Palm Chakras, which allow us to feel the energy around us as a quantifiable essence and heal others. Hands-on healing requires us to channel love energy from Anahata via our Palm Chakras and project it into areas that need healing. Love energy is the ultimate healer of mind, body, and Soul.

In Anahata, we understand our life's work and purpose. Since the essence of the Air Element is thought, Anahata fuels both the Fire and Water Elements and gives them life. If this Chakra is inactive, we turn to selfishness and satisfying the Ego.

Anahata has twelve petals, and its colour is green. Foods that correspond with Anahata Chakra are the wide variety of green coloured fruits, vegetables and herbs, and leafy greens. Challenges in this Chakra relate to the clarity of thought. Are we engrossed in fantasy and illusive thinking too much, or are our thoughts based on truth? Are we using our imagination to help us achieve our goals? Are our thoughts of a higher nature in the direction of helping others or of a lower quality, where our focus is only to tend to ourselves?

When Anahata is open and active, we are compassionate and friendly with others, enabling us to have harmonious relationships. We have an understanding of our Spiritual nature which makes us virtuous and ethical in our words and actions. As such, we become forgiving, kind, and charitable. Essentially, our behaviour becomes motivated by unconditional love as opposed to Self-love.

When Anahata is underactive, we tend to be emotionally cold and distant. We get too ingrained in the lower Chakras, which makes us Egotistical instead of exalting our Spiritual nature. We tend to ourselves and our needs and desires without regard to other people. If this Chakra is overactive, on the other hand, we smother others with love, often for selfish reasons.

Vishuddhi Chakra

The fifth Chakra, Vishuddhi, is located in the centre of the neck; hence it is called the Throat Chakra. Vishuddhi is of the Element of Spirit (Aethyr); it works in conjunction with the following two Chakras above and the Chakras below it. Vishuddhi is related to the verbal, subtle, and written expression of one's thoughts. It corresponds with the

Planet Mercury, which rules communication and the speed of thought. Vishuddhi generates the vibration of the spoken word on an energetic and physical level.

Vishuddhi also controls discernment and intellect. It has sixteen petals, and its colour is blue. Vishuddhi Chakra rules all liquids that we bring into the body. Foods that correspond with this Chakra include blue coloured fruits and vegetables, salt, sage, and peppermint. Challenges in Vishuddhi relate to whether we express what is on our minds and how well we communicate with others. Do we talk too much, or does what we say have substance? When we talk, do we project power with our vocal cords, or do we come off meek and timid?

When Vishuddhi is open and active, we speak our truth to others creatively. We are Self-expressive and use words as anchors to convey our reality to others. Not only are we great talkers but listeners too, since communication works both ways.

When Vishuddhi is underactive, we tend to be quiet and introverted generally. We lack confidence in speaking our truth, which may arise from Solar Plexus Chakra issues. If we don't convey our truth because we feel unworthy, we might have problems in Anahata. Speaking our inner truth aligns us with the Divine while lying aligns us with lower, Demonic entities.

When Vishuddhi is overactive, we tend to talk too much, which clouds our ability to listen to other people. This situation usually occurs because of the Ego's desire to domineer others due to an unbalanced Manipura Chakra. If we become chatterboxes and lack substance in our speech, other people generally distance themselves from us. Therefore, it is essential to have a balanced Throat Chakra if we desire to thrive in life and have meaningful relationships.

Ajna Chakra

The sixth Chakra, Ajna, is located in the brain's centre, in the Third Ventricle. (More on the Third Ventricle in a later chapter.) Its more immediate access point is slightly above the centre of the eyebrows. Ajna is often referred to as the Mind's Eye Chakra, the Third Eye, or the Brow Chakra. It relates to the Element of Spirit or Aethyr.

Ajna corresponds with the Moon. Although the Moon is classified as a satellite while the Sun is our central Star, the Ancient people included both as part of their Seven Ancient Planets framework, referring to them as Planets. The Moon is our centre of clairvoyance and intuition. It gives us insight into the Unknown because it receives information from the Higher Realms above, through Sahasrara, the Crown Chakra. Ajna is our psychic centre. It gives us wisdom and understanding concerning the mysteries of the Universe. We obtain this knowledge through Gnosis, our ability to channel information from Divine energies directly. This sixth Chakra gives us the sixth sense of knowing beyond the Self.

Ajna is the essential Chakra concerning the Spiritual and Astral Worlds. As such, it is the centre of dreaming. Through this Chakra, we reach the Crown/Sahasrara and exit out of our physical bodies to travel to different dimensions of Time and Space. These Lucid Dream travels occur in the Inner Worlds or Planes—we use our Light Body as the vehicle.

Ajna has two petals and is the colour indigo. Foods that correspond with Ajna Chakra are indigo or dark bluish coloured fruits and vegetables, red wine, caffeine, chocolate, juniper, and lavender. Challenges in this Chakra relate to whether we receive higher information from Sahasrara or is our Mind's Eye closed up? Do we spend too much time in our heads, focusing on our intellect to guide us or are we in touch with our intuition? Are our dreams vivid and filled with life or bland and uneventful?

When Ajna Chakra is open and active, we have a good intuition that serves as our guiding force in life. When our intuition is strong, so is our faith since we can perceive reality beyond the Third Dimension. A strong intuition is usually connected with being a consciously aware Spiritual human being.

When Ajna is underactive, we tend to lose touch with the Spiritual reality. As such, we begin to rely too much on our intellect and Ego to guide us in life. Confusion sets in about our true essence, making us look for existential answers from people of authority.

When Ajna is overactive, we tend to live in a fantasy world. We lose touch with the reality of who we are and may even experience psychosis. Someone who uses hallucinogenic drugs too often will invariably overstimulate their Ajna Chakra.

Sahasrara Chakra

The seventh Chakra, Sahasrara, is located at the top, centre of the head. As such, it is otherwise known as the Crown Chakra. Sahasrara is our source of Enlightenment, Oneness, truth, and Spiritual wisdom and understanding. It corresponds with the Sun, the Star of our Solar System. The Crown Chakra is the highest Chakra of the Spirit/Aethyr Element, and it serves as a gateway to the Divine Planes represented by the Transpersonal Chakras above the head.

Sahasrara is the highest in human consciousness and the ultimate in understanding and knowledge of the Universe. Traditionally, this centre is described as a wheel with one thousand (countless) petals or vortices. When all the petals are open, the individual obtains a permanent link to Cosmic Consciousness, achieving transcendence.

Since Sahasrara is the source of everything, it is also the source of all the powers and their totality. The colour of Sahasrara is white since white is the source of all the colours. Its other colour is violet as the first colour in the White Light spectrum, and one following indigo. Foods that correspond with Sahasrara are white, violet, and Lavender coloured foods. Also, purified water, fresh air, and sunlight align us with the energy of Sahasrara, as well as fasting, detoxing, and breathing and meditation techniques.

White Light comes into the Body of Light through Sahasrara, and depending on how much Karma there is in the lower Chakras, this Light gets dimmer. Therefore, the dimmer the Chakras below Sahasrara, the more the Ego is present, and the lesser the Higher Self.

The source of the Higher Self is Sahasrara. Awakening the Kundalini and raising it to Sahasrara will allow you to gain a direct connection with your Higher Self. Once achieved, the Higher Self becomes your own master and teacher for the rest of your life. There will never be a need for an outside teacher again since you will be the teacher and student in one. The challenge, though, is to purify the Chakras so that you can easily be guided and taught by your Higher Self.

An open and active Sahasrara centre imparts on us the understanding that we are Spiritual beings living a human existence and not the other way around. Embracing our Spirituality allows us to recognize that the physical reality is merely an illusion. Our essence is Soul and consciousness, which are Eternal and cannot be annihilated. Spiritual people don't regard physical death as the end but merely the beginning of something new and different. A Spiritual worldview creates a sort of detachment from taking this reality too seriously, which brings joy and happiness that accompanies people who have embraced the Spirit energy within them.

If you are closed to the Spiritual reality of things, your Sahasrara centre is most likely inactive. You tend only to the physical body, which makes you align with the Ego and its needs and desires. Embracing the Ego while negating the Soul attracts lower, Demonic entities to feed off our energy. The consciousness becomes hijacked and remains so until we recognize that we are not separate from the world and that there is a Spiritual reality that underlies everything.

On the other hand, an overactive Sahasrara may result in ignoring bodily needs and overintellectualizing. If Light only pours into the higher Chakras, there is no grounding, and the individual becomes very cerebral. Remember, this world is an illusion but one that we need to respect since our physical body is our vehicle for manifesting the reality we desire. Balance of mind, body, and Soul is the key to Enlightenment, not discarding one aspect for another.

SEVEN CHAKRAS AND THE NERVOUS SYSTEM

The Sushumna channel carries the Kundalini energy through the spinal cord and into the brain. The spinal cord and brain constitute the Central Nervous System (CNS). Emanating from the spinal cord are nerves that reach outwards like the branches of a tree, where Sushumna acts as the central trunk. These nerve fibres constitute the Sympathetic Nervous System (SNS) and Parasympathetic Nervous System (PNS) which are part of the Autonomic Nervous System (ANS).

The Autonomic Nervous System operates mainly unconsciously and regulates essential processes such as breathing, digestion, and the beating of the heart. For example, during a Spiritual awakening, the heart begins to race, thus involving the Autonomic Nervous System, which is regulated by the emotional networks in the brain.

The Sympathetic Nervous System and Parasympathetic Nervous System do opposite things in most cases—the Sympathetic Nervous System prepares the body for action and activity while the Parasympathetic Nervous System enables the body to relax. The Autonomic Nervous System is responsible for creating a healthy balance between the two, promoting a calm and peaceful mind.

The areas where the Sympathetic Nervous System and Parasympathetic Nervous System meet are centred around major body organs and endocrine glands. Referred to as "Plexuses," these convergence areas in the body's cavities form the most vital grouping of nerve cells. The Plexuses connect the significant bodily organs to the spinal cord. These are also the areas where the Major Chakras are located at the front of the body.

The Major Chakras interact with the physical body through the nervous system and the endocrine glands and organs. Each Chakra is associated with particular bodily functions, controlled by its Plexus and the endocrine glands and organs related to it.

In the centre of each of the Major Chakras is a stem-like channel (Figure 23). Each channel extends towards the spinal cord and merges with it—Sushumna powers each of the Major Chakras by providing them with their vital energy. Chakric stems bend downwards near the Pharyngeal Plexus (Throat), Cardiac and Pulmonary Plexuses (Heart), Splenic and Celiac Plexuses (Solar), Pelvic Plexus (Sacral) and Coccygeal and Sacral Plexuses (Root). Above the Carotid Plexus (Mind's Eye), the Chakric stem bends upwards, while for Sahasrara Chakra, it rises to the top of the head through the Cerebral Cortex.

The Pharyngeal Plexus "innervates" (supplies organs or other body parts with nerves) our palate and vocal cords. Since Vishuddhi (Throat) Chakra governs communication and expression, it is no wonder the throat and inside of the mouth are powered by it. Its Chakric channel extends from the spinal cord between the second and third cervical vertebrae (C2-3) to the centre of the throat.

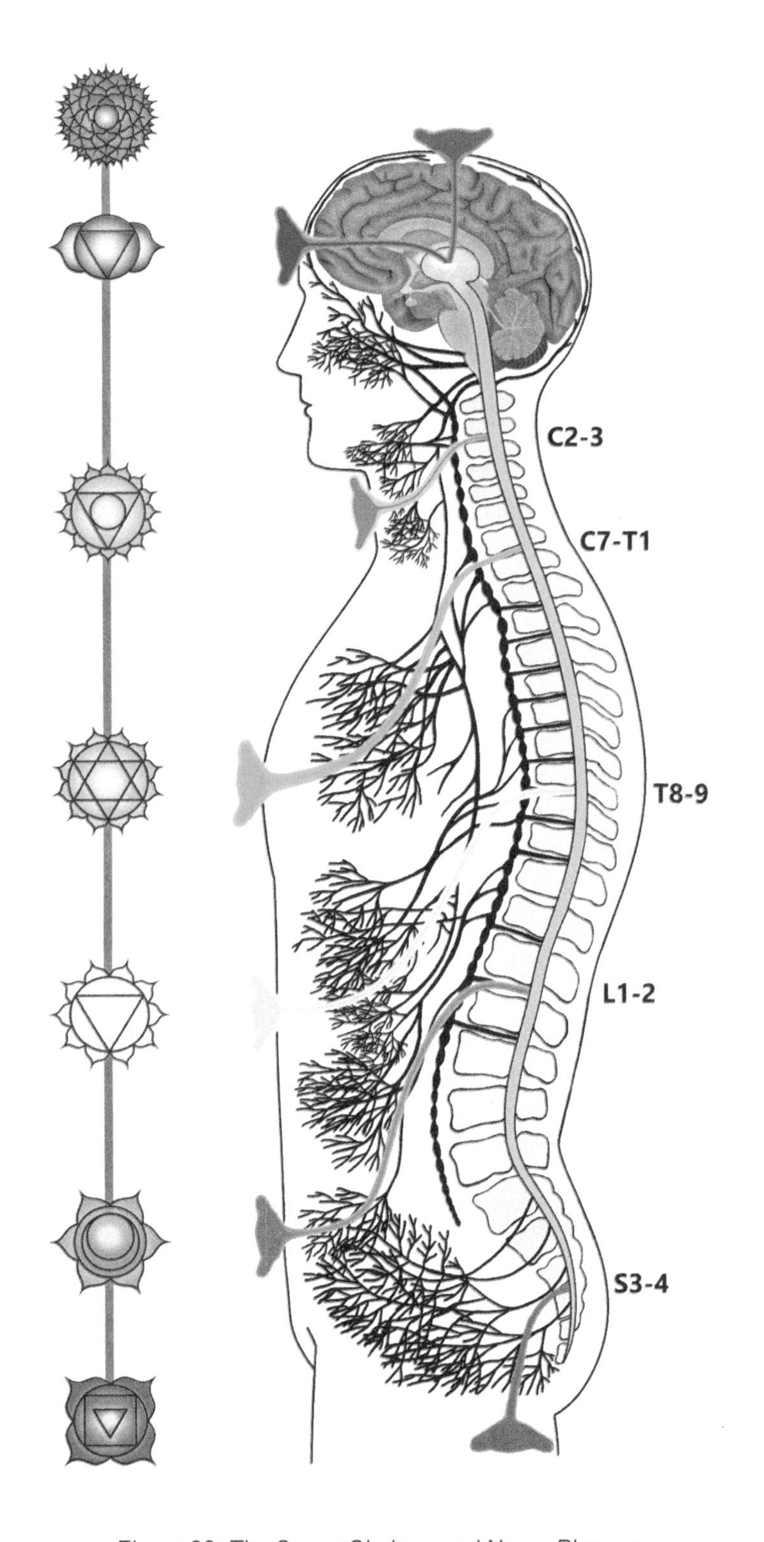

Figure 23: The Seven Chakras and Nerve Plexuses

The Pulmonary Plexus is in continuity with the Cardiac Plexus—located above the aortic of the heart, about midway in the chest. The Cardiac Plexus innervates the heart, the organ associated with our capacity for love and compassion and our connection with all living and non-living things. These are all attributes of the Anahata (Heart) Chakra that powers it. Anahata's Chakric stem-like channel extends from the spinal cord between the seventh cervical and first thoracic vertebrae (C7-T1) to the centre of the chest.

Branches from the Celiac Plexus and Vagus Nerve form the Celiac Plexus in its entirety. (More on the importance of the Vagus Nerve in a later chapter.) Known as the Solar Plexus in scientific and Spiritual circles, the Celiac Plexus is located at the base of the ribs near the stomach. Its nerves innervate the pancreas, gall bladder, upper intestines, liver and stomach. Manipura (Solar Plexus) Chakra governs our willpower, vitality, and digestion, powered by the organs mentioned above. Its Chakric channel extends from the spinal cord between the eighth and ninth thoracic vertebrae (T8-9) to the centre of the upper abdomen.

The Pelvic Plexus governs the eliminative and reproductive functions and consists of the superior and inferior Hypograstric Plexuses. The superior Hypogastric Plexus innervates the ovaries in women and testicles in men. Its location is in the lower abdomen, and it correlates with Swadhisthana (Sacral) Chakra, which is associated with reproduction and fertility.

The inferior Hypogastric Plexus is a continuation of the superior one, located right below it in the lower pelvic region. It innervates the uterus and cervix in women and the prostate in men. It also is connected to the rectum and bladder. Swadhisthana's Chakric stem-like channel extends from the spinal cord between the first and second lumbar vertebrae (L1-2) to the lower abdomen centre.

The Coccygeal Plexus consists of the coccygeal nerve and the fifth sacral nerve, innervating the skin in the coccyx (tailbone) region. The Sacral Plexus is a network of nerves that emerge from the lower lumbar and sacral vertebrae and provide motor control to and receive sensory information from most of the pelvis and legs. The largest nerve in the Sacral Plexus is the Sciatic Nerve that innervates the thigh, lower leg, and foot.

Muladhara Chakra's stem-like channel extends from the sacrum between the third and fourth sacral vertebrae (S3-4), and it droops down to the area between the perineum and coccyx. The Root Chakra points downward towards the Earth as it is tasked with grounding our Chakric system. The energy channels in the legs are our energetic connection with the Earth Star Chakra below our feet. They also power the Ida and Pingala Nadis, which begin in Muladhara, but get their feminine and masculine currents through each of the leg energy channels.

PURIFYING THE CHAKRAS

After a full and permanent Kundalini awakening, once the Body of Light has been built up through food intake, the next step is attuning your consciousness to its highest aspect, the Spiritual Body. This part is challenging because you will have to purify your lower Chakras first, which will allow your consciousness to rise naturally. Your consciousness will be weighed down by Karmic energy in the lower Chakras until you do so. This process of Spiritual Ascension is systematic in this respect.

The lowest and most dense energies must be overcome before the higher vibrational energies can permeate the Self. The negative Karmic energy of fear is the part that keeps most of us vibrating at a lower frequency. Since fear energy binds the Ego to the lower Four Elements, these Elements must be purified and consecrated to allow your consciousness to elevate and operate from the higher three Spiritual Chakras—Vishuddhi, Ajna and Sahasrara.

Once your Body of Light is built up, you will have occasional experiences of these rapturous states in certain moments where you lose sight of your Ego. However, since you have to remove the clutches of the Ego to integrate the Spiritual Body fully and absorb your consciousness into it, the Four Elemental Chakras below the Spiritual Chakras must be worked through. There is no other way, and you can't take any shortcuts in this process. It may take many years, and it does in most cases, but it has to be accomplished.

In *The Magus: Kundalini and the Golden Dawn*, I offer Ceremonial Magick ritual exercises for working on the lowest four Chakras of Muladhara, Swadhisthana, Manipura and Anahata. Whoever needs to work on their Chakras will find this work invaluable on their journey towards Spiritual Ascension. *The Magus* focuses on working with all the Chakras and purifying them through particular ritual exercises that invoke the Elemental energies of Earth, Water, Fire, Air, including Spirit.

Once you break down the parts of the Lower Self through working with the Four Elements, you will have fine-tuned the corresponding aspects of your psyche. The next step is to re-integrate those parts of the Self through the Spirit Element. These ritual invocation techniques serve as powerful tools to attune the Seven Chakras and raise your consciousness so that you are channelling the maximum amount of Light energy into your Aura.

The purpose of the ritual work with Ceremonial Magick is to gain an everlasting connection with your Holy Guardian Angel, which is another term for the Higher Self. It is the part of you which is of God-the Divine. By cleansing and purifying your Chakras, you align yourself to your Higher Self and distance yourself from your Lower Self-the Ego.

The full Kundalini awakening (whether it happened all at once or gradually) and permanent localization of the Kundalini energy in the brain is considered the highest achievable state of Spiritual awakening. There is no other form of Spiritual awakening or initiation that is higher or greater in scope. But awakening the Kundalini is merely the beginning of your journey towards Enlightenment. The next step is purifying your Chakras and raising the vibration of your consciousness. And to do it successfully in a shorter period, you will need some form of Spiritual practice to aid you on your journey.

BRAIN EXPANSION

The six Chakras, Muladhara, Swadhisthana, Manipura, Anahata, Vishuddhi, and Ajna, have different counterparts in respective areas of the brain (Figure 24). This means that once a Chakra is entirely opened through a Kundalini awakening, the part of the brain associated with that Chakra becomes permanently activated. The activation of the brain is necessary to facilitate the expansion of consciousness. Also, as different brain areas open up, it will begin to feel transparent and weightless, as if you are losing touch with the Matter that comprises it. As Matter's effect drops away in your consciousness, your brain becomes an antenna to receiving vibrations from the outside Universe through the Crown Chakra, Sahasrara, right above it.

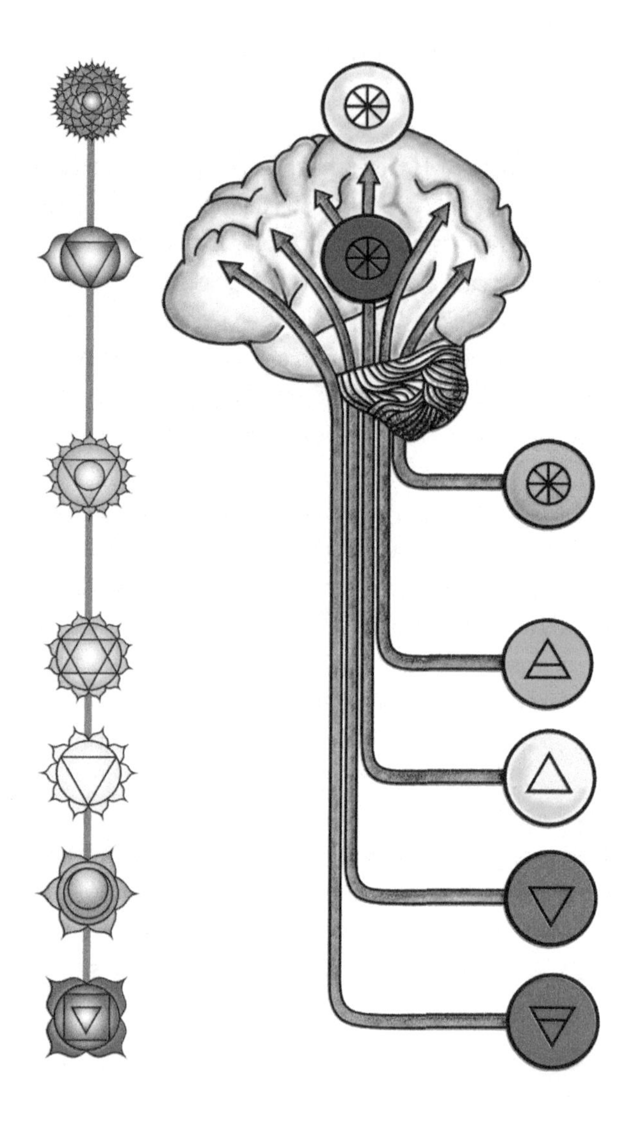

Figure 24: Brain Expansion and Chakric Correspondences

As this numbing effect occurs in the brain, you begin to feel a connection to Cosmic Consciousness. The Light inside your head is felt as a quantifiable essence. Your inner Light is connected to the Great White Light that is the foundation of all existence and is the essence of Cosmic Consciousness. It is through this connection that your psychic powers develop.

As your Body of Light optimises over time, small pockets of energy in different areas of the brain open up, which will feel like a liquid substance that is moving through your brain. This substance is liquid Spirit energy, which activates and enlightens different areas of your brain. As you bring food into your system, it transforms into Light energy, which becomes a liquid substance in your brain area. As such, you will feel your consciousness and your brain expanding daily. This process is similar to a plant receiving its nutrients from the ground and developing and growing over time. Its growth and development depend entirely on the nutrients it gets from the ground. Sometimes there is a lot of pressure in different parts of the brain and head as this development process occurs, resulting in headaches. If this happens, it is a sign that you are not bringing enough nutritious food into your system or are not eating frequently enough.

Keep in mind that what I am describing only happens if you have had a permanent Kundalini awakening which means that this energy has risen into your brain and resides there permanently now. As soon as this occurs, the brain starts to become remodelled by this newfound Light permeating it. And as mentioned, this will also be accompanied by a vibratory sound heard inside your head whose pitch level depends on the food you bring into your body. This is because you are now like a battery of Divine Light energy, which is bio-electric.

CONSCIOUSNESS EXPANSION PHENOMENA

As the brain expands, another sense develops—the awareness of the Silent Witness, the moment-to-moment record-keeper of reality. The Silent Witness is the part of the Self that stands apart in consciousness and watches the actions of the physical body as an impartial witness of it. It can read the energy created by the body language as a quantifiable essence and keep you informed on what you are putting out into the world with your actions like a supercomputer.

The Silent Witness develops as the Kundalini energy expands the brain. This new ability to perceive reality results in a complete detachment from the Ego, as you experience yourself radically different than before the Kundalini awakening took place. I believe that one of the major purposes of the Kundalini transformation is to exalt the silent watcher within, the True Self, and allow it to rise out of the physical body via the activated Kundalini circuit and hover above you, recording your movements.

The silent observer, or Silent Witness, is the part of you which is Spirit, which is God. It is the part of you that is pure, undifferentiated consciousness that forms part of the Cosmic Consciousness. In reality, we are all One and the part of us that stands aside and silently observes our actions are the same for everyone; it is God. But with a Kundalini awakening, there is an incredible distinction between that part of you and your Ego. You become more attuned to the silent observer aspect of your being than the Ego since it enables you to control your reality and manifest your desires.

The Silent Witness watches and prompts you to go about your day and perform your daily tasks, almost like a director who directs the movie of the main character—you. Your notion or concept of Self uses the physical body to accomplish the desired purpose of the Silent Witness.

When I developed this sense, I began to see outside of myself, and the world around me began to seem like a video game, with me as the main character. This phenomenon is ongoing and will continue to be present for the rest of my life. It enables me to see my facial expressions and the energy they evoke in others, and based on this perception, I can have complete control over the type of vibrations I put out into the Universe. As such, I have a high degree of control over what others feel in my presence since I am navigating their emotions with my body language and the energy I put out. As I am in this state, I am generally neutral with my feelings where nothing gets me overly excited or down, but I am in a tranquil and balanced state of mind.

By being in this elevated state of mind, I feel a strong connection with sound, where everything I hear makes an impression on my consciousness. It took some time to get used to it, and I had to re-learn how to concentrate when

I am focusing on getting something important done so that I am not swayed by the sounds coming from my environment. I also had to implement earplugs early on in my Kundalini transformation process since it was difficult to induce sleep because of this powerful connection to sound. I learned to go inwards when necessary, instead of allowing my consciousness to project outwards, as is my natural state now.

As the years went by, my consciousness continued to expand, as did my ability to see more from outside myself. It came to a point where I could project high up in the clouds and look down at the world below me from a birds' eye point of view. To be clear, I only leave my physical body in Spirit. Since my consciousness has expanded and has no limits or barriers now in terms of size, I can turn my attention to anything I see before me, no matter how far away, and connect with it through my Spirit. At that moment, my consciousness will vault out of my physical body and project to that spot or location. As it does so, high levels of histamine will release into my body, numbing it temporarily and allowing my consciousness to leave my body.

Even as my consciousness is out of my physical body, I still have complete control over it, and I can leave the transcendental state I am in at any moment. It is a mystical experience to project my consciousness in such a way since I feel a sense of unity with everything I see before me. Along with seeing Light in everything I look at, this is my favourite gift I received from the Divine after awakening the Kundalini energy.

THE MINOR CHAKRAS

THE HEAD CHAKRAS

The head contains Minor Chakras that are separate from the Seven Major Chakras. Because of where these Minor Chakras are located, they create a crown-like pattern on the head. It is no coincidence that representations of Spiritual figures often wear crowns on their heads in many traditions. For example, in Christianity, Jesus Christ is often depicted wearing a crown that alludes to him being a King of Heaven. As he said, we can all be Kings and Queens of Heaven; meaning we can all wear this metaphoric crown once we attain it through evolving Spiritually. The crown also represents the attainment of the Crown Chakra, Sahasrara, the highest Major Chakra and our connection to the Divine Light.

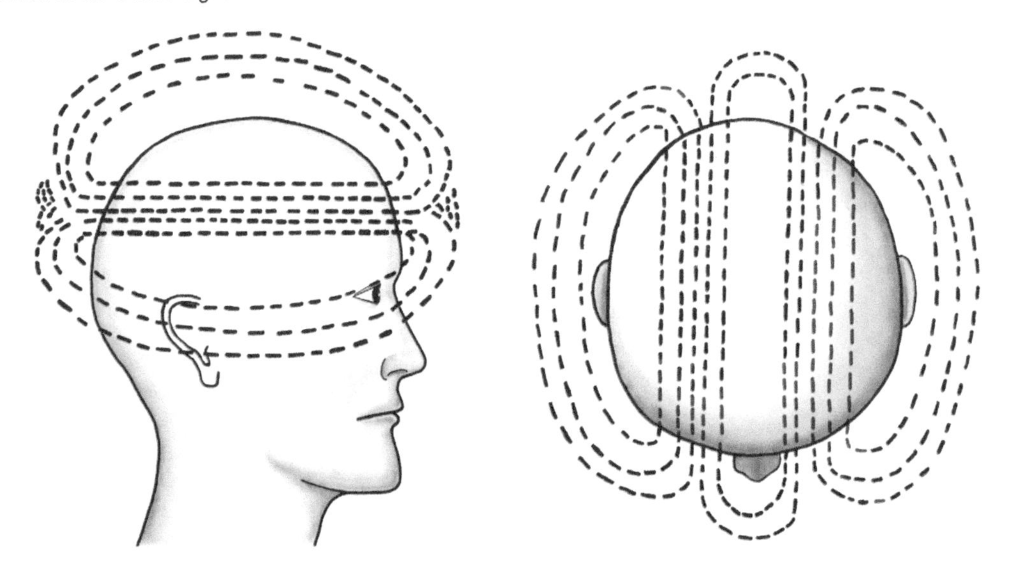

Figure 25: Halo Around the Head

The symbolic crown represents the awakened Chakras in the head and, therefore, the expansion of consciousness. The halo around the head of Jesus, the Saints, and other significant Spiritual figures, signifies that the Spiritual crown has been activated—Sahasrara Chakra is entirely open, and the individual consciousness has been expanded. Light in, over and around the head represents someone who is Enlightened (Figure 25). The very term "Enlightened" originates from this process of Light manifesting and permeating the area around the head.

On the diagram below (Figure 26), Chakra 1 is known as the Seventh Eye. It is an important minor Chakra on the head that, along with the Bindu (Chakra 6), works to power the circuit of the Kundalini within the Body of Light. These two Chakras carry the energy that connects the Self to Eternity and Non-Duality, allowing the awakened individual to feel the rapture of the Spiritual Realm and connection with the Divine. Also, since the Spiritual Realm is the contact point for the Divine Realm above it, it is not uncommon to have otherworldly experiences when Chakras 1 and 6 are active and functioning at their maximum capacity.

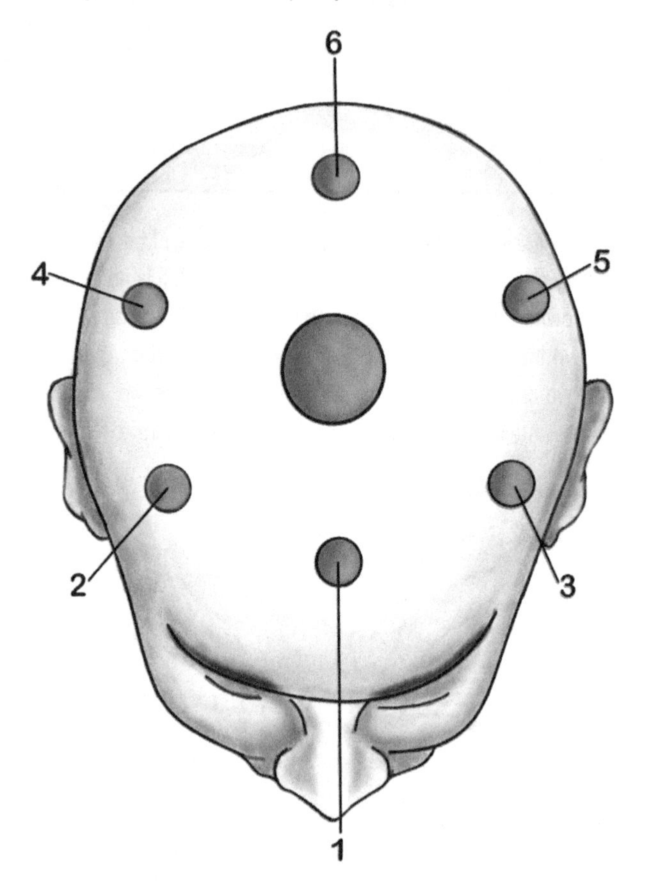

Figure 26: The Minor Head Chakras (Crown)

The Bindu is likened to the "Void," or the Abyss. In the Qabalah, the Abyss is the Eleventh Sphere of Daath on the Tree of Life, representing death—the death of the Ego. By entering the Void, the Self finds its True or Spiritual Self, and the duality of the mind ceases to exist. The Void of Bindu is our entry into the Spiritual Plane of Unity. The Bindu is like a "Lake of Fire," which unites all opposites and purifies all impurities. The mind experiences the duality of thoughts and ideas, and through this duality, the pain of separation is created. In the Bindu Chakra, all dual thoughts or ideas are reconciled by their opposites. This process allows us to bypass the mind and experience the purity and Oneness of the Spiritual realm. This energetic mechanism has been left in us by our Creator. It marks the next stage of our Spiritual Evolution and our return to the Garden of Eden.

Chakra 3 in the diagram is directly linked to Ida, the feminine channel in the body, while Chakra 2 is linked to Pingala, the masculine channel. Once Chakra 2 is completely opened, you begin to feel a connection with the right side of the body, through which the Pingala channel flows. Over time, the Spiritual Heart awakens, which feels like a spherical pocket of energy through which Pingala crosses. Its location is to the right of the physical heart. It contains a soothing flame since the Pingala Nadi is related to the Fire Element of the Soul. As the physical heart regulates the circulation of blood in the physical body, the Spiritual Heart governs the flow of Pranic energy in the Body of Light. The Spiritual Heart is transcendental, and it regulates thoughts and emotions that are of a Non-Dual quality.

Chakra 3, when fully opened, will form the connection to the left side of the body and the feeling of openness and expansion in the physical heart. A sense of tranquillity in your emotions characterizes it, which belong to the Water Element. Having an open heart makes you a better feeler and receiver of the vibrations from the outside world. In addition, it increases your capacity for empathy.

Chakras 4 and 5 are the next ones to open during the sublimation/transformation of Light, or Pranic energy in the body. They give a stronger connection to the Bindu (Chakra 6) and allow the individual's consciousness to leave the physical body when in meditation. Having these two Chakras fully open enables the fully Kundalini awakened individual to get absorbed in anything they view with their physical eyes when they give it their attention. These two Chakras help individual consciousness achieve Oneness.

You can know that the six Minor Chakras in the head are opening up and aligning when you feel a liquid substance moving through your brain in snake-like patterns. It infuses the channels that connect with each of the six Minor Chakras in the head. This phenomenon is characterized by a pleasant, tranquil feeling in your brain as it occurs.

You can know that Bindu is aligning and opening up more once Chakras 4 and 5 are opening. Consequently, once Chakras 2 and 3 are opening, an alignment occurs in the Seventh Eye (Chakra 1). One trinity of Chakras works together while the other trinity also works together. For this reason, Adepts in the Western Mysteries often wear a kippah on their heads, containing an image of the Hexagram, or Star of David as the Hebrews call it. The upwards and downwards triangles of the Hexagram represent the two trinities of minor Chakras in the head.

THE FOOT CHAKRAS

Along with the Seven Major Chakras that run vertically through the body, we have a web of auxiliary energy centres, or Minor Chakras in the feet and the hands, that provide a broad spectrum of energy influx into our system. Unfortunately, the Minor Chakras in the feet and hands are often ignored and neglected by Spiritual teachers even though they serve a crucial role in the energy framework of our bodies.

Each toe, including the middle of the foot and heel area, is governed by one of the Major Chakras (Figure 27). The big toe corresponds with Manipura, index toe with Anahata, the middle toe with Vishuddhi, the fourth toe to Ajna, the little toe with Swadhisthana, the middle of the sole to Sahasrara, and the back of the heel with Muladhara.

One of the functions of the toes is to discharge excess energy that has been accumulated in the Major Chakras through our regular, daily activities and body functions. This surplus energy is released and transmitted into the

Earth, facilitating grounding in our consciousness. When the Minor Chakras in the feet function well and are in harmony with the Major Chakras, there is a constant connection and flow of communication between Earth energy grids and our energies.

As per their location and connection with the Earth, the Foot Chakras also serve to channel energy from the Transpersonal Earth Star Chakra (below the feet) and transmit it into the Major Chakras via the energy channels in the legs. In this case, the Foot Chakras serve as energy conduits or connectors that allow the Earth Star to be in direct communication not only with Muladhara Chakra but with the other Major Chakras as well.

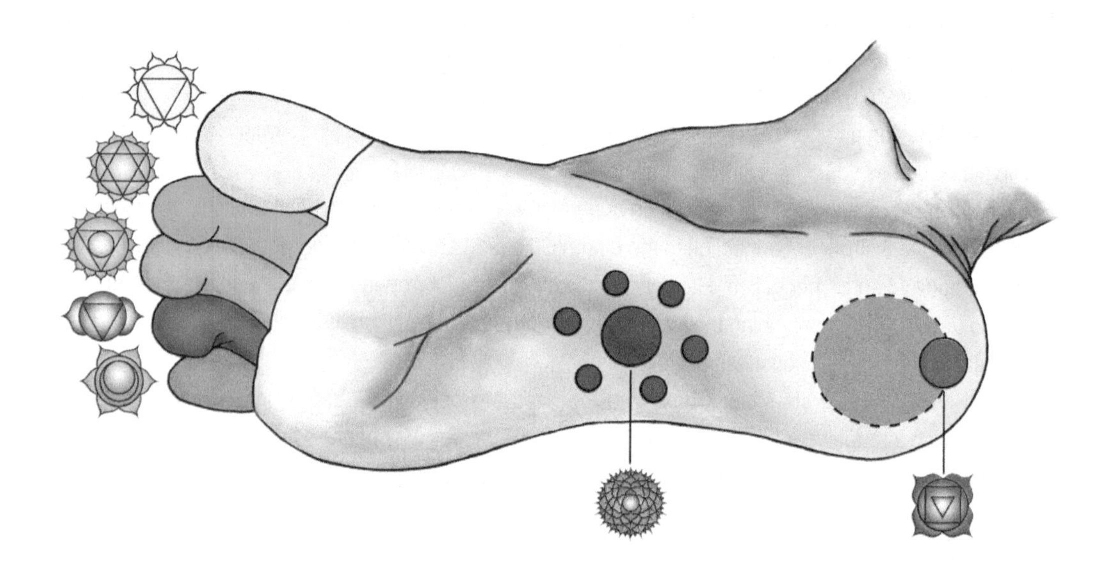

Figure 27: The Foot Chakras

The Foot Chakras also help facilitate the balancing and assimilation of the Kundalini energy that comes from the Earth through its magnetic currents. They work as energy transformers, regulating the quantity and intensity of energy coming into the Body of Light from the Earth.

The "Sole" Chakra is located in the middle of the foot and is related to Sahasrara, the Crown. The Sole Chakra is the most important of the Foot Chakras. If we examine its structure, we can see that its six secondary points directly reflect the Minor Chakras in the head, related to Sahasrara.

The relation between the Sole Chakra and Sahasrara is best described by the axiom of "As Above, So Below." These two sets of Chakras allow the initiate to have their feet on the Earth and their head in Heaven simultaneously. Interestingly, the feet symbolize the duality of the World of Matter, while the head represents the singularity of the Spiritual Realm.

Another important Foot Chakra is the Heel Chakra, related to Muladhara. This Minor Chakra helps us feel grounded since our heels are the first ones that touch the Earth every time we take a step. The Heel Chakra is directly connected to Muladhara via the energy channels in the legs. The primary energy channels in the legs power the feminine and masculine Ida and Pingala Nadis that begin in Muladhara. In men, Ida and Pingala are energized by the testes, while in women, by the ovaries. Numerous other Nadis run alongside the primary energy channels in the legs, connecting the toes to other Major Chakras.

THE HAND CHAKRAS

The Seven Major Chakras find their correspondence in the feet but also the hands (Figure 28). The thumb corresponds with Manipura, index finger with Anahata, middle finger with Vishuddhi, ring finger with Muladhara, little finger with Swadhisthana, middle of the palm to Sahasrara, and wrist point to Ajna Chakra.

The Chakras are perfectly balanced on the hand as the ring and little fingers are feminine in quality while the thumb and index finger are masculine. Moreover, a central line runs from the wrist point through the middle of the palm and up to the middle finger, corresponding with the Spirit Element, which reconciles the opposing gender principles.

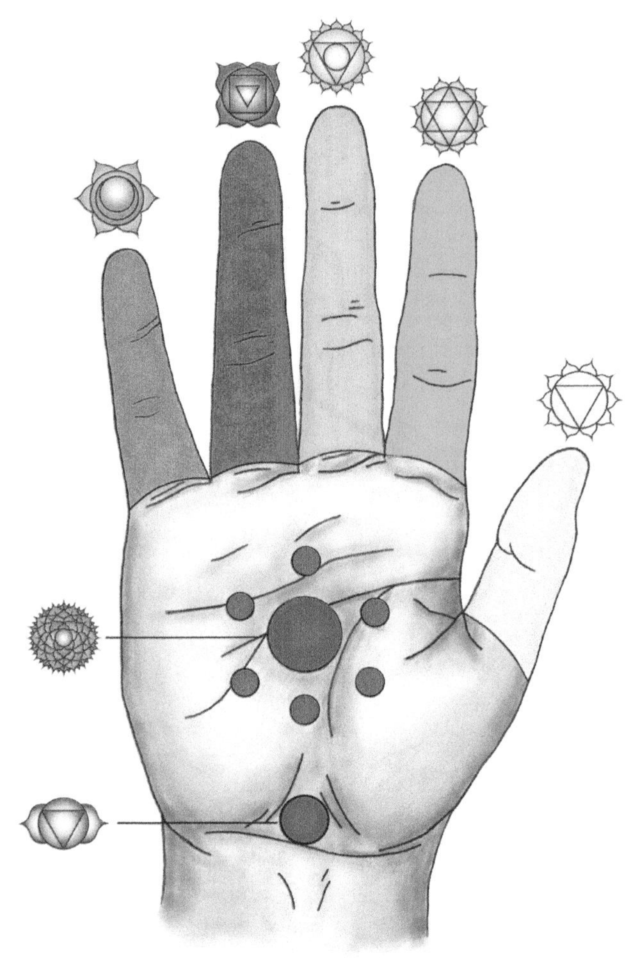

Figure 28: The Hand Chakras

Hand Chakras are essential for healing and receiving energetic information from the Universe. Our hands allow us to interact with the world on both a physical and energetic level. The fingers serve as sensors while the palms serve to channel healing energy. Your dominant hand sends out energy while the non-dominant hand receives it.

While the feet relate to the Earth Element and the physical body, the hands correspond with the Air Element and the mind since they are literally suspended in the air before us. As such, the Hand Chakras very much affect the information that comes into our minds.

For this reason, society has adopted the handshake as the primary greeting between people. By shaking someone's hand, your palms touch, allowing you to intuit who they are as a person since you make direct contact with their energy.

The middle of the palm contains an essential Minor Chakra, which is related to Sahasrara, the Crown. Otherwise called the "Palm" Chakra, it is the most important of our Hand Chakras since it is used for healing purposes. You will notice that the Palm Chakra mirrors the Sole Chakra, which reflects the Minor Chakras at the top of the head. All three sets of Chakras correspond with Sahasrara and the Spirit Element. Their function is crucial in the Kundalini transformation process since they infuse the Spirit energy into the body.

Figure 29: Healing Energy Generation and Transmission (Palms)

The Hand Chakras are connected to the Throat Chakra, Vishuddhi, via the energy channels in the arms. Therefore, to fully open the Hand Chakras and maximize their functional abilities, one must awaken the Throat Chakra as it is the first Chakra of the Spirit Element. The Spirit Element also includes the two Chakras above Vishuddhi, Ajna and Sahasrara.

Healing energy is generated in Anahata, which is sent out through the Palm Chakras via Vishuddhi (Figure 29). The Throat Chakra is used to intuit the energetic impressions around you because of its connection with Ajna Chakra, the psychic centre, which has a corresponding energy point in the wrist area. These impressions are often received through the Hand Chakras, which we can use like energy sensors through intention alone.

Awareness and activation of the Hand Chakras can make a significant difference in the quality of your life. The average person has the Minor Chakras in their hands open to some extent meaning that healing energy is continually flowing in and out of them. Only people who are entirely turned to evil will be completely closed off from healing energy until they can reopen their hearts to love and goodness again. Then there are those people who have outstripped the masses concerning Spiritual evolution. These people have their Heart and Throat Chakras fully open. Their consciousness is much higher in the degree of vibration, which means that their Hand Chakras are optimally functioning and sending out and receiving healing energy.

A fully Kundalini awakened person will have all of their Chakras open, including the Hand and Foot Chakras. They will be natural healers, empaths and telepaths. Much of the outside information comes in through the hands. The mere act of touching an object will result in receiving energetic knowledge about that object. When the Hand Chakras are fully open, the fingertips become extra sensitive to receiving information and sending it into the body for evaluation.

HEALING WITH THE HANDS

The Hand Chakras can be used to receive energy but also to send it out; it all depends on your intention. When you are receiving energy, the fingertips are involved, while when you are sending it out, you do so mainly through the Palm Chakras (Figure 30).

The most common use for the receiving function in the Hand Chakras is to scan the Aura of an individual and look for "hot spots" and other information that can help you intuit the state of their overall energy. The Hand Chakras can willingly be used as sensors that inform you what the energy is like in your environment.

You can use the sending function of the Hand Chakras to channel healing energy to someone, clear the room of stagnant energy, charge a Crystal or another object, or even bless or offer protection to an individual or group of people. You can also use your energy to heal yourself and your Chakras, although this could be draining. It helps to heal oneself using a Gemstone instead, for example.

Although it is crucial to know how to build up your chi in your Hara Chakra (more on this in the following chapter on Transpersonal Chakras), it is far more efficacious for healing work to learn how to bring in the Spiritual energy and allow it to flow through you. As long as you are coming from a mental place of unconditional love (a characteristic of Anahata Chakra), your intention alone should be enough for you to call in the Spiritual energy and channel it through your Hand Chakras for healing purposes.

It is essential to remain neutral regarding specific outcomes from your healing session and not impose your will. For most of the healing session, you are merely making yourself into a channel, a conduit of Spiritual energy. Therefore, you should only involve your Higher Will when moving and removing energy blockages. To do so, you can either comb the area in the Aura that contains negative energy or push out this negative energy with healing energy from your Palm Chakras. In the latter, you can intensify the magnitude of the healing energy channelled through your Palm Chakras by employing your willpower and focused attention.

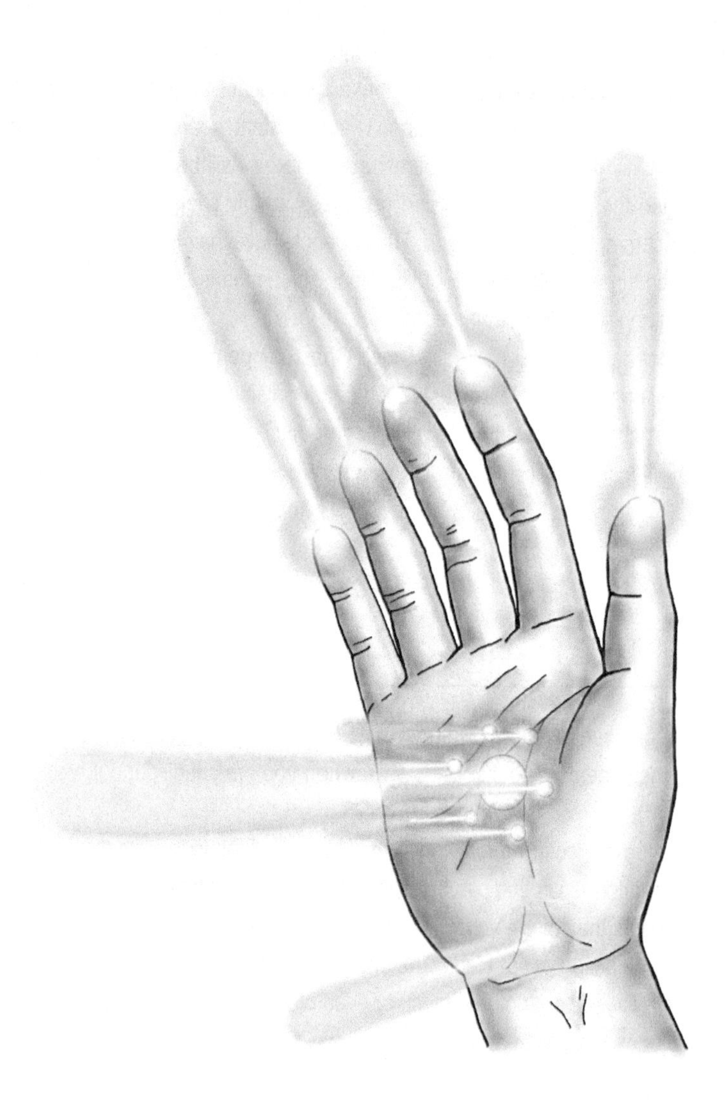

Figure 30: Healing Energy from the Hands

INFUSION OF SPIRIT ENERGY

The purpose of the Kundalini purification process is to make your body a vessel for the Spirit. Of course, nothing happens to your physical body during this process, although it feels like it does to your consciousness. The Kundalini allows your consciousness to rise as high as the Spiritual Body and align with its vibration by purging the Chakras.

The body must be infused by the Spirit energy carried out by the Sole and Palm Chakras. These Minor Chakras become fully activated once the Kundalini reaches Sahasrara in the process of awakening. It usually takes some time for the consciousness to prepare itself for the infusion of Spirit since the Chakras require cleansing. Once it is ready, though, the Spirit energy rises into the body via the Sole and Palm Chakras. This experience feels like a gust of wind has entered the limbs and made them feel transparent. This Divine breath can then permeate the torso entirely, enabling the individual consciousness to feel weightlessness in the body, especially the arms and legs. It feels like the physical body has become hollow from the inside to the experiencer.

When the Spirit comes into the body, the individual begins to experience the overall numbness of the whole body. It again takes some time for this part of the Kundalini transformation to manifest. As I mentioned before, it was in year seven of the awakening that this took place for me. It felt like the physical body had received a permanent shot of Novocaine, a numbing agent.

The numbness sensation occurs so that the consciousness can lose its connection with the physical body, making it easier for it to localize within the Body of Light fully. By losing consciousness of the physical body, the Soul is ultimately released from its shackles. The individual consciousness is united with Cosmic Consciousness, ending the pain of division between the two.

THE PSYCHIC EYES

Besides the two physical eyes, there are five additional Spiritual eyes in our heads (Figure 31) that give us expanded awareness when our consciousness is heightened. Also, the two physical eyes have functions beyond ordinary seeing abilities worth mentioning. The right eye is primarily used to see the forms of objects; it aids in the perception of detail. The left eye relates to our emotional Self. It gives us a sense of the relationship between objects through their colour and texture.

The Third Eye, or Mind's Eye, is located slightly above and between the eyebrows. It serves as an energy portal that allows us to intuit the energetic form of the objects in our Third Dimension. The Third Eye gives us insight into the Unknown as our window into the Astral World. The actual location of Ajna Chakra, though, is in the centre of the brain, in the Third Ventricle area, as will be discussed in a later chapter. The psychic eyes described below have auxiliary functions to the Mind's Eye. They serve as energy portals, each with specific powers that, when awakened, give us expanded awareness and understanding since they are distinct components of Ajna Chakra as a whole.

The Fourth Eye is right above the Third Eye, and it allows us to comprehend the relationships between people while promoting belief in the Creator. It is the higher sense of what the left physical eye perceives as it enables us to understand the Source of Creation. The Fourth Eye is the builder of faith.

The Fifth Eye is right in the middle of the forehead, and it aids in our understanding of Universal truths and ideals. Through it, we receive concepts of the workings of Universal Laws that govern reality. It allows us to see the larger picture of life and our place within it. The Fifth Eye activates the higher mind and our creative thinking. It also allows us to view our past lives.

The Sixth Eye is right above the Fifth Eye, and its function is to give us true inner sight and the understanding of our Soul's purpose. The Seventh Eye is right where the hairline is, on the opposite side of the Bindu. It aids in understanding the totality and purpose of the Universe as a whole. We can communicate with Angelic Beings from the Divine Plane of existence through it.

The Seventh Eye is paramount in the Kundalini transformation process since it acts as the exit point of the Kundalini, the same as the Bindu. The Seventh Eye and the Bindu act like funnels for the Kundalini circuit when fully active and integrated. If there is a blockage in the Seventh Eye, the Kundalini circuit becomes inactive, and one loses touch with the Bindu and the Spiritual and Divine Planes of existence.

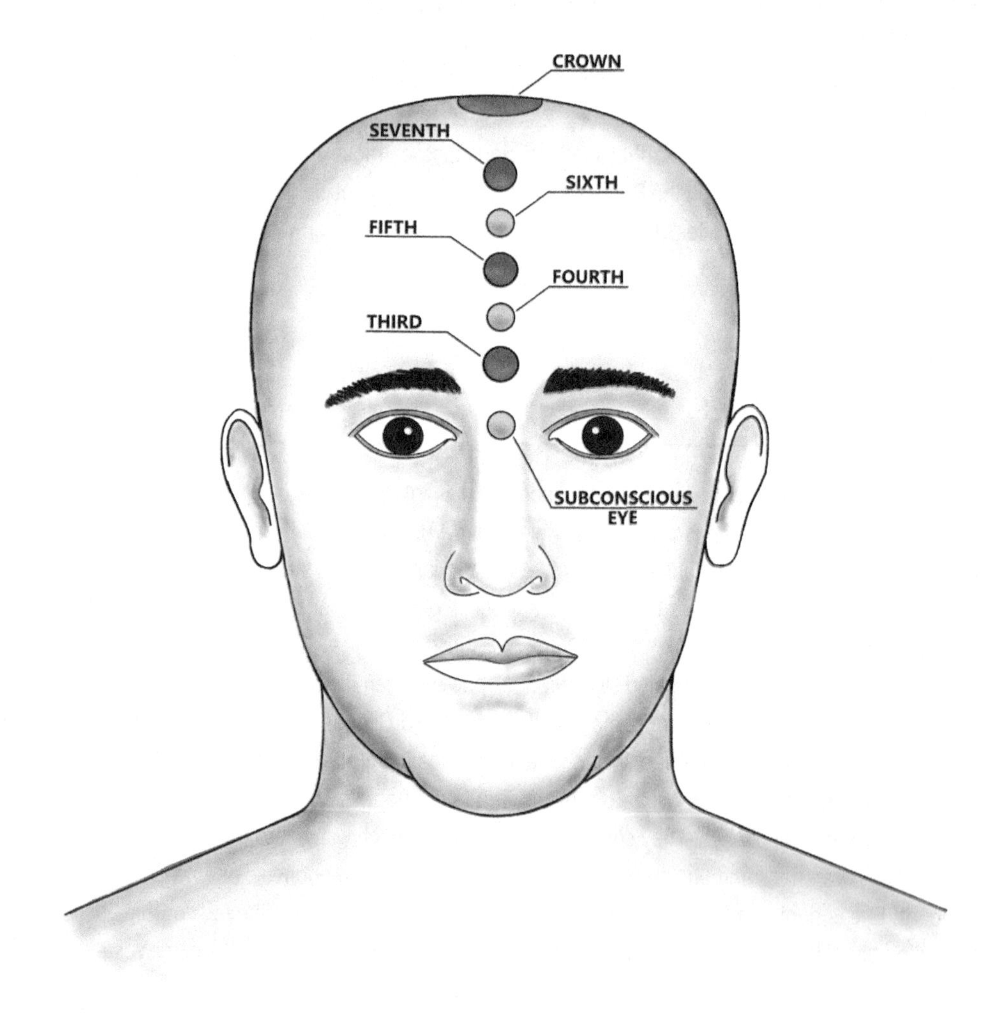

Figure 31: Location of the Psychic Eyes

It is crucial to understand that all of the psychic eyes develop over time when undergoing a Kundalini transformation after a full awakening. Once they are all created and consciousness gains the ability to utilize their functions, the Fifth Eye becomes the "command centre" of the consciousness, instead of the Third Eye, since it is the middle of the five psychic eyes and can receive impressions from each of them.

There is another psychic centre called the "Subconscious Eye", and it lies right between the two physical eyes, at the bridge of the nose. The subconscious mind is the centre of our primitive and basic living and gut-level feelings. Its function is survival; thus, it relates to the necessities in life, such as food, water, and shelter. Fear also plays a crucial part in survival as we learn to avoid those things that can hurt us, either physically or emotionally. The subconscious mind becomes a storehouse of all those things that caused us pain over time, containing the fear energy that limits us in life.

Once the Kundalini has entered the brain and pierced Ajna Chakra, the Subconscious Eye is fully awakened. Since a full Kundalini awakening bridges the conscious and subconscious minds, all the negative energy stored in the subconscious is released to be dealt with and transformed. As such, the Subconscious Eye allows us to see everything that used to be hidden from us psychically.

The Subconscious Eye allows us to see the workings of the subconscious mind to become more efficient Co-Creators with our Creator. Once we overcome the negative energy stored in the subconscious mind, we can utilize this psychic centre to mould our thoughts, making us masters of our realities. However, the Subconscious Eye is merely a window, or portal into the subconscious mind, whose location is at the back of the head. In contrast, the conscious part of the mind is at the front of the head.

THE TRANSPERSONAL CHAKRAS

According to many Spiritual schools of thought, other than the Major and Minor Chakras, there are also Transpersonal Chakras. These are Chakras outside of the Light Body that the human being is connected to energetically. Transpersonal means that they transcend the realms of the incarnated personality. Also, in Chakric science, they add the second, crucial piece of the puzzle, next to the Major and Minor Chakras, in understanding our energetic makeup.

The primary purpose of the Transpersonal Chakras is to connect the physical body and the Major and Minor Chakras to other people, Ethereal Beings and other sources of Divine and higher energies. Most Spiritual schools of thought say there are five Transpersonal Chakras, although this number may vary. It is also common to see many Chakric systems use only the two opposite Transpersonal Chakras, the Soul Star and the Earth Star.

The Transpersonal Chakras exist along the Hara Line, which is an energetic column that contains the seven primary Chakras. When we extend this energetic column upwards and downwards, past the seven primary Chakras, we encounter various Transpersonal Chakras above Sahasrara and one below Muladhara called the Earth Star Chakra (Figure 32).

The Transpersonal Chakras hold the keys to the Spiritual development and understanding of the dynamics of Creation. Through the Chakras above Sahasrara, we can connect with the more subtle vibrations in the Cosmos. In *The Magus*, I have referred to these higher vibratory states of consciousness as the Divine Planes of existence.

In terms of the Qabalistic Tree of Life, the Transpersonal Chakras around and above the head area are part of the Kether Sephira and not within the Three Veils of Negative Existence (Ain Soph Aur). And since Kether is the White Light, these Transpersonal Chakras deal with how this Light filters into the Body of Light and the Seven Major Chakra centres.

Unless your Seven Major Chakras are adequately balanced and your vibration is heightened, I highly discourage you from attempting to work with the three highest Transpersonal Chakras. Trying to use these potent power sources before making yourself into a proper conduit will be futile since you won't be able to access their power. As such, save working with these higher Chakras for once you have sufficiently developed yourself Spiritually. The only Transpersonal Chakra that you can work with safely is the Earth Star since this Chakra relates to grounding.

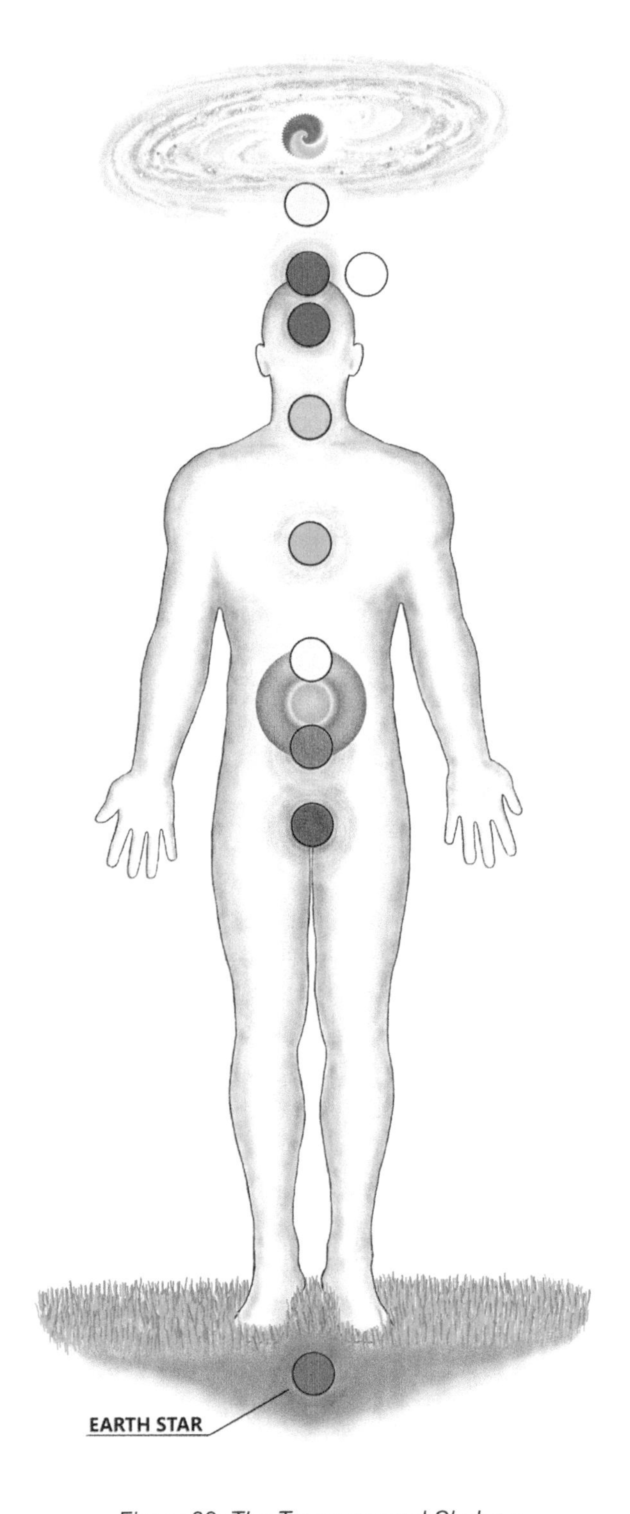

Figure 32: The Transpersonal Chakras

EARTH STAR CHAKRA

The Earth Star Chakra, Vasundhara (Sanskrit for "Daughter of the Earth"), is approximately six inches below the feet. Otherwise called the "Super-Root", this Chakra assists in grounding and connecting us to Planet Earth since it makes direct contact with the ground. The Earth Star acts as a bridge between our consciousness and the collective consciousness of Planet Earth. Thus, this Chakra deals with nature awareness. The Foot Chakras are the medium of communication between the Major Chakras and the Earth Star.

The Earth Star also enables us to connect with the denser terrestrial energies of our Planet. The terrestrial/telluric energy rises through the legs' energetic channels via the Foot Chakras until it reaches the Root Chakra, Muladhara. Muladhara Chakra is the foundation of our Chakric system, its root—hence how this Chakra got its name. Muladhara and the Earth Star have a direct relationship—they are both related to the Element of Earth and serve to channel its energy. Qabalistically, their function corresponds with the Sephira Malkuth, placed directly at the feet. However, the Earth Star represents the Spiritual aspect of Earth, vibrating at the Fourth Dimension of Vibration or Energy.

The Earth Star is essential to anchor us to the Physical Plane of existence. One of the functions of the Earth Star is to root the personal and transpersonal parts of the Soul to the magnetic core of Planet Earth through its electromagnetic field. Since the human being's energy system can be likened to a tree, the Earth Star serves as its roots.

The Earth Star allows us to stay grounded despite all day-to-day activities that unground us. Having a solid connection with this Chakra enables us to remain firm in our life's purpose and not be swayed by the thoughts and emotions of other people around us. These external energies are cleared out from our Aura when our connection with our Earth Star is strong. As such, our relationship with our Earth Star gives our Soul security for it to express itself and its purpose.

The Earth Star has its own Auric layer extending past the Sahasrara Chakra layer. It serves as an Etheric blueprint connecting the in-between Auric layers to our Lower Astral Body (Etheric Body), the first Subtle Body beyond the Physical Plane. Due to its placement below the feet, this Chakra grounds the Subtle Bodies and the entire Chakric system, including the Transpersonal Chakras above Sahasrara.

The Earth Star is also directly involved in stimulating the Kundalini into activity because of its relationship with Muladhara. Without its assistance, the awakening process would be impossible since human consciousness is inextricably linked with Earth consciousness. Changes in Earth consciousness affect human consciousness on a collective and personal level.

For a Kundalini awakening to occur, we must create a powerful energy current in Muladhara Chakra. Creating this energy begins in the Earth Star since these two Earth Element Chakras work together. In other words, energy in Muladhara is generated from the Earth Star Chakra. The Earth Star acts as a battery for Muladhara; it sends Planetary energies into it via the positive and negative currents represented by the two energy channels in the legs.

Our life story is recorded inside the matrix of our Earth Star. This Chakra is responsible for our personal development on the material plane and the paths we take to move forward in life. It embraces all of our Ancestral history and DNA patterns. This Chakra is also the record keeper of all past life incarnations and Karmic lessons learned.

The Earth Star connects us with all of humanity on a terrestrial level. When balanced, this Chakra allows us to feel a deep connection with our inherent inner powers and work for a greater cause. Earth Star's ultimate goal is to further the collective consciousness of our Planet and the Universe we are a part of. A balanced Earth Star also allows us to feel grounded, protected, and secure as our Divine connection with Mother Earth (Gaia) is strengthened.

An unbalanced Earth Star creates mental and emotional instability in life. By being ungrounded with Mother Earth, we lose touch with our Spirituality, making us lose our sense of purpose over time. On a physical level, an unbalanced Earth Star can cause problems with the legs, knees, ankles and hips since these parts of our body ground us with Mother Earth.

The colour of the Earth Star is black, brown, or magenta (when activated). Gemstones attributed to this Chakra are Smoky Quartz, Onyx, Black Obsidian, and Magnetite (Lodestone).

HARA CHAKRA (NAVEL)

Hara is a Japanese word that means "sea of energy." Its name is fitting since Hara Chakra acts as a gateway into the Astral Plane. Through this Plane, one can access all the inner Cosmic Planes. As such, Hara Chakra is our access to the infinite ocean of energy in the Universe. It is not necessarily a Chakra but is in a league of its own because of its size and scope. However, Hara is part of the Transpersonal Chakras model in many New Age Chakric systems. Its location is between Swadhisthana and Manipura, at the belly button (Figure 33), about two inches inwards.

Around the Hara is an Etheric ball of energy, about the size of a soccer ball, called the "Dantian," or "Tan Tien." The Dantian's energy is chi, qi, mana, Prana, which is Life energy. This ball of energy interacts with the nearby organs involved in food processing since ingested food transforms into Life energy, whose essence is Light energy. This energy is filled from the Hara, as that is its centre. Once Light Energy is generated in the Dantian through the Hara Chakra, it is then distributed throughout the body.

Hara Chakra has a direct relationship with Swadhisthana since it acts as a portal into the Astral Plane and a generator of Life energy. The distinction between the two is that Swadhisthana's function is to generate sexual energy (along with Muladhara), while Hara generates Life energy. In reality, though, the two work together as a battery, just like Muladhara works with the Earth Star Chakra. On the Tree of Life, the function of Hara and Swadhisthana Chakras corresponds with the Sephira Yesod.

Hara Chakra gives us sustenance and strength, which is dependent on Muladhara and the Earth Star being sufficiently grounded. Our source of power is in the Hara and our regenerative ability. While the Earth Star and Muladhara Chakras are drawing up the Earth energies, the Hara uses the sexual energy of Swadhisthana to power the will. To achieve this, it uses the raw Fire energy of Manipura, which lies directly above it. Manipura is directly involved in the process of transforming ingested food into Light energy. Many Spiritual traditions recognize the existence of Hara Chakra but cannot distinguish whether it is related to Swadhisthana or Manipura, or both—as is the case.

The efficiency of Hara Chakra is also dependent on how well the Earth Star and Root Chakra are grounded. These two Chakras draw in the Earth's energies, while the Hara uses that energy, along with the energy from Swadhisthana and Manipura Chakras, to power the entire energy system. Hara Chakra is essentially our core and foundation. Its colour is amber, as it is a mix of the yellow of Manipura and orange of Swadhisthana.

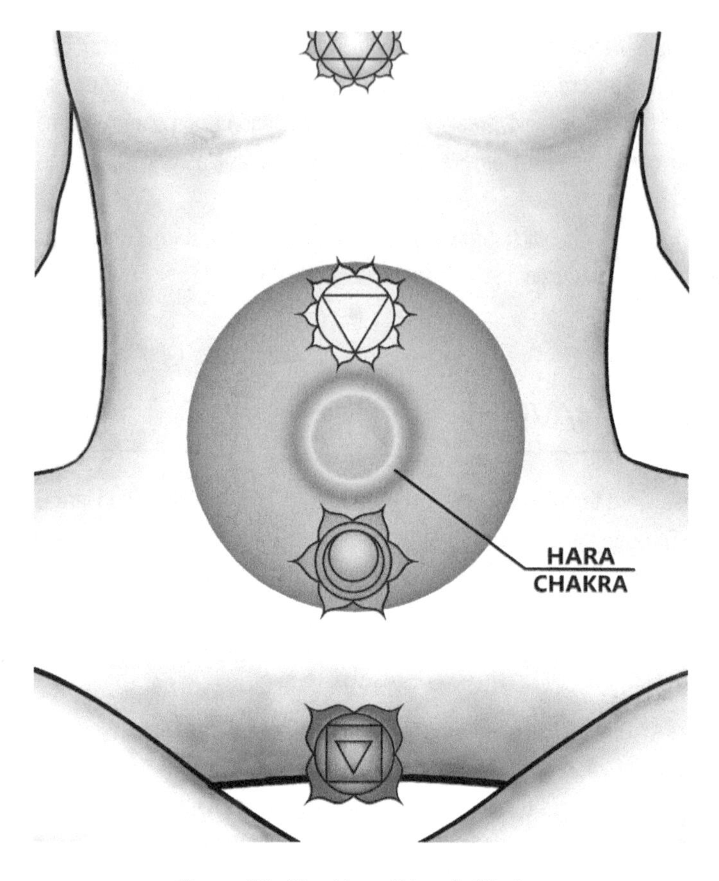

Figure 33: The Hara (Navel) Chakra

Although Swadhisthana is often referred to as the Navel Chakra in Spiritual traditions, Hara is the actual Navel Chakra because of its placement and function. As a fetus, we were all fed through the navel as our Subtle Bodies were being formed. Once we were born and the umbilical cord was cut, we were cut off from the Etheric source of energy. As such, we stopped drawing in energy through the Hara. Through conditioning and the forming of the Ego, we lost sight of this portal and began channelling energy into our heads from overthinking. To remedy this, we should focus on our core and draw in energy through our Hara Chakra, which will expand our Dantian.

Hara and the Dantian (Tan Tien) are often referred to in Qigong, Tai Chi and other martial arts. All martial arts disciplines that attempt to work with energy realize the power of the Hara centre and building up the Dantian, which they consider the centre of gravity. But to do so, one must have a firm connection with their Etheric Body; otherwise, they will be unable to channel their inner energies. In many of these martial arts systems, the Hara is only one of the Dantians, referred to as the Lower Dantian. The Middle Dantian is in the heart area (Anahata), while the Upper Dantian is in the head area, at the level of Ajna Chakra. This breakdown of three main energy centres in the human body allows martial artists to best use the natural flow of their energies to optimize their fighting power.

Hara Chakra must be open and the Dantian (Lower) full of energy if one is to have good health and an abundance of vitality. If the Hara is closed or inactive, it can cause many addictions, especially to food. Overeating is an attempt to feel full despite having the Hara blocked and the Dantian empty. Tantric Sex practice is one way to open the Hara and become aware of your Dantian. Tantric Sex focuses energy into the abdomen, incorporating the use of our sexual energy as well as our willpower, thereby involving both Swadhisthana and Manipura Chakras.

CAUSAL CHAKRA (BINDU)

The Bindu serves as the gateway to the Causal Chakra, which is approximately two to three inches away from the top back of the head once you project a straight line from the Thalamus (Figure 34). Then, it lines up with Sahasrara Chakra, which lies directly in front of it. The Causal Chakra is one of the three Transpersonal Celestial Chakras around the head area, including the Soul Star and the Stellar Gateway.

The Bindu at the top-back of the skull (from the inside) acts as a doorway to the Causal Chakra. The Bindu is the door, while the Causal Chakra is the house. You can't have the door without the house, though, nor the house without the door—the two go together. For this reason, the characteristics of the Bindu Chakra mirror those of the Causal Chakra in the Transpersonal Chakras model.

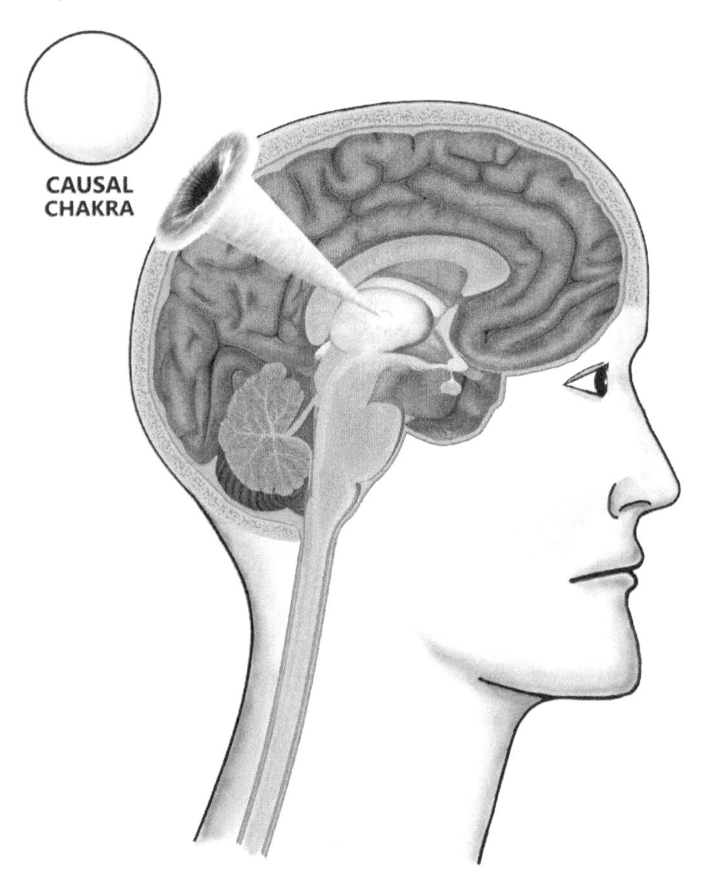

Figure 34: The Causal/Bindu Chakra

The Causal Chakra is concerned with eradicating the Ego and transforming the personality. It gives us the notion of the continuity of life beyond physical death. We are Eternal Beings of Light that will continue living past this momentary physical existence. This Chakra serves to silence the Ego and make the mind still, enabling the individual to explore the Spiritual Plane and the Divine Planes.

The Causal Chakra is a point of entry into the Divine Planes, which can be experienced through the Soul Star and the Stellar Gateway Chakras that lie above the Crown Chakra. Causal Chakra also assists in the higher activations of the Spiritual Chakras (Crown, Mind's Eye, and Throat), which facilitate the exploration of the Spiritual Plane.

Since the Causal/Bindu Chakra is referred to as the Moon Chakra, it is feminine in quality. When awakened, the feminine qualities of love, compassion, creativity, and intuition are heightened in the individual. This Chakra absorbs and radiates the Lunar Light, thereby illuminating the thoughts we receive directly from the Cosmic Consciousness.

Through the Causal Chakra, we receive information from the Divine Planes and the higher Spiritual Plane; information that can only be accessed when we are detached from our Ego and personality. As such, one of the main properties of this Chakra is that it allows us to explore higher wisdom and mysteries of the Cosmos.

The Causal Chakra vibrates at the Fourth Dimension, the Dimension of Vibration or Energy. It receives the energies from the two Fifth Dimensional Chakras above the head (Soul Star and Stellar Gateway) and filters them into the Aura. The Causal/Bindu Chakra is our link with those two higher frequency Chakras as it allows us to accept the gradating dosages of White Light that the Divine Planes emit.

Higher Spiritual Beings from the Divine Realms can communicate to us through the Causal Chakra. As information comes in through this Chakra, it is brought into the lower Chakras, where we can access it through the Subtle Bodies respective to those particular Planes.

The Causal Chakra plays the most crucial role in the Kundalini awakening process, as its opening results in enhanced clarity of psychic and telepathic communication. It enables the individual to "read" the energy around them through their intuitional capacity. The Causal/Bindu Chakra works with Ajna Chakra to accomplish this feat. The individual uses the various Mind's Eye portals to "see" the information that is being channelled into the Causal Chakra from the Cosmic Consciousness.

The Causal/Bindu Chakra naturally opens and stays open as part of the Kundalini transformation process. When this Chakra is unlocked, and the mind and Ego are silenced, our Higher God-Self can communicate to us directly. This communication is an immediate process that doesn't require any conscious effort. The individual gets absorbed in meditation from one waking moment to the next and becomes a living embodiment of the unity of all existence. However, this experience only happens when the Kundalini has been awakened and raised to Sahasrara Chakra.

Although you can access the energies of the Causal/Bindu Chakra through different Spiritual practices (such as the use of Gemstones), the only way to open it and keep it open permanently is through a Kundalini awakening. As mentioned, Kundalini's two exit points are the Bindu and the Seventh Eye centre. Once the Kundalini system is active in the Body of Light after the awakening, the Bindu regulates the Light energy that circulates within it, nourishing the Seventy-Two Thousand Nadis or energy channels. As these channels get infused with Light energy, consciousness expands. The Bindu opens further, allowing the individual to streamline more information from the Spiritual Plane and the Divine Planes above.

The Causal/Bindu Chakra is white, suggesting a deep and intimate connection with the Spirit Element and the Moon. Gemstones attributed to this Chakra are Moonstone, Angel Aura Quartz, Celestite, Kyanite, and Herderite.

SOUL STAR CHAKRA

The Soul Star Chakra, Vyapini (Sanskrit for "All-Pervading"), is located about six inches above the top of the head, lining up directly with the Crown Chakra below it (Figure 35). The colour of this Chakra is golden-white. The Soul Star serves as our connection with the Cosmic energies of our Solar System, while the Stellar Gateway serves as our connection with the Milky Way Galaxy as a whole. The Soul Star also moderates the very high vibrational energy from the Stellar Gateway and beams it down (via the Causal Chakra) into the Seven Major Chakras within the Body of Light. As such, we are enabled to assimilate these galactic energies into our physical existence.

The Soul Star Chakra is of the Fifth Dimensional frequency, representing the energy of love, truth, compassion, peace, and Spiritual wisdom and awareness. It corresponds with the lowest Divine Plane of existence. According to Ascension teachings, the Earth and humanity are in the process of shifting into a whole new level of reality, which is the Fifth Dimension.

We can only experience the Cosmic energies of the Fifth Dimension through the unity of individual consciousness with Cosmic Consciousness. When one achieves this connection, they gain access to the Akashic records, a memory-bank within Cosmic Consciousness that contains all the human events, thoughts, emotions, and intentions of the past, present, and future. As such, one becomes a clairvoyant, psychic, or seer. Therefore, part of the Kundalini transformation process is fully activating the Bindu/Causal Chakra, which connects us with the Soul Star and Stellar Gateway, allowing us to become one with Cosmic Consciousness.

The Soul Star Chakra is where we connect with our Higher God-Self. However, this connection is integrated through the Causal/Bindu Chakra and the Spirit Chakras (Vishuddhi, Ajna, and Sahasrara). These Chakras serve to ground the experience of connecting with our Higher Self. As the Soul Star represents Divinity in all its forms, it partakes of unconditional love, Spiritual selflessness and compassion, and unity in all things. It is the origin of our quest for Ascension and Enlightenment.

As the Causal/Bindu Chakra is referred to as the Moon Chakra, the Soul Star would be our Sun Chakra since it is the origin of our Souls. It has an intimate connection with the Star of our Solar System (the Sun) and Manipura Chakra, the Seat of the Soul and the Sun of the Light Body. Hence, where the Soul Star gets the golden aspect of its colour, which is a higher vibration of the yellow colour of Manipura.

Since the Soul Star corresponds with the Divine Plane, it is above Karmic energy since Karma belongs to the Lower Planes of existence. The Soul Star regulates the Karma of the Soul, though, by imparting the necessary life lessons through Manipura Chakra and the Fire Element. These Karmic energies have built up through many lifetimes, and they block us from manifesting our desires. Therefore, by developing our willpower, we enlighten Manipura Chakra and gain a stronger connection with our Soul Star.

The Soul Star works with the Stellar Gateway, allowing us to see the Cosmic connectedness between ourselves and the Universe we live in. When the Soul Star is in alignment with the Chakras below, we feel a strong sense of purpose and a zest for life. The Soul Star is our True Will in life and the bridge between our impersonal essence and the personal, physical reality.

To avoid being spaced out and ungrounded, one must activate the Earth Star before working with the Soul Star. Those who spend too much time working on their higher Transpersonal Chakras while ignoring the Earth Star will be too spacey and ethereal. The Soul Star and Earth Star function together to accomplish the work of the central

Star of our Solar System—the Sun. Gemstones attributed to the Soul Star are Selenite, Kyanite, Nirvana Quartz, and Danburite.

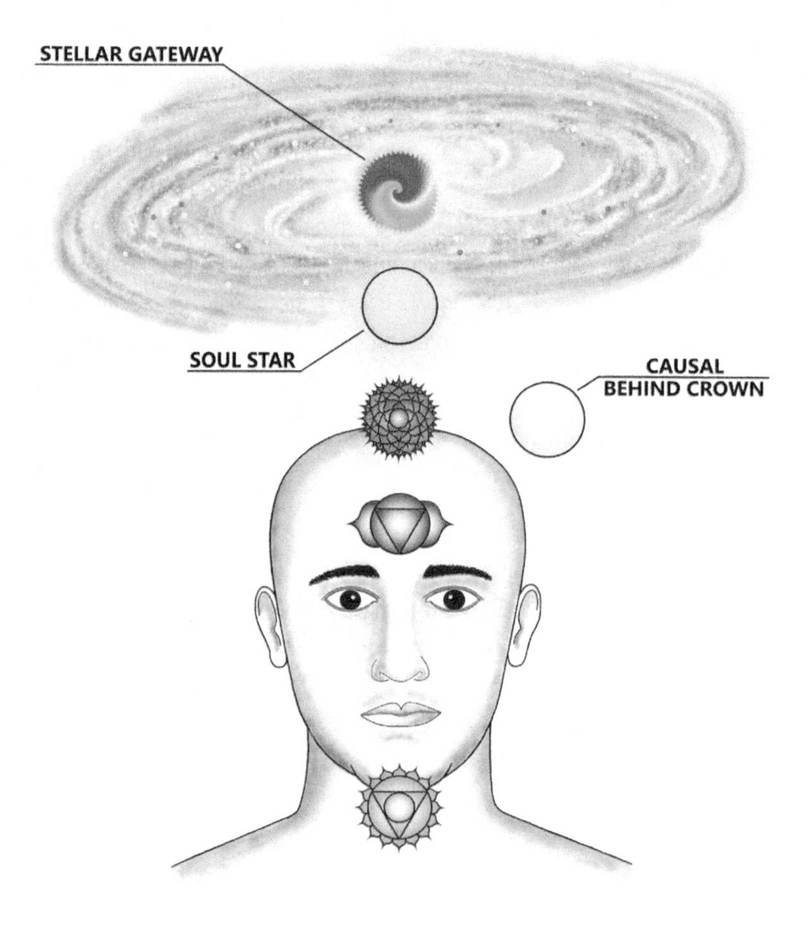

Figure 35: The Transpersonal Chakras Above the Crown

STELLAR GATEWAY

The Stellar Gateway Chakra, Vyomanga (Sanskrit for "Heavenly Being"), is about twelve inches above the top of the head, directly above the Soul Star and Crown Chakra (Figure 35). The colour of this Chakra is pure gold or rainbow (when activated). The Stellar Gateway, as its name implies, is a doorway or portal to the Stars of the Milky Way Galaxy. Simply put, it is the Chakra of Cosmic Consciousness.

The Stellar Gateway is the highest in vibration from all the Transpersonal Chakras. It is the highest of the Fifth Dimensional Chakras and our ultimate connection with the source of all of Creation. The Stellar Gateway corresponds with the higher Divine Planes of existence.

The Fifth Dimension represents conscious Oneness with the Creator (Godhead). The Soul Star gives us the understanding that we have Eternal Souls, which originate from the central Star (the Sun) in our Solar System.

However, the Stellar Gateway gives us the understanding that our Eternal Souls originate from the same source as other Souls from other Solar Systems in our Milky Way Galaxy. Thus, the Stellar Gateway represents the highest level of the Fifth Dimension, which is Oneness with all Sparks of Light in the Galaxy.

The Fifth Dimension is the very source of the White Light we all partake of. It not only unites us with terrestrial Beings but Extraterrestrial Beings as well. No matter what Solar System you are from, we are all One since our Creator is the same, and so is the Cosmic Hologram we all participate in. As such, the Fifth Dimension relates to ultimate peace and harmony between all things and the Divine love energy that connects everything.

The Stellar Gateway is a Spiritual barometer that moderates the intensity of White Light that pours into our Aura. The Soul Star is the filter through which the Light is measured, while the Earth Star grounds this Light and our consciousness to the consciousness of Planet Earth.

The Stellar Gateway is humanity's Interstellar connection, which is timeless. As it is timeless, it holds all of our experiences from all our past lives. So whenever you recall a past life, you connect with the Stellar Gateway Chakra.

The Stellar Gateway is the apex of the Kundalini transformation experience and the highest state of consciousness attainable by human beings. This Chakra emits the highest vibrational energies that human virtues are built upon. Enlightenment is only achievable once the individual fully connects with the Stellar Gateway Chakra. Gemstones attributed to the Stellar Gateway are Moldavite, Stellar Beam Calcite, Azeztulite, and Selenite.

THE HARA LINE

The Hara Line is a major energy conduit connecting the Transpersonal Chakras column. It is a channel that allows Light energy to pass from the Stellar Gateway to the Soul Star, into the Causal Chakra, down to the Hara Chakra and connect with the Earth Star below the feet. This energy passes through the central part of the human body, along the Sushumna channel, where the Seven Major Chakras are located.

The Hara Line aims to bring Light into the Seven Major Chakras through the Causal Chakra and into Sahasrara. This Light is then distributed throughout the lower six Major Chakras. Finally, the Hara Chakra collects this Light and sends it down through the perineum (Muladhara Chakra) to the Earth Star, thereby connecting the Major Chakras and the Transpersonal Chakras.

The Hara line also directs the flow of energy in the Major Chakras. Since each of our Seven Major Chakras takes in and gives out energy to Chakras above and below, the Hara Line serves as an invisible axis that subtly directs and distributes the flow of that energy.

The Hara Chakra serves as the centre of the Hara Line energy conduit since it is the container of Life energy (Prana, chi, qi, mana). The Hara Line is wholly activated and invigorated when the Kundalini is awakened and risen to the Crown Chakra. The Kundalini serves as the force that connects the Transpersonal Chakras with the Major Chakras. This connection is then anchored to Mother Earth (Gaia) through the Earth Star.

Since the Hara Line is concerned with channelling Light energy into the Major Chakras and then distributing it, it is the essence of our Divinity. This Light energy is guided by the Soul Star Chakra, our Divine essence. The Soul uses the Hara Line axis as a freeway, ascending and descending the Light energy from one Chakra to the next. The Soul Star serves as the command (control) centre to accomplish this task.

When the Transpersonal Chakras and Seven Major Chakras are adequately balanced, an Alchemical phenomenon occurs where all of the Chakras are unified and fused as one. This occurrence on an energetic level represents the highest point of Enlightenment. For this experience to occur, both the Soul Star and Earth Star must be activated and working together. These two Transpersonal Chakras work like the negative and positive poles of a battery, where Light energy is bounced back and forth between them.

THE FIFTH DIMENSION

Most religions and Spiritual traditions agree that the Fifth Dimension is the highest realm a Soul can reach and the final frontier in human consciousness. The Fifth Dimension is the dimension of the White Light that underlies all of manifested Creation. It is the "Mind of God," otherwise called Cosmic Consciousness. Our manifested Universe exists within this White Light, which is limitless, timeless, and Eternal.

The White Light is the First Mind, while the manifested Universe is the Second Mind. In reality, the two are One, as the Forms in the Second Mind depend on the Force projected from the First Mind to give them life. The White Light is the Kether Sephira on the Tree of Life, which depends on Chokmah (Force) and Binah (Form) for Creation to manifest. These two Sephiroth manifest Soul and consciousness in the Universe.

The White Light is the Source of love, truth, and wisdom. We incarnate on this Planet as luminous Beings of Light, but over time, as our Ego develops, we lose touch with our Soul and our Spiritual powers. As our consciousness devolves, it becomes imperative that we get back in touch with our Souls so that we can Spiritually rise again and realize our full potential. Awakening the Kundalini is our method of achieving Spiritual Realization. Our Creator left the Kundalini trigger in us by design. Most people are unaware of this fact, which is why people like me serve as messengers of the Kundalini energy's existence and potential.

A full Kundalini awakening activates the Seven Major Chakras, each of which resonates with the vibration of one of the colours of the rainbow. We find these rainbow colours when we shine White Light through a prism. We have red, orange, yellow, green, blue, indigo, and violet, in sequence.

When the Kundalini rises through the spinal column and into the brain, it seeks to reach the Crown Chakra and break open the Cosmic Egg. Doing so activates the Seventy-Two Thousand Nadis of the Body of Light, thereby awakening all of its latent potential. As all the petals of Sahasrara open with the Kundalini's upwards rise, the individual consciousness is expanded to the Cosmic Level. Since Sahasrara is the gateway to the higher Transpersonal Chakras, the awakened individual gains access to their powers as well over time.

A full Kundalini awakening begins the Spiritual transformation process, which is meant to align our consciousness with the two Fifth Dimensional Chakras above the head, the Soul Star and the Stellar Gateway. When we have access to these Chakras, we rise above physical pain, fear, and duality in general. We begin to function fully on intuition and live in the present moment, the Now. Once the mind is bypassed, the Ego is conquered, since it exists within the mind only.

Through a Kundalini transformation, the pain of separation is overcome since we experience the Oneness of all Creation by taking part in the Fifth Dimension. All of our actions are based on love and truth, which builds wisdom over time. We gain access to unlimited knowledge of Creation's mysteries, received through Gnosis.

With the full activation of our Body of Light, we gain Immortality. We realize that we will die physically, yes, since we cannot avoid this, but we know internally that this life is one of many since our Souls can never be annihilated.

THE MERKABA-VEHICLE OF LIGHT

The word "Merkaba" is derived from Ancient Egyptian. It refers to an individual's vehicle of Light which allows for Interdimensional and Interplanetary travel. "Mer" relates to two counterrotating fields of Light spinning in the same space, while "Ka" refers to the individual Spirit and "Ba" to the physical body. The two opposite Tetrahedrons within one another represent the two poles, or aspects of Creation, Spirit and Matter, in complete equilibrium.

The Merkaba has a prominent place in Jewish mysticism as well. In Hebrew, the word "Merkabah" (Merkavah or Merkava) means "chariot," and it refers to the Divine chariot of God described by the prophet Ezekiel in one of his visions (*The Old Testament*). Ezekiel's visions are reminiscent of visitations from other-dimensional or otherworldly Beings described through metaphors that contain symbolic imagery.

Figure 36: Metatron's Cube and the Merkaba

In his vision, Ezekiel describes a Divine vehicle that had "wheels within wheels," which sparkled like "diamonds in the sun" and rotated around one another like a gyroscope. Jewish mystics and Spiritual people interpret Ezekiel's vision as a reference to one's interdimensional vehicle of Light—the Merkaba. It is a known fact in Spiritual circles that Ascended Masters and Beings beyond our realms and dimensions manifest into our reality via their Merkaba.

The Merkaba is a geometrical depiction of the optimized torus, one's "dynamic doughnut," which includes the Auric field and the Electromagnetic Field of the heart. As mentioned, the torus has a central axis with a north and south pole that circulates energy in a spiral fashion. After a full Kundalini awakening, energy begins to circulate within the torus at a higher velocity, affecting the rate of spin of the Merkaba.

The Merkaba becomes fully activated as the torus becomes optimized, enabling travel through consciousness. Metatron's Cube is a symbol that contains every known sacred geometrical shape in the Universe. Attributed to the Archangel Metatron, the representative of the Spirit Element, Metatron's Cube serves as a metaphor for the manifested Universe and the harmony and interconnectedness of all things. Among the myriad of geometric shapes we can find in Metatron's Cube is the Merkaba, viewed along the vertical plane from above or below (Figure 36).

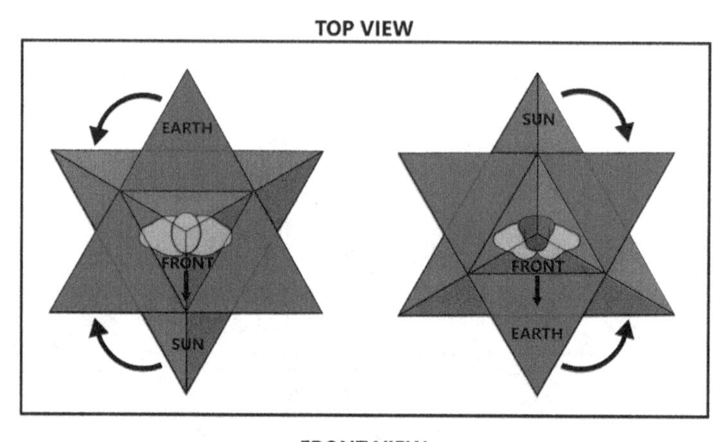

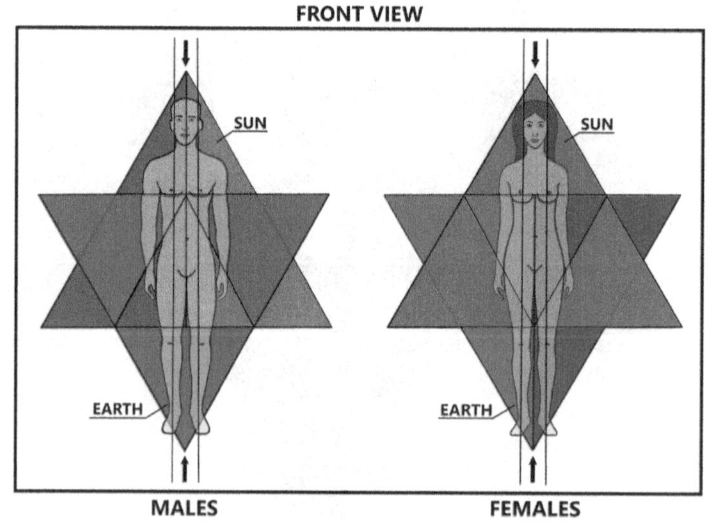

Figure 37: Orientation of Tetrahedrons in Males and Females

When viewed from the side, along the horizontal plane, the Merkaba's two Tetrahedrons intersect along the middle and point in opposite directions—one points up and the other points down. The upward-pointing Tetrahedron in the Merkaba is the male Sun principle, related to the Fire and Air Elements and electric energy. The downward-pointing Tetrahedron is the female Earth principle corresponding with the Water and Earth Elements and magnetic energy. Together, the two opposite, intertwined Tetrahedrons create the "Star Tetrahedron," an eight-pointed object that is a Three-Dimensional extension of the Hexagram, the Star of David.

The Sun Tetrahedron rotates clockwise while the Earth Tetrahedron rotates counter-clockwise. In males, since the masculine energy is dominant, the Sun Tetrahedron is oriented towards the body's front, while the Earth Tetrahedron is oriented towards the back. In females, the orientation is interchanged, and the Earth Tetrahedron faces the front (Figure 37).

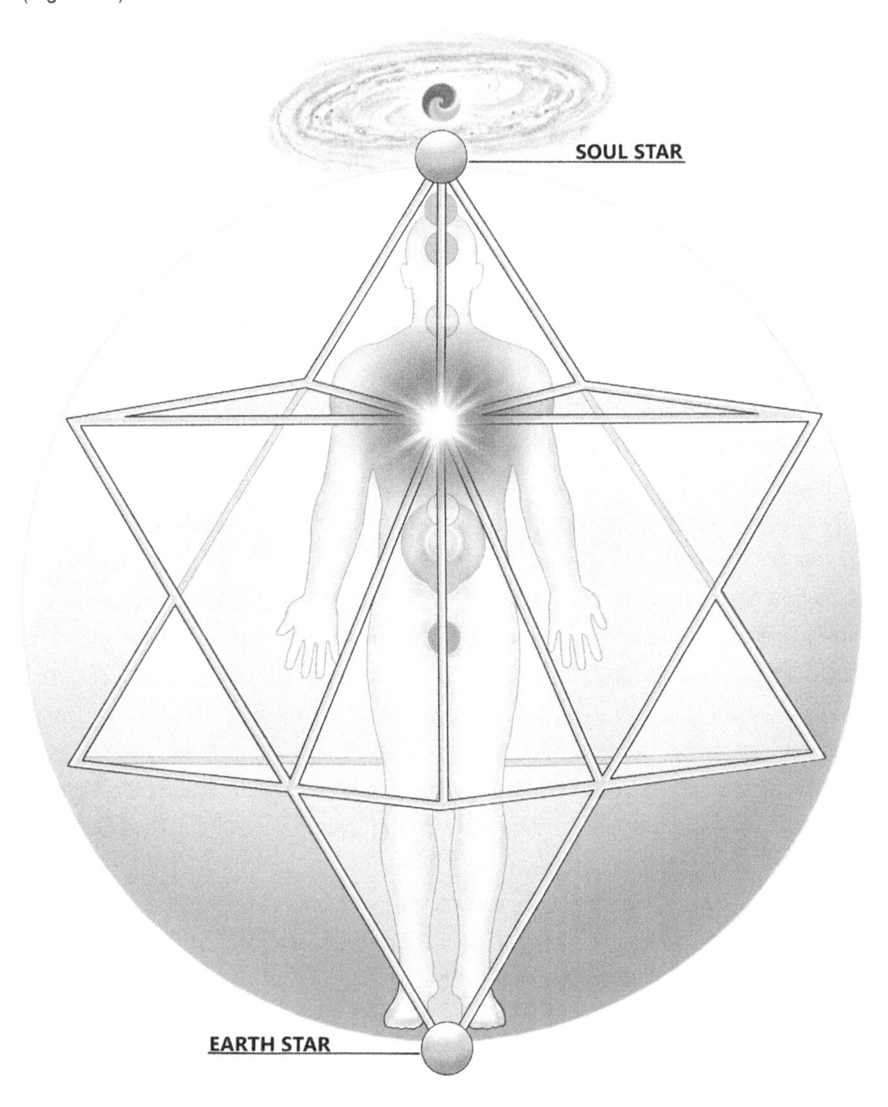

Figure 38: The Merkaba: Vehicle of Light (in Males)

The Sun Tetrahedron is powered by the Soul Star Chakra, six inches above the head at its apex. Conversely, the inverted Earth Tetrahedron is powered by the Earth Star Chakra—situated six inches below the feet. The Earth Star Chakra is the apex of the inverted Earth Tetrahedron. Light energy bounces back and forth between the Soul Star and Earth Star, along the Hara Line, powering the two Tetrahedrons of the Merkaba and making them spin in opposite directions.

When the Merkaba is optimized, the Light field generated around its spinning spherical shape can stretch out 50-60 feet in diameter in proportion to someone's height. If you were to look at a fast-spinning Merkaba with appropriate instruments, you would see a saucer-like shape around the person that expands out horizontally. It is not the Merkaba itself that is so big, but the Light it emits that creates its outstretched form, diffusing along the horizontal plane.

The Chakric system's centre is in the Heart Chakra, Anahata; the two counterrotating Tetrahedrons of the Merkaba are suspended at its level (Figure 38). The Light emanating from the Heart Chakra causes the Merkaba Tetrahedrons to spin. For this reason, there is a correlation between Merkaba activation and one's Being resonating with the energy of unconditional love. In other words, the more love you carry in your heart, your Merkaba spins faster.

People who love unconditionally have enhanced creative abilities, including psychic abilities such as transposing their Spirit into objects and other people. Their fast-spinning Merkaba allows them to transcend the barriers of their physical body through their imagination.

The Heart Chakra is the centre of our Being that receives Light energy from the Soul Star and distributes it to the lower Chakras before grounding it in the Earth Star. Our physical and etheric hearts interface with the world around us as receivers of energies. As I will describe in the next section on Kundalini and anatomy, the heart works in tandem with the brain to guide our reality.

When the Kundalini is awakened, it travels upwards through the Sushumna channel. In contrast, Ida and Pingala travel along the spine in a spiral fashion, opposite one another, resembling the DNA molecule's Double Helix. When the Kundalini reaches the top of the head at Sahasrara, it expands this centre exponentially, allowing the Light energy from the Soul Star to pour into our Chakric system below. As each of the Chakras become infused with the Light, the toroidal energy field becomes optimized, activating the latent potential of the Merkaba.

A full Kundalini awakening energizes the Body of Light, maximizing Merkaba's capacity (Figure 39). When Light is infused into the Aura, the counterrotating Tetrahedrons of the Merkaba begin to spin faster, forming a Sphere of Light around the physical body. The Soul, which is also spherical, now has a vehicle that supports its shape, with which it can leave the physical body to travel within other dimensions of Space/Time. Seeing Light orbs is a common Spiritual phenomenon of looking at the spinning Merkabas of Beings beyond the Third Dimension who want to interface with human beings through consciousness.

One of the main functions of the Merkaba is to allow the individual to explore the deeper meanings and layers of life in the Universe. By optimizing your Merkaba function, you become a Fifth Dimensional Being of Light who can utilize the higher Transpersonal Chakras to your benefit.

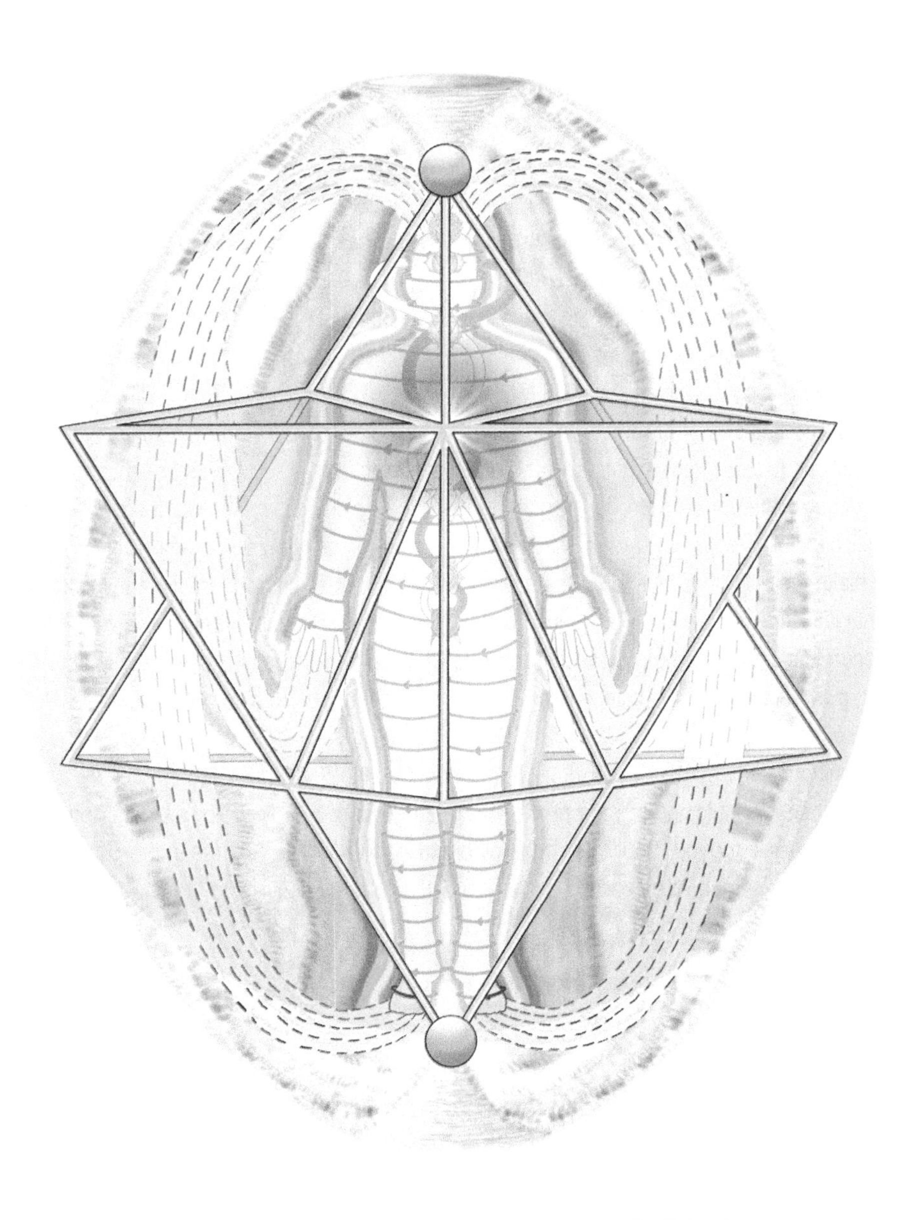

Figure 39: Kundalini Awakening and Merkaba Optimization

THE RETURN TO THE GARDEN OF EDEN

The torus shape strikingly resembles an apple which is an interesting correlation that brings us back to the Garden of Eden story from the *Old Testament* and humanity's acquisition of knowledge. The mischievous serpent is the one who went against God-the Creator by tempting Eve to do the one thing she and Adam were told not to do—eat from the Tree of Knowledge of Good and Evil.

The serpent said that if Adam and Eve disobey God, they will become "as the Gods and know duality" (Genesis 3:4-5). Knowledge is received through life experience in the World of Matter, built on the duality of Light and Darkness, good and evil.

Adam and Eve eating the forbidden apple from the Tree of Knowledge of Good and Evil can be seen as a reference to humanity obtaining a toroidal energy field, which allows our consciousness to experience the World of Matter. By materializing in the Third Dimension, our consciousness became engrained in Matter, making us lose touch with the Spiritual Plane, our inherent birthright.

The Garden of Eden is a metaphoric representation of the Spiritual Plane, the source of our primordial innocence. As mentioned before, everything that has a form in the World of Matter has a toroidal energy field around it. The toroidal energy field supports the existence of Matter in the Third Dimension of Space/Time.

The torus is comprised of the Major and Transpersonal Chakras that form our Inner World and give us the cognitive functions to learn from experience and grow in intellect. It also allows us to contemplate God's Creation and the mysteries of the Universe through the inner Cosmic Planes and dimensions corresponding with the Chakras.

After being expelled from the Garden of Eden for their act of disobedience, God-the Creator said that Adam and Eve could make their way back into the Garden only if they "eat the fruit from the Tree of Life," which would give them Eternal life. As explored in my previous book, eating the fruit from the Tree of Life refers to awakening the Kundalini energy and progressing upwards through the Chakras to achieve Spiritual Enlightenment. Consequently, the serpent, a symbol for the Kundalini energy, is also involved in the "coming home" process. He is found in the cause but also the effect.

By awakening the entire Tree of Life within yourself through the Serpent Power, the Kundalini, you integrate the Light within your Being. In doing so, you optimize the rate of spin of your Merkaba's counterrotating Tetrahedrons, which provide a vehicle for your Soul to travel in other dimensions of Space/Time. More importantly, however, by unifying the positive and negative energies within yourself, you regain entry into the Garden of Eden and become Immortal and Eternal, like the Gods.

THE SOLAR FLASH EVENT

Many Ascension stories from Ancient traditions and religious scriptures say that there will come a time when the Earth, along with all its inhabitants, will transform into a Fifth-Dimensional Light Body. They say that our Planet will have a physical shift that will transfigure its dense material body into a Body of Light. Some people believe that the Earth will become a Star, but I don't think this. Instead, I think that the Earth will retain its properties, which will only be enhanced as the vibration of its consciousness heightens. And, of course, with this shift in Earth consciousness, human consciousness will be affected.

After many years of research and one powerful prophetic dream in early 2019, I have concluded that an Ascension event will occur in our near future. It will be an actual moment in time when something significant happens on a Cosmic level. According to the Mayan tradition and prophecy, it was supposed to happen in 2012. However, many Cosmic insiders who claim contact with Extra-Terrestrials invested in our Spiritual Evolution believe that humanity was not ready then, and the event was delayed. So if I had to predict an actual year, I would say between 2022-2025, but it really depends on how primed humanity will be.

The Sun will be the activating force behind this grand event, which will usher humanity into the much-anticipated Golden Age. The Sun will perform a type of activation from within, which will change the frequency of its Light. In one moment, as the activation takes place, the Sun will give off a flash, which may be catastrophic for the Earth's surface, as it will knock out our electromagnetic grid and cause massive forest fires. Regardless of its physical ramifications, this event will cause a significant shift in Earth's consciousness, resulting in mass Kundalini awakenings for all of humanity.

Once our society stabilizes after this event, a new way of living will begin for us all. Evil will be eradicated on a mass scale, as goodness will prevail. From having gone through a Kundalini awakening myself, I can safely say that once you experience it, you no longer have the choice but to turn to the Light. And as you do, the darkness within you burns away through the transformational fire of the Kundalini.

I believe that some people who have been so evil their whole lives, the repeat murderers and rapists, for example, will be utterly consumed by this fire and will not physically survive. The sudden shift in consciousness will be too much for them to integrate, and as they try to cling to their evil ways, the fire will devour their hearts. On the other hand, most people who have only dabbled into darkness but have not allowed it to take complete control over their Souls will become purified by the Holy Fire of the Kundalini.

Although my belief may sound Christian, understand that Jesus Christ was a Kundalini awakened individual, a prototype of the experience others were meant to emulate. Other central religious figures like Moses of Judaism and the Buddha of Buddhism were also Kundalini awakened. However, due to my Ancestry and upbringing, I aligned with Jesus Christ and his teachings but studied both from an esoteric perspective, not a religious one. For this reason, I mention Jesus' teachings often.

However, don't confuse my agenda and think I am promoting Christianity or Catholicism. On the contrary, I believe that all central figures of religions have an esoteric nature that reveals the essence of their actual teachings before being polluted by dogmatic views of their respective religions. These are the teachings I was always interested in since each one contains some kernel of truth of our existence.

The prophecy of Jesus' Second Coming is a metaphor for a time in the future when humanity will integrate his Christ Consciousness as their own and become as he was, a Being of Light. Jesus' Second Coming falls in line with the prophecies of the Ancients that speak of the collective human Ascension. It does not mean that Jesus will reappear in physical form, whether he even existed or not, which is a debate left for another time.

The word "Christ" is based on the Greek translation of "Messiah." As such, Jesus of Nazareth was given the title of "Christ" to denote his Godhood. Christ Consciousness represents a state of awareness of our true nature, as Sons and Daughters of God-the Creator. In this state, the integration of Spirit within Matter and equilibrium between the two is implied, experienced through an influx of love energy via the expanded Heart Chakra.

Christ Consciousness is akin to Cosmic Consciousness, the Fifth Dimension, which is the ultimate destiny of the human race. And as humanity learns to function at the Fifth Dimensional level, love, truth, and wisdom will be our guiding force. We will not require governments and other control structures but will be guided by the newly awakened Light within us. Instead of countries fighting with one another, we will unify and focus our energies on exploring space as we become true Intergalactic beings.

PART IV: KUNDALINI ANATOMY AND PHYSIOLOGY

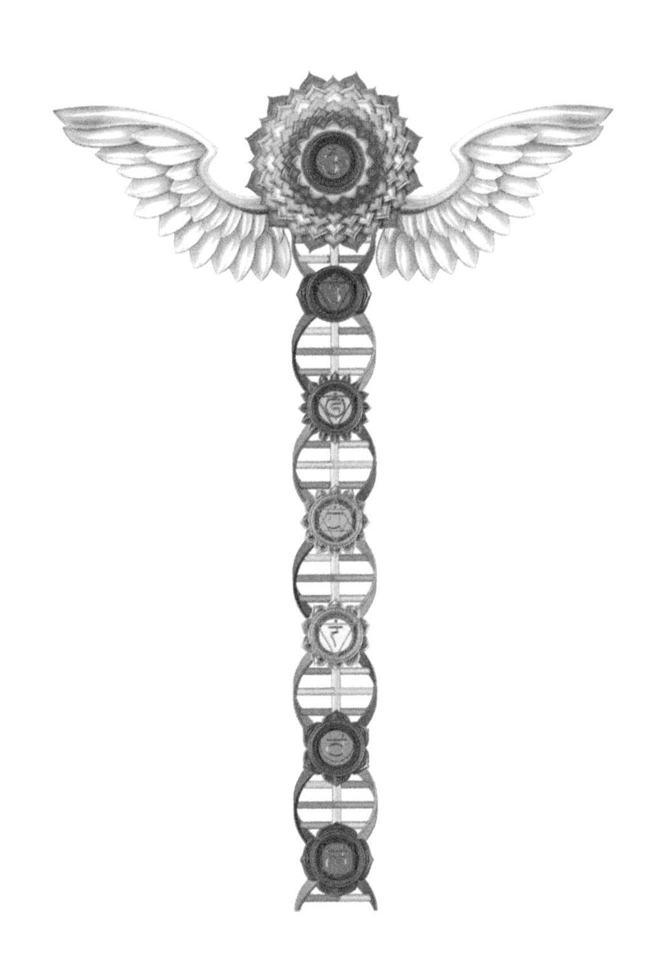

AWAKENING THE MIND'S EYE

The Mind's Eye or Third Eye is an energy portal or "doorway" within the brain that provides perception beyond ordinary sight. It is an invisible eye or window into the inner Cosmic Planes and higher states of consciousness. The Mind's Eye is often associated with clairvoyance, the ability to see visions, observe Auras, precognition, and even have Out-of-Body Experiences. Individuals that claim to have the capacity to utilize their Mind's Eye are known as "seers." Awakening or activating your Mind's Eye goes hand-in-hand with Spiritual Evolution and the path towards Enlightenment.

As described in *The Magus*, The Mind's Eye is located in-between the eyebrows, just above eye level at about 1/5 of the way towards the hairline. It features a small, circular portal, whose location is one centimetre inside the head when looking up at this point with closed eyes. A magnetic pull occurs when we focus on it that puts us into a calm, meditative state. By holding our attention on the Mind's Eye portal, the Ego becomes silent, and we begin to receive visions and images streaming across this area as if on a movie screen.

Although the Mind's Eye portal is located slightly above the centre of the eyebrows, the actual location of Ajna Chakra is in the Third Ventricle of the brain. Ajna is not a single Chakra but an arrangement of energy centres in the brain and along the forehead. Ajna Chakra is often called the Mind's Eye or Third Eye, although the latter terms insinuate the portal of Ajna, whereas the actual Chakric location is in the centre of the brain.

Ajna is best described as the movie projector, while the movie screen is the Mind's Eye. Therefore, the name "Third Eye" has an association with the Third Ventricle of Ajna but also its location; between the two physical eyes, in the brain's centre. Also, the Third Eye gives us the ability to perceive our reality psychically, with our minds, thereby bypassing ordinary physical sight; hence, it is called the Mind's Eye.

Although some Ancient traditions assert that Ajna Chakra is the Thalamus, my research has led me to discover that the Thalamus, Hypothalamus, and the Pineal and Pituitary Glands all contribute to the workings of Ajna. These four primary endocrine and neurological switchboards of the brain work in synchronicity with one another.

The Third Ventricle is filled with Cerebrospinal Fluid (CSF), which acts as the medium for carrying information from one part of the brain to the next. The sacrum pumps the CSF up the spinal cord and into the brain. The sacrum is also responsible for the awakening of the Kundalini, which lies coiled in the coccyx. The bioelectrical Kundalini current charges up the spine and into the brain through the CSF as the medium. I will describe the role of the CSF and sacrum in more detail later on in this section.

The Hindu tradition speaks widely of the connection between the Mind's Eye and Sahasrara, the Crown, otherwise called the Thousand-Petalled Lotus. The former is the receiver for the energies experienced and projected from the latter. Qabalistically speaking, Kether (the White Light) can only be experienced when Chokmah (Force) projects its omnipotent power into Binah (Form). Binah serves as the feminine receiver, the "Me" component of the

Self that receives its impetus from the masculine projector, the "I." As Binah relates to intuition and understanding, Chokmah is the All-Knowing force that projects into it to give us wisdom. The workings of Chokmah and Binah constitute the operation of Ajna Chakra, while Kether corresponds with Sahasrara. The three Supernal Sephiroth work together and cannot be subtracted from one another.

In the Tantra Yoga system, the Mind's Eye is associated with the sound "Om." The Om sound is the primordial sound of the Universe, which refers to the Atman (Soul) and Brahman (Spirit) as One. However, when pronounced correctly, it sounds more like "Aum," whose three letters embody the Divine energy of Shakti and its three main characteristics of creation, preservation, and liberation. After all, Ajna Chakra is feminine in nature, which is why it relates to the Moon.

Taoism teaches that by practising Mind's Eye training exercises, one can tune in to the correct vibration of the Universe and gain a solid foundation on which to reach more advanced meditation levels. They teach that the Mind's Eye portal expands up to the middle of the forehead when the Fifth Eye centre opens. It is one of the primary energy centres of the body, forming part of the principal meridian, which separates the left and right hemispheres of the body and brain.

Ajna Chakra is the Lunar storehouse of Prana, while Manipura is the Solar Prana depository. Ajna Chakra is female and nurturing, and its primary mode of operation is to serve as a receptor of higher vibratory energies projected from Sahasrara. Ajna, just as Vishuddhi, is sattvic, meaning it contains the qualities of positivity, truth, goodness, serenity, peacefulness, virtue, intelligence and balance. Sattvic qualities draw the individual towards Dharma (meaning "Cosmic Law and Order" in Buddhism) and Jnana (knowledge).

As Ajna has two petals, it indicates the number of major Nadis that terminate at this Chakra. Ajna has the lowest number of Nadis but the most important two, Ida and Pingala. Sushumna is excluded since it is the middle energy channel that powers the Central Nervous System and sustains all the Chakras.

Ida is the Lunar channel powering the right-brain hemisphere and the Parasympathetic Nervous System (PNS). Pingala is the Solar channel that powers the left-brain hemisphere and the Sympathetic Nervous System (SNS). The PNS inhibits the body from overworking and restores it to a calm and composed state—all qualities of the Water Element brought on by the cooling Ida Nadi. The SNS readies the body for activity and prepares it for a "fight or flight" response when a potential danger is recognized. The SNS is characteristic of the Fire Element and heat, induced by the Pingala Nadi.

THE SEVEN CHAKRAS AND THE ENDOCRINE GLANDS

Each of the Major Chakras is paired with an endocrine gland(s), and they govern their functions (Figure 40). In many cases, the individual Chakras affect the organs surrounding those glands as well. The endocrine system is part of the body's primary control mechanism. It comprises several ductless glands that produce hormones, which serve as the body's chemical messengers that act on different bodily operations and processes. These include cognitive function and mood, development and growth, maintenance of the body's temperature, metabolism of food, sexual function, etc.

The endocrine system works to adjust hormone levels in the body. Hormones get secreted directly into the bloodstream and are carried to organs and tissues to stimulate or inhibit their processes. Hormonal balance is a delicate process, and a slight lack or excess of hormones can lead to disease states in the body. If one experiences any physical ailments, it means that problems exist either with the endocrine glands, the Chakras that governs them, or both. Never forget that all physical manifestations result from energetic changes in the Inner Planes—As Above, So Below. This Hermetic Principle or Law is Universal and is always in operation.

Muladhara/Adrenal Glands

The Root Chakra, Muladhara, governs the Adrenal Glands, which are situated on top of the kidneys and aid in this Chakra's function for self-preservation. The Adrenals produce the hormones adrenaline and cortisol that support our survival mechanism by stimulating the "fight or flight" response when we are faced with a stressful situation. In addition, the Adrenals also produce other hormones that help regulate our metabolism, immune system, blood pressure, and other essential life functions.

Since the Root Chakra deals with grounding, it governs the support of the physical body, including the back, hips, feet, spine, and legs. It also regulates the rectum and the prostate gland (in men). An unbalanced Muladhara Chakra can lead to issues such as sciatica, knee pain, arthritis, constipation, and prostate issues for men.

Swadhisthana/Reproductive Glands

The Sacral Chakra, Swadhisthana, governs the Reproductive Glands, including the testes in men and ovaries in women. The Reproductive Glands regulate our sex drive and support our sexual development. The ovaries produce eggs while the testes produce sperm, both of which are essential for procreation. In addition, the ovaries produce the female hormones estrogen and progesterone, which are responsible for aiding in the development of breasts at puberty, regulating the menstrual cycle, and supporting a pregnancy. The testes produce the male hormone testosterone, which is responsible for helping men grow facial and body hair at puberty and for stimulating the growth of the penis during sexual arousal.

Swadhisthana Chakra also governs the other sexual organs, bowels, bladder, prostate, lower intestine, and kidneys. As such, issues with these organs and their performance are linked to an unbalanced or inactive Sacral Chakra. Note that in many Spiritual systems, the correspondences are reversed—Muladhara Chakra governs the Reproductive Glands, while Swadhisthana Chakra governs the Adrenal Glands. Credible arguments can be made for either case. The ovaries and Adrenal Glands are connected in women. If a woman's menstrual cycle is affected, it could be a sign of Adrenal fatigue.

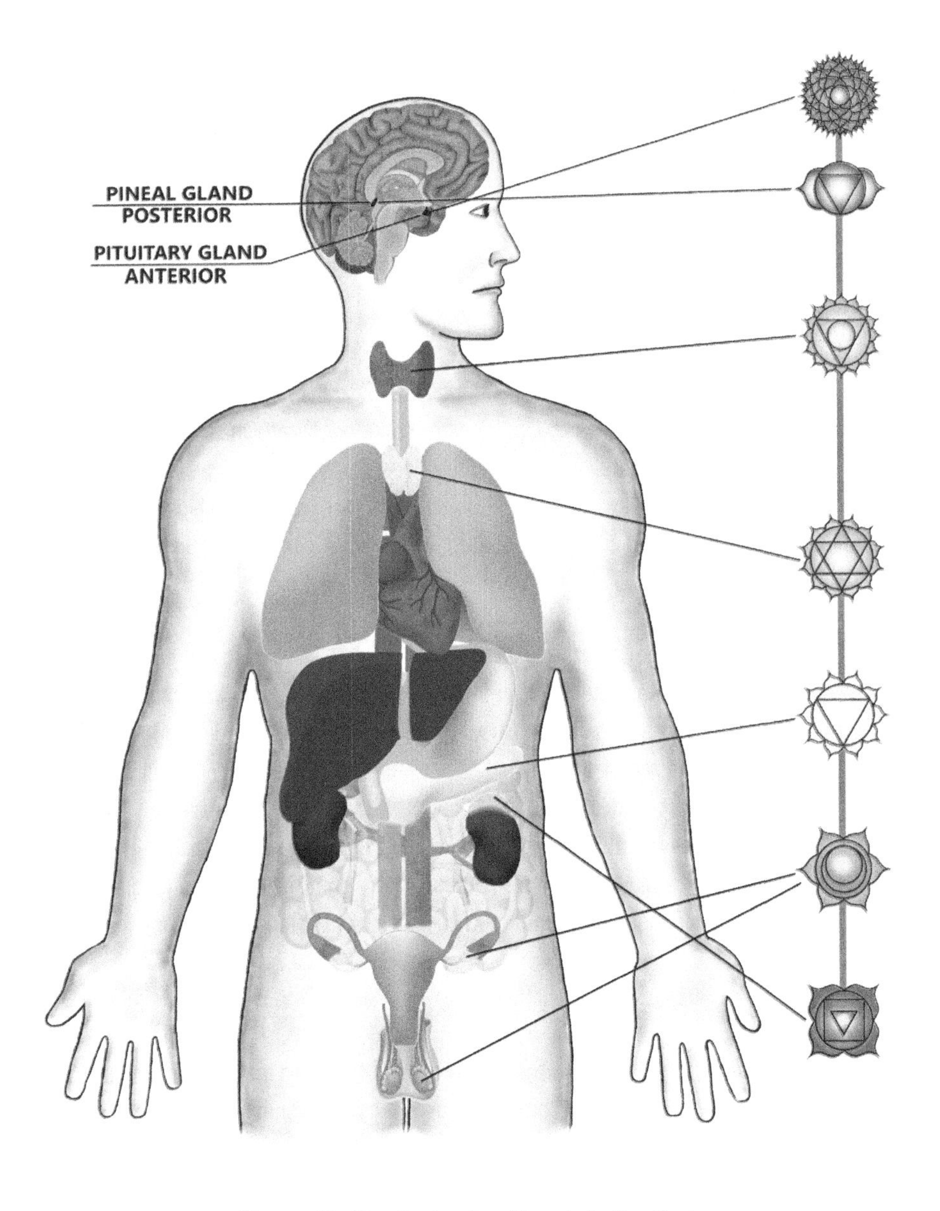

Figure 40: The Endocrine Glands in the Body

Manipura/Pancreas

The Solar Plexus Chakra, Manipura, governs the Pancreas, which regulates the digestive system. Organs and body parts ruled by Manipura include the liver, gall bladder, upper spine, upper back, upper intestines and stomach. The Pancreas is located behind the stomach in the upper abdomen. It produces enzymes that break down sugars, fats, and starches to aid digestion. It also produces hormones that help regulate the level of glucose (sugars) in the blood. Diabetes is a sign of a malfunctioning Pancreas resulting from an unbalanced Manipura Chakra. When Manipura is over-stimulated, excess blood glucose can occur, which causes diabetes. When Manipura is under-stimulated, hypoglycemia (low blood glucose) can occur as well as stomach ulcers. An unbalanced Manipura Chakra can also lead to digestive and gallbladder issues.

Anahata/Thymus Gland

Anahata Chakra governs the Thymus Gland while regulating the immune system. The Thymus Gland is located in the upper part of the chest—behind the sternum and before the heart. The Thymus is crucial in keeping our immune system working correctly. Its function is to produce white blood cells (T-lymphocytes) that serve as the body's defence system against viruses, bacteria, and cancer cells. In addition, the white blood cells fight infections and destroy abnormal cells.

Anahata Chakra also regulates the function of the heart, lungs, and blood circulation. Also known as the "Heart" Chakra, Anahata is associated with Spiritual and physical healing. It is considered the centre of our being since it produces love energy that heals us on all levels, mind, body, and Soul. Feelings of compassion and unconditional love are expressed through the Heart Chakra. On the other hand, our Heart Chakra weakens when we engage in negative emotions, such as anger, hate, jealousy, and sadness, which affects the Thymus Gland, lowering the immune system's disease-fighting ability. An unbalanced Heart Chakra can lead to high blood pressure, poor blood circulation, respiratory and breathing difficulties, heart problems, and a lowered immune system.

Vishuddhi/Thyroid Gland

The Throat Chakra, Vishuddhi, governs the Thyroid Gland, located at the base of the neck. The Thyroid releases hormones that control metabolism, the rate at which the body converts food into useable energy. These hormones also regulate body temperature, breathing function, heart rate, cholesterol levels, digestion processes, muscle tone, and menstrual cycles in women. As such, the Thyroid Gland is one of the essential glands in the body.

A dysfunction in the Thyroid Gland causes significant problems such as debilitating fatigue, weak muscles, weight gain or loss, memory impairment, and irregular menstrual cycles (in women). The Throat Chakra's function also controls the vocal cords, bronchial tubes, and all areas of the mouth, including the tongue and oesophagus. An unbalanced Throat Chakra can lead to sore throat or laryngitis, jaw pain, lung issues, pain or stiffness in the neck, and vocal cord problems.

Ajna/Pineal Gland

The Mind's Eye Chakra, Ajna, governs the Pineal Gland, which regulates the biological cycles. Besides releasing the hormone melatonin, which is responsible for making us sleepy, the Pineal Gland also secretes serotonin, the body's "happy" chemical.

The Pineal Gland's location is posterior (in the back) of the brain, directly behind the Thalamus and slightly above eye level. The Pineal Gland is the size of a grain of rice (5-8mm) in humans and is pinecone-shaped (hence its name). It governs and inhibits the Pituitary Gland's function. These two glands work in partnership with one another to achieve the overall balance in the body. Creating a healthy balance between the Pineal and Pituitary Glands helps facilitate the opening of Ajna Chakra—the Third Eye.

Ajna is our psychic centre since it gives us inner vision. Mental and emotional disorders such as insomnia, bipolar, schizophrenia, personality disorder, and depression result from an unbalanced Ajna Chakra and the over or under-stimulation of the Pineal Gland. Ajna also controls the function of the spinal cord, brainstem, pain centres, and nerves. Therefore, an unbalanced Ajna Chakra can also be responsible for epileptic seizures and other neurological disorders.

Sahasrara/Pituitary Gland

The Crown Chakra, Sahasrara, governs the Pituitary Gland and produces hormones that control the rest of the endocrine system. As such, The Pituitary is called the body's "Master Gland." It is slightly bigger than a pea and housed within a bony hollow, just behind the bridge of your nose. It is anterior (in the front) of the brain and is attached to the Hypothalamus by a thin stalk. The Pituitary connects to the Central Nervous System via the Hypothalamus. Organs regulated by Sahasrara include the eyes and brain.

Issues such as headaches, vision and some neurological problems are associated with an imbalanced Sahasrara Chakra. Note that in some Spiritual systems, the Pineal Gland is associated with Sahasrara, while the Pituitary Gland relates to Ajna. Since the Pineal Gland is at the back of the brain, it relates to the subconscious, the Moon, and the Water Element (feminine), which are associated with Ajna Chakra. The Pituitary is at the front of the brain, which relates to the conscious Self, the Sun, and the Fire Element (masculine). Therefore, I believe these are the correct correspondences of the Pituitary and Pineal Glands. (More on the Pineal and Pituitary Glands and their various functions in a later chapter.)

***

Since each of the Chakras is related to one of the Subtle Planes, negative energy in those Planes will manifest as disturbances in the corresponding glands and organs. All physical symptoms are manifestations of the quality of the Chakric energies. Since Chakras are energy centres that influence our Being on many levels, we need to keep them in balance if we are to be healthy in mind, body, and Soul.

Physical afflictions may occur whenever one of our energy centres is filled with negative energy or is blocked. Chakra tuning then is of crucial importance for our physical well being. My first book, *The Magus,* focuses on energy work through Ceremonial Magick, the Western method of healing the Chakras. In *Serpent Rising*, I am focusing on Eastern techniques such as Yoga, Tattvas, Mantras, while implementing New Age practices such as Gemstones (Crystals), Aromatherapy, and Tuning Forks.

It is essential to understand that negative energy in one Chakra is felt at the level of that specific Chakra and other Chakras connected with its function. After all, our thoughts affect our emotions and vice versa. And these, in turn, affect our willpower, imagination, level of inspiration, etc.

CHAKRA HEALING AND THE ENDOCRINE GLANDS

Endocrine glands are helpful reference points for Chakra healing since they represent the connection between the energy of the Chakras and the physical and physiological functions of the body. The nervous system and its multiple nexuses are also associated with glands and organs. Therefore, knowledge of the nervous system and its parts is crucial as it can aid healing sessions. For this reason, I have included a chapter on it in this book. Relaxing and balancing the nervous system allows for more effective healing to a gland or specific region of the body.

There are various methods for optimizing the function of the Chakras. One such method that an entire section in this work is devoted to is the Eastern practice of Yoga. Yoga is comprised of postures (Asana), breathing techniques (Pranayama), chanting (Mantra), meditation (Dhyana), as well as the performance of specific physical gestures for energy manipulation (Mudras). Some of these gestures involve the entire body, while others only involve the hands. Besides balancing the energetic system, Yoga is an excellent form of physical exercise that will leave you feeling and looking great.

Diet is also an essential component in Yogic practice. After all, you are what you eat. The physical body requires certain nutrients throughout the day to function and perform at its most optimal level. By supporting good health through diet and exercise, the Chakras become healed on a subtle level. In turn, our thoughts, emotions, and overall Spiritual well-being are positively affected. Also, by working on one Chakra, other Chakras are impacted since the entire system is interdependent on its various components.

SPIRITUAL AWAKENING AND BRAIN ANATOMY

THE PITUITARY GLAND

The two glands that regulate the overall glandular and biological function of the body are the Pituitary Gland and the Pineal Gland. These are the two most essential glands in the human body. They orchestrate and control the entire endocrine system.

Pituitary Gland's primary function is to regulate body chemistry. Just like the Pineal Gland expresses its dual nature by controlling the day/night cycles, the dual nature of the Pituitary Gland is expressed in the two lobes it is comprised of (Figure 41). The Frontal Lobe (anterior) accounts for 80% of the Pituitary Gland's weight and is the dominant lobe.

Various Ancient traditions assert that the anterior lobe is associated with the intellectual mind, logic and reason. In contrast, the back/rear (posterior) lobe relates to the emotional mind and imagination.

As mentioned, the Pituitary Gland controls the activity of most other hormone-secreting glands, including the Thyroid, Adrenals, ovaries and testicles. It secretes hormones from the anterior and posterior lobes, whose purpose is to carry messages from one cell to another through our bloodstream. Because of its immense role in our lives, it has been said that removing the Pituitary Gland from the brain will cause physical death in three days.

The Hypothalamus is situated immediately above the Pituitary Gland and is connected to it. Directly in front of it is the Optic Chiasm which transmits visual information from the Optic Nerves to the Occipital Lobe at the back of the brain.

The Hypothalamus governs the Pituitary Gland by sending messages or signals. These signals regulate the production and release of additional hormones from the Pituitary, which, in turn, send messages to other glands or organs in the body. The Hypothalamus is a type of communication centre for the Pituitary Gland.

The Hypothalamus works with the Medulla Oblongata. The Medulla and Hypothalamus control the involuntary, autonomic processes in the body, such as regulating the heartbeat, breathing, and body temperature. In addition, the Medulla is essential in the transmission of nerve impulses between the spinal cord and higher brain centres. It is essentially the doorway between the spinal cord and brain.

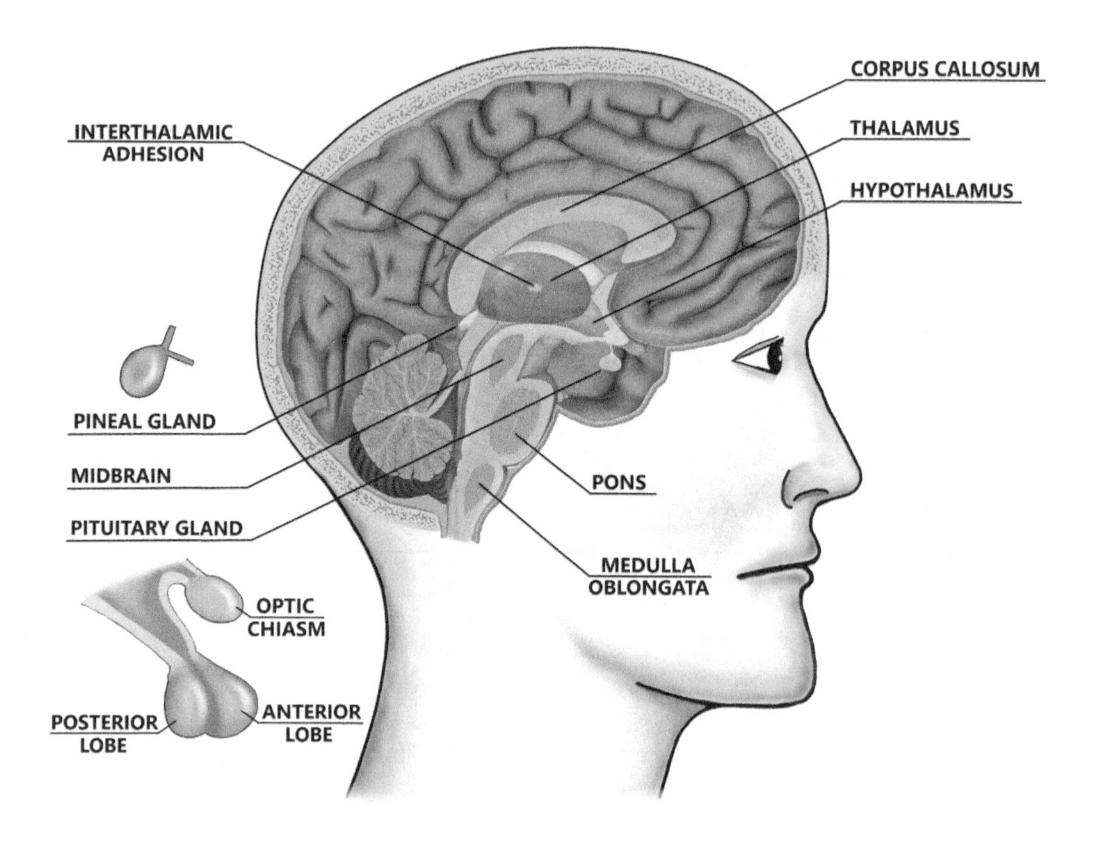

Figure 41: The Major Brain Centres

THE PINEAL GLAND

The Pineal Gland is in the geometric centre, deep within the brain. It produces the hormone serotonin and its derivative melatonin, essential to our function and well-being. Serotonin is a chemical and neurotransmitter that controls our moods, social behaviour, appetite and digestion, memory, and sexual desire and function. Serotonin contributes to our level of happiness and mental and emotional well-being—low serotonin levels have been linked to depression, anxiety and other mental and emotional disorders. With some of these issues, medical doctors usually prescribe anti-depression medication (SSRI's), which are designed to boost serotonin levels in the brain.

During the day, in response to sunlight received by the eyes, the Pineal Gland secretes and stores a large amount of serotonin. When the night comes and darkness sets in, the Pineal Gland begins to convert the stored serotonin into the hormone melatonin, which gets released into the brain and blood, inducing sleepiness throughout the night. Melatonin is the only hormone synthesized by the Pineal Gland, and it affects our wake/sleep patterns and the functions of the seasons. As such, it is often referred to as the "hormone of darkness."

Around the Summer Solstice (the longest day of the year), people experience the most sunlight and are happiest and most joyous since their Pineal Gland secretes the most serotonin. Conversely, around the time of the Winter Solstice (darkest day of the year), there is the least amount of sunlight, meaning that the Pineal Gland receives the least amount of serotonin, leading to the "winter blues," the time in the world when people are most down and depressed.

The "Hypnagogic State," otherwise called the "Trance State" or "Alpha State," is produced when consciousness finds itself at a point between being awake and asleep. One is conscious and unconscious at the same time but alert. Brain activity slows down, but not enough to put you to sleep. The ultimate purpose of meditating is to reach this state since the Mind's Eye is utilized during it, resulting in the ability to see visions and have mystical experiences. The Alpha State also is known to induce Lucid Dreams if one reaches it during a sleep cycle.

The Ancients readily used the Hypnagogic state to contact the Spirit World and receive messages from the Divine. We can reach it with Spiritual practices and methods but also through the use of certain drugs.

DMT (Dimethyltryptamine) is also produced from the Pineal Gland via similar pathways as melatonin. Often called the "Spirit Molecule," DMT is widespread throughout the plant kingdom, but there are also trace amounts of it in mammals.

DMT-containing plants such as ayahuasca are commonly used in Shamanic rituals. Its use can produce powerful, mystical, psychedelic, and near-death experiences. DMT is hypothesized to be released at birth, death, and vivid dreams. DMT is found in the blood, urine, faeces, lungs, and kidneys in humans. Its highest traces, though, are found in the Cerebrospinal Fluid.

THE PINEAL GLAND AND SPIRITUALITY

The word "Pineal" is derived from the Latin word "pinealis," referring to a pinecone, the gland's shape. Ancient traditions widely depicted the Pineal Gland in their art and sculpture. However, its meaning and role were veiled from the profane through symbology, as was most esoteric knowledge passed down through the ages. By examining the symbols of the Ancients associated with the Pineal Gland (most notably the pinecone), we can get a better idea of its Spiritual role in our lives.

Interest in the Pineal Gland can be traced to Ancient China during the reign of the Yellow Emperor, Huangdi, the oldest of the five legendary Chinese emperors. In the Ancient Hindu scriptures, *The Vedas*, the Pineal Gland was one of seven Chakric points, purportedly connected to Sahasrara, the Crown. This viewpoint evolved over time as other Yogis and Sages began to relate the Pineal Gland to Ajna Chakra instead. As mentioned, depending on the school of thought, Ajna and Sahasrara's correspondences to the Pineal and Pituitary Glands are interchanged. So keep this in mind as you read about brain anatomy and the Chakras.

Ancient Greek philosophers and scientists perhaps made the most significant impact on our understanding of the Pineal Gland's Spiritual function. Their discovery journey began with philosophical and theological debates about the Seat of the Soul, in reference to the area of the body where the Soul operates from. They referred to this concept as "Phren," the Ancient Greek word for the location of thought or contemplation.

More than 2000 years ago, Plato and Aristotle wrote about the Soul and agreed that the Soul operated from the heart but did not reside within the body. They highlighted the three types of Soul, the nutritive, sensible, and rational, and concluded that the heart was their control centre. Hippocrates refuted this claim and believed that the Soul resided in the body and operated from the brain, not the heart, since the brain is concerned with logic, reason, and feelings.

Then came the Greek physician Herophilus, considered by many to be the father of anatomy. He was the first scientist to discover the Pineal Gland in the brain since he was the first to systematically perform scientific dissections of human cadavers (corpses). He was also the first to describe the brain ventricles and believed them to be the "Seat of the Mind." Furthermore, he concluded that the Pineal Gland regulates the flow of psychic "Pneuma," an Ancient Greek word for "breath," through these brain ventricles.

Pneuma also refers to the Spirit and Soul from a theological and religious perspective. It is an Ethereal substance in the form of air that flows from the lungs and heart into the brain. Pneuma is necessary for the systemic functioning of vital organs. In addition, it is the material that sustains the body's consciousness—referred to as the "first instrument of the Soul." Herophilus believed that the Pineal Gland regulated one's thoughts and memories in the form of psychic Pneuma.

Galen, the Greek philosopher and doctor, refuted Herophilus and said that the Pineal Gland is simply a gland that regulates blood flow and nothing more. Instead, he advocated that the Cerebellum vermis controlled the psychic Pneuma in the cerebral ventricles. Since Galen was the supreme medical authority until the 17th century, his views and beliefs about the Pineal Gland nature remained relatively unchallenged until Rene Descartes, the French mathematician and philosopher, started examining these subjects.

Descartes concluded that the Pineal Gland was the medium between the Soul and body and the source of all thought. He refuted Galen and said that since the Pineal Gland was the only structure in the brain that wasn't duplicated, it was the Soul's Seat. His position held that since the vermis of the Cerebellum has two halves, it could not be a suitable candidate for this task. Descartes believed that the Soul was beyond duality and had to have a single counterpart symbolic of its function.

Descartes thought that the mind could be separate from the body but can take over the animal instincts through the Pineal Gland. The Soul controls the mind, which, in turn, governs the system of actions carried out by the body by way of the Pineal Gland. Descartes believed that the Pineal Gland was the Soul in physical form. Since the scientific community widely respected Descartes, most did not dare challenge his views, and so the idea that the Pineal Gland was the Seat of the Soul remained intact for the next three centuries.

In recent years, scientists have determined that the Pineal Gland is an endocrine organ intimately linked to the body's perception of Light. However, its Spiritual function is still left to debate, although most scholars still agree that it plays a significant role.

In *The Magus*, I have referred to the Seat of the Soul as being in Manipura, the Solar Plexus Chakra, as the Soul's source energy. Manipura is the source of our willpower—the Soul's highest expression. In addition, the Soul needs Pranic energy for existence which it receives through food digestion (related to Manipura) and respiration/oxygen intake (related to Anahata). As such, the Soul is situated (seated) in our Sun centre, the Tiphareth Sphere, located between Manipura and Anahata Chakras.

On the other hand, the Pineal Gland could very well be the Soul's physical connection with the body. However, my research and intuitive insight have led me to conclude that the dynamic between the Pineal and Pituitary Glands and the Thalamus and Hypothalamus regulates consciousness and Spirituality and not one gland or brain centre in particular.

THE THALAMUS

The Thalamus is in the brain's centre, sitting atop the brainstem, between the Cerebral Cortex and the Midbrain, with vast nerve connections to both of them that allow hub-like exchanges of information. The Thalamus is our central control system, the command centre of consciousness regulating sleep, alertness, and cognition. Its name is derived from Greek, meaning "inner chamber."

The Thalamus acts as a relay station that filters information between the brain and body. It receives vibrations (data) from the outside world via all the sensory receptors (except olfactory) and transmits them to different parts of the brain. The Thalamus affects voluntary movement by communicating motor signals to the Cerebral Cortex. It also relays information concerning arousal and physical pain.

Along with the Hypothalamus, the Amygdala and the Hippocampus, the Thalamus is part of the Limbic System (Figure 42) that regulates emotions and memory. The Limbic System governs the autonomic and endocrine functions, which deal with responses to emotional stimuli, such as "fight or flight." The Limbic System is often referred to as the "Reptilian Brain," as it governs our behavioural responses and survival motivations. Our sense of smell directly affects the Limbic System; odours are received through the Olfactory Bulbs that register neural input detected by cells in the nasal cavities.

Interestingly, the Thalamus doesn't seem to distinguish between what is outside and what is inside of us. It gives emotional meaning to everything we take in through the senses, including our Spirituality and God-the Creator concepts. In essence, the Thalamus is our interface with the reality around us. It mediates to us our impression of what we accept as real.

The Thalamus has two lobes, known as the "Thalamic Bodies," which look like a smaller version of the two brain hemispheres. They are also comparable to two small eggs joined together. Applying the Hermetic Principle of Correspondence (As Above, So Below), we find a reflection of the Thalamic Bodies in a male's testicles and the female's ovaries, which are also dual and egg-shaped. While the Thalamus contributes to creating our mental reality (the Above), the testicles and ovaries are tasked with generating our offspring on the Earth Plane (Below). As such, the egg shape relates to creation on all levels of reality.

In 70-80% of human brains, the two Thalamic lobes are connected by a flattened band of tissue called Massa Intermedia or Interthalamic Adhesion (Figure 41). This tissue contains nerve cells and fibres. Around the Massa Intermedia, the two Thalamic bodies are separated by the Third Ventricle, which continually pumps Cerebrospinal Fluid into this area of the brain.

The Thalamus is the nucleus of our brain, the medium of communication between the different parts of the neocortex. Researchers and neurologists believe that the Thalamus is the centre of our consciousness. According to scientific studies, if the Thalamus gets damaged, it will knock out the consciousness, leading to a permanent coma.

Many Ancient traditions, including the Egyptians, regarded the Thalamus as the Third Eye centre. As the Kundalini rises up the spinal column (Sushumna), it reaches the Thalamus at the top of the brainstem. According to Yoga and Tantra, the Ida and Pingala Nadis meet at the Third Eye and unify. Their unification represents the complete opening of the Third Eye. The Caduceus of Hermes represents this same concept, namely the two snake heads facing one another in the upper part of the staff. The Caduceus is humanity's Universal symbol representing

Kundalini energy's awakening process. However, most people don't know the deep esoteric meaning behind this symbol and only link it to medicine.

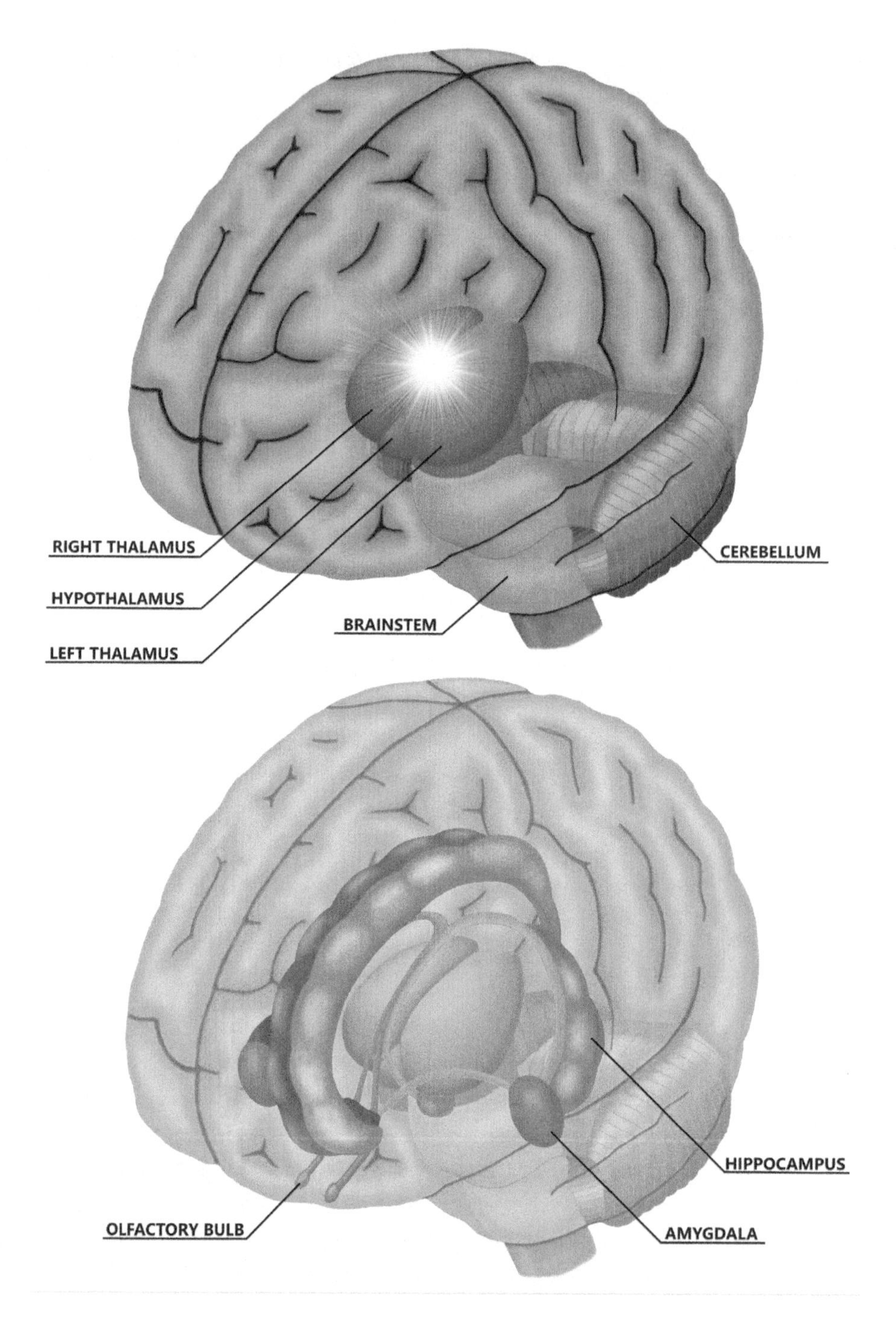

Figure 42: The Limbic System

In Yogic traditions, the brain's central area where the Thalamus lies plays an essential role in Spiritual awakening. The massive nerve bundles emerging from the spine and brainstem pass through the Thalamus before being distributed through the Corpus Callosum. The Corpus Callosum (Figure 41) is a large, C-shaped nerve fibre bundle beneath the Cerebral Cortex that connects the left and right brain hemispheres. The nerve fibres contained therein branch upwards throughout the neocortex until they reach the top of the head. The millions of neurons along the head's crown correlate with Sahasrara Chakra and its designation as the Thousand-Petalled Lotus.

Next to the Thalamus are the Pituitary and Pineal Glands and the Hypothalamus, which play a central role in meditation practices and Spiritual awakening. During meditation, the Light from Sahasrara is drawn into the brain's centre, resulting in a substantial and permanent shift in one's perception of Self and the world. The Thalamus is essentially our centre of Spiritual transformation and the expansion of consciousness.

Since the Thalamus focuses our attention, it is involved in the filtering process of the numerous impulses that stream into our brain at any given moment. It acts like a valve that prioritises the vibratory messages our brain receives from the outside world. For this reason, when a person undergoes a Kundalini awakening, their Thalamus becomes optimised so that more information can be received and processed at once.

The Thalamus' transfiguration results in one receiving and experiencing a heightened version of reality through enhanced senses. As such, psychic powers like clairvoyance, clairaudience, and clairsentience become a part of everyday life. As the Thalamus becomes optimised, latent DNA is activated within the Self, resulting in the permanent transformation of consciousness at a cellular level.

The Thalamus is also the gateway between the conscious and subconscious parts of the Self, a filter that keeps our Karmic energies at bay. When a person undergoes a full Kundalini awakening and Light enters the brain permanently, a bridge is formed between the conscious and subconscious minds, allowing our negative, repressed energies to stream into the consciousness. Instead of serving as a filter, the Thalamus no longer operates as such. Instead, its function goes into hyperdrive, allowing our consciousness to experience all the energies within us at once. Part of the reason for this phenomenon is to open our consciousness fully so that we can purify our Karmic energies through the Kundalini Fire and Spiritually evolve.

THE RETICULAR FORMATION

The Reticular Formation (Figure 43) is an intricate network of neurons and nerve fibres that extends from the spinal cord to the lower brainstem, through the Midbrain and Thalamus, splitting into multiple radiations to different parts of the Cerebral Cortex. The Reticular Formation is a conduit for transmitting information from the various sensory pathways and transmitting them to parts of the brain via the Thalamus. Its other name is the Reticular Activating System, or RAS for short.

The Reticular Formation is critical to the existence of consciousness since it mediates all of our conscious activity. As the Thalamus is our central control box, the Reticulating System is the wiring that connects that box to the brainstem below and the Cerebral Cortex above. It is involved in many states of consciousness that engage the Thalamus.

The Reticular Formation allows the Thalamus, Hypothalamus, and Cerebral Cortex to control which sensory signals reach the Cerebrum (uppermost part of the brain) and come to our conscious attention. As such, it is the focusing mechanism of our minds.

The Reticular Formation is also involved in most Central Nervous System activities. Pain sensations, for example, must pass through the Reticular Formation before reaching the brain. In addition, the Autonomic Nervous System, which deals with automatized behaviour such as breathing, beating of the heart, and arousal, is also regulated by the Reticular Formation.

Meditation alters our consciousness to allow higher brain regions to control sensory impulses and environmental stimuli. During meditation, the Hypothalamus and Reticular Formation become partially inhibited, explaining some of the physiological effects of meditation, such as decreases in blood pressure and respiration rate.

When we can suspend the Reticular Formation's function and stop the flow of distracting and irrelevant sensory information, the brain begins emitting Alpha waves, resulting in a calm and relaxed state of mind. As such, overcoming the effects of the Reticular Formation is associated with conscious awareness and mindfulness.

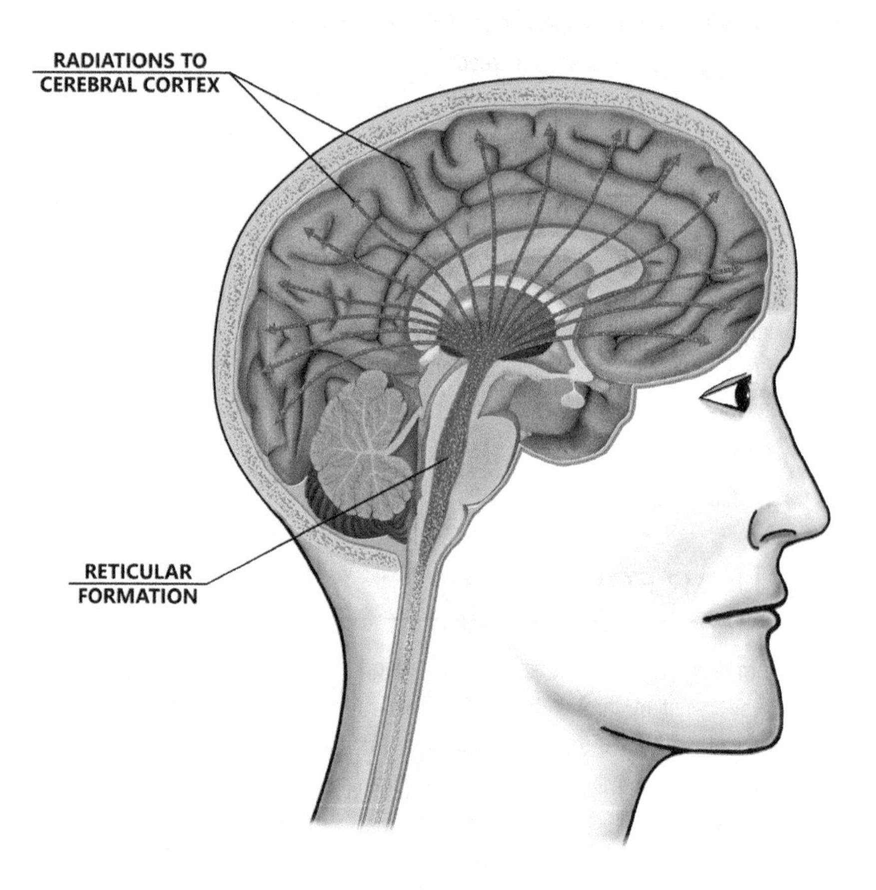

Figure 43: The Reticular Formation

The Reticular Formation directs our impressions of life and its activities, which results in Self-identifying with those impressions. The Self anchors to the physical body's sensations, whether good or bad and our consciousness drops to the level of the Ego. Over time, the consciousness becomes hijacked by the Ego. By aligning with it, we lose touch with the Soul on the opposite end of the spectrum.

After a full Kundalini awakening, as the voltage of one's bioelectricity increases, the Thalamus becomes optimized, and the Reticular Formation becomes permanently disengaged. This experience results in feeling the Body of Light's radiance through all the body cells at once instead of having individual Spiritual moments or encounters. By bypassing the mind and Ego, the individual begins to operate through the heart, which allows them to experience the field of energy around them more substantially.

The skull sits atop the Atlas, the first cervical vertebra (C1). Atlas is also the name of a Titan from Greek mythology who holds up the celestial heavens or sky. Visual images of Atlas portray him as holding the Planet Earth atop his shoulders. We see here a connection between the skull and brain, the world, and the Heavens. The cervical Atlas holds up the head, which contains the brain that regulates our reality concept. Our brain is also the connecting link to the Heavens, or God-the Creator, popularly portrayed by the artist Michelangelo in a fresco painting called "The Creation of Adam," forming part of the Sistine Chapel's ceiling.

The first grouping of neurons in the Reticular Formation begins in the area between the Medulla Oblongata and the top of the spinal cord, represented by the Atlas. This area is the primary point of entry of Pranic energy into the body for the Kundalini awakened individuals. The highest concentration of the Life Force is stored in Sahasrara, our White Light centre, the principal reservoir of Prana in those people whose consciousness is expanded. Pranic energy flows downwards from Sahasrara into the significant brain centres, thereby powering them. Afterwards, it moves down the spine and into the nervous system, followed by the organs and muscles. As such, the body becomes nourished by the Light energy. For this reason, Spiritually awakened individuals don't require a lot of Pranic energy from food and the Sun like the unawakened—they get everything they need from Sahasrara Chakra.

Consequently, this same area where the Reticular Formation begins is where a crucial and mysterious hidden Chakra is located, called Lalana or Talu Chakra. The Kundalini must pierce Lalana Chakra on its upward rise before entering the brain. Then, with Lalana Chakra's full activation, the Kundalini can reach Ajna in the brain's centre, followed by Sahasrara at the top of the head.

Lalana is the main switchboard that controls the entrance, storage and distribution of Pranic energy. The Life Force must pass through Lalana before reaching the five Chakras below it, passing on the Pranic power to the major organs and endocrine glands through the Peripheral Nervous System (PNS). Compared to Lalana, the lower Chakras are but minor distribution centres of the Life Force. Lalana connects with Hara Chakra in the navel, representing the location where the Self first anchored into the physical body upon conception.

Lalana is esoterically called the "Mouth of God" or the "Golden Chalice" as our Ascension Chakra—it relates to the "Three-Fold Flame of the Soul" (Hebrew Letter Shin). Once Lalana is pierced, the Kundalini continues to rise towards the brain's centre, where the three channels of Ida, Pingala, and Sushumna unify into one energy source. Their unification results in the energetic fusion of the Pineal and Pituitary Glands and the Thalamus and Hypothalamus. The Reticular Formation's effect on the consciousness detaches once the individual begins to operate from the Source energy present in their brains' centre.

When Ajna and Sahasrara Chakras are fully open, the consciousness expands to the Cosmic level, resulting in a permanent experience of the Spiritual reality. After the Body of Light is fully activated, a brain rewiring occurs over time, awakening its latent potential. The transformed individual becomes a receiver of Cosmic Wisdom as their intelligence is expanded. Once they align with these higher vibrations, the individual gradually disassociates with the physical body, which lessens the Ego's hold over the consciousness.

Once the Reticular Formation is disengaged, the Self can overcome the Ego much easier since consciousness is naturally elevated to a higher level. Physical pain is one of the critical factors that align the Self with the physical body. After a full Kundalini awakening, one's conscious connection with physical pain is severed permanently. As I have described this phenomenon previously, one can still feel pain since it is impossible to fully overcome it while living in the physical body. Instead, they develop the ability to consciously disassociate from experiencing the pain's negative energy by rising to a substantially higher Cosmic Plane than the Physical Plane where the pain is occurring.

PARTS OF THE BRAIN

The brain is divided into three main parts: the Cerebrum, Cerebellum, and Brain Stem. I have already discussed the Brain Stem, which includes the Midbrain, Pons, and Medulla Oblongata. The Midbrain is continuous with the Diencephalon, our "interbrain," consisting of the Thalamus, Hypothalamus, Pituitary Gland (posterior portion) and Pineal Gland. The Diencephalon encloses the Third Ventricle.

The Cerebrum is the largest part of the brain and comprises the right and left-brain hemispheres, joined together by the Corpus Callosum. The right half of the brain controls the left side of the body, while the left half controls the right side. Each hemisphere contains four lobes on its external surface: Frontal, Parietal, Temporal and Occipital Lobes (Figure 44). The brain's outer layer is called the Cerebral Cortex, which forms the brain's grey matter, while the inner layer is the white matter.

Each of the four lobes is associated with a set of functions. For example, the Frontal Lobe is in the front section of the brain. The Prefrontal Cortex is the Cerebral Cortex that covers the front part of the Frontal Lobe. The Frontal Lobe is concerned with higher cognitive functions such as memory recall, emotional expression, mood changes, language and speech, creativity, imagination, impulse control, social interaction and behaviours, reasoning and problem solving, attention and concentration, organization and planning, motivation, and sexual expression.

The Frontal Lobe is also responsible for primary motor function and movement coordination. It is the most prominent lobe in the brain and is most frequently used by the Self daily. Since it is at the front of the head, directly behind the forehead, the Frontal Lobe is the most common traumatic brain injury region with potentially the worst side effects because it affects your cognitive abilities and motor function. In addition, damage to the Frontal Lobes can set off a chain reaction that can negatively affect other brain areas.

The Parietal Lobe is located near the brain's centre, behind the Frontal Lobe. This brain area is the primary sensory area where impulses from the skin related to temperature, pain, and touch are processed and interpreted. The left Parietal Lobe is concerned with handling symbols, letters, and numbers, and interpreting Archetypal information. The right Parietal Lobe is tasked with interpreting spatial distance in images.

The Parietal Lobe is concerned with all spatial information, allowing us to judge size, distance, and shapes. It provides us with an awareness of the Self and other people in the space before us. Interestingly, neuroscientists have determined that a person experiences increased activity in the Parietal Cortex during a Spiritual experience. The boundary between the Self and objects and people around us gets broken since most Spiritual experiences involve some "out of body" element. As the individual experiences a sense of unity with their environment, they transcend their physical surroundings.

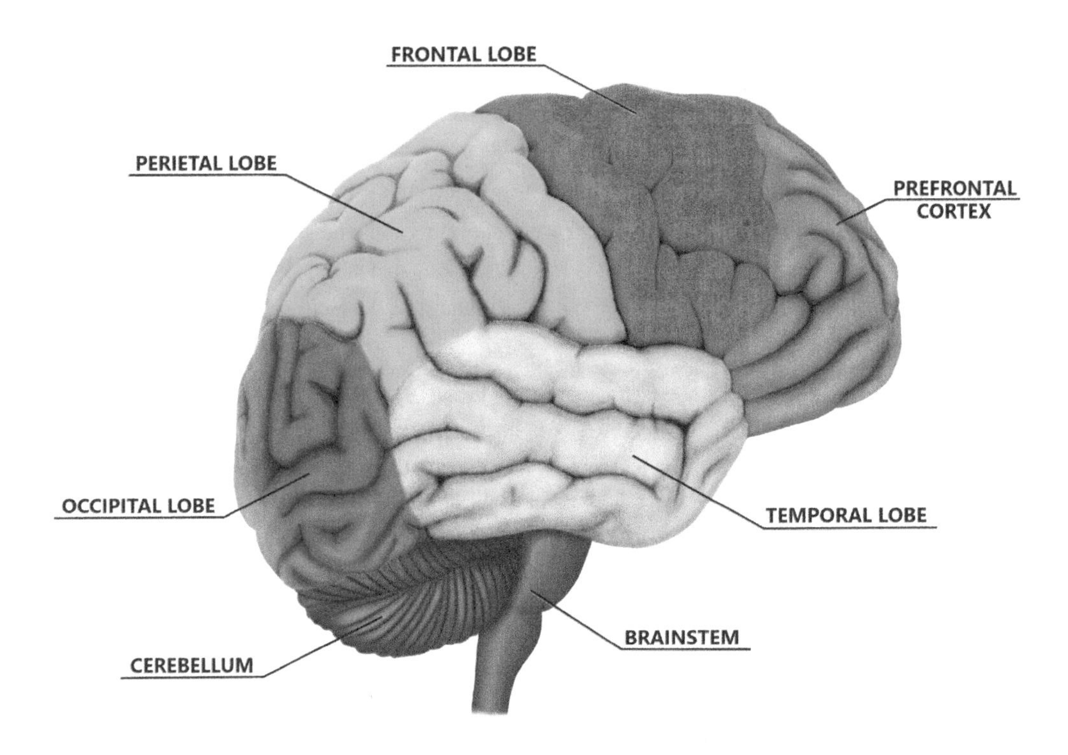

Figure 44: The Parts of the Brain

The Temporal Lobe sits behind the ears and temples of the head. It holds the Primary Auditory Cortex, which is concerned with processing sound and encoding memory. It also plays an essential role in processing emotions, language, and some aspects of visual perception. Temporal Lobe consists of structures vital for conscious memory relating to facts and events. It communicates with the Hippocampus and is modulated by the Amygdala.

The Occipital Lobe is located on the rear part of the upper brain. It contains the Primary Visual Cortex, a brain region that receives input from the eyes. The Occipital Lobe generally deals with interpreting distance, colours, depth perception, object and face recognition, movements, and memory information.

The Cerebellum is at the back of the head, and it controls the coordination of muscular activity. It helps us maintain posture, balance, and equilibrium by coordinating different muscle groups' timing and force to produce fluid body movements. The Cerebellum also coordinates eye movements, as well as speech.

The founder of psychoanalysis, Sigmund Freud, associated the Cerebellum with the personal unconscious, the repressed part of the Self that is hidden from the conscious mind. Although Freud coined the term "unconscious" mind, he often interchanged it with the "subconscious" mind, the former being a deeper layer of the latter. This aligns with Ancient wisdom teachings that associate the subconscious mind with the back of the head and the Moon. However, the scope of the subconscious mind involves most parts of the brain, including the Limbic System. Excluded is the Prefrontal Cortex, which represent the conscious mind and the Sun.

With a full Kundalini awakening, as the energy rises through the spinal cord, large amounts of high-octane energy reach the brain. This energy flows from the Reticular Formation to the Thalamus and into the Cerebral Cortex, awakening dormant, inactive parts of the brain, especially in the Frontal Lobe. Afterwards, the entire brain begins to pulse as a cohesive unit, generating coherent, high amplitude brainwaves within all frequency bands. This brain-power augmentation process is coupled with consciousness expansion once the Kundalini pierces Sahasrara Chakra.

The Alpha band of frequency reaches maximum amplitude in the Occipital Lobe, creating changes in perception of the world around us. Things that used to appear one way get transformed before your very eyes once the Occipital Lobe's potential is maximised, combined with the influx of Astral Light in the head.

Increased brain activity unifies the conscious and subconscious minds, represented Alchemically as the Sun and Moon energies conjoined in Holy Matrimony. The Cerebellum is also affected by the heightened activity of the brain as the individual gains access to repressed feelings, thoughts, desires, and hidden memories to be integrated and transformed.

Large amounts of electrical activity occur in the Beta and Gamma frequency bands in the Frontal Lobe, maximising the potential of the Prefrontal Cortex and other essential parts. As a result, the Kundalini awakened individual develops the ability to control their thoughts, emotions, and behaviour, allowing them to master their reality. In addition, their cognitive skills, including imagination, creativity, intelligence, communication, critical thinking, and the power of concentration, are all vastly enhanced, enabling them to become the powerful and efficient Co-Creators with the Creator they are destined to be.

THE NERVOUS SYSTEM

The nervous system is made up of all the nerve cells one has in their body. We use our nervous system to communicate with the outside world and control the various mechanisms of our body. The nervous system assimilates information through the senses and processes it, thereby eliciting reactions in the body. It works in conjunction with the endocrine system to respond to life's events.

The nervous system connects the brain with every other organ, tissue and body part. It contains billions of nerve cells called neurons. The brain itself has 100 billion neurons that act like information messengers. These neurons use chemical signals and electrical impulses to transmit information between different parts of the brain as well as the brain and the rest of the nervous system.

The nervous system consists of two parts with three distinct divisions. Firstly and most importantly, we have the Central Nervous System (CNS), which controls sensation and motor functions. The Central Nervous System includes the brain, Twelve Pairs of Cranial Nerves, the spinal cord, and thirty-one pairs of spinal nerves. All of the nerves of the Central Nervous System are safely contained within the skull and the spinal canal.

Two types of nerves serve the brain: motor (efferent) nerves, which execute responses to stimuli, and sensory (afferent) nerves, which transmit sensory information and data from the body to the Central Nervous System. Spinal nerves serve both functions; hence they are called "mixed" nerves. Spinal nerves are connected to the spinal cord via ganglia which act like relay stations for the Central Nervous System.

The head and brain serve as organs of the Soul and Higher Self. Since it is at the top of the body, the head is nearest to the Heavens above. The brain allows us to experience the world around us through the five senses of sight, touch, taste, smell and sound. It also allows us to experience reality through the sixth sense of psychism, received through the Mind's Eye.

The Peripheral Nervous System (PNS) connects the nerves emanating from the Central Nervous System to limbs and organs. All the nerves outside the brain and spine are part of the Peripheral Nervous System (Figure 45). The Peripheral Nervous System is further sub-divided into three separate subsystems: Somatic Nervous System (SNS), Enteric Nervous System (ENS), and Autonomic Nervous System (ANS).

The Somatic Nervous System is the voluntary nervous system whose sensory and motor nerves act as a medium of transmission of impulses between the Central Nervous System and the muscular system. The Somatic Nervous System controls everything about our physical body, which we can consciously influence. The Enteric Nervous System acts involuntarily, and it functions to control the gastrointestinal system. It is an autonomous nervous system that regulates bowel motility in the digestion process.

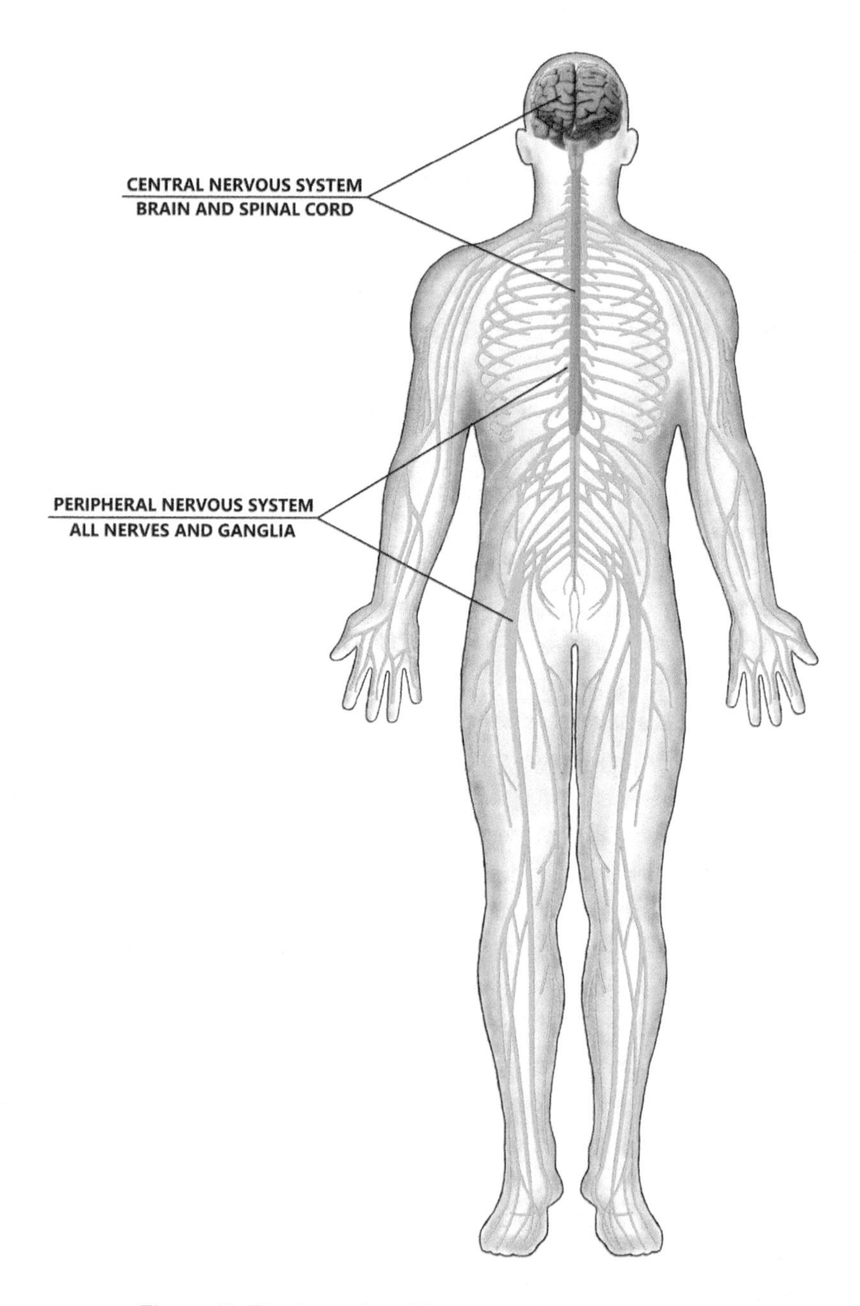

Figure 45: The Central and Peripheral Nervous Systems

The Autonomic Nervous System is also an involuntary system that acts mostly unconsciously. It regulates our heart rate, breathing, metabolism, digestion, sexual arousal, urination and pupil dilation/constriction. Both the Autonomic Nervous System and Enteric Nervous System are always active, whether we are awake or asleep. The involuntary nervous system reacts quickly to changes in the body, allowing it to adapt by altering its regulatory processes.The Autonomic Nervous System is controlled by the Hypothalamus and can be broken down into the Sympathetic Nervous System (SNS) and the Parasympathetic Nervous System (PNS). The Sympathetic Nervous System and Parasympathetic Nervous System usually do opposite things in the body. The Sympathetic Nervous System is powered by the body's masculine (Yang) energy, while the Parasympathetic Nervous System is powered by the feminine (Yin) energy.

The Sympathetic Nervous System prepares the body for mental and (or) physical activity. It is activated in emergencies (fight or flight) to create useable energy. It increases heart rate, dilates pupils, opens airways to breathe more easily, increases blood supply to muscles, and inhibits digestion and sexual arousal. The Parasympathetic Nervous System, on the other hand, is passive. It is activated when the body and mind are in a relaxed state. The Parasympathetic Nervous System lowers the heart rate, constricts pupils, stimulates digestion and urination, triggers various metabolic processes, and promotes sexual excitement.

STRONG/WEAK NERVOUS SYSTEMS

Stress and anxiety are common problems in today's fast-paced society. Therefore, people often talk about the importance of having a strong nervous system when facing adversity in life. A person with a robust and resilient nervous system faces reality head-on, the good and the bad. In contrast, someone with a weak nervous system gets intimidated easily and shelters themselves from reality to avoid negativity.

As a Co-Creator with the Creator, you cannot control what comes your way 100% because there are always external factors that even the most acute minds cannot think of, but you can choose through Free Will whether to allow yourself to face everything that comes your way. That choice often depends on how you handle fear energy, which either strengthens or weakens your nervous system over time.

Think of the nervous system as a container. People with weak nervous systems have small containers since there is a limit to how much anxiety, stress, or physical pain they can withstand. People with strong nervous systems have substantially larger containers and can deal with whatever comes their way. They experience and process adverse events much faster and aren't shaken in their poise. People with robust nervous systems have the attitude of facing fear and adversity, no matter how scary things may appear on the surface. The result is becoming a master manifester of your reality and maximizing your personal potential. People with strong nervous systems live their dreams and get the most out of life.

The strength of your nervous system depends on how well you use your willpower and how much you can overcome your emotions. Emotions are fluid; they fluctuate from positive to negative at all times. Sometimes it takes time for things to turn negative, but they inevitably do, and eventually, they come back to being positive again.

The Principle of Rhythm (from *The Kybalion*) states that the pendulum of rhythm manifests its swing between all opposites found in nature, including emotions and thoughts. Therefore, nothing ever remains static, and all things are constantly undergoing a process of change and transformation from one state into another. As such, this Principle is always in play. You cannot overcome it unless you learn to vibrate your willpower so strongly that you rise above the Astral Plane of where the emotional swing is occurring and into the Mental Plane.

Another key to a robust nervous system is learning to relax the body and mind when dealing with a stressful situation. Stress and anxiety immediately activate the Sympathetic Nervous System, which puts you into survival mode—applying mindfulness and breathing techniques when under pressure and not letting your emotions rule you will switch off the SNS and turn on the Parasympathetic Nervous System. As such, even when dealing with an adverse situation, you can be cool, calm, and collected, which will enhance your problem-solving skills and yield the best outcome in any situation.

Letting your emotions be the guiding force in your life will always bring chaos and despair, while if you attune to your willpower and let it guide you, you will triumph in life. Emotions are dual and void of logic and reason. On the Tree of Life, they belong to the Netzach Sphere, while logic and reason correspond with its opposite, Hod. Emotions are naturally opposed to logic and reason until one learns to utilize their higher Sephiroth. By implementing willpower (Geburah) and imagination (Tiphareth), tempered by memory (Chesed), you can rise in consciousness and control your reality much more efficiently than by being a slave to your emotions.

To rise even higher on the Tree of Life, you need to bypass duality altogether, which means your consciousness needs to be attuned to intuition. Intuition belongs to Ajna Chakra, which is powered by Binah (Understanding) and Chokmah (Wisdom). To function fully through intuition, you either need to have had a permanent Kundalini awakening or have mastered meditation and gained the ability to resonate with the Spiritual Plane at will. As mentioned, a Kundalini awakening will naturally attune you to the Spiritual Plane over time. Thus, it is the desired experience for all that know about Kundalini's transformative power.

YOGA AND THE NERVOUS SYSTEM

The Sympathetic and Parasympathetic Nervous Systems switch from one to another many times throughout the day, especially in people whose emotions dominate their life. Thus, for one to be balanced in mind, body, and Soul, they need to have a balanced Autonomic Nervous System. When one half of the Autonomic Nervous System is overly dominant, it causes problems for the other half.

People who are prone to stress, for example, utilize the Sympathetic Nervous System more so than is healthy for the mind and body, which causes a detriment to the Parasympathetic Nervous System over time. As such, the person is always tense and under mental pressure, unable to relax and be at peace.

Psychological stress also affects the immune system, so the quality of our Autonomic Nervous System makes the difference in how prone we are to disease. Chronic degenerative diseases such as heart disease, high blood pressure, ulcers, gastritis, insomnia, and Adrenal exhaustion result from an unbalanced Autonomic Nervous System.

How we manage the two complementary halves of the Autonomic Nervous System depends on diet and nutrition but also lifestyle and living habits. We must learn to balance activity and rest, sleep and wakefulness, and our thoughts and emotions.

Yoga helps regulate and strengthen the Autonomic Nervous System by its effect on the Hypothalamus. Yoga is very efficient in helping the body and mind relax through breathing exercises (Pranayama) and meditation. Breathing is an interface between the Central Nervous System and Autonomic Nervous System. Through the practice of Pranayama, one can learn to control their autonomic functions. By controlling the lungs, we gain control of the heart. Yogic postures (Asanas) aim to balance the masculine and feminine energies within oneself, which promotes a healthy and robust nervous system.

Anulom Vilom (Alternate Nostril Breathing), for example, works directly on the Sympathetic Nervous System or Parasympathetic Nervous System, depending on which nostril you are breathing through. When you breathe through the right nostril, metabolism increases, and the mind becomes focused externally. When you breathe through the left nostril, metabolism slows down, and the mind turns inwards, which enhances focus.

KUNDALINI AWAKENING AND THE NERVOUS SYSTEM

A nerve impulse is an electrical phenomenon, just like a lightning strike. So when there is an abundance of bioelectricity in the body after a full Kundalini awakening, it puts the entire nervous system in overdrive. A complete transformation occurs over time as the nervous system augments itself, building new circuits daily to adjust to the inner changes.

Firstly, as the Kundalini Light activates and invigorates all the latent nerves, the Central Nervous System begins operating at maximum capacity. Higher activity levels are shown in the brain as it works extra hard to register the vibration impulses coming in from the hyperactive Peripheral and Autonomic Nervous Systems. Other than adjusting to the expanded consciousness, the brain must also work to build new neural pathways to accommodate this bioenergy expansion and synchronize with the rest of the nervous system.

The initial stages of rebuilding your nervous system are taxing on the mind and body. Since the entire process is new to the consciousness, the body goes into "fight or flight" mode to protect against potential harm. As such, the Sympathetic Nervous System dominates for the time being while fear energy is present. As many Kundalini awakened people know firsthand, Adrenal exhaustion from stress is common in these initial stages.

However, in the latter stages of the rebuilding process, once the new neural pathways have been built up, the mind becomes more accepting of the process, allowing it to relax. As a result, the Sympathetic Nervous System switches off, and the Parasympathetic Nervous System takes over. The Vagus Nerve also plays a role during this process, as it contributes to bringing coherence to the body. Although it might take many years to complete the transformation overall, the result will be a substantially stronger nervous system that allows one to navigate potentially stressful situations in an unprecedented way.

VAGUS NERVE FUNCTION

The Twelve Cranial Nerves come in pairs and help link the brain with other body areas such as the head, neck, and torso. The Vagus Nerve (Figure 46) is the longest of the Cranial Nerves (tenth nerve) as it runs from the brainstem to a part of the colon. It has both motor and sensory functions.

The word "Vagus" means "wandering" in Latin, which is appropriate since it is a winding, serpentine-like bundle of motor and sensory fibres that primarily links the brainstem to the heart, lungs, and gut. The gut is the digestive system (gastrointestinal tract) that consists of the mouth, oesophagus, stomach, liver, small intestine, large intestine, and rectum (anus).

The Vagus Nerve also branches out to interact with the liver, spleen, gallbladder, ureter, uterus, neck, ears, tongue, and kidneys—its nerve fibres innervate all the internal organs. Although the brain does communicate with the body's organs via the Vagus Nerve, 80% of information is directed from the organs to the brain. Out of all the organs in the body, the stomach uses the Vagus Nerve to communicate with the brain the most—it sends signals to it related to satiety (hunger), satiation (fullness), and energy metabolism.

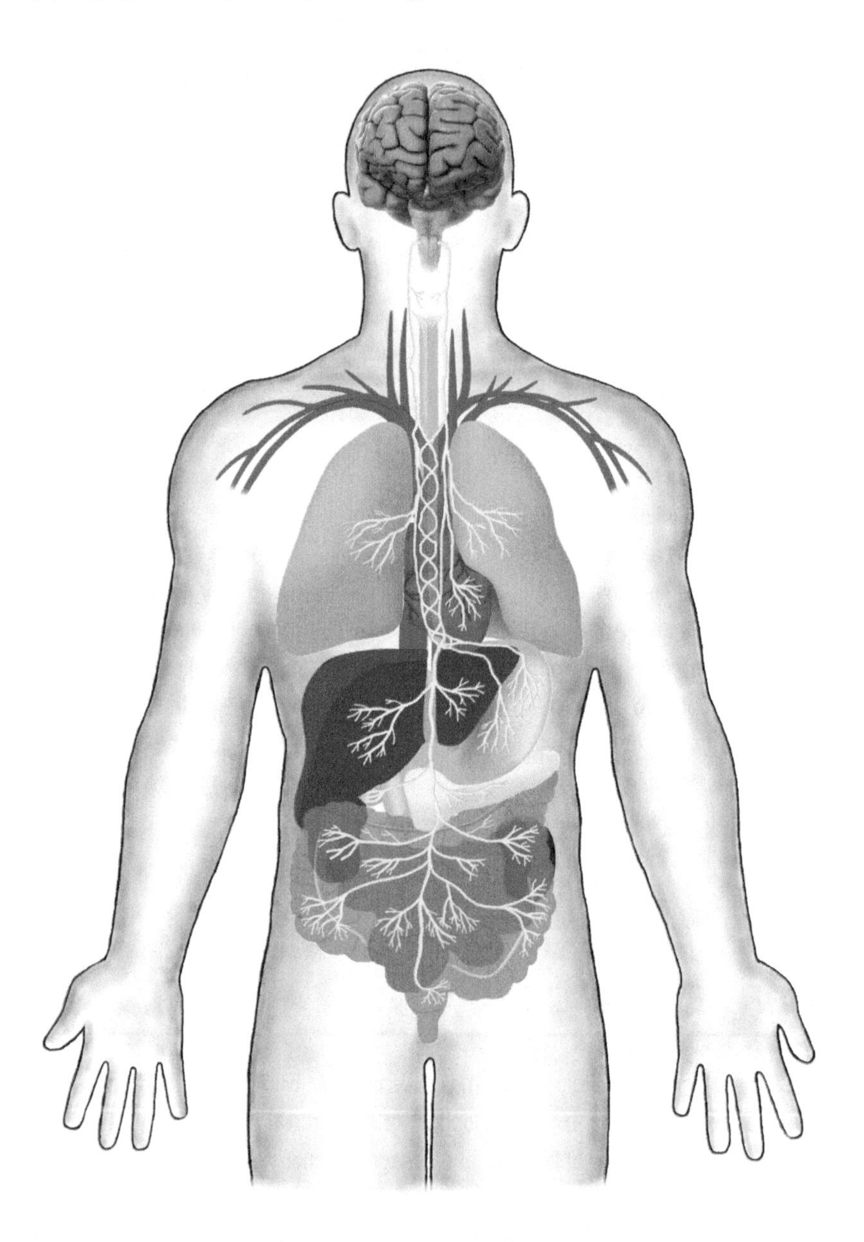

Figure 46: The Vagus Nerve

The processing and management of emotions occur via the Vagus Nerve between the heart, brain, and gut. The Enteric Nervous System has a mesh-like system of neurons that govern the gut's function and communicate with the brain via the Vagus Nerve. When you hear someone saying they have a "gut feeling" about something, this sense of knowingness is a real nervous signal in the gut. For this reason, we have a powerful gut reaction to intense mental and emotional states. The Enteric Nervous System is often referred to as our "second brain" centred in our Solar Plexus area, and the Vagus Nerve is often called the "gut-brain axis."

The Vagus Nerve activates the Parasympathetic Nervous System, which controls the body's unconscious "rest and digest" functions. The Vagus Nerve serves to calm down the body after eating so that we can process food easier. One of its key roles, though, is to act as the "reset" button that counteracts our automatic, internal alarm system, the "fight or flight" response of the Sympathetic Nervous System.

The neurotransmitter that the Vagus nerve uses to communicate with the body, acetylcholine, is responsible for feelings of calm, peace, relaxation, and learning and memory functions. People whose Vagus Nerve is underactive are plagued by chronic anxiety and have poor learning abilities and memory recall. It is crucial for these people to stimulate the Vagus Nerve, either naturally or with an artificial electrical device. Doing so can lead to positive health benefits, including overcoming stress and depression and reducing inflammation caused by emotional pain.

Vagal tone is measured by tracking the heart rate alongside the breathing rate. When we breathe in, our heart rate speeds up, while when we breathe out, our heart rate slows down. People with high Vagal tones have a more extended period between their inhalation and exhalation heart rates, meaning that their body can relax faster after a stressful event.

High Vagal tone improves the function of many of the body's systems—it reduces the risk of stroke by lowering blood pressure, aids in digestion and blood sugar regulation, and enhances one's overall mood and resistance to stress. Low Vagal tone, on the other hand, does the opposite to the body—it is associated with cardiovascular conditions, diabetes, cognitive impairment, chronic anxiety, and depression. Low Vagal tone also makes the body more susceptible to autoimmune diseases resulting from high inflammatory states.

Vagus Nerve is known to promote love, compassion, trust, altruism and gratitude, all of which add to our overall happiness in life. One of the most effective, natural methods of stimulating the Vagus Nerve and improving the Vagal tone is through the Pranayama technique of Diaphragmatic Breathing. When you breathe slowly and rhythmically through your abdomen, the diaphragm opens up, allowing more oxygen into the body. As a result, the Parasympathetic Nervous System gets activated, calming the mind.

Diaphragmatic Breathing encompasses the whole of the nervous system and the Seven Major Chakras, allowing us to ground our energies instead of allowing them to run frantically in the chest area, causing unnecessary stress and anxiety. (For a complete description of the Diaphragmatic Breathing technique and its benefits, turn to "Pranayama Exercises" in the Yoga section.)

Since the Vagus Nerve is connected to the vocal cords, singing, humming, and chanting is also associated with improving one's Vagal tone. Oral communication is beneficial, and people who talk a lot are generally of a good disposition. Communicating with others promotes positive emotions and brings social closeness, which improves Vagal tone.

Research has shown that Yoga increases Vagal tone, reduces stress, and improves recovery from emotional and mental trauma. Pranayama and meditation activate the Parasympathetic Nervous System and calm down the mind, stimulating the Vagus Nerve. Asanas (Yogic postures) balance the masculine and feminine parts of Self, creating harmony in the body and promoting mindfulness. Other Yogic techniques also have tremendous physical and Spiritual health benefits. For this reason, I have devoted an entire section to the science, philosophy, and practice of Yoga.

THE VAGUS NERVE AND THE KUNDALINI

There are interesting similarities between the Vagus Nerve and the Kundalini worth examining. After seeing the correspondences, it will be self-evident that the Vagus Nerve complements the Kundalini awakening process and may even be a physical representation of the Kundalini itself.

Firstly, the Vagus nerve runs from the colon area (Muladhara) to the brain (Sahasrara). In contrast, the Kundalini lies coiled at the base of the spine in Muladhara, right beside the anus. Once awakened, it rises upwards to the brain's centre and finally the top of the head to complete the process.

People refer to the Vagus Nerve as one, but in reality, they are two nerves that operate as one. Here we see a correlation with the Ida and Pingala Nadis, the dual serpents that, when balanced, function as one channel (Sushumna).

The Vagus Nerve interacts with all the organs and glands in the body directly. Its role is to collect information from the organs and glands and carry it to the brain for examination. Similarly, the Kundalini connects with the body's organs and glands and communicates their state to the brain via the nervous system.

The Kundalini moves through the spinal cord, while the Vagus Nerve runs more centrally through the body. When we activate the Kundalini, all the organs and glands begin to work in synchronicity with one another, bringing coherence to the body. The Vagus Nerve also, when stimulated, creates a unifying effect in the organs and glands where they begin to function in harmony with one another.

Since the Vagus Nerve connects with the digestive system, impairment in the Vagus Nerve will result in stomach problems. In contrast, the Kundalini's power centre is in Manipura, and when it is not activated or its energy is blocked, digestive and stomach problems will ensue.

The heart and brain are closely connected, and they communicate a great deal via the Vagus Nerve. The Heart Chakra is also in direct communication with the two highest Chakras in the brain, Ajna and Sahasrara. In the Kundalini system, the Heart Chakra is the centre of the Self, the part of us that assimilates and harmonizes energies from the other Chakras. On a physical level, the heart is the most powerful generator of electromagnetic energy in the body and our primary interface with our environment (See chapter "Power of the Heart" for more detail on this topic.)

The subject of Kundalini originated in the East and is part of Yogic and Tantric practices. Both Yoga and Tantra involve Pranayama, Asanas, meditation, and other techniques, which involve the Vagus Nerve response to relax the body and calm the mind. Many Yogis recognize the Vagus Nerve's role and power in the body and mind and consider it the anatomical counterpart to the Sushumna Nadi. As such, the Vagus Nerve demands our utmost attention.

THE TWELVE PAIRS OF CRANIAL NERVES

The Twelve Pairs of Cranial Nerves (Figure 47) connect your brain to different parts of your head, neck, and trunk. As such, they relay information between your brain and body parts, especially to and from the head and neck regions. These Cranial Nerves govern sight, smell, hearing, eye movement, feeling in the face, balance, and swallowing. The functions of the Twelve Pairs of Cranial Nerves are sensory, motor, or both. Sensory nerves are concerned with seeing, hearing, smelling, tasting, and touching. On the other hand, motor nerves help control movements in the head and neck regions.

Each of the Twelve Pairs of Cranial Nerves has corresponding Roman numerals between I and XII based on their location from front to back. They include the Olfactory Nerve (I), Optic Nerve (II), Oculomotor Nerve (III), Trochlear Nerve (IV), Trigeminal Nerve (V), Abducens Nerve (VI), Facial Nerve (VII), Vestibulocochlear Nerve (VIII), Glossopharyngeal Nerve (IX), Vagus Nerve (X), Spinal Accessory Nerve (XI), and Hypoglossal Nerve (XII). The Olfactory Nerve and Optic Nerve emerge from the Cerebrum while the remaining ten pairs arise from the brainstem.

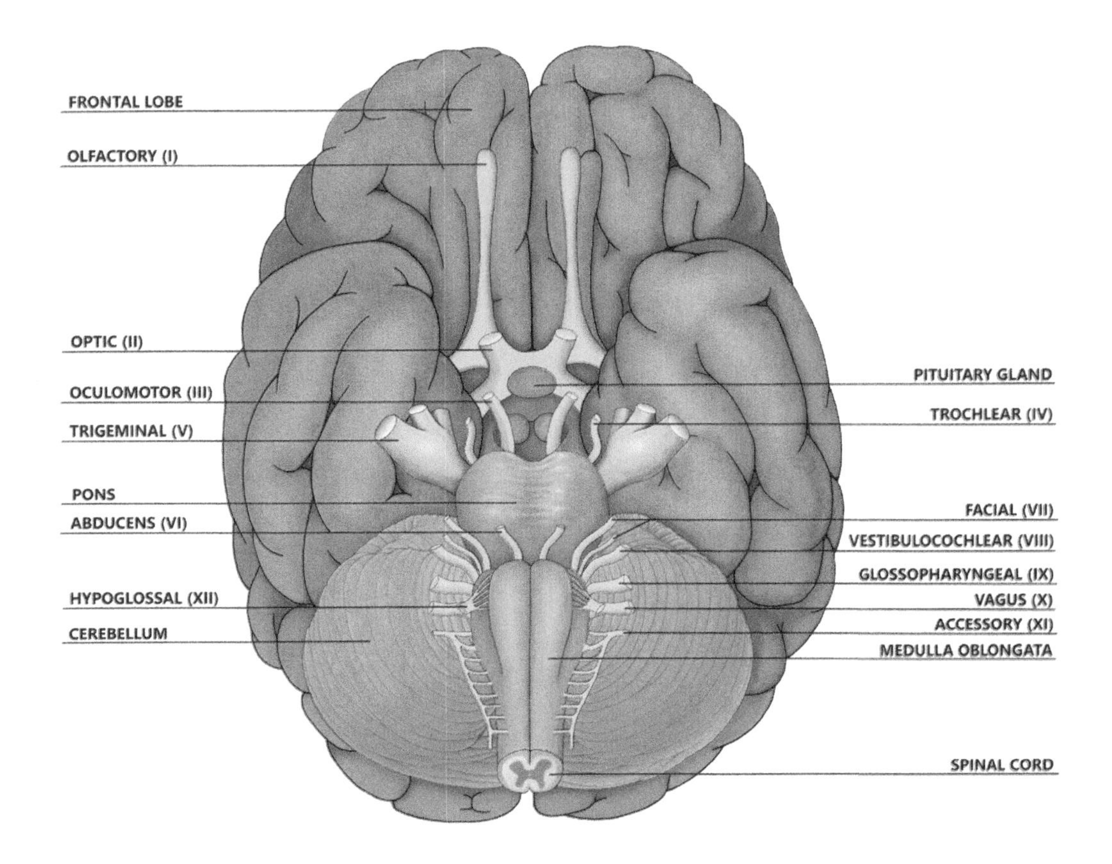

Figure 47: The Twelve Pairs of Cranial Nerves

The Olfactory Nerve transmits information to the brain regarding the individual's sense of smell, while the Optic Nerve relays vision information. The Oculomotor, Trochlear, and Abducens Nerves are concerned with eye movements. The Trigeminal Nerve governs sensation and motor function in the face and mouth. The Facial Nerve controls the muscles of facial expression and conveys taste sensations from the tongue. The Vestibulocochlear Nerve transmits sound and balance from the inner ear to the brain. The Glossopharyngeal Nerve is concerned with the sense of taste received from the part of the tongue and throat area. The Vagus Nerve has many functions, which I have already described. The Spinal Accessory Nerve controls muscles of the shoulder and neck. And finally, the Hypoglossal Nerve controls tongue movements concerning speech and swallowing of food.

The Twelve Pairs of Cranial Nerves correspond with the Twelve Zodiacal Constellations. As such, they exemplify the Hermetic Principle of "As Above, So Below." There are twelve "pairs" since we live in a world of Duality where there are two of everything. The World of Duality, the material world, reflects the Unity of the Spiritual World, which powers the Twelve Zodiacal Constellations (groupings of Stars) by emitting its White Light through them.

Keep in mind that the Sun of our Solar System is just one such Star, and there are millions of Stars in the Milky Way alone, with Solar Systems of their own. The Ancients named the ones that we see in our night sky according to the shapes and images their groupings made, giving us the band of Twelve Zodiac. Consequently, the Twelve Zodiacal Constellations are reflected in the Twelve Pairs of Cranial Nerves, either a grand coincidence or part of a larger mystery. This master plan has much to do with our Spiritual Evolution and optimizing our personal power.

The Cranial Nerves inform the human mind (Below) of all that happens in the manifested Universe they are a part of (Above). They are responsible for how we interact with and interpret material reality. As our interface with the outside world, the Twelve Pairs of Cranial Nerves help define our reality. They allow us to receive external information and express our responses to this information through body language, including facial expressions and eye movements.

The Cranial Nerves affect how others perceive us by affecting our bodily responses to outside stimuli. Since 93% of our communication is non-verbal, the Cranial Nerves are tasked with expressing our inner energies, although most of this communication occurs on a subconscious level.

When a person undergoes a full Kundalini awakening and optimizes their Chakras, they gain complete control over their vibrations and what signals they put out into the Universe through their body language. As the Silent Witness of one's Self awakens, it enables the awakened individual to see themselves from the third-person. I believe this gift of the awakening is connected to the expansion of the radius of one's Mind's Eye inner portal, allowing the individual to leave their body at will and observe their body's processes, including facial gestures and eye movements that reveal their internal state. By gaining conscious control over the Twelve Pairs of Cranial Nerves' otherwise involuntary functions, the individual's is well on their way towards Self-mastery.

CEREBROSPINAL FLUID (CSF)

Cerebrospinal Fluid (CSF for short) is a clear liquid substance that bathes the spaces within and around the spinal cord as well as the brainstem and brain. It plays a crucial role in sustaining consciousness, coordinating all physical activity, and facilitating the Kundalini awakening process.

There are about 100-150 ml of CSF in the normal adult body (on average), which is about two-thirds of a cup. The body itself produces approximately 450-600ml of CSF per day. The CSF is continually produced, and all of it is replaced every six to eight hours.

The cavities in the brain are fluid reservoirs called "ventricles," which create the CSF. The brain ventricles serve as passageways or channels for consciousness. When these passageways are obstructed or blocked, loss of consciousness occurs. The most significant brain ventricle is the Third Ventricle which encompasses the central area of the brain, containing the Pineal and Pituitary Glands and the Thalamus and the Hypothalamus. The CSF also bathes the outside of the brain, providing buoyancy and shock-absorption.

After serving the brain and brainstem, the CSF travels downwards through the spinal cord's central canal as well as outside of it (Figure 48). The central canal is a hollow space that is filled with CSF that goes all the way down the spine. Even though the spinal cord ends between the first and second lumbar vertebrae (L1-2), right above the waist area, the CSF goes down through the sacrum. Once it reaches the bottom of the spine, the CSF gets absorbed into the bloodstream.

The Central Nervous System is contained in the brain and spinal cord. It is submerged in the CSF at all times. It serves as the medium through which the brain communicates with the Central Nervous System. The actual circuitry is the white and grey matter (butterfly shape) that make up the spinal cord. Once the Central Nervous System integrates information from the brain, it sends it out to different parts of the body.

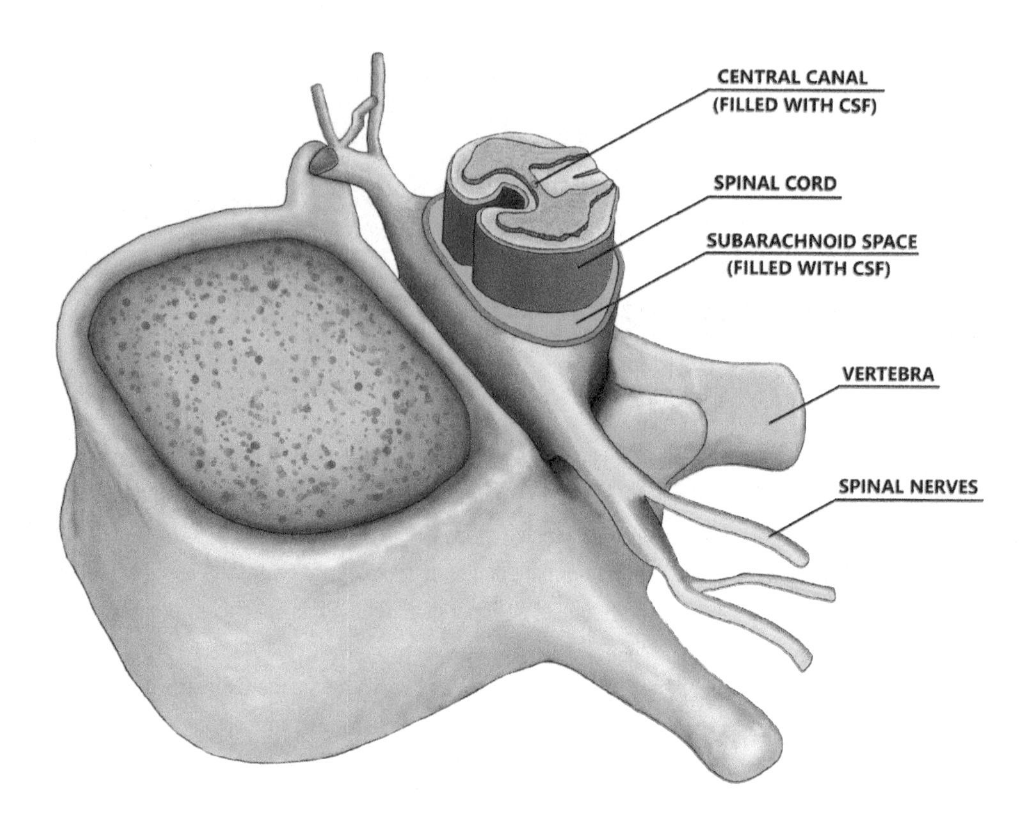

Figure 48: The Spinal Cord (Cross-Section)

The CSF is contained within the subarachnoid spaces in the brain and spinal cord. The brain and spinal cord are protected by three membranes (meninges): pia mater, arachnoid space, and dura mater. The subarachnoid area is the connective tissue between pia mater and arachnoid space. It has a spiderweb-like appearance and serves as the cushioning for the Central Nervous System, the spinal cord, and the brain. Most importantly, it serves as the channel for the CSF.

The CSF can transmit Light, vibrations, movement, and molecules. It transports nutrients and hormones to the entire nervous system and brain. The CSF serves to protect both of them and the spinal cord. It also eliminates all waste from these three parts of the body. On a more fundamental level, the CSF regulates circadian rhythms and appetite.

The CSF is essential for keeping the physical body vibrant, healthy and balanced. In addition, it facilitates the free-flowing movement of the spinal column and head by providing mobility.

The CSF provides essential growth and survival factors to the brain, from its embryonic stage to adulthood. It is critical for stem cell multiplication, growth, migration, differentiation and our overall survival.

BRAIN VENTRICLES

The Third Ventricle (Figure 49) is a perfectly centreline structure that contains the Pituitary Gland on the front end and the Pineal Gland on the back end. In the middle of it are the Thalamus and Hypothalamus. It is the connecting point between the rational upper parts of the brain and the survival-based functions of the lower brain.

The Ancients have revered the space in-between the Third Ventricle from time immemorial because of its Spiritual qualities. Daoists called it the "Crystal Palace," while the Hindus referred to it as the "Cave of Brahma." The Third Ventricle is essentially the foundation of the mind-body-Spirit connection. Deep feelings of bliss, peace, and Oneness with the Source originate in the Third Ventricle, which serves as our portal to Universal knowledge.

The Third Ventricle brain cavern is the space that gives us a unified awareness of our true essence. Many people believe that the CSF fluid in the brain transmits the Spirit energy once the Pineal and Pituitary Glands and Thalamus are activated. As such, the Third Ventricle allows for the transformation of consciousness.

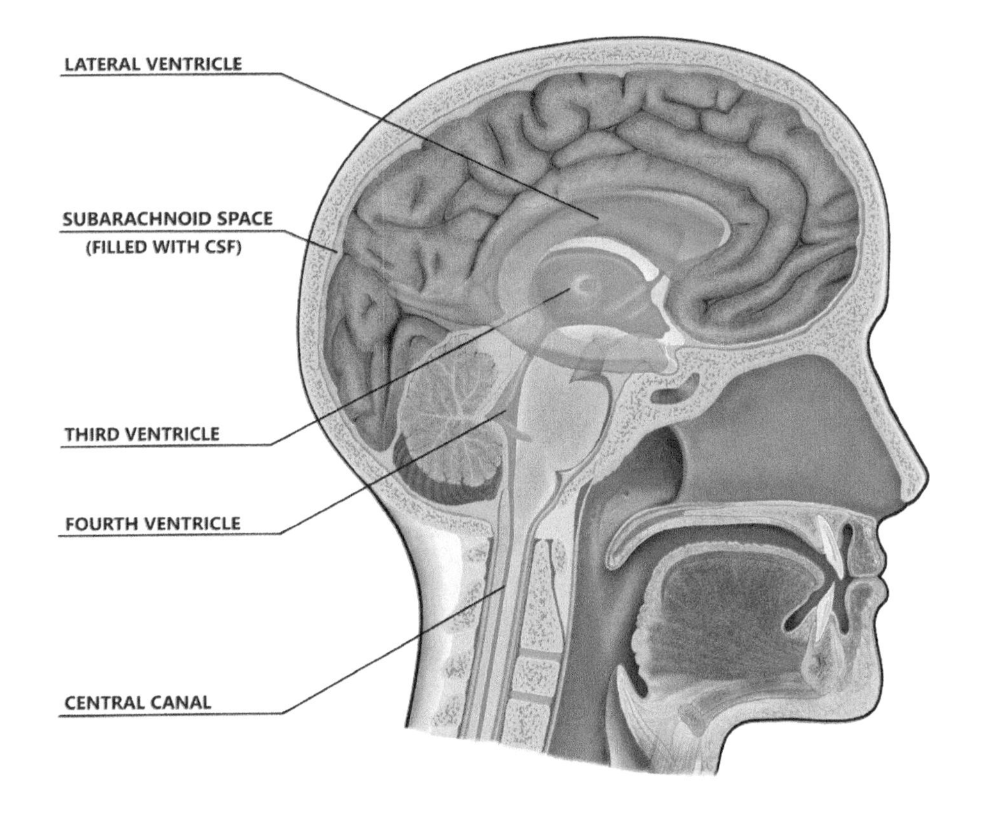

Figure 49: CSF and the Brain Ventricles (Lateral/Side View)

The Lateral Ventricle contains two horns (Figure 50) that make contact with the Frontal Lobe, the Parietal Lobe, the Occipital Lobe, and the Temporal Lobe. The posterior horn makes contact with the visual areas of the brain.

The Fourth Ventricle makes contact with the Cerebellum, Pons, and Medulla. It is situated between the Third Ventricle and the central canal within the brainstem and spinal cord. The CSF produced and (or) flowing into the

Fourth Ventricle exists in the subarachnoid space at the bottom of the skull, where the central canal enters the brainstem.

The CSF serves as a vehicle for transmitting information to the brain. It absorbs, stores, and transmits vibrations from the outside world to different brain receptors. For this reason, all the control areas of the brain, including the spinal cord (Central Nervous System), are submerged in the CSF at all times.

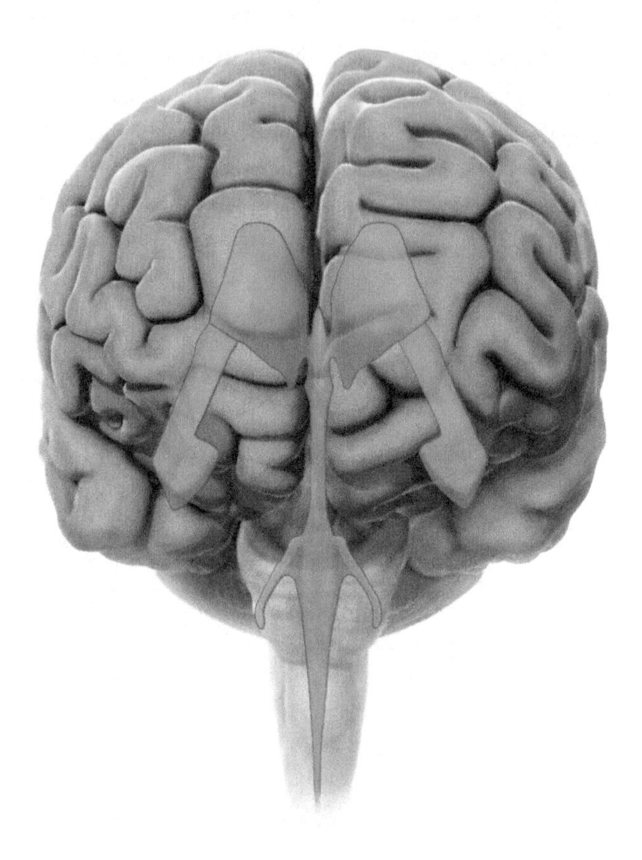

Figure 50: The Brain Ventricles (Front View)

CSF AND KUNDALINI AWAKENING

The three Nadis of Ida, Pingala, and Sushumna meet at the Third Ventricle, this CSF-filled radiant space in the middle of our heads. Once the Kundalini and the activated Nadis enter the Third Ventricle area, the Pineal and Pituitary Glands become electrified through the CSF as the medium. The Kundalini awakening and Chakric activation happen on a subtle, Etheric level, while the electrified CSF invigorates the nervous system and activates latent potential in the major brain centres.

Since the Pineal and Pituitary Glands represent the feminine and masculine components of the Self, the emotions and reason, their simultaneous activation represents the unification of the right and left-brain hemispheres. As such, the Thalamus begins to function at a higher level, facilitating the opening and optimization of Ajna Chakra.

Sushumna operates through the CSF in the spinal cord. At the point where the spinal cord ends between the first and second lumbar vertebrae (L1-2), called Conus Medullaris, a delicate filament called Filum Terminale begins and ends at the coccyx (Figure 51). It is approximately 20cm in length and is without nervous tissue. One of the purposes of Filum Terminale is to transport the CSF to the bottom of the spine.

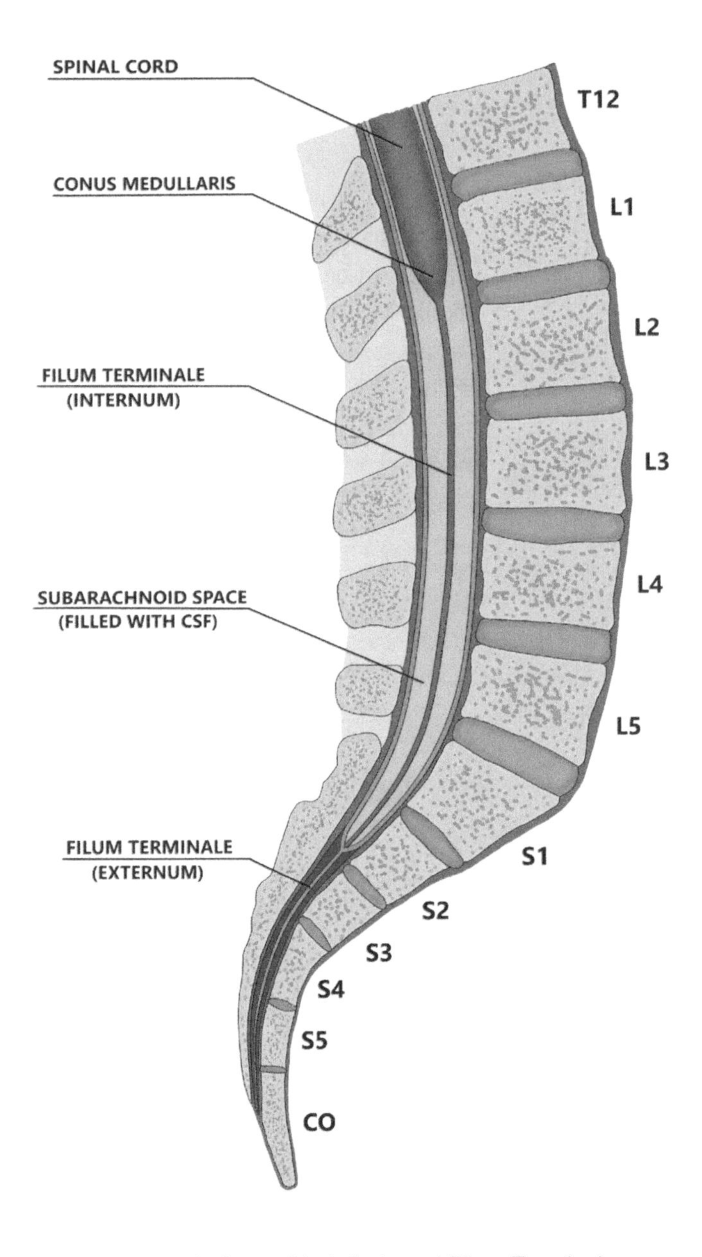

Figure 51: Conus Medullaris and Filum Terminale

Scientists believe that another tiny fibre runs through the central canal in the spinal cord that is made of condensed CSF protein. This fibre serves as a filament that lights up when electrically charged. Since one of the CSF purposes is to carry Light energies, it serves as the conduit through which the awakened Kundalini travels up the spine and into the brain.

Sushumna begins in the coccyx and runs up the Filum Terminale until it reaches Conus Medullaris. It continues through the fibre in the central canal, past the Fourth Ventricle, and ends in the Third Ventricle area, namely the Thalamus and Hypothalamus that connects to it. The CSF gets electrically charged by awakened Kundalini energy, which rises up the spinal cord, systematically activating the Major Chakras until it reaches the higher brain centres. The CSF is the key to the anatomical changes that occur in the brain upon a Kundalini awakening. The nervous system transforms as well through the invigoration of the spinal nerves. The organs are affected by this infusion of Light energy, which explains why so many Kundalini awakened individuals report anatomical changes in their insides.

When the Kundalini enters the brain through the Sushumna channel, it terminates in the Thalamus, energizing it. Simultaneously, the Ida and Pingala Nadis energize the Pineal and Pituitary Glands. Since Ida and Pingala terminate in the Pineal and Pituitary Glands, their activation creates a magnetic effect that projects a vibratory stream of energy towards the Thalamus. The unification of these masculine (Yang) and feminine (Yin) powers in the Thalamus enables a full opening of Ajna Chakra, followed by Sahasrara at the top of the head.

Once the Kundalini reaches the Crown, the "I Am" component of the Self, the Higher Self, awakens in our consciousness. The potential of the Thalamus is maximized, making this brain centre a perfect antenna to outside vibrations. The consciousness expands to the Cosmic level, and instead of taking in only 10% of the stimuli from the environment, it can now experience the full 100%.

MULADHARA AND KUNDALINI

THE SACRUM AND COCCYX

The sacrum and coccyx (Figure 52) play a significant role in the Kundalini awakening process. The sacrum, or sacral spine, contains five fused vertebrae. It is a large triangular bone between the hip bones and the last lumbar vertebra (L5). In Latin, the word "sacrum" means "sacred." The Romans called this bone "os sacrum" while the Greeks termed it "hieron osteon," the meaning of both being "Holy bone."

Interestingly, the word "hieron" in Greek also translates as "Temple." The sacrum was considered sacred because within its bony concavity lay the ovaries and uterus in females. The Ancients believed the female reproductive organs to be Divine as the womb is the origin of Creation.

The sacrum is our Holy Temple since it houses and protects the genital organs, plexuses, and lower subtle energy centres, all of which are involved in activating the Kundalini awakening process. The sacrum is also responsible for pumping the CSF upwards into the brain. This fluid sustains consciousness and plays a crucial role in activating the higher brain centres upon Spiritual awakening.

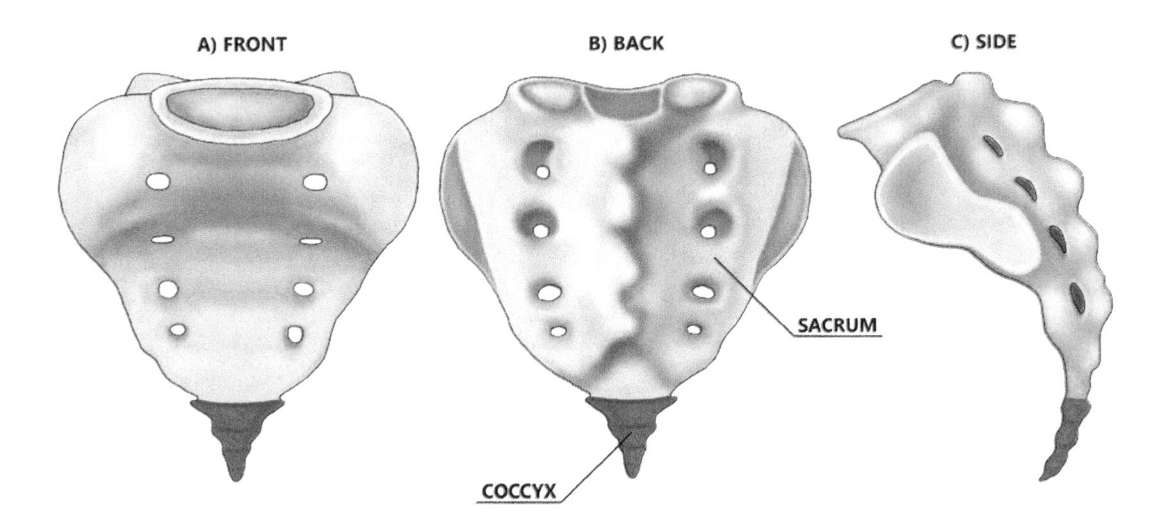

Figure 52: The Sacrum and Coccyx

In the Egyptian tradition, the sacrum was sacred to Osiris, the God of the Underworld. The Egyptians believed that Osiris' backbone, referred to as the Djed Pillar, represented the Kundalini energy whose awakening process began in the sacrum. The coccyx (tailbone) is another small triangular bone attached to the bottom of the sacrum.

As mentioned, in its state of potential, the Kundalini is coiled three and a half times in the coccyx. Muladhara Chakra, the source Chakra of the Kundalini energy, is located between the coccyx and perineum. When the Kundalini energy is released, it travels through the hollow tube of the spinal cord like a snake (Figure 53), accompanied by a hissing sound that a snake makes when it is moving or about to strike.

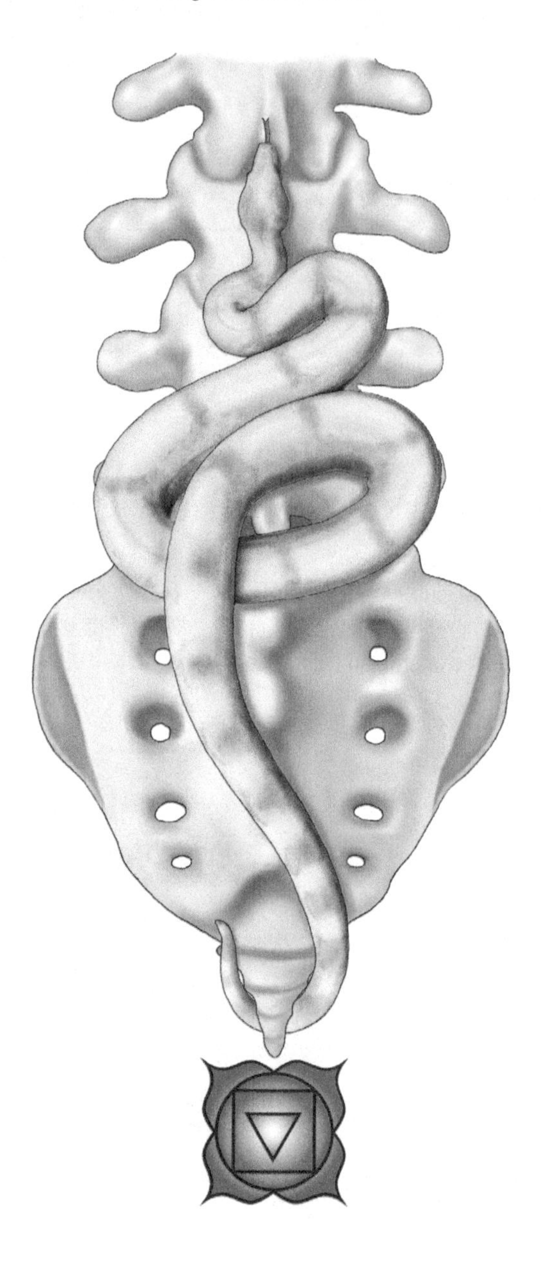

Figure 53: The Uncoiled Kundalini

Coincidentally, the coccyx is composed of three to five fused coccygeal vertebrae or spinal bones. The coccyx is the remnant of a vestigial tail on a physical level. In the context of human evolution, it is believed that all humans had a tail at some point in time, as most mammals do today.

The word "coccyx" originates from the Greek "cuckoo" since the bone itself is shaped like a cuckoo's beak. Interestingly, the cuckoo is a bird renowned for its sound that brings forth change in one's life. Its call is symbolic of a new fate or event that unfolds in one's life. Remember that the Caduceus of Hermes, symbolic of the Kundalini awakening process, originated in Greece—the Greeks were well aware of the coccyx' Spiritual potential since they knew it housed the transformative Kundalini energy.

In the Egyptian tradition, the God of Wisdom, Thoth (Tehuti), has an Ibis bird head with a long beak whose shape resembles the coccyx. Thoth is the Egyptian counterpart to the Greek Hermes and Roman Mercury. These three Gods have almost identical attributes and correspondences, and all three are associated with the Kundalini energy and awakening process.

In *The Koran* (also spelt Quran), the Prophet Muhammad stated that the coccyx never decays, and it is the bone from which humans will be resurrected on the Day of Judgment. The Hebrews held the same idea, but instead of the coccyx, they believed it was the sacrum that was indestructible and was the nucleus of the human body's resurrection. They referred to the sacrum as the "Luz" bone (Aramaic for "nut"). The sacrum has a pattern of dimples, which, along with its overall shape, resembles the almond shell. In *The Zohar,* the book of Jewish esoteric and mystical teachings, the Luz is the bone in the spine that appears like a snake's head. Given that both the coccyx and sacrum are triangular shaped, some Rabbis believe it is the sacrum that is sacred, whereas others believe it to be the coccyx.

SACRAL PLEXUS AND SCIATIC NERVE

Another two essential factors in the Kundalini awakening process are the Sacral Plexus and Sciatic Nerve (Figure 54). The Sacral Plexus is a nerve plexus that emerges from the lower lumbar vertebrae and sacral vertebrae (L4-S4). It provides motor and sensory nerves for the posterior thigh, the pelvis, and most of the lower leg and foot.

Below the Sacral Plexus is Muladhara Chakra, located between the coccyx and perineum. Muladhara's flower head projects downwards towards the Earth and is situated near the Coccygeal Plexus. Muladhara's Chakric stem, though, originates between the third and fourth sacral vertebrae (S3-4), a part of the Sacral Plexus.

The Pelvic Plexus is located in the abdominal region, right in front of the Sacral Plexus. The Pelvic Plexus innervates the organs associated with Swadhisthana and Muladhara Chakras, namely our sexual organs.

There is a connection between the Earth and Water Elements and the Planet Earth below our feet. It is not a coincidence that our lowest two Major Chakras, Muladhara and Swadhisthana, relate to the only two passive Elements concerned with receiving energy. As Muladhara is a receptacle of the Earth energy generated by the Earth Star below the feet, Swadhisthana is our emotional container, the Chakra of the subconscious mind and instincts.

Swadhisthana represents the emotions, including our sexual energy, which fuels creativity. Sexual energy, when turned inwards, is proven to have a transformative effect on consciousness. In my personal experience, I was generating a tremendous amount of sexual energy through an inadvertent Tantric sex practice I was performing, which led to continuous internal orgasms that culminated in a full Kundalini awakening.

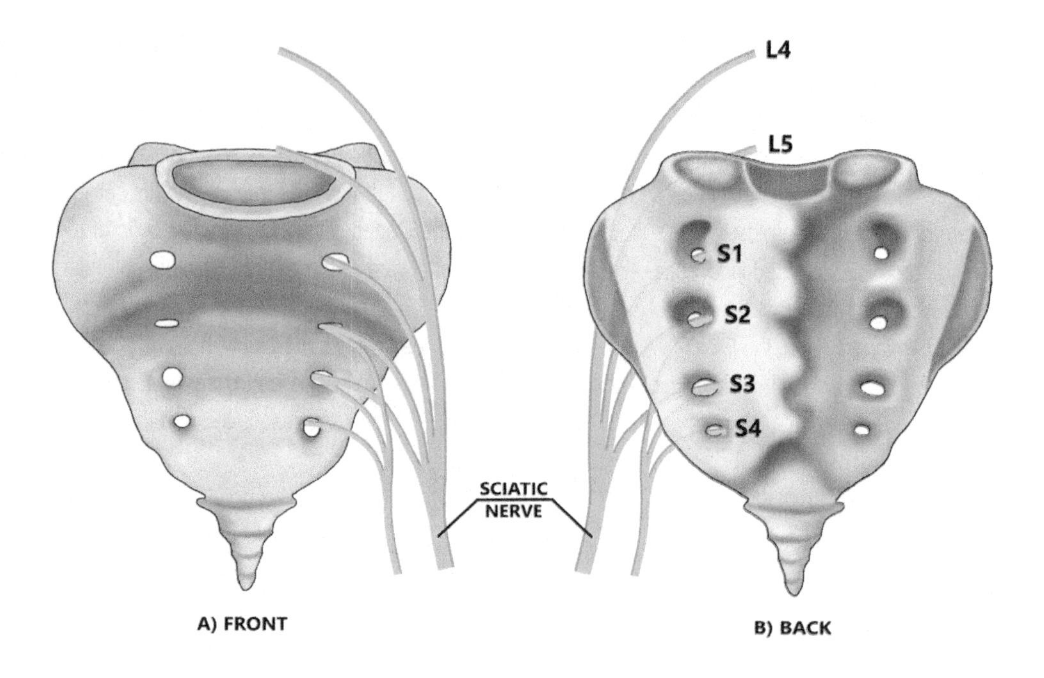

Figure 54: The Sacral Plexus

The Sciatic Nerve is the largest peripheral nerve in the human body formed by the union of five nerve roots from the Sacral Plexus. It is 2cm in diameter and runs through the thigh and leg, down to the sole. The Sciatic Nerve functions as a root for the nervous system by grounding us to Planet Earth. Since there are two legs, two Sciatic Nerves are running through them. The Sciatic Nerve splits into two major branches in the knee area (tibial nerve and common peroneal nerve).

As the Vagus Nerve is a physical representation of the Kundalini energy, the Sciatic Nerves are a biological equivalent of the legs' energy channels that connect us to the Earth Star via the Foot Chakras (Figure 55). Although the Ida and Pingala Nadis begin in Muladhara, their power source comes from the two energy currents in the legs, the negative and the positive.

Ida is attributed to the left side of the body, and it gets its negative energy current from the left leg, while Pingala runs through the right side of the body, getting its positive energy current from the right leg. The two legs carry the feminine and masculine energies from the Earth Star into Muladhara, thereby supplying the entire Chakric system with these dual forces. As mentioned, the Earth Star operates as a battery for Muladhara—the energy channels in the legs serve as the negative and positive currents that transmit Earth energies from our Planet.

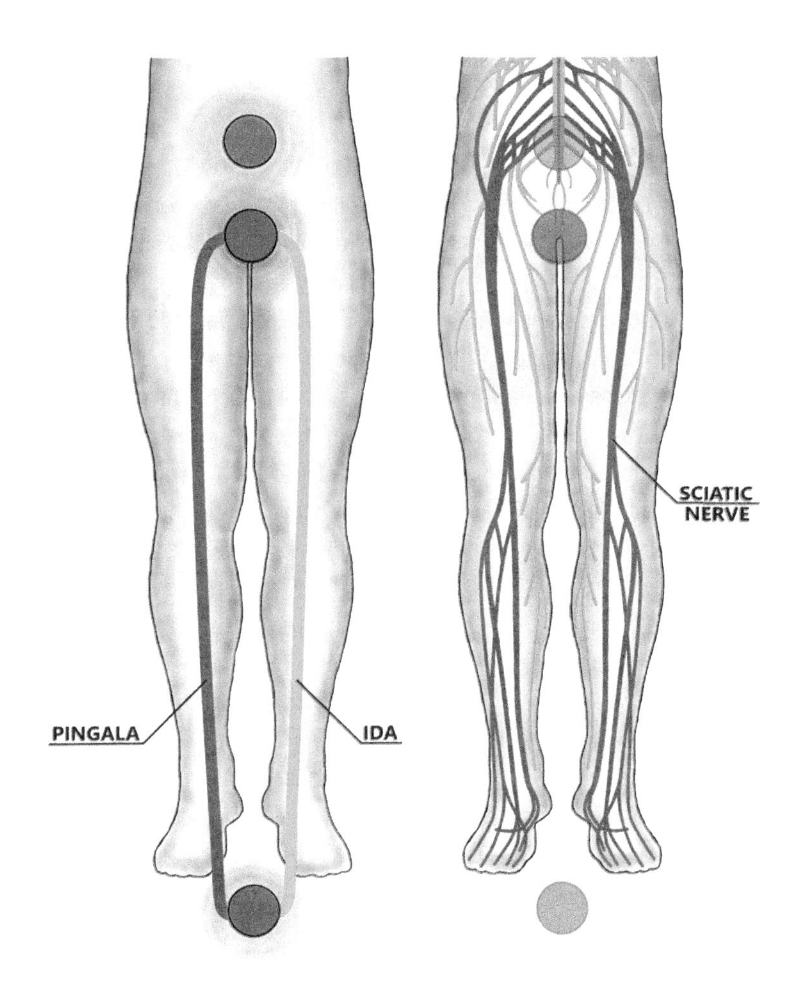

Figure 55: The Sciatic Nerves and Energy Channels in the Legs

BRINGING IT ALL TOGETHER

To stimulate the Kundalini into activity and awaken it from its slumber, we must create a powerful energy current in Muladhara, which involves many factors working together. Stimulating the Ida and Pingala Nadis begins in the Earth Star, the root of our overall energy system, represented by the Hara Line. When the Earth Star becomes energized, through meditation or other practices, it projects an energetic current through the energy channels in the legs via the Heel Chakras. Simultaneously, the Sciatic Nerve is stimulated, energizing the Sacral Plexus area where Muladhara's Chakric stem begins.

As I will describe in more detail in the Yogic science section, we must stimulate both Muladhara and Swadhisthana Chakras to awaken the Kundalini. Swadhisthana Chakric stem begins between the first and second lumbar vertebrae (L1-2), corresponding with where the spinal cord ends and Filum Terminale begins. The Kundalini awakening process has much to do with energizing the CSF, which starts in Filum Terminale and runs through the spinal cord until it reaches the Third Ventricle and the central Thalamus and Hypothalamus. By energizing the Third Ventricle, the surrounding brain lobes also become stimulated. The entire process of brain-power expansion involves the Third Ventricle and the electrified CSF.

Awakening the Kundalini in Muladhara involves the Five Prana Vayus, the five movements or functions of Prana, the Life Force. When three of these Prana Vayus change their directional force to meet in Hara Chakra, an activation occurs that involves the generation of heat in the Navel centre. This immense heat is accompanied by a feeling of ecstasy in the abdomen, likened to intensified sexual excitement, which then electrifies the Sushumna Nadi, making it light up like a light bulb. Once Sushumna lights up, the Kundalini is awakened at the base of the spine. (I will explain this part of the process in more detail in "The Five Prana Vayus" chapter).

In my experience, the awakened Kundalini manifested as a ball of Light energy, emanating an electrical field about a golf ball's size. When it awakened, it created pressure in the bottom of the spine, which was not physical but could be felt regardless at a subtle level. The Kundalini ball of Light travels upwards through the CSF in the spinal cord. Simultaneously, the Earth Star generates tremendous energy, which gets transmitted towards Muladhara Chakra via the legs' energy channels, thereby energizing the Ida and Pingala Nadis.

On a physical level, the testes (men), ovaries (women) and the Adrenals are involved in the Kundalini awakening process since they generate the sexual energy needed to power Ida and Pingala and make them rise. Ida corresponds with the left testicle and ovary, while Pingala relates to the right. Once the Kundalini begins to rise through Sushumna, Ida and Pingala, powered by the sexual energy, rise in an undulating motion, adjacent to the spinal cord, crossing each other at each of the Chakric points along the spine.

As the Kundalini ball of Light energy systematically reaches each of the Chakric stems, it combines with the balanced feminine and masculine currents from Ida and Pingala, electrifying and sending a beam of Light energy through each of the Chakric flower stems. Once each Chakric stem gets infused with Light energy, the Chakric flower at the front of the body begins to spin faster, fully awakening each Chakra and optimizing its flow.

After piercing Brahma and Vishnu Granthis and awakening the first five Chakras, the Kundalini energy enters the brain's centre, terminating in the Thalamus, which lights up from the inside. Conversely, the electrified Ida and Pingala Nadis end in the Pineal and Pituitary Glands. Once fully activated, the Pineal and Pituitary Glands become magnetized and project an electrical current unifying in the central Thalamus as a single Light source. As the Thalamus receives Ida and Pingala's energies, it Lights up more than ever via the Pineal and Pituitary Glands, as the three main Nadis become integrated.

The unification of the Sushumna, Ida, and Pingala Nadis in the Thalamus sends a current of Light energy through the Chakric stem of Ajna until it reaches its flower head which lies in the centre of the eyebrows (slightly above). If the stream of Light energy being projected from the Thalamus is powerful enough, it will expand Ajna's Mind's Eye portal. I likened this part of the process to the circular portal of Ajna growing from a doughnut size to a car tire. As I mentioned, though, this part of the process was not Universal, which means that it only happens to those individuals who generate an exceptional amount of Light energy in the centre of their brains, as it happened with me.

The next phase of the Kundalini awakening process involves the unified Light current of Ida, Pingala, and Sushumna Nadis rising through the cerebral cortex to the top, centre of the head. Along the way, Rudra Granthi is pierced, which is necessary for the awakening of Sahasrara since this is the final knot that binds consciousness to duality. (More on the Granthis and their role in the Kundalini awakening process in "The Three Granthis" chapter).

If the Kundalini current is powerful enough once it reaches the top of the head, the Cosmic Egg blows open, resulting in the "electrocution" phenomenon, which involves the infusion of Light energy into the Seventy-Two

Thousand Nadis. This experience represents the full activation of the Body of Light. The next and final step of the Kundalini awakening process is fully opening the Thousand-Petalled Lotus of Sahasrara, optimizing one's toroidal energy field and unifying their consciousness with Cosmic Consciousness. (Figure 56 is a symbolic representation of the Kundalini awakening process and its association with the Caduceus of Hermes and DNA's Double Helix.)

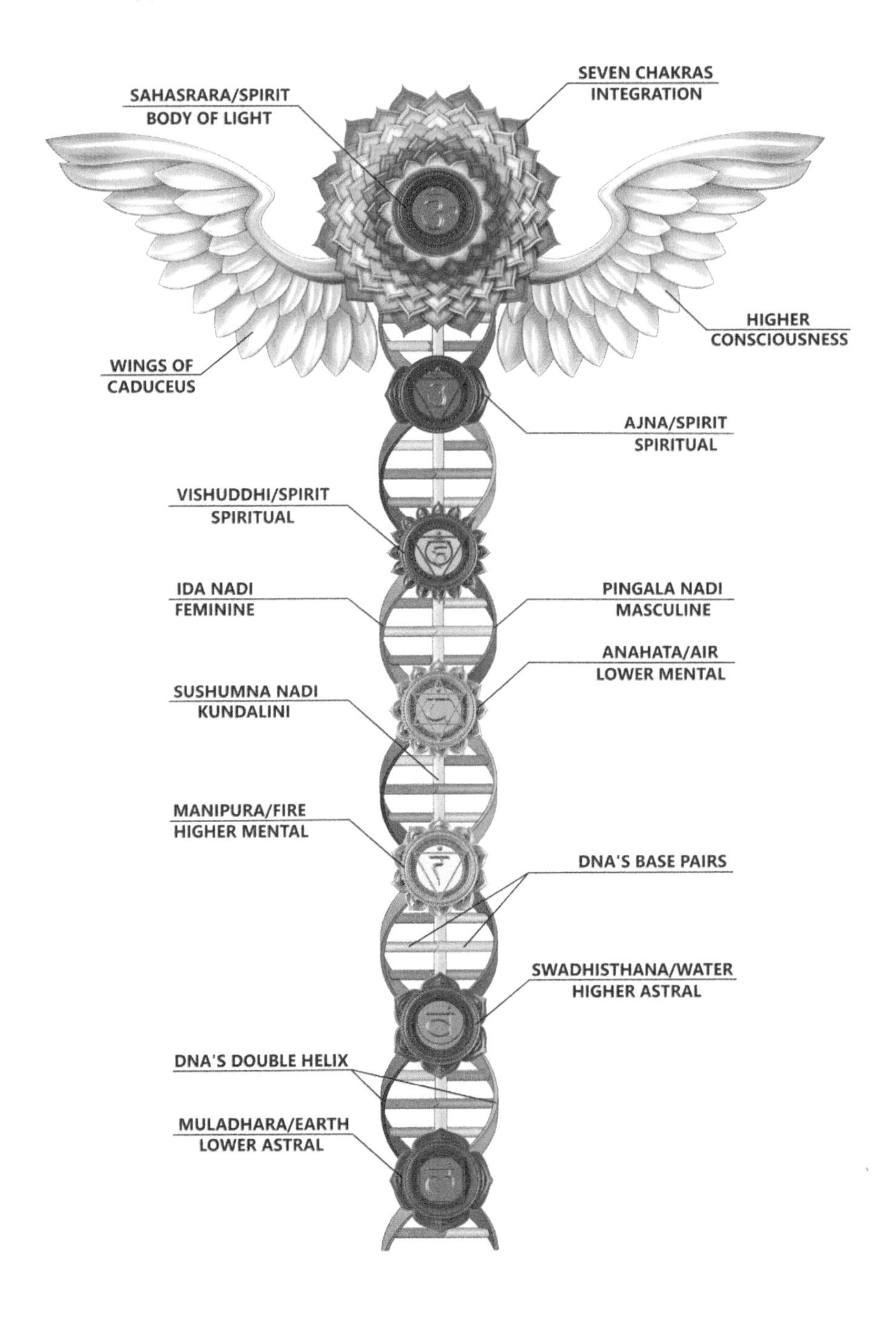

Figure 56: Kundalini/Caduceus of Hermes/DNA's Double Helix

THE POWER OF THE HEART

The HeartMath Institute has been conducting research for the past two decades on the power of the human heart. They have determined that the heart is the most powerful electromagnetic energy generator in the human body. Its electrical field is about 60 times greater in amplitude than that of the brain. The heart's magnetic field, on the other hand, is 5000 times greater in strength than the field generated by the brain.

The heart's Electromagnetic Field (EMF) is toroidal in shape (Figure 57), and it envelops every cell of the human body. Our heart EMF extends out in all directions and directly affects other people's brainwaves that are within eight to ten feet (on average) of where we are. People further away (up to 15 feet) are also affected but in more subtle ways. The heart EMF, just like the Auric field, fluctuates in size along the horizontal plane, expanding and contracting like a living, breathing organism.

Since HearthMath's discoveries about the power of the heart are relatively new, many researchers have suggested that the heart EMF and the Auric field are the same thing since both are toroidal in shape, and both are expressive of our electromagnetic energies. My belief, formed through extensive research and Divine guidance, is that they are two-separate but interconnected electromagnetic fields.

The Auric field is a composite of the different subtle energies that express the Major and Transpersonal Chakras, which vibrate at various electromagnetic frequencies. The Auric field also contains other subtle fields that connect us to other living beings, the Planet Earth and the Universe. Since the Auric field extends to approximately five to six feet and the heart EMF is substantially larger, we are clearly talking about two different things.

I believe that the Auric field sits inside the heart EMF, and they are two parts to a whole. The heart EMF's purpose is to register vibrations from the environment and send them to the brain and the rest of the body. As a result, the inner Cosmic Planes are affected, influencing the Chakric energies. The Chakras, in turn, elicit certain responses in the consciousness based on their corresponding inner faculties. For this reason, the heart EMF affects us on all levels, Spiritual, mental, emotional, and physical. It acts as our interface with the environment, sending information into the Auric field, which powers the consciousness.

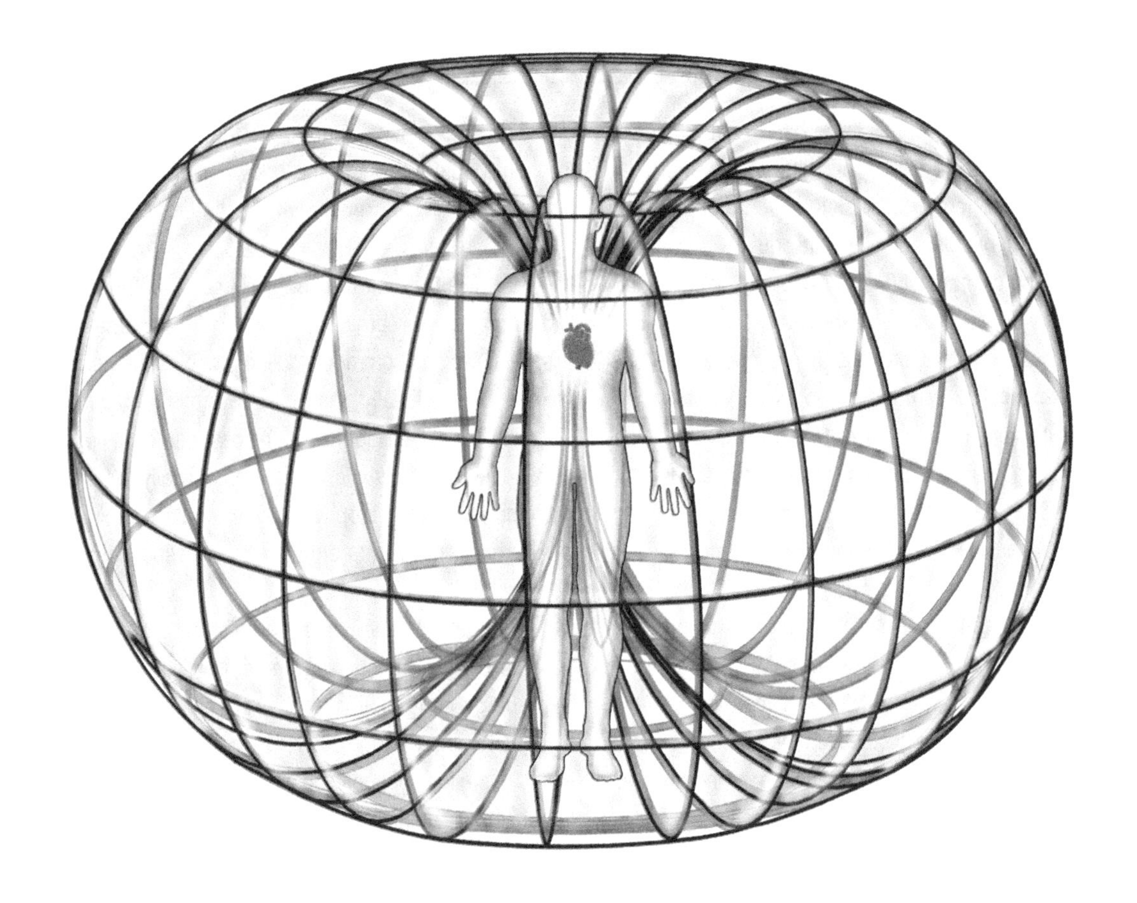

Figure 57: The Electromagnetic Field of the Heart

The heart EMF is related to the Heart Chakra, which corresponds with the Air Element and the Lower Mental Plane. Due to its placement, the heart EMF acts as the intermediary between the higher and lower Cosmic Planes. Subtle vibrations from the environment are picked up and transmitted into the Higher Mental and Spiritual Planes above and Astral and Physical Planes below.

The Heart Chakra is the fourth Major Chakra positioned between the higher three Chakras of the Spirit Element and the lower three Chakras (Fire, Water, and Earth). The Air Element is esoterically known as an intermediary between Spirit and Matter, compared to how the air-containing atmosphere separates the Heavens above and Earth below. Air relates to breath and oxygen, sustaining all of life. We cannot survive for more than a few minutes without the act of breathing, as it is essential to our survival. In this way, the heart EMF serves the Soul and mind, the go-betweens of Spirit and Matter.

HEART-BRAIN CONNECTION

In fetal development, the heart is the first organ that forms—it begins to beat before the brain even develops. The heart is the central part of the Self, the foundation upon which the rest of the body is created in the womb. Neurocardiologists have determined that the heart contains many similar components to the brain, allowing for a dynamic, ongoing, two-way dialogue.

Approximately 60-65% of heart cells are neural cells, much like those in the brain. These 40 000 neurons are clustered in groups in the same way as neural groupings of the brain and contain the same ganglia, neurotransmitters, proteins, and support cells. The "heart-brain," as it is commonly called, enables the heart to act independently from the cranial brain. As it processes life events emotionally, the heart develops decision-making abilities and memory. Over time, the heart develops its own emotional intelligence that helps guide us in life.

The heart and brain communicate neurologically (through the nervous system) and energetically (through their EMFs). They also communicate hormonally and through pulse waves (biophysically). Vibratory energies that continuously flow between the heart and brain assist with processing events and emotional responses, sensory experience, reasoning, and memory.

The heart is our primary interface with the world around us that works in unison with the Thalamus and brain. The brain and heart relate to the Mind and Soul, which are partners in maintaining and governing consciousness. As the brain contains the ventricles which channel Spirit energy and consciousness, the heart also has subtle passageways that accomplish the same. If there is a disruption in the harmonious flow of communication of Spirit and consciousness between the brain and heart, it can result in the loss of consciousness.

Our heart EMF continuously receives signals from the environment, but most of that information never reaches the conscious mind. Instead, the data gets stored in the subconscious. The subconscious mind is associated with 90% of the brain's neural activity and substantially impacts our behaviour more than the conscious mind. For this reason, most of our instinctual responses, such as expressions of body language, are automatic without us being consciously aware of having initiated them.

The conscious mind uses the Prefrontal Cortex of the brain to process information. It can process and manage only 40 nerve impulses per second. In comparison, the subconscious mind operating from the backside of the brain can process 40 million nerve impulses per second—the subconscious mind's processor is 1 million times more powerful than the conscious mind's.

After a full Kundalini awakening, when the inner Light enters the brain's centre and localizes there permanently, the conscious and subconscious minds become one, resulting in a permanent upgrade of one's CPU. As such, the individual gains full access to all the information read by their heart EMF, which increases their awareness, optimizing their decision-making abilities.

BODY COHERENCE

The human heart is a hollow muscle, the size of a fist, that beats at 72 beats a minute and is the circulatory system's centre (Figure 58). The heart is located in the head and torso's centre, in the centre of the chest (slightly offset to the left), allowing for the most optimal connection to every organ that powers the body.

The circulatory system is made up of blood vessels (arteries) that carry blood away from and towards the heart. The heart's right side receives oxygen-poor blood from the veins and pumps it to the lungs, where it picks up oxygen and discards carbon dioxide. The heart's left side gets the oxygen-rich blood and pumps it through the arteries to the rest of the body, including the brain. Of all the organs, the brain is one of the most significant consumers of oxygen-rich blood, and insufficient cranial supply can cause significant brain fatigue.

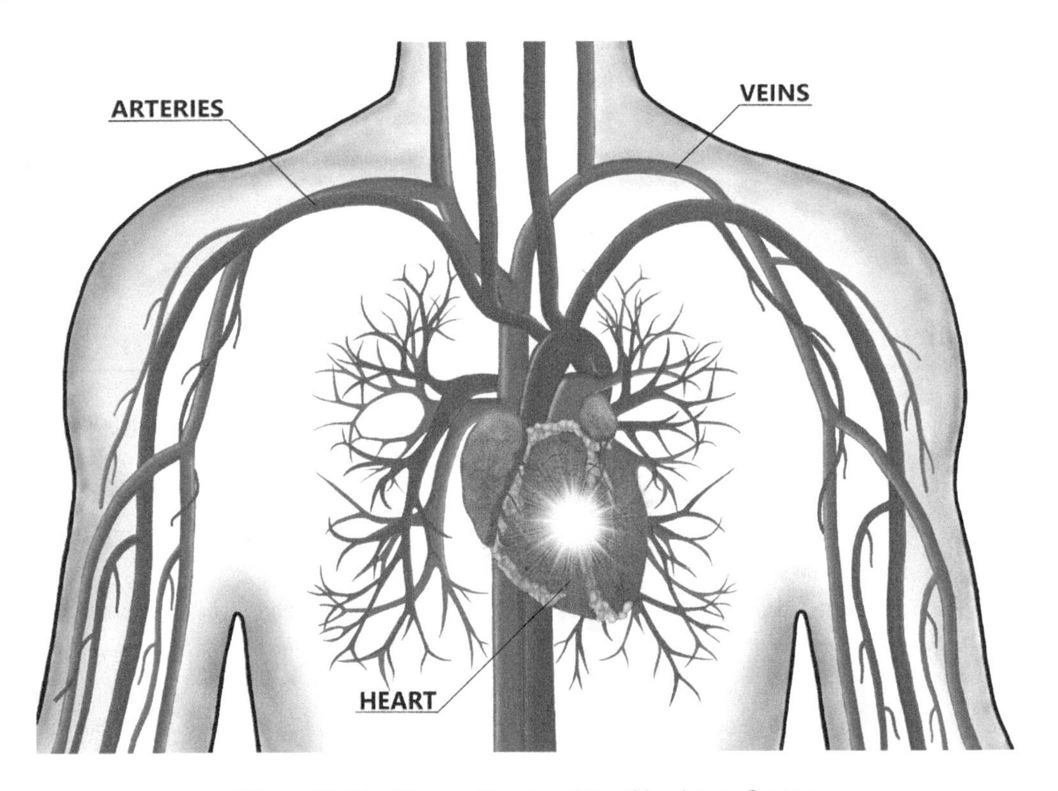

Figure 58: The Human Heart and the Circulatory System

The heart has a significant influence on the physical body on a cellular level. Not only does the heart pump oxygen and nutrients to every cell in the body through the circulatory system, but it also produces hormones that impact the physiological function of the body and brain. As mentioned, one of the ways the heart and brain communicate is hormonally, and this is because the heart serves as an endocrine gland.

Through electromagnetic frequencies and chemical releases, our heart entrains the brain's rhythms, along with the various systems in the body (respiratory, immune, digestive, circulatory, endocrine, etc.). Body coherence is achieved when harmonious and balanced interaction is created in all of the body's systems.

If we experience positive, loving emotions, body coherence occurs, slowing the brainwaves and balancing the Parasympathetic and Sympathetic Nervous Systems. Our heartbeat slows down and becomes smooth and balanced. Our minds become clear, allowing us to tune into the inner Light of our Souls. As such, our creativity, imagination, intuition, and inspiration become heightened, enabling us to tap into our innermost potential as Spiritual human beings.

Conversely, if we experience negative, fearful emotions, our body falls out of harmony and stress and anxiety set in. Our brainwaves speed up, making us more alert. The heartbeat also speeds up, and we often experience rhythmic contractions resulting from our minds processing negativity. Our Sympathetic Nervous System overrides the Parasympathetic one, and we lose touch with our Souls, which severs our connection to inspiration and creativity. Our ability to think becomes clouded by the negative state we are in, and we rely on our Egos to rationalise our existence.

Breathing through your stomach by expanding the diaphragm (Diaphragmatic Breathing) is perhaps the most useful way to neutralise negative energy and calm down the interior. This Yogic breathing technique (Pranayama) allows one to regain control over their bodily rhythms and achieve body coherence again. Diaphragmatic Breathing is a pre-requisite for meditation, which is another method for raising the vibration of consciousness that optimises the body's health.

THE HEART AND VIBRATIONS

According to the Hermetic Principle of Vibration, all things in the Universe (including living organisms, thoughts, emotions, etc.) are in a state of vibratory motion on a sub-atomic level. Quantum physics now also affirms what the Ancients have been saying for thousands of years. Not only is Matter made up of vibratory energies, but vibration is the basis of all communication in the Universe, whether orally or through more subtle levels—we are all continually inducing one another through our vibes.

The Earth's magnetic resonances vibrate at the same frequency as our heart rhythms and brainwaves—As Above, So Below. All living organisms broadcast unique vibratory energies while the heart is the receiver that "reads" the energy fields around us. Our heart EMFs constantly receive vibratory signals from the environment, which allows our cells to interact with the outside world. Scientific analysis reveals that the heart, not the brain, initiates the first response to incoming information from the outside. For this reason, you hear people often say, "I like this person's vibes," relating to their impression of them received through the heart.

Interestingly, with the plethora of stimuli present at any given time, the heart primarily registers information that resonates with one's inner vibes. This phenomenon is a manifestation of the Law of Attraction which states that positive or negative thoughts and emotions bring positive or negative experiences in a person's life. In other words, we experience that which our minds and hearts focus on.

For example, a person who occupies their minds and hearts with thoughts and feelings of love will attune to information from the environment that pertains to love energy. Their heart EMF will focus on and amplify all signals from the environment related to love. Someone who only thinks of fear and experiences fearful emotions will access environmental data relating to fear. And even if we are thinking about not thinking something, we focus on that thing regardless, which manifests in our minds and hearts. Thus, we continuously register and hear what we are programmed to hear.

Each person's heart has an electromagnetic wave pattern as unique as their fingerprint. It not only contains data about the body's current state but also has encoded memories stored within the heart's two distinct networks of nerves. You can find proof of the heart-memory phenomenon in heart transplant recipients. It is common for someone who received another person's heart to develop changes in their personality, likes, dislikes, and preferences, brought on by old memories stored in the heart.

THE HEART AND RELATIONSHIPS

Upon meeting someone, we undergo a heart-brain synchronization with that person. Our mental and emotional state immediately induces the other person since they psychically read our intentions on an energetic level. For example, when we come from a place of love, truth, and respect, then another person's heart will naturally open to us, and they will reciprocate our good intentions. If we come from a place of Ego, and our intentions aren't pure, such as when we are trying to manipulate someone for selfish gains, then the other person will naturally go on the defence. Their hearts will remain closed to us, and instead, their brains will take over to try and rationalize the situation.

If we are under stress and agitated, we naturally repel other people around us while we attract them when we are calm and at peace. People are drawn to positivity because we intuitively know that we are continually communicating telepathically and are inducing each other with our thoughts and emotions. This knowledge is something we are born with, even though we might not recognize it with our Egos.

Considering the heart's electromagnetic power and the impact that loving, positive energy has on people we encounter, it is no wonder why we naturally crave being social and forming bonds with others. We nourish and heal each other when our hearts are open and when our intentions are good. With good intentions alone, we can penetrate through the Ego barrier and the personality and reach the Soul of another human being. Conversely, when our intentions are selfish, we trigger one another emotionally and can cause harm at a deep level. In the latter case, the Ego takes over, and there is no exchange of Soul-healing energies.

When you are in a quarrel with someone, the best way to resolve your differences is to speak from the heart to that person, who will most often reciprocate this action. Truth has a way of clearing all obstacles as it neutralizes all negative energy so one can get to the "heart of the matter," as the saying goes. When there is an openness in the heart between two people, not only do differences become resolved, but the loving bond between them becomes stronger. For this reason, living from the heart and being honest at all times allows one never to have regrets and live with a clear conscience.

Isolating oneself from others and lacking human contact on a physical and emotional level is painful and often numbing if too much time passes. We need human connections, including friendships and intimacy, to help us on our Spiritual Evolution path. Romantic relationships are the most healing, especially if they involve sex since sex is the physical act of unification that creates the most powerful bond when an open heart and loving intentions are applied.

HUMAN BEHAVIOUR AND CAUSE AND EFFECT

As I have described in *The Magus,* if you want to develop true personal power, you have to be familiar with your Demons so you can use their energies productively when the situation requires it. For example, when someone is trying to manipulate you, you will recognize their intention instead of being blind to it and can exact an equal and opposite reaction to neutralize the Law of Karma.

When I speak of Demons, I refer to the negative, fear energy that is not of the Light per se but can further the Light's agenda. Although what I am saying may sound counter-intuitive (since many of you were taught that Demonic energies are bad), it is not. Negative energy is not something you should run from but should seek to tame within you. Through the application of Free Will, you can readily use negative energy to obtain a positive outcome. Doing so gives your Demons wings, metaphorically speaking.

Being familiar with your Demonic energies allows you to realize when you are energetically attacked by others, weigh the type of attack, and mobilize your inner forces to get on the offence. Remember, we must punish all evil; otherwise, we become evil's accomplices. The Law of Karma requires us to be vigilant and strong when faced with any adversarial energy and exact Severity when it is required of us. In doing so, we subtly teach others to behave correctly, per the Universal Laws. We each have a sacred duty we owe to our Creator to treat each other with love and respect and protect one another from all evil.

If we run away from negative energies, we fail to build our personal power, which takes away our God-given abilities over time. Every time we don't punish evil out of fear of confrontation, that fear gets magnified within us, severing us more and more from the Light in our Souls. And since the Law of Karma is cyclic, we continue to face the same challenges, time and again, until we get it right.

The "Eye for an Eye" Law of Moses from *The Torah (The Old Testament)* contains the underlying principle that punishment must fit the crime. It is in line with Newton's Third Law of Cause and Effect, based on the much earlier Hermetic Cause and Effect Law, "For every action (Force) in nature, there is an equal and opposite reaction." Cause and Effect is the foundation of the Law of Karma, and it essentially implies that what you put out into the Universe, you will get back.

"You reap what you sow," as the saying goes—if you do bad things, bad things will happen to you, while if you do good things, then good things will happen to you. From a human relations perspective, if you are positive and loving to other people, you will get that back from them, while if you are selfish and evil, others will return the favour. We are all inherently tasked with expressing the Law of Cause and Effect and being the effect of other people's causes.

A similar maxim with the same underlying energy came from Jesus, who said, "You live by the sword, you die by the sword," meaning that the quality of your life and choices you make will determine your life course. On an even deeper level, Jesus' saying implies that you attract the kind of life that corresponds with the quality of your heart. If you exhibit courage, strength, and fortitude, you can live up to your potential as a Spiritual human being. Whereas, if you live in fear, you will never be satisfied with your life's quality and will continuously make excuses and feel victimized. And the most optimal way to curb fear energy is to face it instead of running away from it. Therefore, we need to become responsible Co-Creators with our Creator and integrate both Angelic and Demonic powers within us and master them.

Jesus' "Turn the Other Cheek" phrase from the Sermon on the Mount (*The New Testament*) refers to responding to injury without revenge or allowing more harm. On a more subtle level, it relates to forgiving the transgressions of others and not standing up for oneself since "God will handle it." This phrase became the backbone of how the Christian Church taught its followers to behave. In retrospect, though, the Church implemented it for political reasons.

It became clear that the Christian Church indoctrinated its followers to have power and control over them while not having any repercussions for their evil actions in much of the Dark Ages and beyond. The Church taxed their people immorally and otherwise oppressed them while burning those at the stake that defied their laws. They kept the people dumbed down while waging religious wars and destroying pagan areas to convert them to Christianity forcefully.

The "Turn the Other Cheek" phrase, incorrectly used by the Christian Church as a Universal Law, creates weak and timid people who are "doormats" for others to use since they are taught never to defend their honour and punish evil being done to them. It leaves all actions in the hands of God-the Creator, with the hope that justice will arrive naturally and that we don't need to take part in exacting justice.

The Christian Church taught its followers that Jesus is the Saviour, whereas Jesus' original teachings were that we are each our own Saviour. In other words, we are conscious Co-Creators with the Creator and have a responsibility in manifesting Creation by using our God-given powers and respecting the Law of Cause and Effect. The Church's misinterpretation was again for political reasons to take personal power away from the people and make itself the sole governing force.

According to Qabalistic teachings, one must always maintain a proper balance between Mercy and Severity. Unbalanced Mercy yields weakness of mind while unbalanced Severity creates tyranny and oppression. Although he was erroneously depicted as being only a Pillar of Mercy, Jesus exacted Severity when necessary. Let us never forget that when he entered the Temple in Jerusalem and saw merchants and money-changers using it for financial profit, he turned their tables in a fit of rage to get his point across that the Temple is a Holy place.

Jesus' "Turn the Other Cheek" Law can be used effectively, as was shown to us by Mahatma Gandhi, who used non-violence to extricate the hostile British out of India. The idea behind Jesus' Law is that negative energy, when projected, bounces right back to you if the other person becomes neutral by applying love energy and forgiving the transgression as it's happening. One is meant to become a product of their own negativity if other people energetically neutralize their immoral treatment.

Jesus' Law can obtain the desired effect if the person applying it is a highly Spiritually evolved Being like Jesus and Gandhi were who don't become emotionally triggered when someone disrespects them. However, this is an impossibility for the commoner since their emotions are instinctual, and their consciousness experiences duality. Therefore, the common person must always balance Mercy with Severity and apply each force when necessary. By punishing evil, we maintain the integrity of the Light in the world, which furthers the Spiritual Evolution of all of humankind. We are all each other's judges, healers, and teachers, and this is because we are all interconnected at the deepest level through the electromagnetic power of our hearts.

OPENING THE HEART CHAKRA

Throughout Ancient history, mystics, Sages, Yogis, Adepts, and Spiritually advanced humans alike, considered the physical heart the centre of the Soul. Our Soul is our inner guiding Light, which is linked to the fiery Star of our Solar System, the Sun. Although the Fire Element corresponds with the Solar Plexus Chakra, the interplay between Manipura and Anahata Chakras initiates Solar consciousness. In the Qabalah, Solar consciousness is represented by the Tiphareth Sephira, whose location is between the Heart and Solar Plexus Chakras, as it shares correspondences with both.

The physical heart corresponds with the Heart Chakra, Anahata, located in the middle of the chest. The Heart Chakra is our centre of inner peace, unconditional love, compassion, truth, harmony, and wisdom. It is our centre of healing energy which can outwardly be applied through hands-on healing practices such as Reiki and Ruach Healing. Healing energy is harnessed in the Heart Chakra but is sent out via the Throat Chakra, which connects to energy channels in the arms that radiate out to the Palm Chakras.

The Heart Chakra is our Spiritual centre through which we can access higher vibrational energies. Since the Heart Chakra is between the higher Spirit Chakras and the lower, Elemental Chakras, the broad spectrum of these higher vibrational energies becomes fully available to us when our lower and higher Chakric centres are fully activated, purified, and balanced. For example, if the higher centres are still relatively closed, less Light will pour into the lower Chakras from Sahasrara, preventing them from functioning at their optimal level. As a result, you will have access to unconditional love, for example, but won't be able to feel it at the deepest levels of your Being.

The Heart Chakra is the centre of the Seven Major Chakras, which harmonizes our masculine and feminine energies. It is our first Chakra of Non-Duality through which we can experience the Silent Witness within us that is our Higher Self, or Holy Guardian Angel. The Holy Guardian Angel resides in Sahasrara but can be experienced through the Heart Chakra if Vishuddhi and Ajna are open.

Although Manipura (Fire Element) is the Seat of the Soul, unless Anahata (Air Element) is awakened, the Soul can only experience lower vibrational energies of Swadhisthana (Water Element) and Muladhara (Earth Element). As such, the Soul becomes too ingrained in Matter, dimming its Light and allowing the Ego to take over. When Anahata is awakened, the Soul obtains access to the Spirit Element, allowing it to undergo a Spiritual transformation if the higher Chakric centres are open.

If we transpose the Transpersonal Chakras model and the Seven Major Chakras, we can see that the Heart Chakra is the centre of the entire Chakric system. Our Cosmic energy source is the Stellar Gateway, which relates to the Milky Way Galaxy that contains our Solar System among tens of billions of other Solar Systems. The Milky Way Galaxy is a spiral galaxy, as are more than two-thirds of all observed galaxies in the Universe.

Cosmic energy emanates from the Stellar Gateway spirally (Figure 59), encompassing the Earth Star and Soul Star before reaching the Major Chakras. Our entire Chakric system reflects our Source energy, which is the Stellar Gateway and the Milky Way Galaxy. We tap into this Fifth Dimensional Source energy through the Heart Chakra at the centre of the spiral.

Figure 59: The Heart Chakra Center

When our Heart Chakra is open, we remember our Divinity, which is deeply inherent. We also recognize the Divinity in all living things around us, including other humans, animals, and plants, and develop unity consciousness. Each living thing has a Soul, an individual cell in the body of a tremendous Cosmic Being that expresses through our Solar System with the Sun as its centre. In the Qabalah, we refer to this grand Being as *Adam Kadmon*, akin to Cosmic Consciousness. Adam Kadmon is the sum of all the Souls manifested on Earth as the higher consciousness that unites us.

With an open Heart Chakra, we realize that our current existence is part of a never-ending chain of lives since our Souls are Eternal and will continue living past physical death. We have lived many different lives before and will continue to do so once our physical body perishes. We were born with this knowledge, which allows us to re-integrate faith as part of our existence when re-activated. And when one has faith and love, they immediately subdue fear since fear is the absence of faith and love.

Healthy, balanced relationships require us to be open with one another. An open Heart Chakra makes us generous and kind in word and deed since we are Spiritual human beings at our core. By experiencing the Spirit energy through the Heart Chakra, we develop a genuine understanding of other people's hardships, allowing us to become merciful and forgiving. Conversely, an open Heart Chakra gives us the courage to exact severity when the situation requires it, a term we call "tough love." If we see someone engaging in immoral activities, taking them off the Spiritual path, we naturally want to help them, which requires us to use mercy or severity, depending on the situation.

By becoming Spiritual, we bring joy and bliss into our lives. We also learn to love and accept ourselves, the good and the bad, which is the first step towards personal transformation. If we hide from who we are, we lose our sense of identity, which makes us lose touch with our Souls. As such, we identify with the Ego and operate solely through its low-level consciousness.

The Ego represents the part of us that is separate from the world. It lacks empathy and engages in vices, while the Soul is virtuous since it is part of the Oneness of all of existence. By opening the Heart Chakra, we regain our connection with the state of Oneness, activating healing within. As such, all personal traumas, including abandonment, rejection, betrayal, physical and emotional abuse, begin being purged to integrate Spiritual consciousness within our hearts.

By healing our inner energies, we also heal issues with the physical body since diseases are a manifestation of Chakric energy blockages. We can consciously send healing energy from the Heart Chakra to any part of the body to heal any imbalances. When we are experiencing physical problems, it is a sign that our hearts are not open enough; either we don't love ourselves enough or we aren't sufficiently loving towards other people. Instead of focusing on the disease or ailment, we need to focus on channelling love energy and becoming a beacon of the Light in the world.

Opening the Heart Chakra allows us to exhibit patience and not expect immediate rewards for our actions. Patience is a sign that faith has come into our lives, and we are following a higher path. Integrity, ethics, and a moral compass become our guiding force instead of being led by the Ego and its desires. When our hearts lead us, we walk the path of the Light with our inner truth as our greatest ally. Inner wisdom is awakened, taking us away from mere logic and reason to rationalize our existence. Instead, we see the big picture: our ultimate purpose on Earth is to Spiritually evolve and attune our vibrations with the Cosmic Consciousness of God-the Creator.

KUNDALINI AND HEART EXPANSIONS

When the Kundalini blows open the Heart Chakra on its upwards rise, it maximizes one's heart EMF, which feels like the Self has expanded in all directions. The immediate effect is a heightened sense of perception and an awakening of silence's unstruck sound.

The inner sound of silence is an underlying stillness compared to white noise, a steady humming sound. It is the sound of nothingness, the Void of Space, which is calming and relaxing when we tune into it. We tune into the sound of silence when we are deep in meditation, although, with a Heart Chakra awakening, it becomes more accessible.

As mentioned, the Heart Chakra is the first Chakra of Non-Duality—when the Kundalini enters it, we become awakened to the present moment, the Now. This experience immediately takes us out of our heads and into the heart. We develop a higher sense of awareness, which is quite transcendental at first, but something we get used to as time goes on.

If the Kundalini rises into the Heart Chakra but not higher, it will drop back down to Muladhara only to rise again in the future until it pierces the higher Chakras and completes the awakening process. Once a full Kundalini awakening occurs, and the energy has penetrated Sahasrara, one's toroidal field is maximized, resulting in the expansion of consciousness and complete remodelling of mind, body, and Soul. Since the heart and brain are partners in the governance and maintenance of consciousness, a transformation in both follows.

I have already spoken about the process of brain-power activation once the Kundalini permanently rises into its central area. The brain feels like it opens up from the inside, awakening latent parts of it. A complete upgrading process occurs in our CPU as the major brain centres begin to function at a higher level. The feeling of transparency and weightlessness accompanies this process, which feels like the head has expanded in all directions.

Heart expansions occur once intense bliss and love enter into the heart. It is usually not an immediate process since the lower Chakras first have to be cleansed. If one experiences a spontaneous Kundalini awakening, the inner fire will naturally purge the lower Chakras over time, allowing the Spiritual energy to descend into the heart.

Heart expansions relax the muscles and the nervous system, which may cause a nauseous feeling in the pit of the stomach and weakness in the arms and legs. The heart EMF can feel so big since the concept of Cosmic Consciousness is no longer an idea but a permanent part of one's reality. The Soul feels like it is no longer in the body but present everywhere. One develops heightened awareness and presence of the environment they are in. The moment they place their attention on an external object, they become absorbed in it and can read its energy psychically. This phenomenon results from the heart EMF expanding exponentially, enabling it to receive a substantially greater degree of information from the environment.

The increased heart EMF causes a transfiguration in the body, activating one's latent DNA. Over time, once the body has adjusted to the inner changes occurring in the consciousness, the heart EMF stabilizes but is now permanently functioning at a higher level (Figure 60).

The heartbeat becomes more powerful as the body and brain process more information and work overtime to support the newly expanded consciousness. During heart and brain expansions and upgrades, it helps to ground one's electromagnetic field with the Earth's energy field. Being inside the house can be detrimental since it cuts us off from nature and the Sun's rays, which boost our vitality and the body's healing ability. Walking barefoot in nature under the open sky, lying on the grass, and being beside a body of water are all beneficial in preventing physical fatigue and supporting a smooth transformation process.

Proper nutrition is crucial, as one should incorporate fruits and vegetables into their diets to align them with the Planet's energies. Furthermore, everything natural and organic should be embraced, while that which isn't should be avoided.

Stimulants such as alcohol and drugs will cause an imbalance in the nervous system and should be avoided. The intake of coffee should be moderated as well, even though a cup a day can aid in grounding.

The Thymus Gland plays a significant role in awakening the Heart Chakra and heart expansions. As mentioned, the Thymus Gland forms part of our lymphatic system and sits between the heart and sternum. When the Heart Chakra opens, our immune system is boosted, optimizing our body's disease-fighting ability. The body no longer needs to spend extra energy reserves on healing itself but can use that energy to purify the Spiritual system.

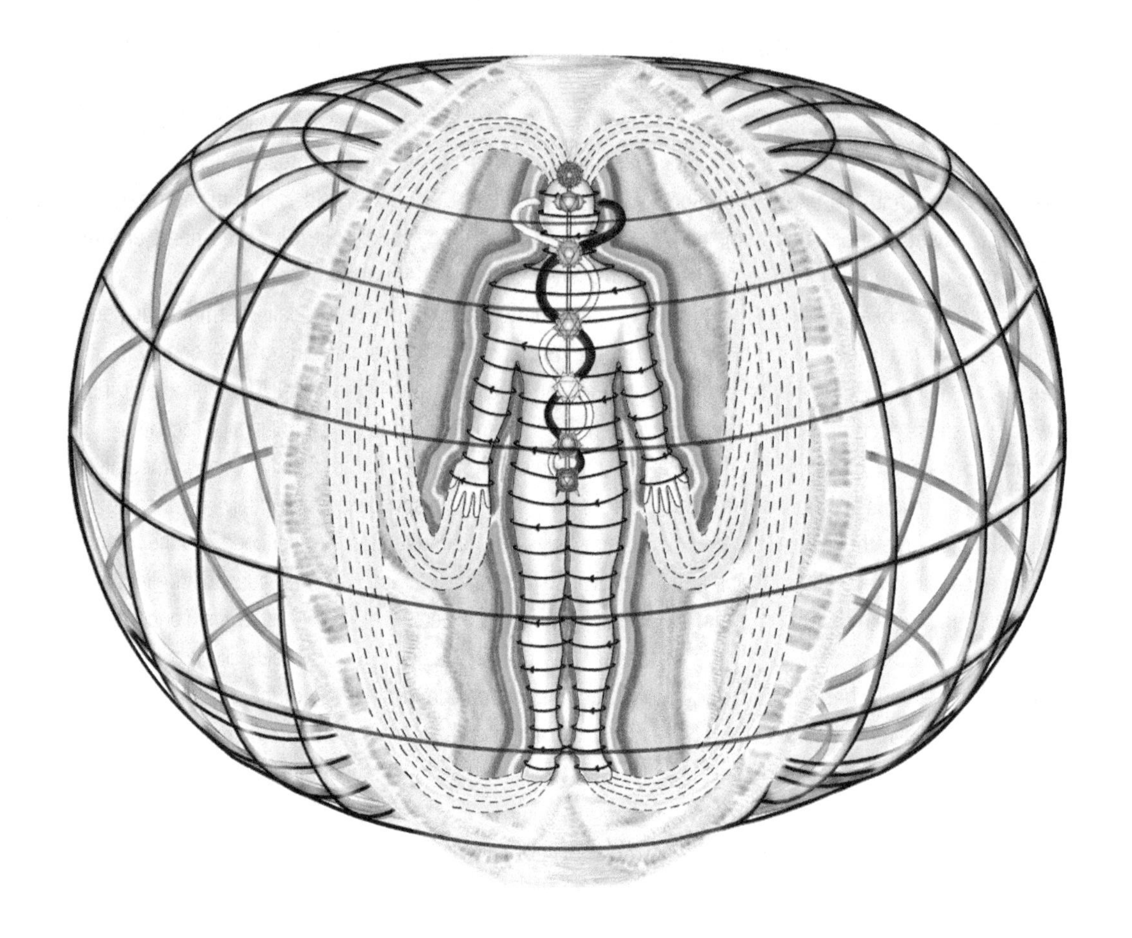

Figure 60: Kundalini Awakening and the Heart EMF

The Thymus Gland wakes up significantly during heart expansions, often causing immense pressure in the chest. We can alleviate this pressure by merely tapping the Thymus Gland rhythmically. As the heart is experiencing an influx of Spirit energy, relaxation and euphoria sweep the body, often coming in undulating waves. Blood pressure tends to drop in these instances while histamine and serotonin levels heighten. This situation signals a time for us to break from everyday life and tend to ourselves and our needs. Expecting ourselves to perform at 100% will be impossible; therefore, instead of fighting the process, it is best to accept it and adjust accordingly.

Heart expansions usually come in phases and can last for weeks, sometimes months. They may occur once during the Kundalini transformation process, although it is more common for them to appear multiple times. The body's equilibrium phase follows heart expansions. The nervous system balances itself out by raising adrenaline, dopamine, and serotonin levels and increasing the heart rate, blood pressure and blood glucose.

Whatever is happening to your body, and no matter where you are in the Spiritual transformation process, always remember that it is best to surrender to it. Being relaxed in mind, body, and Soul during this process is a must since it is futile to rationalize or control it. Complete and absolute surrender will help us reach the finish line in the shortest time possible and facilitate the smoothest ride.

PART V:
SEVEN CHAKRAS HEALING MODALITIES

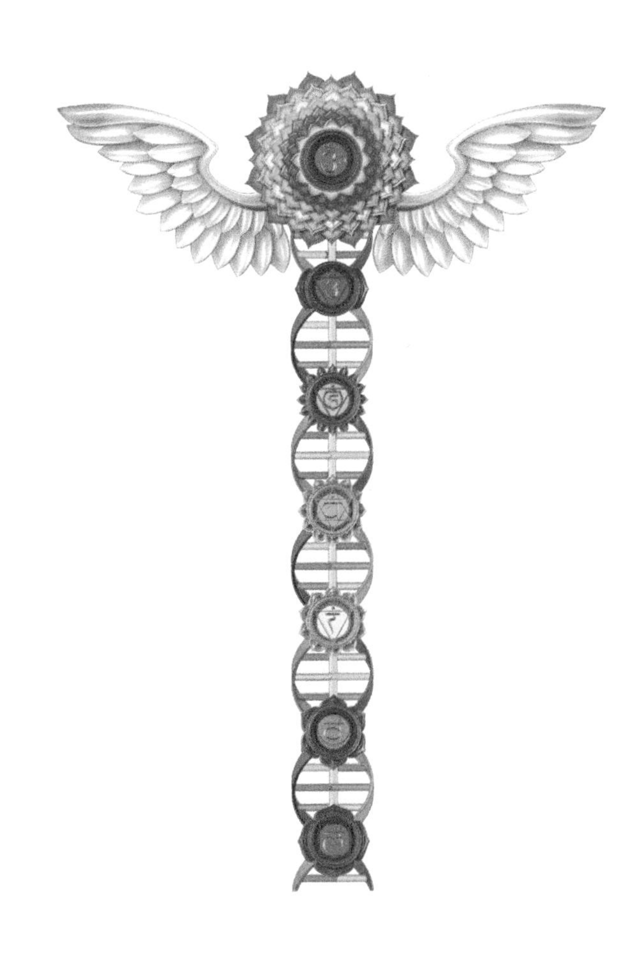

MALE AND FEMALE CHAKRAS

The Principle of Gender from *The Kybalion* states, "Gender is in everything; everything has its Masculine and Feminine Principles, Gender manifests on all Planes." This Principle implies that every human being has a dual-energy dynamic, a masculine and feminine component—expressed through their Seven Major Chakras.

Each of the Major Chakras is associated with masculine or feminine energy, representing the quality of their essence. Male (Yang) energies represent active, projective energy, while female (Yin) energies represent passive and receptive energy. These binary energies are a manifestation of Shiva and Shakti, the Divine Source of the Masculine and Feminine Principles. In scientific terms, male energy is comprised of protons, while female energy is composed of electrons.

Similarly, as all Beings in the Universe have a masculine and feminine component (regardless of their Soul's gender), so do the Chakras. In other words, a Chakra is never wholly masculine or feminine but contains aspects of both. However, each of the Seven Chakras is dominant in one gender as they express either a positive or negative pole. The two gender poles define the Chakra's nature and function, which are reversed in the Chakric system of male and female Souls. I am distinguishing between gender Souls and bodies since it is not uncommon for a female Soul to be born in a male body in our modern-day society, and vice versa.

Figure 61 is a schematic that describes the Seven Chakras system and its various parts and functions. A central energy column inside the body channels the Light and beams it back and forth between Sahasrara and Muladhara. Sahasrara projects upwards towards the Soul Star, while Muladhara projects downwards towards the Earth Star.

Each Chakra between Sahasrara and Muladhara has a front and back portion that projects outwards. When the Chakra is working well, it casts further out, while when its energy is stagnant, its projection reaches a shorter distance. The Chakra stops its spinning when it is blocked, and its projection is closer to the body. Use the Figure 61 schematic as a reference for the Spiritual Healing methods in this section, namely energy work with Crystal Wands and Tuning Forks.

Since each Chakra is a wheel of spinning energy, it can rotate either clockwise or counterclockwise, spiralling outwards at a ninety-degree angle to the body. The direction in which a Chakra spins is something inherent in us since birth. The origin of the opposite spin of male and female Chakras begins in Sahasrara, alternating as we go downwards through the Chakras. As such, each of us is either positive or negative, male or female energy dominant. The males reside more in their First, Third, and Fifth Chakras, in which they are dominant, while females operate from their Second, Fourth, and Sixth Chakras.

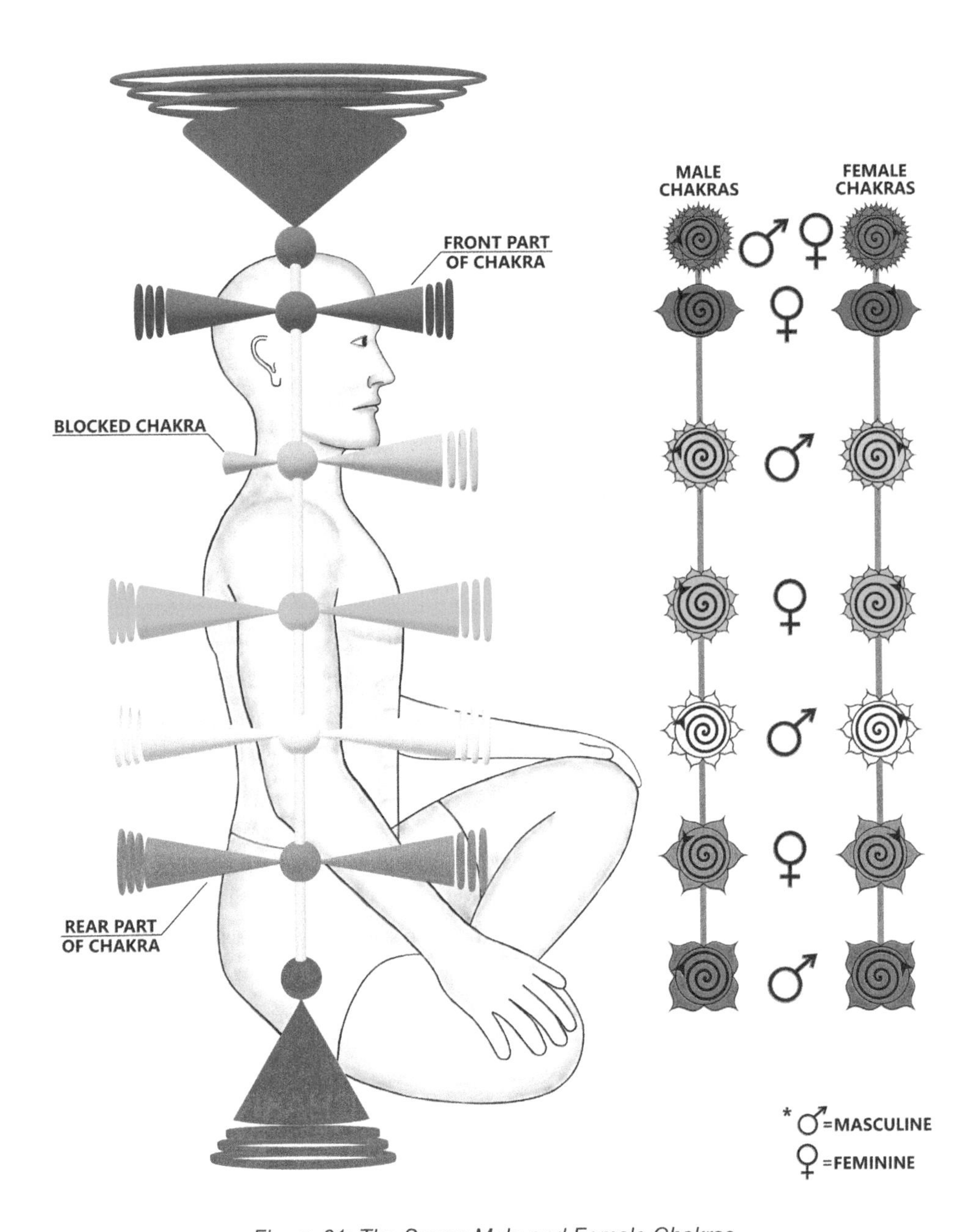

Figure 61: The Seven Male and Female Chakras

Keep in mind, though, the direction of spin of our male and female Chakras is not fixed. Any Chakra can either be in the act of projecting or receiving, which affects its direction of spin. Chakras are like cogs in a machine where each wheel relates to every other wheel. They work together as parts of an engine or a clock, where every piece of machinery affects every other component, and everything must be in synch to make the device work. Similarly, each Chakra must spin smoothly and at a similar speed as every other Chakra to give coherence to the whole energy system.

The challenge for males and females is to bring their Chakras into balance by working with their non-dominant Chakras. We can achieve Chakric balance through Spiritual Healing methods but also by falling in love. When two people of opposite Soul polarities fall in love, their complementing energies allow them to achieve unification in their masculine and feminine polarities, giving rise to a higher state of consciousness. Falling in love is highly beneficial to one's Spiritual Evolution, which explains why it is so sought after in our society.

Whether a Chakra is of a masculine or feminine quality, its power gets optimized when it spends more time spinning clockwise. As you see in Figure 61, the Chakra is dominant when the spin is in the clockwise direction. Energy is projecting outwards in a clockwise spin, allowing the inner Light to flow through the Chakric system more efficiently. The inner Light is essentially what powers the Chakra—the more Light one carries, the more powerful their Chakras will be. Conversely, when a Chakra is receiving energy, it rotates counterclockwise. In this case, its power doesn't get fully utilized since it is drawing energy from the environment instead of using its own energy source.

For the Chakras to be kept healthy and balanced, one should never spend too much time pulling in energy from the outside since unknown, foreign energies can easily block a Chakra, especially if they have a low vibrational frequency. A blocked Chakra causes stagnation in the energy flow of the Aura and can even cause physical disease over time. Conversely, constantly projecting energy outwards without spending the necessary time grounding and Self-reflecting can deplete one's Aura of vital Pranic energy, exhausting the mind, body, and Soul.

In the case of a full Kundalini awakening, however, when the individual has established a permanent connection with Sahasrara, they channel a greater degree of Light energy into their optimized six Chakras below, enabling them to be a natural healer to others. Individuals are naturally drawn to Kundalini awakened people—one is being healed simply by being in their presence.

On a side note, to maintain healthy relationships, there should always be an equal give and take energetically. We should feel rejuvenated by spending time with others instead of feeling depleted. Those people that take too much energetically without giving anything back (whether they are doing it consciously or not) are termed "energy vampires." The concept of vampirism came from this type of selfish energy exchange between people; if we are open to taking love energy from others, we should be open to giving our love energy back to them as well.

GENDER CHARACTERISTICS OF THE CHAKRAS

As the source of the raw energy of physicality and action, Muladhara, the Root Chakra, is masculine (positive) in nature, spinning clockwise in males and counterclockwise in females. For females, Muladhara is in the receiving mode; for males, however, it is in the act of giving out energy. For this reason, males are generally the more dominant gender involved in physical activities such as manual labour and competitive sports.

Swadhisthana, the Sacral Chakra, the source of one's emotions, is feminine (negative) in nature; it spins counterclockwise in men and clockwise in women. Swadhisthana is in the receptive mode for males and projective mode for females. Since Swadhisthana is more dominant in females, it is no wonder they are generally the more emotional of the two genders.

As the source of willpower, Manipura, the Solar Plexus Chakra, is of the masculine (positive) energy, spinning clockwise in men and counterclockwise in women. Manipura is in the receiving mode for women, while it gives out energy for men. Manipura's dominance in males has led to an obsession with power and control, as shown historically in the history of wars males have waged with one another. On a positive note, the male warrior energy has made them the protector and provider in the family household since time immemorial.

The source of compassion and love, Anahata, the Heart Chakra, is feminine (negative) in nature, and it spins counterclockwise in men and clockwise in women. Anahata is in the act of receiving for males and the mode of projecting for females. Females are associated with nurturing and caregiving. They can go with the flow of life instead of controlling every facet of their existence. Since females dominate the Heart and Sacral Chakras, intimacy is much more accessible to them than males. Most females are generally the heart of their romantic relationships, while males struggle with their feelings.

Vishuddhi, the Throat Chakra, the centre of one's expression, is of the masculine (positive) energy; it spins clockwise in men and counterclockwise in women. Since males are dominant in the Throat Chakra, it is not uncommon for them to be more aligned with purpose and expression than females, who tend to be more introverted.

Being the centre of one's intuition, Ajna, the Mind's Eye, is feminine (negative) in nature, spinning counterclockwise in men and clockwise in women. In men, Ajna is in the act of receiving, while in women, it is in the mode of giving out. As such, females are known to have higher psychic senses than males. Throughout history, it is no wonder that women were the seers and Oracles since they were a better channel for energies from the Higher Planes.

Sahasrara is gender-neutral as it is the source of Divine Light. The positive and negative poles merge into one unified energy, making Sahasrara the only Major Chakra that is Non-Dual. In males, this Chakra spins clockwise, while in females, it spins counterclockwise. Sahasrara is the source of the Divine Masculine and Divine Feminine energies. For both genders, Sahasrara is in the act of giving out the Divine Light energy and projecting it into the Chakras below.

The roles and designations between the genders mentioned above are in no way fixed, nor do they determine a human being's strengths and weaknesses. Many male and female individuals have optimized the Chakras they aren't naturally dominant in and thrive in areas that are less common for people of their gender. Free Will supersedes all energetic dispositions and societal conditioning; with focus and determination, human beings can develop themselves into anything they want to be.

BALANCING THE CHAKRAS

When it comes to Spiritual Healing, it helps to know which Chakras we are naturally dominant in. We can develop our non-dominant Chakras and achieve greater balance in our overall energy system by having this knowledge. After all, the key to maximizing one's potential is to balance the masculine and feminine energies within the body. With that in mind, when working with the Chakras through Spiritual Healing practices, females should focus on the masculine, odd Chakras (First, Third, Fifth), while males should focus on the feminine, even Chakras (Second, Fourth, Sixth).

When a Chakra is overactive (in excess of energy) or if a Chakra is underactive and deficient in energy, we can apply the masculine and feminine principles to bring that Chakra into balance. For example, since Swadhisthana Chakra has feminine energy, an imbalance in this Chakra means that one has either an excessive amount of feminine energy or is deficient in masculine energy. If the individual feels overly emotional, they need to apply masculine energy in their Sacral Chakra for balance. If they are cold and aloof and out of touch with their emotions, they should use feminine energy.

Since Manipura Chakra has a masculine quality, if the individual feels an excess of energy that makes them agitated and angry, it is a sign that the Chakra is overactive and needs feminine energy applied to bring it into balance. Conversely, if the individual is out of touch with their willpower, they need to use the masculine energy to restore its balance.

Whether masculine or feminine, every Chakra spins in the clockwise direction when it is overactive and counterclockwise when it is underactive. Therefore, to optimize a Chakra, we must find the correct balance between its projective and receptive functions. However, as mentioned, for the individual to channel their inner Light, the Chakras should be projecting energy more than receiving. Doing so will strengthen the connection with the Soul.

ASTROLOGY AND THE SEVEN CHAKRAS

Astrology is an Ancient science that examines the movements and relative positions of the Heavenly bodies (Planets) in our Solar System. Astrology was at the heart of all sciences, philosophy, medicine, and Magick for our early Ancestors. According to them, the outer Universe (Macrocosm) was reflected in the human experience (Microcosm)—As Above, So Below. They believed that by studying the Star Constellations and the Planets, they could divine human affairs, heal the body, and even predict events here on Earth.

Astrologers believe that every human being is influenced by the Planets and the Zodiac signs they were in when they were born. They call the blueprint of these energetic influences our Horoscope, or Birth Chart. Our Horoscope gives us a map of the energies that comprise our overall Self. At birth, Zodiacal energies become locked into our Aura, powering the Chakras and influencing our desires, aspirations, motivations, likes and dislikes, and behavioural tendencies. The Stars provide us with the Karmic lessons we need to Spiritually evolve in this lifetime.

The essence of Astrology lies in understanding the meaning of the Planets since they rule the Zodiac Signs and Twelve Houses. In other words, the forces of the Star Constellations manifest through the Planets. Every human being is made up of different combinations and degrees of the Planets' energies. The Seven Ancient Planets act as relay stations for the reception and transmission of Stellar energies. They correspond with the Seven Chakras, while the Twelve Zodiac signs represent the masculine and feminine, day (Solar) and night (Lunar) aspects of the Seven Ancient Planets (Figure 62). Therefore, by gauging our Birth Chart, we can determine the characteristics of our Chakras that shape our character and personality.

The Birth Chart is a snapshot in time, a blueprint of who we are and who we can become. When examining the Birth Chart, one needs to pay particular attention to the Sun, Moon and Rising (Ascendant) Signs. These three signs give us extraordinary insight into our Chakric focus in life, the strengths we can build on, and weaknesses and limitations we can improve and overcome to evolve Spiritually.

An individual's Elemental breakdown in their Birth Chart also determines how much masculine or feminine energy they embody, which impacts their psychology. However, their physical appearance is affected by their Ascendant and the Planets that fall in the First House. For example, if someone has Jupiter in their First House, the individual may struggle with weight gain, while if they have Mars, their physical body will be toned and muscular. These associations have much to do with the ruling Chakras of the Planets, which will be explored in detail in this chapter.

WESTERN ASTROLOGY VS. VEDIC ASTROLOGY

Since the advent of Astrology, which is as old as humanity itself, many Astrological systems have been invented to study and divine the Stars. However, the two most notable ones that have stood the test of time are Western Astrology and Vedic Astrology.

Vedic, Hindu, or Indian Astrology, otherwise called "Jyotish Shastra" ("Science of Light" in Sanskrit), is different and more complex than Western Astrology. Vedic Astrology is rooted in the Vedas and is at least 5000 years old. It uses the Sidereal Zodiac, which is based upon the position of Star Constellations in the night sky that serve as a backdrop for the moving Planets. Ancient cultures like the Egyptians, Persians, and Mayans used the Sidereal system to predict future events accurately.

In contrast, Western Astrology is based on the Tropical Zodiac, which is geocentric; it follows the Earth's orientation to the Sun, where the Zodiac Signs are set upon the ecliptic. Western Astrology is aligned with the changes in seasons; Aries is the first Zodiac since it coincides with the first day of spring on the Vernal (Spring) Equinox, as the Sun crosses the celestial equator going north. So, Aries starts off the Solar year, while Pisces finishes it year in and year out. Most of the modern world has adopted the Tropical or Solar calendar to count time because of its consistency in matching the changes in seasons.

Therefore, Western Astrology evaluates a person's birth using the alignments of the Stars and Planets from the Earth's perspective, instead of in space like in Vedic Astrology. Western Astrology originated in Ancient Greece with Ptolemy approximately 2000 years ago. However, it was a continuation of Hellenistic and Babylonian traditions.

Since the Earth wobbles and tilts around 23.5 degrees from the equator, it causes a 1 degree shift every 72 years, which we refer to as the "Precession of the Equinoxes." This means that the Vernal Equinox comes 20 minutes early every year and one day early every 72 years. While Vedic Astrology accounts for this variance, Western Astrology does not. So, while Vedic Astrology is moveable and gives results basically in "real-time" of the configuration of Star Constellations, Western Astrology is fixed and doesn't account for these changes in the night sky.

Here is where it gets tricky, though. Although the two systems were aligned at the advent of the Tropical Zodiac some 2000 years ago, the dates for the Sun Signs have changed over the years in Vedic Astrology, while in Western Astrology, they stayed the same. So, for example, at present, Aries begins on April 13th (this number varies) in the Sidereal Zodiac, while in the Tropical Zodiac, Aries maintains its arrival on March 21st.

Therefore, although the Twelve Zodiacal Signs share the same characteristics and traits, since their dates differ, you may get an entirely different readout in your Birth Chart. Also, although not an official part of either system, since its Constellation touches upon the ecliptic, Ophiuchus the "Serpent-Bearer" has sometimes been suggested as the thirteenth Zodiac Sign in Sidereal Astrology. It falls between Scorpio and Sagittarius from November 29th to December 18th.

Another essential difference between the two systems is that Western Astrology utilizes the three outer Planets in our Solar System, Uranus, Neptune, and Pluto, as part of the Planetary framework. In contrast, Vedic Astrology (mirroring Ancient Alchemy and Hermetic Qabalah) only focuses on the Seven Ancient Planets. However, it includes the North and South Nodes of the Moon (Rahu and Ketu), for a total of nine Heavenly bodies (Deities), called the "Navagrahas" (Sanskrit for "Nine Planets."). According to Hindu beliefs, the Navagrahas influence humanity collectively and individually. Therefore, it is not uncommon to see Hindus worship the Navagrahas in their homes to overcome adversity or misfortune arising from past Karmas.

Western Astrology emphasizes the position of the Sun in a specific Sun Sign. At the same time, Vedic Astrology emphasizes the position of the Moon and the Ascendant (Lagna in Sanskrit). In addition, it includes the "Nakshatras" (Lunar Mansions), which is unique to this system. Also, the Twelve Houses are part of the Vedic Astrology Birth Chart, while they are secondary in Western Astrology. The Solar-based system of Western Astrology is arguably better at evaluating the personality and characteristics of a person and the Planetary influences on behaviour and perceptions. In contrast, the Lunar-based Vedic Astrology system is better at giving one insight into their destiny and fate because of its accuracy in predicting the future. In other words, the Western Astrologer is more of a psychologist, while the Vedic Astrologer is more of a seer or diviner.

As a final note on this topic, having studied Western Astrology my entire life, I can attest to its validity and accuracy concerning my own personality traits and characteristics and other people I have come across. Also, since Hermeticism is the primary influence on all my work, I recognize the importance of the Sun's Light and its effects on life on Earth and our inner Spiritual nature and give it precedence over all things. For this reason, the seasonal attribution of the Zodiacal Signs always made sense to me since their placement reflected the metaphoric life, death, and rebirth of the Sun from the Earth's point of view.

My interest in Astrology has always been a form of transpersonal psychology instead of predicting future events in my life. As such, Western Astrology has been of great benefit to me. However, if your interest in Astrology is primarily as a form of divination, you will find Vedic Astrology more beneficial. Having said that, I think that neither system has the ultimate answers. Therefore, to fully understand Astrology, you should familiarize yourself with both systems, which many earnest Astrologers do.

THE SEVEN ANCIENT PLANETS

The Seven Major Chakras correspond with the Seven Ancient Planets in the following way: Muladhara relates to Saturn, Swadhisthana to Jupiter, Manipura to Mars, Anahata to Venus, Vishuddhi to Mercury, Ajna to the Moon, and Sahasrara to the Sun (Figure 62).

By placing the Planets in their Chakric positions, we get an almost exact sequence of their order in our Solar System. The only variance is the Moon, placed second after the Sun instead of being between Venus and Mars, alongside the Earth.

On the Qabalistic Tree of Life, the Moon is the first Sephira (Yesod) we encounter when going inwards. Since it reflects the Sun's Light, it corresponds with visual thoughts projected through the Mind's Eye—our doorway or portal into the inner Cosmic Planes or Realms. The Moon represents the Astral Plane, reflecting the Spiritual reality that the Sun generates on the other end of the spectrum.

In Alchemical symbology, the Moon and Sun were always pictured together as representatives of the Universal feminine and masculine energies. The interplay of Sun and Moon energies is found at the foundation of all Creation as Soul and consciousness—the Fire and Water Elements.

Consequently, the placement of the Seven Ancient Planets on the Chakric tree almost mirrors their arrangement on the Qabalistic Tree of Life, although in reverse. If we substitute the Planet Earth in place of the Sun, we have the Moon next, followed by Mercury, Venus, Mars, Jupiter, and Saturn.

As mentioned before, the Light of the Sun is the origin of our Souls. The association between the Earth and the Sun implies that the Spiritual reality is reflected in the material reality and vice versa. The two are merely opposite aspects of the One.

If the Sun represents the Soul, then the Planets are the Soul's higher powers that manifest through their associated Chakras. They are the various components of the inner Self and the source of all virtues, morals, and ethics that comprise our character. As stated in *The Magus*, through our connection with the Planets and their cycles around the Sun, we are a "perfect Microcosm of the Macrocosm—a Mini Solar System which reflects the grand Solar System in which we have our physical existence."

As each of the Seven Ancient Planets corresponds with one of the Seven Chakras, each Chakra displays the nature of its ruling Planet. This association is helpful to know when examining our Horoscope or Birth Chart. Since life is continuous, the positioning of the Planets reflects the required powers we need to overcome our Karmic energy from previous lifetimes.

Depending on which Zodiac Sign a Planet was aligned with the moment an individual was born, some Planets are malefic, while others are benign in one's Birth Chart. This is because of the relationship between Planets and the rulers of the Zodiac Signs in which they are located. Planets are strong in signs of their friends while being neutral in strength in neutral Signs. Conversely, they are weak in the Signs of their enemies. As such, the Planetary, Cosmic radiations can either positively or negatively impact their associated Chakras in the Body of Light. If any of our Planets are weak in our Birth Chart, its corresponding Chakra will also be weak. When Chakras are weak and (or) blocked, health issues related to that Chakra are caused.

On a final note, most Western Astrologers include the outer Planets in their Horoscope models. They equate Pluto to the feminine side of the Mars Chakra (Scorpio), Neptune to the feminine side of the Jupiter Chakra (Pisces), and Uranus to the masculine side of the Saturn Chakra (Aquarius).

The North and South Nodes of the Moon are often included as well. They are called Caput and Cauda Draconis in Latin—the Head and Tail of the Dragon. Generally speaking, the North Node relates to our fate and destiny in this life, while the South Node relates to the Karma we bring into this incarnation from past lives.

The following is the description of the Planetary powers with relation to their associated Chakras. For a more thorough exposition on Western Astrology's Planetary and Zodiacal correspondences, consult *The Magus*. The Astrological knowledge presented herein complements the information on the same subject in my previous book.

Saturn/Muladhara

Saturn (Shani in Sanskrit) is the slowest moving Planet in our Solar System, which is why it is associated with lessons in life that relate to the passage of time. It is the Planet of self-control, responsibility, diligence, and discipline, all of which give structure to our lives. Its energy is grounding, like the Earth Element it represents. Saturn represents the masculine Muladhara Chakra.

Saturn allows us to see the truth of the matter and align with it. As such, it is very much concerned with integrity. Saturnalian energy affects our ability to manifest our life's dreams and goals, inspiring us to take on the world head-on. It also affects our boundaries and restrictions, allowing us to live within society's constraints in a healthy yet productive manner.

Saturn contains an Airy quality; it stimulates intuition and a deep knowingness of a higher reality that rules over the Universe. After all, it is the Planet of faith and Karma. A strong influence of Saturnalian energy enables us to prioritize our Spiritual Evolution over material gains.

In terms of the body, Saturn governs all things related to our physical structure, including the skeletal system, teeth, cartilage, glands, hair, and skin. Too little Saturnalian energy in Muladhara will make us ungrounded and unable to support ourselves. A lack of discipline and ambition can make us inert and internally conflicted, preventing us from achieving the goals we set for ourselves. On the other hand, too much Saturn and a person can become overly ambitious, selfish, inflexible, and pessimistic.

Saturn has a friendly relationship with Mercury and Venus in a Birth Chart while being enemies with Mars and neutral with Jupiter. In addition, it rules the two steadfast and trustworthy signs in the Zodiac, Aquarius (Kumbha in Sanskrit) and Capricorn (Makara in Sanskrit). Aquarius represents the masculine energy of Saturn, while Capricorn represents its feminine energy. While Aquarius is concerned with the expression of the conservative force in life, Capricorn is involved in stabilizing it.

If either of these two signs is prominent in your Birth Chart, mainly if they are found as your Sun Sign, Moon Sign, or Rising Sign (Ascendant), you should pay attention to Muladhara Chakra. Aquarius' and Capricorns often receive either too much or too little Saturnalian energy and require Spiritual work on Muladhara to balance it.

Jupiter/Swadhisthana

The Planet Jupiter (Brihaspati or Guru in Sanskrit) is an expansive and bountiful Planet that brings good fortune, abundance, and success. It is related to the Water Element and represents the higher qualities of consciousness whose base energy is unconditional love. Jupiter corresponds with the feminine Swadhisthana Chakra.

Jupiter's benevolent energy inspires Self-confidence, optimism, cooperation with others, and the protective impulse. Jupiterian energy builds virtues that shape our character and connect with our Higher Selves. It gives us a strong sense of morality and ethics and allows us to grow in society and be an asset to others. Jupiter instils a sense of compassion, mercy, and generosity within us, making us just and honourable in our words and actions. Luck, happiness, and good health are all aspects of Jupiter. It governs the growth of the physical body, including cellular development and the preservation of soft tissues.

Jupiter is the teacher that gives us inner wisdom and inspires us to develop a philosophical outlook in life. Its positive energy makes us friendly, cheerful, and generally well-liked by others. It allows us to see the positive in all situations, which gives success in business ventures.

If Swadhisthana is deficient in Jupiterian energy, suppression of emotions and sexuality ensues, negatively affecting creativity, self-confidence, and one's sense of personal identity. Too little Jupiterian energy can make us pessimistic, dishonest, timid, shy, and generally unlucky in life. Conversely, too much Jupiter can make us blindly optimistic, extravagant, and lazy. The downside of things coming too easy in life is that we cannot develop strength of character.

In a Birth Chart, Jupiter is friends with the Sun, Moon, and Mars, while enemies with Mercury and Venus and neutral with Saturn. In addition, Jupiter rules Sagittarius (Dhanus in Sanskrit) and Pisces (Mina in Sanskrit), both highly moral signs. Sagittarius represents the masculine energy of Jupiter, while Pisces represents its feminine energy. While Sagittarius manifests the creative energy in life, Pisces expresses it. People who have either of these two signs in their Birth Chart should pay attention to Swadhisthana Chakra and its functioning. If they are unbalanced in their intake of Jupiterian energy, they may require Spiritual work to optimise this Chakra.

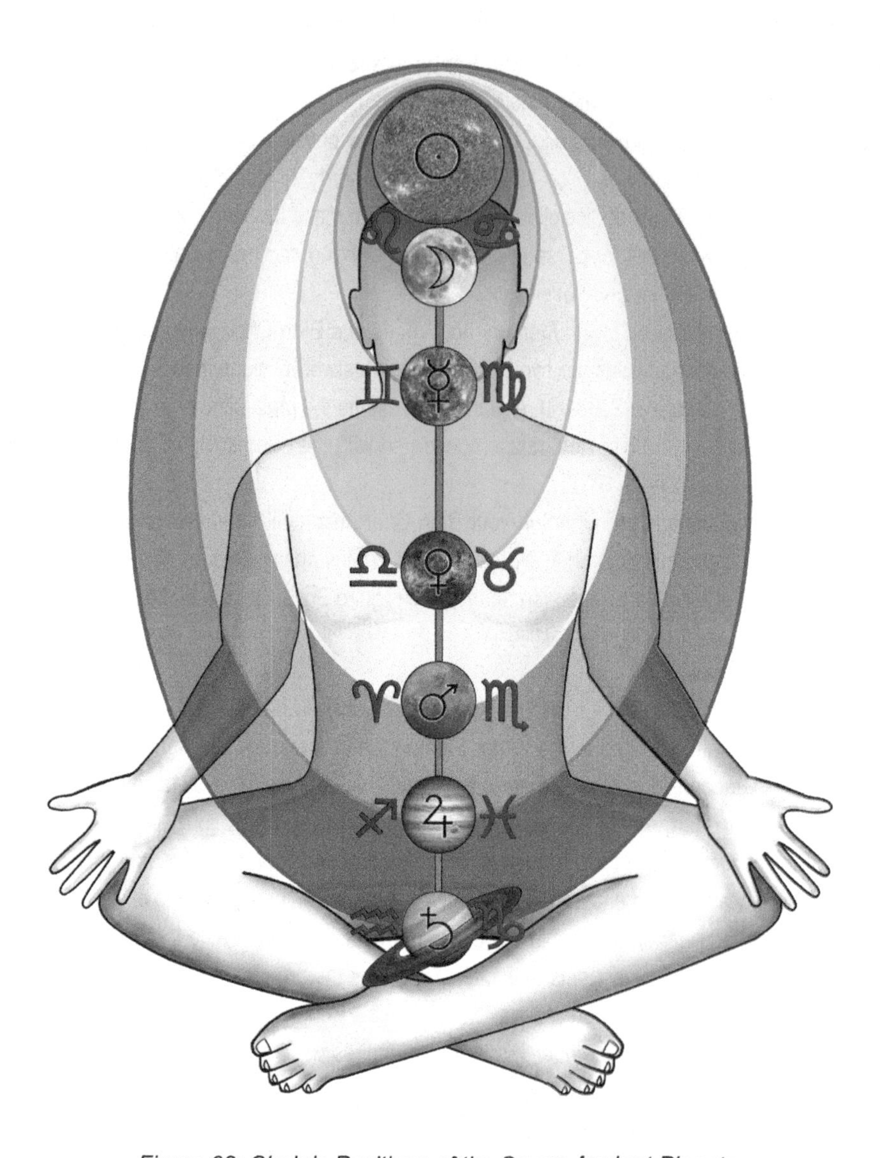

Figure 62: Chakric Positions of the Seven Ancient Planets

Mars/Manipura

The Planet Mars (Mangala, Angaraka, or Kuja in Sanskrit) is the fuel of the willpower which initiates action and change. It represents the Fire Element, corresponding with the masculine Manipura Chakra. Mars is the Planet of physical energy that governs the sex drive. It is the source of our personal power that provides strength and courage to the mind, body, and Soul.

Mars is exciting and dynamic; it gives us mental fortitude and makes us competitive with other human beings. Moreover, since it is the Fire Element, it allows us to build strong beliefs that aid in finding our life's purpose and the drive to carry it out.

Mars also gives us enthusiasm, passion, and the ability to take on challenges in life and overcome them through determination and persistence. It facilitates inner growth and the change necessary to continue to evolve. Martian energy is heavily focused on inner transformation since the Fire Element consumes the old to make room for the new.

As the Red Planet, Mars governs the red blood cells and oxidation in the body. If Manipura receives too much Martian energy, individuals can become destructive to themselves and others. As such, they may turn to anger, rage, tyranny, oppression and even violence. Therefore, Jupiter should always balance Mars—the Ego must be held in check by the Soul and its higher aspirations. Conversely, too little Martial energy results in being intimidated, apprehensive, cowardly, doubtful, overly changeable in personal beliefs, lacking passion and drive, and generally indifferent to life's outcomes.

In a Birth Chart, Mars has a friendly relationship with the Sun, Moon, and Jupiter, while being enemies with Mercury and neutral with Venus and Saturn. In addition, the two very ambitious and action-driven signs, Aries (Mesha in Sanskrit) and Scorpio (Vrishchika in Sanskrit), are ruled by Mars. Aries represents the masculine energy of Mars, while Scorpio represents its feminine energy. While Aries governs our projection of vitality, Scorpio affects its preservation. If either of these two signs is prominent in your Birth Chart, you should give attention to Manipura Chakra and ascertain its level of functioning. To optimise Manipura, you will require a balanced ray of Martian energy.

Venus/Anahata

The Planet Venus (Shukra in Sanskrit) is the Planet of love, desire, and pleasure. Venus is a joyful and benign Planet that brings luck in friendships and romantic relationships. It rules over our capacity to accept and express affection and enjoy beauty. Its energy gives us sex appeal since it rules the seductive arts. Since love affects our level of inspiration and imagination, Venus fuels right-brained, abstract thinking. It governs artistic expressions such as music, visual arts, dance, drama, and poetry.

Venus relates to the feminine Anahata Chakra and the Air Element, which governs our thoughts. Desires are either the by-product of lower vibrational thoughts of the Ego or higher-vibrational thoughts of the Soul. Venus has an affinity to the Fire Element; desire can easily turn into passion which fuels creativity. It also has an affinity to the Water Element since love is a powerful emotion. Remember, Air fuels both the Fire and Water Elements and gives them life.

Since Anahata is the bridge between the lower three Elemental Chakras and the higher three Spirit Chakras, Venus teaches us to love without attachment to transcend our individuality and merge with the Spirit whose essence is Divine Love. Venetian energy allows us to clear the emotional attachments to money, sex, and power created by the lower three Chakras. Doing so facilitates exploring the Spirit Element's expansive qualities that we can experience through the higher three Chakras, giving us more profound levels of understanding.

Venus is a tactile Planet, so it governs the body's sensory organs. A low dose of Venetian energy in Anahata Chakra results in unhealthy relationships, extreme attachment to worldly things, self-indulgence, and creative blockages. A deficiency in Venetian energy creates the fear of not being loved, making us insecure.

When the higher Chakras are utilized, the individual can love unconditionally. However, when the lower Chakras are dominant, love turns to lust which can be destructive to the Soul if not balanced by Mercury and its reasoning powers.

In a Birth Chart, Venus is friends with Mercury and Saturn, being enemies with the Sun and Moon and neutral with Mars and Jupiter. In addition, the two social and pleasure-oriented signs, Libra (Tula in Sanskrit) and Taurus

(Vrishabha in Sanskrit) are ruled by Venus. Libra represents the masculine energy of Venus, while Taurus represents its feminine energy. While Libra represents our capacity to express emotions, Taurus governs our emotional receptivity. If either of these two signs is influential in your Birth Chart, be mindful of Anahata Chakra to ensure it is receiving an equilibrated ray of Venetian energy.

Mercury/Vishuddhi

Mercury (Budha in Sanskrit) is the Planet of logic, reason, and communication, corresponding with the masculine Vishuddhi Chakra and the Spirit Element. Since it relates to thought processes, Mercury has an affinity to the Air Element; its correct designation would be Air of Spirit. Mercury also rules travel and the desire to experience new environments.

As Mercury rules intelligence, it influences how a person thinks and the characteristics of their mind. Mercury tempers Venus and gives structure to creative thoughts and ideas. Both hemispheres of the brain are affected by Mercury, although it is dominant in the left hemisphere that deals with linear thinking through logic and reason.

Mercury rules the brain, nerves, and respiratory system. Since it governs verbal and non-verbal communication, such as body language, Mercury affects our ability to express our thoughts. A strong influence of Mercury gives us good memory and excellent speaking and writing skills. It turns us into captivating storytellers and clever and cunning bargainers. Since it rules the voice, it gives us the power to speak and perform in public.

Mercury reflects how we see, hear, understand, and assimilate information. Too little Mercurial energy renders Vishuddhi inactive, closing ourselves off from the subtle intuitive information imparted to us by the higher Chakras. People who are low in Mercurial energy lose the ability to express their inner truth, making them lose touch with reality and live in illusion.

A deficiency in Mercurial energy often results in wrong decision making since we must think intelligently before acting. Also, if we don't balance our emotions with logic and reason, neurotic behaviour can ensue. Our ability to plan things out in our minds affects how well we can manifest our goals and dreams and whether our results will be fruitful.

Conversely, too much Mercury can make individuals sarcastic, argumentative, manipulative, and overly critical of themselves and others. Lies and deceit indicate an unbalanced Mercury, which blocks Vishuddhi Chakra while speaking the truth optimizes it.

Mercury has a friendly relationship with the Sun and Venus in Astrology while being enemies with the Moon and neutral with Mars, Jupiter, and Saturn. In addition, Mercury governs the two highly communicative signs of Gemini (Mithuna in Sanskrit) and Virgo (Kanya in Sanskrit). Gemini represents the masculine energy of Mercury, while Virgo represents its feminine energy. While Gemini is involved in the expression of ideas, Virgo governs our intake of impressions. Pay attention to Vishuddhi Chakra if you have either of these two signs in your Birth Chart. It indicates the utilization of Mercurial energy and this Chakra's need for equilibrium.

The Moon/Ajna

The Moon Planet (Chandra in Sanskrit) is the Planet of instincts, illusions, and involuntary emotions projected by the subconscious. It is highly influential on higher mental abilities such as introspection, contemplation, self-examination, and intuition because it reflects deep thoughts and emotions. The Moon affects our perceptions of reality since everything we take in must pass through the subconscious mind. Its influence affects the five senses of sight, hearing, taste, smell, and touch.

The Moon corresponds with the feminine Ajna Chakra and the Spirit Element. However, it is affiliated with the Water Element—its correct designation would be Water of Spirit. Ajna has an intimate connection with Swadhisthana, as both carry out the subconscious mind's functions that control the voluntary and involuntary emotions.

The Moon rules the night as the Sun rules the day. It governs dreams, giving clarity to visual images. As such, it impacts our imagination and creative thinking as well. The Moon is nurturing with a strong influence on growth, fertility, and conception. It is highly changeable; one moment, we can be cold and aloof while under the Moon's control, and the next moment we become intensely passionate.

In the Horoscope, the Moon Sign reflects our inner, emotional Self and is second in importance only to the Sun Sign. As the Sun is expressive of our character, the Moon expresses our personality. Since it regulates the ebb and flow of all bodies of water, the Moon rules all bodily fluids and affects the fluctuations in emotions.

The Moon is our inner core that experiences emotional reactions to environmental stimuli. Since it represents the subconscious, the Moon is the part of our personality that we may find disturbing about ourselves. It gives rise to strange, often immoral fantasies and daydreams and elicits instinctual reactions like hate and jealousy. On the other hand, the Moon also affects our call for spontaneity and desire for sensual pleasures. As two feminine Planets, the Moon and Venus have an affinity.

If the individual's Ajna Chakra is deficient in Lunar energy, their visual thoughts become dim and unclear, negatively impacting imagination, creativity, and level of inspiration. A low powered Ajna Chakra severs one's connection with intuition and deep emotions, allowing fear and anxiety to take over. The individual no longer has inner guidance, which renders them incapable of learning from life's experiences, bringing a general sense of hopelessness and depression. Low Lunar energy in Ajna Chakra also negatively impacts dreams as they become dull, blurred, and otherwise obscure. An efficient method of receiving Lunar energy is to spend time outside on a full Moon.

In Astrology, the Moon is friendly with the Sun and Mercury while neutral with Venus, Mars, Jupiter, and Saturn. It has no enemies. The Moon governs the intuitive and sensitive sign, Cancer (Kataka in Sanskrit), which is of a feminine energy quality. If Cancer is prominent in your Birth Chart, pay attention to Ajna Chakra and its functioning. It may require balancing the ray of Lunar energy through Spiritual Healing practices.

The Sun/Sahasrara

The Sun Planet (Surya in Sanskrit) is the Planet of imagination, inspiration, Spirituality, and transcendence. The Sun is the source of Pranic energy that gives life, Light, and warmth to all living things in our Solar System. All Souls in our Solar System emanate from and rely upon the Sun for sustenance.

The Sun corresponds with the Non-Dual Sahasrara Chakra and the Spirit Element. As the Sun is the Light source for our Solar System, Sahasrara is our Chakric Light source. The White Light is our source of Oneness, truth, and Universal wisdom. It represents the conscious mind, as the Moon represents the subconscious.

The Sun not only generates Light but also heat. Hence, it is affiliated with the Fire Element; its correct denomination is Fire of Spirit, implying that although it is beyond duality, it has a propensity towards the projective, masculine principle.

Love energy generates a calm and steady heat, whose essence is White Light. Therefore, when we use the term "Cosmic Consciousness," we refer to Sun-consciousness as our Solar System's source of love, Light, life, and Divine bliss.

The Sun is the fundamental expression of the individual's identity—the I. As such, it is the most critical influence in our Horoscope. It represents who we are and the essence of our Soul. Therefore, the Sun Sign is our foundational energy that influences our character and highest aspirations.

The Sun gives one excellent leadership abilities. It governs the heart, regulating our circulatory system. The Sun also gives us vitality, harmony, and equilibrium, as it balances all the opposite energies in the body. If we are deficient in the energy of the Sun, we experience blockages in Sahasrara, negatively affecting our entire Chakric system. Low levels of Light energy in the Chakric system slow down the Chakras' spin, manifesting mental, emotional, and physical issues.

The ideal way to receive Sun energy is to spend time outside on a sunny day and allow the Sun's rays to nourish your Chakras, fueling your Aura with Pranic energy. The Sun is our energy system's battery source; without it, we would perish. A full Kundalini awakening optimises Sahasrara Chakra, maximising our connection with the Sun, allowing us to access our Sun Sign's full potential.

In the Zodiac, the Sun has a friendly relationship with the Moon, Mars, and Jupiter, while enemies with Venus and Saturn and neutral with Mercury. The Sun rules the authoritative sign, Leo (Simha in Sanskrit), whose base energy is of a masculine quality. Cancer and Leo, the signs of the Moon and the Sun, represent the basic polarity of the mind in terms of emotions and reason, the subconscious and conscious Self. Notice if you have Leo in your Birth Chart and how Solar energy is affecting Sahasrara Chakra. You may need Spiritual Healing to balance your Solar current and optimise this essential Chakra.

SPIRITUAL HEALING AND EVOLUTION

As we enter the Age of Aquarius, Spiritual Evolution (Figure 63) has become of utmost importance to humanity. Since the advent of the internet and free information sharing, our collective consciousness has evolved to understand that God is not outside of us but within. As a result, existential questions that relate to our purpose in life and how to achieve real and lasting happiness have taken precedence over our quest for accruing material wealth.

The major world religions have become outdated, as all religions do after some time. They no longer hold the answers for the new generation of humans, and many are looking for alternate Spiritual methods and techniques to connect with God-the Creator. Irrespective of what religion they are born into, people have become open to trying new and old Spiritual healing practices, so long as those practices provide the results they seek.

Falling into the heading of "healing modalities," these alternative therapeutic techniques aim at balancing the mind, body, Soul in an integrative way while promoting Spiritual Evolution. Therefore, they are very appealing to Spiritual people and those looking for alternate methods to treat issues at both energetic and bodily levels.

Even though we all have the same energetic foundation, we have different inclinations. Some of us are drawn to certain Spiritual healing practices while being repelled by others. Our Ancestral energy has much to do with this propensity, as does our environmental conditioning. For this reason, it has been my goal the past four years to present the most optimal Western and Eastern Spiritual healing modalities in *Serpent Rising* and *The Magus*. I wanted to give people options and give them the most practical instructions on applying these Spiritual practices in their everyday lives.

Before covering the science and philosophy of Yoga, I want to focus on other Spiritual practices that recalibrate the Major Chakras. By healing the Chakras at a deep level, you optimise their energy flow, maximising how much Light energy the Aura can hold. The more Light is present, the higher one's vibration of consciousness is, improving the mind, body, and Soul quality and furthering one's Spiritual Evolution.

The four healing modalities that I will focus on in this section are Gemstones (Crystals), Tuning Forks, Aromatherapy, and Tattvas. These are the healing modalities I found most attractive to work with and learn about on my Spiritual journey and the ones that had the most significant impact on me. Other healing methods include but are not limited to Reiki, Acupuncture, Qigong, Tai Chi, Reflexology, Biofeedback, Ruach Healing, Past Life Regression, Hypnosis, Transcendental Meditation, and Neuro-Linguistic Programming.

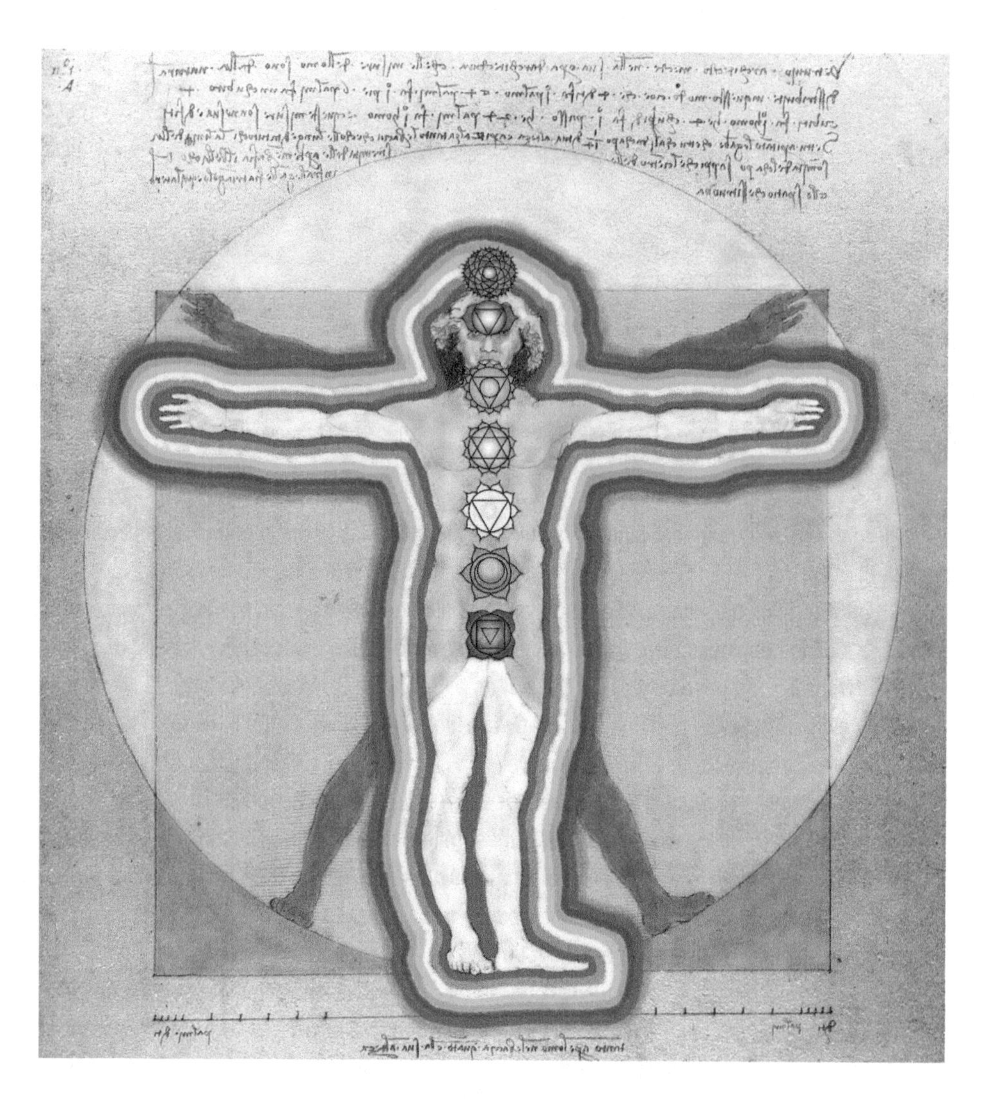

Figure 63: Spiritual Evolution

GEMSTONES (CRYSTALS)

Formed within the heart of the Earth over Aeons of time, Gemstones (Crystals) embody intense concentrations of energy. Their therapeutic use dates to approximately 5000 years ago; old Chinese texts on traditional medicine mention Gemstones, as do Ayurvedic texts from India. We find evidence of the use of Gemstones going back to before history was written—even *The Holy Bible* has over 200 references to Gemstones and their healing and protective properties.

Many Ancient civilizations and traditions, including the Olmecs from Mesoamerica and the Egyptians, used Gemstones in their sacred sites, where we found evidence of energy generation and manipulation. The practice of using Gemstones to heal the mind, body, and Soul and protect the Aura from negative energy influences continues today since they are still being used as a form of alternative healing by Spiritual practitioners alike.

A Gemstone is a precious or semi-precious stone produced by nature, found in rock formations. They are the Earth's DNA—containing records of the development of the Earth over millions of years. Most Gemstones are mineral Crystals—semi-precious stones that occur more widely in nature than precious stones. To clarify, precious stones (Ruby, Sapphire, Diamond, and Emerald) are considered Gemstones but not Crystals, whereas all Crystals in existence can be referred to as Gemstones. Also, there are certain occasionally organic materials that are not minerals (Amber, Jet, Coral, and Pearl) but are deemed Gemstones also. Because of their rarity, colour, and composition, precious stones are much more expensive on the market than semi-precious stones.

"Crystal Healing" is the term used in the Spiritual community for the therapeutic use of Crystals—the semi-precious Gemstones. Many Crystals have their molecules arranged in such a way so that they create a geometric pattern in some way, making them great energy generators and conductors for use in healing sessions. One healing session can have positive effects that last for days, including heightened awareness, inner peace and calm, increased intuition, empathy, intellectual capabilities, and a sense of love and acceptance for oneself and others.

Gemstones are generally easy to use, which makes them quite attractive to beginners in the field of Spiritual healing. However, one needs a correct understanding of the correspondences of each stone to get the most out of them since many Gemstones relate to multiple Chakras. For this reason, it is not uncommon to see authors on this subject presenting inconsistent relations between the Gemstones and the Chakras.

As mentioned, there are hundreds of Gemstones in existence, and each one has its unique vibration and specific energetic properties determined by its colour and other factors. By learning about the varieties of Gemstones and their application, you can harness their full healing potential. Gemstone energy medicine uses the body's inherent healing force to nourish and heal the energies in the Aura. When placed on the body, the Crystal's vibration induces the Lower Astral Body (Etheric Body) sheath—the lowest and most dense Subtle Body after the Physical Body and one that links us with the higher Subtle Bodies of the Elements of Water, Fire, Air, and Spirit.

The Physical Body and the Lower Astral Body relate to the Earth Element—the contact point for Crystal energies to enter into our Aura. Quarried from deep within our Planet, all Crystals have an Earthy component, even if their properties relate to other Elements. For this reason, Crystal work is very effective in treating ailments associated with the physical body. However, although we can use Crystals and other stones to cure mental issues, emotional disorders, or acute illnesses, their ultimate purpose is to help us reach our highest potential as Spiritual human beings.

As our Chakras vibrate at a specific frequency, it makes us naturally receptive to the vibrations of Gemstones since we can align our vibrations with theirs. Gemstones have the most potent vibratory effect when placed directly on the body in areas that correspond with the Major Chakras. The energy emitted by the Gemstone directly affects the Chakra, thereby removing any blockages or stagnations within it. Thus, the Chakras regain their optimal functioning, which, in turn, facilitates the free flow of energy in the Nadis. In essence, this is how the practice of Crystal Healing works.

Gemstone use does not begin and end with Spiritual Healing, though. We can also incorporate Gemstones to enhance the power of other energy healing modalities and even help us manifest a desire or goal. For example, if you want an energy boost while meditating, simply hold a Gemstone in your hand with corresponding properties you are trying to induce into your Aura. Or, if you desire to attract romantic love or want a new job or career, you can devise a ritual where you infuse your intention into a Gemstone with properties that can attract those things to you. In fact, since they relate to the Earth Element, Crystals are powerful tools to aid in manifestation.

Gemstones are essentially like batteries with different properties that we can use in various ways. Another example of their use is to add protection to a room or to infuse positive energy into it, making it a sacred space. To raise the vibration of an area, place Gemstones with specific properties in certain parts of the room, especially the corners or in front of a window where Light comes in. However, be careful with Clear Quartz in front of a window since it focuses the Sun's rays and may start a fire.

Placing various Gemstones around a space creates a grid-like energy pattern that connects them, beaming energy back and forth to provide the desired effects and influence anyone that comes into this space. This use of Gemstones has existed since time immemorial which is why we find them strategically placed in many Ancient sites from various cultures and traditions.

Although Gemstones have many uses, in this section, we will focus primarily on Chakric Healing and using Crystals to aid in the Spiritual Evolution process. Remember that by healing one's energy at a deep level, their mental, emotional and physical state improves and their ability to manifest the life they desire.

CRYSTAL FORMATIONS AND SHAPES

Crystals can be found in many shapes and forms with many natural formations such as Geodes, Clusters, Freeform Crystals, and others that humans quarried and cut into specific shapes (Figure 64). Geodes are rounded rock formations that expose a beautiful crystalline interior once they are broken in half. Clusters, however, are groups of Crystals extracted from Geodes. Each Cluster is special and unique, making no two Clusters the same.

Both Geodes and Clusters have powerful vibrational energies since they contain many Crystal points combined. Unlike Clusters, though, Geodes have all of their terminations located on the inside. Both varieties also come in different shapes and sizes and are often used in decoration because of their visual appeal. Clusters are more often used during healing sessions to amplify and focus their natural energies.

Freeform Crystals, or "Rough" Crystals, as they are called, are irregularly shaped, unpolished chunks of semi-precious stone. They have been cut and carved instead of polished to show off the natural beauty of the individual Crystal. The smaller cut Freeform Crystals can be used in healing sessions. In contrast, the larger ones are more often used to add positive, protective energy to a space or simply as decorative elements.

Tumbled stones are the standard cut and polished shape of Crystal on the market, with forms that vary in size and shape. Generally, they are on the smaller side, though, up to one inch in diameter, making them useful for Crystal Healing since they can be placed directly on the body to generate and manipulate energy.

Next, we have Crystals that are carved and polished into different geometric and symbolic shapes. This custom has existed for thousands of years within various Ancient traditions and cultures. Since all geometric shapes direct energy in different ways, by carving a Crystal into a shape, we change its energy output and enhance specific properties, allowing us to work with the stone in more ways. Some of the more widely produced Crystal shapes are the Crystal Points, Wands, Hearts, Spheres, Eggs, Pyramids, and Shards. Other less commonly made Crystal Shapes include Rods and Slabs, to name a few.

Crystal Points (Towers) are generally larger stones that terminate at a point, generating more directed energy. They are often six or eight-sided and shaped like Crystal Wands but bigger. Crystal Points occur naturally in many Cluster types, including Amethyst, Clear Quartz, and Citrine. They are usually cut at the base to stand upright and sought after by energy healers since they carry more natural energy. Larger pieces of Rough Crystals can also be cut to a point to direct energy. These are less expensive than Towers, making them more desirable to energy healers.

Crystal Wands come in a variety of shapes, sizes, and types. Like Crystal Points, Wands are cut to a point to help amplify and direct the energy of a Crystal. Some Wands are double terminated with a point at each end of the Crystal. In contrast, Massage Wands are fully rounded and smooth at each end. Crystal Wands are typically used to heal different parts of the Aura. We can also use them to optimize the spin of a Chakra, as will be given in a Chakra Healing technique at the end of this chapter.

Crystal Hearts are heart-shaped stones that come in various sizes. Generally, they have properties that relate to the Heart Chakra, such as the Rose Quartz, Malachite, and Green Aventurine. They emit energy in a loving and gentle manner, giving us a sense of peace and harmony. Crystal Hearts symbolically remind us to balance and centre ourselves by tuning into Anahata Chakra and allowing our Soul to guide us in life. When used in a healing session, the Crystal Heart become the central focus since it serves to infuse the Spirit into the lower Elements, bringing about a complete transformation of mind, body, and Soul.

A Crystal Sphere is a Three-Dimensional object with every point on its surface being the same distance from the centre. Spheres are reflective, emanating energy outwards in equal directions, making them perfect tools for scrying, otherwise called "Crystal Gazing." The purpose of scrying is to receive Divine downloads or visions of things that will happen in the future or to obtain information concerning something happening right now that we are unaware of consciously.

Crystal Eggs are similar to Crystal Spheres since they emit energy from all sides but with a focal point at the top. Crystal Eggs contain a symbolic component that relates to personal transformation and renewal. They help tune us into our feminine energy, our receptive, passive side of Being connected to the Water Element. Crystal Eggs are known for tuning us into our subconscious mind, where the Spiritual transfiguration first begins to take place.

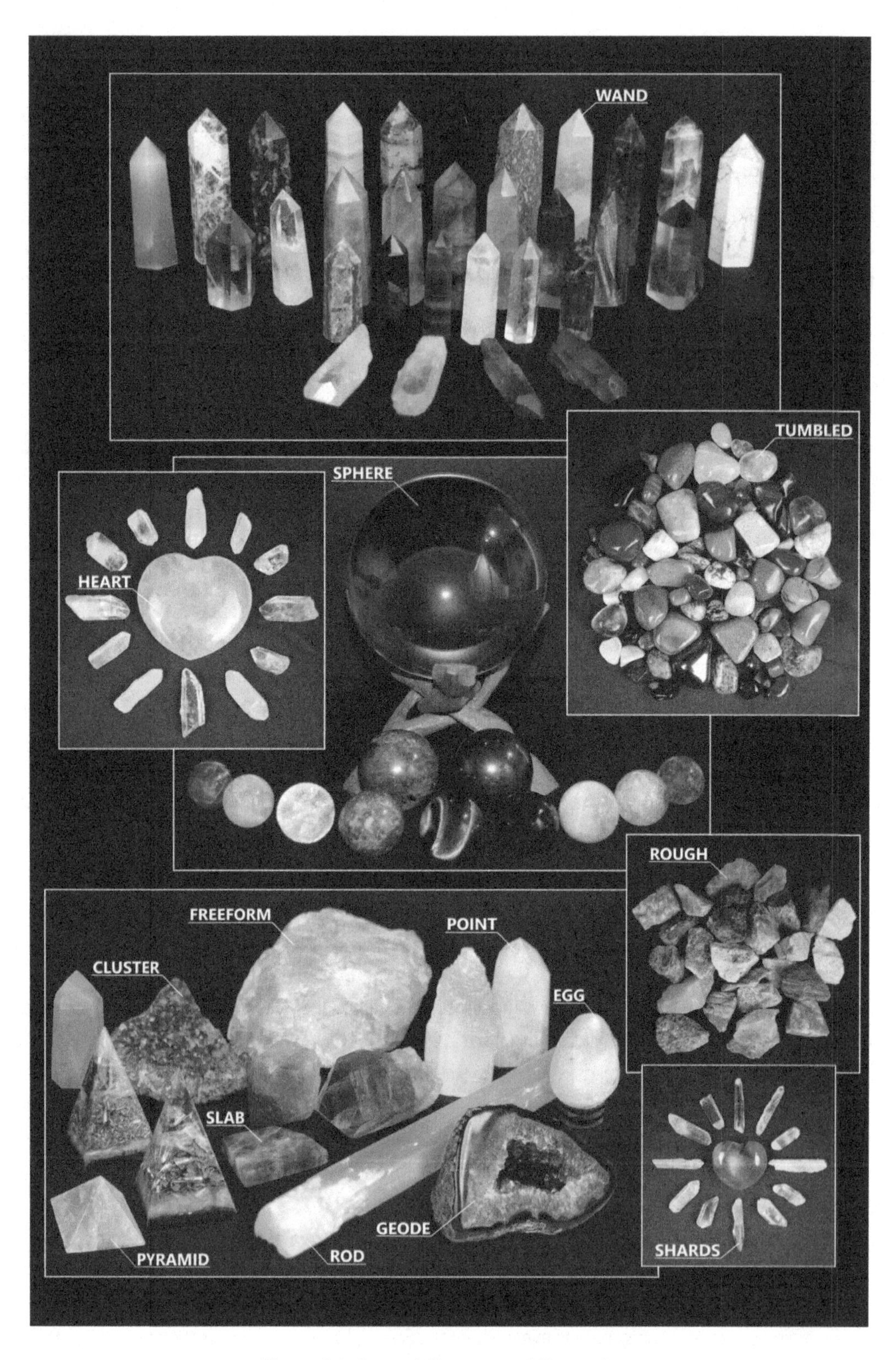

Figure 64: Crystal Shapes and Formations

Crystal Pyramids are Three-Dimensional figures with a flat base and four sides that meet at a point. They draw energy from the Earth and project it upwards through the termination point. They can be made of an individual Crystal type or a combination of different Crystals, such as in Orgonite Pyramids that are often used to absorb and shield from electromagnetic radiation.

Crystal Shards are stick-like smaller pieces of rough Crystal, most frequently used to add energy to other stones during healing sessions. The three most common types of Crystal Shards are Clear Quartz, Amethyst, and Rose Quartz. Crystal Rods (Sticks) are unpolished and raw pieces of Crystal cut into a staff-like shape that vary in size. Since Selenite is quite brittle and hard to shape by machines, it is usually sold in this form. And finally, Crystal Slabs are cut and polished slices of Crystal with rough sides that preserve the natural look of the stone. The larger sizes are generally used in decoration, while we can use the smaller ones (up to 2" diameter) for healing purposes.

TWENTY-FOUR SIGNIFICANT GEMSTONE TYPES

Amber

This stone is created by fossilized resin from ancient trees; it comes in various yellow, gold, and brown shades. Amber has properties of the Fire Element, making it a powerful healer and cleanser of the body, mind, and Spirit. It renews the nervous system while balancing our inner energies. It also absorbs negative energy while grounding and connecting us to Ancient wisdom. Amber is associated with Manipura Chakra and the Sun Planet. It relates to the Taurus and Leo Zodiac Signs. Amber helps us overcome depression while stimulating the intellect and promoting self-confidence, altruism, self-trust, decision-making, and inner peace. This stone also gives us the courage to establish healthy boundaries in our relationships while protecting us from people who drain our energy.

Amethyst

A transparent purple stone that enhances Spiritual awareness by unlocking a higher level of consciousness. Vibrating at a high frequency, Amethyst has Spirit Element properties that create a ring of protection around one's Aura, blocking lower frequencies and energies. Amethyst also aids in meditation while increasing one's intuition, inner guidance, and wisdom. It boosts our psychic abilities by stimulating the Third Eye and Crown Chakras. In addition, Amethyst promotes emotional and mental balance by clearing out negativity and confusion. It is known for warding off nightmares and encouraging positive dreams. Amethyst is related to the Aquarius and Pisces Astrological Signs with an affinity to Uranus and Neptune Planets and the Air and Water Elements.

Aquamarine

This green-blue transparent to opaque stone has calming energies that reduce stress while quieting the mind and bringing Spiritual awareness. It connects us with the powers of Water and Air since it is associated with the Planet Jupiter while having an affinity to Uranus and Neptune. Aquamarine is known for boosting brainpower and intellect. Relating directly to Vishuddhi Chakra, this stone improves our communication abilities while giving us the courage to express our inner truth. It soothes our fears and increases our sensitivity to the energies in our environment. Aquamarine sharpens our intuition while clearing creative blockages. It helps us build tolerance and responsibility while improving our problem-solving abilities. This stone aligns the Chakras while shielding the Aura from negative energies. It clears the consciousness of emotionally charged thoughts, promoting harmony and balance, making it an excellent tool for meditation. Aquamarine relates to the Gemini, Scorpio, and Pisces Zodiac Signs.

Black Obsidian

This dark black reflective stone comes from molten lava that has cooled so quickly that it didn't have the time to crystallize. Related to the Earth Element, this stone has a grounding and calming effect on the mind and the emotions, helping us stay centred and focused on the task at hand. Its black colour draws the user inwards to the void of space, where our inner truth lies. As such, this truth-enhancing stone has reflective qualities that expose one's blockages, weaknesses, and flaws. It acts as a mirror for the Soul that gives us vitality to find our life's purpose. The Black Obsidian's energetic properties keep negative thoughts at bay, promoting a positive outlook on life. We can also use it to deflect the negative energies of others and remove unwanted Spiritual influences. This stone relates to the Earth Star Chakra and the Planet Earth, with an affinity to Pluto and the Fire Element. Its energy is also characteristic of the Scorpio Zodiac Sign.

Bloodstone

This dark green to black stone with red blood-like spots helps remove energy blockages from the Aura while boosting vitality, motivation, courage, creativity, stamina, endurance, and overall energy. Associated with the Planet Mars and the Fire Element, the Bloodstone purifies and cleanses the lower three Elemental Chakras while equilibrating the Heart Chakra. It has grounding properties, reducing stress, irritability, impatience, and aggression, allowing us to live in the present moment. It also protects one from harmful environmental energy, such as disruptive electromagnetic frequencies. In addition, this stone is excellent for improving blood circulation and balancing hormones, bringing coherence to the physical body. Ancient soldiers used the Bloodstone to ward off evil and to invoke the warrior's energy. The Bloodstone is associated with Aries and Pisces, the two Zodiac Signs ruled by Mars. It has an affinity with the Earth Element.

Carnelian

This translucent orange to brownish-red stone stimulates creativity and imagination, helping us give birth to new projects. Carnelian has a powerful effect on emotions, so it is directly related to Swadhisthana Chakra. Known as a stone of action and moving forward in life, Carnelian aids us in finding solutions when experiencing emotional blockages. It has properties of the Fire Element, motivating us to achieve success in business and other matters. It also helps us in processing negative emotions such as anger, jealousy, fear, sadness, confusion, loneliness while protecting us from other people's projected negative energies. Carnelian can also be used as a tool to get us involved in creative expressions such as visual art, music, dance, or writing. This stone is associated with Aries, Leo, and Virgo Zodiac Signs. In addition, it has an affinity with Mars and the Sun.

Citrine

This transparent yellowish-orange stone brings vitality, confidence, courage, happiness, and joy to one's life. Since it relates to Hara and the Solar Plexus Chakras, Citrine is a very energizing stone, boosting one's Pranic energy, creativity, motivation, and problem-solving skills. Citrine works well for one's self-respect while promoting the expression of our inner truth. It has properties relating to the Air and Fire Elements. Its golden light rays draw out insecurities stemming from a negative mindset and replace them with positivity. This stone also relates to the Gemini Astrological Sign and the Planet Mercury. It has an affinity with the Sun, which is why we can use it to energize all the Chakras.

Clear Quartz

This transparent stone carries the full spectrum of Light within it, making it a master healer on all levels. Relating directly to the Spirit Element, the Clear Quartz can be used for meditation, channelling, dreamwork, energy healing while connecting us with our Higher Selves. Due to its deep cleansing properties, the Clear Quartz clears any stagnant and negative energy out of the Aura. It promotes positivity, mental and emotional clarity, and focus. The Clear Quartz enhances one's metaphysical abilities and attunes us to our Spiritual purpose and True Will. Since its healing uses are wide range, this stone works on all the Chakras. However, as it is very high vibrational, the Clear Quartz works best on Sahasrara Chakra and the Transpersonal Chakras above the head. Its energy also amplifies the positive aspects of all the Astrological Signs. We can use clear Quartz to purify, cleanse, and boost the energy of other Crystals. Since it is easily programmable with intention and thoughts, it can also be used as a talisman to attract whatever one desires.

Fluorite

This transparent stone is a mix of purple, blue, green, and transparent colours. It is excellent for neutralizing negative energy, detoxing the mind, and bringing harmony to mind, body, and Soul. Fluorite brings out one's inner genius by stabilizing the Aura and heightening focus. Associated with Ajna Chakra, this stone grounds and integrates Spiritual energies, heightening psychic powers and intuition. Since it raises one's consciousness to the Spiritual Plane, Fluorite is a good stone for meditation and deep sleep. Its properties relate to the Air, Water, and Spirit Elements, invoked by its colours: its green energy infuses the Air Element, purifying the heart, the blue brings in the Water Element, calming the mind, while the purple colour integrates the metaphysical properties of the Spirit Element. The clear, transparent energy, the guiding force of the stone, realigns all the Chakras and Elements into an integrated whole, enabling one to function mentally, emotionally, and physically at their optimal capacity. Besides its profound healing properties, Fluorite is one of the most stunning crystals on the market, making it a popular stone in households.

Garnet

This transparent to translucent ruby-red stone boosts vitality, courage, creativity, determination, change, and the ability to manifest your goals. Associated with Mars and the Fire Element, Garnet cleanses all the Chakras while re-energising them. It activates and strengthens the survival instinct while invoking unconditional love, passion, and Spiritual devotion. It grounds one's chaotic energy, balancing the emotions and creating expanded awareness of oneself and surroundings. It is the stone of Spiritual awakening whose energy is known to stir the Kundalini into activity when used side-by-side with Yogic practices designed to awaken this energy. Garnet also has strong links with the Pituitary Gland as it promotes body regeneration while boosting metabolism, the immune system, and one's sex drive. This stone is associated with Aries, Scorpio, and Capricorn Zodiac Signs.

Green Aventurine

This translucent green stone is known for manifesting prosperity and wealth. It amplifies one's intentions to create more abundance in life. Associated with the Heart Chakra and the Planet Venus, Green Aventurine brings harmony to all aspects of Being. It balances one's masculine and feminine energy, promoting a feeling of well-being. It also reinforces leadership qualities and decisiveness while fostering compassion and empathy. Green Aventurine enhances creativity while enabling one to see different alternatives and possibilities. It stabilizes the mind, soothing emotions and calming irritation and anger. This stone protects one from psychic vampires. Since it aids in manifestation, Green Aventurine has powerful Earth Element properties.

Hematite

This metallic black to steel grey stone provides a grounding and balancing energy that helps dissolve mental limitations. Hematite uses the magnetic qualities of our Yin-Yang energies to balance the Nadis and bring stability to the nervous system. It removes chaotic energies from the Aura while repelling the negative thoughts from other people. It also gives us a feeling of security while boosting self-esteem, courage, and willpower. Hematite's calming vibrations make it the perfect stone for people suffering from anxiety, stress, and nervousness. This stone is known to help overcome compulsions and addictions. Its relaxing effect on the physical body enhances our connection to Planet Earth. Hematite is related to Muladhara Chakra and the Earth Element with an affinity to Mars and the Element of Fire. Because it stimulates concentration, focus, and original thoughts, Hematite has specific properties akin to the Aries and Aquarius Zodiac Signs.

Kyanite

This deep blue stone instantly aligns all the Chakras and Subtle Bodies. Associated with the Causal and Soul Star Chakras, Kyanite balances our Yin-Yang energies while removing blockages and restoring Prana to the body. Kyanite brings peace and serenity; it eliminates all confusion and stress and improves communication and the intellect. Kyanite also balances the Throat Chakra since it encourages self-expression while aligning us to our inner truth. It awakens our psychic faculties, activating our innate ability to communicate telepathically. Kyanite's soothing blue colour opens us up to the Spiritual and Divine Realms, allowing us to contact our Spirit guides, whether through meditation or dreams. Its energy is Fifth-Dimensional while having certain properties akin to the Air Element. Kyanite is a powerful transmitter and amplifier of high-frequency energies that awakens us to our True Self and purpose in life. This stone never requires energetic clearing since it cannot retain negative vibrations.

Lapis Lazuli

This opaque deep dark blue stone with metallic gold flecks opens the Third Eye, improving intuition, Spiritual insight, inner guidance, and psychic abilities. Mediums often use Lapis Lazuli to contact higher Cosmic Planes and enhance their channelling ability. This stone is suitable for improving memory and is often used in dreamwork. Lapis Lazuli has Water Element properties that have a calming effect on the nervous system, improving concentration and focus. Its use is beneficial with studying and learning since it enhances one's ability to digest knowledge and understand things deeply. One can also use it to overcome addictions and trauma since it promotes emotional healing. As it harmonizes all aspects of the Self, Lapis Lazuli helps one overcome stress and anxiety, facilitating inner peace and promoting deep sleep. Lapis Lazuli is related to Ajna Chakra and the Planet Jupiter.

Malachite

This opaque dark-green stone with light and dark green and blue-green bands protects one against negative energies while releasing unhealthy emotional patterns that prevent our Souls from further advancement. Associated with the Heart Chakra and the Planet Venus, Malachite realigns the mind with the heart, helping one grow Spiritually. It invokes love, compassion, and kindness into our lives, healing past trauma while raising our empathic abilities. Malachite teaches us to take responsibility for our actions, thoughts, and feelings while encouraging risk-taking and change. It is known to guard against radiation while clearing electromagnetic pollution. Malachite has an Earthy, grounding component; it has an affiliation with the Capricorn Zodiac Sign.

Moldavite

This olive green or dull green stone takes us beyond our limits and boundaries to otherworldly dimensions. It is technically a Tektite, which is a group of natural glasses formed by meteorite impacts. As such, Moldavite is quite literally out of this world. Its energetic properties are Fifth Dimensional; they relate to the higher Divine Planes of consciousness, which we can contact through complete transcendence. Moldavite allows us to communicate with our Higher Selves, Ascended Masters, and other high-vibrational Beings. This stone is also reported to open us up to Extraterrestrial contact through consciousness. Associated with the highest Transpersonal Chakra, the Stellar Gateway, Moldavite's metaphysical properties enable us to transcend Time and Space. As such, it can be used to obtain knowledge related to our past lives and to clear any unwanted baggage that we carried into this incarnation. On a more temporal level, Moldavite helps us uncover emotions that keep us stuck in unhappy situations in life. It allows us to move forward towards finding out our Soul's purpose.

Moonstone

This milky-white stone with a luminescent glow is great for boosting one's feminine energy, enhancing intuition, psychic abilities, and balancing our emotions. It is related to the two feminine Major Chakras, Swadhisthana and Ajna, while directly connected to the Causal/Bindu Chakra. With Water Element properties, the Moonstone keeps us in emotional balance, enabling us to go with the flow of life without being too attached. It invokes passivity, receptivity and reflection, allowing us to perceive the world around us without judgement. The Moonstone is also known to improve negative belief patterns while enhancing our empathic abilities. Its use promotes a higher sense of consciousness and Spiritual growth. The Moonstone is related to the Cancer Zodiac Sign and the Moon Planet; its energy is more potent when the Moon is waxing (increasing) than waning (decreasing). When it is a full Moon, the Moonstone is known for inducing Lucid Dreams. Ancient people used the Moonstone to help with female reproductive system issues.

Red Jasper

This red stone is excellent for providing protection and stability to the Aura while absorbing negative energy. It can neutralize radiation and other forms of electromagnetic and environmental pollution as well. Its red-hot vibration increases our energy levels, inspiring a positive attitude while grounding all undesired energies. Red Jasper provides courage to be assertive and mental endurance to complete any tasks. It has Fire Element characteristics; Red Jasper is associated with Muladhara Chakra and the Aries Zodiac Sign, with an affinity to Saturn. This stone sustains and supports us through stressful times, bringing about emotional stability and peace of mind. It stimulates our imagination, motivating us to put our ideas into action. Since it fires up our energy system, the Red Jasper also regenerates and rejuvenates our passions and sex drive.

Rose Quartz

A transparent to translucent pink coloured stone that balances the Heart Chakra with its loving and peaceful energy. It invokes Divine Love, mercy, compassion, tolerance, and kindness into the Aura. The stone's pink colour vibration activates a bridge between the upper three Spirit Chakras and the lower three Elemental Chakras. Creating this bridge is crucial to synthesizing the Spiritual Self with the human physical Self. With properties of the Water Element, the Rose Quartz makes one receptive, teaching us to love ourselves and others through trust, forgiveness, and acceptance. Its use is beneficial during traumatic times since it soothes emotions at a deep level. It is calming to the entire nervous system, reducing stress and anxiety. Rose Quartz is the ideal stone to help one attract a romantic partner into their life since it increases one's level of unconditional love in the Heart Chakra. It is related to the Libra and Taurus Astrological Signs and the Planet Venus. The Rose Quartz can also be used as a sleep aid and heal any issues related to the physical heart.

Selenite

This reflective, milky-white stone is a powerful tool to attune us to Spiritual and Divine Planes of consciousness. Its use provides Ethereal energy that connects us with our Body of Light which we can use to contact high vibrational Beings such as Angels, Archangels, and Ascended Masters in these Heavenly Realms. Associated with the Greek Goddess of the Moon, Selene, this calming stone with Spirit Element properties heals us on all levels: physical, emotional, and mental. Attributed to Sahasrara Chakra and the Soul Star Chakra, one can use Selenite to connect with their Divine purpose and anchor it to their lower consciousness. In addition, we can use this stone to tune in with our innate wisdom and realign our consciousness with love and Light. Selenite connects us with the Moon cycle and our Guardian Angels and Spirit Guides.

Smoky Quartz

This translucent light to dark brown stone maintains one's protective energies while deflecting negative vibes. Smoky Quartz is known for creating a protective circle around oneself during Spiritual ceremonies and rituals. We can also use it for deflecting electromagnetic frequencies emitted by electronics. With Earth and Air Element properties, the Smoky Quartz grounds all mind chatter while raising concentration, making it a perfect companion to meditation. This stone helps eliminate fear, nervousness, and anxiety while giving us a feeling of security. It is known to amplify masculine energy and survival instincts. The Smoky Quartz is often recommended for treating depression and emotional stress since it drives out darkness while bringing in positive energy. Smoky Quartz is associated with the Earth Star Chakra and the Planet Saturn. It also relates to the Capricorn Zodiac Sign.

Sodalite

This opaque dark blue with white and black streaks stone is excellent for improving intuition, psychism, creative expression, and communication. Related to Vishuddhi and Ajna Chakras, Sodalite raises one's consciousness to the Spiritual Plane, which brings the higher mind to the physical level. By raising one's Spiritual perception, Divination and meditative practices become intensified. With properties related to the Air and Water Elements, Sodalite is a good study aid as it removes mental confusion while raising concentration, focus, and the ability to recall information.

In addition, it increases one's reasoning abilities, objectivity, and discernment. Sodalite also stabilizes the emotions, bringing inner peace, making it a good tool for overcoming panic attacks. In addition, it enhances self-esteem, self-acceptance, and trust in oneself. It has an affinity to the Planet Jupiter and the Sagittarius Zodiac Sign.

Tiger's Eye

This opaque brown and gold stone with lighter bands of those two colours combines Solar and Earth energies to invoke confidence, courage, motivation, protection, and emotional balance. Tiger's Eye supports integrity, pride, security and aids us in accomplishing our goals and dreams. It is associated with Swadhisthana Chakra while having an affinity with Muladhara (Earth) and Manipura (Fire) Chakras and the Elements that rule them. Since its energy is directly related to the Sun, Tiger's Eye sparks the imagination while keeping us grounded in our Spiritual and material aspirations and pursuits. It connects us to our Souls, which empowers us and opens us up to our fullest potential. Its use lightens up our outlook on life, bringing mental clarity and positivity, even when faced with adversity. Tiger's Eye helps us master our emotions while releasing negative feelings towards others, such as jealousy. It has an affinity with the Capricorn and Leo Zodiac Signs.

Turquoise

This opaque bluish-green to greenish-blue stone is excellent for communication since it aids in articulating inner feelings while removing blocks to self-expression. It relates to Vishuddhi, the Throat Chakra, where the masculine and feminine energies become balanced through the Spirit Element. Turquoise is beneficial for connecting us with our inner truth while shielding us from people's negative emotions. With properties of the Air, Water, and Fire Elements, Turquoise balances mood swings while boosting inspiration that aids us mentally when experiencing creative blocks. In addition, it helps with channelling higher wisdom and expressing it verbally or through the written word. Turquoise is related to Jupiter and Mercury Planets and the Gemini, Virgo, and Sagittarius Zodiac Signs. It has been a prevalent stone used in jewellery throughout the ages because of its striking colour and energy properties. Native Americans, especially, have been wearing it for thousands of years to connect with Cosmic energies.

CLEANSING GEMSTONES

Gemstones become programmed with energy over time. It is their nature to do so, mainly if they have been handled by other people or even yourself when you were in an unbalanced state of mind. Therefore, before using Gemstones for healing purposes, it is crucial to "clear" them of any residual energy. Clearing a Gemstone will return it to its optimal, neutral state, which is essential, especially when doing a healing session on someone new. But even if you are performing healing on yourself, it helps to clear the Gemstones often as they are most potent when their energies are reset.

I will discuss a few methods that I found work best to clear Gemstones. Keep in mind that if you are familiar with how to clear the energy of Tarot Cards as outlined in *The Magus,* you can utilize those same methods to clear Gemstones as well. The Full Moon Cleanse is especially useful since the rays of the Moon are very efficient to dispel old energies from Gemstones and return them to their optimal vibration.

The quickest, most popular, and perhaps most efficient way to cleanse a Gemstone is to place it in saltwater. Water by itself, especially from a natural stream, works well to cleanse a Gemstone, but when you pour it in a glass (not metal or plastic) and add sea salt, it makes for a more powerful cleanse. Be sure to use sea salt only since table salt contains aluminium and other chemicals.

Make sure that the Gemstone is wholly submerged in the water and leave it in there for 24 hours so it has time to reset completely. A Gemstone that requires a much deeper and thorough cleansing can be left in there for up to one week. Afterwards, rinse your Gemstones in cool running water to remove any remaining salt. It is recommended to dispose of the saltwater after since it would have absorbed the negative unwanted energies.

Keep in mind that even though saltwater is the most optimal method of cleansing a Gemstone, it can have a harmful effect on some Gemstones and even change their appearance and properties. For example, porous stones that contain metal or have water in them should not be left in saltwater. Gemstones that should be kept away from salt include Opal, Lapis Lazuli, Pyrite, and Hematite, to name a few.

PROGRAMMING GEMSTONES

Other than being used for energy healing, Gemstones can also be programmed with a specific intention to manifest a goal. Gemstones are known throughout history to be used as tools to help connect conscious thoughts with the body. Thoughts are powerful because they direct energy. When one uses a programmed Gemstone, its frequency helps to magnify the thoughts and intentions, thereby aiding the manifestation process.

Although many people use Gemstones to manifest material things for them, such as a new girlfriend or a car, I have always believed that focusing on your Spiritual transformation instead would be more propitious in the long run. After all, attracting something to yourself that your Ego wants but that does not further your Soul's progression will stagnate your Spiritual Evolution progress since you will have to discard that thing eventually to move ahead. Therefore, if you focus on Enlightenment instead and programme Gemstones to reach this goal, your material life will fall into place in due time.

You can programme a Gemstone to focus its energy on something you desire to achieve or alter within yourself, thereby magnifying your intent. Thus, the Gemstone becomes a talisman, a self-generating energy device (battery) that adds the necessary fuel to your willpower to achieve your goal.

Find a place where you can be on your own for this exercise. Before beginning the process of programming a Gemstone, you must make your intention or purpose clear in what you are trying to achieve through its help. Construct a simple sentence with your desire ingrained within it, framed from the affirmative viewpoint. If you want help with developing better memory, for example, or increasing your creativity or inspiration, make your intention clear in your sentence. Refer to Table 1 at the end of this chapter for the correspondences between the Gemstones and human expressions/powers.

You must then cleanse the Gemstone and remove any pre-programmed energies from it. To do so, perform one of the cleansing techniques previously mentioned. Afterwards, hold the Gemstone in your hand and connect with it by going into a meditative state. Feel its energy pouring into your Heart Chakra through your palms become one with it. Once you have made a connection, you can begin to programme it.

Speak to the stone out loud as you would to a friend. Make it clear what you need help with. If you feel its energy becomes negative concerning what you are asking of it, you will need to find another stone. The connection between you and the stone must be positive for this to work.

Now begin to repeat your sentence, which you will use like a Mantra. Your sentence is Magickal since you will use it to manifest the reality you desire. Keep repeating the Mantra for a few minutes and feel the stone heat up in your hand while charging it. Once you feel you have charged the stone sufficiently with your willpower, end the exercise.

You now have a potent device that will help you achieve whatever it is you need help with. Store the stone in white linen and carry it with you until what you asked of it manifests. If you feel you need to reprogram the stone or add more charge to it, you can always hold it in your hand, make a connection, and repeat your Mantra to programme it further.

CHAKRA HEALING WITH GEMSTONES

The following Crystal Healing technique can be done on yourself or on other people. When doing it on yourself, create a space in which you can relax and meditate without being disturbed. If you want to burn some incense to get you in the right mind-state, then do so. You will need to be lying down comfortably for this exercise, so use a pillow if you wish. You should be in a relaxed and meditative state of mind, practising mindfulness.

Breath control is one of the essential components for entering a meditative state of mind, which is a prerequisite when working with all Spiritual Healing modalities. For optimal results, use the Four-Fold Breath (Sama Vritti) technique that you can find in the "Pranayama Exercises" chapter in the Yoga section of this book. This breathing exercise will calm down your inner energies and raise the vibration of your consciousness, opening you up to receiving the healing. You can use it in isolation for a few minutes before the healing session and during the healing session to keep yourself balanced.

If you are performing Crystal Healing on someone else, you can include a hands-on healing component to this exercise for optimal results. However, it would be helpful if you determined which Chakras require extra attention before starting the Chakra Healing exercise. This information can then also be applied if you wish to add the use of Crystal Wands to optimise the spin of Chakras.

Scan each Chakra using the palm of your non-dominant hand to intuit whether it is functioning well or its energy feels stagnant. Well-functioning Chakras have a ball of energy with steady heat emanating from them that you can feel on your scanning hand as pressure intensifies the more conscious contact you make with it. However, Chakras that are stagnant will create very little to no pressure on your scanning hand.

Chakra Healing with Gemstones Method (with Optional Added Elements)

To begin the exercise, place a corresponding Gemstone on each of the Seven Major Chakra points (on the front of the body) while laying down. (Use Table 1 to obtain this information.) For Sahasrara, place a Gemstone above the head. For Muladhara, you can place a Gemstone on your genitals or right below, in the area between your perineum and coccyx. If you are working with the Transpersonal Chakras, place the Soul Star Crystal six inches above the top of the head while placing the Hara Crystal directly on top of the navel (Figure 65). The Earth Star

Crystal should be placed six inches below the feet. If you are doing this exercise by yourself and are having a challenging time placing the Crystals on your body, you may get assistance from another person.

Once the Gemstones are placed, close your eyes and relax, quieting your mind for 10-30 minutes. The longer you give this exercise, the more healing energy you will obtain. It is essential to do at least 10 minutes for the energy in the Gemstones to infuse the Chakras efficiently. This exercise has a quantifiable effect, meaning that the longer you do it, the more healing you will receive. For starters, best to start with less time and then add more time as you repeat the exercise. Ideally, it would be best if you repeated this exercise daily. Let your Higher Self guide you in this process.

During the healing session, practise becoming aware of any of your body's responses to the healing treatment. Your attention may be drawn to one or more of the Gemstones where they may feel hot or cold, heavy or light. You may experience tingles, or electrical zaps, usually in the areas where the Gemstone is placed but even in other areas of the body. Simply notice them and let go. Do not dwell on what you are experiencing. This exercise should make you feel calm and relaxed but also grounded. Gemstone energy will stimulate your thoughts and emotions. Regardless, focus your attention on keeping your mind still.

Figure 65: Gemstone Placement on the Chakras

Option#1-Crystal Shards

A powerful technique for amplifying the healing in a specific Chakra (or Chakras) is to add four, eight, or twelve Clear Quartz Crystal Shards around a Chakra Gemstone to intensify its healing properties. The more Quartz Crystal Shards you add, the greater the effect will be. You can use this part of the exercise on yourself or other people. Each Quartz Crystal Shard should be pointing towards the central Gemstone, which will focus the energy into the chosen Chakra more efficiently, greatly amplifying and intensifying the healing power.

Figure 66: Amplifying a Crystal with Clear Quartz Shards

For example, you can boost the power of the Crystal placed on the Heart Chakra, such as a Rose Quartz or Malachite, since this is the Chakra of the Air Element that harmonizes the lower three Chakras of Fire, Water, and Earth while infusing the Spirit Element. Using a Heart Crystal for this purpose can be beneficial, especially a larger one that becomes the focus of the Crystal Healing session. It can also be beneficial to amplify the power of a Hara Chakra Crystal (Figure 66), like a Citrine or a Sunstone. Doing so will increase the quantity of Prana in your body, which can be used for various purposes like powering the mind or healing the body.

Option#2-Hands-on Healing

If you are performing Crystal Healing on someone else, you can use the time while they are lying down in silence to practise hands-on healing on their Chakras (Figure 67). Using your Palm Chakras, you can intentionally send healing energy into any Chakra that needs work or on all the Chakras by spending a few minutes on each if you aim to balance them.

When doing hands-on healing, it is necessary to generate Pranic energy in the chest, which requires you to bring attention to its centre and breathe from the lungs. Channel this energy now through your hands by imagining healing energy beaming out of your Palm Chakras and infusing the targeted Chakra. You should feel the heat coming from your hands and occasional zaps on your palm's surface if you are doing it right.

Figure 67: Sending Healing Energy through the Palms

Option#3-Crystal Wands

A powerful method of optimizing the spin of Chakras is to use Crystal Wands. This technique can be used on yourself or other people. If you are doing a Crystal Healing session on someone else, you can incorporate this technique on Chakras that need extra attention. It helps if you have already scanned each of the Chakras before starting the exercise. Since you will need to move the Crystal Wand circularly to optimize the spin of a Chakra, you will also need to determine whether the Chakra you want to work on spins in a clockwise or counterclockwise direction. (Use the diagram in Figure 61 to obtain this information.)

Place the Crystal Wand in front of the Crystal that sits atop the body over the targeted Chakra. Ensure that the Crystal Wand's properties correspond with the Chakra or use one that can be used on all the Chakras, like a Clear Quartz Wand. Now, begin to move it either clockwise or counterclockwise. When working closer to the body, your circles should be smaller in diameter than if you are working further away since every Chakra projects outward in a cone-like fashion. You can also pull outwards in a spiral-like manner, tracing the outside of the projecting Chakra.

By making contact with the Chakra's flowerhead, you create a vortex of energy in the Aura whose movement optimizes the spin of that particular Chakra. For best results, spend five to ten minutes on each Chakra that needs work. Unless you are performing this technique on yourself, you can work on two Chakras at a time (Figure 68).

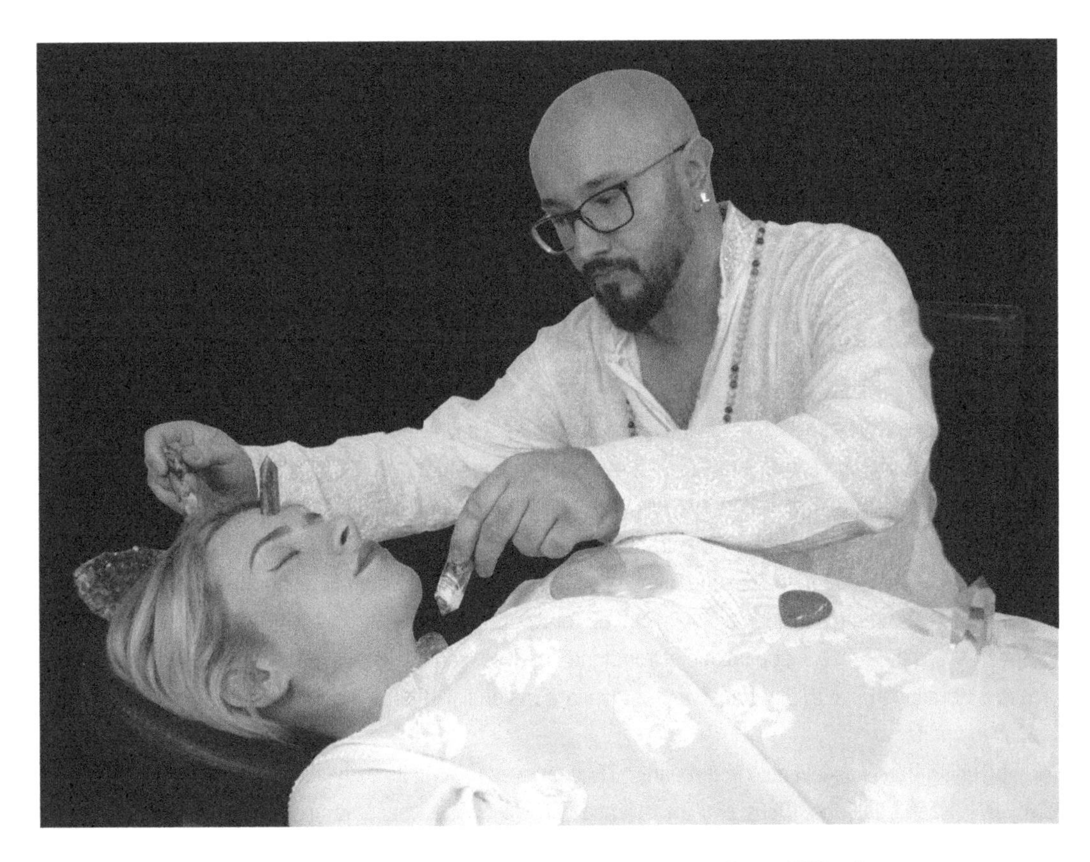

Figure 68: Optimising the Spin of Chakras with Crystal Wands

Once the Crystal Healing exercise is complete, remove the Gemstones from your body. Your Chakras will be infused with new energy, which you may feel strongly for the rest of the day. Any excess energy will dissipate during sleep while your Chakras retain some of the energy into the next day or two. Your consciousness may notice a shift in your energy immediately depending on how sensitive you are psychically. Considering you are tuning the Seven Major Chakras in this exercise, you will become balanced in mind, body, and Soul. This effect is only temporary, though, which is why I advise you to perform this exercise often.

TUNING FORKS

For thousands of years, all cultures and traditions spoke of a Universal Energy Field that connects everything in existence. *The Kybalion* refers to it as "The All" and further adds that everything within this all-encompassing Field is in constant vibration and motion. *The Holy Bible* refers to the vibration of the Universe as "the Word," while in Hinduism, it is sounded as the sacred Mantra "Om."

Within our Solar System and beyond, everything is essentially made up of Light and sound. Pythagoras taught that all the Planets create a melody of sound in their rotational movement, a vibration he referred to as the "Music of the Spheres." While Light is made up of electromagnetic waves, sound is made of mechanical waves. A mechanical wave is a vibration in Matter that transfers energy via a material like a Tuning Fork, which emanates perfect sine-wave sound patterns.

The Tuning Fork was invented in the early 1700s but was used in its early stages to tune musical instruments. However, it wasn't until the 1960s that the science of Tuning Forks became applied to the human body and its energies. As such, Tuning Forks became a powerful modality used in Sound Healing.

Sound therapy is based on the sympathetic resonance principle—one vibrating object sends out impulses through the air, thereby causing other objects in its vicinity to vibrate in harmony with it. Tuning Forks are mainly used on or around the body, sending waves of sound into targeted areas. For Chakric healing, the focus is the front of the body where the Chakric energy centres are found, or the back along the spine, again targeting the Chakric points. The Chakric energy centres happen to be where the nerve centres are found along the spine that send impulses to different body organs. For this reason, by energizing the Chakric centres, we are also stimulating the organs and optimizing their health.

Our sense of hearing that detects sound is associated with the Element of Spirit or Aethyr. For this reason, the use of Tuning Forks in Sound Healing has an immediate impact on our consciousness, as opposed to the use of other healing modalities mentioned in this section which require a more extended application period to feel their energetic effects.

The length of time a healing modality requires to impact the consciousness depends on which of the five senses it filters through and the Cosmic Plane level of its corresponding Element. Crystals, for example, since they are associated with the Earth Element, require a longer period of use during one healing session to impact the consciousness than Aromatherapy, which is related to the Water and Air Elements that are higher on the scale. Conversely, the use of Tattvas has an even more immediate impact on the consciousness than Crystals and Aromatherapy since it is associated with the Fire and Air Elements.

There are many Tuning Forks and sets on the market used for Spiritual healing. Each Tuning Fork is calibrated to emit a particular sound frequency that relates to our physical, mental, emotional, and Spiritual well-being. Some of the more widely used Tuning Fork sets include the Sacred Solfeggio, DNA activation, Tree of Life Sephiroth, and Planetary energies. In all cases, Tuning Fork sets are calibrated to match the particular energies they are meant to produce. Using these specific sounds changes our internal vibration, enabling deep cellular healing to occur.

TUNING FORK TYPES AND USE

There are weighted and unweighted versions of all Tuning Fork Sets. Weighted Tuning Forks have a round weight at the end of each prong. The heavier the Tuning Fork, the stronger or heavier its vibration is. Weighted Tuning Forks have a more robust vibration and can be used around the body and directly on it with the end of the fork, the stem, sitting upright. Unweighted Tuning Forks do not provide the same frequency as the weighted ones and are best used around the body and ears.

The Tuning Fork sets we will concern ourselves with in this book relate directly to Major and Transpersonal Chakras. The process of Chakric healing with Tuning Forks is simple. All one has to do is strike a Tuning Fork and place it on its corresponding area. Then, by listening to the Tuning Fork's vibration until it dies away, the related Chakra becomes entrained with its sound, thereby returning to its optimal, healthy state.

Since Tuning Forks are a form of Sound Healing, it is imperative to hear their vibration undisturbed, especially if you are using unweighted Forks. But I have found that even if you wear earplugs when you are in the vicinity of vibrating Tuning Forks, the soundwave induces the Aura and causes an inner change. Its intensity, however, is less than it would be if you were listening to the vibration as well.

In my experience, there is no other method as powerful and efficient to balance the Chakras as working with Tuning Forks. And this is because Sound Healing directly impacts the Spiritual Plane, which affects the Planes below it. Ceremonial Magick ritual exercises from *The Magus* are the most efficient practice of isolating each Chakra and working on it. At the same time, Tuning Forks are most optimal for balancing all the Chakras at once.

Chakra Tuning Forks also provide a renewed vitality and sense of well-being while calming and relaxing the nervous system. Balancing the Chakras silences the Ego since impulses from lower parts of the Self are neutralized. With balanced Chakras, peace of mind is obtained. In turn, this balanced state of mind enables the consciousness to connect with the Higher Self, bringing inspiration, creativity, and purposeful living into one's life.

Connecting with the Higher Self enables one to live in the moment, improving cognitive abilities and raising awareness of one's environment. Living in the Now is a rapturous process that allows us to tap into our highest potential as Spiritual human beings.

CHAKRA TUNING FORK SETS

There are two sets of Tuning Forks for the Chakras on the market, which I will discuss. Both sets work to balance and tune the Major Chakras, although the effects produced are slightly different. The first is the Seven Chakra Set (Figure 69), which often includes the Soul Star and Earth Star Forks. This Tuning Forks set is designed to contact the higher Cosmic Planes, including one's inner Spiritual energy. Through the Hermetic Principle of Correspondence

(As Above, So Below), the lower Planes will be affected, including emotions and thoughts. The Seven Chakra Tuning Fork Set is based on the rotation of the Planets around the Sun.

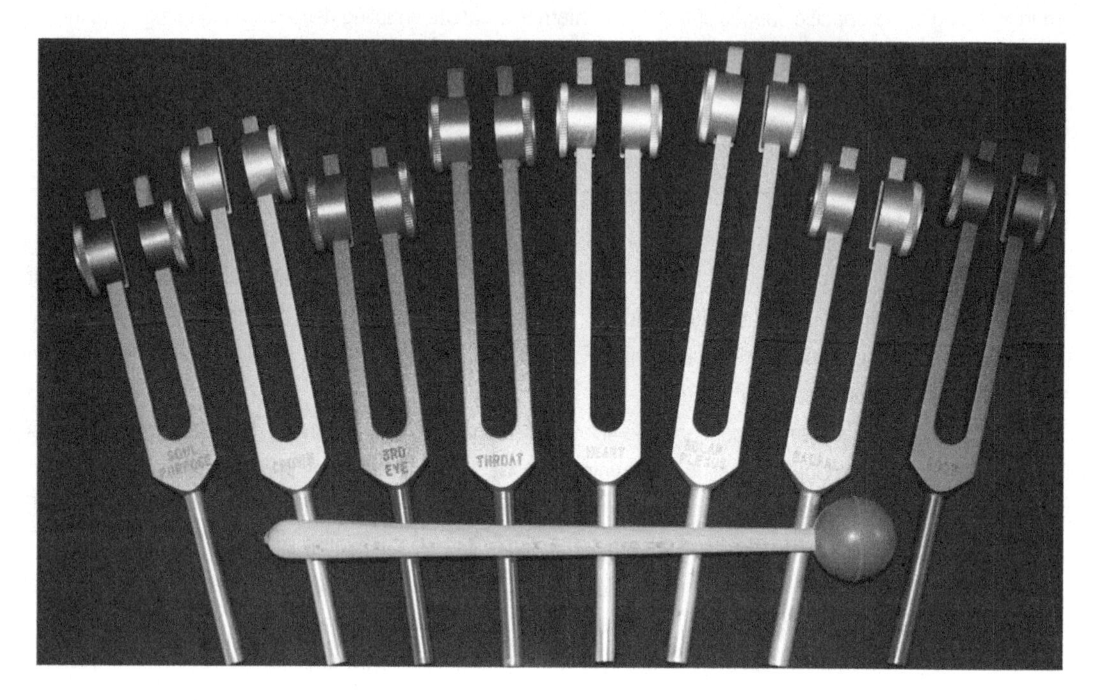

Figure 69: Seven Chakras Tuning Fork Set with Soul Star (Weighted)

The Seven Chakra Set uses precise mathematical formulas of our Solar System's Planetary cycles, connecting to our Cosmic Multi-Dimensional Selves. It essentially allows us to connect to our Higher Self and utilize its powers. Working with these Tuning Forks balances the Chakras and neutralizes the Ego. The immediate result is an inspired state of mind and clarity of thought. Being able to tune the Soul Star and Earth Star Transpersonal Chakras allows one to ground the entire Chakric system, which aligns the consciousness with the Higher Will. It enables one to be in harmony with the Planet Earth.

The second set of Chakra Tuning Forks is called the Harmonic Spectrum Set (Figure 70). This is a complete octave of eight Tuning Forks (C,D,E,F,G,A,B,C) derived from Pythagorean mathematics, which is essentially the ascending musical scale. In comparison to the Seven Chakra Set, the Harmonic Spectrum Set works more at a physical level, directly affecting cognitive function. Since the Physical Plane is denser and lower in vibration than the Spiritual Plane, the physical body is affected first, which then affects the inner Cosmic Planes through the Principle of Correspondence.

The Harmonic Spectrum Set is more centred around the five human senses; the tissues, fluids, organs, bones, etc., of the physical body, are affected. They are the traditional Chakra frequencies from the Hindu tradition with two C notes corresponding with the Root Chakra, D the Sacral Chakra, E the Solar Plexus, F the Heart Chakra, G the Throat Chakra, A Ajna Chakra, and B the Crown.

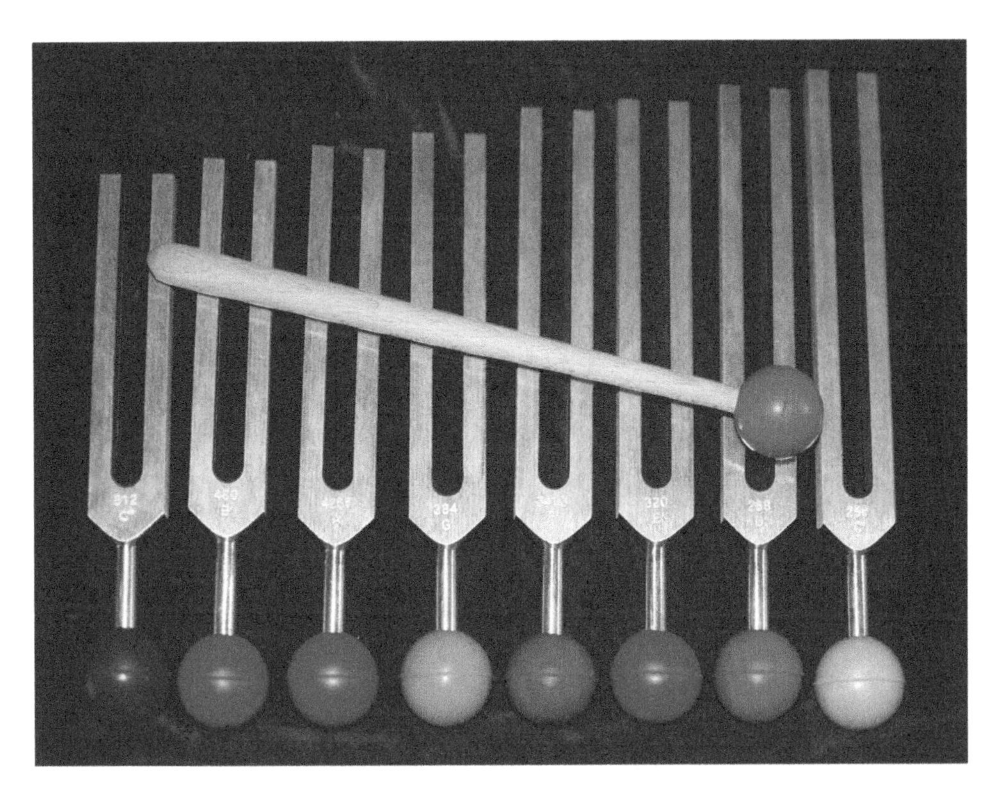

Figure 70: Harmonic Spectrum Tuning Fork Set (Unweighted)

TUNING FORK CHAKRA HEALING

You can perform Tuning Fork Healing on yourself if you wish to target the Chakric points on the front of the body (Figure 72). For the Chakric points along the spine, you will need help from another person. Keep in mind that the person helping you will also be receiving the healing since Tuning Forks work through soundwaves—all one has to do is listen to the sound a Tuning Fork makes or be in the same vicinity, and the vibration will induce their Aura.

If you are performing Tuning Fork Healing on yourself, you should be sitting in a Lotus position comfortably or on a chair. Ensure that you have some privacy when performing Tuning Fork Chakra Healing. As with all Spiritual practices and exercises, relaxation, focus, and peace of mind are of primary importance. As such, you should start every session by performing the Four-Fold Breath for a few minutes with your eyes closed to calm down your interior and enter a meditative state of mind. Remember to keep using this breathing technique during the healing session as well for optimal results.

Tuning Fork healing is best done on an empty stomach since that is when the Ego is least active, and the mind is most focused. Also, I teach my students never to work with energy invoking or balancing exercises right before sleep since, in many instances, it is challenging to induce sleep afterwards. In the case of Tuning Fork Chakra Healing, you will find that your vitality and overall raw energy will heighten after the exercise, which will make you unable to fall asleep for at least a few hours. It is best to perform this practice right in the morning before a meal and set the tone for the day by being energetically balanced.

Tuning Fork Chakra Healing-Basic Method

Begin the exercise at the lowest Chakra, the Earth Star, if you have its corresponding Tuning Fork. If not, start with the Root Chakra, Muladhara, and strike its Tuning Fork with the rubber mallet that came with the set. If you did not receive a rubber mallet, you could use a hockey puck instead. Many practitioners prefer using the hockey puck since it is more versatile.

You will employ two techniques on each Chakra in this Basic Healing method. The first technique involves using the vibrating part of the Tuning Fork, the prong, in unweighted Forks and the round weight in the weighted ones and placing it about half an inch away from the body over the Chakra. Another method you can use only with weighted Tuning Forks is to stand it on its stem (end part) and place it upright directly on the Chakra so that the vibration induces the body. (Make sure not to touch the prongs of the Tuning Fork so as not to disturb its vibration.)

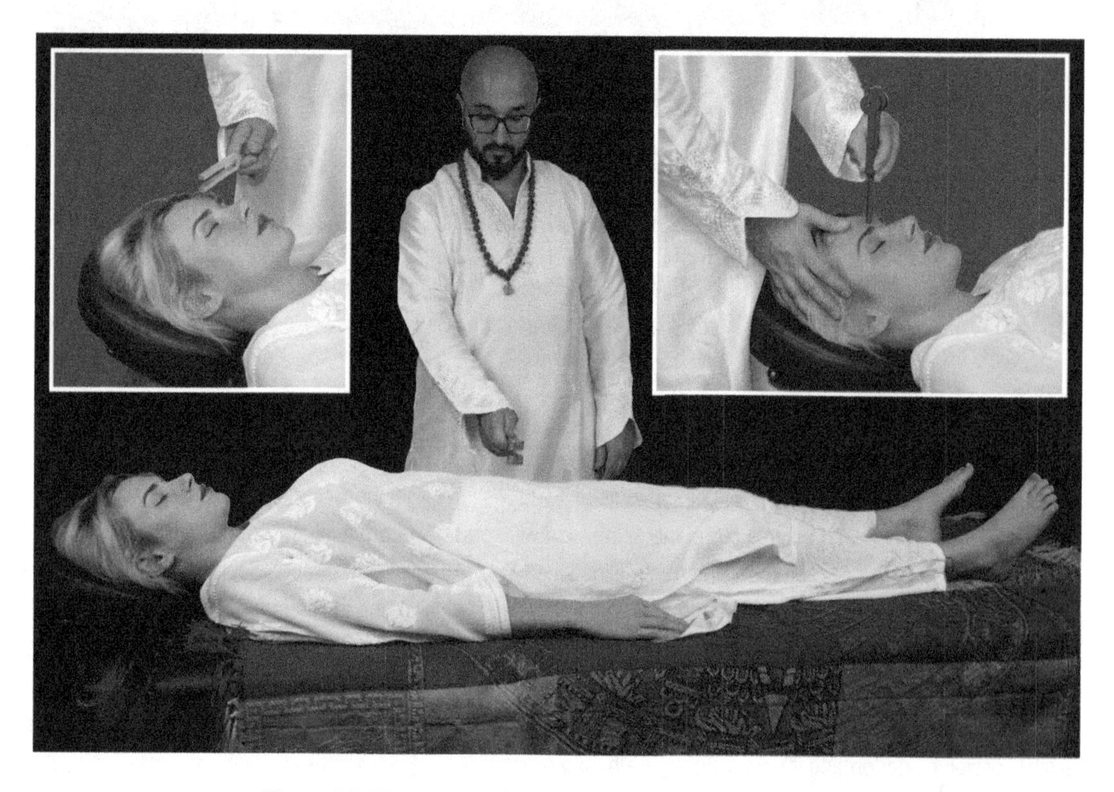

Figure 71: Placement of Tuning Forks in Chakric Healing

The Tuning Fork should be held in position and listened to for twenty seconds. You will need to strike the Fork two, maybe three times, since the sound dies away after ten seconds or so. Figure 71 shows the positioning of the Tuning Forks in Chakric healing, whether weighted or unweighted.

The Earth Star Tuning Fork is to be placed six inches below the feet or at the feet if you are standing, while the Soul Star should be placed six inches above the top, centre of the head. For the Root Chakra, you should place its

Tuning Fork on or directly below the perineum, while for the Crown Chakra, place it on or directly above the top centre of the head. The idea behind this first healing technique, whether you are using the Tuning Fork on the body or an inch away from it, is to allow the vibrating Fork to induce the Chakra and make it vibrate in resonance with it.

The second technique is similar to the Crystal Wands method of optimising a Chakra's spin. With this method, you will focus only on the Seven Major Chakras. Depending on your Soul's gender, determine the direction of movement of your Root Chakra's flowerhead. (Again, use Figure 61 in the previous chapter to find out which of your Chakras are spinning clockwise and which are spinning counterclockwise.) Then, use the Root Chakra Tuning Fork and gradually move it circularly in the same direction as the corresponding Chakra's spin. You can keep the Tuning Fork parallel to the body as you do this or have it at a 45-degree angle. As you circle the Tuning Forks, move them outwards in a pulling motion for the Chakras that project perpendicular to the body. In contrast, for the Crown and Root Chakras that project parallel to the body, circulate their corresponding Forks upwards and downwards in a spiral-like fashion. Be mindful to always focus on the centre of where the Chakric energy is emanating from.

You are to use both healing techniques with the Tuning Forks and interchange them, spending approximately two to three minutes working on each Chakra. Keep in mind that this exercise has a cumulative effect. The longer you spend on each Chakra, the more you will be tuning it. If you want to spend more than three minutes on each Chakra, the choice is yours. Be mindful of being consistent with all the Chakras—if you spend a certain amount of time on one Chakra, then spend an equal amount of time on all the other ones since the purpose of this exercise is to tune the Chakras but also to balance them.

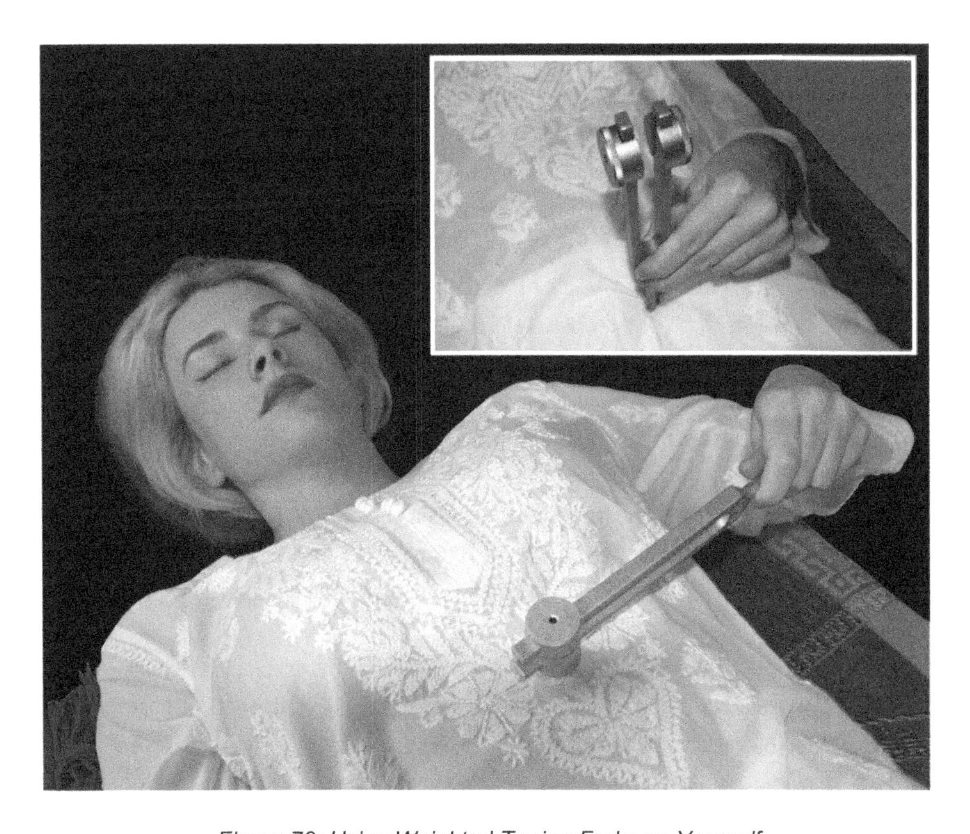

Figure 72: Using Weighted Tuning Forks on Yourself

Next, pick up the Tuning Fork for the Sacral Chakra, Swadhisthana, and follow the same procedure. Keep in mind that if your Root Chakra is spinning clockwise, your Sacral Chakra rotates counterclockwise and vice versa. Therefore, once you get the direction of spin of your Root Chakra, the Chakra above will spin in the opposite direction, interchanging as you go upwards until you reach Sahasrara.

Be consistent with your technique variation while being clear-minded and focused on the task at hand. Allow all outside thoughts to dissipate and leave your Aura without you getting attached to them. The key is to keep the mind silent and only focus on the energy within you as you are tuning your Chakras. Doing so will allow for the most optimal healing to occur.

Next, pick up the Tuning Fork for the Solar Plexus Chakra, Manipura, and repeat the same procedure with the two techniques mentioned above. Then, do the same for the other Chakras. Note that if you are working with the Earth Star and Soul Star Chakras, you are to start with the Earth Star and end with the Soul Star since they are the two lowest and highest Chakras you are working with. Also, when working with the Transpersonal Chakras, you are only to employ the first healing technique since these Chakras emanate outwards from their centre instead of projecting horizontally or vertically.

Once you are finished with the exercise, spend a few minutes meditating on your energy and allowing the healing to permeate all levels of your consciousness. You will find that Tuning Fork Chakra Healing will not only tune and balance the Chakras but also connect you with your Higher Self. As a result, your inspiration and creativity will heighten, as will neutrality in your emotional state. There is no more efficient way to balance your Chakras than with the use of Tuning Forks.

Tuning Fork Chakra Healing-Advanced Method

A more advanced method of performing Tuning Fork Chakra Healing is to use multiple Forks simultaneously (Figure 73). The idea behind this technique is to connect two Chakras in sequence. This technique is best performed on the Major Chakras, although you can also do it to join the Earth Star with Muladhara and the Soul Star with Sahasrara.

If you are working only on the Major Chakras, pick up the Root and Sacral Chakra Tuning Forks in one hand and strike each one. While they are vibrating, place one of the Tuning Forks in the other hand and position each one above their respective Chakras. After about five seconds, take the Sacral Chakra Tuning Fork and move it over to the Root Chakra in a brushing movement. Now move back up to the Sacral Chakra area, again in a brushing motion. Repeat this process a few times with the Sacral Chakra Tuning Fork, going up and down while holding the Root Chakra Tuning Fork in place.

Next, take both Tuning Forks into one hand and strike each one with the rubber mallet or hockey puck. Repeat the same process; only this time hold the Sacral Chakra Tuning Fork in place while moving the Root Chakra Tuning Fork up and down in a brushing movement. Repeat this procedure a few times, spending approximately three to five minutes on each set of Chakras.

Now, put down the Root Chakra Tuning Fork and pick up the Solar Plexus one. Repeat this same procedure for the Sacral and Solar Plexus Chakras, spending the equal amount of time on this set of Chakras as you did the first set. Then, put down the Sacral Chakra Tuning Fork and pick up the Heart Chakra one. Repeat the same process. Do this for the remaining Chakras, making sure to be consistently working with each pair. When you are finished, spend a few minutes in silence meditating on the invoked energies before ending the exercise altogether.

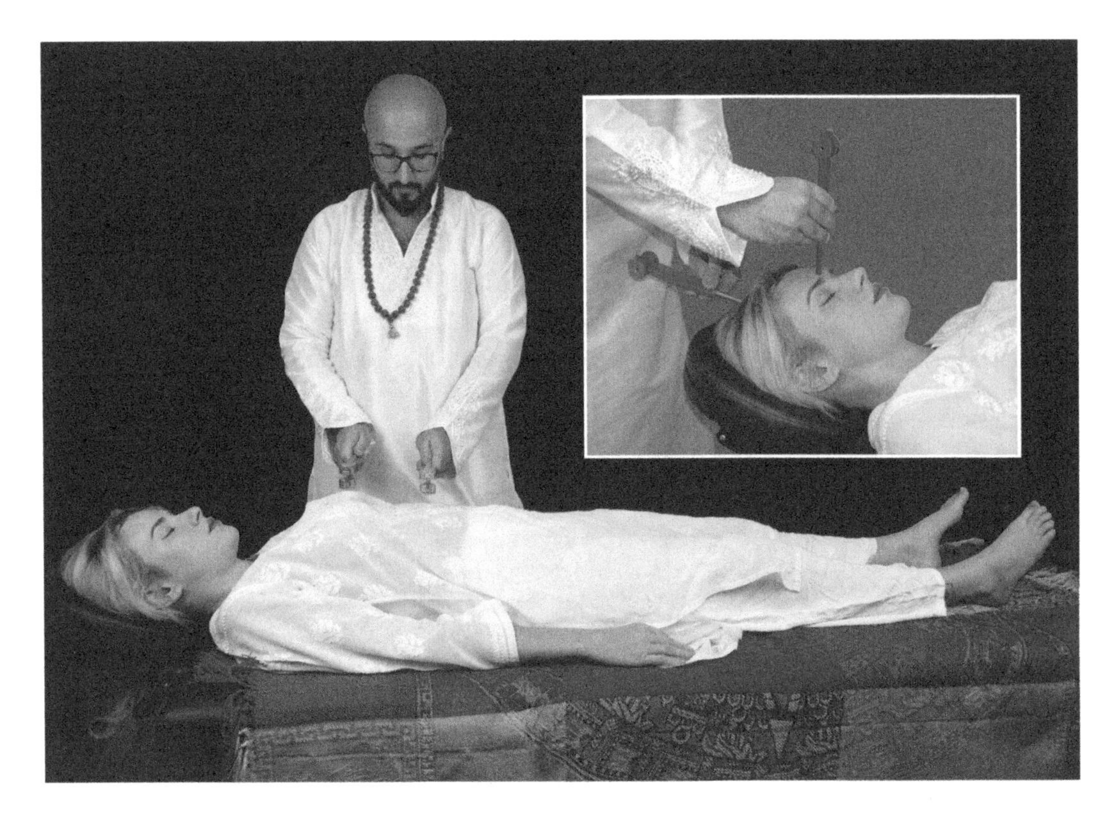

Figure 73: Working with Two Tuning Forks at the Same Time

SACRED SOLFEGGIO TUNING FORKS

Sacred Solfeggio frequencies date back hundreds of years. They are believed to have originated with Gregorian Monks who chanted these frequencies in harmony during religious masses to bring about a Spiritual awakening. These sound frequencies make up a six-tone scale where each frequency attunes different parts of the Self on physical, emotional and Spiritual levels.

As there are six original frequencies, three more missing notes have been added in recent times to complete the entire scale. Together, the Sacred Solfeggio frequencies heal and balance the whole Chakric System. Seven of the nine frequencies are attributed to one of the Seven Major Chakras, while the other two Tuning Forks correspond with the Earth Star and Soul Star Chakras (Figure 75).

When used in Sound Healing, the Sacred Solfeggio Tuning Forks are best applied 0.5-1 inch away from the ears, thereby making direct contact with the Etheric Plane, the first Auric layer from the body related to the Earth Star and Muladhara Chakras. The Earth Star also has a Transpersonal layer that is like an Etheric blueprint containing the entire Chakric system while connecting with the energies of the three highest Transpersonal Chakras. Thus, by targeting the lowest Auric layer, the Etheric Plane, we can induce any of the layers higher than it contained within this Etheric blueprint. Remember, the higher layers interpenetrate the lower ones—As Above, So Below.

Each Auric layer of the Major Chakras is about 1 inch apart in width from the one that comes before or after it (Figure 74). (This number varies depending on the school of thought.) The four Auric layers of the Transpersonal Chakras are more comprehensive than the seven Major Chakra ones. Each one is at least 3-4 inches wide, maybe more.

Although the Causal/Bindu Chakra has its own Auric layer, placed between the Earth Star's Etheric blueprint and the Soul Star, it generally serves as our contact point between the Spiritual and Divine Planes. Then we have the Stellar Gateway Auric layer and other subtle fields overlapping it. However, in using the Sacred Solfeggio Tuning Forks, we will only be working with the first seven Auric layers related to the Physical, Astral, Mental, and Spiritual Planes, while using the Soul Star Fork to open our consciousness to the high vibration of the Divine Plane.

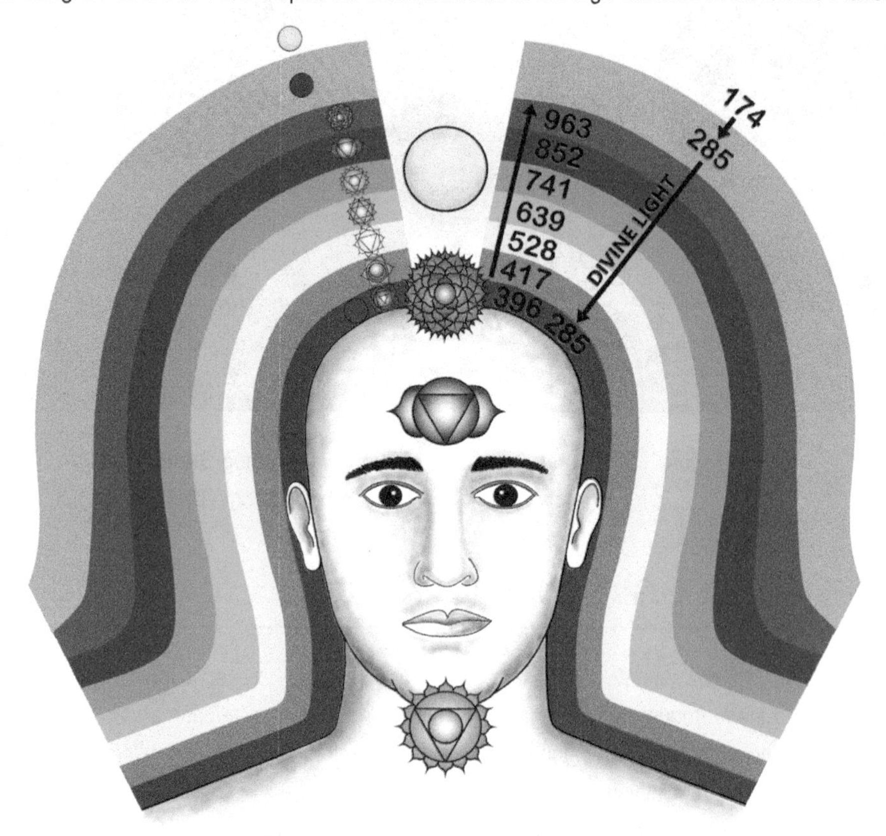

Figure 74: Sacred Solfeggio Frequencies and the Layers of the Aura

When using the Sacred Solfeggio Tuning Forks (Figure 76), you begin with the lowest frequency, 174Hz (Soul Star), followed by the 285Hz (Earth Star) frequency. The low frequency of the Soul Star Tuning Fork doesn't connect you with the Divine Plane by raising the vibration of your consciousness to it. Instead, it tranquillizes your consciousness so that you become open to the loving energy of the Fifth Dimension, which projects downwards from the Soul Star. Then, the Earth Star Fork picks up this high vibration and grounds and anchors it deep into the Aura. Afterwards, you gradually begin to move outward through the seven Auric layers in sequence by utilizing their corresponding frequencies related to the Seven Major Chakras. You are to end the progression with the final frequency, 964Hz, related to Sahasrara Chakra.

Compared to the two sets I previously described, the Sacred Solfeggio Tuning Forks have a significantly higher and more ethereal vibration. They open the mind to the Divine Plane and allow its Light to pour into the consciousness. They give one a glimpse of the Spiritual or religious experience of God. Below, I will describe each of the nine Sacred Solfeggio frequencies and their attributes and powers.

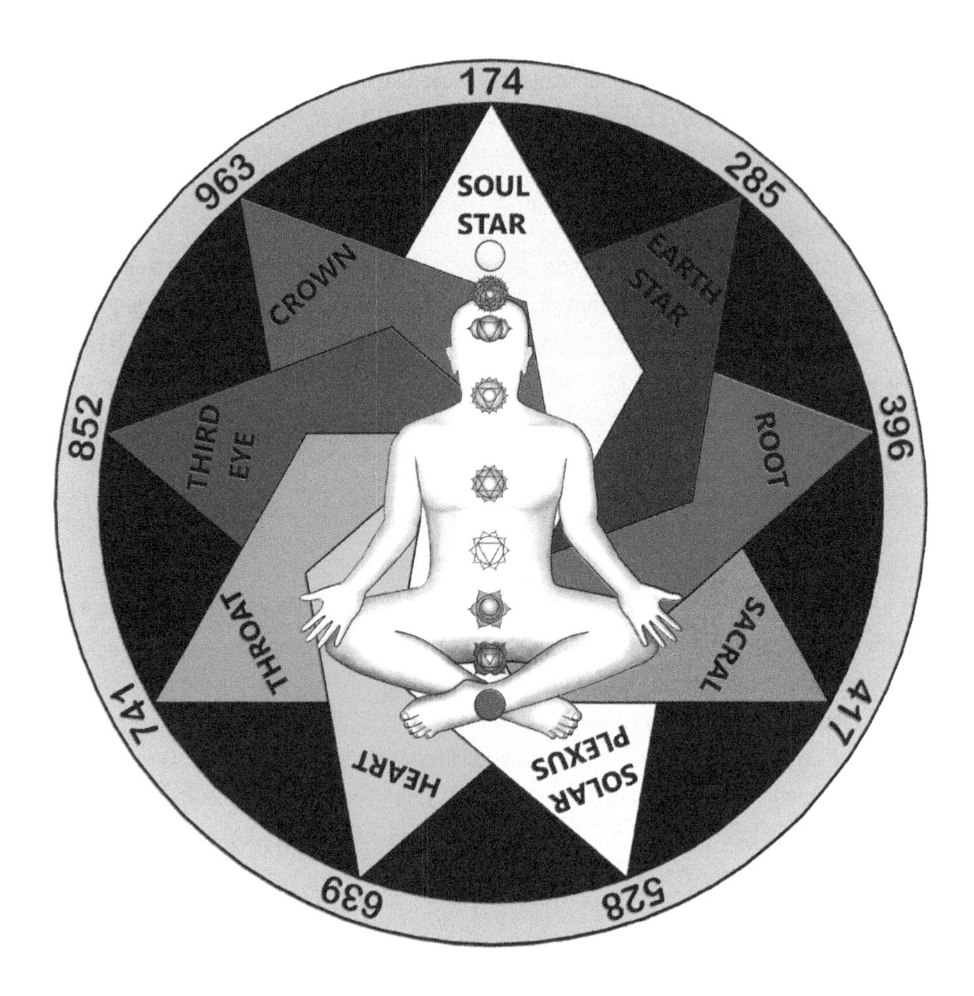

Figure 75: Sacred Solfeggio Frequencies and the Chakras

174 Hz/Soul Star

As the lowest vibration in the Sacred Solfeggio scale, the 175 Hz vibration acts like an energetic anaesthetic—any pain in the physical body or the Aura will be diffused by it. Its low soothing vibration gives our organs a sense of security, safety, and love, and returns them to their optimal state. It makes us feel comforted and nurtured by heightening our connection with the Soul Star Chakra.

285 Hz/Earth Star

The 285 Hz frequency grounds the consciousness to Mother Earth as it has an intimate relationship with the Earth Star Chakra. This particular frequency addresses any holes in the Aura and imbalances in the Chakras. It helps repair damaged tissue by sending messages to corresponding energy fields, telling them to restructure the tissue and return it to its original form. 285 Hz is the frequency of choice for many energy healers.

396 Hz/Muladhara

As it is related to Muladhara, the Root Chakra, 396 Hz frequency is used to realise our goals in life. Its energy tunes us into the Earth Element, which the consciousness uses to manifest our desires into reality. Since it grounds the emotions and thoughts, the Earth Element also grounds our guilt, fear, and trauma. The 396 Hz is a liberating frequency that creates a powerful magnetic field that clears any obstacles to realization.

417 Hz/Swadhisthana

This particular frequency relieves tension and stress and facilitates positive change and creativity. It is associated with Swadhisthana, the Sacral Chakra, corresponding with the Water Element. It has a cleansing effect on the emotions as it clears out destructive influences from past events stored in the subconscious. 417 Hz restructures DNA to function most optimally by clearing limiting beliefs that hold us back from being the best version of ourselves. On a physical level, this frequency increases physical mobility by alleviating tightness in the joints and muscles as we get an influx of the Water Element's energy. 417 Hz is a Soul-cleanser that begins the process of attuning us to the Light.

528 Hz/Manipura

Since it is related to the Solar Plexus Chakra (Manipura) and the Fire Element, the 528 Hz frequency is concerned with transformation on all levels. By optimizing our Life energy and vitality, this frequency brings about heightened awareness, clarity of mind, inspiration and imagination. It gives us the raw energy for creative expressions and makes us excited about life's opportunities. The 528 Hz frequency has been linked with DNA reparation and rewiring neural pathways in the brain. It opens our hearts further to the power of the Light and brings on profound Spiritual experiences and miracles in our lives. This frequency helps neutralize anxiety and physical pain while facilitating weight loss.

639 Hz/Anahata

This frequency is related to Anahata, the Heart Chakra, and the Air Element. Best known as the frequency of love and healing, 639 Hz helps us create harmonious interpersonal relationships in our lives, whether with family, friends, or romantic partners. The frequency inspires compassion, creating deep and profound connections with others. It enhances tolerance, patience, understanding and communication. In romantic relationships, the 639 Hz frequency will enable us to become vulnerable, which improves intimacy. On a mental and emotional level, this frequency is very healing as it allows us to tune into our Souls and away from the Ego and its inhibitions.

741 Hz/Vishuddhi

This frequency deals with empowerment and speaking one's truth. Since it is related to Vishuddhi, the Throat Chakra, the 741 Hz frequency improves communication by facilitating clear thinking and speaking, which increases self-confidence. In addition, this frequency brings about an influx of the Spirit Element which allows us to tune into our intuition and our Higher Self. Doing so leads to a simpler and healthier life filled with new opportunities. On a physical level, the 741 Hz frequency brings about a change in diet towards foods with harmful toxins. Also, this frequency has been known to clear out any bacterial, viral, and fungal infections in the body.

852 Hz/Ajna

As it is related to Ajna Chakra, the Mind's Eye, this frequency has to do with inner sight, intuition, deep dreams (often Lucid ones), awareness, and cutting through illusions. By bringing on an influx of the Spirit Element, the 852 Hz frequency allows us to reconnect with Spiritual thinking and mystical experiences. It brings order to our lives by establishing a link with the Higher Self so that it can communicate easily with our consciousness. As such, the 852 Hz frequency gives us a deeper understanding of the mysteries of Creation. It transforms the DNA and raises its vibration, thereby fully attuning us to the Light and our Souls.

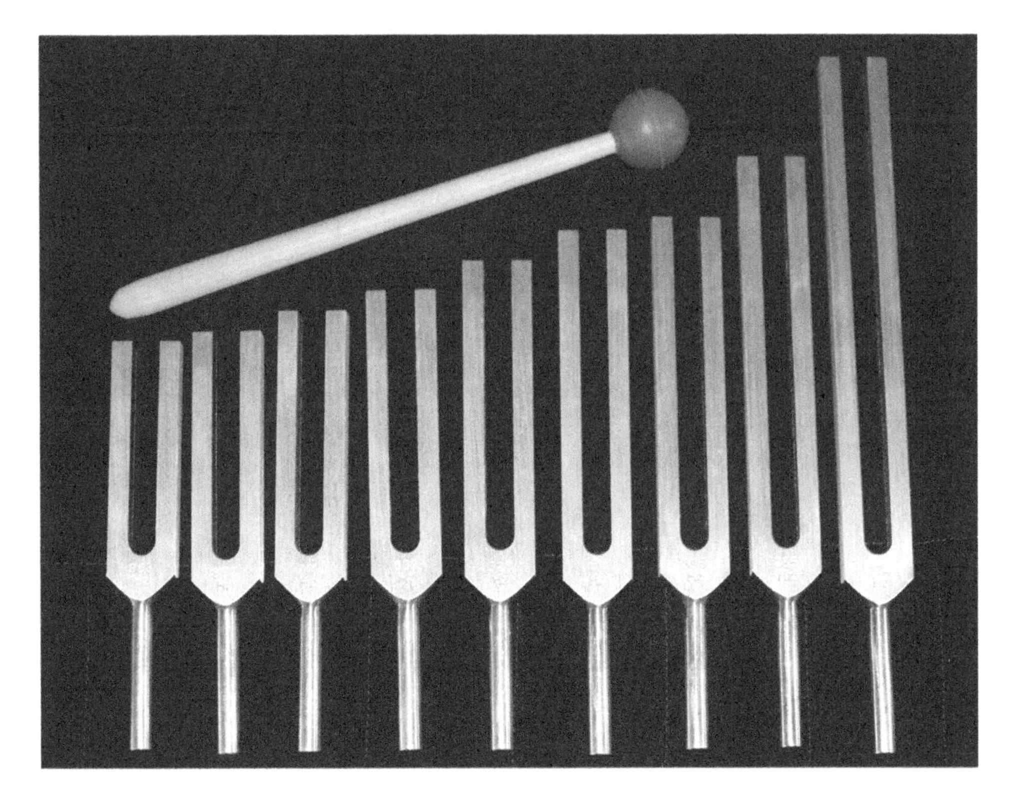

Figure 76: Sacred Solfeggio Tuning Forks (Unweighted)

963 Hz/Sahasrara

This particular frequency corresponds with Sahasrara, the Crown Chakra, and it deals with Oneness. It connects us to Cosmic Consciousness and the Fifth Dimension, resulting in direct experiences of the Spiritual and Divine Planes. As the 852 Hz frequency gave us an understanding of inner truths concerning our reality, the 963 Hz frequency imparts on us Universal wisdom and knowledge. Through this frequency, Ascended Masters can make contact with our consciousness and teach us through Gnosis. It is also not uncommon for us to channel information received from higher Planes. The 963 Hz frequency gives us the most substantial connection with our Higher Self by bringing us closest to the Mind of the Creator.

Sacred Solfeggio Tuning Forks Healing Method

The following exercise is to be used with the unweighted Sacred Solfeggio Tuning Forks, although you can use any unweighted Tuning Forks set with a descending scale, like the Harmonic Spectrum Set I described. The idea is to start with the lowest frequency and move upwards in the scale until ending with the highest frequency. You will find this healing method straightforward to complete since it only requires that you listen to the vibrations of the Tuning Forks (Figure 77).

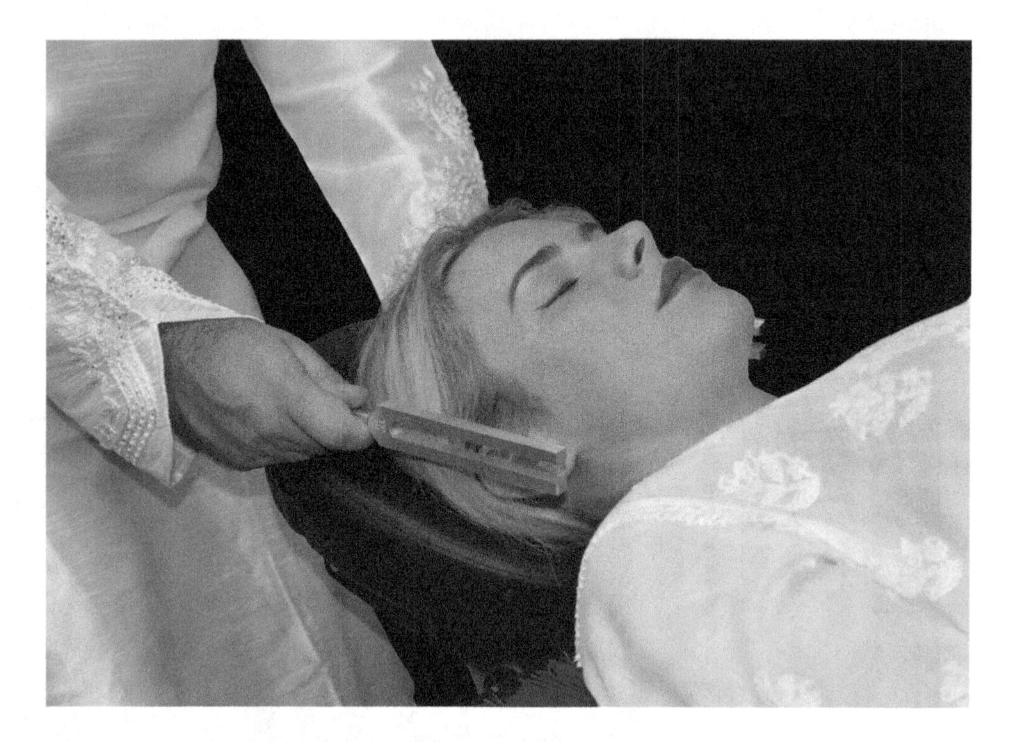

Figure 77: Placing Tuning Forks by the Ears

You can perform this exercise on yourself or someone else. The person accepting the healing should either be sitting or lying down. Begin by calming down your inner energies and entering a meditative state of mind. This healing method has two different sequences that can be performed multiple times in the day, although not simultaneously.

In the first sequence, you are to listen to each Sacred Solfeggio frequency one at a time, from the lowest (174Hz) to the highest (963Hz). Place the vibrating Tuning Fork by the left ear first (0.5-1 inch away) and listen to its sound undisturbed for twenty seconds. You will need to strike the Fork at least two times since the sound dies off after ten seconds. Then, place the vibrating Tuning Fork beside the right ear and listen for twenty seconds before moving on to the next Tuning Fork in sequence. Work through the ascending scale by repeating the same process until finishing with the 963Hz frequency, thereby completing the scale.

In the second sequence, you listen to two Tuning Forks simultaneously, one by each ear, following their order in the scale. Begin with the 174Hz and the 285Hz, placing one by the left ear and the other by the right. Then, switch ears. Next, pick up the 285Hz and 396Hz and repeat the process. And so on, until you have finished with the 963Hz and 174Hz frequencies, thereby completing the cycle. Spend a few minutes in silence after each sequence, meditating on the energies you invoked before ending the exercise altogether.

***

It is not uncommon for unresolved issues to come to the surface to be dealt with as is the case with any energy healing. Remember, you are tuning your Chakras, which means you must heal the Karmic energy they carry. This process can be unpleasant for some and welcoming to others who are determined to get through it. Focus on facing your issues instead of running away from them. Permanent and lasting healing only happens when you have accepted something about yourself and are ready to make a change.

It would be best if you become flexible in changing your beliefs about yourself and the world you live in. Otherwise, every healing session will only be temporary for you until you fall right back into your old programming. Your consciousness must align with your Higher Self who is of the Light, if you desire to realize and live your true Spiritual potential in this lifetime.

TABLE 1: The Twelve Chakras and their Correspondences

Chakra Name (Sanskrit & English)	Location and Colour	Element, Cosmic Plane	Expressions/ Powers	Tuning Fork Hz- Cosmic/ Musical	Gemstones
Earth Star, Super-Root	6 Inches Below Feet, Black, Brown, Magenta	All Elements, Etheric Blueprint/Lower Astral (Etheric)	Energetic Foundation, Past Lives, Nature Awareness, Karmic Records	68.05, -	Smoky Quartz, Onyx, Black Obsidian, Magnetite
Muladhara, Root or Base	Between Perineum and Coccyx, Red	Earth Element, Lower Astral (Etheric) Plane	Survival, Grounding, Security, Physicality, Kundalini (Origin)	194.18, 256.0 & 512.0	Hematite, Black Tourmaline, Red Jasper, Snowflake Obsidian
Swadhisthana, Sacral or Spleen	Lower Abdomen, Orange	Water Element, Higher Astral (Emotional) Plane	Emotions, Fear Energy, Subconscious Mind, Sexuality, Personality (Ego)	210.42, 288.0	Carnelian, Orange Calcite, Tiger's Eye, Septarian
Hara, Navel	Navel, Amber	All Elements, Astral Plane	Astral Gateway, Pranic Source, Sustenance, Regeneration	-	Fire Agate, Citrine, Sunstone
Manipura, Solar Plexus	Solar Plexus, Yellow	Fire Element, Higher Mental Plane	Willpower, Creativity, Vitality, Motivation, Self-Esteem, Conscious Mind, Character (Soul)	126.22, 320.0	Amber, Yellow Citrine, Golden Topaz, Yellow Jasper and Opal
Anahata, Heart	Between Breasts (Centre), Green	Air Element, Lower Mental Plane	Thoughts, Imagination, Love, Compassion, Affection, Kindness, Healing, Harmony, Group Consciousness	136.10, 341.3	Green Aventurine, Green Jade, Malachite, Rose Quartz
Vishuddhi, Throat	Throat, Blue	Spirit Element, Spiritual Plane	Communication, Intelligence, Self-Expression, Truth, Discernement	141.27, 384.0	Amazonite, Aquamarine, Blue Lace Agate, Blue Topaz, Turquoise, Sodalite, Angelite
Ajna, Brow, Mind's Eye, Third Eye	Between the Eyebrows (Slightly Above), Indigo	Spirit Element, Spiritual Plane	Clairvoyance, Intuition, Psychic Senses, Dreaming, Gnosis	221.23, 426.7	Lapis Lazuli, Sapphire, Azurite, Sodalite, Fluorite, Labradorite
Sahasrara, Crown	Top of Head (Centre), Violet or White	Spirit Element, Spiritual Plane	Oneness, God Self & Cosmic Consciousness (Link), Transcendence, Understanding, Wisdom	172.06, 480.0	Amethyst, Diamond, Clear Quartz, Rutilated Quartz, Selenite, Azeztulite
Causal/Bindu	Top & Back of Head (2-3 Inches Out), White	All Elements, Spiritual/Divine Plane	Union, Ego Death, Life Continuity, Cosmic Exploration, 4th Dimension	-	Moonstone, Angel Aura Quartz, Celestite, Kyanite, Herderite
Soul Star	6 Inches Above Top of Head, Golden-White	All Elements, Divine Plane	Solar Self, Spiritual Awareness, Life Purpose, True Will	272.2,-	Selenite, Kyanite, Nirvana Quartz, Danburite
Stellar Gateway	12 Inches Above Top of Head, Gold or Rainbow	All Elements, Divine Plane	Galactic Self, Cosmic Consciousness & God Self (Source), Divinity, Eternity, 5th Dimension	-	Moldavite, Stellar Beam Calcite, Azeztulite, Selenite

AROMATHERAPY

Aromatherapy uses natural plant extracts to create essential oils, incenses, sprays, and mists, which we can use Spiritually, therapeutically, ritualistically, and for hygienic purposes. This practice has been around for thousands of years in various Ancient cultures and traditions—written records going back to about 6000 years ago mention the use of essential oils.

In Ancient Mesopotamia, the cradle of civilization, the Sumerian people used essential oils in ceremonies and rituals. Immediately after them, the Ancient Egyptians developed the first distillation machines to extract oils from plants and used them in their embalming and mummification process. The Egyptians were also the first to create perfumes from essential oils, which we still do today in the cosmetics industry.

The vast array of essential oil fragrances not only have pleasant scents but they give off specific vibrations with healing properties that impact our consciousness when breathed in through the olfactory canal or applied directly onto the skin. Ancient Chinese medicine was the first to use essential oils holistically, while the Ancient Greeks used essential oils topically to fight diseases and heal the body. Even the Ancient Romans used essential oils for their fragrance as part of personal hygiene.

Aromatherapy is an excellent method of using the elements of the natural world to heal the mind, body, and Soul. Its health benefits include easing stress, anxiety, and physical pain, improving sleep, increasing vitality, and boosting feelings of relaxation, peace, and happiness.

Essential oils are the most widely used plant extracts in Aromatherapy, concentrated tinctures made from flower, herb, and tree parts, like bark, roots, peels, and petals. The cells that give a plant its fragrance are considered its "essence," which becomes an essential oil when extracted from a plant. The three main extraction methods of extracting essential oils from plant extracts are distillation, cold-pressing, and supercritical CO_2 extraction.

On a subtle level, essential oils have a healing effect on the Aura and the Seven Chakras. They can be used independently or combined with Crystals, Tuning Forks, Mudras, Mantras, and other tools given in this section for energy invocation/manipulation.

USING ESSENTIAL OILS

Aromatherapy is vibrational healing based on metaphysical principles and the physiological and physical benefits of the chemical components of each fragrance. While Crystals impact our consciousness through physical contact (touch) and Tuning Forks work through sound, essential oils work through our sense of smell to affect our inner energies.

The three most popular methods of using essential oils are topical use, diffusion, and inhalation. Topical use requires blending essential oils with carrier lotions or oils and applying them directly onto the skin. Essential oils have powerful chemical components with antiseptic, antibacterial, and antiviral properties that have been used for centuries to prevent and treat diseases when used directly on the skin.

Diffusion and inhalation require that you use your nose to breathe in the essential oil's scent to obtain a healing effect. When using essential oils for their subtle properties, you will need a lot less than topical application. Generally speaking, the smaller the amount of oil that is being used, the more potent its subtle effect.

In diffusion, you combine essential oil drops with cold water into a diffuser machine (Figure 78), gradually releasing mist into the environment. When diffused, the vast array of fragrances not only affect our mental and emotional state, they also help remove unwanted odours from the surrounding atmosphere and purify it of harmful contaminants.

The use of essential oils is generally safe, although some side effects can occur, including eye, skin, and nose irritation. These are "concentrated" extracts where it takes an enormous amount of plant matter to make just one drop of essential oil, and every drop contains the condensed chemical components of all the plants that went into it. Therefore, using too much essential oil can cause adverse effects, just like using too much medicine.

In addition, some fragrances can cause mild allergic reactions in people with sensitivities to plants. As such, inhalation is the most widely used method by healing practitioners, which requires smelling the essential oil directly from the bottle to obtain the desired effects. It gives one complete control over how much of the fragrance they want to inhale, making it the most low-risk method of applying essential oils during a healing session. For example, if someone were to have an allergic reaction with a diffuser, they might need to leave the space entirely, thus halting or even having to end the healing session.

Essential oils can also be used to prepare an aromatic bath as part of a ritual cleansing process. Use only six to eight drops of an essential oil in ritual baths and combine with burning candles in corresponding colours to the effect you are trying to produce. Keep in mind that intent is fundamental, so choose your essential oil carefully and practise mindfulness while in the bath. Ritual baths are an excellent way to cleanse your energies and should be performed often, especially as a precursor to meditation, Ceremonial Magick, Yoga, and other Spiritual Healing practices.

There are some precautions to be mindful of with the use of essential oils. For one, essential oils should never be swallowed. Certain oils are considered toxic when ingested, which can cause harm to the body and organs. For this reason, make sure to keep all of your essential oils out of reach from children. Secondly, pregnant women should avoid using essential oils, especially during the first trimester. The same goes for children under the age of six. And lastly, it is not recommended to use essential oils on animals because they could have adverse reactions to the potency of some fragrances and even die. For example, using essential oils on birds can prove to be fatal in many instances.

Figure 78: Essential Oils and a Diffuser

HOW ESSENTIAL OILS WORK

Essential oil fragrances use the air around us as a transmission medium to carry molecules into the nasal passage (Figure 79), thereby triggering an emotional response. At the same time, the essential oil's particles are delivered to the lungs with each breath where they enter the bloodstream, directly impacting the nervous system and other organs. As such, Aromatherapy is directly associated with the Air Element. However, since our sense of smell is tied to our Limbic System, which regulates emotions, behaviours, memories, and memory, Aromatherapy also has a relation to the Water Element.

There is a symbiotic relationship between the Water and Air Elements, exhibited by nature's processes. For example, the water molecule (H2O) contains one part oxygen. This close relationship is also found in our mental processes since every time we experience a feeling (Water Element), a thought (Air Element) precedes it.

In the Samkhya (also spelt Sankhya) school of Indian philosophy, the sense of smell is associated with the Earth Element, which fits in this case since plants are organic solids that come from the Earth. However, we can change the solid state of plants with the application of heat and turn them into liquid forms to create essential oil tinctures. We cannot change the solid state of Crystals, though, which is why their energies are denser than the energies of Aromatherapy fragrances.

Aromatherapy scents are known for activating old memories and restoring our emotions to their peaceful state. Many fragrances are also known for improving our overall mood since they stimulate the Hypothalamus to send messages to the Pituitary Gland to create feel-good brain chemicals like serotonin. When we are calm and happy, the mind becomes tranquil, raising the vibration of our consciousness. For this reason, burning incense or diffusing oils is beneficial before starting meditation as it cleanses the space and calms us down, enabling us to go deeper within ourselves.

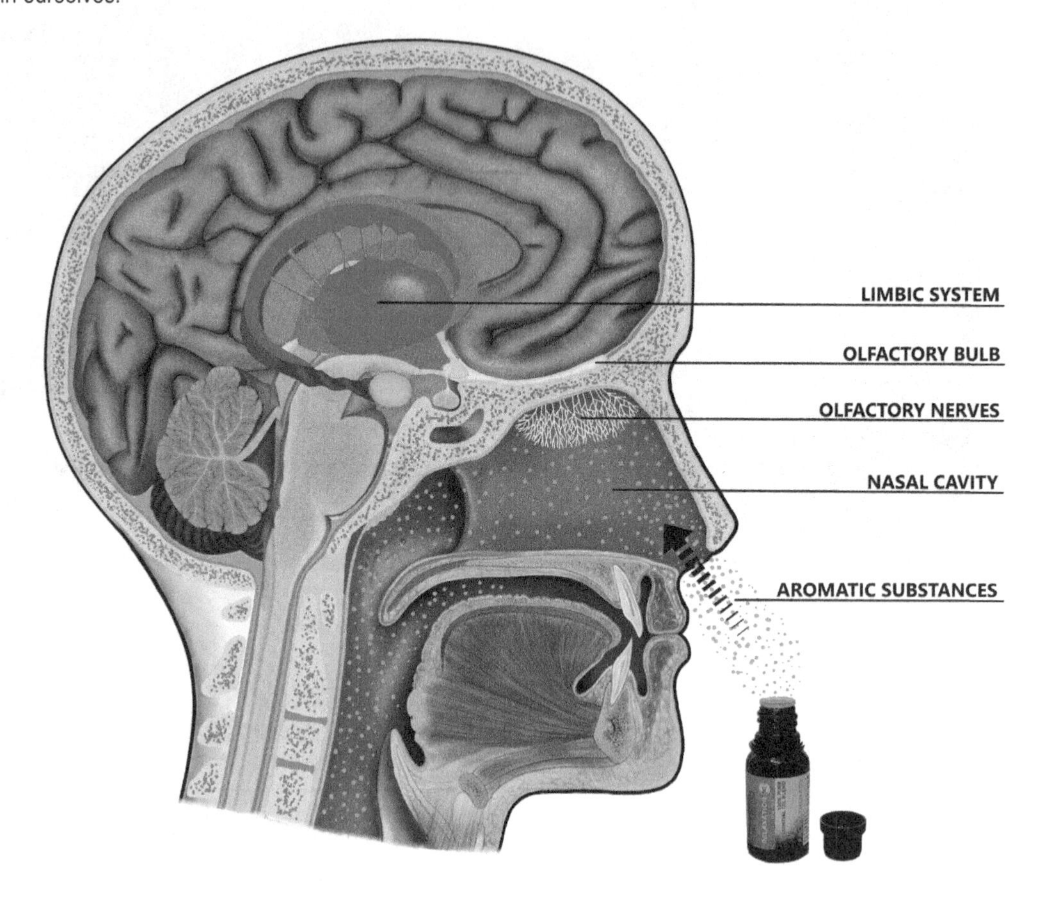

Figure 79: Aromatherapy and the Limbic System

When we apply essential oils topically, while the scent enters the lungs and nostrils, even more molecules are absorbed into the skin directly, providing immediate physical benefits. In addition, we can use the topical application of essential oils to cure skin-related issues, including healing a rash or minor wound, stopping an infection, soothing pain from a sunburn, or alleviating itching from bug bites. Massage therapists like using essential oils directly on the skin to relax the muscles and manage pain.

ESSENTIAL OILS FOR THE SEVEN CHAKRAS

Every Chakra has unique properties that correspond with certain essential oils. Therefore, we can use essential oils on the body to promote balanced Chakra functioning. The method described below can be used on one Chakra at a time to optimize its energy flow or on multiple Chakras that require healing. You can also apply this method to all Seven Chakras at the same time to bring alignment to the entire Chakric system. However, since essential oils have to be applied onto the body where the Chakras are located, we cannot target the Transpersonal Chakras with this particular application method.

When using essential oils to heal and balance the Chakras, never apply them directly on the skin without diluting them first with a carrier oil. Essential oil blends enhance and maximize the therapeutic and medicinal effects. There are a variety of carrier oils you can use to make essential blends for the Chakras, including jojoba oil or fractionated coconut oil. The ratio to keep in mind is two to three drops of an essential oil per one teaspoon of carrier oil. The essential oil blends are best applied with a standard 10ml roll-on bottle. If you are using a different type of bottle, you can use your finger to apply the oil instead.

To apply an essential oil blend, rub some of it onto the front or back of the body where the Chakra is located. Use just enough to cover an area of about 1.5"-2" in diameter. Once applied, you may leave it on your body for the entirety of the day to obtain maximum therapeutic effects. The only way to stop the continued healing influence of the essential blend(s) is to wash them off your body with a strong soap, although some of the mixture usually lingers on the skin's surface.

Keep in mind that once you have applied the essential oil blend for more than an hour, changes in your energy will have already taken place, even though your consciousness may need more time to integrate them. Therefore, it helps to meditate immediately after application to speed up the integration process.

Use Table 2 to find the most appropriate essential oil(s) to use on each Chakra. Certain essential oils have an energizing effect on a Chakra, while others have a calming one. Balancing oils are good to bring Chakras into equilibrium, whether they are underactive or overactive. When the Chakra is underactive, the vibration emitted by the chosen essential oil will accelerate the spin of the Chakra, returning it to its optimum velocity. When it is overactive, the vibration will slow down the spin of the Chakra and bring it into balance.

Use a carrier oil to make an essential oil blend for each Chakra you want to work on. Your intention is of utmost importance, as it is to be consistent and follow the correspondences given in Table 2. You can make a collection of essential oil blends for Chakric healing in this way, which you can use in your future healing sessions.

You can also make single blends of multiple oils, so long as they correspond with the Chakra you are targeting and whether you are trying to energize, calm, or balance it. For example, if you are making a 10ml oil blend (two teaspoons) to balance an overactive Muladhara Chakra, you should use four to six essential oil drops of a combination of calming oils pertaining only to this Chakra. Experiment with mixing the essential oil blends using the Table below for reference.

TABLE 2: Essential Oils for the Seven Chakras

Chakra Name (Sanskrit & English)	Energizing Oils	Calming Oils	Balancing Oils	Application on Body (Front/Back)
Muladhara, Root or Base	Cinnamon, Cardamom, Black Pepper, Ginger, Cypress	Vetiver, Patchouli, Cedarwood, Myrrh, Basil	Sandalwood, Frankincense, Geranium	Between Perineum and Coccyx, Bottom of Feet, or Both
Swadhisthana, Sacral or Spleen	Orange, Mandarin, Lemon, Bergamot	Rosewood, Ylang-Ylang, Clary Sage, Neroli	Neroli, Jasmine, Helichrysum, Sandalwood, Elemi	Lower Abdomen (Below Navel), Lower Back, or Both
Manipura, Solar Plexus	Grapefruit, Lemon, Lemongrass, Ginger, Lime, Juniper	Vetiver, Bergamot, Fennel, Rosemary	Black Pepper, Spikenard, Helichrysum	Solar Plexus, Mid Back, or Both
Anahata, Heart	Palmarosa, Pine, Rosewood, Bergamot	Rose, Marjoram, Cedarwood, Eucalyptus	Jasmine, Melissa, Sandalwood, Geranium	Between Breasts (Centre), Upper Back, or both
Vishuddhi, Throat	Peppermint, Cypress, Lemon, Spearmint, Sage	Roman Chamomile, Basil, Rosemary, Bergamot	Coriander, Geranium, Eucalyptus	Middle of Throat, Back of Neck, or Both
Ajna, Brow, Mind's Eye, Third Eye	Clary Sage, Pine, Lavender, Myrrh Sandalwood, Juniper	German Chamomile, Basil, Patchouli, Cedarwood, Thyme	Frankincense, Helichrysum, Jasmine	Between the Eyebrows, Back of Head, or Both. Also, Middle of Forehead (Fifth Eye)
Sahasrara, Crown	Lavender, Saffron, Palo Santo	Rosewood, Thyme, Cedarwood, Neroli, Lotus	Frankincense, Myrrh, Helichrysum, Sandalwood	Top of Head (centre)

THE TATTVAS

Tattva, or Tattwa, is a Sanskrit word meaning "principle, "truth," or "reality." It signifies "thatness," which can be understood further as the "essence which creates the feeling of existence." In *The Vedas*, Tattvas are sacred formulas or reality principles that denote the identity of the individual Self and God-the Creator. They represent the body of God, which is the Universe itself, and our own body that experiences nature through consciousness.

There are five primary Tattvas (Figure 80), representing nature's essence that manifests as the Five Elements. The five Tattvas are known as Akasha (Spirit), Vayu (Air), Tejas (Fire), Apas (Water), and Prithivi (Earth). The first four Tattvas (Prithivi, Apas, Tejas, Vayu) represent modes or qualities of the Solar energy of Prana in varying degrees of vibrations. They are a consequence of Light and sound emanations, which merge into the final Tattva, or principle—Akasha, the Spirit/Aethyr Element.

The Tattvas are primal and simple in form; they assume the five main shapes within the range of human perception—the square, crescent moon, triangle, circle, and egg. Tattvas are presented on cards with a white background that brings out their shape and colour. They are classified as "Yantras"—tools for mental concentration and meditation. Yantras are mystical diagrams from the Tantric tradition and Indian religion that come in many geometric shapes and configurations, often very complex. Other than using them as meditation tools, Hindu people often use Yantras to worship Deities in Temples or at home. They also use them as talismans for protection or to bring good fortune.

Tattvas are perhaps the simplest Yantras in existence. In the simplicity of their shapes and colours, however, lies the potential to make a powerful connection with the primordial Five Elements that exist on a Microcosmic level. As such, we can obtain a connection into the Macrocosmic level—As Above, So Below. Therefore, by mastering the Elements within ourselves, we develop the ability to alter and change reality with our thoughts, becoming master manifesters.

Kundalini Shakti is the subtlest form of energy (feminine) and an inseparable part of pure consciousness (masculine)—represented by Lord Shiva, Shakti's consort. Although energy and consciousness have separated and diversified to give rise to Creation, they are forever striving to re-unite. This process is exemplified by Kundalini energy rising from the bottom of the spine to the top (Crown) of the head.

The purpose of a Kundalini awakening is not only Enlightenment for the individual in whose body this process takes place but for Shakti and Shiva to re-experience the Cosmic unity from which they evolved. However, as the Kundalini rises, the individual experiences the full awakening and infusion of Light into the Seven Chakras, whose energies can be broken down into the Five Elements, represented by the five primary Tattvas. As such, by working with the Tattvas, you are working on tuning your Chakras and healing the Karmic energy contained therein.

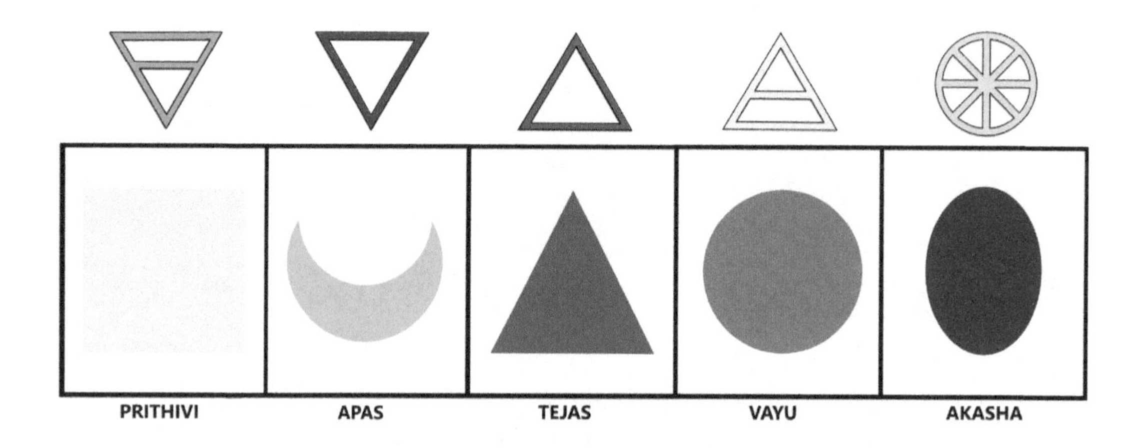

Figure 80: The Five Major Tattvas

THE PROCESS OF CREATION

During the process of Creation, the infinite White Light gradually lowered its vibration, manifesting the Five Elements in successive stages. Each of the five primary Tattvas represents one of the creative processes, beginning with Spirit, followed by Air, Fire, Water, and then Earth as Creation's final materialisation. According to the Eastern and Western Esoteric Mysteries regarding this subject, each Element (Tattva) is part of a connected series in which each successive Element (Tattva) is derived from its predecessor. Also, all the Tattvas should be regarded as an extension of pure consciousness and not as individual principles that exist separately.

The first Tattva, Akasha (Spirit), is an amalgamation of energy and Matter that contains an infinite amount of potential energy in the Sea of Consciousness. As Akasha's energy began to vibrate in the evolution process, it created movement that manifested the Tattva Vayu (Air). Vayu's particles have the maximum freedom of movement since Air is the least tenuous of the lower Four Elements. As the creative process continued, the perpetual motion of Vayu generated heat, causing the emergence of the next Tattva, Tejas (Fire).

Since the movement of the energy of Tejas was less than Vayu, it enabled it to expel part of its radiative heat, which cooled down to create the Apas Tattva (Water). With Apas, the Spirit, Air, and Fire particles became confined within constricted space, with limited but fluid motion. As the vibration of Creation's manifestation further lowered, however, Apas solidified into the Tattva Prithivi (Earth), the next and final stage in the process of Creation. Prithivi is the equivalent of the Malkuth Sephira on the Tree of Life, representing the World of Matter, the physical reality.

It should be noted that during the creative process, subtle states gave rise to grosser, denser states that are lower in vibration than the preceding state. The higher the vibration, the higher the state of consciousness and the Element it corresponds with. Also, keep in mind that the cause is an essential part of the effect. Earth contains the Elements of Water, Fire, Air, and Spirit, since it evolved out of them, while Spirit does not since it precedes all the Elements.

I described in *The Magus* that when you work with one Element's energy, by the time you have completed its Spiritual Alchemy process, the next Element in sequence unveils itself before you. Therefore, there is no fine line where one Element ends and the other begins, but all five are connected as part of one sequence.

You will notice that the Eastern sequence of emanation of the Elements is slightly different than the Western one—the Air Element comes immediately after Spirit, instead of the Fire Element. According to the Eastern Spiritual system, the Air Element is less dense and more ethereal than Fire, so Ancient Rishis put Air before Fire in the sequence of Creation's manifestation. I will discuss this variation between the Eastern and Western systems in depth in the following Yoga section, specifically "The Five Koshas" chapter.

THE THIRTY TATTVAS SYSTEM

Each of the five Tattvas has five Sub-Tattvas that relate to different Planes of the main Tattva they pertain to. For instance, a Fire Tattva has five Sub-Elements: Fire of Fire, Spirit of Fire, Water of Fire, Air of Fire, and Earth of Fire. By working with the Sub-Elements of the Tattvas, we have a more precise way to tune into the exact energy we desire.

The principal energies that affect our Solar System, Planetary and Zodiacal, can all be broken down into Sub-Elements, corresponding with different parts of the Self. They relate to the connecting paths of the Tree of Life (Tarot Cards) and energies that filter one state of consciousness into another. These states of consciousness are ten in number, represented by the ten Spheres of the Tree of Life in the Qabalah.

There are six main schools of thought on Tattvic philosophy in India. The original Tattva system was developed by the Vedic Sage Kapila in the sixth century BC as part of his Samkhya philosophy, which heavily influenced the science of Yoga. Samkhya philosophy uses a system of twenty-five Tattvas, while Shaivism recognises thirty-six Tattvas. The Hermetic Order of the Golden Dawn uses the thirty Tattvas system since this particular breakdown corresponds with the Elements and Sub-Elements found on the Qabalistic Tree of Life. This system includes the five primary Tattvas and the twenty-five Sub-Elemental Tattvas (Figure 81). Considering that I have the most extensive experience with this particular system, it is the one I will adhere to in this book.

Since working with Tattvas requires our sense of sight that perceives colours and shapes in the environment, this vibrational healing modality is associated with the Element of Fire and the Higher Mental Plane. Thus, it enables us to go deeper within ourselves than with other healing modalities presented in this book. And since Fire relies on Air for sustenance, there is an Air Element component also in working with the Tattvas, corresponding with the Lower Mental Plane.

Therefore, the Mental Plane that utilizes our willpower and thoughts is our contact point for reaching the Higher and lower Cosmic Planes, represented by the Tattvas. Moreover, this symbiotic relationship between the Elements of Fire and Air is evident in nature's processes. For example, the physical fire, or flame, requires oxygen for sustenance; without it, it dies. In the same way, intention and willpower cannot succeed in any undertaking without thoughts and imagination.

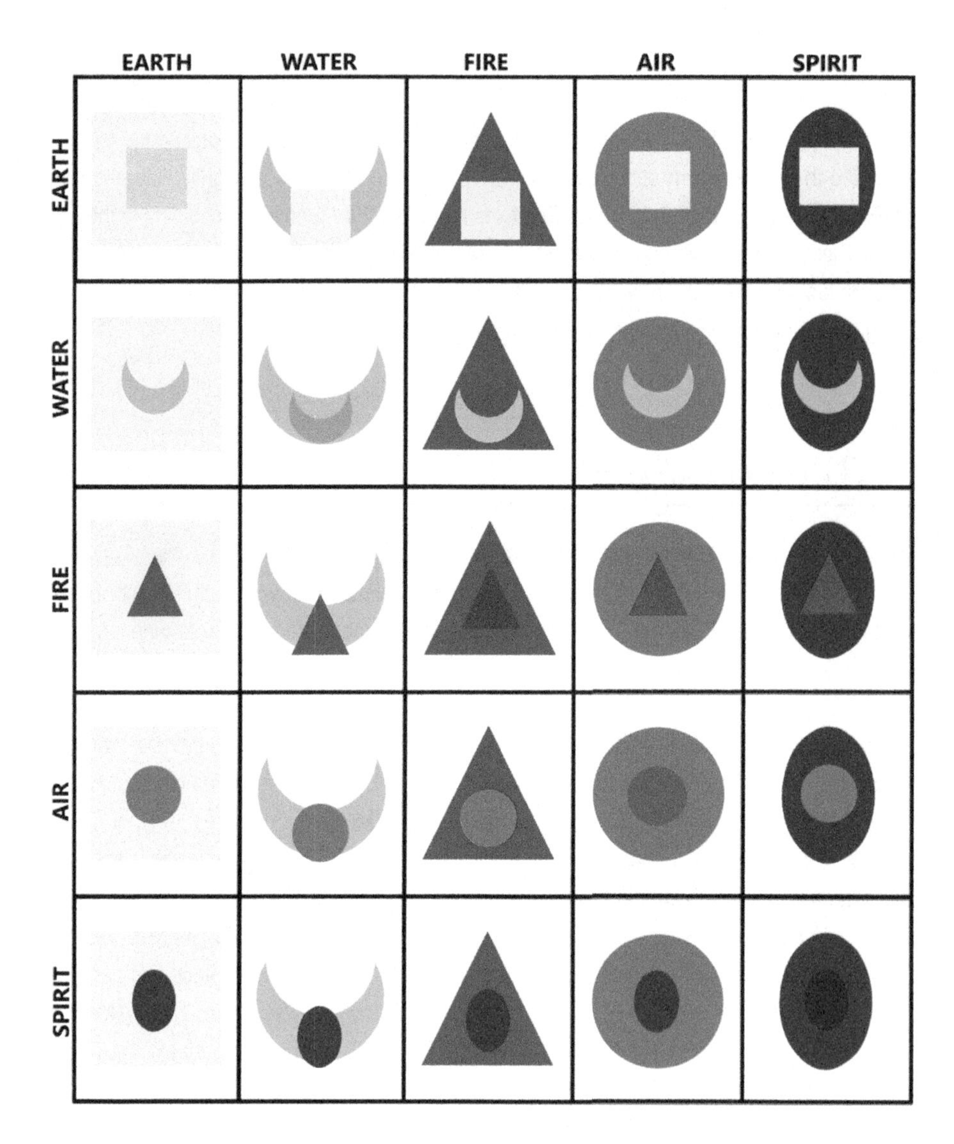

Figure 81: The Twenty-Five Sub-Elemental Tattvas

As mentioned earlier, working with the Tattvas is akin to working with the Elements through Ceremonial Magick ritual exercises presented in *The Magus*. However, Ceremonial Magick deals mainly with invocations, or calling in particular energies from the outside Universe into your Aura, while working with Tattvas constitutes as an evocation, meaning that you access or "draw out" a specific type of energy within yourself for introspection.
Hence, Ceremonial Magick ritual exercises invoke a more significant amount of Elemental energy into the Aura while Tattvas only work with our inner, natural energies.

However, the benefit of Tattvas over Ceremonial Magick ritual exercises is that you can zero in on the Sub-Elements effortlessly using their respective Tattva cards (Yantras). In contrast, the only ritual exercises in Ceremonial Magick that enable you to accomplish the same goal are Enochian Keys which are very advanced and carry a lot of Karmic energy specific to that egregore. I left warning notes in multiple pages of *The Magus* concerning working with

Enochian Magick because it requires over a dozen months of preparation with other, more basic Elemental invocations. With Sub-Elemental Tattvas, however, you can jump right in.

THE FIVE MAJOR TATTVAS

Akasha Tattva (Spirit Element)

The first Tattva, Akasha, corresponds with the Spirit Element. Akasha represents the void of space, the Aethyr, symbolized by a black or indigo ovoid, or egg. Spirit and Aethyr are interchangeable terms that stand for the same thing—the Akasha. The black colour of Akasha reflects the darkness of the void, which we can see in the vast space between the Heavenly bodies (Stars and Planets) in the Universe. When we close our eyes, we also mentally see this same darkness of space before us, implying that Akasha is within us as well. Although blackness is the absence of Light, it contains all the colours of the spectrum within itself. As such, it is infinite in potential and scope. For example, one black hole in the Universe contains more mass than millions of Stars combined.

Akasha is equated with the White Light principle that stretches out infinitely in all directions. Hermeticists refer to it as the First Mind of God-the Creator (The All). Another name is the "Monad," which means "singularity" in Greek. The darkness of space is merely a reflection of the White Light on a physical level, manifested by the Second Mind, which was generated (birthed) by the First Mind through the process of differentiation. Although we cannot enter the First Mind while living, we can experience its potential by awakening the Cosmic Consciousness within us (via the Kundalini), which bridges the First and Second Minds.

The manifested Universe, including all the Galaxies and Stars in existence, are contained within the Second Mind. Matter is a by-product of the Spiritual energy that is invisible to the senses but permeates all things. As the essence of everything, Akasha's vibration is so high that it appears motionless, unlike the other Four Elements, which are constantly in motion and can be experienced through the physical senses. Akasha is undifferentiated Matter containing an infinite amount of potential energy. In other words, Matter and energy exist in their dormant potential state within the Spirit Element at the very heart of Creation. Akasha was never born, and it will never die. It cannot be subtracted from nor added to.

The Spiritual energy of the First Mind manifests into the Second Mind through the Stars as visible Light. However, Spirit is said to travel faster than the speed of Light, having the highest velocity known to humanity. This would explain why information channelled via the Cosmic Consciousness is instantaneously transmitted anywhere in the Universe. And why Spiritually evolved people need to merely think of an object or place, and they immediately experience what it is like to be that object or be in that place through thought.

Since it travels faster than the speed of Light, Spiritual energy transcends space and time according to Einstein's Theory of Relativity. As such, it is not uncommon for Spiritually awakened people to develop the sense of precognition or prescience, enabling them to see into the future via the sixth's sense (psychism). Spiritual consciousness allows one access to the Akashic Records.

In Hermetic Alchemy, Akasha is the Quintessence. It is all-penetrating since everything in existence evolved out of Akasha, and into Akasha, everything will eventually return. Akasha relates to the principle of sound vibration. It provides the medium for sound to travel through space. Akasha is the source of the other Four Elements that evolved through Creation's manifestation process.

The Planetary energy of Saturn influences Akasha, exemplified by the colours indigo and black that correspond with both. In the Qabalah, Saturn relates to the Sephira Binah, one of the Supernals representing the Spirit Element. Binah is the Astral blueprint of everything in existence, the subtle, ethereal forms of all things that are invisible to the physical senses but that we can experience through the Mind's Eye. The vibration of Akasha can only be accessed when the mind is silenced, and the Ego is transcended. In Yogic and Hindu philosophy, its realm of experience is the Plane of consciousness, termed "Jana Loka," the abode of the liberated mortals who dwell in the Heavenly Realm.

Akasha is attributed to the three Chakras of Vishuddhi, Ajna, and Sahasrara (Figure 82). At the level of Sahasrara, Akasha is best expressed by the Infinity symbol, a figure eight on its side, representing the concept of Eternity and limitlessness. At Ajna's level, Akasha is best symbolized by the Taoist Yin/Yang symbol, representing duality, the feminine and masculine forces, Ida and Pingala, that unite at Ajna Chakra. Vishuddhi is the traditional representative of the Akasha Tattva in Tantra and Yoga, at its most accessible level that connects it with the lower Elements and Chakras.

Akasha's Bija Mantra is "Ham." (More on the Bija Mantras in the following section on Yoga.) Experiencing the energy of Akasha Tattva resembles the effect of Spirit Element ritual invocations and Saturnalian energy, although the latter can be best described as the Earthy aspect of Akasha. The Sub-Elements of Akasha are Spirit of Spirit, Fire of Spirit, Water of Spirit, Air of Spirit, and Earth of Spirit.

Vayu Tattva (Air Element)

The Hindu religious text, *The Upanishads*, teach that the first principle or Tattva to evolve out of Akasha is Vayu, symbolized by a blue circle. "Vayu" comes from the same Sanskrit root word for "motion" and is consequently attributed to the Element of Air. Having the nature of wind, Vayu takes on a blue colour of the clear sky.

As the void of Akasha became influenced by motion during the creative process, Light energy was created, manifesting the Vayu Tattva. However, Vayu is not physical Light but kinetic energy in its diverse forms: electrical, chemical, and vital energy (Prana). As Akasha was motionless, Vayu is all-pervading motion.

All gases within the Earth's atmosphere, including oxygen, encompass the Vayu Tattva. Although invisible to the naked eye, Vayu is the first Tattva that can be felt tangibly on the skin. As such, it relates to the sense of touch. The essence of Vayu is expressed through contraction and expansion. In the physical body, Vayu controls the five vital "airs" called the Prana Vayus: Prana, Apana, Samana, Udana, Vyana.

Vayu is attributed to Anahata, the Heart Chakra. It relates to the mind, thoughts, and imagination, powered by the breathing process—bringing Pranic energy into the body. The constant motion of Vayu Tattva creates change, causing instability, inconsistency, volatility, and fickleness in the individual and the environment. Such is the nature of the Air Element. Its realm of experience is the Plane of consciousness, termed "Maha Loka," the home of the great Sages and Rishis.

The Bija Mantra of Vayu Tatva is "Yam." Its energy is comparable to Air Element ritual invocations and invocations of the Planet Mercury with aspects of Sun energy. After all, Vayu is an extension of Pranic energy, whose source is the Sun. The Sub-Elements of Vayu are Air of Air, Spirit of Air, Fire of Air, Water of Air, and Earth of Air. The Sub-Element Air of Air is akin to the energy of the Aquarius Zodiac, while Fire of Air is similar to Libra and Water of Air to Gemini.

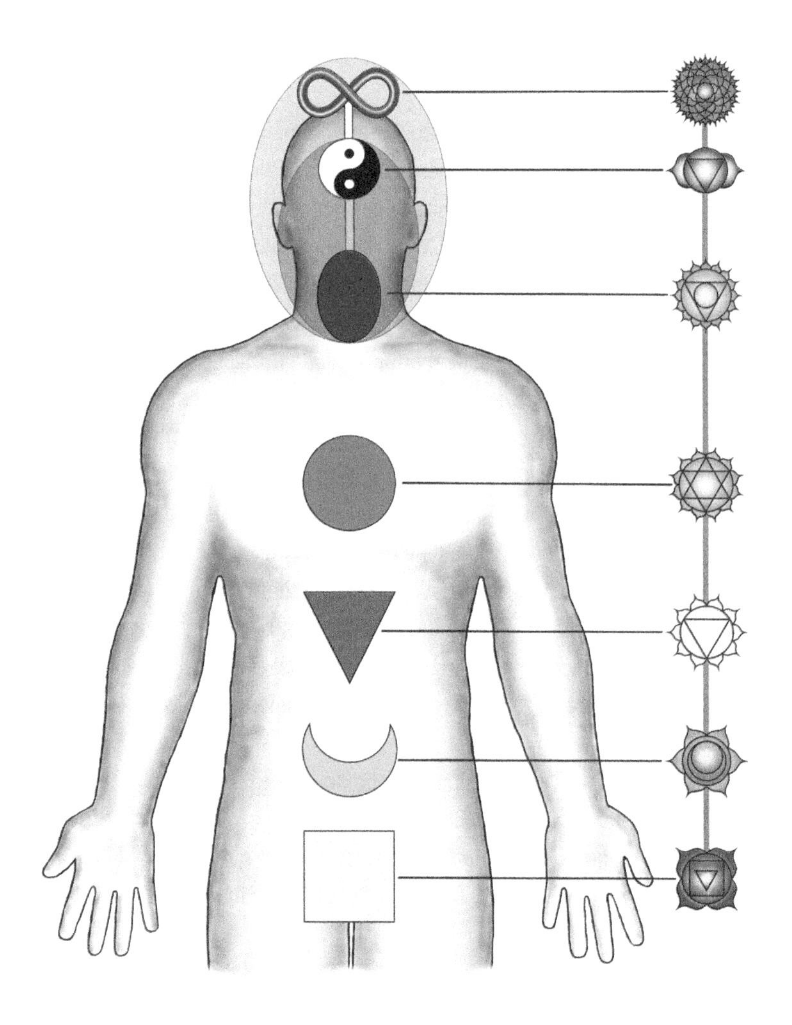

Figure 82: The Tattvas and the Chakras

Tejas Tattva (Fire Element)

Tejas, or Agni (fire), is the Fire Element Tattva. Tejas means "sharp" in Sanskrit; its meaning translates to "heat" or "illumination." Tejas Tattva is symbolized by an upwards red triangle whose colour is associated with its Archetypal energy. However, when placed on the body, the triangle points downwards towards the Apas (Water) Element (Figure 82). The concept of "Water up, Fire Down" explains our body's natural energy flow.

As Fire is the source of heat and Light, it is the first principle whose form is visible to the naked eye. After all, it is by the appearance of Light we perceive forms in our environment. Thus, Tejas is the quality that gives definition or structure to the different expressions of kinetic energy represented by Vayu Tatva, from which Tejas has evolved.

The birth of form is closely connected with the advent of the Ego—the Soul's antithesis. The Ego was born when we recognized something outside of ourselves for the first time. As we acclimatized to the material world in our early years, we became attached to forms we saw in the environment, which allowed the Ego to grow, taking a firm hold over the consciousness. Thus, Samskaras developed over time, a Sanskrit term implying mental impressions, recollections, and psychological imprints. Samskaras are the root of Karmic energy that holds us back from Spiritually evolving until we overcome it.

The Ego's development continues into our teenage years, forming our personality over time. The Ego doesn't stop growing and expanding for the rest of our life here on Earth since it is tied to the physical body and its survival. The only way to halt the Ego's growth is to recognize and embrace the deeper Spiritual reality that underlies the physical one—one which is void and therefore form-less. When our attention focuses on Spiritual Evolution instead of feeding the Ego, the Soul finally takes over, and we begin building character that transcends our material existence.

As mentioned before, the Ego and the Soul cannot co-exist as drivers of consciousness; one always has to assume the passenger seat. That choice is determined by us and which aspect of the Self we give our attention to in any given moment since we have Free Will. Therefore, Tejas relates to both the Soul and the Ego. The Fire Element is the willpower we use to express our Free Will principle in either direction, powered by Manipura, the Solar Plexus Chakra. Its realm of experience is the Plane of consciousness, termed "Swar Loka," the region between the Sun and the Polar Star, the Heaven of the Hindu God Indra.

Tejas Tattva has often been described as a devouring force that consumes everything in its path. However, destruction is a catalyst for transformation since nothing ever dies but only changes its state. As such, the Fire Element is crucial to Spiritual Evolution since it enables us to remake our beliefs about ourselves and the world, allowing us to tap into our highest potential. Tejas' destruction, therefore, results in new creations propitious to the Soul's growth.

Tejas' Bija Mantra is "Ram." This Tattva's energy is comparable to a ritual invocation of the Fire Element and the energy of Planet Mars with aspects of the Sun's energy. Tejas is masculine and active as it stimulates the individual's drive and willpower. The Sub-Elements of Tejas are Fire of Fire, Spirit of Fire, Air of Fire, Water of Fire, and Earth of Fire. The Sub-Element Fire of Fire is akin to the energy of the Aries Zodiac, while Air of Fire is similar to Leo and Water of Fire to Sagittarius.

Apas Tattva (Water Element)

The next Tattva in the sequence of manifestation is Apas, symbolized by the silver crescent moon. Apas is intensely active Matter that emerged out of the Fire Element because of decreased motion and condensation. It is confined within a definitive space while in a state of fluidity.

Apas is the physical Universe still arranging itself before it materializes as the next Tattva. It represents order arising out of chaos. The arrangement of atoms and molecules in Apas take up very little space with limited freedom of movement, unlike the Fire, Air, and Spirit Elements. For example, hydrogen and oxygen behave differently than those same molecules in vapour.

Apas is feminine and passive; it is attributed to Swadhisthana, the Sacral Chakra. Apas relates to the Moon's effect upon the tides of the sea and the Element of Water within us. Considering our own physical body is made up of 60% water, the importance of the Water Element in terms of our biological system is obvious.

Since Apas is Matter that is still being created, it represents the creative impulse within our psyche. It relates to the emotions that are fluid and changeable, like the Water Element that represents them. Our sexuality is also expressed emotionally as desire, serving as a powerful motivator in our lives. The Moon cycles not only have a strong influence on our emotions but our sexuality as well.

Apas has the quality of contraction and the principle of taste. It's Bija Mantra is "Vam." Experiences of Apas are similar to ritual invocations of the Water Element. Its Planetary correspondence is with the Moon and Jupiter and aspects of Venus since all three Planets are associated with emotion and feelings.

The Sub-Elements of Apas are Water of Water, Spirit of Water, Fire of Water, Air of Water, and Earth of Water. The Sub-Element of Water of Water is akin to the energy of the Pisces Zodiac, while Fire of Water is similar to Cancer and Air of Water to Scorpio. Apas' realm of experience is the Plane of consciousness termed "Bhuvar Loka," the area between the Earth and the Sun and home to celestial beings known as Siddhas.

Prithivi Tattva (Earth Element)

The fifth and final Tattva is Prithivi, symbolized by a yellow square and related to the Element of Earth. The last Element that evolves in the process of Creation results from a further decrease in vibration that causes the Water Element to solidify and become motionless. Prithivi is the densest of all the Tattvas, as it represents the concrete World of Matter whose molecules are fixed in place. It represents the qualities of solidity, weight, and cohesion, bringing stability and permanence on all levels.

Although the yellow colour typically represents the Air Element in the Western Mysteries, in the Tattvic system, it is associated with Earth. Yellow relates to the yellow Light of the Sun that allows us to perceive the World of Matter. Prithivi's correspondence is with the Root or Muladhara Chakra and the sense of smell. Its Bija Mantra is "Lam."

Prithivi's energy is similar to the ritual invocations of the Earth Element. The Sub-Elements of Prithivi are Earth of Earth, Spirit of Earth, Fire of Earth, Water of Earth, and Air of Earth. The Sub-Element of Fire of Earth's energy is akin to the Capricorn Zodiac, while Water of Earth is similar to Virgo and Air of Earth can be compared to Taurus. Prithivi's realm of experience is the Plane of consciousness termed "Bhu Loka," the Physical World of gross Matter.

TATTVA SCRYING

Tattvas are easy to use and very effective in tuning you into the desired Elemental energies. One simply needs to hold a Tattva in their hand and "scry" it by gazing, or looking deeply into it, to unlock its power. Scrying Tattvas is instrumental in developing psychic powers such as clairvoyance. It is one of the easiest, fastest, and most effective methods of exercising and improving your clairvoyant abilities.

The Tattva Scrying method can also facilitate a full Out-of-Body Experience since it includes an Astral Projection component whose technique is akin to Shamanic journeying and pathworking. However, you need to be cautious when attempting Astral Projection, especially if you suffer from anxiety or nervousness. It can be quite a jolt for the mind to experience things beyond the physical, especially your first time. Therefore, you should be sufficiently energetically balanced before attempting Astral Projection, which you can achieve with the use of Spiritual Healing modalities presented in this book.

Before starting this exercise, you will need to print out the Tattva cards in colour from my website at www.nevenpaar.com by following the "Tattva Cards" link in the main navigation. The cards in the PDF document are five by six inches, which is their ideal size for scrying purposes, with the symbols around three to four inches in height. If you already own Tattva cards, proceed to work with them so long as they fall within the given parameters.

However, the most optimal Tattva cards should be self-constructed out of cardboard. You should cut out the symbols separately, paint them by hand, and glue them onto the cards to provide a Three-Dimensional perspective. Figure 83 shows the Tattva cards I constructed many years ago when I was in the Golden Dawn Order.

Figure 83: The Author's Tattva Cards

There are two parts of the Tattva Scrying method as presented by the Hermetic Order of the Golden Dawn. The first part is called "Scrying in the Spirit Vision," which involves tuning into the Elemental and Sub-Elemental energy within your Aura, which isolates your Chakras so you can work with them. The second part is optional, and it is a continuation of the first, called "Travelling in the Spirit Vision." After evoking the Elemental or Sub-Elemental energy and amplifying it in your Aura, your consciousness becomes immersed in it. This is an excellent opportunity to perform an Astral Projection into its Cosmic Plane using a visualisation technique that involves your imagination and willpower.

Before starting the Tattva Scrying exercise, find a quiet space where you will be undisturbed during its performance. Since the practice involves going inwards, it is advisable to burn some incense to clear your space of negative energies and make it sacred. If you are familiar with the Ceremonial Magick Ritual exercises from my first book, perform the Lesser Banishing Ritual of the Pentagram and the Banishing Ritual of the Hexagram to banish adverse energy influences and centre yourself.

These two ritual exercises are instrumental for protection when doing Astral work, including Astral Projection which opens the consciousness to direct contact with Spiritual Intelligences within the inner Cosmic Planes. Other than basic Elementals, these can be Angelic or Demonic entities or Spirits that lodged themselves in the layers of your Aura and their respective Chakras sometime in the past. They are responsible for many of our moods and feelings, whether positive and constructive ones, as in the case of Angels, or negative and destructive ones as influenced by Demons.

Demons are more elusive than Angels since people generally avoid dealing with them. Often, they become locked away deep in the subconscious mind out of fear of having to face them. However, Demons will remain attached to you until you confront them with courage and learn their true nature, thereby fully integrating their powers and releasing them back into the Universe. In doing so, you are healing and optimising the Chakras while mastering their corresponding Elements within your psyche. Remember that whatever Spiritual Intelligence you may encounter in your scrying session, if you confront it with poise and love in your heart, they will be at your service.

Tattva Scrying Method-Part 1 (Scrying in the Spirit Vision)

Begin the exercise by sitting comfortably in the Lotus position or on a chair while facing the cardinal direction of the Element you are scrying. (Use Table 3 to obtain all relevant information you will need to scry the Tattvas.) You should have a white surface in front of you, such as a wall, or screen, or some sort of background since you will need to transpose the Astral imprint of the Tattva onto it as part of the exercise. The white surface also ensures no distractions for the mind when concentrating on the Tattva card. If you have hanging pictures or furniture close to your working area, remove them.

Perform the Four-Fold Breath for a few minutes with your eyes closed to get yourself into a meditative state of mind, which is essential for success in this work. Next, open your eyes and take up the Tattva. Hold it in your hand at arm's length so that the image is at eye level. Begin gazing at it comfortably, blinking as little as possible. Ensure that you see the Tattva card and the white background before you and nothing else. Don't allow your eyes to wander. Instead, get absorbed into the Tattva while keeping your mind empty of all thoughts. Allow its image to fill your consciousness as you imagine being soaked in the energy of its associated Element or Sub-Element.

You should gaze at the Tattva for twenty seconds to one minute initially and then lengthen your duration as you become more proficient at this exercise. Make sure not to strain your eyes at any point. After some time, the Tattva will begin to "flash" out of the symbol you are gazing at, like you are seeing its energy imprint or Aura. Experience will teach you how long it takes to get to this point.

The next step is to put down the Tattva card and smoothly switch your gaze onto the plain white surface in front of you. You will notice the transference of the symbol into its "flashing" or complementary colour to the Tattva. For example, if you are scrying Prithivi, its complementary colour will be violet. If you are scrying a Sub-Elemental Tattva, you will see two complementary colours flashing in front of you.

Now gaze at the flashing symbol before you. If it starts to drift, bring it back into focus in front of you. Once it vanishes in your physical sight, close your eyes and focus on what remains of its mental imprint. Let your physical vision transition into Astral vision as if the back of your eyelids is a movie screen replaying the image back to you.

It is advisable to practise transferring the Tattva card visually onto the white background three to four times since this part of the exercise is most important for the next step of Astral Projection. However, simply by gazing at the Tattva, you are unlocking its associated energy in your Aura, which you should feel immediately (if you are sensitive to energies) as a quantifiable essence. Note that the longer you gaze at the Tattva, the more of its corresponding energy permeates the Aura.

Tattva Scrying Method-Part 2 (Travelling in the Spirit Vision)

After the Astral image vanishes, use your imagination to bring it back in your Mind's Eye in the complementary colour of the Tattva you are working with. Imagine the image becoming enlarged to the size of a door. Next, visualize your Astral form and see it standing right before this doorway. Take a moment to note all the details of your Astral Self, including your wardrobe, facial expressions, etc. If it helps your visualization, imagine yourself wearing the same clothes you are wearing while doing the exercise. Note that you should be looking at yourself in the third-person in your mind for this part of the exercise like you are both the director and the star of the movie as one.

Next, you need to transfer your seed of consciousness into your Astral Self. This part is tricky and is where most students need practise. To do it successfully, you need to stop viewing yourself in the third-person and switch your perspective to first-person. Imagine your entire essence entering your Astral Self as you exit your physical body, which remains sitting quietly with eyes closed. Take a moment now by opening your eyes as your Astral Self and observe your hands and feet as if you just woke up inside of a Lucid Dream. Next, look at the doorway in front of you, your portal to another dimension. When you are ready, pass through the doorway. If you are familiar with the ritual exercises from *The Magus*, you can project your Astral Self through the doorway with the Sign of the Enterer while sealing yourself in the corresponding Cosmic Plane with the Sign of Silence. If you are unfamiliar with these gestures, simply step through the doorway.

The moment you step into the projected Cosmic Plane, allow your imagination to go on autopilot. This part is crucial to success with Astral Projection since everything up to this point was a guided visualization using your willpower and imagination. Now you must stop controlling the experience so that your imagination gets its impression from the Elemental or Sub-Elemental energy that you amplified in your Aura with the Tattva gazing technique. If done correctly, you should obtain a vision of the Cosmic Plane.

TABLE 3: Tattva Correspondences

Element (English & Sanskrit)	Direction	Elementals	God Name (Hebrew)	Archangel	Angel
Earth, Prithivi	North	Gnomes	Adonai ha-Aretz	Auriel	Phorlakh
Water, Apas	West	Undines	Elohim Tzabaoth	Gabriel	Taliahad
Fire, Tejas	South	Salamanders	YHVH Tzabaoth	Michael	Aral
Air, Vayu	East	Sylphs	Shaddai El Chai	Raphael	Chassan
Spirit, Akasha	Up/Down, East (default)	-	Eheieh	Metatron	Chayoth ha-Qadesh

Observe the scenery around you, noting every little detail you can see. Use your Astral senses to take in the sights, sounds, tastes, smells, and tactile sensations of the Cosmic Plane. If things appear dull and unanimated, you can vibrate the Divine Names of the corresponding Element three or four times each as per Table 3. The sequence to follow is God Name, Archangel, and Angel. Doing so should bring things to vivid colour and movement. If it does not, then you may need more practise transferring your consciousness into your Astral Self and allowing yourself to "let go" long enough to experience a vision in the Astral Plane. Don't despair if this does not work the first few times; most people need more practise with Part 1 of the Tattva Scrying Method before engaging in Part 2.

After vibrating the appropriate Divine Names, it is not uncommon to see a Spiritual guide appear before you. This entity is often an Elemental whose characteristics represent the qualities of the Element you are visiting. You can also summon a guide to help you explore the place, which is recommended, especially if you are new to this practice.

Observe the entity's appearance and test it by asking its purpose in assisting you, which will help you determine whether it is benevolent or malevolent. Sometimes you may not see an entity but feel its presence, which can often be more trustworthy than the use of Astral sight or other senses.

If the entity appears malevolent, you can use the Divine Names of the Element you are working with to banish it. You can also draw a banishing Pentagram of Earth (as instructed in *The Magus*) to dismiss the entity, unless you are working with Prithivi Tattva, which will cause a banishing of both positive and negative aspects of Earth. If for some reason you don't want the assistance of a guide, you can use the banishing Pentagram of the Element you are working with to send them away, which works in most cases.

Assuming that your guide is a positive Spirit that wants to help you, allow it to lead you around so that you can explore the scenery. Ask your guide any questions about what you are seeing on your journey or the nature of the Element pertaining to the Cosmic Plane you are exploring. After all, this work aims to develop knowledge and mastery over the Elements which are parts of your psyche.

When exploring Sub-Elemental Cosmic Planes, it is not uncommon to be passed onto a second guide who will show you around a different scenery altogether. In this case, you need to test them again to determine the quality of their Being, including vibrating the Divine Names of the secondary Tattva you are visiting. When leaving the first guide behind, grant them the courtesy of a goodbye, especially if they treated you with respect.

If you feel that the environment has become chaotic with your presence, you can use the Divine Names to bring harmony and peace to the Cosmic Plane you are visiting and restore its original constitution. Remember always to be respectful but firm with your guides and not let them get out of line since they are there to assist you. You must always maintain composure and control over the situation.

The method of leaving the Cosmic Plane and returning to ordinary, waking consciousness is the exact reversal of the initial process. Firstly, thank the guide and bid them farewell. Then you must retrace your footsteps back to the doorway from whence you came. Once you step through the doorway, your journey will be complete. If you used the Sign of the Enterer and Sign of Silence to enter the doorway, then use it again to leave it.

Next, you need to transfer your seed of consciousness from your Astral Self to your physical Self. In doing so, feel your Being switching from an internal to an external perspective as you shift your attention from your Astral senses to your physical ones. Take a few deep breaths now as you focus on listening to any sounds in your environment. When you are ready to end your Tattva Scrying experience, slowly open your eyes. If you started this exercise with the Lesser Banishing Ritual of the Pentagram and the Banishing Ritual of the Hexagram, repeat them to centre yourself and banish any unwanted influences.

It is crucial never to simply end the experience by opening your physical eyes while your Astral Self is still within the Cosmic Plane you are visiting. There should never be a merging of an Elemental Plane into the Physical Plane of consciousness since doing so can be detrimental for the psyche. The immediate side-effects are feeling confused, disoriented, and spaced out. The more lasting side-effects include chaotic and destructive manifestations in your life, which can go on for weeks, months, and even years, until becoming resolved. Therefore, take your time with this "returning home" process and follow all the steps, even if you do them in a fast-tracked manner.

***

As a beginner, start by practising with the primary Tattvas of Prithivi, Apas, Tejas, Vayu, and Akasha, in that order. Focus on the first four until you gain some experience before moving to Akasha Tattva. Perform each scrying session with an individual Tattva card once a day, not more. You can perform this exercise anytime, although mornings and afternoons are best, preferably on an empty stomach. If you scry the Tattvas right before sleep, anticipate that the operation will affect your dream content.

After a few weeks of experimenting with primary Tattvas, and once you have obtained satisfactory results with Astral Projection, you can move on to the Spiritual Alchemy Program I devised for the more ambitious aspirants of this work. This advanced Tattva operation will provide optimal results when exploring the Elements, Sub-Elements, and their corresponding Chakras. It follows the sequence of entering the layers of the Aura from the Lower Astral (Earth) to Higher Astral (Water), followed by Lower Mental (Air), onto Higher Mental (Fire), and finally to the Spiritual Plane (Spirit).

I am presenting the Western sequence of the emanating Elements, which puts the Fire Element after the Air Element, instead of before, as the Eastern system. In my experience, this sequence of progressively working with the Cosmic Planes from the lowest to the highest is most effective in Spiritual Healing and raising the vibration of consciousness.

The entire Spiritual Alchemy Program with the Tattvas will take you one month to complete. Afterwards, you can either repeat the cycle or work with individual Elements and Sub-Elements to master those parts of the Self. You can also revisit specific Cosmic Planes you found most exciting and revelatory that either called to you or that you felt needed further exploration.

Working with the Tattvas is an excellent opportunity to use a Magickal Journal, a notebook or a diary to record your experiences. This is essential to improving your scrying abilities and memory recall and to give you insight into particular symbols, numbers, and events you experienced during a session. By documenting your experiences over time, you will begin to recognize patterns and derive metaphoric meanings from your sessions that are part of a larger picture of who you are and what you need to work on to further your Spiritual Evolution.

In conclusion, remember to be patient, determined, and persistent with this work, especially when starting out. It is easy to get deterred from the Astral Projection component of this practice when you are not getting the results you anticipate. However, keep in mind that developing inner clairvoyance is no easy task. Tattva Scrying is hard, strenuous work that often takes months or even years to become proficient. But with perseverance, your visions will grow from vague, slightly indistinguishable pictures to vivid, dynamic, and powerful Magickal experiences.

Spiritual Alchemy Program with the Tattvas

Lower Astral Plane—Earth/Muladhara:
Day 1—Earth/Primary Earth
Day 2—Earth/Earth of Earth
Day 3—Earth/Water of Earth
Day 4—Earth/Air of Earth
Day 5—Earth/Fire of Earth
Day 6—Earth/Spirit of Earth

Higher Astral Plane—Water/Swadhisthana:
Day 7—Water/Primary Water
Day 8—Water/Earth of Water
Day 9—Water/Water of Water
Day 10—Water/Air of Water
Day 11—Water/Fire of Water
Day 12—Water/Spirit of Water

Lower Mental Plane—Air/Anahata:
Day 13—Air/Primary Air
Day 14—Air/Earth of Air
Day 15—Air/Water of Air
Day 16—Air/Air of Air
Day 17—Air/Fire of Air
Day 18—Air/Spirit of Air

Higher Mental Plane—Fire/Manipura:
Day 19—Fire/Primary Fire
Day 20—Fire/Earth of Fire
Day 21—Fire/Water of Fire
Day 22—Fire/Air of Fire
Day 23—Fire/Fire of Fire
Day 24—Fire/Spirit of Fire

Spiritual Plane—Spirit/Vishuddhi, Ajna, Sahasrara:
Day 25—Spirit/Primary Spirit
Day 26—Spirit/Earth of Spirit
Day 27—Spirit/Water of Spirit
Day 28—Spirit/Air of Spirit
Day 29—Spirit/Fire of Spirit
Day 30—Spirit/Spirit of Spirit

PART VI: THE SCIENCE OF YOGA (WITH AYURVEDA)

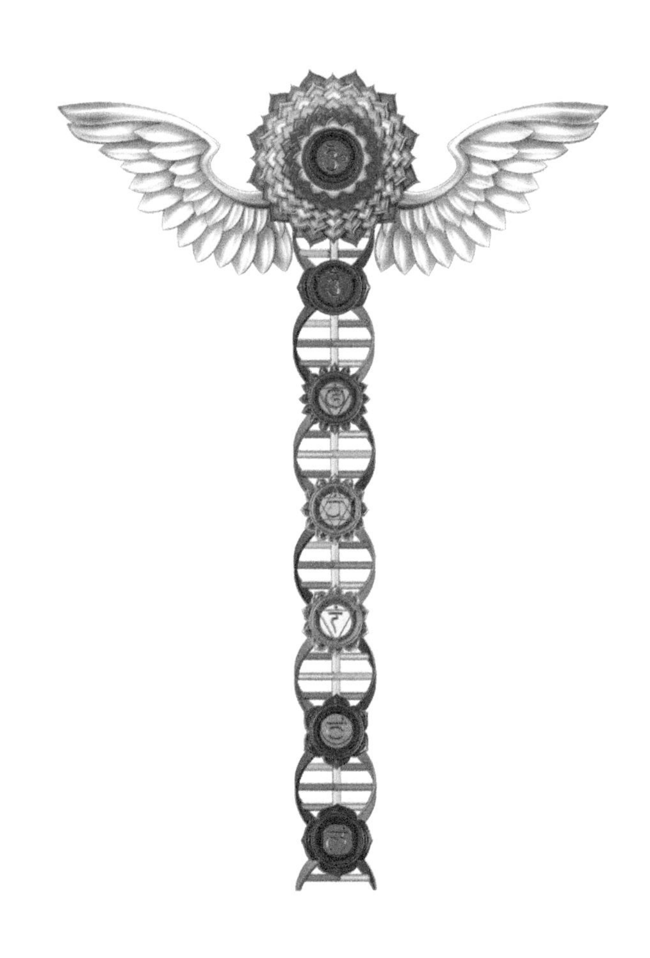

THE PURPOSE OF YOGA

Yoga is a group of physical, mental, and Spiritual practices, disciplines, and techniques that originated in Ancient India approximately 5000 years ago. Yoga was mentioned in the ancient Hindu texts, *The Rig Veda* and *The Upanishads*, although its actual development only occurred in the fifth and sixth centuries BC. *The Yoga Sutras of Patanjali*, the most influential Hindu text on Yoga, is dated around the second century BC. In the 20th century, this text was translated into English, which sparked a strong interest in Yoga in the Western world.

Although most people in the West believe that Yoga is a mere physical exercise consisting of bodily postures (Asanas), this could not be further from the truth. Asanas are the physical aspects of what is a profound science of unfolding the Spiritual potential of human beings. There was very little Asana practice as part of Yoga in the olden days. Its original forms were mostly of a transcendental and meditative nature. Yoga used to be about accessing states of pure consciousness and bliss (Samadhi) and overcoming the burdens of the material reality. Asana practice, which is the core of Hatha Yoga, came out of Tantra approximately 1000 years ago.

The word "yoga" in Sanskrit means "union," and it refers to the union of the individual consciousness with the Cosmic Consciousness. For there to be a union between the two, though, there must first have been a separation. In reality, there never was. Separation is an illusion that occurs through the mind with the birth and growth of the Ego. Yoga then aims to transcend the Ego and become a Self-realized human being. By practising a time-tested system of working with their energy field, an individual can overcome the limitations of their mind and reach the highest of their Spiritual potential.

According to Patanjali, Yoga requires the cessation of the mind's fluctuations, which results in the union of the observer, observing, and observed. The ultimate purpose of Yoga is Enlightenment and the integration of the Spirit within the body. To get its practitioners there, Yoga aims to balance the energetic system and gradually awaken the Kundalini at the base of the spine. Once Kundalini Shakti rises up the spinal column to meet Shiva at the Crown, a Divine Marriage occurs, expanding the individual consciousness. When the two opposing masculine and feminine forces become one, The Soul is released from the body and exalted over the Ego. The individual becomes a Yogi or liberated Soul, a God-man. They transcend duality and the Elements within themselves, represented by the lower Cosmic Planes, and attune their consciousness to the Spiritual Plane which is Non-Dual.

Because Yoga is our most ancient method of balancing the energetic system and awakening the Kundalini energy, I have decided to dedicate a whole chapter to its science. Although this section is a mere primer on Yoga, there is much to be gained from the practices presented herein, and they form part of the Eastern Spiritual system.

TYPES OF YOGA

The practice of Yoga is very diverse, as there are many different branches. All of them are ultimately meant to lead to the experience of union with the Godhead. Below are the main branches of Yoga, although there are many more that are not listed here. Some of those are considered part of the main ones, although unique in and of themselves.

Hatha Yoga

Tantra emerged around the sixth to eighth centuries AD, and it is its historical development in practice that later generated Hatha Yoga (14th century). Hatha Yoga is the type that is generally practised in Western society. There are slight variations in philosophies, practices, and terminology that allow the different schools of Yoga in the West to fit the individual practitioners, but they all include the practice of Asanas (physical postures) and Pranayama (known as breathing techniques but more accurately designed for the expansion of Prana).

The word "Hatha" is translated from Sanskrit to mean "Sun and Moon," with "ha" indicating Sun energy, while "tha" signifies Moon energy. Hatha Yoga means the harmony or balance between the Sun and Moon, Pingala, and Ida Nadis, two opposite and complementary aspects of our Being. Hatha Yoga's higher purpose is optimizing one's health by purifying the energetic channels in the body and maximizing the function of the Chakras. It attempts to harmonize the physical body so that it can be transcended. Hatha Yoga also gives one control over their internal states so that they gain better awareness and concentration for the purpose of developing and refining the meditative practices of Yoga, termed Dharana and Dhyana. Meditation is a crucial component in all Spiritual practices, including Yoga.

Mudras and Bandhas are also classified as part of Hatha Yoga. Mudras are physical gestures or body positions that induce psychological and mental changes in one's Being. Bandhas are physical energy locks that perform the same function as Mudras. Bandhas are primarily used to pierce the Three Granthis, or psychic knots, that lie along the Sushumna Nadi. The ultimate goal of Hatha Yoga is awakening the Kundalini and reaching Samadhi. There are many methods and techniques in Hatha Yoga to accomplish this goal. Many of these are presented in this work.

Kundalini Yoga

The system of Yoga focused on awakening the Chakric centres to induce a higher state of consciousness. Kundalini Yoga involves repetitive movements of the body, synchronized with the breath, coupled with chanting and meditation. It is meant to keep the mind busy by combining several Yogic practices simultaneously. Kundalini Yoga's ultimate goal is to awaken the Kundalini energy at the base of the spine, which activates the Major Chakras on its upward rise. Its discipline involves simple Asanas, which allows the practitioner to focus on their energy and have optimal awareness of their body and mind. Kundalini Yoga includes specific techniques from Kriya Yoga, Hatha Yoga, Bhakti Yoga, Raja Yoga, and Shakti Yoga.

Karma Yoga

The "Yoga of Action." Karma Yoga is the system of attaining Self-awareness through activity. Its ideals are altruistic as it involves selfless service to others as part of one's larger Self, void of attachment to results—the individual aims to align their willpower with the Will of God. As such, all of their actions are performed from a higher sense of consciousness. Karma Yoga involves being involved in the present moment, which allows one to transcend the Ego. It aids in making the mind more calm and peaceful by overcoming personal emotions. Since Karma Yoga is more of a way of life than anything else, there have been many notable individuals in the past who were Karma Yogis, even unknowingly. Jesus Christ, Krishna, Mahatma Gandhi, Mother Teresa, Rumi, are just a few examples.

Mantra Yoga

The "Yoga of Sound." Sound vibrations have an incredible effect on the mind, body, and Soul, and they can also produce a change in the material world. Mantra Yoga uses the power of sound to induce different states of consciousness through the process of repetition of certain Universal sounds, which becomes a Mantra. These Universal sounds are to be vibrated or "chanted" with our vocal cords for added effect. Mantras are found in every tradition and often include the names and powers of Gods, Goddesses, Spirits, and other Deities. Using Mantras invokes/evokes energy into the Aura, which affects one's consciousness. Many Mantras aim at producing mental and emotional tranquillity, thereby raising awareness of the inner processes of the mind. The name itself, "Mantra," means to "transcend the working mind." There are three ways to chant Mantras: Bhaikari (Normal audible intonation—voiced), Upanshu (Soft audible intonation—Whispering), and Manasik (Not audible—silently/mentally). Mantra Yoga is a powerful method of introspection as well as aligning one's consciousness with Divine forces. Through it, the ultimate aim of Yoga (union with the Godhead) can be achieved.

Jnana (Gyana) Yoga

The Yoga or path of Self-inquiry, also known as the path of Intuitive Knowledge. Although many people think that Jnana Yoga is the path of the intellect, perception is predominantly through the Vijnanamaya Kosha (the intuitive mind) and not the Manomaya Kosha (the rational intellect), which is the direct experience of the Divine and develops Gnosis. Jnana Yoga aims to develop an awareness of one's Higher Self to achieve illuminative knowledge of the mysteries of the Universe. It seeks to discern between Maya (illusion) and the real world of the Spirit. Jnana Yoga's components include the study of sacred texts, introspection, philosophical discussions, and debates. Notable Jnana Yogis include Swami Vivekananda, Sri Yukteswar Giri (Yogananda's Guru) and Ramana Maharshi, to name a few. Some of the Greek philosophers, including Socrates and Plato, were also Jnana Yogis.

Bhakti Yoga

The Yoga of devotion. Bhakti Yoga focuses the love of the Divine through devotional rituals. Examples of practices involved in Bhakti Yoga are prayer, chanting, dancing, singing, ceremony and celebrations. The emotions are given an outlet instead of suppressing or dissipating them in different directions. By becoming wholly absorbed in their object of devotion, the Bhakti transcends their Ego. As the lower emotions are diminished, the mental problems disappear. As such, one's concentration and awareness increases, leading to Self-realization.

Raja Yoga

The Yoga of introspection through meditation. Raja Yoga is the Royal Path as "raja" means king. It encompasses the essence of many other Yoga paths, namely Karma, Bhakti, and Jnana Yoga. Raja Yoga's focus is the internal analysis of the workings of the mind for the sake of quieting it and going beyond it. It attempts to transcend the Ego and the outer environment of the physical body and attune to the inner Self of the Soul and Spirit. It is the path towards Enlightenment.

Patanjali Yoga

Patanjali Yoga is often identified with Raja Yoga directly because it is introspective. The system of Patanjali consists of eight limbs (Sanskrit term "Ashtanga") or steps of Yoga (Figure 84), which the individual must master on their path to Self-realization. Think of the eight limbs as parts of the great tree of Yoga where each limb (branch) connects to the trunk. Each limb has leaves that express its life and are the techniques of the science of Yoga. The eight limbs or steps of Yoga are outlined in the *Yoga Sutras*, which was compiled by the Sage Patanjali. They are Yamas (Self-restraints), Niyamas (Self-observances), Asana (postures), Pranayama (breathing), Pratyahara (withdrawal of the senses), Dharana (concentration), Dhyana (meditation), and Samadhi (Self-identification with the Cosmic Consciousness).

Figure 84: The Eight Limbs of Yoga

Kriya Yoga

The Sanskrit word "kriya" means "action" or movement." Kriya Yoga is the science of controlling the Prana in the body. One of its aims is to decarbonize the human blood and recharge it with oxygen which is meant to rejuvenate the brain and spinal centres. The Ancient system of Kriya Yoga consists of many levels of Pranayama, Mantra, and Mudra, based on techniques intended to rapidly accelerate your Spiritual Evolution and lead to communion with one's Higher, God-Self. Kriya Yoga gained popularity in the world through Paramahamsa Yogananda's book *Autobiography of a Yogi*.

Dhyana Yoga

The Yoga of meditation. Dhyana Yoga primarily involves the seventh limb of Yoga mentioned in the *Yoga Sutras of Patanjali*. It concerns itself with quieting the mind and enabling greater focus and awareness, which is achieved through the practices of Asana, Pranayama, Mantra, and Dharana (concentration). Dhyana Yoga trains you to keep your mind off the unnecessary things in life and concentrate on what matters. Meditation cuts through illusion, leading to the truth of reality, enabling Self-knowledge.

***

In conclusion, many other forms of Yoga are excellent systems in and of themselves, but that fall within one of the primary groups mentioned. They include Siddha Yoga, Shiva Yoga, Buddhi Yoga, Sannyasa Yoga, Maha Yoga, and others. Since there are many styles or types of Yoga, each slightly different from the other, the average person has many options to choose from that best suits their psychological and physical makeup. However, most types of Yoga include the same elements and practices, which I will examine in detail in this section.

THE FIVE KOSHAS

According to Yoga and Ayurveda, the human energy system is comprised of five Subtle Bodies or "sheaths," called the Koshas (Figure 85), which cover and hide our essential nature—Atman, the Universal Self (Soul). The Koshas are essentially the gateways to the Soul. They account for the different dimensions and vibratory states of consciousness that humans partake of. The Koshas relate to the Five Elements (Tattvas) and the Seven Major Chakras, with the highest Kosha (Anandamaya) encompassing the three Spirit Chakras. (Note that Figure 85 is an abstract schematic of the Five Koshas, not their actual depiction in the Aura.)

The Koshas are synonymous with the Subtle Bodies of the inner Cosmic Planes of the Western Mystery Tradition. However, instead of seven, there are five layers of the Aura in the Yogic system, which are interconnected, constantly interacting with one another. The Koshas emanate in sequence, starting with the densest, with each subsequent layer being more subtle and higher in vibration than the one that came before it.

Annamaya Kosha

The first layer or sheath is called Annamaya Kosha, and it relates to the conscious mind and the physical body. It is the grossest and most dense Kosha and one with which we identify the most. Built up by the food we eat, Annamaya Kosha corresponds with the first Chakra, Muladhara, and the Earth Element (Prithivi Tattva). Regular Asana practice and a healthy diet can keep our physical body in optimal condition so that we can experience life free of disease.

Pranamaya Kosha

The second sheath is Pranamaya Kosha; the vital energy body made up of Life energy. Pranamaya Kosha, as the name says, deals with the Prana in the body; hence it can be termed our Pranic Body, which is absorbed through the breath, food, and the Universal Life Force that surrounds us, permeating our Aura. It flows through the intricate system of Nadis in the body, of which it is said there are Seventy-Two Thousand. Pranamaya Kosha can be controlled by the breath, although it is more subtle of a force than the air we breathe. It relates to the second Chakra, Swadhisthana, and the Water Element (Apas Tattva). Pranamaya Kosha links Annamaya and Manomaya Koshas as it relates to both the body and the mind. The practice of Pranayama aids in keeping the Life Force flowing freely in Pranamaya Kosha, keeping the body and mind healthy.

Figure 85: The Five Koshas

Manomaya Kosha

The third sheath is Manomaya Kosha, the mental/emotional body in the Yogic system, related to the subconscious mind. Manomaya Kosha includes thought patterns and feelings, permeating the vital and food sheaths. It corresponds with the third Chakra, Manipura, and the Fire Element (Tejas Tattva). Becoming aware of our daily thoughts and emotions and dissolving them through sense-withdrawal (Pratyahara) and one-pointed concentration (Dharana) can help keep our mind pure and unburdened by the pain of duality.

Vijnanamaya Kosha

The fourth sheath is Vijnanamaya Kosha, and it is the psychic or higher mental body that enables intuition. In Yoga, Vijnanamaya Kosha is the "wisdom body" that reveals personal insights. It links the subconscious and the unconscious minds, giving us inner knowledge, including gut reactions to life events. Vijnanamaya Kosha relates to the fourth Chakra, Anahata, and the Air Element (Vayu Tattva). Through the practice of Yamas (Self-restraints) and

Niyamas (Self-observances), and with the use of Yogic practices, we can purify our minds and hearts to connect with our intuition, enabling us to live a happier and more Spiritual life.

Anandamaya Kosha

Lastly, the fifth sheath is Anandamaya Kosha, which is considered as the transcendental or bliss body, the Body of Light. Its experience can be described as a state of total absorption into a blissful state, achieved through the silence of the mind. The sweetness and beauty of life we experience when the mind is still is known as Sat-Chit-Ananda (Truth-Consciousness-Bliss in Sanskrit), the subjective experience of the ultimate unchanging reality—Brahman.

Ananadamaya Kosha can be experienced through daily meditation (Dhyana) or via a full Kundalini awakening. Although Anandamaya Kosha allows us to experience the super-conscious state of Samadhi, there still exists the duality between subject and object. Therefore, to become one with Brahman (The All), we need to reach the layer above Ananadamaya Kosha, the nameless Divine layer.

In The Upanishads, Anandamaya Kosha is known as the Causal Body. It relates to the unconscious mind, a reservoir of feelings, thoughts, memories, and urges outside of our conscious and subconscious awareness. The unconscious mind controls many of the automatic processes in the body that ensure our physical survival. Anandamaya Kosha corresponds with the Spirit Element (Akasha Tattva) and the three highest Chakras of Vishuddhi, Ajna, and Sahasrara. It is the state of consciousness where our Holy Guardian Angel, our Higher Self, resides.

THE SUBTLE BODIES IN THE EAST AND WEST

The Five Koshas of the Eastern Spiritual system of Yoga correspond with the Subtle Bodies of the inner Cosmic Planes of the Western Esoteric System: the Physical, Astral, Mental, and Spiritual, with the Astral and Mental containing the Lower and Higher aspects. However, one minor difference between the two systems requires our attention.

In the science and philosophy of Yoga, the Subtle Bodies emanate with respect to the sequence of the first five Major Chakras, starting with Muladhara and ending with Vishuddhi. As mentioned, the three Spirit Chakras are attributed one Auric layer, for a total of Five Koshas. In contrast, the Western Mystery Tradition, whose foundation is the Qabalistic Tree of Life, follows the sequence of emanation of the Divine Light of Ain Soph Aur (Limitless Light) as pertains to the Five Elements. In the Qabalah, the Divine Light manifests as Spirit, Fire, Air, Water, Earth, where each of the subsequent Elements is less in Spiritual quality than the one before it.

As you can see, the two systems are almost identical concerning this subject, with one exception. In Yoga, the Fire (Manomaya Kosha) and Air (Vijnanamaya Kosha) Elements are interchanged since Manipura Chakra is below Anahata in the Chakric system. In Qabalistic philosophy, Fire is the first Element that manifested out of Spirit and is higher in Spiritual quality than the Air Element, irrespective of its positioning on the Chakric system. Western Mystery Schools teach that willpower (Fire) is higher than thought (Air) in the process of manifestation.

Both Spiritual systems give compelling arguments regarding this subject. The Western system argues that our Word, which links us with the Creator, is motioned by willpower. Its medium of expression is the mind (thoughts), but its impetus is a Force projected from the Soul deep within. The Soul is a Fire, and its origin is our Sun (Sol).

Theosophists, who belong to the Western Mystery Tradition, refer to the Plane of the Soul as the Buddhic Plane, which they position between the Mental and Spiritual Planes. To it, they attribute the Fire Element. Theosophists were heavily influenced by Hermeticism and its branch of Alchemy, the latter of which was impacted by the works of Plato and Aristotle. Therefore, the Theosophists adopted the Eastern Chakric system but modified it according to their psychic experiences of the Subtle Planes. In their view, Spiritual Alchemy clearly defines the Fire Element as higher in Spiritual quality than the Air Element.

Although Air is more subtle than Fire, since it is invisible like the Spirit, Hermeticists believe that the Air Element vibrates between the Fire and Water Elements since both partake of it and require it for sustenance. According to its placement on the Chakric system, the Air Element emanates from the Spirit. Still, its positioning in the expression of the subtle energy in our Aura would be between the Higher Mental Plane (Fire) and Higher Astral Plane (Water). For this reason, the Air Element is used more by the Ego, while the Soul uses the Fire Element to express itself.

The Ego also uses the Fire Element, but it filters through the mind, partaking in duality. The Fire Element, though, reaches into Non-Duality of the Spirit, as it reconciles all opposites within itself in the same way as combustion, Fire in its physical state, consumes all things. For this reason, Fire is the Element of action since it bypasses the mind and deals strictly with applying willpower.

Willpower does require imagination, however, which in the Qabalah is related to the Tiphareth Sephira, located between the Heart and Solar Plexus centres and corresponding with the Air Element. You see then that according to Qabalistic philosophy, both the emotions (Water) and willpower (Fire) require Air (thoughts) to manifest. They both partake of it, which is why in the Cosmic Planes model, its energetic sheath or Subtle Body lies between the two instead of above them.

Another argument for Qabalistic philosophy is that, according to their Four Worlds (YHVH) model, the Fire Element is Atziluth, the highest of the worlds. This world relates to Archetypes as the highest Plane below Spirit, while the Air Element is the third World (Yetzirah), relating to the visual images our minds form. According to Qabalists, Atziluth (Fire) is formless, while Yetzirah (Air) does have form.

The Fire Element is responsible for abstract thinking, while the Air Element is responsible for logical or rational thinking. Abstract thoughts exhibit higher intelligence than logical thoughts. For example, the Ego uses logic and reason to relate to the world around it, where its primary impetus is survival and the fear of death. On the other hand, the Soul uses abstract thinking as well as what we call intuition, which is an internal recognition of truth in reality. We don't know how or why we know what we know, but we are confident that we know it.

Abstract thinking and intuition are motivated by unconditional love, which is an expression of the Fire Element acting on the Water Element. For this reason, when we experience love in our hearts, there is a warmth that accompanies it. And according to most world religions and philosophies, the highest conception of God-the Creator for humanity is unconditional love. Hence, the highest of the four lower Elements, and one closest to God, is the Fire Element and not the Air Element.

Although I am a Qabalist first Yogi second, my thoughts naturally align with the Western Mystery Tradition, as do my beliefs. Ceremonial Magick, the Spiritual practice of the Western Mysteries, has provided me with direct experience of the Elemental energies for many years, and I have witnessed firsthand the Qabalistic system's accuracy. Likewise, my experiences with Enochian Magick, especially the Thirty Aethyrs operation that systematically enters the Aura layers, have given me Gnostic insight that validates and supports the Western Tradition's claims about the Elements in terms of Spiritual progression.

Regardless, I must remain respectful to the Yogi who has practised the Eastern Spiritual system for 20-plus years, who may also feel the same sense of certainty concerning its validity. The emanation of the Eastern Tattvas, for example, follows the Earth, Water, Fire, Air, Spirit sequence. And in the explanations of the Tattvas and how each manifested into existence, it is evident that the Air Element is more etheric and therefore less dense than the Fire Element. It is invisible to the senses, while Fire is visible as combustion or flame. Also, one cannot negate the sequence of manifestation of the Chakras, their correspondences, and their locations in the body. Thus, I recognize that arguments can be made for Western and Eastern systems concerning this subject.

Does the Subtle Body related to the Fire Element come before the Subtle Body associated with the Air Element or after it? We can debate this topic ad nauseam and won't get anywhere because both the Eastern and Western systems make valid claims from their respective viewpoints. But since *Serpent Rising* is my brainchild and I can only speak about the things I have experienced to be accurate, its philosophy concerning the emanation and the sequence of the Cosmic Planes will remain aligned with the Qabalistic system until I am convinced otherwise.

ASANA

According to the *Yoga Sutras of Patanjali*, Asana is defined as "that position which is steady and comfortable." In Sanskrit, the word "asana" means "sitting down," a sitting posture, or meditation seat. Its most literal meaning is "posture," whether a sitting or standing posture. For this reason, Asanas are called "Yoga poses" or "Yoga postures" in English.

Asana aims to develop the ability to sit or stand comfortably in one position for an extended period. The purpose of Asana is to influence, integrate, and harmonize all levels of one's Being, including physical, mental, emotional, and Spiritual. Although it may seem at first that Asanas are concerned mainly with the physical body, they have profound effects at every level of Being if one practices awareness during the process.

Asana is one of the eight limbs of Yoga. On a subtle level, Asanas are used to open energy channels and psychic centres. Their use facilitates the free-flow of Prana through the Nadis of the Subtle Bodies, thereby stimulating the Chakras and the Kundalini energy. As such, Asanas aid considerably in the Spiritual Evolution of an individual. One of its more immediate results is an improvement in one's flexibility and strength and the reduction of stress and the mental and emotional conditions that relate to it.

By developing control over the body, one gains control over the mind as well—As Above, So Below. Thus, the practice of Asanas integrates and harmonizes the physical body and the mind. It releases tensions or knots in both. Mental stresses are released by dealing with them on the physical level through holding the physical postures. Physical tension, such as muscular knots, is eliminated as well, thereby restoring the health of the body. After just one Yoga Asana session, the practitioner has more vitality, vigour and strength, while the mind is more joyful, creative, and inspired.

The 15th century *Hatha Yoga Pradipika*, the central text of Hatha Yoga, identifies 84 Asanas that provide both Spiritual and physical benefits. Because of its power as a tool for developing higher awareness, the practise of Asana is introduced first in Hatha Yoga practice, followed by Pranayama, and then Mudras, etc. While practising Asana, the individual should always breathe through the nose unless they are given specific instructions to do otherwise. The breath should always be coordinated with the Asana practice.

It has been proven that the practice of Yogic postures (Asanas) increase the feel-good chemicals in the brain, such as serotonin, dopamine, and endorphins. As the stress hormone cortisol decreases, mental relaxation is restored, and awareness and focus are heightened. By combining physical exercise and meditation, the body's metabolism becomes balanced. The practice of Asanas strengthens and tones the muscles resulting in not only feeling good internally but looking great on the outside.

THE THREE MEDITATION ASANAS

The purpose of meditation Asanas is to allow the individual to sit for an extended period without movement of the body or discomfort. Once the physical body is bypassed through the application of a meditation Asana and single-pointedness of the mind, one can experience a deeper state of consciousness.

When you are in a meditation Asana, your spinal column should be straight, which will allow Prana to circulate through the Nadis and Chakras most optimally. Also, since it is easy to lose control over the muscles while in deep meditation, it is best if the legs are immobilized in some way while the torso makes contact with the ground.

Sukhasana, Siddhasana, and Padmasana (Figure 86) are practised most when one wants to get into a deep meditation. These poses are the sitting down, cross-legged Asanas that the Ancient Gods from the East are commonly depicted in. The mechanics of each of these meditation Asanas will be described below.

Lying down in what the Yogis refer to as Shavasana (Figure 94), the Corpse Pose, is not recommended for meditation since there is a tendency to drift off into sleep. Sukhasana, Siddhasana and Padmasana satisfy all the requirements of meditation while making the individual alert and focused on the task at hand. These three meditation Asanas also allow the bottom of the spine to make contact with the ground, which achieves proper grounding of one's inner energies. As such, the chatter of the mind can be overcome.

When the practitioner can sit in a meditation Asana for a full three hours without the body jolting or shaking, they will have achieved mastery over it. Only then can they practise the higher stages of Pranayama and Dhyana. It is imperative to attain a steady meditation Asana if one wants to progress in meditation practice. The chatter of the Ego must be overcome, and the mind calmed if the individual is to find their inner bliss.

Achieving mastery over a meditation Asana is just one part of the process of entering deep meditation. The other part of the process is having your eyes closed and focusing on the space between your eyebrows, which activates the Mind's Eye. The Mind's Eye is the doorway or entry-point to Sahasrara, which represents one's higher state of consciousness. Sahasrara is, in fact, our contact point with Cosmic Consciousness.

Before beginning with a meditation Asana, it helps to do some basic stretching. Doing so will allow the practitioner to avoid muscle cramps and joint pain which can deter from the task at hand. Also, it helps to avoid meditating on a full stomach since there might be too much movement of one's inner energies as the food is being synthesized.

Sukhasana

This is the standard sitting cross-legged pose. It is called the "Easy Pose" because everyone can do it rather effortlessly. The back is to be straight and shoulders relaxed. The hands are placed on the knees, with the index fingers and thumbs touching in either Jnana or Chin Mudra. (For how to perform Jnana and Chin Mudras, see the "Mudra: Hasta (Hand Mudras)" chapter.) When meditating, the eyes should be closed, and one should focus on the point between the eyebrows, which is the location of the Mind's Eye.

Although this pose is considered the easiest of the meditation Asanas, if not done correctly, a backache can develop. It is imperative that the knees are kept close to or on the ground and the spine straight. It is common to see practitioners place a cushion under their buttocks for support.

Note that it is good to start your meditations with Sukhasana but not make it your end-goal. Instead, it would be best if you progressed to being able to accomplish Siddhasana and even Padmasana as they offer more support for your body and are optimal for long-term meditations.

Figure 86: The Three Meditation Asanas

Siddhasana

As the more advanced sitting cross-legged pose, Siddhasana is otherwise called the "Accomplished Pose." In Siddhasana, you are to tuck your feet into your thighs (between thighs and calves), so your genitals will be between your two heels. Your feet will be side by side, thus keeping your knees wide apart. The back is to be straight, and the hands are to be placed on the knees, in either Jnana or Chin Mudra. This pose is called "Accomplished" because it is more advanced than Sukhasana, and it requires the practitioner to be more flexible to have their hips open.

Siddhasana directs the energy from the lower Chakras upwards through the spine, thus stimulating the brain and calming the entire nervous system. As the lower foot is pressed against the perineum, Muladhara Chakra is activated, enabling Mula Bandha. Also, the pressure to the pubic bone pushes the trigger point for Swadhisthana, automatically triggering Vajroli Mudra. These two psycho-muscular locks redirect sexual nervous impulses back up the spine and into the brain. They give the practitioner control over their reproductive hormones, which allows them to practise sexual continence or abstinence. (For a description of Mula Bandha and Vajroli Mudra, see the "Mudra: Bandha (Lock Mudras)" and "Mudra: Adhara (Perineal Mudras)" chapters.)

Padmasana

The most advanced sitting cross-legged meditation pose, Padmasana, is commonly referred to as the "Lotus Pose." Although you have heard the term "Lotus Pose" frequently used in meditation circles, Padmasana is the only correct Lotus pose, while the previous two are less advanced variations of it. In Padmasana, you are to sit with your feet on top of your thighs, tucked close to the hips. It is the closed-knee pose that can only be done successfully when the hips are more open than the other two meditation Asanas or postures. One should not attempt Padmasana until sufficient flexibility of the knees has been developed.

Padmasana allows the body to be held entirely steady for long periods of time. Once the body is steadied, the mind can become calm. Padmasana directs the flow of Prana from Muladhara to Sahasrara Chakras, heightening the experience of meditation. Applying pressure to the lower spine through this posture has a relaxing effect on the nervous system as well. Blood pressure is reduced, muscular tension decreases, and the breath becomes slow and steady.

HATHA YOGA VS. VINYASA YOGA

Hatha Yoga is an umbrella term for many of the most common forms of Asana practice taught in the West. Hatha Yoga emphasises controlled breathing and posture, which builds core strength while providing the psychological benefits associated with the practice of Asanas. In Hatha Yoga, you move your body slowly and deliberately from one posture to the next while focusing on mindfulness and relaxation.

Vinyasa is an approach to Yoga in which you smoothly transition from one pose into the next. There is a flow in a Vinyasa Yoga session where the transitions are coordinated with your breathing, giving you the feeling that your breath moves with your body. Fast-paced Vinyasa sessions are physically challenging. They provide a cardio workout that makes you sweat more and is more physically demanding than Hatha Yoga sessions.

Hatha and Vinyasa are two different styles or approaches to Asana practice that incorporate the same poses and are beneficial in their own way. While Hatha is a more static approach, Vinyasa is dynamic. Since Vinyasa moves at a faster pace from one posture to the next, it requires more significant breathing control than Hatha Yoga. Conversely, Hatha Yoga allows for more stretching and meditation since the poses are held for longer.

While Hatha Yoga is better for stress reduction, Vinyasa provides a better strength training and cardio workout. You can apply either approach to your Asana practice to yield different results. However, for optimal results, it would be best to determine your specific mind/body constitution, or Dosha, to know which style is best suited for you. Guidelines for Yogic practices, including Asanas, and to determine which of the Three Doshas is dominant in your life are given in the chapter on Ayurveda in the latter part of this section.

PREPARING FOR ASANA PRACTICE

Before starting your Asana practice, set aside a specific time in the day for its performance. For example, dawn and dusk are traditionally the best times of the day to practise Yoga because of our body and mind's natural connection with the energy of the Sun. However, if you find it impossible to practise at this time, then find another time in the day and be consistent with it throughout the week when you are planning your Yoga sessions.

If you decide to practise Yoga in the morning so that you can prepare your body and mind for the day, keep in mind that your muscles and bones will be stiffer than later in the day. Therefore, exercise caution when entering postures and don't overexert yourself. Conversely, an evening practice allows you to relax after completing your daily obligations. In addition, your body is more flexible in the evenings enabling you to go deeper into your postures with less resistance.

Find a place where you will be undisturbed for the duration of your Asana practice. This should be an area that has an even, flat surface. Make sure that you have enough room to move around you since many poses require that you extend your arms and legs freely. It is best to practise Asanas in an open environment to avoid the distraction of nearby objects.

If you are practising indoors, as most people do, ensure that the room is well ventilated and has a comfortable room temperature. Keep in mind that your body will generally heat up, so ensure that there is no draft, or the room is too cold since cold air affects your muscles and joints and makes them stiffer. For this reason, it is common for Yoga classes to be held in hot environments but never cold ones.

Fresh air adds additional benefits to the breathing component of performing Asanas. After all, breathing is one of the keys to successful Yoga practice. If you are burning incense or diffusing essential oils to help elevate the mind and attain a meditative state, make sure not to overdo it in a way where it will interfere with the air quality and your breathing. Although essential oils and incense have been an integral part of many Yoga classes over the years, some practitioners avoid it since scent can be a distraction.

The same rule applies to playing music during your Yoga sessions. Relaxing, calming music in the background can help you get in the right mood, but it can also be distracting. If you decide to play music, make sure it is not too loud since your focus should be on going inwards during your practice.

As is the case with all energy invoking or manipulating practices, including the Spiritual Healing modalities in this book, avoid practising Yoga on a full stomach. In other words, give yourself at least an hour after a snack or two to three hours after a heavy meal before starting your Yoga practice. After your practice, it is advisable to drink a protein shake or have a complete, well-balanced meal so that your muscles can begin to repair themselves. You can also drink a meal-replacement smoothie to bring nutritious elements into your body.

Make sure to have a water bottle handy to avoid becoming dehydrated. It is advisable to avoid drinking water during the Asana practice to avoid losing concentration, but if you find yourself thirsty, you may do so. After all, being dehydrated can be more distracting than taking a few sips of water. However, it is best to drink water before and after the Yoga session.

You should wear loose, comfortable, light clothing made of natural fibres like cotton. Your clothing should not restrict your movements. Remove any jewellery and ornaments and take off your shoes and socks since Yoga is practised with bare feet. Also, please turn off your phone and place it away from you to avoid distractions.

Lastly, get a Yoga mat that provides padding and a non-slip surface to practise on. Your Yoga mat will become your unique ritualistic item that will contain your energy, so make sure not to share it with others. Get a cushion and keep it handy if you need extra support while engaging in meditation Asanas. Meditation Asanas are prerequisites for most other Yogic practices like Pranayama, Mudra, Mantra, and meditation.

Although the above preparation guidelines are for Asana practice, they also apply to other Yogic practices. For a complete session that yields the most optimal Spiritual results, you should structure your Yoga practice to include a combination of Asanas, Pranayamas, Mudras, Mantras, and meditation.

TIPS FOR YOUR ASANA PRACTICE

Before starting your Asana practice, you should do a basic warm-up to prepare the body for physical activity and prevent injury risk. Begin by rolling your joints in a circular fashion for a few minutes, clockwise and counterclockwise, to awaken your body and provide natural lubrication for better mobility. You can perform head, wrist, ankle, and shoulder rolls on the ground while sitting on your mat. Then, stand up on your mat and transition into arm, leg, and lower back rolls.

Next, you should do some basic stretches for a few more minutes to ensure that you don't pull a muscle during your practice. Start by stretching your back while standing up. Then, as you sit back down, transition into the shoulder, arm, leg, and head stretches. Your entire warm-up should take five to seven minutes.

Begin and end every Asana practice by lying in Shavasana, the Corpse Pose. For example, you can do a shorter Shavasana to start and a longer one when you finish your Asana sequence. When you begin with your Asanas, keep in mind always to move from one posture to the next calmly and deliberately. As you do so, coordinate your breath so that you inhale as you move into an Asana and exhale as you move out of it.

Although there are mixed thoughts on this point, there is no definitive amount of time that an Asana should be applied. You should hold it as long as it is comfortable and does not cause pain or discomfort. Get a good stretch and work whatever part of the body the Asana targets. As a beginner, don't overexert yourself but gradually increase the duration with time. For example, you can start with 20-60 second intervals while practising deep breathing. The average time for optimal results is about one to three minutes per Asana.

To prevent back injury, practice an equal number of Asanas that bend the back forwards as those that bend it backwards. If your back becomes tight, or if pain develops in your back, especially your lower back, you can assume the Balasana (Child's Pose) to get relief. Also, when you feel tired or weak during your Asana practice, lie in Shavasana or Balasana for a short time to get some rest. You can then resume your practice.

Remember to perform all Asanas slowly and with control. You will progress much faster in your Yoga practice if you take things slow while concentrating on breathing and mindfulness. Also, learn to let go of any tension, stress, or negative thoughts. The key to unlocking the power of Yoga in your life is to be consistent and determined in your practice while exhibiting patience by not expecting instant results. Listen to your body and let it guide you by never forcing things. Finally, have fun and enjoy the process. Yoga will bring more happiness to your life if you let it.

Figure 87: Beginner Asanas (Part I)

Figure 88: Beginner Asanas (Part II)

Figure 89: Beginner Asanas (Part III)

Figure 90: Intermediate Asanas (Part I)

Figure 91: Intermediate Asanas (Part II)

Figure 92: Advanced Asanas (Part I)

Figure 93: Advanced Asanas (Part II)

PRANAYAMA

Pranayama is a term used for various breathing techniques that work with Pranic energy in the body. It consists of two words, "prana" and "ayama." Prana is the vital energy or Life Force that is in constant motion and which exists in every animate and inanimate thing in the Universe. Although it is closely related to the air we breathe, Prana is more subtle than mere oxygen, though we as human beings can manipulate it through breathing techniques.

"Ayama" means "extension" or "expansion." The word "Pranayama" then can be said to imply the "extension or expansion of Prana." The essence or purpose of Pranayama is to utilize breathing methods to influence the flow of Prana throughout the various Nadis in the Body of Light. As the movement of Prana in the Light Body Body is increased, the function of the Chakras is optimized.

Both Yoga and Tantra say that the basis of existence depends on the forces of Shiva (consciousness) and Shakti (energy). Ultimately, instead of two, there is only one force, as Shakti is the creative force or energy of Shiva. Shakti is also a direct reference to one's Kundalini energy which is sublimated Prana. The ultimate purpose of Hatha Yoga is to realize Shiva or Cosmic Consciousness through the manipulation of one's Shakti. Raising the Kundalini energy to the Crown Chakra is the goal of all human beings, which is synonymous with Shakti and Shiva becoming One in a Divine Marriage at the Crown.

Pranayama is considered as one of the eight limbs of Yoga. In Hatha Yoga, Pranayama commences once the individual has regulated the body through the practice of Asana and a moderate diet. Eating is a direct means of obtaining Prana in the body. All foods contain different Pranic vibrations, and the quality of the food we eat has an immediate effect on our body and mind.

The practice of Pranayama works primarily with the vital energy body, otherwise known as the Pranamaya Kosha, along the Astral Plane. It directly affects the Five Prana Vayus, which, in turn, affect the Nadis and the Chakras. The mind follows the breath while the body follows the mind. By controlling the energy body through the breath, we gain control over our minds and physical bodies—As Above, So Below.

Pranayama is beneficial in regulating brain waves and calming the mind and emotions. Through Pranayama, we can still our minds and create a meditative state of consciousness that will give us mental clarity and enhance concentration and focus. It is for this reason that breathing techniques are a prerequisite in most ritual work.

Pranic energy provides vitality to all systems that support our consciousness. By increasing the storehouse of Prana in the body through breathing methods, our mind is elevated, and we can achieve higher vibratory states of consciousness. Its more physical goals are to aid in the recovery from illness and to maintain our health and well-being.

Natural Breathing

Natural breathing is essentially the awareness of the breath. It is the most basic Pranayama exercise that introduces practitioners to their breathing patterns and respiratory system. Being aware of the process of breathing is enough to slow down the respiratory rate and initiate a calmer rhythm. It is relaxing for the mind and will put one into a meditative state. Natural Breathing can be practised at any time, irrespective of where you are and what you are doing.

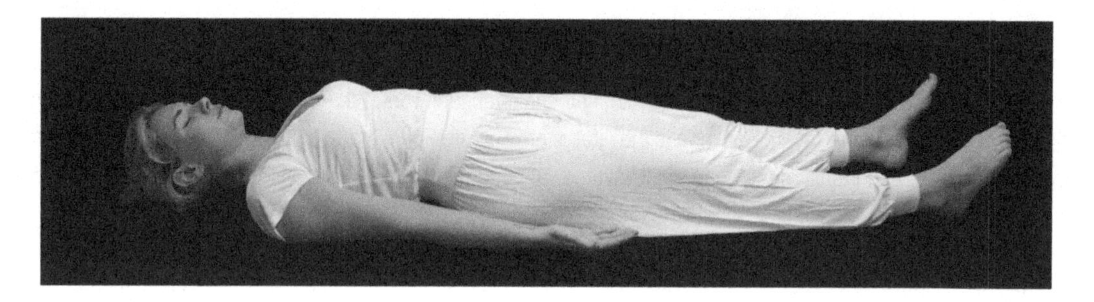

Figure 94: Shavasana

To begin the exercise, sit in a comfortable meditation Asana or lie in Shavasana (Figure 94). Close your eyes and allow your body to relax. Go within your mind and become aware of your natural breathing. Feel the breath flowing in and out of your nose while keeping your mouth closed the whole time. Notice if the breath is shallow or deep, and examine whether you are breathing out of your chest or stomach. Notice if there is any sound when you are breathing and become aware of its temperature as it is going in and out. The breath should be cooler on the inhale and hotter on the exhale.

Be aware that the lungs expand and contract as you breathe. Notice the effect your breathing pattern has on your body and if it is causing any strain. Observe its rhythm with complete detachment. The key to this exercise is awareness and attention. Do not try to control your breath in any way but develop total and absolute awareness of it by going inwards. Perform this exercise for as long as you want. Then, end it by bringing your awareness back to your entire body and opening your eyes.

Abdominal/Diaphragmatic Breathing

Abdominal breathing is the most natural and efficient way to breathe. Utilizing it and making it a natural part of your daily life will improve your physical and mental well-being. The purpose of Abdominal or Diaphragmatic Breathing is to increase the use of the diaphragm and decrease the use of the ribcage.

The diaphragm is a thin skeletal muscle located at the base of the chest that separates the abdomen from the chest. During inhalation, the diaphragm moves downward, which pushes air into the abdomen, thereby expanding it. During exhalation, the diaphragm moves upwards as air is emptied from the abdomen, contracting it in the process. The lungs naturally inflate and deflate on the inhale and exhale as well.

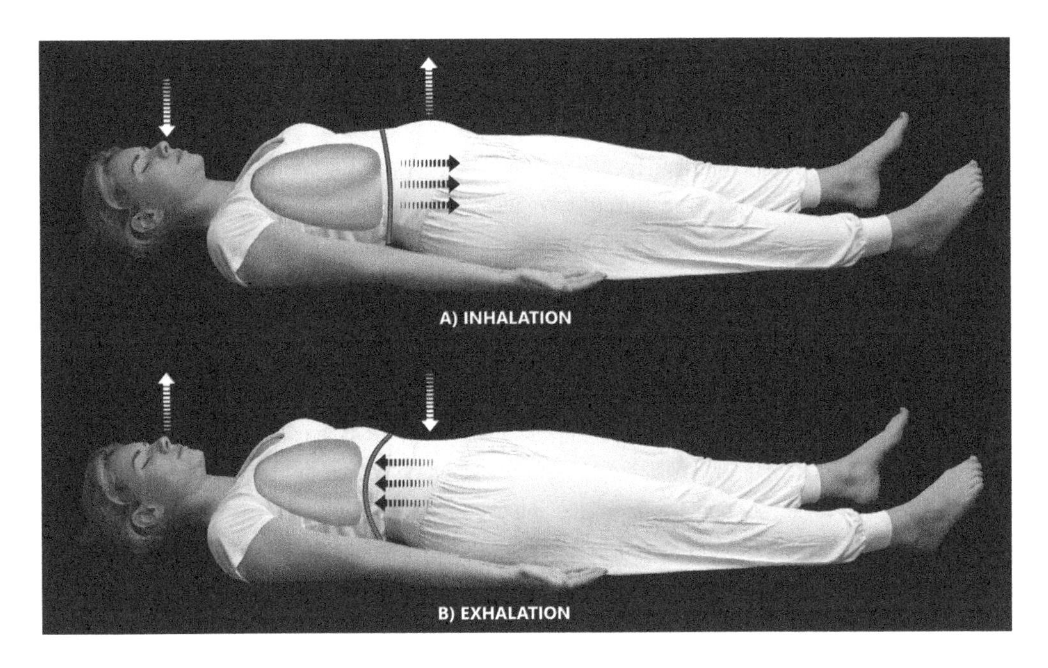

Figure 95: Abdominal/Diaphragmatic Breathing

To begin, sit in a comfortable meditation Asana or lie in Shavasana to relax the body. Close your eyes and get into a calm, meditative state. Place the right hand on the abdomen just above the navel, while placing the left hand over the centre of your chest. Observe your natural breathing without trying to control it in any way. Notice if you breathe out of your chest or belly.

Now take control over the breathing process by inhaling deeply through the nose and sending the breath into your abdomen, making it expand outward. As you exhale through the nose, your abdomen moves downward until the air is emptied from it (Figure 95). Feel as though you are trying to breathe through the navel alone.

All the movement should be in your right hand, as it moves up with inhalation and down with exhalation. Your left hand should remain unmoved since you are trying to not involve the ribs in the breathing process. Repeat the inhalation and exhalation while breathing slowly and deeply. When expanding the abdomen, do so comfortably without causing any strain on the body.

Perform this exercise as long as you want, with a minimum of a few minutes. Once you are ready to end it, bring your awareness back to your physical body and open your eyes.

Note that Diaphragmatic Breathing increases the use of the lower lobes of the lungs, improving their efficiency and providing a positive effect on the heart, stomach, liver and intestines. People who breathe through the diaphragm are less prone to stress and anxiety and have better overall mental health. As such, make all efforts to make this type of breathing a regular part of your life.

Thoracic Breathing

Thoracic breathing employs the middle lobes of the lungs by expanding and contracting the ribcage. This type of breathing expends more energy than Abdominal breathing but brings oxygen quicker into the body. As such, it is the preferred breathing method when performing physical exercise or dealing with stressful situations.

Many people who are prone to anxiety have made Thoracic breathing a regular part of their life. However, breathing this way in tense situations perpetuates stress further since negative energy does not neutralize or "ground" itself in the abdomen. As mentioned, Abdominal or Diaphragmatic breathing is the most optimal method of breathing naturally. If one begins Thoracic breathing, they need to make a conscious effort to switch back to Abdominal breathing soon after to preserve and conserve their vital energy and keep their mind balanced.

To begin the exercise, sit in a comfortable meditation Asana or lie in Shavasana. Close your eyes and get into a calm, relaxed state. Place your right hand on the abdomen just above the navel while placing your left hand over the centre of your chest. Become aware of your natural breathing pattern without trying to control it at first. Notice which hand is moving up and down as you breathe.

Discontinue using the diaphragm now and begin to inhale by expanding the ribcage slowly. Draw the air into the lungs and feel them as they inflate and widen. Expand your chest as much as is possible, comfortably. Now exhale slowly and draw the air out of your lungs without causing any strain on your body. Your left hand should move up and down on this motion while your right hand remains unmoved.

Repeat the inhale again by expanding your ribcage, being mindful not to utilize the diaphragm whatsoever. Control the breathing process by making sure that only your left hand is moving. Continue Thoracic breathing for as long as you want, with a minimum of a few minutes. Notice how breathing in this way makes you feel and the thoughts that enter your mind. Once you are ready to end the exercise, bring your awareness back to your physical body and open your eyes.

Clavicular Breathing

Clavicular Breathing follows Thoracic breathing and can be done in combination with it in periods of significant stress or strong physical exertion. If someone is experiencing obstructive airways, such as under an asthmatic attack, they tend to breathe in this way. Clavicular Breathing allows maximum ribcage expansion on inhalation, bringing the most air into the lungs.

Clavicular Breathing is performed using the sternum and neck and throat muscles to pull the upper ribs and collar bone upwards, engaging the upper lobes of the lungs. We can combine this breathing technique with Thoracic and Abdominal Breathing to form Yogic Breathing.

Lie in Shavasana or sit in a comfortable meditation Asana to begin the exercise. The body should be relaxed, as with all Pranayama exercises. Close your eyes and get into a meditative state, becoming aware of your natural breathing pattern. Next, perform Thoracic Breathing for a few minutes. Take another breath into the chest; only this time inhale a little more until an expansion is felt in the upper portion of the lungs. Notice the shoulders and collar bone moving up slightly. Exhale slowly by relaxing the neck and upper chest first, followed by bringing the ribcage back to its original state as air completely expels out of your lungs.

Repeat this exercise as many times as you want, with a minimum of a few minutes. Observe the effects on the body of this type of breathing technique. When you are ready to complete the exercise, bring your awareness back to your physical body and open your eyes.

Yogic Breathing

Yogic Breathing combines the previous three breathing techniques to maximize oxygen intake and to balance the Elements within. It is commonly known as the "Three-Part Breath" because it involves the abdomen, chest, and clavicular region for maximum inhalation and exhalation (Figure 96). Yogic Breathing greatly benefits the vital organs and Chakras that can become constricted or stagnant with physical and emotional tension from stress and anxiety. In addition, this exercise revitalizes the body, mind, and energy system through the Pranic energy we get from the air around us.

Yogic Breathing relieves anxiety, refreshes the psyche, and activates the Parasympathetic Nervous System to bring about a calmer, more balanced state of consciousness. As such, this exercise should be practised often, for at least ten minutes at a time, preferably on an empty stomach. Yogic Breathing is recommended before and during more advanced Pranayama techniques and to correct poor breathing habits.

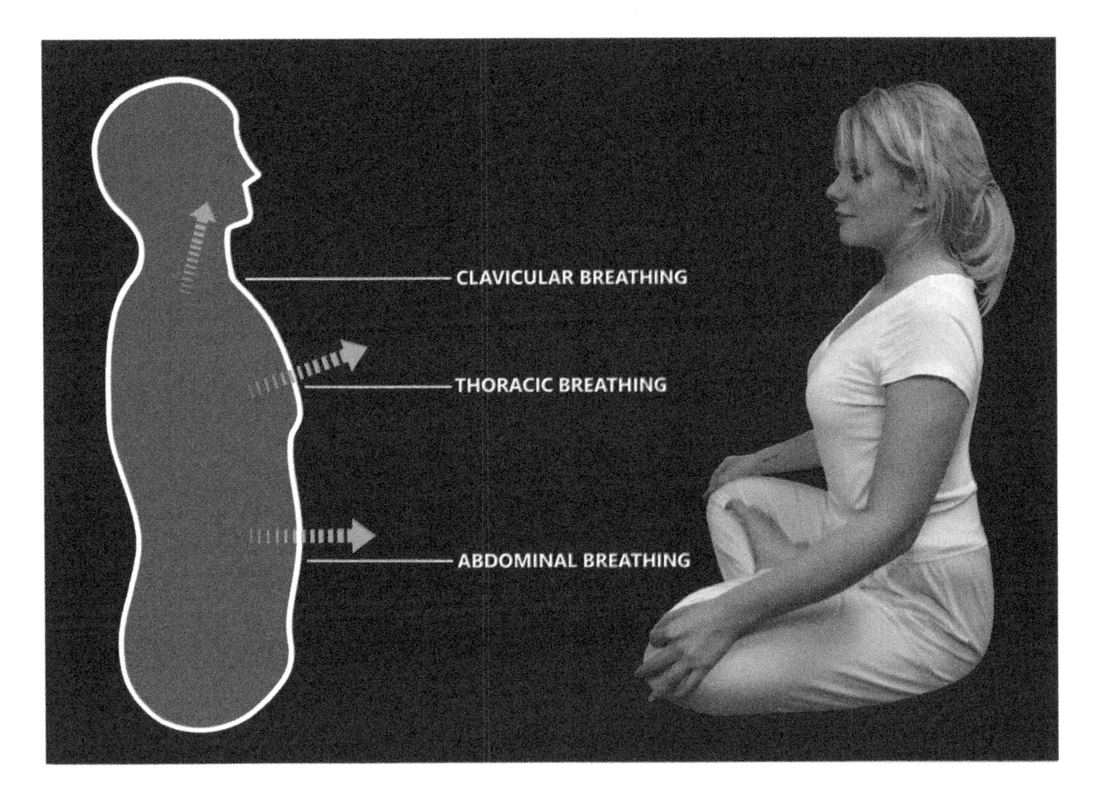

Figure 96: Yogic Breathing (Three-Part Breath)

To begin the exercise, sit in a comfortable meditation Asana or lie in Shavasana. Inhale slowly and deeply, allowing the abdomen to expand fully. When the belly cannot receive any more air, extend the chest outwards and upwards next. After the lower and middle portions of the lungs have maximized their air intake, inhale a little more so that the collar bones and shoulders move up slightly, filling up the upper lobes of the lungs. There will be some tension in the neck muscles while the rest of the body should remain relaxed.

The sequence is to be reversed on the exhale; the collar bones and shoulders move downward first, freeing air out of the upper chest, followed by the ribs contracting in the mid-torso. Finally, the breath is released from the lower abdomen as the belly contracts and draws inwards towards the spine. One round of Yogic Breathing includes one complete inhalation and exhalation.

The inhale and exhale should be one fluid, continuous movement without any transition points unless you practise rhythmic breathing, such as the Four-Fold Breath, where you pause on the in and out breaths. At no point in time should the Yogic Breathing exercise cause any strain on the body.

After repeated Yogic Breathing cycles, you will notice that Abdominal breathing takes in approximately 70% of the breath. The more you practise Yogic Breathing, you will adjust your natural breathing to utilize your abdomen most constructively and alleviate stress. Practise the Yogic Breathing technique for as long as you want; when you are ready to complete the exercise, bring your awareness back to your physical body and open your eyes.

Note that the primary requirement of all Pranayama exercises is for respiration to be comfortable and relaxed. Any strain on the body brings agitation in the mind. Once awareness and control over the breathing process have been established in the Yogic Breathing method, the Clavicular technique is abandoned while emphasis is placed on Abdominal and Thoracic breathing. This alteration makes the Yogic Breathing method more natural in filling up the abdomen and lungs with air without causing any strain on the body.

Sama Vritti (Four-Fold Breath)

Sama Vritti (Sanskrit for "equal breathing") is a powerful relaxation exercise that allows individuals to clear their minds, relax the body, and enhance focus. It utilizes equal ratio breathing, where the inhalation (Puraka), internal retention (Antara Khumbaka), exhalation (Rechaka), and external retention (Bahya Khumbaka) are all the same length. Sama Vritti promotes mental balance by activating the Parasympathetic Nervous system, alleviating stress, and raising consciousness.

Otherwise known as the Four-Fold Breath, Sama Vritti is the foundational breathing technique in *The Magus*, a prerequisite for meditation and Ceremonial Magick ritual work. It calms down the individual within minutes and shifts their consciousness into the Alpha State, activating the higher brain centres. It has been my primary breathing technique for over sixteen years and one that I teach to all Kundalini awakened individuals.

The Four-Fold Breath should be performed with Yogic Breathing on the inhale and exhale for maximum air intake. If you feel too much of a strain on the clavicular region during the Yogic breath, just focus on Diaphragmatic and Thoracic breathing. This exercise can be performed at any time and anywhere. You do not need to close your eyes during the exercise, although it helps if you are meditating or are in the midst of a healing session.

To begin the exercise, sit in a comfortable meditation Asana or lie in Shavasana. Breathe in through your nose, slowly counting to four. Fill up your abdomen with air first, followed by your lungs. Both should reach their maximum air intake as you get to the four-count. Hold your breath now and count slowly to four again. Next, begin to exhale to the count of four, allowing your chest and abdomen to relax back to their natural state. The exhale should be unforced and even. Hold now again to the count of four, thereby completing the first breath cycle.

Continue the exercise for as long as you require, with a minimum of a few minutes. The breath cycles should be continuous and smooth, without breaks or interruptions. Repeat the exercise as many times as you need throughout the day. It helps to perform the Four-Fold Breath before encountering any potentially challenging situations since it optimizes your mental and emotional state so you can perform at your highest capacity.

Anulom Vilom (Alternate Nostril Breathing)

Anulom Vilom, commonly known as Alternate Nostril Breathing, involves inhaling through one nostril while exhaling through the other nostril. The left nostril corresponds with the Lunar Ida Nadi, while the right nostril relates to the Solar Pingala Nadi. Anulom Vilom purifies the Ida and Pingala Nadis while creating a sense of well being and harmony within the mind, body, and Soul.

Alternate Nostril Breathing stimulates the Chakras and major brain centres to work at their optimum capacity by balancing the masculine and feminine energies. This Pranayama technique gives vitality to the body while clearing Pranic blockages and balancing the brain's two hemispheres. Its regular use stimulates the Sushumna Nadi and can even cause a Kundalini awakening.

Figure 97: Alternate Nostril Breathing

Anulom Vilom is often recommended for stress-related issues, such as headaches or migraines. It nourishes the body through the extra supply of oxygen, benefiting the brain and respiratory system. It also purifies the blood of any toxins, which aids the cardiovascular and circulatory systems.

To begin the exercise, choose one of the three meditation Asanas. Keep your spine and neck straight while closing your eyes. Next, with either your left or right hand, make the Pranava Mudra called Vishnu Mudra, which involves bending the index and middle fingers towards the palm (Figure 97). While doing so, place your other hand on your knee in either Jnana or Chin Mudra.

Pranava Mudra allows you to block one nostril with the thumb or ring finger while breathing in through the other nostril and then alternate as you breathe out. (When blocking with the ring finger, the little finger serves as support.) With this method, you can go back and forth while targeting one nostril for the inhale and the other for the exhale.

Anulom Vilom should be used in combination with Yogic Breathing on the in and out breaths. Start by inhaling slowly to the count of four through the left nostril while keeping the right nostril closed. Now switch and close the left nostril while exhaling to the four-count through the right nostril.

Reverse the process now and inhale to the count of four through the right nostril while keeping the left nostril closed. Next, switch and close the right nostril as you exhale through the left nostril to the four-count. The first round or cycle is now complete.

Remember to always start Anulom Vilom by inhaling with the left nostril, which calms the inner Self, putting you in a meditative state. Keep your inhalations and exhalations equal and in rhythm. You should not feel any bodily strain nor be out of breath at any point.

Start with the four-count on the inhale and exhale and move on to five and six, up to ten. The higher you can go on the count while keeping the inhale and exhale equal, the more control you will obtain over your breath. If you are having trouble counting to four, count to three or even two instead. I found that the most optimal results occur with the four-count, so I always introduce it as the baseline.

As you inhale and exhale, pay attention to the corresponding nostril and notice the inner emotional changes as they are happening. Being mindful during this Pranayama technique will enable you to draw the most power from it.

A powerful and effective variation of Anulom Vilom is Nadi Shodhana, which includes internal breath retention (Khumbaka). You can incorporate the internal Khumbaka to hold your breath for the same count as the inhale and exhale. You can also include the internal and external Khumbakas, where you hold your breath after the inhale and the exhale. Think of this second method as Samma Vritti with the addition of the Alternate Nostril Breathing technique. Again, I suggest starting with the count of four and moving upwards from there, all the way to ten.

Another variation of Anulom Vilom is breathing through one nostril at a time, referred to as the Lunar Breath and Solar Breath. The Lunar Breath involves keeping the right nostril closed and breathing out of the left nostril. Since it is associated with the Ida Nadi and the passive Water Element, it can be utilized to cool down the body, lower metabolism, and calm the mind. The Lunar Breath invokes an introverted mind state, making its practice beneficial before inner contemplation, deep meditation, and sleep.

The Solar Breath involves keeping the left nostril closed while breathing out of the right nostril. Being associated with the Pingala Nadi and the active Fire Element, performing the Solar Breath warms the body, raises metabolism, and accelerates bodily activities. Since it strengthens willpower, the Solar Breath is useful when you need to invoke concentration, determination, and fortitude. Its use makes the individual extroverted, which aids in work and physical activities.

Bhastrika Pranayama (Bellows Breath)

Bhastrika means "bellows" in Sanskrit, which refers to a bag-like device with handles that blacksmiths use to blow air onto a fire to keep the flame burning. Similarly, the Bhastrika Pranayama increases air flow in the body, fueling the inner fire and producing heat at the physical and subtle levels. This Pranayama technique is known to balance the Three Doshas of Ayurveda.

Bhastrika Pranayama pumps a higher quantity of oxygen in the body, which raises the heartbeat, increasing one's energy levels. When done regularly, it removes blockages from the nose and chest, including toxins and impurities. Bhastrika helps with sinus, bronchitis, and other respiratory issues. Since it stokes the gastric fire, it also improves appetite and digestion. You can practise Bhastrika Pranayama with internal breath retention (Khumbaka) to keep the body warm in cold and rainy weather.

To begin the Bhastrika Pranayama exercise, sit in one of the three meditation Asanas. Close your eyes and relax the body while keeping your head and spine straight. Next, place your hands on your knees in either the Jnana or Chin Mudra.

Take a deep breath in and breathe out forcefully through the nostrils without strain. Then, breathe in again with the same force. On the inhalation, you should fully expand the abdomen outwards, allowing your diaphragm to descend. On the exhalation, the abdomen pushes inwards, while the diaphragm moves upwards. You should perform the movements with exaggeration and vigour, which will cause a strong nasal sound.

One round of Bhastrika Pranayama equals ten cycles. Practise up to five rounds to start while taking a deep breath in and breathing out slowly. Do this at your own pace while always keeping the force of inhalation and exhalation equal. If you feel dizzy, slow it down to a more comfortable pace. When you gain some proficiency in the exercise, gradually increase the speed while keeping the breath rhythmical.

Bhastrika Pranayama reduces the level of carbon dioxide in the blood, which balances and strengthens the nervous system, inducing peace of mind and energetic tranquillity. It is an excellent exercise to prepare one for meditation.

A variation of this exercise is Kapalbhati Pranayama, a Yogic breathing technique that is considered a Kriya, or internal purification practice (Shatkarma). Kapalbhati comes from the Sanskrit root words "kapal," meaning "skull," and "bhati," meaning "shining." Therefore, it is called the "Skull Shining Breath" in English. This Pranayama technique is meant to cleanse all parts of the skull and head through strong air exhalations, improving one's clarity of mind and focus while sharpening the intellect.

Unlike Bhastrika, Kapalbhati involves force only on the exhale while keeping the inhale a natural, passive process. While Bhastrika engages the chest and lungs, Kapalbhati only engages the abdominal muscles. Kapalbhati Pranayama reverses the normal breathing process, which involves active inhalation and passive exhalation. This Pranayama technique is known to have profound effects on the nervous system. Many Yogis also practise it to clear the Nadis.

Since Bhastrika is the more advanced of the two Pranayama techniques, it is wise to begin with Kapalbhati and transition into Bhastrika. Both have similar effects on the body and mind. You can also practise internal and external retention (Khumbaka) with both exercises for added benefits.

Ujjayi Pranayama (Ocean Breath)

Ujjayi Pranayama is a soft, whispering breath, often called the Ocean Breath, as it resembles the sound of the waves coming to shore. Its other name is the Victorious Breath since Ujjayi in Sanskrit means "one who is victorious." The Ujjayi technique allows us to become victorious in Pranayama by constricting the breath to make its distribution into the targeted areas easier. It builds a soothing internal heat while calming the mind and nervous system. This Pranayama technique has a profoundly relaxing effect on a psychic level since it mimics deep sleep breathing.

With Ujjayi Pranayama, you are to breathe in and out of the nose with the lips closed while contracting the glottis inside the throat to produce a soft, snoring sound. The glottis is the middle part of the larynx where the vocal cords are located that expands with forced respiration and closes when you are speaking. The glottis should contract but not close all the way so that it feels like you are breathing out of a drinking straw in your throat (Figure 98). You will feel the breath stroke the back of your throat on the inhale and exhale.

Ujjayi Pranayama's breathing should be slow, calm, and deep. You should implement Yogic Breathing on the inhale and exhale for maximum air intake. (The diaphragm should control the length and speed of the breath.) The inhalations and exhalations should be equal in duration without causing any strain on the body. While practising Ujjayi, focus on the sound produced by the breath in the throat, which should only be audible to you.

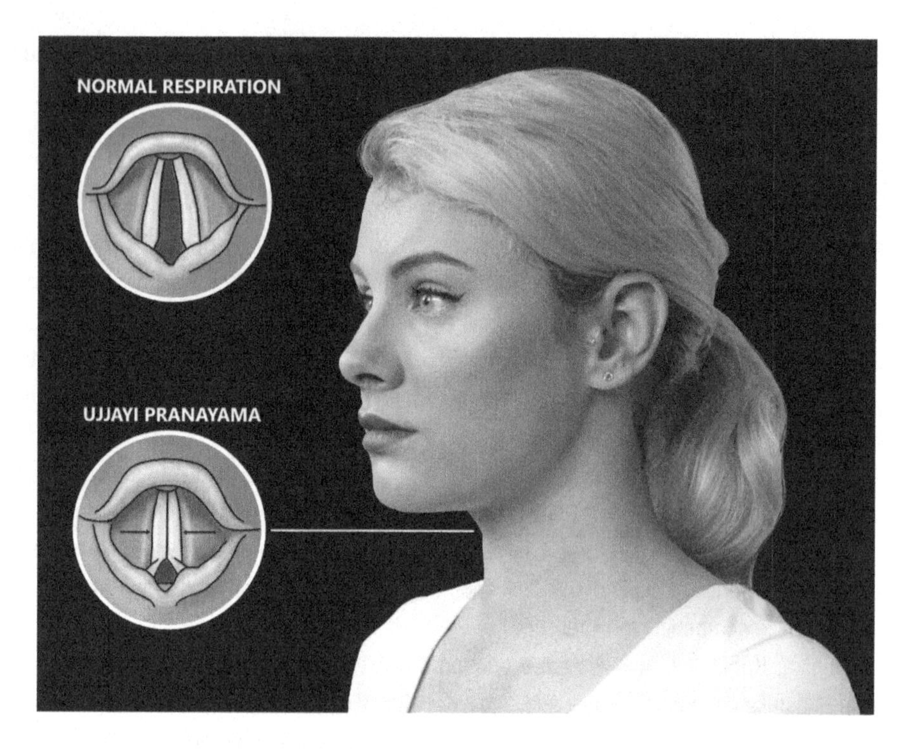

Figure 98: Ujjayi Pranayama (Glottis Position)

Start the exercise with ten to fifteen breaths and slowly increase to five minutes for optimal effects. As you get some experience with Ujjayi Pranayama, you may integrate Khechari Mudra for added benefits. (For the Khechari Mudra technique, refer to the "Lalana Chakra and Amrita Nectar" chapter in this section.) Khechari Mudra can be practised independently or as part of Asanas and advanced Pranayama techniques.

Bhramari Pranayama (Humming Bee Breath)

Bhramari Pranayama derives its name from the Indian black bee called Bhramari since the exhalation of this Pranayama resembles the typical humming sound. The humming sound vibrations have a natural calming effect on the nerves and psyche, making this Pranayama technique excellent for alleviating mental tension, stress, anxiety, and anger. Its performance strengthens the throat and voice box and is beneficial for the Thyroid Gland and overcoming any physical issues related to it.

Bhramari Pranayama stimulates the Parasympathetic Nervous System, inducing muscular relaxation and lowering blood pressure. Its health benefits make it advantageous to perform before sleep since it helps with insomnia.

Begin the exercise by sitting in one of the three meditation Asanas. Keep the spine straight and close your eyes. Place both hands on your knees in either Jnana or Chin Mudra while allowing your body and mind to relax. Bring the awareness to the centre of the forehead, where Ajna Chakra is located. While performing the exercise, be mindful to keep your attention in this area. You will find that with repeated use, the Bhramari Pranayama increases psychic sensitivity and awareness of subtle vibrations, which is helpful for deep meditation.

Next, raise your arms while bending the elbows and bringing your hands to the ears. Use the index finger on each hand to plug your earholes or press against the ear flaps without inserting the fingers (Figure 99). You should block out all outside sounds, which allows you to focus entirely on your interior.

Take a moment now to listen to the sound of silence within you while keeping your breathing steady. Before starting the controlled breathing method, close your lips while keeping your teeth separated slightly, which will allow the sound vibration to be heard and felt more inside of you.

Inhale slowly and deeply through the nose. On the exhalation, make a deep "mmmm" sound, resembling the humming sound of a bee. Your exhale should be longer than the inhale with a continuous, smooth, and even sound vibration. You should feel the vibration strongly inside your mouth and larynx, which has a soothing effect on the brain. The first round is now complete.

Continue the exercise for as long as you want with a minimum of a few minutes while practising Yogic Breathing throughout for maximum air intake. Observe the effects of the exercise on the body and mind. When you are ready to end Bhramari Pranayama, bring your awareness back to your physical body and open your eyes.

Figure 99: Humming Bee Breath

Sheetali Pranayama (Cooling Breath)

In Sanskrit, the word "Sheetali" roughly translates as "that which has a soothing or cooling effect." Sheetali Pranayama or Cooling Breath is a Pranayama technique that calms down the mind and body with the performance of a powerful cooling mechanism on inhalation.

Sheetali Pranayama is especially beneficial in the summertime when we feel an excess of the Pitta's main qualities. Hot weather produces hot flashes, fevers, skin conditions, inflammation, acid indigestion, high blood pressure, general agitation due to heat, and overall physical exertion, which throw the mind-body out of balance. Sheetali Pranayama aids in the adverse effects of hot weather by releasing body heat, harmonizing Pitta's qualities and leaving the body and mind feeling calm, cool and relaxed.

To begin the Pranayama exercise, sit in one of the three meditation Asanas. Close your eyes and relax the whole body while keeping your spine straight. Place your hands on your knees in either the Jnana or Chin Mudra.

Open your mouth and extend the tongue as far out as it can go, curling the sides of it towards the centre to form a tube. Purse your lips to hold the tongue in this position (Figure 100). Practise a long, smooth, controlled inhalation through the rolled tongue. After the inhalation, draw the tongue while closing the mouth and exhale through the nose. The first round is now complete.

Figure 100: Sheetali Pranayama

Continue the exercise for as long as you want with a minimum of a few minutes. Observe its effects on the body and mind while paying particular attention to the tongue and the sound and cooling sensation of the inhaled breath. Remember to practise Yogic Breathing throughout the exercise. When you are ready to end Sheetali Pranayama, bring your awareness back to your physical body and open your eyes.

The in-breath should produce a sucking sound with a cooling sensation on the tongue and roof of the mouth. Although you should begin with an equal ratio of in and out breaths, as you get more advanced with Sheetali Pranayama, the duration of the inhalation should gradually become longer to increase the cooling effect.

The Cooling Breath effectively restores temperature balance after practising Asanas or other Yogic practices that heat the body. As such, you should make it a part of your daily practice, especially during the summer months.

Sheetkari Pranayama (Hissing Breath)

In Sanskrit, the word "Sheetkari" implies a form of breathing that produces the "shee" (hissing) sound; hence it is often referred to as the Hissing Breath. Just like Sheetali Pranayama, this exercise is designed to cool down the body and mind. The only difference between them is that in Sheetali, you inhale through a folded tongue, while in Sheetkari, you inhale through closed teeth. As with Sheetali Pranayama, Sheetkari is quite beneficial in hot weather and to restore temperature balance after heating the body via physical exercise.

Figure 101: Sheetkari Pranayama

To begin Sheetkari Pranayama, sit in one of the three meditation Asanas and close your eyes. Keep your spine straight, and body relaxed while placing your hands on your knees in either the Jnana or Chin Mudra. Hold the teeth lightly together without strain on your jaw. The lips should be separated, thus exposing the teeth (Figure 101). Keep your tongue flat against the soft palate in your mouth, or even perform Khechari Mudra.

Inhale slowly and deeply through your teeth. At the end of the inhalation, close your mouth and exhale through the nose in a controlled fashion. The first round is now complete. Remember to practise Yogic Breathing throughout the exercise. The in and out breaths should be slow and relaxed. Be mindful of the cooling sensation on your teeth and inside your mouth and the hissing sound produced. Perform the exercise for as long as you want, with a minimum of a few minutes. When you are ready to end Sheetkari Pranayama, bring your awareness back to your physical body and open your eyes.

This Pranayama technique and the previous one can be used to control hunger or thirst since bringing in cool air satisfies the body. Both exercises allow Prana to flow more freely through the body, relaxing the muscles and, consequently, emotions. Both cooling practices balance the endocrine system and purify the blood of toxicity. Finally, both exercises are helpful before going to sleep or in cases of insomnia.

Avoid Sheetali and Sheetkari Pranayamas if you have low blood pressure, asthma, respiratory ailments, or excessive mucous, as with a cold or flu. Due to the cooling effect on the body, avoid both exercises in cold climates or if you are experiencing general cold sensitivity. With Sheetkari Pranayama, avoid if you have problems with your teeth or gums.

Moorcha Pranayama (Swooning Breath)

The word Moorcha in Sanskrit means "fainting" or "loss of sensation." Moorcha Pranayama's other name is the Swooning Breath, referring to the dizziness one experiences while performing this exercise. Moorcha Pranayama is an advanced technique that should be practised only by those individuals who have developed mastery over the previous Pranayama exercises. When it is performed correctly, the individual can experience intense and prolonged periods of inner bliss that accompany being semi-conscious.

There are two methods of practising Moorcha Pranayama; in the first, you are to lean your head slightly back, while in the second, you are to rest your chin on the base of your throat (Jalandhara Bandha). In both methods, you are to practise internal breath retention (Khumbaka) while gazing at the centre between the eyebrows where the Mind's Eye tunnel is located (Shambhavi Mudra). Doing so induces the void mind-state while the connection with Ajna chakra allows you to experience deep, contemplative thoughts.

One of the reasons that the individual becomes lightheaded while performing Moorcha Pranayama is the reduction of oxygen supply to the brain during extended breath retention. Another reason is the pressure they put on the blood vessels in the neck, which cause fluctuations in the pressure within the skull. Finally, the carotid artery gets continually compressed, which further induces a swooning sensation.

Moorcha Pranayama can be performed at any given time during the day, as is the case with all Pranayama exercises. However, it is most effective early in the morning and in the evening when the Ego is least active. Overcoming the Ego's hold over the consciousness is crucial in facilitating the desired effect of this exercise. The sensation of near-fainting can be so powerful that it makes you feel entirely out of your body, like you are floating in space.

Overcoming the boundaries of the physical body allows us to separate from the Ego in consciousness and feel the rapture of Spiritual awareness. Moorcha Pranayama helps alleviate stress, anxiety, anger, and neuroses while raising the level of Prana in the body. This exercise is highly recommended for people who want to awaken their

Kundalini energy. It allows them to understand the Oneness that Out-of-Body Experiences can bring, connecting them with Sahasrara Chakra.

To begin the exercise, sit in one of the three meditation Asanas while keeping your head and spine straight. Place your hands on your knees in either the Jnana or Chin Mudra while relaxing the body. Some people like to hold their knees instead of adopting Jnana or Chin Mudras. Doing so allows them to press on their knees while locking their elbows when they lean their head back or forward, giving them better support during this crucial part of the exercise. You may try both options and see what works best for you.

Method#1

With eyes open, focus on the space between your eyebrows. Take in a few deep and slow breaths to calm down the mind. Perform Khechari Mudra, then slowly inhale through both nostrils with Ujjayi Pranayama as you gently bend the head back (Figure 102). Hold your breath now for as long as you can without strain while maintaining eyebrow centre gazing the entire time. You should feel slight dizziness as you hold your breath. Exhale slowly now while bringing the head back to its upright position. Close your eyes and relax for a few seconds. Allow yourself to experience the lightness and tranquillity in the mind and body. The first round is now complete.

Figure 102: Moorcha Pranayama (Method#1)

Method#2

Focus your eyes on the space between the eyebrows while taking a few deep breaths to calm down your interior. Implement Khechari Mudra, then slowly inhale through both nostrils with Ujjayi Pranayama as you gradually bend your head forward until your chin touches your throat cavity (Figure 103). Pause your breathing for as long as you can without tension while allowing yourself to become united with the Mind's Eye. Hold this position until you begin to feel a loss of consciousness. Exhale slowly now while returning your head to its upright position. Close your eyes and relax for a few seconds while allowing yourself to experience the intense feeling of nonexistence brought on by near-fainting. This completes the first round.

Repeat the breathing pattern in either method as many times as you are comfortable. It helps to start with 5-10 breaths and move on to 15-20 as you get more familiar with the exercise. Remember always to discontinue the practice as soon as the fainting sensation is felt. The goal is to induce a swooning sensation, not to lose consciousness entirely.

Figure 103: Moorcha Pranayama (Method#2)

As a final note, you can combine Method#1 and Method#2 in the same practice where on the first breath, you perform one method while on the second breath, you perform the other one. Before doing so, however, please spend some time getting familiar and comfortable with both techniques separately.

THE THREE GRANTHIS

Granthi is a Sanskrit term that means "doubt" or "knot," more explicitly meaning "a difficult knot to untie." This term is often used in Yogic literature, referring to psychic knots which block the flow of Pranic energy in the Sushumna Nadi. In Kundalini Yoga, there are Three Granthis which are obstacles on the path of the awakened Kundalini. These Granthis are called Brahma, Vishnu, and Rudra (Figure 104).

The Three Granthis represent levels of awareness where the power of Maya or illusion (concerning our ignorance of the Spiritual reality and attachment to the material world) are particularly strong. For you to awaken all the Chakras and raise the Kundalini to the Crown, you must transcend these barriers. Our limiting beliefs, personality traits, desires, and fears result from us being entangled by the Granthis.

The Three Granthis are obstacles on our path to higher knowledge and Spiritual Evolution. They obscure the truth of our essential nature. However, by applying knowledge and Spiritual practices, we can untie the knots and transcend their restrictions.

In Yoga, there are various ways to untie the Granthis. Bandhas (energetic locks) of Hatha Yoga aid the flow of Prana and can also be used to overcome the Three Granthis. (I will discuss Bandhas in the following chapter on Mudras.) Bandhas block off energy flow to a specific body area, causing the energy to flood more strongly when the Bandha is released. Bandhas are powerful tools that we can use to raise the Kundalini energy to Sahasrara Chakra by overcoming the Three Granthis along the way.

Brahma Granthi

Commonly referred to as the Perineal Knot, Brahma Granthi operates in the region between Muladhara and Swadhisthana Chakras, along the Sushumna Nadi. This first knot is caused by anxiety about survival, the urge to procreate, instinctive tendencies, lack of grounding or stability, and the fear of death. Brahma Granthi creates an attachment to physical pleasures, material objects as well as Ego selfishness. It binds us to the ensnaring power of Tamas—inertia, inactivity, lethargy, and ignorance.

Tamas, meaning "darkness," is one of the Three Gunas found at the core of Hindu philosophy and psychology. Yogic texts consider the Three Gunas-Tamas, Rajas, and Sattva, to be the essential qualities of nature. They are present in every individual but vary in degree. Brahma Granthi can be transcended through the Mula Bandha, the "Root Lock." When Brahma Granthi is pierced by the Kundalini on its upwards rise, the instinctual patterns of the personality are overcome, resulting in the Soul's liberation from the described attachments.

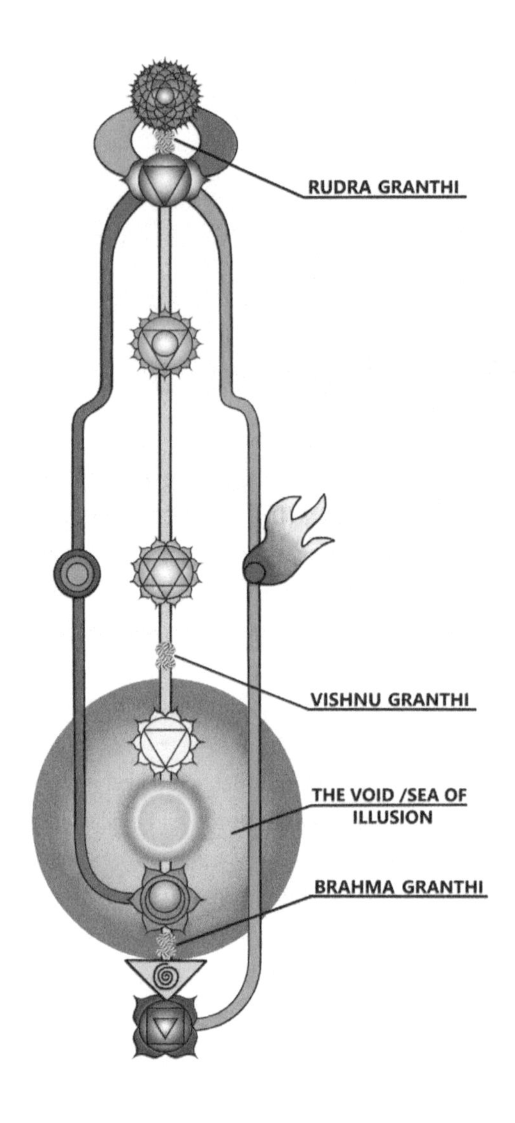

Figure 104: The Three Granthis

Vishnu Granthi and the Void

Although its placement is higher than the navel region, Vishnu Granthi is referred to as the Navel Knot. It functions in the area between Manipura and Anahata Chakras, along the Sushumna Nadi. This Granthi is caused by clinging to the Ego and seeking personal power. Pride, as well as an emotional attachment to people and outcomes, also causes this knot. Vishnu Granthi is connected with Rajas—the tendency towards passion, assertiveness, and ambition. These are all negative expressions of the Manipura Chakra related to the improper use of willpower. The willpower must serve the Higher Self instead of the Ego for Vishnu Granthi to be untied.

A Void surrounds the second and third Chakra called the "Sea of Illusion." Within this Void are found our negative behavioural patterns resulting from outside influences, including the Karmic effects of the Planetary and Zodiacal forces. Hara, the Navel Chakra, creates the Void and the ball of Life energy it generates, which is our gateway into the Astral Plane. Karmic forces affect us through the Astral Plane, which binds our Ego to the lower Chakras surrounding the Hara centre. As such, our Ego becomes entangled in the Sea of Illusion, blocking the vision of our true Spiritual nature.

Overcoming the Vishnu Granthi takes our awareness out of the Void and into our hearts, wherein lies the true Self, the Eternal Spirit. It allows us to experience unconditional love in Anahata Chakra and the higher Spirit Chakras of Vishuddhi and Ajna. Untying the Vishnu Granthi makes the individual a Master of the Self, and all the innate Laws of nature are awakened within them. Such a person becomes honest and truthful in all their expressions. Their charisma heightens naturally, which makes them great leaders of humanity.

To transcend the Vishnu Granthi, one must surrender to the energy of unconditional love. True discrimination, knowledge, and faith in the unity of all things in the Cosmos allow one to raise their consciousness to the higher Spheres and transcend the Ego's limitations as well as its desire for power. The performance of Uddiyana Bandha, the "Abdominal Lock," aids in untying the Vishnu Granthi.

Rudra Granthi

Referred to as the Shiva Granthi ("Knot of Shiva") or the "forehead knot," Rudra Granthi functions in the region between Ajna and Sahasrara Chakras. This knot is caused by attachment to Siddhis (psychic powers), the separateness of Self from the rest of the world, and dualistic thinking. Rudra Granthi is connected with Sattva—the inclination towards purity, wholesomeness, and virtue. One must surrender their Ego and transcend duality to untie this knot. To do so, they must become virtuous and pure in mind, body and Soul, wholly devoting themselves to God-the Creator.

We must see that Siddhis are just an expression of our connection with the Universal Mind and not something to be gained for personal use. When we attach ourselves to Siddhis, we bring them down to the material world level. Instead, we should be detached, allowing Siddhis to merely express through us without attempting to control the process. When we pierce the Rudra Granthi, Ego consciousness is left behind, and the truth of Oneness is revealed. Jalandhara Bandha, the "Throat Lock," can be applied to untie this knot so that we can transition to a higher level of consciousness.

***

Once the Kundalini has been awakened in Muladhara Chakra, and for it to complete its journey and pierce Sahasrara, all Three Granthis must be unlocked. If there is a blockage along Sushumna Nadi, it is usually in the area of one of the Three Granthis. By untying them through the application of willpower and pure thoughts, or with the use of energetic locks (Bandhas), the Kundalini can rise to Sahasrara. As such, the individual consciousness will unite with Cosmic Consciousness as the two become One. This transformation is permanent, and the individual will no longer be bound by the Granthis for the duration of their life here on Earth.

MUDRA

We often see visual depictions of Ancient Gods and Goddesses from the Eastern part of the world sitting in meditation and holding their hands in certain positions. These hand gestures are called Mudras. They are esoteric hand gestures that activate a specific power within us through the manipulation of energy. Performing a Mudra, we are also directly communicating to Deities and aligning ourselves with their energies or powers.

There are over 500 different Mudras in existence. Mudras are used cross-culturally in many Spiritual systems but especially in Hinduism, Jainism, and Buddhism. In Sanskrit, Mudra means "seal," "mark," or "gesture." Mudras are essentially psychic, emotional, devotional and aesthetic gestures that link the individual Pranic force with the Universal Cosmic force. Performing a Mudra alters one's mood, attitude, and perception while deepening awareness and concentration.

Although most Mudras are simple hand positions or gestures, a particular Mudra may involve the whole body. Hatha Yoga Mudras, for example, use a combination of Yogic techniques such as Asana (body positions), Pranayama (breathing techniques), Bandha, and visualization meditations. They involve the performance of internal actions that engage the pelvic floor, throat, eyes, tongue, diaphragm, anus, genitals, abdomen, or other parts of the body.

Hatha Yoga Mudras are geared towards particular Yogic aims, including affecting Prana's flow to awaken the Kundalini, facilitating the piercing of the Three Granthis by the Kundalini, directly activating the Bindu, utilizing the Amrita or Ambrosia nectar dripping from the Bindu, or reaching transcendence or Enlightenment. Examples of Hatha Yoga Mudras are Khechari Mudra, Shambhavi Mudra, Nasikagra Drishti, Vajroli Mudra, Maha Mudra, and Viparita Karani.

Hatha Yoga Pradipika and other Yogic texts consider Mudras to be an independent branch of Yoga which is only introduced after some proficiency has been attained in Asana, Pranayama, and Bandha. They are higher practices that can lead to the optimization of the Chakras, Nadis, and even awakening Kundalini Shakti. When performed through dedicated practice, Mudras can bestow psychic powers (Siddhis) on the practitioner.

Mudra practice is meant to create a direct link between Annamaya Kosha (Physical Body), Pranamaya Kosha (Astral Body) and Manomaya Kosha (Mental Body). It is meant to assimilate and balance the first three Chakras of Muladhara, Swadhisthana, and Manipura and allow for an opening of the fourth Chakra, Anahata, and beyond.

I have grouped the different types of Mudras into the Hand, Head, Postural, Bandhas (energy locks), and Perineal Mudras. Hasta (Hand Mudras) are meditative Mudras that redirect the Prana emitted by the hands back to the body, generating an energy loop that moves from the brain to the hands and back. Their performance allows us to connect with Archetypal powers within our subconscious mind.

Mana (Head Mudras) are powerful gestures that utilize the eyes, ears, nose, tongue, and lips. They are significant in meditation because of their power to awaken major brain centres and their corresponding Chakras, and access higher states of consciousness.

Kaya (Postural Mudras) are specific physical postures that are to be performed with controlled breathing and concentration. Their use allows us to channel Prana to particular areas of the body and stimulate the Chakras.

Bandha (Lock Mudras) combine Mudra and Bandha to charge the system with Prana and prepare it for a Kundalini awakening. They also allow us to ensure that the Kundalini pierces the Three Granthis when awakened. Bandhas are closely related to nerve plexuses and endocrine glands which relate to Chakras. Lastly, Adhara (Perineal Mudras) redirect Prana from the lower body centres to the brain. They also allow us to sublimate our sexual energy located in the groin area and lower abdomen and utilize it for Spiritual awakening purposes.

HASTA (HAND MUDRAS)

Hasta (Hand Mudras) allow us to direct and seal Pranic energy into specific channels in the Aura. Since most of the major Nadis either start or finish in the hands or feet, Hasta (Hand Mudras) are particularly effective in cleansing these subtle channels of impurities and removing obstructions, facilitating a free flow of energy. Their regular use promotes physical, mental, and emotional healing, furthering our Spiritual Evolution journey.

As each finger relates to a Chakra, you influence the corresponding Chakras by positioning the fingers in specific ways. The Palm Chakra also serves as an interface between the Heart Chakra and the Chakras above and below it. As such, Hand Mudras not only affect the flow of Prana in the Aura, but they allow us to tap into Anahata's healing energy and distribute it to Chakras that require cleansing.

Since there are five fingers and Five Elements, there is a correspondence between them (Figure 105). For example, the thumb relates to Fire (Agni), the index finger to Air (Vayu), the middle finger to Spirit or Space (Akasha), the ring finger to Earth (Prithivi), and the little finger to Water (Jal). The two passive Elements of Water and Earth and the two active Elements of Fire and Air are reconciled by the central Spirit Element.

You will notice that the thumb is most often used in Hand Mudras, which has more Pranic currents running through it than the other fingers. Relating to Manipura Chakra and the Fire Element, the thumb fires up and activates all the other Elements and Chakras. In Ayurveda, where these correspondences come from, the thumb is said to stimulate Pitta Dosha, the energy responsible for transformation. Manipura is also the Seat of the Soul, and so when the thumb is involved in a Hand Mudra, the Soul is the guiding force that enacts change.

There are five primary finger and hand positions to be aware of when implementing a Hand Mudra. The first position involves joining your thumb to a fingertip, which stimulates stability in the associated Element. The second position involves touching the back of a finger on the nail or knuckle, which decreases the related Element's influence. In the third position, you are to bring the thumb to the finger's base, which also stimulates the corresponding Element. Next, depending on the Mudra you are activating, when your palm faces outward, you open yourself to receiving energy. When your palm faces downward, however, you are grounding yourself.

Because they are simple to perform, Hand Mudras can be practised at any time, whether at home or on the go. Yogis often perform Hand Mudras as part of meditation practice, before or after other techniques such as Asanas, Pranayamas, or Bandhas.

Figure 105: The Fingers and the Five Elements

Steps for Performing Hand Mudras

When doing Hand Mudras, make sure your hands are clean. Since these are Divine gestures designed to connect you with higher powers, cleanliness is crucial. You can practise Hand Mudras while standing, kneeling, lying down, or sitting in a chair. However, you should sit in a comfortable meditation Asana and keep your back and head straight for optimal results. In addition, the hands and arms should remain relaxed during the entire practice. Hand Mudras are generally performed at the level of the navel, the heart, or placed on the knees while in a meditation Asana.

Start by rubbing your hands together gently for seven to ten seconds to charge them with Pranic energy. Next, place your right hand on your Hara Chakra and your left hand on top of the right. You will begin to feel a warm energy flow generated in Hara, your body's Pranic centre. Stay in this position for a minute or so to obtain the necessary connection.

Always perform each Mudra one at a time, allotting the required amount of time for each one. Remember that the outcome is cumulative, so the longer you do a Mudra, the greater the effect on your energy. To manage chronic issues, hold one Mudra daily for forty-five minutes or three fifteen-minute periods.

When performing a Mudra, don't exert any pressure but merely connect the hands and fingers in the required manner to manipulate the desired energy flow. Also, perform each Mudra with both hands since doing so promotes harmony and balance while maximizing the desired effect. Finally, it is ideal to practise Hand Mudras on an empty stomach, as is the case with all energy invoking/manipulating techniques.

Jnana Mudra

Jnana Mudra is one of the most widely used Hand Mudras, especially during meditation practice. Its name is derived from the Sanskrit "jnana," meaning "wisdom" or "knowledge." The knowledge being referred to is the enlightened wisdom the Yogi seeks to attain in the Yogic path.

To perform this Mudra, touch the tip of the index finger and thumb together, thereby forming a circle, while the remaining three fingers are extended and kept straight (Figure 106). A variation of Jnana Mudra is to tuck in the index finger under the tip of the thumb. The front of the hand should rest on the thighs or knees, with the palm facing downwards.

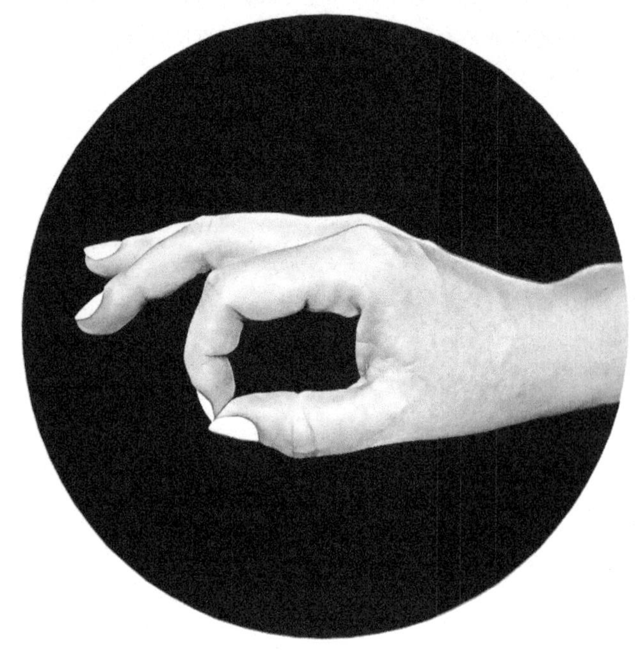

Figure 106: Jnana Mudra

According to Ayurveda, Jnana Mudra balances the Elements of Fire (Agni-thumb) and Air (Vayu-index finger) within the body. As such, practising this Mudra during meditation stabilizes the mind while promoting concentration and facilitating higher states of consciousness.

There is further symbolism in the practice of Jnana Mudra across various Spiritual traditions such as Hinduism, Buddhism, and Yoga. The thumb is believed to symbolize the Supreme Soul, or universal consciousness (Brahman), while the index finger represents the individual Soul, the Jivatma. By connecting the thumb and index finger, we are uniting these two realities. The remaining three fingers, however, represent the three qualities (Gunas) of nature—Rajas (middle finger), Sattva (ring finger), and Tamas (little finger). For consciousness to advance from ignorance to knowledge, we must transcend these states.

By connecting the index finger to the thumb, we produce a circuit that redirects Pranic energy through the body, sending it up to the brain instead of releasing it into the environment. Since Jnana Mudra points to the Earth, the effect is grounding to one's energy, calming the mind while soothing the emotions. This Mudra is also known to improve memory.

Chin Mudra

Chin means "consciousness" in Sanskrit, and this Mudra is often referred to as the "psychic Mudra of consciousness." Chin Mudra is otherwise known as Gyan Mudra. ("Gyan" is Sanskrit for "knowledge" or "wisdom".) Chin Mudra is to be performed in the same way as Jnana Mudra, the only difference being that the palm faces upwards instead of downwards (Figure 107) so that the back of the hand can rest on the thighs or knees.

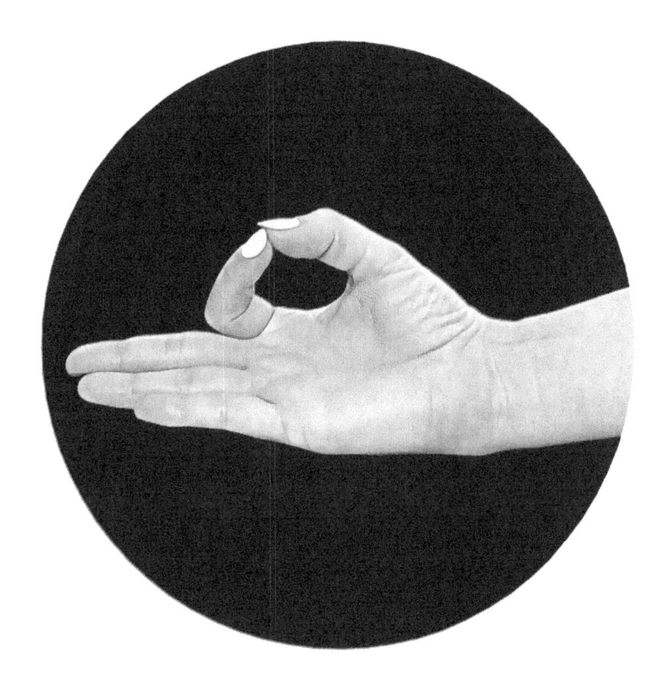

Figure 107: Chin Mudra

Since they are almost identical, the symbolic elements of Chin Mudra are the same as in Jnana Mudra. As Chin Mudra points to the Heavens above, the upward-facing position of the hand opens up the chest, making the practitioner receptive to energies from the Higher Planes. As such, Chin Mudra boosts intuition and creativity while relieving stress and tension and improving concentration. It is also helpful in overcoming insomnia.

Both Jnana and Chin Mudras facilitate going inwards, a prerequisite for deep meditation and reaching higher states of consciousness. In addition to their use in meditation, Jnana and Chin Mudras can be used to enhance the effects of Mantra chanting and other Yogic practices like Asanas, Pranayamas, and Bandhas.

As a final note, it is not uncommon for Yoga practitioners to perform Jnana Mudra on one hand while performing Chin Mudra on the other. Doing so enables one to receive energy from a higher source while at the same time grounding the experience.

Hridaya Mudra

Hridaya means "Heart" in Sanskrit, as this Mudra improves the heart's vitality by increasing the flow of Prana. Hridaya Mudra is known to have the ability to save a person from a heart attack by reducing chest pain instantly and removing blockages within the arteries. It is also known as "Mrit Sanjeevani," a Sanskrit term implying that this Mudra has the power to snatch us back from the jaws of death.

Hridaya Mudra is also called Apana Vayu Mudra because it combines two Mudras—Apana and Vayu. To assume the Mudra, fold the index finger and press on the knuckle with the thumb (Vayu Mudra), which reduces the Air Element's influence, relaxing the body and mind. Then, you are to join the thumb tip with the middle and ring fingers (Apana Mudra), thus activating the Spirit, Earth, and Fire Elements (Figure 108).

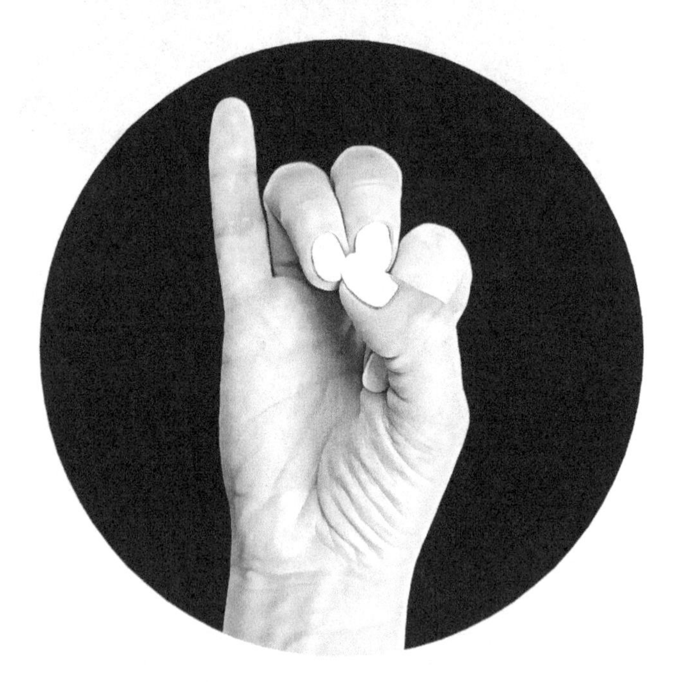

Figure 108: Hridaya Mudra

As Vayu Mudra cures heart irregularities, including rapid heartbeats and perspiration, Apana Mudra reduces excess gas from the stomach while promoting blood circulation to the heart. Acidity and heartburn are also relieved with the performance of Hridaya Mudra.

Since the heart is the centre of emotions, Hridaya Mudra also helps release pent-up feelings that cause stress and anxiety. As such, it is beneficial to practise this Mudra during emotional conflict and crisis. Another common benefit of Hridaya Mudra is overcoming sleep issues, such as insomnia. Hridaya Mudra can be done for ten to fifteen minutes at a time or longer and repeated as often as necessary.

Shunya Mudra

Shunya means "emptiness," "spaciousness," or "openness" in Sanskrit; hence its other name, the "Heaven Mudra." This Mudra is designed to decrease the Spirit (Space) Element in the body (middle finger) while increasing the Fire Element's energy (the thumb).

To assume Shunya Mudra, fold the middle finger and press on the knuckle with the thumb. The remaining three fingers should stay extended (Figure 109). Regular use of Shunya Mudra during meditation awakens intuition while increasing willpower and calming the mind. In addition, its long-term practitioners report gaining the ability to hear Anahata's unstruck sound of silence, which makes one feel like they are on a different Planet, in another dimension of space-time. Thus, regular practise of this Mudra paves the way to obtaining Eternal bliss and transcendence.

Figure 109: Shunya Mudra

On a physical level, Shunya Mudra is known to relieve a range of hearing and internal balance issues, including motion sickness, vertigo, body numbness, and ear disorders. It is also known to cure heart and throat diseases. Practise this Mudra for ten to fifteen minutes at a time, or longer if necessary. Repeat as often as you like.

In Ayurvedic medicine, Shunya Mudra is beneficial for Vata Dosha dominant people, which is the energy associated with movement, including blood circulation, respiration, and the nervous system.

Anjali Mudra

Anjali means "salutation" or "to offer" in Sanskrit. Anjali Mudra is commonly accompanied by the word "Namaste," which forms a type of greeting used frequently by Spiritual people in the Western world. This gesture, however, originated in India and has been a part of its culture for thousands of years. It consists of holding both palms held erect together in front of one's breasts (Figure 110), often accompanied by a slight bow.

Figure 110: Anjali Mudra

In Sanskrit, "Nama" means "bow" while "as" means "I" and "te" means "you." Therefore, Namaste means "I bow to you." Namaste represents the belief in a Divine spark of consciousness within each of us located in the Heart Chakra, Anahata. By performing it, we recognize one another as Divine Souls from the same source—God-the Creator.

Anjali Mudra can also be offered as a sacred greeting when trying to establish contact with a higher power. This powerful hand gesture has been adopted as the prayer position in the Western world for over two thousand years. Its performance allows us to connect with our Holy Guardian Angel. By bringing the hands together at the Heart Chakra centre, you symbolically and energetically unify all opposites within you, allowing your consciousness to rise to a Higher Plane.

Anjali Mudra reconciles our masculine and feminine energies while uniting the left and right brain hemispheres. The result is coherence in the mind and body on all levels. Its other health benefits include: improving focus, calming the mind, promoting mindfulness, and relieving stress.

Yoni Mudra

Yoni means "womb," "source," or "receptacle" in Sanskrit, and it is an abstract representation of Shakti, the dynamic feminine power of nature. Yoni also refers to the female reproductive system in general. Performing Yoni Mudra balances the opposing but complementary energies in your body, especially the two brain hemispheres.

To assume Yoni Mudra, place the palms of the hands together at the level of the navel. The fingers and thumbs should be straight and pointing away from the body. First, turn the middle, ring and little fingers inwards so that the backs of the fingers are touching. Next, interlock the middle, ring, and little fingers while keeping the tips of the index fingers and thumbs together. Finally, brings the thumbs towards the body as you point the index fingers to the ground, thereby forming the shape of the womb with the thumbs and index fingers (Figure 111).

Figure 111: Yoni Mudra

In its final position, the elbows naturally tend to point to the side, opening up the chest. You can do Yoni Mudra for ten to fifteen minutes at a time to obtain the desired effect. Repeat as often as you like throughout the day.

The downward-pointing index fingers stimulate the flow of Apana, the subtle energy that cleanses the body, mind, and emotions. Yoni Mudra has a calming effect on the nervous system as it reduces stress and brings about peace and harmony within. In addition, Yoni Mudra attunes us to the feminine, intuitive aspect of our Being. Like a fetus in the womb, its practitioner experiences bliss by becoming passive mentally and emotionally.

Bhairava Mudra

Bhairava means "fearsome" in Sanskrit, and it refers to the ferocious manifestation of Shiva the Destroyer. Bhairava Mudra is a symbolic, ritualistic gesture of the hands that harmonises the body's energy flow during meditation or other Yogic practices. This common Yogic practice gives an instant feeling of peacefulness, enabling the higher qualities to emerge.

To perform Bhairava Mudra, place the right hand on top of the left, with the palms facing up (Figure 112). If performed in a meditation Asana, the hands should be on one's lap as the spine and head are held straight. When the left hand is placed on top of the right, the practice is called Bhairavi Mudra, the feminine (Shakti) counterpart of Bhairava.

Figure 112: Bhairava Mudra

The two hands represent the Ida (left hand) and Pingala (right hand) Nadis, the feminine and masculine energy channels that become unified when one hand is placed on top of the other. Depending on which hand is on top, however, this gender principle becomes the expressive quality. For example, when the left hand is on top, the Water Element is dominant, activating the principle of consciousness and manifestation. Conversely, when the right hand is on top, the Fire Element dominates, invoking strength and power and destroying one's Egoism as the Divine Light absorbs into the Aura. Thus, this Mudra is also said to cure all bodily diseases.

Do Bhairava Mudra for ten to fifteen minutes at a time or longer and repeat as often as you like. Within Tantric and Yogic texts, Bhairava Mudra is considered the ultimate Hand Mudra because its performance unifies the individual Soul with the universal consciousness—the inward and outward Selves become One.

Lotus Mudra

Lotus Mudra is designed to open the Heart Chakra, Anahata. It is a symbol of purity and positivity, representing the Light emerging from the darkness. As such, Lotus Mudra has powerful healing effects on mental, emotional, and physical levels. Its performance relaxes and stabilizes the mind while creating a more loving attitude towards other people. On a physical level, Lotus Mudra is known to treat ulcers and fevers.

To perform Lotus Mudra, start by bringing the hands together in front of the heart centre in Anjali Mudra. Next, spread the index, middle, and ring fingers like a lotus flower opening while keeping the thumbs and little fingers together (Figure 113). Remain in this position now and feel the effects of this Mudra on your Heart Chakra. Lotus Mudra can be performed as often as you like, for a minimum of ten minutes at a time to feel its effects.

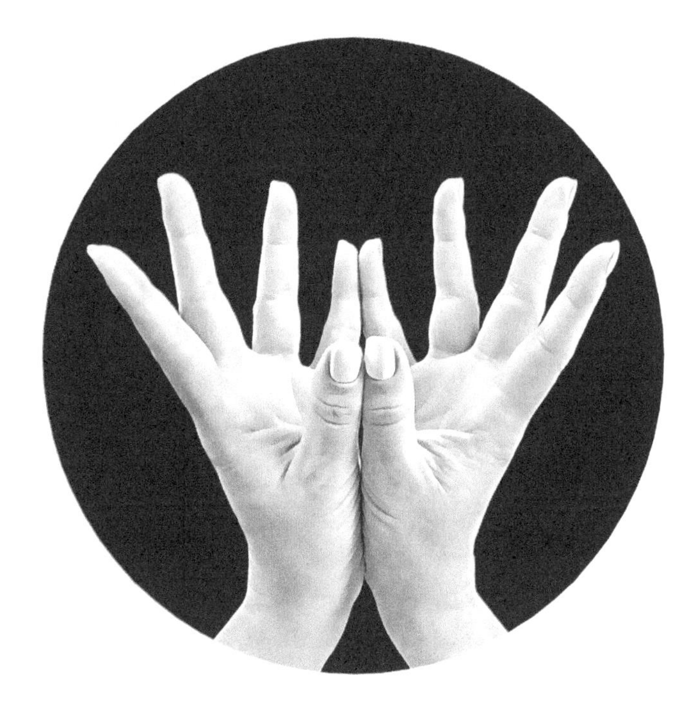

Figure 113: Lotus Mudra

As the roots of a lotus flower remain firmly embedded in the muddy bottom of a pond, its flower head faces the sun, receiving its healing rays. In the same fashion, Lotus Mudra teaches us to stay connected to our roots as we open our hearts to the Divine Light. It teaches us to keep our thoughts pure and accept others, even if our feelings are negative towards them. In doing so, we connect with the grace and beauty present within us when our Heart Chakra is open.

Shiva Linga Mudra

Shiva Linga Mudra is a powerful hand gesture representing the God Shiva and the Goddess Parvati, his consort. The Lingam is emblematic of male creative energy, the phallus, worshipped in Hindu Temples. It is represented symbolically by the upright thumb of the right hand in Shiva Linga Mudra, while the palm on which it rests represents the feminine energy, the receptacle. As such, this Mudra denotes the integration of Shiva and Shakti (Shiva's feminine energy). Its English name is the "Upright Mudra."

To assume Shiva Linga Mudra, place your left hand at the abdomen level in a bowl shape, keeping the fingers together. Next, place your right fist on top of your left palm. Finally, extend the thumb of the right hand upward (Figure 114). Feel the grounding effects of this Mudra in your Aura.

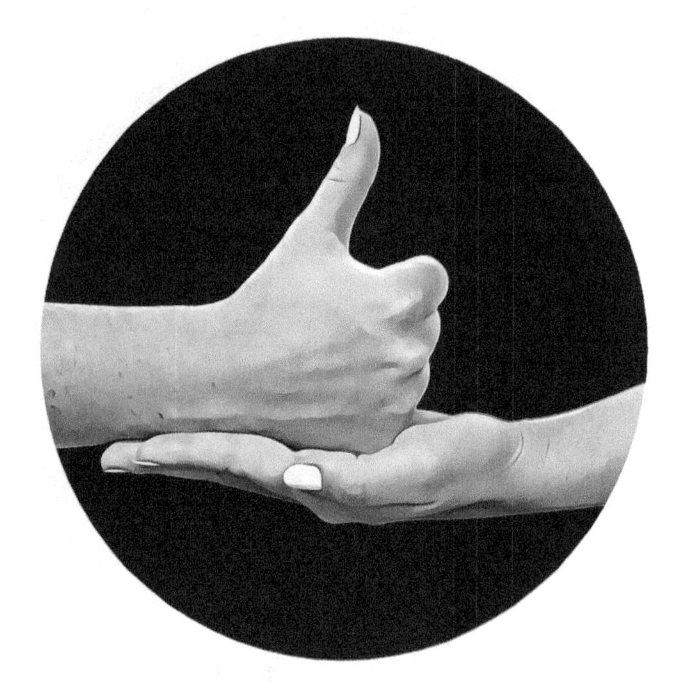

Figure 114: Shiva Linga Mudra

Shiva Linga Mudra's focus is on Muladhara Chakra, the abode of the Lingam. This Mudra relieves anxiety and stress by calming the mind and charging the body with the dense Earth energy. It not only addresses physical and mental fatigue by energizing the body but it increases self-confidence and improves intuition. Because of its powerful effects in grounding one's energy, Shiva Linga Mudra should be done no more than two to three times a day for ten minutes at a time.

Kundalini Mudra

Kundalini Mudra awakens the sexual force, stimulating creativity and regeneration. This Mudra is known to activate dormant sexual desires and heal any issues with the reproductive organs. On a subtle level, performing Kundalini Mudra unifies the masculine and feminine principles within the Self, which facilitates the awakening of the Kundalini at the base of the spine.

To perform Kundalini Mudra, make a loose fist at the navel level with both hands. Next, extend the index finger of the left hand while you wrap the four fingers of the right hand around it. The tip of the left hand's index finger should connect to the right hand's thumb (Figure 115).

Figure 115: Kundalini Mudra

The left index finger represents the individual Soul and mind, while the four fingers of the right hand symbolize the outside world. Finally, the right thumb is the sacred power of the Kundalini. The Kundalini Mudra, as a whole, represents the union of the individual Self with the Universe. Because of its potent effect on one's sexual energy, the Kundalini Mudra should be practised no more than two to three times a day for ten minutes at a time.

MANA (HEAD MUDRAS)

Shambhavi Mudra (Eyebrow Centre Gazing)

Shambhavi Mudra is a highly regarded practice in Yoga and Tantra because of its power in stilling the mind and experiencing higher states of consciousness. It is a powerful technique of awakening Ajna Chakra since it involves gazing at the eyebrow centre where the Mind's Eye tunnel is located. Shambhavi Mudra nullifies all positive and negative thoughts when applied correctly and brings about a state of Void (Shoonya) or thoughtlessness/emptiness. Its other name is Bhrumadya Drishti, where "bhru" means "eyebrow centre" and "drishti" means "gazing" in Sanskrit.

The word "Shambhavi" originates from the Sanskrit "Shambhu," which is a reference to Lord Shiva as one who is "born from happiness or bliss." Shambhavi is the feminine aspect of Lord Shiva—the Kundalini Shakti. Shambhavi Mudra not only activates Ajna Chakra but focusing on the eyebrow centre stimulates Ida and Pingala Nadis to converge at this point, which directly affects the Kundalini at the base of the spine and can facilitate a rising.

Shambhavi Mudra is beneficial for overcoming fearful, negative thoughts, which originate from the subconscious mind. Focusing on the eyebrow centre causes attention to be placed to the front of the head, where the conscious mind operates from. In Hermeticism, the front of the head represents the Solar, masculine aspect, while the back of the head represents the Lunar, feminine aspect. On the Qabalistic Tree of Life, the path of Qoph (The Moon Tarot card), which literally means "the back of the head," represents the subconscious mind. Conversely, the path of Resh (The Sun Tarot card) means "head," referring to the front of the head and the conscious mind.

To begin the Shambhavi Mudra exercise, sit in one of the three meditation Asanas while relaxing the body and keeping your spine straight. Place your hands on your knees in either the Jnana or Chin Mudra. Close the eyes and relax all the muscles in the face, forehead, eyes, and behind the eyes while taking a few slow and deep breaths. Now gradually open your eyes and look ahead of you at a fixed point. For best results, implement Khechari Mudra as part of the practice, although it is recommended to start without it until you get more familiar with the exercise.

Figure 116: Shambhavi Mudra

Look upwards and inwards now as you focus your eyes on the eyebrow centre while keeping the head and whole body still (Figure 116). If performed correctly, the curve of the eyebrows will form a V-shaped image whose apex is at the eyebrow centre. If you do not see the V-formation, then your gaze is not directed upward and inwards correctly.

Concentrate on the point between the eyebrows without blinking for a few seconds. Then, relax your eyes by moving them to their original position before repeating the practice. It is crucial to hold the gaze for only a few seconds at first and gradually increase the duration as you get more comfortable with this exercise. There should never be too much strain on the eyes. If you feel discomfort in your eyes, you can warm up your hands by rubbing them together and covering the eyes to infuse healing energy and remove tension.

As you get more experience with this exercise, fixing your gaze on the eyebrow centre will come naturally as the muscles that control the eyes become stronger. When you perform the Shambhavi Mudra exercise, practise being mindful while implementing Yogic Breathing on the inhale and exhale for optimal effects.

Shambhavi Mudra can be incorporated as part of Asana practice and Pranayama exercises such as Sama Vritti and Moorcha Pranayama. When practised on its own, start with five rounds and gradually increase to ten over a period of five months. Note that if you are having any health issues with your eyes, you should not perform this exercise.

You can also practise Shambhavi Mudra with your eyes closed once you get some experience with it. The closed-eyes variation of this exercise is the all-important Mind's Eye Meditation from *The Magus*. I discuss the mechanics of this internal Shambhavi Mudra as part of the Kundalini Meditations from the "Troubleshooting the System" chapter of this book.

Nasikagra Drishti (Nosetip Gazing)

Nasikagra Drishti is similar to Shambhavi Mudra, except that the eyes focus on the nose tip instead of the eyebrow centre. The term comes from the Sanskrit words "nasagra," meaning "nose tip" and "drishti," which translates as "gazing." Nasikagra Drishti is excellent in strengthening the eye muscles, developing concentration, and taking the practitioner to higher states of consciousness during meditation. This exercise is known to activate Muladhara Chakra, which is connected to the brain's Frontal Lobe.

To practise nose tip gazing, hold your index finger upright at arm's length at the level of your nose. Fix your gaze upon it and slowly start moving it towards the tip of your nose while keeping your head steady. When your finger reaches the end of your nose (the eyes should still be focused on it), drop the finger and transfer the focus of your eyes to your nose tip. After a few seconds of holding your gaze there, close your eyes and relax them before repeating the practice. Spend no more than three to five minutes a day on this exercise for the first two weeks. After it becomes straightforward to fix your gaze on your nose tip at will, you are ready for Nasikagra Drishti.

To begin Nasikagra Drishti, sit in one of the three meditation Asanas while relaxing the body and keeping your spine and head straight. Place your hands on your knees in either the Jnana or Chin Mudra. Close the eyes and relax all the muscles in the face while taking a few deep, slow breaths. Gradually open your eyes now and focus them on the nose tip (Figure 117). Refraction of light that forms a V should be seen just above the tip of the nose if performed correctly. Hold your gaze there for a few seconds before closing your eyes and repeating. Spend no more than five to ten minutes a day on this exercise and increase the duration after a few months.

You can implement Khechari Mudra as part of Nasikagra Drishti, although it is recommended to start without it for the first little while. Always be mindful not to put too much strain on your eyes; if you feel discomfort in your eyes, you can warm up your hands by rubbing them together and covering the eyes to infuse healing energy. Practise

Nasikagra Drishti with Yogic Breathing on the inhale and exhale for optimal effects. Individuals who have health issues with their eyes or are suffering from depression should not perform this exercise.

You can also practise Nasikagra Drishti with your eyes closed. I discovered the closed-eyes nose tip meditation on my Spiritual journey and its power to optimise the Kundalini circuit once it collapses. Later on, once I got into Yoga, I found out about Nasikagra Drishti and its similar mechanics. I have found that by focusing on the tip of your nose, you connect with the Subconscious Eye psychic centre that lies in-between the two physical eyes, one centimetre outside of the head.

Figure 117: Nasikagra Drishti

An energy channel runs along the front of the nose from the Subconscious Eye to the nose tip. The tip of the nose serves as a release point for the Subconscious Eye. If this psychic centre becomes blocked, there is an increase of negative energy and fear inside the mind, usually resulting from a collapsed Ida channel. Focusing on the nose tip allows you to open or reopen this channel if it becomes blocked, alleviating disturbing, fear-based thoughts and emotions. Refer to the Kundalini Meditations for more information on this exercise (Middle of the Eyes/Nose Bridge Meditation).

Shanmukhi Mudra (Closing the Seven Gates)

Shanmukhi Mudra is made of two root Sanskrit terms, "Shan" meaning "six," and "mukhi" meaning "face" or "gate." As such, Shanmukhi Mudra refers to the six gates of perception through which we sense the external world—

the two eyes, two ears, and the nose and mouth. This exercise involves closing the six openings of perception to block the body's five senses—sight, sound, smell, and touch.

According to the *Yoga Sutras of Patanjali*, Shanmukhi Mudra is considered a practice of Pratyahara (sense withdrawal)—the preliminary stage of Dharana (concentration) and Dhyana (meditation). Shanmukhi Mudra is excellent for focus and introspection since by cutting ourselves off from the external world, we gain deeper insight into our inner Self. It also calms the mind and nervous system and relaxes and rejuvenates the eyes and facial muscles through the energy and heat from the hands and fingers.

To begin the Shanmukhi Mudra exercise, sit in one of the three meditation Asanas while keeping your spine straight. Place your hands on your knees in either the Jnana or Chin Mudra. Close your eyes and take a few deep breaths to relax your body. Allow yourself to feel your environment before you are to become detached from it.

For maximum benefit and to potentially awaken the Kundalini at the base of the spine, this exercise should be accompanied by Mula Bandha's application. As such, place a small cushion beneath your perineum to apply pressure to this area, thus activating Muladhara Chakra.

Raise the arms and elbows at shoulder level with your palms facing you. One by one, start closing your sense organs with your fingers. Close the ears with the thumbs, eyes with the index fingers, nostrils with the middle fingers, and the mouth with the ring and little fingers (Figure 118). Release the pressure of the middle fingers (partially) so that you can breathe through the nostrils. The rest of the sense organs apply mild pressure to ensure that they remain closed during the exercise.

Figure 118: Shanmukhi Mudra

Inhale slowly and deeply through the partially blocked nostrils using the Yogic Breathing technique. At the end of the inhalation, close your nostrils with the middle fingers and hold your breath. The longer you can comfortably hold your breath, the more substantial effects you will receive from this exercise. Release the pressure of the middle fingers now and exhale slowly through your nostrils. This completes the first round.

Start with five minutes of practice and build it up to thirty minutes over three months. When you are ready to end the exercise, lower your hands to your knees while keeping your eyes closed. Spend a few moments becoming aware of your surroundings before opening your eyes and concluding the practice.

For optimum effects with Shanmukhi Mudra, focus on the space between your eyebrows with the eyes closed to connect with Ajna chakra. Pay attention to your breathing as you become detached from the external world. With every breath, you should be going deeper into your inner Self. As you do so, notice how it makes you feel and the changes in your Heart Chakra. It is not uncommon to hear different sounds from your interior, such as subtle vibrations emanating from Bindu Chakra.

You can practise Shanmukhi Mudra at any time during the day, although it is optimal right in the morning or before going to sleep. As with all Yogic exercises that bring on an introverted state of mind, people suffering from depression should not practise Shanmukhi Mudra.

KAYA (POSTURAL MUDRAS)

Viparita Karani-Inverted Psychic Attitude

Viparita Karani comes from the Sanskrit words "viparita," meaning "inverted," or "reversed," and "karani," meaning "a particular type of practice." The purpose of this Postural Mudra is to reverse the downflow and loss of the Amrita (the life-giving Ambrosia Nectar that secretes from the Bindu) through the use of gravity. (You can learn more about the use and purpose of the Amrita in the "Lalana Chakra and the Amrita Nectar" chapter in this section.) Its other goal is to create a sublimation of energy from bottom to top of the body and balance its Pranic energy flow. Because the attention should be placed on Manipura and Vishuddhi on the inhale and exhale, Viparita Karani serves to optimize these two Chakras as well.

To come into the Viparita Karani pose, bring your legs over the head while supporting your hips with your hands. You should hold your torso as close to a 45-degree angle as possible while the legs are straight up (Figure 119). Your eyes should look upwards at your feet while your toes point to the sky. Keep your elbows close to each other while being mindful to keep your chin from pressing against your chest. In the final position, the body's weight rests on the shoulders, neck, and elbows. If you have issues coming into this pose, you can use a wall and pillows to support your legs and torso. Close your eyes now and relax your whole body.

Apply Jiva Bandha (tongue on the roof of the mouth) or Khechari Mudra for the entire practice. Then, inhale slowly and deeply with Ujjayi Pranayama while placing your awareness on Manipura Chakra. On the exhale, move your attention on Vishuddhi Chakra. This completes the first round.

Practise up to seven rounds at first, switching your attention from Manipura on the inhale to Vishuddhi on the exhale and vice versa. If you feel the pressure build-up in the head or other discomfort arises, end the practice immediately.

Gradually increase the number of rounds from seven to twenty-one over three months. Your inhalation and exhalation should be the same duration during this practice. As you get more comfortable with it, work on increasing the duration while keeping the same ratio.

To end the practice, slowly lower the spine, vertebra by vertebra, while keeping your head on the floor. After your buttocks are lowered, bring down your legs while keeping them straight. Spend a few moments in Shavasana now to allow your consciousness to ground itself. It is also advisable to perform an Asana counterpose afterwards to balance your energies.

Viparita Karani is best practised in the morning. Incorporate this exercise at the end of your daily Asana practice program and/or before meditation. Note that people suffering from high blood pressure, heart disease, neck or back pain, or excessive toxins in the body should not perform Viparita Karani. Also, since performing this exercise for an extended period increases the metabolic rate, avoid it for at least three hours after a meal.

Figure 119: Viparita Karani

Pashinee Mudra-Folded Psychic Attitude

Pashinee Mudra is derived from the Sanskrit term "pash," meaning "noose." The word "Pashinee" refers to being "bound in a noose," which this position resembles. Practising this Mudra provides tranquillity and balance to the nervous system and induces Pratyahara. It stretches the neck as well as the spine and back muscles.

To begin the Pashinee Mudra exercise, assume Halasana (Plough Pose) but separate the legs about one and a half feet. Bend the knees and bring your thighs towards your chest until your knees are on the floor. In the final position, the knees should be as close as possible towards the shoulders and ears (Figure 120).

Relax the body and close your eyes. Take slow and deep breaths. Maintain this position as long as comfortably possible. Now, gently release the arms and come back to Halasana. Lower the legs and relax in Shavasana for a few moments to allow your consciousness to ground itself.

As with Viparita Karani, it is advisable to perform a counterpose to balance out your energies, which would be a backward bending Asana. Note that people suffering from a spinal condition or neck injury should avoid this Mudra. Also, menstruating or pregnant women should skip this practice.

Figure 120: Pashinee Mudra

Tadagi Mudra

Tadagi is derived from the Sanskrit term "tadaga," meaning "water body" or "water pot-like structure, similar to a lake or pond. This Mudra technique involves moulding the abdomen into a barrel shape through deep abdominal breathing, hence its name. Tadagi Mudra stimulates Manipura and Hara Chakras, raising the level of Prana in the body. In addition, it encourages blood circulation to the abdominal organs while relieving any held tension from the pelvic floor.

Sit on the floor or a yoga mat with legs stretched out straight and the feet slightly apart. (The legs should remain straight throughout the exercise.) To assume Tadagi Mudra, begin by placing the hands on the knees while keeping the head and spine straight. Next, close the eyes and relax the entire body while breathing normally. Bend forward now and wrap the thumbs, index, and middle fingers over your big toes (Figure 121).

Inhale slowly and fill your abdomen with oxygen, allowing it to expand fully. Retain the breath for an extended period comfortably. There should not be any strain on your body at any time during this exercise. You can release the toes between breaths to adjust and make yourself more comfortable.

Exhale slowly and deeply, letting the belly relax while maintaining a hold on your toes. One round is now complete. Repeat the rounds five to ten times. When you are ready to end the practice, release the toes and return to the starting position. Note that pregnant women and people suffering from a hernia or prolapse should avoid this exercise.

Figure 121: Tadagi Mudra

Manduki Mudra-Gesture of the Frog

Manduki means "frog" in Sanskrit, and it mimics the posture of a frog at rest. Its other name is the "Gesture of the Frog," or "Frog Attitude." This Mudra stimulates Muladhara Chakra and balances the Pranic energy flow in the body. It calms the mind, balances Ida and Pingala Nadis, and enhances levels of insight. Since it involves a powerful Yoga Asana, it enhances the strength of the hips, knees, and ankles and makes them more flexible.

Begin in a simple kneeling position where both of the knees are touching the ground. Then, to perform Manduki Mudra, adjust your legs so that your toes are pointing outward and your buttocks are resting on the floor (Figure 122). If this position is uncomfortable for you, sit on a cushion instead, placing your legs and feet in the same position.

You should feel pressure being applied to the perineum, thus triggering Muladhara Chakra. Next, place your hands on your knees in either the Jnana or Chin Mudra. You should hold your spine and head straight during this exercise. If you find yourself naturally leaning forward from this position, hold your knees and straighten your arms for support. Close your eyes now and relax your whole body.

Open your eyes and perform Nasikagra Drishti. Start by placing your tongue on your palate (Jiva Bandha) for a minute or two and then transition to Khechari Mudra. Your breath should be slow and rhythmic. If you feel discomfort in your eyes, close them for a few seconds and then resume the practice. Practise Manduki Mudra with Yogic Breathing on the inhale and exhale for optimal effects.

Start with doing this exercise for two minutes once a day, preferably in the morning. As you get more familiar with it, gradually increase up to five minutes for optimal effects. The senses should become drawn inwards when performed correctly.

Manduki Mudra is an advanced version of Nasikagra Drishti. As such, it should be practised in mild light so that the tip of the nose can be seen clearly. Follow the precautions for practising Nasikagra Drishti. People with problems with the ankles, knees, or hips should exercise caution when performing Manduki Mudra since it requires these body parts to be flexible.

Figure 122: Manduki Mudra

BANDHA (LOCK MUDRAS)

Mula Bandha (Perineum Contraction)

Mula Bandha is the first of three major energy locks used in Yogic practices to control the flow of Prana in the body along with Uddiyana and Jalandhara Bandhas. Each of the three Bandhas (locks) seals a specific part of the body, sending the Prana inwards and upwards through Sushumna Nadi. When all three Bandhas are used together, the practice is called Maha Bandha, meaning the "Great Lock" (Figure 132). Each Bandha can also be used to untie one of the Three Granthis (psychic knots), which obstruct the Kundalini energy on its upwards rise.

Mula Bandha means "Root Lock" in Sanskrit, referring to the process of harnessing energy in Muladhara, the Root Chakra and sending it upwards through Sushumna. Mula Bandha is the initial energy lock used to stir the Kundalini into activity at the base of the spine.

Performing Mula Bandha involves the contraction of specific muscles between the anus and genital organs in the perineum region where Muladhara's flower head is located. The exact contraction point for males is between the anus and testes, while in females, it is behind the cervix, where the uterus protrudes into the vagina (Figure 123).

Since it is the junction point for the nerves, the perineum area is where our nervous system starts. Contracting the perineum with Mula Bandha has a calming effect on the nervous system, promoting peace of mind while increasing concentration.

On a Pranic level, Mula Bandha redirects the energy of Apana, the aspect of Prana within the body that flows downward from the navel. Reversing the direction of Apana's flow coupled with stimulating the three Nadis that commence in the Muladhara region can have a powerful effect at awakening the Kundalini from its slumber in the coccyx region.

During a Kundalini awakening, Mula Bandha can be used to transcend Brahma Granthi that exists between Muladhara and Swadhisthana Chakras. In doing so, the Soul is liberated from particular attachments that bind it to the World of Matter. Overcoming Brahma Granthi is essential to raising the Kundalini into the Chakras above Muladhara.

On a physical level, Mula Bandha strengthens the muscles of the pelvic floor. It prevents premature ejaculation in men, while for women, it soothes the pain of menstruation. Psychologically, Mula Bandha aids in regulating hormones and promoting healthy mental and emotional growth and development. This timeless technique balances the male and female sex hormones—testosterone and estrogen. It regulates thyroxine, which helps in metabolic activities, as well as serotonin, the mood-elevating hormone. Mula Bandha is very effective in treating mental issues such as mania, hysteria, phobias, neuroses, and general depression.

To begin the Mula Bandha exercise, choose one of the three meditation Asanas, preferably Siddhasana, which allows you to press on your perineum with your heel. Keep your spine and neck straight while closing your eyes and relaxing the whole body. For added effect, you may place your hands on your knees in either the Jnana or Chin Mudra.

Become aware of the natural breath as you focus your awareness on the perineal region. On the next inhale, contract this region by pulling up the pelvic floor muscles, lifting them towards the spine. On the exhale, release and relax the pelvic muscles. Breathe slowly and deeply. Continue contracting and relaxing the perineal/vaginal region in a controlled, rhythmic manner, timing it with the inhale and exhale. Do this exercise for a few minutes as preparation for the following step.

Instead of letting go of the next contraction, hold it tightly for a few seconds while maintaining relaxation in the rest of the body. Focus on the pelvic floor and ensure that you have contracted only the perineal muscles related to the Muladhara region and not the anus or urinary sphincters. Hold for a few seconds. Release the contraction now, allowing the pelvic muscles to relax. Repeat the exercise for as long as you want with maximal contraction followed by total relaxation of the pelvic muscles.

The final stage of Mula Bandha involves breath retention (Khumbaka). Inhale deeply as you contract the perineum muscles. Hold the breath now as long as you can comfortably while maintaining the contraction. As you exhale, release the contraction while relaxing the entire pelvic region. Take a few normal breaths before commencing with the next contraction coupled with breath retention. Repeat the exercise as long as you want. When you are ready to end the practice, open your eyes.

Mula Bandha can be performed with different Asanas, Pranayamas, Mudras, and Bandhas, for optimal effects. When practised on its own, it should be performed as a precursor for meditation.

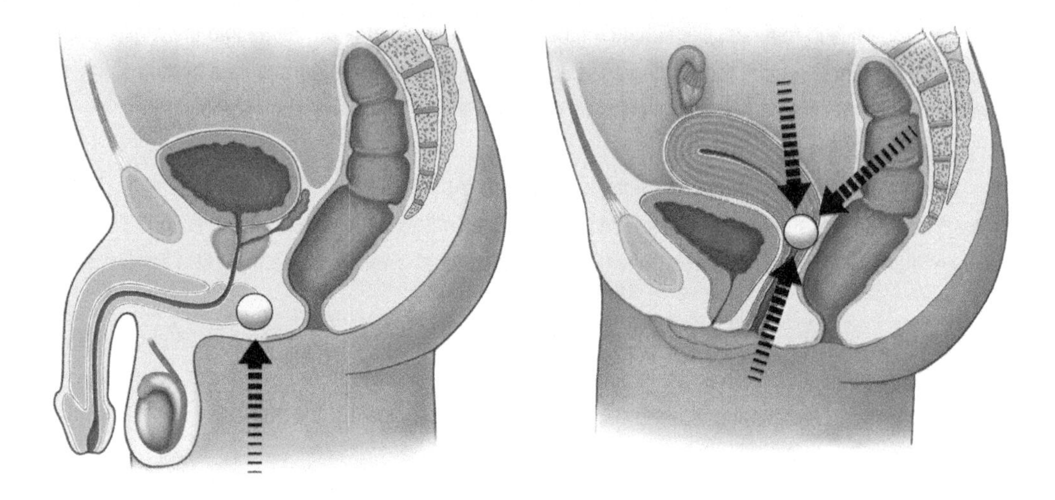

Figure 123: Mula Bandha Contraction Point

Uddiyana Bandha (Abdominal Contraction)

Uddiyana in Sanskrit means "Upwards Flying," relating to the technique of locking Pranic energy in the abdominal region and directing it upwards through Sushumna Nadi. This "Abdominal Lock" involves contracting and lifting the abdominal wall inside (towards spine) and upwards (towards ribcage) at the same time. When applied correctly, the diaphragm rises towards the chest. Keep in mind that this exercise is performed with external breath retention only.

The best time to practise Uddiyana Bandha is in the morning on an empty stomach and with empty bowels. This exercise prepares your stomach for better digestion throughout the day since it kindles the digestive fires while purifying toxins from the body. It massages and cleanses the abdominal organs while toning the deep interior muscles in this area. Uddiyana Bandha allows for more optimal blood circulation to the abdominal organs by creating a vacuum in your chest. It also balances the Adrenal Glands, removing tension and easing anxiety. Many Yogis have noted that performing Uddiyana Bandha stops the ageing process and makes older people feel young again.

On an energetic level, performing Uddiyana Bandha charges Hara Chakra with Pranic energy while stimulating Manipura Chakra, which strongly influences the distribution of energy throughout the body. The suction pressure created by Uddiyana Bandha reverses the energy flow of Apana and Prana, uniting them with Samana. When combined with Mula Bandha and Jalandhara Bandha as part of Maha Bandha (Great Lock), this exercise can not only trigger a Kundalini awakening but can help raise the Kundalini to the Crown. (More on this in a later chapter.)

During a Kundalini awakening, Uddiyana Bandha can be used to transcend Vishnu Granthi that exists between Manipura and Anahata Chakras. Overcoming Vishnu Granthi allows us to experience unconditional love in Anahata Chakra that the higher Spirit Chakras fuel. Reaching the Heart Chakra is crucial in the Kundalini awakening process since we awaken the Guru within—our Higher Self.

You can practise Uddiyana Bandha in the standing or sitting positions. The standing position makes it easier to focus and control the abdominal muscles if you are a beginner. You then want to progress to a sitting position when comfortable with the mechanics of this exercise.

Figure 124: Standing Uddiyana Bandha

To begin Uddiyana Bandha in a standing position, keep your spine straight and bend your knees slightly, keeping a distance of one-and-a-half feet between them. Lean forward now while putting your hands on your thighs, slightly above the kneecaps. The spine should be horizontal while the arms are straight as the fingers point inwards or downwards, whatever is more comfortable. You should slightly bend the knees as they support the weight of the upper body (Figure 124).

Relax now while taking a few slow and deep breaths, in through the nostrils and out through the mouth. There should be an automatic contraction of the abdominal region occurring while in this position. Bend the head forward but don't press the chin against the chest as that triggers Jalandhara Bandha.

Take a deep breath now, and as you exhale, straighten the knees, which will automatically contract the abdomen upwards and inwards towards the spine, activating Uddiyana Bandha. When you are ready, inhale deeply and release the Abdominal Lock as you relax your belly and chest. Raise the head and torso now to the upright position. Remain in the standing position until your breath comes back to normal. The first round is now complete.

Figure 125: Sitting Uddiyana Bandha (With Jalandhara Bandha)

To begin Uddiyana Bandha in a sitting position, get into Padmasana or Siddhasana, where the knees make contact with the floor. Relax the body while keeping your spine straight. Place the palms of the hands flat on the knees. Take a few deep breaths while maintaining relaxation of the body.

Inhale deeply now through the nostrils. As you exhale, lean forward slightly and press down on your knees with your hands as you straighten your elbows and raise your shoulders, allowing further extension of the spinal cord.

Next, bend the head forward and press the chin against the chest, triggering Jalandhara Bandha. As part of the same motion, contract the abdominal muscles inward and upward towards the spine, activating Uddiyana Bandha. Hold without breath as long as you can comfortably and without strain.

When you are ready, inhale deeply and release the Abdominal Lock as you bend the elbows and lower the shoulders. Raise your head now on the exhale, releasing Jalandhara Bandha, and remain in this position until your breathing returns to normal. This completes the first round.

Note that you need to exhale completely to get into Uddiyana Bandha since the abdominal contraction depends on having an empty stomach. As you hold your breath, be mindful not to inhale at all, as doing so can minimize the effects of Uddiyana Bandha.

Start the practice with three to five rounds initially and gradually increase to ten rounds over a few months. Uddiyana Bandha is ideally performed in combination with different Asanas, Pranayamas, Mudras, and Bandhas. When practised on its own, it should be performed as a precursor to meditation. Note that you can practise Uddiyana Bandha in conjunction with Jalandhara Bandha (Figure 125) but also without it. Work with both methods to get familiar with the effects of each.

People suffering from high blood pressure, hernia, stomach or intestinal ulcer, heart disease, or other abdominal issues should not practise Uddiyana Bandha. Also, women should not practise Maha Mudra during menstruation or pregnancy.

Jalandhara Bandha (Throat Lock)

In Sanskrit, "Jal" means "throat," while Jalan means "web" or "net" and "dharan" means "stream" or "flow." Jalandhara Bandha controls and captures energy in the throat through the nerves and vessels in the neck area. It is quite simple to perform as it requires the practitioner merely to bring the chin down and rest it on the chest, thus restricting the breath to go down. This powerful exercise stretches the spinal cord in the neck area while having powerful, subtle effects on an inner level.

Jalandhara Bandha targets the Throat Chakra, Vishuddhi, which is the lowest of the three Spirit Chakras. Obstructing the flow of Prana to the head by locking the throat supercharges the lower four Elemental Chakras. It stimulates the upper body organs while the other two Bandhas, Uddiyana and Mula, target the lower body.

To begin Jalandhara Bandha, sit in a meditative pose that allows the knees to touch the floor. You can also practise this exercise standing, such as in the Mountain Pose. While sitting, you may place your hands on your knees in either the Jnana or Chin Mudra as you close your eyes and relax the entire body. Inhale deeply and hold your breath. Bend the head forward now and press the chin tightly against the chest. Straighten the arms and lock them into position, which will raise the shoulders upward and forward slightly. Bring your awareness to your throat and hold it there.

Stay in this pose while retaining the breath (internal Khumbaka) as long as possible, feeling the effects of this exercise. When you are ready to release the energy lock, bend the arms, allowing the shoulders to relax, followed by slowly raising the head and exhaling, all in one motion. This completes one round. Take a few breaths now, allowing your respiration to return to normal before starting the next round.

Keep in mind that you can also perform this exercise by holding your breath out after an exhalation (external Khumbaka). The procedure is the same except that you bend the head down and hold the breath after the exhale, instead of the inhale. Be mindful never to inhale or exhale until the chin lock has been released and the head is upright. Start the practice with three to five rounds and gradually increase to ten rounds over a few months.

Note that Jalandhara Bandha is best practised in the morning and can be added to various Pranayama exercises and Bandhas. Remember to keep your spine straight; otherwise, you will disrupt the flow of energies through the central channel of the spine. People suffering from high blood pressure, heart problems, or throat and neck issues, should not practise Jalandhara Bandha.

Jiva Bandha

Jiva (or Jivha) Bandha is the fourth Bandha, and one of the most useful tools in Yoga, especially for Kundalini awakened individuals. It can be used on its own or as an alternative to Khechari Mudra during certain Asanas, Mudras, or Pranayamas. Jiva means "Being with a Life Force or Soul" in Sanskrit, and so this Bandha allows the individual to control their Pranic energy. Prana is indestructible, and its origin is the Sun, as is the origin of the Soul. Prana is best described as an extension of Life Energy of the Soul. Jiva Bandha is essential in closing the Kundalini energy circuit in the Body of Light so that sublimated Prana can circulate and nourish the Seven Chakras.

Jiva Bandha involves placing your tongue on the upper palate of your mouth and connecting its tip to the underside of the front teeth (Figure 126). You should not be applying any pressure but merely hold the tongue in this position.

All fully Kundalini awakened individuals should implement Jiva Bandha as the neutral position of their tongues since doing so allows the Kundalini energy to channel upwards towards the Mind's Eye where Ida and Pingala unite, opening the doorway of the Seventh Eye. As described before, the Bindu is the entry point of the Kundalini circuit, while the Seventh Eye is the exit point. Both need to be open for the Kundalini awakened individual to experience the rapturous realm of Non-Duality, the Spiritual Realm. Jiva Bandha facilitates this experience and can also be used to rebuild the Kundalini circuit in awakened individuals.

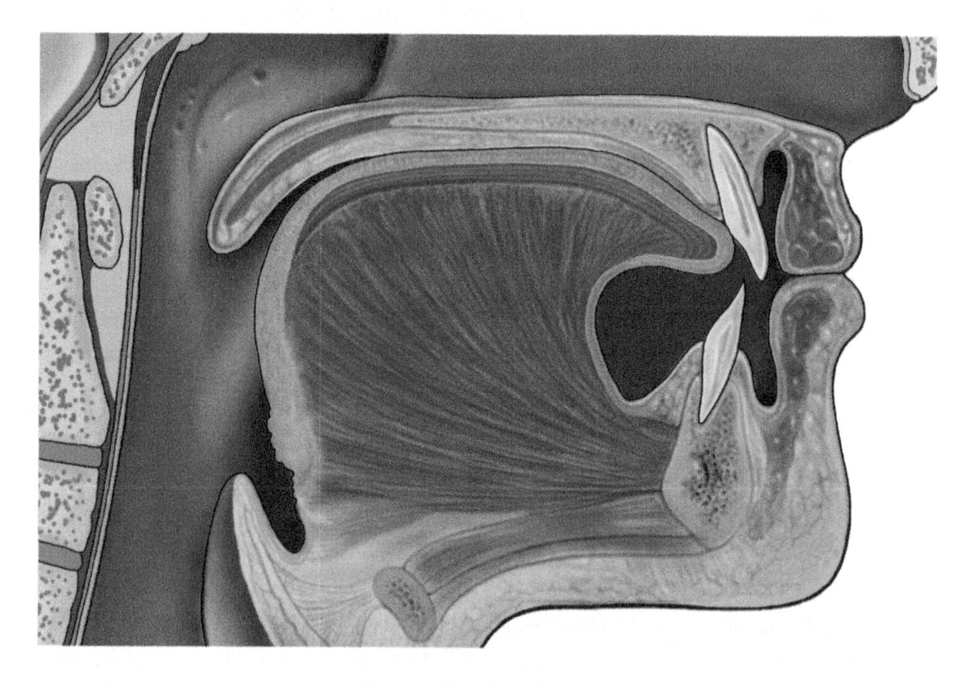

Figure 126: Jiva Bandha

Jiva Bandha can be performed with the mouth closed, as I just described, or the mouth open. Yogis believe that Prana can only be assimilated through the sinuses; therefore, having the mouth open is not vital for breathing and benefiting the consciousness. However, since having the mouth open while practising Jiva Bandha relaxes the jaw, it is also recommended as a practice.

For Kundalini awakened individuals, performing Jiva Bandha with the mouth open as a regular part of the day would be impractical. As such, Jiva Bandha should be practised with the mouth open when the individual is on their own and in a safe space. In both instances, you should be implementing Yogic Breathing with emphasis on Diaphragmatic and Thoracic Breathing. For added benefits, practise Ujjayi Pranayama.

Maha Mudra-The Great Gesture

Maha means "great" in Sanskrit, which is why this Mudra's English name is the "Great Seal," "Great Gesture," or "Great Psychic Attitude." Maha Mudra is called that because it involves various individual Yoga techniques, elevating one's sexual energy potential and facilitating an Alchemical transformation.

Maha Mudra is the first of ten Mudras mentioned in *Hatha Yoga Pradipika*, believed to have the power to destroy old age and death. Apart from its benefits as a Mudra, it is considered a master Asana because it combines all five directional movements of the spine: forward bend, backbend, twist, lateral bend, and axial extension.

Unlike other Yoga Mudras, Maha Mudra is a type of Bandha Mudra (lock gesture) since it involves one or more of the three Bandhas. When all three Bandhas are applied, the top and bottom of the trunk are sealed so that no Prana can release from the body, increasing the potential to awaken the Kundalini energy at the base of the spine.

Maha Mudra is best done in the morning on an empty stomach. There are two notable variations of Maha Mudra. In the first variation, you exert pressure on the perineum with the heel (Mula Bandha) while performing Shambhavi Mudra and practising internal breath retention (Khumbaka). Doing so harnesses the energies of Muladhara, Vishuddhi, and Ajna Chakras. The whole energy system is charged with Prana, which intensifies awareness and facilitates meditation.

A second variation is an advanced form called Maha Bheda Mudra. ("Bheda" in Sanskrit means "piercing.") The second variation contains the same elements as the first with the addition of Uddiyana and Jalandhara Bandhas, which activates the Kundalini to rise through Sushumna, piercing the Seven Chakras along the way.

To begin Maha Mudra, sit on the floor or your Yoga mat with the legs outstretched and your spine straight. Breathe slowly and deeply. Your hands should be placed on the floor by your side. Fold the left leg now and exert pressure on the perineum with the left heel. Your left knee should be touching the floor. The right leg is to remain outstretched throughout the practice. Place both hands now on the right knee as you relax your whole body and implement Khechari Mudra.

Bend forward now and hold the big toe of the right foot with both hands. Your head should be facing forward, and your spine kept as straight as possible (Figure 127). Slowly inhale now while activating Mula Bandha. Tilt and hold the head slightly back. Perform Shambhavi Mudra now while holding your breath for eight to ten seconds.

While holding your breath, cycle your awareness from the eyebrow centre to the throat, down to the perineum, and back again. Mentally repeat "Ajna, Vishuddhi, Muladhara" while maintaining concentration on each Chakra for one to two seconds. As you exhale, release Shambhavi Mudra and Mula Bandha while returning your head to the upright position. Repeat the entire process but with the right leg folded instead. This completes one round, which is equivalent to two complete breaths.

The second variation involves contracting the abdominal region after activating Mula Bandha, which starts Uddiyana Bandha. Next, instead of bending the head back, you move it forward, thus initiating Jalandhara Bandha. Finally, Shambhavi Mudra is performed as you hold your breath for eight to ten seconds. Mentally repeat "Vishuddhi, Manipura, Muladhara" as you concentrate on the throat, abdomen, and perineum, in succession, for one to two seconds each.

When you exhale, release Shambhavi Mudra, followed by unlocking the Bandhas in reverse order. Repeat the same process with the right foot folded, thus completing one full round. In Maha Bheda Mudra, a combination of Asana, Pranayama, Bandha, and Mudra are all involved for optimal Spiritual results.

Start by practising three rounds with the first variation for a few weeks until you get some experience with this exercise. Then you can practise the second, more advanced variation with the Three Bandhas applied. After a few months, increase the number of rounds to five. Maha Bheda Mudra supplements Maha Mudra to supercharge the entire mind-body system.

You should only practise Maha Mudra after an Asana and Pranayama session and before a meditation session. Always complete the Maha Mudra process by practising it on both the left and right sides.

Precautions for Shambhavi Mudra are applied during this exercise. Individuals suffering from high blood pressure, heart problems, or glaucoma should not perform Maha Mudra. Because it generates a lot of heat in the body, it is best to avoid this practice during hot summer days. Also, women should not practise Maha Mudra during menstruation or pregnancy. For Maha Bheda Mudra, precautions for Uddiyana and Jalandhara Bandhas are included as well.

Figure 127: Maha Mudra

ADHARA (PERINEAL MUDRAS)

Vajroli Mudra (Male) and Sahajoli Mudra (Female)

Vajroli Mudra is an advanced Hatha Yoga practice that aims to preserve the semen in males, allowing the sexual energy to sublimate and be used for Spiritual purposes. Sahajoli Mudra is the female counterpart of the same practice that yields similar benefits.

Vajroli is derived from the Sanskrit root word "vajra," which is an indestructible weapon of the Hindu God Indra with the properties of lightning, namely the thunderbolt. Thus, when the practitioner has achieved control over their sexual force in the genital area, it makes it move upwards into the Chakras with the power of lightning. For this reason, Vajroli Mudra is often called the "Thunderbolt Gesture."

Vajra is also a Nadi that begins at the genitals, which engages the sexual energy. Activation of the Vajra Nadi with this Mudra allows the sexual energy to rise upwards into the brain, not only increasing one's vigour but facilitating meditative states. Conversely, Sahajoli comes from the root word "sahaj," which means "spontaneous," relating to the arousal and control of the sexual force in females.

Vajroli Mudra involves contracting the muscles around the base of the penis, strengthening them over time. This practice enables control over the urogenital system, including holding the orgasm through semen retention. As a result, Vajroli Mudra is a powerful exercise that leads to sexual potency even in old age. In addition, its daily practice prevents premature ejaculation, a common issue in men.

Sahajoli is a practice that involves the contraction of the urinary passage to redirect the sexual energy in females and also allow it to move upwards into the Chakras and the brain. This practice provides control over the menstrual flow and helps control ovulation.

On a subtle level, both Vajroli and Sahajoli Mudras stimulate Swadhisthana Chakra, which is involved in the Kundalini awakening process. Both exercises tone the urogenital region while taking care of urinary disorders. In addition, both practices are therapeutic for sexual disfunction.

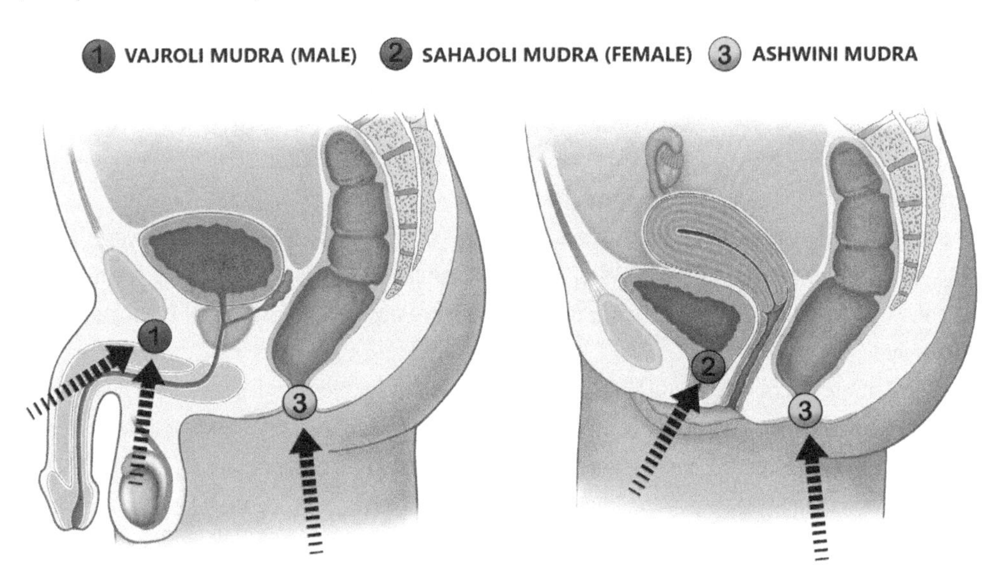

Figure 128: Vajroli, Sahajoli, and Ashwini Mudras Contraction Points

To begin Vajroli or Sahajoli Mudras, sit in any comfortable meditation Asana and keep your head and spine straight. Next, place the hands on the knees in either Jnana or Chin Mudras, close the eyes, and relax the entire body. Your breathing should be normal. Place your awareness on the urethra now (Figure 128). Males should put their attention on the root of their penis, not the tip.

Inhale deeply and hold your breath while drawing the urethra upwards. This action is similar to intensely needing to urinate but holding it back. As you perform this contraction, the testes in men and the labia in women should move up slightly towards the navel. Make sure that your contraction is limited to the urethra alone. Hold the contraction for as long as it is comfortable, and then release it as you exhale the breath. This completes one round. Perform five to ten rounds of Vajroli or Sahajoli Mudras for the first few weeks. As your holding capacity improves, gradually increase to twenty rounds within a few months.

For a more advanced version of these two exercises, enter the Navasana, Boat Pose instead of a meditation Asana. Keep in mind that you will need a strong core to perform this variation. To begin, start in Shavasana as you breathe normally and relax. Then, bring your legs to a specific angle to the ground and keep them straight. Now, raise your chest to form a V-shape with your body, resting all of your weight on your buttocks. You should feel immense pressure on the abdominal muscles during the Boat Pose. Lift your hands straight in front of you now to balance yourself.

From Navasana, follow the same instructions of contracting the urethra and holding the breath after the inhale, and then releasing the contraction as you exhale. If you have difficulties with internal breath retention, you may breathe normally instead during this exercise variation. When you are finished with the exercise, go back into Shavasana for a few minutes to relax before ending the practice. Note that people suffering from medical conditions related to the urinary tract should consult a physician before commencing Vajroli or Sahajoli Mudras.

Ashwini Mudra (Horse Gesture)

Ashwini Mudra is a Tantric practice used to generate and carry Pranic energy upwards through the Sushumna channel. This practice involves rhythmically contracting the anal sphincter, which generates Pranic energy in the Pelvic floor before pumping it upwards. It is an easy practice that stimulates the Kundalini energy, which lies between the perineum and coccyx at Muladhara Chakra.

Ashwini's root word "Ashwa" is the Sanskrit transliteration for "horse." This exercise is referred to as the Horse Gesture because it mimics the peculiar way in which horses contract their anal muscles after they defecate, thereby pulling energy upwards instead of allowing it to flow down.

By contracting the anal muscles with Ashwini Mudra, the energy that usually flows downwards and out of the body (Apana Vayu) gets reversed and flows up towards the internal organs, strengthening them in the process. When Apana Vayu fills the lower organs to full capacity, pressure occurs at the bottom of the spine, making Pranic energy flow through Sushumna Nadi.

Although Ashwini Mudra is similar to Mula Bandha, the muscles involved in the process are different. In Ashwini Mudra, we engage a larger area of the pelvic muscles, which makes it a suitable preparatory exercise for Mula Bandha. While Ashwini Mudra is focused on contracting and releasing the anal muscles, redirecting the natural flow of energy and facilitating its flow upwards, Mula Bandha's focus is on holding the muscles to lock in energy in the pelvic area.

To begin the Ashwini Mudra exercise, sit in any comfortable meditation Asana. Close your eyes and relax the whole body while becoming aware of your natural breathing. Place your awareness on your anus now (Figure 128) and contract your anal sphincter muscles for a few seconds, then relax them. Breathe normally as you do so.

For maximum contraction, apply a little more pressure inside the anus to lift the sphincter muscles upwards. You should feel like you are holding in your bowel movement, then releasing. Perform the contraction ten to twenty times smoothly and rhythmically. Upon completion of the exercise, release the seated posture and then come out of the pose slowly.

For a more advanced variation of Ashwini Mudra, you can practise internal breath retention (Khumbaka) during the contraction phase. Inhale slowly and deeply, then contract the anal sphincter muscles for five seconds while holding your breath. On the exhale, release the contraction. Perform five to ten rounds of this variation of Ashwini Mudra for the first few weeks, up to twenty rounds within a few months.

Note that practitioners can also incorporate Pranayama, Bandhas, and other Mudras with Ashwini Mudra. For example, you can include Jalandhara Bandha and Khechari Mudra along with Diaphragmatic and Thoracic Breathing for maximum effects. Doing so will have a greater impact on the Kundalini at the base of the spine and may facilitate a rising.

Regular use of Ashwini Mudra purifies the energy channels in the body (Nadis), resulting in a more balanced mental and emotional state. On a physical level, its daily use overcomes many ailments related to the lower abdomen and colon. In addition, it gives the practitioner conscious control over their unconscious body activity, resulting in greater control over the autonomic nervous system. For men, the performance of Ashwini Mudra aids in erectile disfunction while regulating the Prostate Gland and clearing any issues related to it.

Pregnant women and people with high blood pressure or heart disease should not perform Ashwini Mudra with internal breath retention. As a final note, be mindful not to contract the anal muscles when your bowels are full of stool or gas.

THE FIVE PRANA VAYUS

Prana is Light energy; a Life Force that interpenetrates every atom of our bodies and the Solar System we are in. Pranic energy originates from the Sun and is directly responsible for our vitality and well-being. As mentioned, we receive Prana from the food we eat, the water we drink, and the air we breathe—it is the Life energy that sustains our mind, body, and Soul.

The very act of breathing is an act of bringing Prana into the body. Each breath replenishes the bloodstream with oxygen and cultivates the fires of cellular metabolism while ridding the body of wastes. Supplying our bodies with food and oxygen creates the foundation for every activity we do.

In the human body, Pranic energy directly affects the Astral Plane, relating particularly to Pranamaya Kosha or the Higher Astral Body of the Water Element. Prana divides into five sub-energies called the Five Vayus. In Sanskrit, Vayu translates to "wind" or "air," concerning the act of breathing. Vayu is also the Air Element Tattva and one of the classical Elements in Hinduism. Breath control and breathing exercises are essential in all Yogic and meditation practices—manipulating Prana in the body can have many effects, one of which is to awaken the Kundalini energy at the base of the spine.

The Five Prana Vayus directly affect the Water Element in the body through the Air Element since water requires air to animate it and give it life. This correspondence is also found in nature since the H2O (water) molecule contains oxygen (air) within itself. In the same way, the act of breathing regulates one's consciousness from one moment to the next.

The Five Vayus are Prana, Apana, Samana, Udana, and Vyana (Figure 129). Each Prana Vayu is regulated by one or multiple Chakras, and each Vayu is responsible for different yet crucial functions in the body. When we understand each Prana Vayu's role, we can comprehend how Prana serves our bodies. The Five Vayus are the different manifestations and processes of Prana in the same way as the various limbs comprise the human body.

To be clear, Prana works through the physical body as well as the Light Body. Food and oxygen are brought in through the physical body, which is then broken down to power the Chakras and nourish the Light Body and its corresponding Subtle Bodies (related to the inner Cosmic Planes). The Light Body requires these different mechanisms that process and put Pranic energy to use. The Five Vayus can be compared to large oceans, where each ocean contains thousands of smaller currents within them.

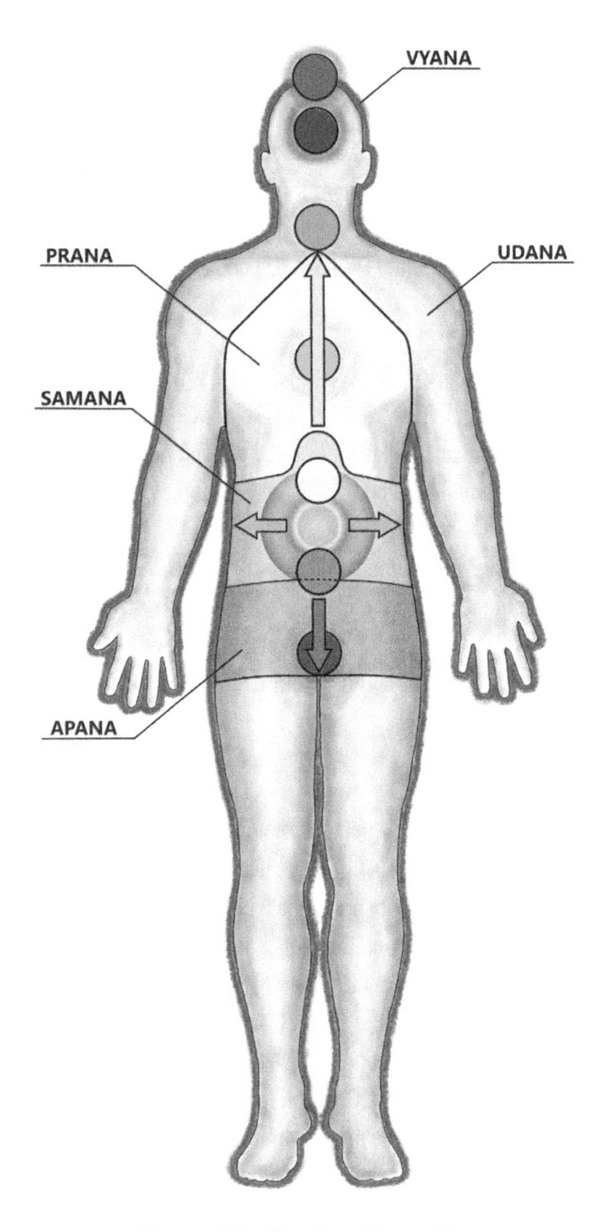

Figure 129: The Five Prana Vayus

Prana Vayu

Operating from the head/chest area as upward-flowing energy, Prana Vayu translates as "forward-moving air." It is responsible for everything that enters our bodies, such as oxygen, food, and sensory information. As such, Prana Vayu refers to how we take in energy, most important of which is the inhale since we cannot live without oxygen for more than several minutes.

Prana Vayu is associated with Anahata Chakra and the Air Element. It regulates our thoughts. It is the most important of the Five Vayus, so the general term "Prana" is used to encompass all of the Five Vayus. Prana Vayu is the fundamental energy in the body that directs the four other Vayus.

Prana Vayu regulates respiration, immunity, vitality, and the heart. It relates to intelligence and the power of sensory and motor functions. The organs it governs are the heart and lungs. Although some schools of thought say that the primary abode of Prana is in the chest/heart area, others say it extends into the head as well. Every time we focus our attention on something, we manipulate Prana in the body and involve Ajna Chakra in the process.

Apana Vayu

Operating from the base of the torso, Apana Vayu translates as the "air that moves away." It is associated with Muladhara Chakra and the Earth Element. Earth is the final Element in the manifestation process, and Apana is the Prana Vayu that represents the elimination of all that our body doesn't need anymore, such as negative energy and bodily waste, like faeces and urine, semen, and menstrual fluid. Apana then represents the downward, and outward-flowing energy and the exhale of the breath.

As the head contains openings suitable for the inward flow of Prana, the base of the torso has openings required for the work of Apana. Apana governs the kidneys, bladder, bowels, and excretory and reproductive systems. Apana also involves Swadhisthana Chakra and the Water Element concerning the elimination of sexual liquids from the body (semen in men and vaginal fluids in women) and the release of negative energy stored in the subconscious mind as harmful emotions.

Samana Vayu

Operating from the navel region, between Prana and Apana Vayus, Samana Vayu translates as "the balancing air." As Prana Vayu is the inhalation and Apana is the exhalation, Samana is the time in between the inhalation and exhalation. Samana Vayu deals with digestion, absorption, assimilation and manifestation. It is associated with Hara, the Navel Chakra, which is fueled by Manipura and Swadhisthana Chakras (the Fire and Water Elements). Samana has a primary connection with the Fire Element, though, since it operates in conjunction with Agni (the digestive fire) and is centred in the stomach and small intestine.

Samana allows mental discrimination between useful and not useful thoughts. It governs the liver, stomach, duodenum, spleen, and small and large intestines. Samana (along with Agni) supplies the internal heat to transform the food we eat into Pranic energy. This energy is then distributed through the other Prana Vayus.

As Prana and Apana are the upward and downward-flowing energies, Samana is the horizontal-flowing energy. All three, though, are said to originate from Hara Chakra, which is essentially the storehouse of Prana in the body.

Udana Vayu

Operating from the throat, head, and arms and legs, Udana Vayu is an upwards-flowing energy that translates as "that which carries upwards." It is associated with Vishuddhi and Ajna Chakras and the Spirit Element. While Udana rises on inhalation, it circulates on the exhalation, nourishing the neck, head, nervous and endocrine systems.

A healthy flow of Udana implies that a person is acting from a higher source. This energy leads us to revitalize and transform our willpower and become realized through the Spirit Element. Udana regulates growth, intuition, memory, and speech. It governs all sensory and action organs, including the hands and feet.

In *The Upanishads*, Prana Vayu is called the "in-breath," Apana the "out-breath," Samana the "middle breath," and Udana the "up breath." Udana is essentially an extension of Samana. Udana drives inhalation, which means that it operates in conjunction with Prana Vayus. Both are upwards-flowing energies, and both are of similar qualities since the Air Element (Prana) is Spirit (Udana) on a lower, more manifest level. At the time of one's death, Udana is the energy that draws the individual consciousness out of the physical body.

Vyana Vayu

Operating throughout the whole body as the coordinating energy of all the Prana Vayus, Vyana Vayu translates as "outward moving air." Vyana is the force that distributes Prana and causes it to flow. It governs the circulatory system and the movement of joints and muscles. Unlike Samana, which draws energy to the navel, Vyana moves energy outward to the body's boundary, expanding on the exhalation.

Most Yogic schools of thought say that Vyana Vayu is associated with Sahasrara Chakra and the Spirit Element because it encompasses and regulates all the Prana Vayus in the same way as Sahasrara is the source of Light to all the Chakras below. However, there are other schools of thought that say that Vyana Vayu corresponds with Swadhisthana Chakra and the Water Element because it governs the circulation in the body. Nevertheless, regardless of its origin and centre, Vyana Vayu encompasses all the Prana Vayus and provides a sense of cohesion, integration and expansiveness for the individual consciousness.

***

One of the most straightforward yet efficient ways to balance the Five Prana Vayus is to practice Hand Mudras particular to each Vayu (Figure 130). In addition to increasing or decreasing the Elements that correspond with each Vayu, each Hand Mudra has added benefits for the mind-body complex. Refer to "Steps for Performing Hand Mudras" on page 312 for instructions on their use.

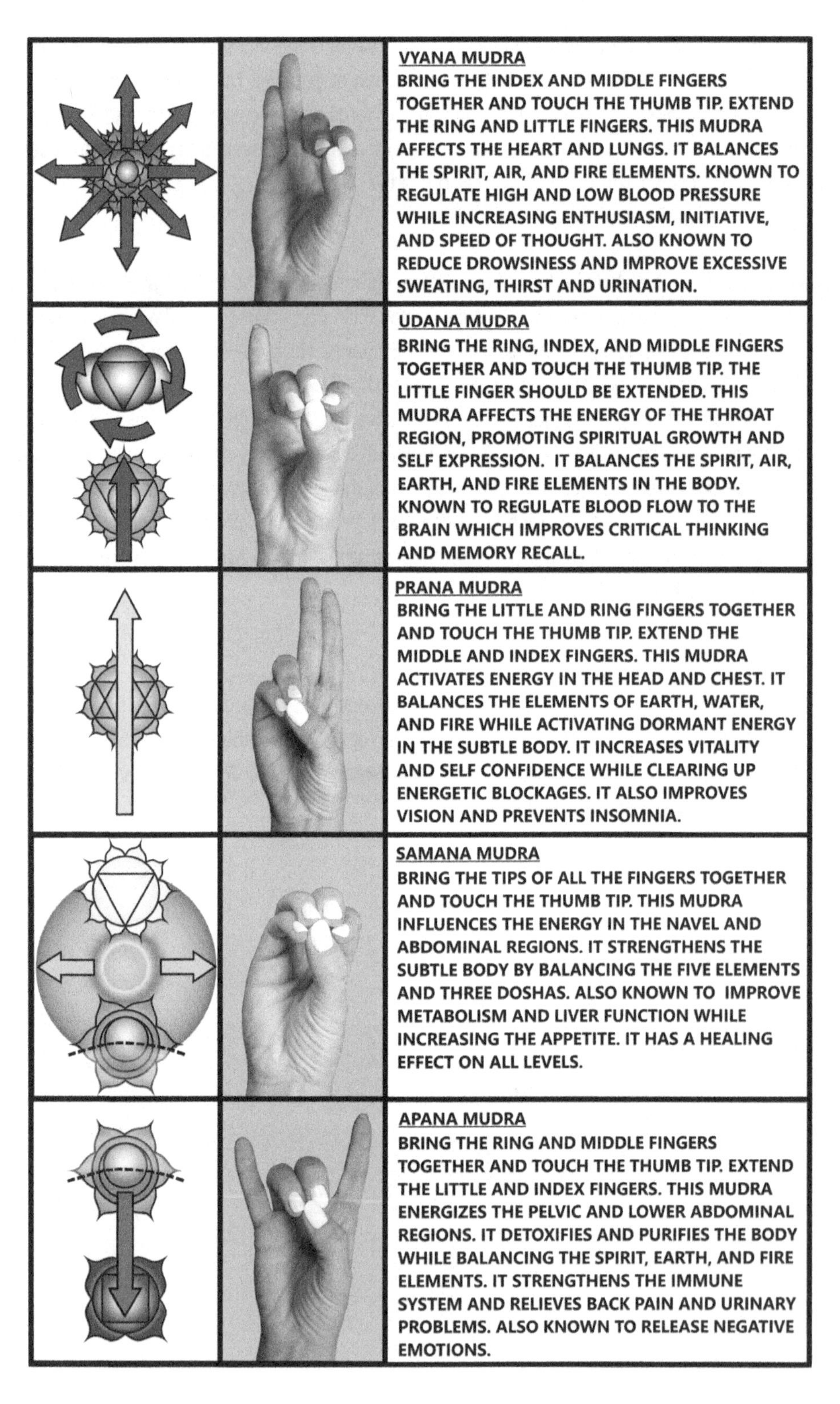

VYANA MUDRA
BRING THE INDEX AND MIDDLE FINGERS TOGETHER AND TOUCH THE THUMB TIP. EXTEND THE RING AND LITTLE FINGERS. THIS MUDRA AFFECTS THE HEART AND LUNGS. IT BALANCES THE SPIRIT, AIR, AND FIRE ELEMENTS. KNOWN TO REGULATE HIGH AND LOW BLOOD PRESSURE WHILE INCREASING ENTHUSIASM, INITIATIVE, AND SPEED OF THOUGHT. ALSO KNOWN TO REDUCE DROWSINESS AND IMPROVE EXCESSIVE SWEATING, THIRST AND URINATION.

UDANA MUDRA
BRING THE RING, INDEX, AND MIDDLE FINGERS TOGETHER AND TOUCH THE THUMB TIP. THE LITTLE FINGER SHOULD BE EXTENDED. THIS MUDRA AFFECTS THE ENERGY OF THE THROAT REGION, PROMOTING SPIRITUAL GROWTH AND SELF EXPRESSION. IT BALANCES THE SPIRIT, AIR, EARTH, AND FIRE ELEMENTS IN THE BODY. KNOWN TO REGULATE BLOOD FLOW TO THE BRAIN WHICH IMPROVES CRITICAL THINKING AND MEMORY RECALL.

PRANA MUDRA
BRING THE LITTLE AND RING FINGERS TOGETHER AND TOUCH THE THUMB TIP. EXTEND THE MIDDLE AND INDEX FINGERS. THIS MUDRA ACTIVATES ENERGY IN THE HEAD AND CHEST. IT BALANCES THE ELEMENTS OF EARTH, WATER, AND FIRE WHILE ACTIVATING DORMANT ENERGY IN THE SUBTLE BODY. IT INCREASES VITALITY AND SELF CONFIDENCE WHILE CLEARING UP ENERGETIC BLOCKAGES. IT ALSO IMPROVES VISION AND PREVENTS INSOMNIA.

SAMANA MUDRA
BRING THE TIPS OF ALL THE FINGERS TOGETHER AND TOUCH THE THUMB TIP. THIS MUDRA INFLUENCES THE ENERGY IN THE NAVEL AND ABDOMINAL REGIONS. IT STRENGTHENS THE SUBTLE BODY BY BALANCING THE FIVE ELEMENTS AND THREE DOSHAS. ALSO KNOWN TO IMPROVE METABOLISM AND LIVER FUNCTION WHILE INCREASING THE APPETITE. IT HAS A HEALING EFFECT ON ALL LEVELS.

APANA MUDRA
BRING THE RING AND MIDDLE FINGERS TOGETHER AND TOUCH THE THUMB TIP. EXTEND THE LITTLE AND INDEX FINGERS. THIS MUDRA ENERGIZES THE PELVIC AND LOWER ABDOMINAL REGIONS. IT DETOXIFIES AND PURIFIES THE BODY WHILE BALANCING THE SPIRIT, EARTH, AND FIRE ELEMENTS. IT STRENGTHENS THE IMMUNE SYSTEM AND RELIEVES BACK PAIN AND URINARY PROBLEMS. ALSO KNOWN TO RELEASE NEGATIVE EMOTIONS.

Figure 130: Hand Mudras for the Five Prana Vayus

PRANA AND APANA

The two energies involved in the Kundalini awakening mechanism are Prana and Apana. These two energies move through our bodies through the Nadis. As mentioned, Prana is represented by the inhale, while Apana is represented by the exhale. Prana and Apana never meet as each moves along its path through the various energy channels.

By practising specific Kundalini Yoga techniques, we create the potential for Prana and Apana to meet. The point at which this magical meeting of Prana and Apana occurs is at Hara (Navel) Chakra, in the navel region. Hara is a significant meeting point of many the energy channels in the body since it is our energetic foundation, our core.

As far as raising the Kundalini is concerned, Prana is the "Vital Air" above the Hara, while Apana is the "Vital Air" below it. The Seventy-Two Thousand Nadis emanate from the Major Chakras and end in the hands and the feet. Most of these Nadis are centred around the Heart Chakra and Hara Chakra regions. Prana is carried to all parts of the body via the Nadis. Ida, Pingala, and Sushumna are the most important of these energetic channels since they transmit the most Prana.

The Ida channel begins at the base of the spine and ends in the left nostril. Conversely, Pingala starts at the bottom of the spine and ends in the right nostril. As mentioned, though, during the Kundalini awakening process, Ida and Pingala terminate in the Pineal and Pituitary Glands. Ida represents the Prana Vayu, while Apana represents the Pingala. The ascension of the Kundalini corresponds with Udana. Samana represents Sushumna. Samana's directional force has to transform for the Kundalini at the base of the spine to awaken. Its development or transformation occurs when Prana and Apana meet at Hara Chakra.

Through inhalation and retention, Prana can be directed down to the Hara Chakra, while through exhalation and retention, Apana is drawn upwards from the Root Chakra to the Hara. As these two energies meet at Hara, Samana begins to change its movement. It no longer is moving away from Hara horizontally but inwards instead, which creates a churning motion exemplified in Figure 131.

During the transformation of Samana, heat begins to generate in the Navel, called Tapas. This heat brings on an ecstatic feeling, likened to euphoric sexual or sensual excitement; the "butterflies in the stomach" one gets when they fall in love, which in this case are more like eagles. Another comparable example is the feeling you get when you recognize the Spirit within you and the immense bliss that accompanies it. For this reason, the type of heat generated in Samana is described as white heat, not hot heat, meaning it is a type of Spiritual rapture.

This intense heat creates pressure which acts on the Sushumna Nadi, thereby activating it. The activation process energizes the Sushumna channel in the spine, making it light up like a light bulb once it receives the necessary electric power. These integrated energies then depart the Navel Chakra and descend to the Root Chakra, thereby stimulating the Kundalini into activity at the base of the spine. As such, the Kundalini begins its journey upwards through the hollow tube of the spinal cord, piercing each of the Chakras as it rises until it reaches the Crown.

Simultaneously, the Ida and Pingala channels rise on opposite sides of Sushumna. They cross each other at each of the Chakric points until they fuse in the Thalamus, which is where Sushumna ends as well. The Pineal and Pituitary Glands also get activated during this process. The next destination for all three channels is to rise as one stream of energy to the top of the head at the Crown Chakra, blowing open the Thousand-Petalled Lotus.

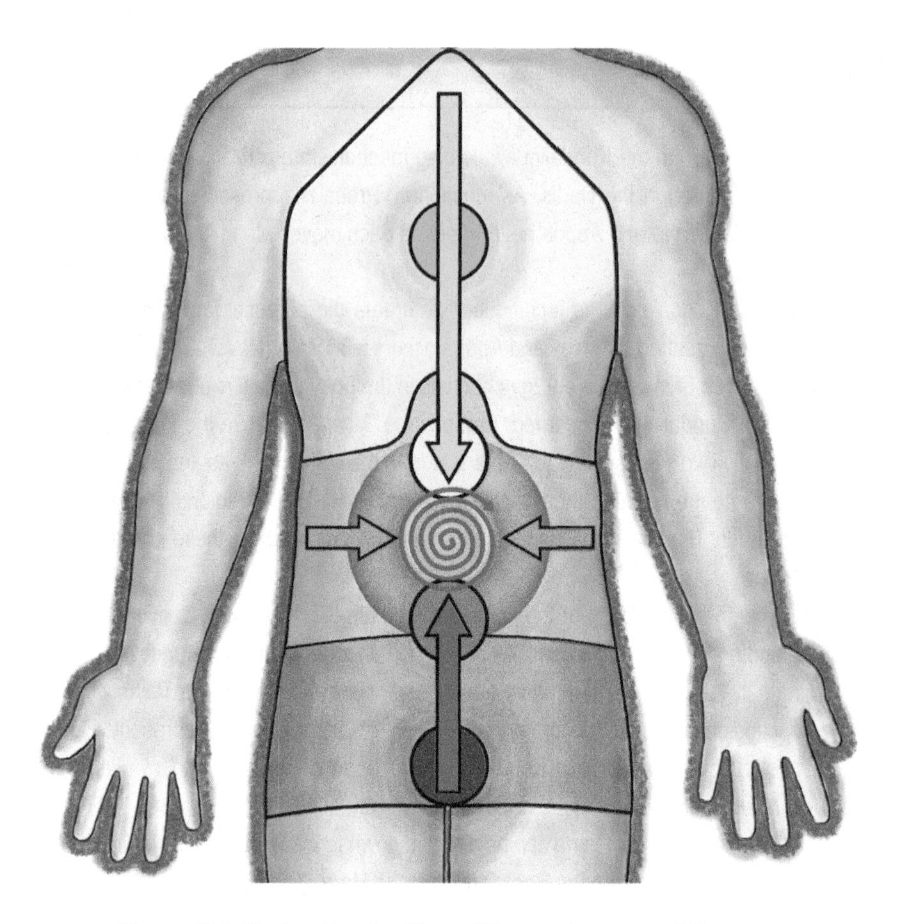

Figure 131: Redirecting the Flow of Prana, Apana, and Samana

AWAKENING THE KUNDALINI

It is necessary to practice proper breath control and mental direction to stir the Kundalini into activity and make it rise and activate the higher centres of consciousness. The application of willpower is key to this process, but so is knowledge since one needs a proven technique that works.

Before attempting to awaken the Kundalini, it is crucial to cleanse the energetic channels and remove any negative energy and impurities in the nerves. Otherwise, if the channels are blocked, Prana will be unable to move through them, and the Kundalini will remain dormant. The techniques employed in Yoga and Tantra work to accomplish this task and awaken the Kundalini.

Yogic and Tantric teachings say that the combination of physical exercises (Kriya/Asana), breathing techniques (Pranayama), energetic locks (Bandha) and Mantra chanting can be used to cause Prana and Apana to meet at Hara Chakra and stir the Kundalini into activity. To raise the Kundalini energy through Sushumna, and Prana (Pingala) and Apana (Ida) along the spine, one can apply hydraulic locks (Bandhas), which require the conscious application of pressure in different parts of the body.

Applying pressure in Muladhara Chakra (Mula Bandha) sends the Kundalini and Prana and Apana energies up to Swadhisthana Chakra. Next, one needs to apply a Bandha in the diaphragm (Uddiyana Bandha), which will send the three energies upwards to the Throat Chakra. From there, the Neck Lock (Jalandhara Bandha) takes the energies into the brain. Applying all three locks simultaneously is called Maha Bandha (Figure 132).

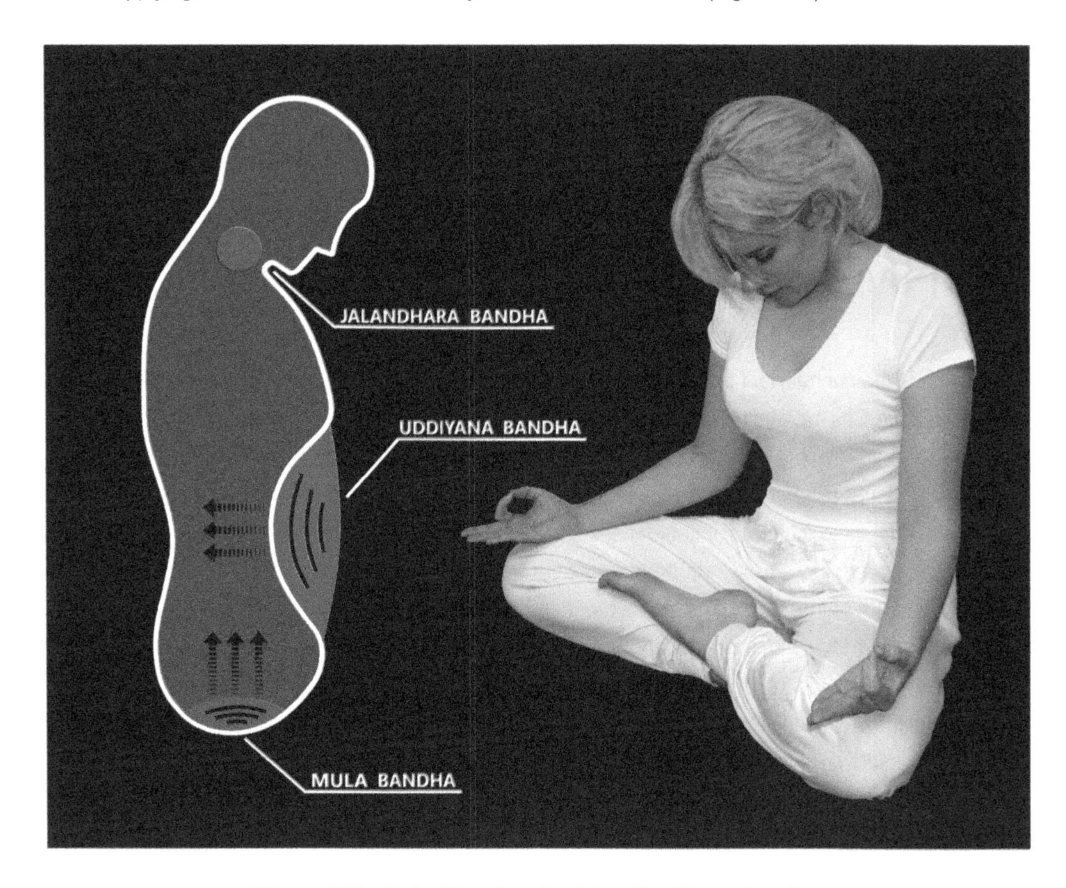

Figure 132: Maha Bandha: Applying the Three Bandhas

The Pineal Gland is connected to the Ida Nadi, while the Pituitary Gland is connected to Pingala. As the Kundalini is rising, the Pineal Gland begins to transmit a beam of radiation and project it towards the Pituitary Gland. The Pituitary thus becomes aroused and projects pulses or flashes of Light towards the Pineal Gland. Once the Kundalini enters the brain through Sushumna, Ida and Pingala cross each other one final time at the Thalamus, where they fuse as opposites. This process awakens Ajna Chakra, activating it entirely, which results in a mystic marriage between the Pineal and Pituitary Glands.

As Ida, Pingala and Sushumna unify as one stream of energy in the Thalamus centre, the gate to Sahasrara becomes open. The Kundalini can then rise to the top of the head and complete its journey. The Soul, which had its seat at the Pineal Gland, leaves the physical body, and a permanent expansion of consciousness occurs.

SUSHUMNA AND BRAHMARANDHRA

Sushumna is the central Nadi that passes through the hollow tube in the spinal column. Its flow begins at the base, at Muladhara Chakra, ending in Sahasrara Chakra at the Crown. Once it enters the head, Sushumna Nadi splits into two streams (at the Thalamus). One stream moves towards the front of the head, past Ajna Chakra as it activates it. It continues moving alongside the front of the head, just within the skull, before reaching Brahmarandhra, the seat of supreme consciousness, located at the top-centre of the head.

The second stream moves towards the back of the head, alongside but just inside the skull, before reaching Brahmarandhra. Both of these energy streams meet at Brahmarandhra, thereby piercing it, resulting in the Cosmic Egg opening, which is the summit directly above it.

In Sanskrit, Brahmarandhra means the "hole or aperture of Brahman." According to Yogic texts, Brahmarandhra is the opening of the Sushumna Nadi at the head's crown. Brahman refers to the Cosmic Spirit in Sanskrit. It connotes the highest Universal Principle, the ultimate reality of the Universe.

When one raises the Kundalini energy to Brahmarandhra, they experience a Spiritual awakening of the highest degree. Brahmarandhra and the Cosmic Egg both relate to the Cosmic energy, and the act of breaking through this centre is the awakening of the Spiritual, Divine Self.

Although both serve to liberate the Soul from the body according to sacred texts, it is unclear whether Brahmarandhra and the Cosmic Egg are one and the same. However, from my extensive research into this topic, coupled with my Kundalini awakening experience, I have concluded that piercing Brahmarandhra with enough force begins the process of breaking the Cosmic Egg. In other words, it is a one-two step process.

Further clues are given to us by the Shiva Linga which contains an egg-shaped cylinder that is said to represent the Brahmanda, whose meaning in Sanskrit is "the Cosmic Egg." Brahma refers to the Cosmos, while "anda" means "egg." Brahmanda is a Universal symbol of the source of the entire Cosmos. The Cosmic Egg is one of the most prominent icons in world mythology that we can find in many Ancient traditions. In almost all cases, a Divine Being resides in the Cosmic Egg who creates himself from nothing and then goes on to create the material Universe.

On its upwards rise, when the Kundalini reaches the top of the head and pierces Brahmarandhra, the Cosmic Egg breaks, and the "yolk" which is sublimated Pranic energy, pours over the body, resulting in the full activation of the Body of Light and the Seventy-Two Thousand Nadis. This experience is akin to inheriting Spiritual "wings," which enable you to travel in the inner Cosmic Planes via the optimised Merkaba. Therefore, breaking the Cosmic Egg results in one becoming an Angelic Being themselves.

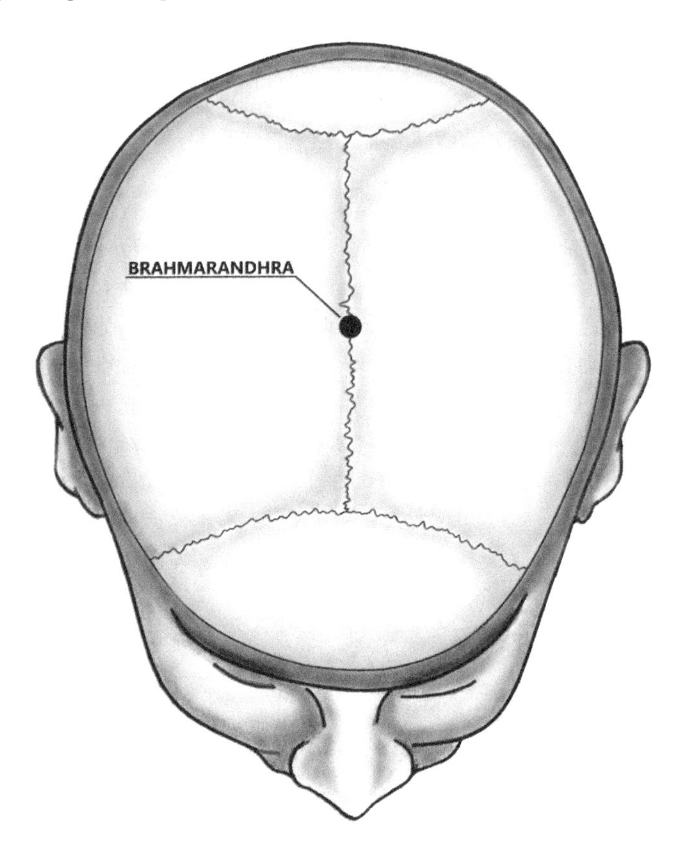

Figure 133: The Brahmarandhra

Brahmarandhra's location is between the two parietal and occipital bones, more specifically in the area of the anterior fontanelle (Figure 133). In a baby, this part of the head is very soft. As the child grows up, the Brahmarandhra closes up with the growth of the bones of the skull. All grown humans are tasked with raising the Kundalini energy into the head and piercing Brahmarandhra if we desire to attain liberation from death. By penetrating Brahmarandhra through a Kundalini activation, we become one with the Spirit as Eternal Beings of Light.

According to *The Upanishads*, once Sushumna pierces the head and goes through the Brahmarandhra, the Yogi attains immortality. The Microcosm and Macrocosm become One, and the Yogi attains illumination. Before this occurs, though, the Body of Light is fully activated, as the Seventy-Two Thousand Nadis are infused with Pranic energy. This process is very intense since the Body of Light experiences getting charged up by what feels like an external energy source. I describe the process as feeling like you are getting electrocuted by a high voltage power line, minus the physical pain, of course.

In my personal experience, once I opened my physical eyes during the Kundalini activation process, I saw my hands and other parts of my body as pure golden Light as if I had undergone a biological transformation.

Furthermore, the room I was in appeared Holographic since the objects around me became semi-transparent and seemingly suspended in mid-air. And this was not a momentary vision but one that I held for over five seconds with my cognitive functions fully operational before the infused energy that now took over my body threw me back onto the bed.

Once Shakti unites with Shiva, the supreme consciousness, the Veil of Maya is pierced, and you can perceive the infinite, living Mind of God. Verily it is true, the nature of our reality is the by-product of the union of energy and consciousness.

While the energy continued rising upwards, even past Brahmarandhra and the Cosmic Egg, my consciousness began entirely leaving my physical body. It felt like I was being sucked out of my body and ceasing to exist. At the apex of this experience, I was at the onset of being united with the White Light. Considering that Brahmarandhra is the centre of energy and consciousness, some people believe that if you go beyond it, you may not be able to return to the physical body. This idea is purely theoretical, but a possibility exists regardless. In other words, had I allowed myself to unite with the White Light during my very intense Kundalini rising experience, I may not have been able to come back to the physical body. The experience was just too intense on every level, and there were many unknown variables, especially since I had no prior knowledge of the Kundalini at that point in my life.

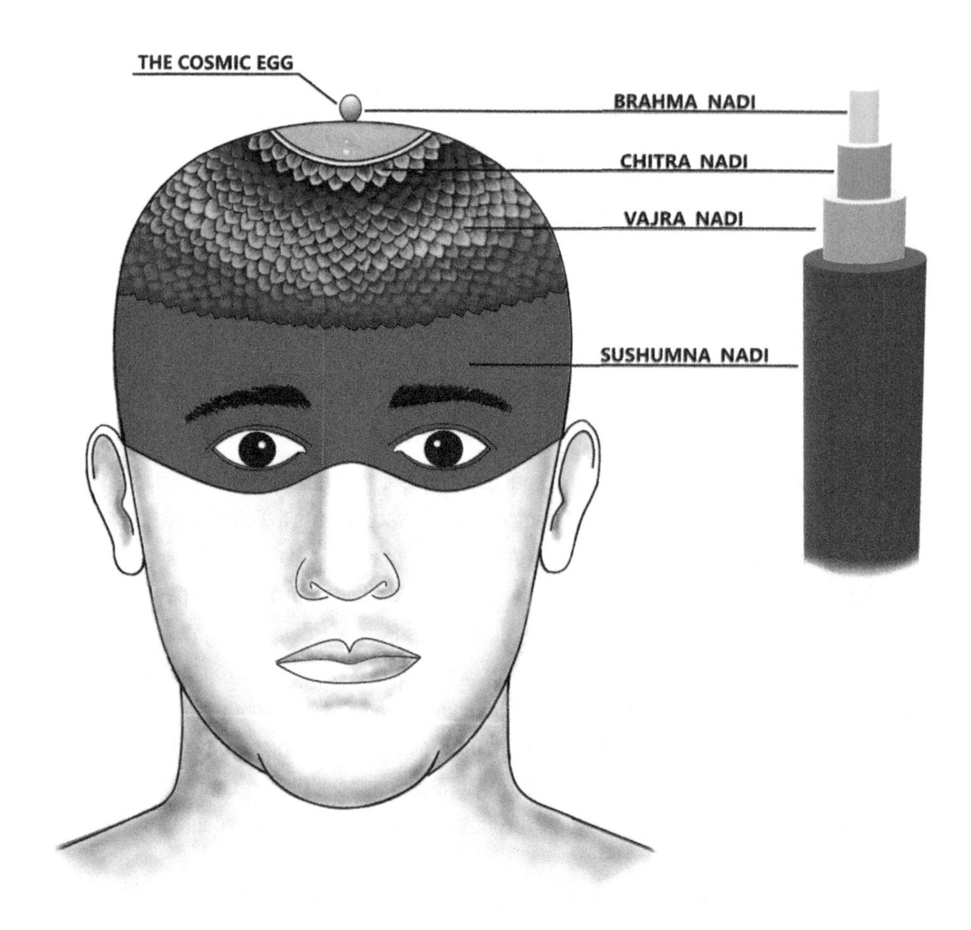

Figure 134: Sushumna Nadi Layers and the Cosmic Egg

Sushumna Nadi has three layers or lesser Nadis that comprise it. Once the Cosmic Egg is broken, Kundalini energy from Sushumna Nadi continues to rise upwards still until the Thousand-Petals of Sahasrara Chakra are opened fully. You have to allow yourself to let go and not try to control the energy as it continues rising upwards. Each of the three Sushumna Nadis or layers have to do its part to make this happen. Once it is complete, the head opens up like a flower. Comprising the symbolic flower are three layers, as portrayed in Figure 134. Those three layers represent the fully awakened Sahasrara Chakra. As such, the human becomes an antenna to the vibrations from the outside.

Sushumna Nadi has an outer layer traditionally considered a brilliant red colour, symbolic of the Kundalini Fire that flows through it. Since the Sushumna Nadi splits into two streams within the head, front and back, it governs the entire middle part of the head.

Sushumna's first layer is called Vajrini or Vajra Nadi. This Nadi starts at the Ajna Chakra and ends in the gonads (testes in men and ovaries in women). Its colour is gold, as it exhibits the nature of Rajas or activity. This layer is the Sun (Surya) Nadi which contains masculine energy that works outside the Sushumna as the Pingala Nadi and within it as the Vajrini. It is believed that Vajrini can be poisonous or toxic.

The second layer is called Chitrini or Chitra Nadi. Silver-white in colour, this Nadi reflects the nature of the Moon (Chandra). It connects us to dreams and visions and is of prime importance to awakened painters or poets. Chitrini exhibits the character of Sattva, which relates to transcendence. It starts in the Bindu Chakra and ends in the Svayambhu lingam in Muladhara. The Chitra Nadi connects to the Chakric stems within the spinal cord. This feminine Nadi works outside of Sushumna as the Ida Nadi and within it as the Chitrini. Chitrini is said to end in Brahmadvara, the door or entrance into Brahma, the Creator. Through the Chitra Nadi, the Kundalini travels to its final resting place within the Seventh Eye, otherwise called Soma Chakra.

The innermost layer is the Brahma Nadi, which is directly related to Brahmarandhra. Brahma Nadi is the stream of purity and the deep essence of the Kundalini energy. When awakened, it energizes the Chakras, infusing them with the Kundalini Light. To have a full awakening, though, you must raise the Kundalini through Brahma Nadi and pierce Brahmarandhra. Anything less than that is not a complete awakening but a partial one.

LALANA CHAKRA AND AMRITA NECTAR

In the Tantra Yoga tradition, it is said that the Bindu Chakra is the point that manifests your entire physical body as well as its point of dissipation. It says that the Bindu holds our Life Force within it, producing the Amrita Nectar. The Amrita Nectar is produced through a synthesis of Light energy one gets from food. In non-Kundalini awakened people, the Amrita drips from the Bindu down to the third Chakra, Manipura, where it is used up for various activities of the body. It gives the body vitality. Over time, the Bindu's Life Force begins to dissipate, thereby ageing the physical body. The skin becomes rougher and dryer, hair begins to fall out, bone tissue and cartilage wear out, and overall vitality lessens.

Yogis say that if one can prevent the Amrita from getting burned up by the Solar Plexus Chakra, they can enjoy its vitalizing and nourishing nectar and stop and even reverse the process of ageing and degeneration of the physical body. To accomplish this, Yogis must stimulate a secret Minor Chakra called Lalana. In *The Upanishads*, Lalana is said to have 12 bright-red petals. Other sacred texts, though, say it has 64 silvery-white petals.

Lalana is a mysterious Chakra, but a critical one, especially in the Kundalini awakened individuals. Utilizing the power of Lalana and Vishuddhi enables one to transform the Amrita into a more fine, Spiritual substance, which is used to energize and nourish the Kundalini circuit. Synthesized Light energy one gets from food that I have said "feeds" the Kundalini circuit, providing the experience of transcendence is the Amrita Nectar spoken of in Yogic traditions. Amrita becomes optimized when it is harnessed and transformed into what I describe feels like a liquid Spirit energy. This cooling substance soothes the mind and heart, removing and washing away any unbalanced thoughts and emotions.

Lalana is a red circular Moon region, which acts as a reservoir for the Amrita nectar. As the Amrita falls from the Bindu, it is stored at Lalana Chakra, ready to be purified by Vishuddhi. If Vishuddhi is inactive, as it is in most non-Kundalini awakened individuals, Amrita falls to Manipura. But if Lalana is somehow stimulated, Vishuddhi becomes active as well. The nectar is thus purified and transformed, becoming the "Nectar of Immortality." As mentioned before, Ancient traditions have referred to this nectar as the "Elixir of Life" and the "Food of the Gods." In Christianity, it is the "Blood of the Christ" that grants Eternal Life. Once the necessary energy centres are opened, the transformed Amrita nectar is then redistributed throughout the Body of Light, enabling the individual to experience true transcendence.

Lalana Chakra is located at the backside of the palate, more specifically, the area where the top of the spinal cord meets the brainstem. In the cross-section of the human brain and skull (Figure 135), its location is between the

Medulla Oblongata and the base of the skull, along the spinal cord's central canal. This area is where the Vagus nerve and other cranial nerves join the first cervical vertebra (Atlas).

Lalana Chakra is about two inches above Vishuddhi and is intimately connected with it. Lalana, which means both "female energy" and "tongue," is also called Talu Chakra, and it is located directly behind the pharynx, at the back of the mouth. The Kundalini energy activates Lalana Chakra as it enters the brainstem. Once it is activated, the Kundalini will then proceed towards the Thalamus, where it will work on opening Ajna next, followed by Sahasrara.

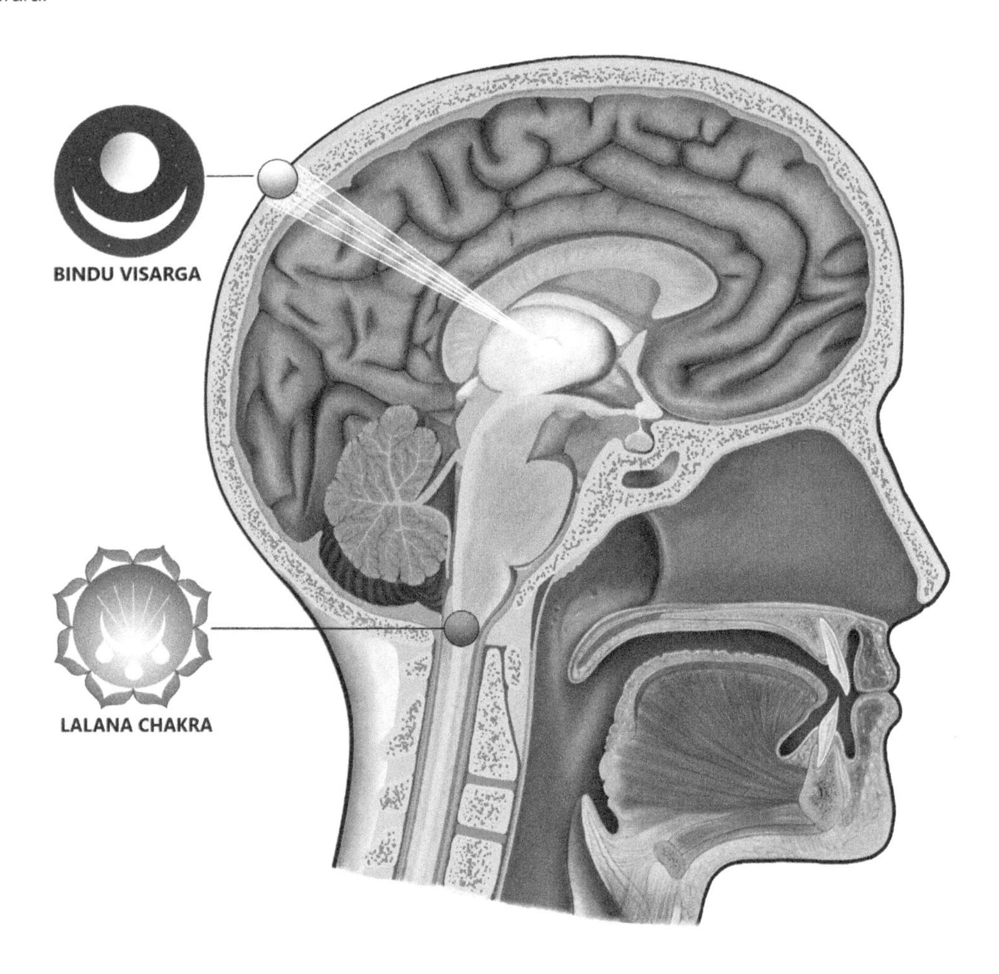

Figure 135: Lalana (Talu) Chakra and the Bindu Visarga

Lalana is also connected to the Bindu at the top-back of the head. Along with Vishuddhi, these three Chakras are responsible for what happens to the Amrita and whether it falls downwards to Manipura, leading to physical degradation, or whether it is harnessed and utilized for Spiritual purposes. Lalana Chakra's powers are best-made use of once the Kundalini has blown open this Chakric centre, but there is another method that Yogis have developed called Khechari Mudra.

KHECHARI MUDRA AND ITS VARIATIONS

Yogis have discovered that they can affect the flow of Amrita from their Bindu with the help of the tongue. Falling under the heading of "Mana: Head Mudras," Khechari Mudra is a powerful technique that uses the tongue to channel energy in the brain. It involves turning the tip of the tongue backwards and attempting to touch the uvula or "little tongue," which directs the flow of energy towards Lalana Chakra.

The tongue is very potent in terms of directing energy into the brain. In Qi Gong, it is essential to put the tip of your tongue on the sensitive area of the roof of your mouth to connect two very important energy Meridians. The end of your tongue is an energy conductor that stimulates whatever it touches. In the case of Khechari Mudra, you are trying to direct the energy flow backwards into Lalana Chakra to activate it.

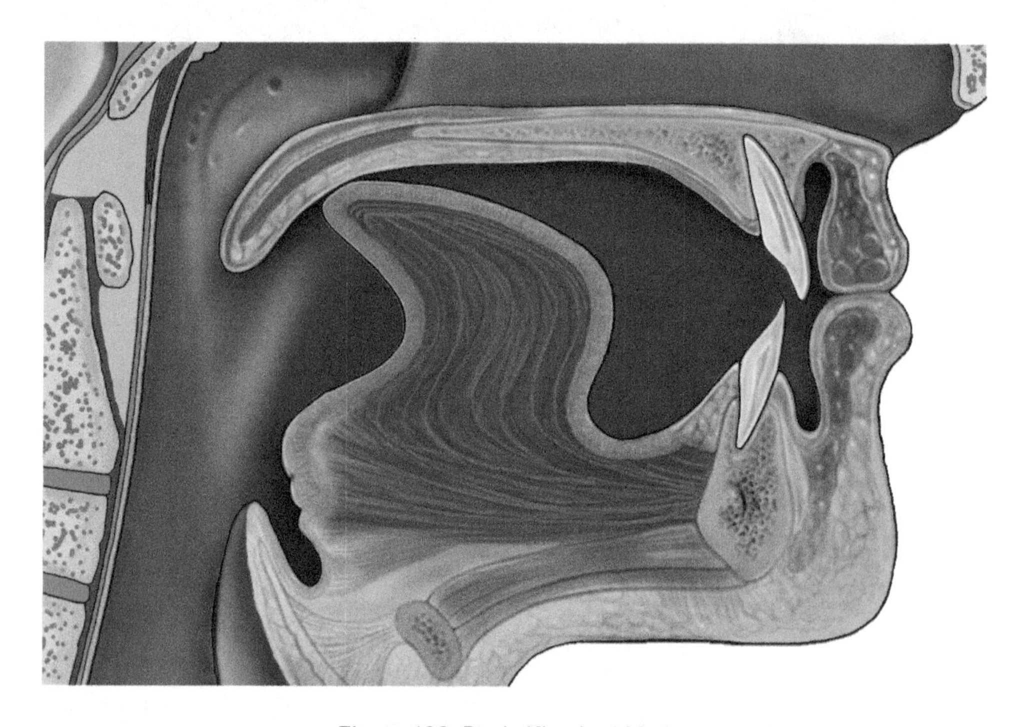

Figure 136: Basic Khechari Mudra

To perform the Basic Khechari Mudra method, you can sit in any comfortable meditative position. With eyes closed, turn your eyes towards the Mind's Eye centre between the eyebrows. Then, with the mouth closed, roll the tongue upward and backwards so that its lower surface touches the upper palate (Figure 136). Stretch the tip of the tongue as far as it will go as you attempt to touch the uvula. There should not be too much strain on the tongue as you do this. Keep it in this position now as long as it is comfortable. If you experience discomfort, relax the tongue by returning it to its neutral position for a few seconds, then repeat the practice.

Khechari Mudra is performed as part of different Asanas, Pranayamas, Mudras, and Bandhas for optimal effects of those exercises. When utilized with the inverted pose, Viparita Karani, it enables the practitioner to retain the Amrita more easily.

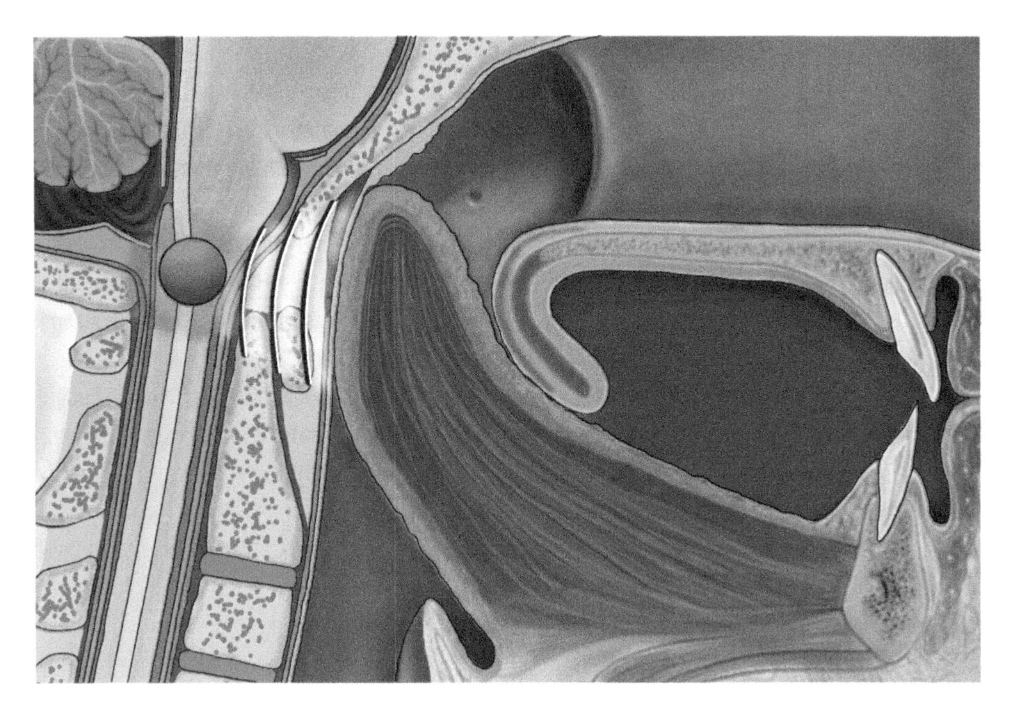

Figure 137: Advanced Khechari Mudra

The Advanced Khechari Mudra involves cutting the bottom of the tissue that connects the underside of the tongue with the bottom of the mouth. Once completed, the tongue can be elongated fully and placed inside the nasal cavity behind the uvula (Figure 137). Doing so puts pressure on the pharynx, which stimulates Lalana and prevents the Amrita from falling to the Solar Plexus. Once Amrita is captured with Khechari Mudra, its healing effects begin to unfold. The Advanced Khechari Mudra method is best practised with the help of a qualified Guru.

When a person undergoes a full and permanent Kundalini awakening, there is a free-flow of Kundalini energy into the Thalamus. From here, the Kundalini flows towards Ajna, Sahasrara, and the Bindu. When the Bindu Chakra becomes involved in the process of Spiritual transformation, it secretes the Amrita down to Lalana Chakra, which is then purified by Vishuddhi and transformed into its most refined form. This nectar is then distributed throughout the Body of Light, nourishing the Seventy-Two Thousand Nadis and expanding the consciousness. As a result, the awakened person begins to have above-average vitality, and their ageing process slows down drastically. They can go for a long time without food and water, as they feel nourished from the inside by the movement of these new energies.

The Amrita nectar is directly involved in the process of Enlightenment. Although we can utilize it through the Yogic practices mentioned above, its real purpose is to play a role in sustaining the Kundalini circuit. The transformed Amrita nectar nourishes the Kundalini circuit, and it relies on the Light energy it gets from food. It provides the emotional tranquillity necessary for one to suspend the ageing process and prolong the health of their physical body. This emotional tranquillity is best described as a state of *Nirvana* which is one of the sought-after goals of the Yogi.

Stress is one of the key factors in ageing. By putting the mind in neutral and utilizing the Amrita nectar to nourish the Body of Light, longevity can be attained.

Over the years, I have discovered another variation of the Khechari Mudra that has become one of the dominant practices in my life. I have found that curving the tongue downwards and pushing it back also puts pressure on Lalana Chakra, which aids in the process of nourishing my Kundalini circuit with the transformed Amrita. To do it correctly, you must touch the tip of the tongue to the Frenulum, which is a fold of mucus membrane located under the centre portion of the tongue that helps anchor it in your mouth and stabilize its movements.

I stumbled upon this technique accidentally, or to be more accurate; it is my Higher Self that led me to find this technique and utilize it. I have never come across this practice in my research of various Spiritual traditions to verify its use, so what I am sharing with you is unique information you won't find elsewhere.

I started practising this technique years ago, seemingly out of nowhere, and often catch myself doing it in front of other people, which sometimes gets a strange reaction from them since I naturally purse my lips when I do it. The front cover of *The Magus* features a younger me as Hermes, portrayed with pursed lips as I am performing this technique. My wife thought it fitting to depict me like this since she often sees me doing it.

The technique I discovered allows me to harness the Light energy I get from food, which turns into a liquid Spirit substance (Amrita) in my brain and is then redistributed along the many Nadis in my Body of Light. It is always accompanied by feelings of warmth like I am kindling a steady fire in my chest, as is the case when Lalana Chakra is being stimulated. Now, keep in mind that the tongue is facing downwards with this variation, which often makes me question its use and to what extent it is benefiting me Spiritually. So, I like to balance it out by performing the Basic Khechari Mudra by turning the tip of the tongue backwards and touching the upper palate. This way, I get the necessary energies streaming upwards into the Cerebrum while keeping Lalana Chakra stimulated.

MANTRA

Mantra is a Sanskrit word that means "a tool of the mind" or "an instrument of thought." It is a sacred pronouncement, a Divine sound, syllable, word, or grouping of words in a sacred language with Magickal power in the invisible world. Mantras are "words of power" that are found in many different Spiritual traditions, Ancient and modern, that serve as tools to invoke or evoke energy into the Aura. Since "manas" means "mind" in Sanskrit, a Mantra's purpose is to transcend the mind. They include but are not limited to the names of Gods, Angels, Spirits, and different Deities from whatever pantheon your chosen Mantra belongs to.

I have already introduced you to the science of Mantras in my previous book, most of which are in the Hebrew language and are used as part of Ceremonial Magick ritual exercises. The Mantras in the Enochian language are stand-alone Mantras that are the phonetic recitation of passages in Enochian. Because of the sacredness and power of Hebrew and Enochian languages, these Mantras are potent in changing one's consciousness through the invocation/evocation of energy.

There are 84 meridian points on the roof of the mouth, which the tongue stimulates by chanting a Mantra. These meridian points, in turn, stimulate the Hypothalamus, which acts on the Pineal Gland, making it pulse and radiate. The Pineal Gland then gives impulses to the entire Endocrine system, enabling the release of hormones that strengthen our immune and neurological systems, putting the body in a state of coherence. Two of the released hormones are serotonin and dopamine, which create emotional bliss that raises one's consciousness to a higher level.

The Mantras I will be presenting in this book are in the Sanskrit language, one of the world's oldest languages (5000 years old). Sanskrit is the Ancient language of Hinduism that was a means of communication and dialogue by the Hindu Celestial Gods, according to legend. Ancient Hindus referred to Sanskrit as "Dev Bhasha" or "Devavani," meaning the "Language of the Gods."

The greatness of the Sanskrit language is in the formation and uniqueness of its vocabulary, phonology, grammar, and syntax, which remains undiluted in its purity to this day. Its fifty letters are comprised of sixteen vowels and thirty-four consonants. Sanskrit letters have never been altered or tweaked throughout time, making it a perfect language for word formation and pronunciation.

Sanskrit Mantras use seed sounds that create the vibratory energy of the words they translate to. By pronouncing a Sanskrit Mantra, its vibration impacts your consciousness which has lasting effects on your mind and body. Therefore, understanding the meaning of a Sanskrit Mantra is paramount to knowing the kind of energetic change it will produce.

The Mantras presented in this section are to be vibrated using your vocal cords in a projective, energizing tone. They should be performed in monotone, natural C, elongating the pronunciation. If you have ever heard Tibetan monks chant, it is to sound similar to that. Vibrating and "chanting" are interchangeable words when it comes to the performance of a Mantra.

THE SACRED NUMBER 108

The standard repetition of a Mantra in many Eastern Spiritual traditions is 108 times. This number is the basis of all Creation, representing the Universe and our existence. Hindus, Yogis, and Buddhists believe that by vibrating/chanting a Mantra 108 times, we align ourselves to the Will of the Creator and its creative energy. They think that by harmonizing our personal vibration with the Universal one, we assume our birthright as Co-Creators, enabling us to manifest whatever reality we desire.

There are many reasons why the number 108 is considered sacred, some found in science and mathematics. For example, the Sun is 108 times the diameter of the Earth, and the distance from the Earth to the Sun is 108 times the Sun's diameter. Also, the distance from the Earth to the Moon is 108 times the diameter of the Moon.

In Astrology, there are twelve Zodiacal Constellations and nine Planets (Seven Ancient Planets plus Uranus and Neptune) in our Solar System. Therefore, twelve multiplied by nine equals 108. Additionally, there are twenty-seven Lunar mansions which are divided into four quarters. When you multiply twenty-seven by four, the result again is 108.

In the Hindu religion, there are 108 Upanishads, which are the sacred texts of wisdom passed down by the Ancient rishis. Each Deity in Hinduism also has 108 names, whose qualities or powers we can invoke through their respective Mantras.

In the Sanskrit alphabet, since there are 54 letters and each letter has a masculine (Shiva) and feminine (Shakti) quality, the total number of variations equals 108. In the Yogic system of Chakras, as well, there are believed to be 108 energy lines (Nadis) that converge at the Heart Chakra, our Body of Light's centre of love and transformation.

In Ayurvedic medicine, there are said to be 108 vital energy points in the body, called Marmas. Working with the Marmas is beneficial to improving our psychological and physiological states. By chanting a Mantra 108 times, we send Divine energy to each Marma point, activating its healing properties.

The holy writings of Tibetan Buddhists also, have been divided into 108 sacred books. In addition, Buddhists believe that the road to Nirvana is paved with exactly 108 temptations. They believe that 108 defilements, or sins, prevent us from living in a perfect, peaceful state.

These are just some of the reasons why the number 108 is sacred. There are many more across not only Eastern religions and Spiritual traditions, but Western ones as well. For example, the number 108 is used in Islam to refer to God. And so on.

JAPA MEDITATION

Traditionally, a Mala bead necklace is used in the traditions of Yoga, Buddhism, Hinduism, Jainism, and Sikhism as part of Mantra practice, which they refer to as a Japa meditation. A Mala has 108 beads and one "Guru" bead, which is used as a marker for the start and end of a cycle. So whether you are chanting out loud or reciting silently, tracing the beads of the Mala with your fingers will help you keep track of your Mantra. Similar implements have been used for generations cross-culturally and across many religions and Spiritual traditions, including the rosary beads used by Christians for prayer.

To perform a Japa meditation, you must obtain a Mala bead necklace to be used with the Mantras presented below. Not only will a Mala allow you to complete 108 repetitions with ease, but it will become a powerful Spiritual item in your life that puts you in the right frame of mind the moment you hold it in your hand.

However, one can work with meditation Mantras without a Mala, so if you can't get one for some reason, don't be deterred from practising Mantras without it. As mentioned before, vibrating/chanting Mantras has a cumulative effect in terms of energy invoked/evoked, so whether you do 108 pronouncements or 100, for example, the outcome will be relatively negligible. Technically, you can even focus on performing a Mantra for a certain amount of time, as in five to fifteen minutes, and time yourself accordingly so you do approximately 100 pronouncements. Having said that, I do believe in the power of traditional practice, especially one with thousands of years of lineage, so before you start tweaking its mechanics, it is better to master its original form and go from there.

Ideally, do your meditation Mantra early in the morning, before eating. If you wish to repeat your Mantra, do so at night, allowing some time between sessions so that the invoked/evoked energy can work on you.

To begin your Japa practice, choose your meditation Mantra from the options given below. Each meditation Mantra affects our energy differently, so read its description carefully so that you can apply each one when needed. Next, find a spot to sit comfortably with your spine straight and eyes closed. One of the meditation Asanas presented so far is ideal. Take a few deep breaths now to align yourself with your intention.

Hold your Mala in your right hand (In India, the left hand is considered impure), draped over your middle finger, as your index finger comfortably extends out (Figure 138). Starting at the Guru bead, use your thumb to count each smaller bead as you pull the Mala towards you with each Mantra pronouncement. Inhale before each pronouncement in a calm and rhythmic fashion.

You are to repeat your Mantra 108 times as you cycle through the Mala beads, finishing at the Guru bead where you started. If you wish to continue your Mantra meditation, reverse the direction and begin the process again instead of passing over the Guru bead. Remember to do complete 108 cycles.

Repetition of Sanskrit Mantras positively affects your nervous system, leaving you calm and relaxed, which is one of the initial side-effects. In addition, these Mantras balance your inner energies, which improves concentration and Self-awareness. However, regular repetition of Sanskrit Mantras works at a deep, subconscious level, creating lasting healing effects on the mind, body, and Soul. Therefore, when you begin this practice, be patient and consistent with it daily to obtain the desired results over time.

Figure 138: Counting Mala Beads

MEDITATION MANTRAS

Om

Pronunciation: *Aaa-Uuu-Mmm*

"Om" is the most universal Mantra in Sanskrit. It is believed to be the first sound heard at the creation of the Cosmos from which all things emerge. "Om" signifies the essence of the ultimate reality, which is Cosmic Consciousness. As such, most Sanskrit Mantras start or end with "Om".

"Om" (pronounced AUM) represents the cycle of life—life, death, and rebirth. It also relates to the Hindu Trinity (Trimurti) of Brahma, Vishnu, and Shiva. "Aaa" represents creation, "Ooo" stands for maintenance or preservation, and "Mmm" is destruction, with relation to overcoming the Ego to achieve Self-realization. Finally, AUM represents the Three Gunas of nature and the four stages of consciousness; the fourth stage represents silence of the mind achieved when the practitioner reaches Samadhi.

Chanting Aaa-Uuu-Mmm (AUM) will help you disconnect from your Ego and reconnect with the Spirit within, which is all-creative and all-encompassing. When you pronounce each syllable fully, you will feel energy lifting from your pelvic floor through to the heart, and finally, the crown of the head. It is the path of the Kundalini, whose purpose is to liberate the Soul from the body in this lifetime.

The sound "Om" vibrates at the 432 Hz vibration frequency, found throughout everything in nature. As such, this sound heals the mind and body at a cellular level, bringing us in tune with our surroundings. It removes all tension and anxiety by calming the mind and harmonizing our inner energies. It also helps improve concentration while enhancing creativity and overall positive energy.

On a physical level, "Om" improves lung function and the digestive system while detoxifying the body. When pronouncing Aaa-Ooo-Mmm, the three unique frequencies should flow naturally as one sound.

ॐ नमः शिवाय

Om Namah Shivaya
Pronunciation: *Aummm Nah-Mahhh Shee-Vah-Yahhh*

"Om Namah Shivaya" translates to "O salutations to the auspicious one," or simply, "I bow to Lord Shiva." This widely used Mantra draws the mind in upon itself to Lord Shiva's infinite, all-pervasive presence—the Cosmic Consciousness principle of the Universe. It is also called "Shiva Panchakshara," meaning the "Five-Syllable Mantra," the essential Mantra in Shaivism that brings silence to the mind.

The five syllables "Namah Shivaya" represent the Five Elements that make up all of Creation: "Na" sound represents Earth, "Ma" is Water, "Shi" means Fire, "Va" is Air, and "Ya" represents Spirit. The "Om" is excluded as it is the first sound of the Universe that stands for peace and love, the energetic foundation of Cosmic Consciousness.

As Shiva is the supreme God of transformation who represents our Higher Self, this Mantra raises our consciousness by harmonizing the Five Elements within the Self. Thus, not only does it bring joy and bliss into our lives, but it also connects us with all of nature, namely the physical representation of the Five Elements that Shiva symbolizes—the land, the sea, the air, and the Sun.

Because it connects us with our Holy Guardian Angel, our God-Self, the Om Namah Shivaya Mantra is said to overcome the effects of the Macrocosm—the fixed Stars and the orbiting Planets that subtly affect us on an energetic level. It builds up transcendental energy in our system that raises consciousness, enabling us to experience the higher Cosmic Planes. As such, this Mantra connects us with the highest Chakra, Sahasrara—the source of all of Creation.

Om Mani Padme Hum
Pronunciation: *Aummm Mah-neee Pahd-mayyy Hummm*

This Sanskrit Mantra is associated with Avalokiteshvara (Sanskrit), the Bodhisattva of compassion. Bodhisattvas are Enlightened, compassionate Beings who assist the Spiritual goals of others. Tibetan Buddhists refer to this same Being as Chenrezig, while the Chinese call it Quan Yin. The regular practice of this Mantra instils a sense of love and kindness towards ourselves and others, which liberates us from the emotional suffering of our mundane existence.

The translation of this Mantra would be "Praise to the Jewel in the Lotus." The jewel itself refers to compassion which purifies the Soul, bestowing it with the bliss of Divine Light. Just as the lotus is not soiled by the mud in which it grows, human beings can use compassion to rise above the oppression of the Lower Self, the Ego, and achieve Enlightenment.

"Om Mani Padme Hum" can be broken down into six syllables, which represent a gradual and progressive path from the mundane into the Spiritual: "Om" is the primal sound of the Universe that brings us in harmony with the Cosmos, "Ma" is our altruistic intention to develop ethics and morals which purifies jealous tendencies, "Ni" builds tolerance and patience, releasing us from our lower desires and leaving us peaceful and content, "Pad" frees us from prejudice and ignorance which bar the way to love and acceptance, and "Me" releases us from attachment and possessiveness, allowing us to cultivate our powers of concentration. Finally, "Hum" liberates us from aggression and hatred, as it represents the unity of all things that opens the door to wisdom and understanding.

The Dalai Lama, whom the Buddhists believe is the current incarnation of Chenrezig, says that every one of the Buddha's teachings resides within this powerful Mantra. To unlock it, however, one must not only chant it but must focus their intention on the meaning behind each of the six syllables.

हरे कृष्ण हरे कृष्ण । कृष्ण कृष्ण हरे हरे ।
हरे राम हरे राम । राम राम हरे हरे

Hare Krishna, Hare Krishna, Krishna Krishna, Hare Hare
Hare Rama, Hare Rama, Rama Rama, Hare Hare
Pronunciation: *Huh-ray Krish-Naaa, Huh-ray Krish-Naaa, Krish-Naaa Krish-Naaa, Huh-ray Huh-rayyy, Huh-ray Ramaaa, Huh-ray Ramaaa, Rama Ramaaa, Huh-ray Huh-rayyy*

The Hare Krishna Mantra, also known as the "Maha," or "Great" Mantra, is a sacred Sanskrit verse whose purpose is to revive God-realization within oneself, known as Krishna consciousness. It is rooted in the Vaishnava tradition of Hinduism and is central to the path of Bhakti Yoga. It has only four lines, composed of Hindu deities' names: Hare, Krishna, and Rama. Hare combines the energy of Hari (Lord Vishnu) and Hara (Krishna's consort, Shakti), while Krishna and Rama are the names of the two avatars, or Divine incarnations, of Lord Vishnu.

Lord Krishna has many parallels to Jesus Christ as both are believed to be sons of God who were fully human and fully Divine. Both teachings emphasised love and peace since their mission was to restore goodness in a morally declining world. By attempting to achieve Krishna Consciousness within ourselves, we refer to Christ Consciousness—a state of awareness in which individuals act in complete harmony with the Divine. This state of consciousness is a precursor, or preparation (in a sense), to reaching Cosmic Consciousness.

The practice of the Maha Mantra activates Spiritual energy within you in the Heart Chakra, whose aim is to transform your consciousness so you can transcend your Ego. The subtle state of awareness that is achieved frees the Self from the illusion of separateness, allowing love energy to take over and harmonise the mind, body, and Soul. As such, Krishna consciousness is achieved, preparing the way for joy and bliss to permanently enter your life.

ॐ शान्तिः शान्तिः शान्तिः

Om Shanti Shanti Shanti
Pronunciation: *Aummm Shanteee Shanteee Shanteee*

The "Om Shanti" Mantra is commonly used in Hindu and Buddhist prayers, ceremonies, and literature; its meaning translates to "Om Peace." "Shanti" comes from the Sanskrit root word "sham," meaning calmness, tranquillity, prosperity, and happiness. It is the root of the word "Shalom" in Hebrew and "Salam" in Arabic, both of which also means "Peace." By chanting this Mantra, not only do you find a profound level of peace within yourself, but you are sending out offerings of peace to the whole world.

Traditionally, the word "Shanti" is chanted three times since it invokes peace and protection on three levels of Self: conscious, subconscious, and superconscious (God-Self). The conscious Self belongs to the Earth, while the subconscious reaches down into the Underworld (Hell), and the superconscious refers to the Heavens (Stars) above. These three can again be broken down into the body, mind, and Spirit or the Physical, Astral, and Spiritual Planes.

"Om Shanti" can also be used as a form of greeting in Yoga. When said aloud to a fellow practitioner, it is a desire for the other person to experience Universal peace. The English translation would be "Peace be with you," or "Namaste"—although the words sound different, the meaning is the same. Be mindful when pronouncing "Shanti" to press the tongue against the teeth instead of on the upper palate—the produced sound "t" should sound different from the English version of "t."

ॐ नमो गुरु देव् नमो

Ong Namo Guru Dev Namo
Pronunciation: *Onggg Nah-Moh Guh-Ruh Devvv Nah-Moh*

This Sanskrit Mantra translates to "I bow to the Creative Wisdom, I bow to the Divine Teacher within." Another translation is "I bow to the All-That-Is," as a Mantra of Oneness. Its other name is the "Adi Mantra," which is often used in Kundalini Yoga at the beginning of its practice, especially in a class setting. It was essential to Yogi Bhajan, the Hindu Spiritual teacher who brought Kundalini Yoga to the West. Many practitioners believe that the Adi Mantra allows one to tune into Kundalini Yoga's particular vibration frequency, unlocking its most profound understanding and purpose.

Chanting this Mantra enables us to humble ourselves and connect with our Higher Self—the inner teacher that channels Universal wisdom and knowledge to us when our minds are in a receptive state. It raises the vibration of our consciousness, allowing us to trust and listen to our inner guidance. It also imparts to us that we are our own greatest teachers in life and that no other teachers are needed.

The "Ong Namo Guru Dev Namo" Mantra enables us to tap into our highest potential as Spiritual human beings. Each word's translation reveals its power to transform our consciousness. To start, "Ong" means infinite creative energy or subtle Divine wisdom. Its pronouncement is similar to saying "Om," with the added advantage of moving the sound in the mouth from the front to the back of the throat, which stimulates different brain parts, especially the Pituitary and Pineal Glands.

"Namo" is equivalent to "Namaha," meaning "my respectful salutations," while a Guru is a Spiritual teacher who guides their disciples on their path towards Enlightenment. "Dev" is a shorter version of the term "Deva," a Sanskrit word for God or Deity. As Deva follows Guru in the Mantra, it implies that the Spiritual teacher is Divine and Holy. And finally, "Namo" at the end reaffirms humility and reverence.

This Mantra refines the energy around and within us, making us a vessel for higher consciousness. By chanting it, one has the wisdom and support of generations of Kundalini Yogis while reinforcing one's connection to their Higher, God-Self.

ॐ गं गणपतये नमः

Om Gam Ganapataye Namaha
Pronunciation: *Aummm Gummm Guh-Nuh-Puh-Tuh-Yehhh Nah-Mah-Haaa*

"Om Gam Ganapataye Namaha" is a powerful prayer and Mantra that praises the beloved Hindu elephant-headed God, Lord Ganesha. Its English translation is "My Salutations to Lord Ganesha." In Hinduism, Lord Ganesha is recognized as the remover of obstacles and master of knowledge. He is known to give good luck, prosperity, and success, especially when undertaking a new venture.

Lord Ganesha is associated with Muladhara Chakra and the Earth Element. He is often invoked to clear one's path when they feel mentally stuck and are in need of a change of perspective. His energy grounds us, helping us overcome challenges and creative blockages. Lord Ganesha empowers us by improving our focus, concentration, and knowledge, facilitating inner peace.

The sound "Gam" is a Bija Mantra for Ganesha, while "Ganapataye" is a reference to his other name—Ganapati. It is said that if one chants the Lord Ganesha Mantra 108 times on a daily basis, all fear and negativity from their hearts will be removed. This is because fear is a by-product of the corrupted Water and Air Elements, which the Earth Element grounds when it is brought in.

ॐ श्री सरस्वत्यै नमः

Om Shri Saraswataya Namaha
Pronunciation: *Aummm Shree Sah-Rah-Swah-Tah-Yahhh Nah-Mah-Haaa*

The "Om Shri Saraswataya Namaha" Mantra invokes the power of the Hindu Goddess, Saraswati (Figure 139), who is associated with wisdom, learning, and the creative arts. The English translation reads, "Salutations to the Goddess Saraswati." Chanting this Mantra stimulates one's creativity while kindling the intellect. Moreover, it inspires us to express ourselves through art, music, and literature. If one chants this Mantra before beginning a new creative endeavour, they will have good luck.

Saraswati is considered the mother of *The Vedas*, the Ancient Hindu and Yogic scriptures. Many educated people believe that regularly chanting the Saraswati Mantra can give them profound knowledge and wisdom concerning the mysteries of Creation that will liberate them from the cycle of death and rebirth (Samsara). They refer to this emancipation process as "Moksha."

In the "Om Shri Saraswataya Namaha" Mantra, Shri is a title of reverence often used before the name of an honoured person or Deity. Saraswati is the consort of the Hindu God Brahma, who is at the head of the Trimurti. Since Brahma represents the creation process, he is related to the Air Element and thoughts, which power and shape the intellect. Saraswati is Brahma's Shakti or creative feminine energy. She represents the passive aspect of the same energy, channelled into the Physical Plane. As such, Saraswati symbolises the inspiration that drives our creative expressions.

Figure 139: The Goddess Saraswati

BIJA MANTRAS AND MUDRAS OF THE SEVEN CHAKRAS

Each of the Seven Chakras has a sacred word or sound associated with it, called a Bija, or "Seed" Mantra. We can use these Mantras in Sound Healing to tune and balance the Chakric energies and return them to their optimal vibration. By correcting the energetic frequency of the Chakras, their dormant potential is released.

When sounding the Bija Mantras of the Seven Chakras, we connect with their corresponding Five Elements. This connection is created by the tongue's position in the mouth when vibrating the Bija Mantras. The Five Elements are attributed to the first five Chakras. At the same time, Ajna represents the duality of the masculine (Pingala) and feminine (Ida) forces in nature, the Yin and Yang, and Sahasrara represents the totality and Oneness of all the Chakras. The Bija Mantras of the Seven Chakras are presented below.

LAM – Muladhara, the Root Chakra – Earth Element – First Bija Mantra
VAM – Swadhisthana, the Sacral Chakra – Water Element – Second Bija Mantra
RAM – Manipura, the Solar Plexus Chakra – Fire Element – Third Bija Mantra
YAM – Anahata, the Heart Chakra – Air Element – Fourth Bija Mantra
HAM – Vishuddhi, the Throat Chakra – Spirit Element – Fifth Bija Mantra
SHAM – Ajna, the Mind's Eye Chakra – Duality – Sixth Bija Mantra
OM – Sahasrara, the Crown Chakra – Oneness – Seventh Bija Mantra

However, these seven are not the only Bija Mantras in existence. Each of the 50 letters of the Sanskrit alphabet has its own Bija Mantra. Consequently, the 50 Sanskrit letters are related to the first six Chakras, whose petals total 50, also found in the Thousand Petalled Lotus of Sahasrara. According to Yogic scriptures, when a Sanskrit letter is sounded in a Mantra, it opens its corresponding petal of the Chakra it is associated with. The Petal Mantras of the Chakras are given in Figure 140.

Bija Mantras have been used in Yogic practices and meditation for thousands of years because of their Spiritual effects on our emotional and mental states of Being. They can be sounded (vibrated silently or chanted aloud) or meditated on by themselves or attached at the beginning of longer Mantras to boost their energetic power. These primordial Mantras do not have a direct translation like other parts of a Mantra do. However, their intense vibrational qualities make them a potent instrument to access higher levels of consciousness.

Figure 140: Bija Mantras of the Chakric Petals

When chanted as part of a longer Mantra, Bija Mantras are generally expressive of that Mantra's foundational energy or essence. For example, OM is the source, or seed, from which all the other sounds in a Mantra precede. Hence, it is the most superior Bija Mantra as the sound of Para-Brahman (the Supreme Brahman); the letters of the Sanskrit alphabet are only emanations from OM, which is their root sound.

OM represents Sahasrara Chakra, the source energy of the other six Chakras below it. Sahasrara is the White Light from which the seven colours of the rainbow emanate in succession, corresponding with the colours of the Seven Chakras. Note that Sahasrara is traditionally white or violet since violet is the highest vibrational colour at the apex of the rainbow.

The seven Hand Mudras from Figure 141 are traditionally used to open the Seven Major Chakras. By combining these Hand Mudras with the Bija Mantras of the Seven Chakras, we have a powerful technique to optimize the energy flow of the Chakras and help awaken the Kundalini at the base of the spine.

Seven Chakras Mudra/Mantra Healing Practice

Begin the Chakra Mudra/Mantra practice by washing your hands. Afterwards, find a comfortable seated position, either in a meditation Asana or on a chair. Next, allow yourself to calm your interior by practising the Four-Fold Breath and silencing the mind. Since this exercise has a visualization component, it helps to have your eyes closed while performing it.

There are two methods of performing this practice, both of which should be used and interchanged often. The first method requires you to begin with Muladhara Mudra and work upwards through the Chakras. This particular sequence mirrors the rising of the Kundalini as well as climbing the Tree of Life, where you begin your journey in the lowest Sphere or Chakra and move upwards in consciousness until you reach the highest.

While performing the Hand Mudra of each Chakra, vibrate/chant its Bija Mantra in an energizing and projective vocal tone. You may spend anywhere from one to five minutes on each Mudra before proceeding further. Be consistent in how long you spend on each Mudra. For example, if you decide to spend two minutes on Muladhara Mudra, then repeat this length of time on the following Hand Mudras as well. The key to any successful Spiritual practice is consistency and balance.

As you are performing a Hand Mudra, and vibrating its corresponding Bija Mantra, focus on the Chakric area. Connect with the Chakra and imagine its complementary colour getting brighter and brighter as Light energy permeates it with every vibration. The visual component of this exercise is beneficial in focusing the energies being invoked through the Mantras.

In the second Chakra Mudra/Mantra practice method, you begin with the highest, Sahasrara, and work your way down in sequence through the Chakras. In this method, imagine Sahasrara as pure White Light instead of the colour violet. After finishing Sahasrara's Mudra/Mantra combo, imagine a beam of Light coming out of it, and connecting with Ajna Chakra below.

Once you are done with Ajna, project this same beam of Light down to Vishuddhi, and so on. You are to visualize a beam of Light projecting from one Chakra to the next until you reach Muladhara. At the end of this exercise, all the Seven Major Chakras will be lit up, connected by a shaft or beam of Light.

Whether you have performed the first or second Chakra Mudra/Mantra practice method, end the exercise by spending a few minutes visualizing your Chakras lit up from inside your Aura in their respective colours. See them brighter than ever. If you performed the second practice method, each of the Chakras would be connected by a Light beam. The Chakra Mudra/Mantra practice is now complete. You may open your eyes and regain full waking consciousness.

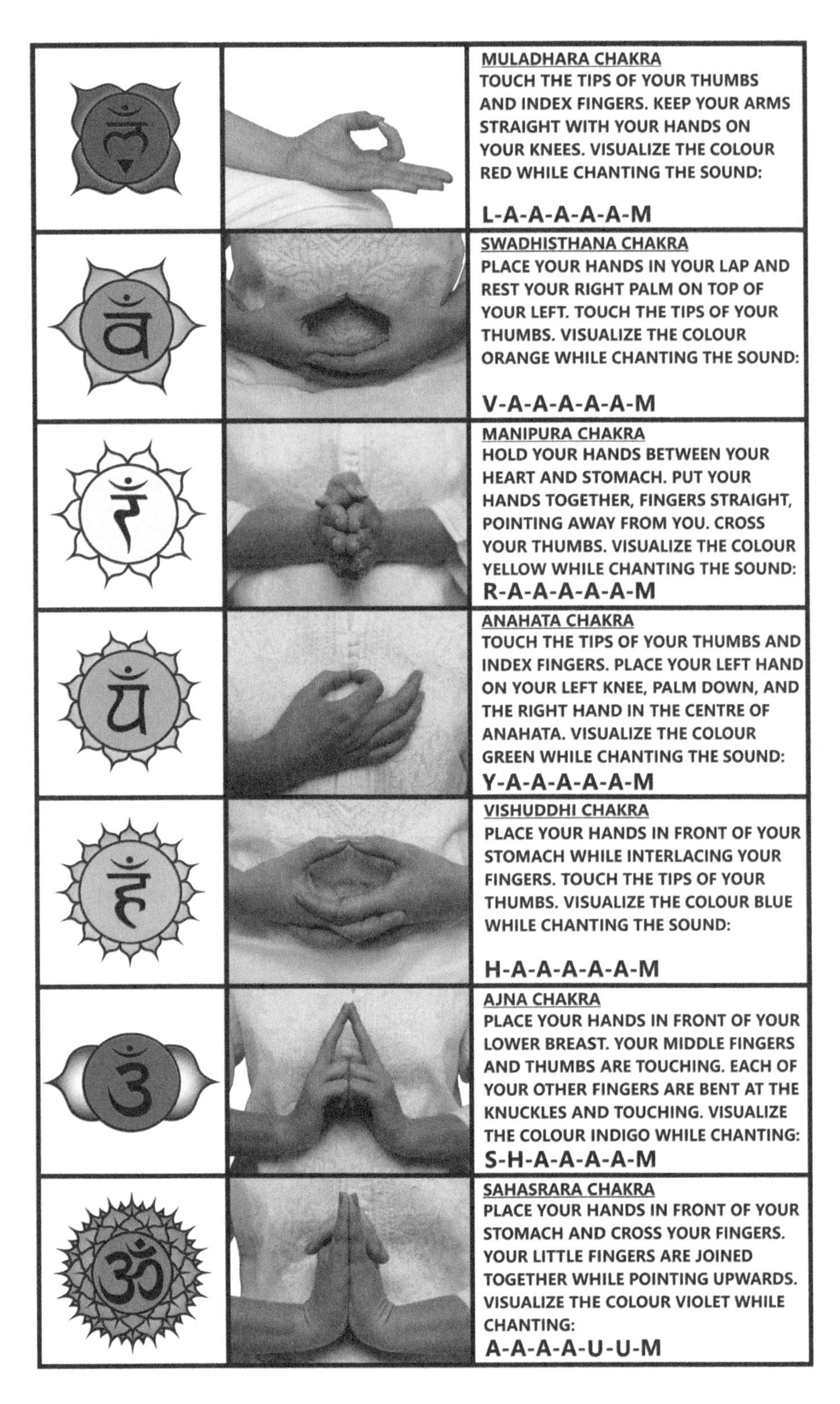

Figure 141: The Seven Chakras Mudras/Mantras

MEDITATION (DHYANA)

The fast-paced, multitasking lifestyle of Westerners has given rise to mental health conditions such as anxiety, depression, and chronic stress. For this reason, holistic mind-body practices such as Yoga and mindfulness meditation have become popular in the West as stress reduction techniques that calm the nervous system and boost dopamine and serotonin levels in the brain. The result is increased happiness and a healthy mind and body.

By dictionary definition, "meditation" means to engage in contemplation or reflection. It involves being mindful and present here and now, which heightens awareness by tapping into the realm of pure consciousness. It is a process that requires us to turn our minds inwards and unify with a higher reality, one that is substantial and wholesome.

Meditation is a journey towards the union of the Self with the inner Spirit. It is a quest for a higher truth that only intuition can grasp, requiring us to overcome our limited intelligence and personal emotions and make a permanent connection with our true essence.

Going within through meditative practice alleviates subconscious conditioning that is preventing us from being the best version of ourselves. Meditation resets the mind, which is helpful in people overcoming bad habits and harmful addictions. We also reconnect with the Soul by going inwards, which redirects our moral compass if we have gone astray.

Meditation brings mental clarity and calms our emotions, which has a healing effect on all aspects of our lives, including personal relationships. It releases inner tension and anxiety and recharges us with new faith in the Universe and love for ourselves and others. On a physical level, meditation lowers the heart rate, improves the immune system, and balances the Sympathetic and Parasympathetic Nervous Systems, bringing coherence to the body.

Meditation helps people achieve mental peace and balance, which is needed to function best in society. This practice has nothing to do with escaping into an Inner World and abandoning one's responsibilities in the material realm but finding our core and reaching genuine and lasting happiness. In doing so, we develop a proper foundation in life that makes everything we do from that point onwards easier.

Meditation is often the result of people coming to a dead-end in their search for happiness through satisfying their Ego's desires. As we become conditioned to associate with the Ego in our teens, this belief stays prevalent into our early adult years until we conclude that reaching ultimate happiness requires us to go beyond the Ego to find the Spirit within. This is what it means to become Spiritual and discern between illusion and reality, and meditation is the most optimal method of reaching that goal.

YOGIC PRACTICE AND MEDITATION

Meditation is the seventh limb or step of Yoga, Dhyana, as outlined in Patanjali's *Yoga Sutras*. Attempting to withdraw the senses (Pratyahara) and concentrate the mind (Dharana) are the fifth and sixth steps of Yoga, which lead to meditation. The third and fourth steps (Asanas and Pranayama) help balance out our masculine and feminine energies and calm down the mind, which leads to going inwards, a prerequisite for meditation.

Once we learn to meditate, we have a technique to contact our inner Self, the Spirit, enabling us to reach the eighth and final step of Yoga—Samadhi—Self-identification with the Cosmic Consciousness. Samadhi implies liberation, or Enlightenment, where the subject and object have become One.

Since meditation requires mental concentration, control over our Pranic energy is crucial. We can achieve this through stabilized meditative postures (Asanas) and breath regulation (Pranayama). People with mental or emotional disorders such as schizophrenia, psychosis, bipolar, PTSD, etc., should focus on Asanas and Pranayama first to balance out their energies, as it is helpful to overcome the negative tendencies of the mind before attempting deep meditation.

Opening new doors of the psyche when the mind is not healthy and strong can be scary for many people. After all, a big part of meditation is detaching from the mind's activities and separating ourselves from our thoughts. It is essential to develop courage and faith to face the unknown, which transmutes fear into positive energy that furthers our Spiritual Evolution. For this reason, Yogic practices such as Asanas, Pranayama, Mudras, and Mantras are often used side-by-side with meditation since they prepare the mind and body for reaching higher states of consciousness.

For example, Mudras help manipulate our inner energies, promoting physical, mental, and emotional wellness while Mantras invoke/evoke transcendental energy into the Aura, raising the consciousness above the level of the body and Ego. Thus, Mantras are paramount in meditation practice, especially when an individual needs assistance in quieting the mind and connecting with a higher power.

Because of their effectiveness, I have devoted most of this section to the Yogic techniques of Asana, Pranayama, Mudra, and Mantra. Their mastery is meant to prepare the body, mind, and Soul for meditation, which leads to unity with the Spirit—the Source energy of the Creator.

Regulation of one's lifestyle, including implementing a healthy diet, is part-and-parcel of preparing the mind for meditation. The first and second steps of Yoga, Yamas (Self-restraints) and Niyamas (Self-observances), require us to be aware of our thoughts, emotions, and actions and control them. As the Ancient Greek aphorism says, "Know Thyself." Only when we have learned the tendencies of our Egos, our automatic inner nature, can we begin to try to change and manage it to open ourselves to the Spiritual energy.

Ultimately, meditation leads to becoming the embodiment of Divine Love. Divine Love is the essence of the Spirit, which we feel tangibly in our hearts as an emotion. For this reason, opening the heart centre, or Heart Chakra is one of the goals of meditation. When Anahata Chakra is readied through Yogic practices coupled with developing morals and ethics, an influx of Spiritual energy pours in from Sahasrara Chakra above, resulting in a permanent transformation of consciousness. When that occurs, the aspirant has reached the ultimate goal of Yoga—union with the Godhead.

THREE MEDITATION METHODS

Just as there are various Spiritual disciplines to reach Enlightenment, there are many ways to meditate. In this chapter, I will mention three primary meditation methods that I have found most useful, although there are many more, some of which I discuss in other sections of this book. Also, meditation doesn't have to be stationary since walking can also be a meditative exercise if you practise mindfulness. Any activity that makes you present here and now and attunes you to the Spiritual energy constitutes a form of meditation.

The first type of meditation that I have found very powerful requires concentrating on a specific object outside of yourself and gazing at it with your eyes opened. The choices of what thing to meditate on are limitless. It helps to start with a simple object such as a candle flame (as given in this chapter) and progress to a more elaborate one, such as a Deity statue.

This type of meditation aims to focus your mind without interruption and become one with the object, which has very positive Spiritual effects. As you concentrate and focus on the object, your attention will be taken away from your subconscious mind and projected outside of yourself, raising your awareness of your surroundings.

This meditation is meant not only to stimulate your Mind's Eye but to awaken it fully and permanently. For this reason, when you focus on a more intricate object, such as a statue of a Deity, you will find that the longer you do this practice, your Astral sense will awaken so that you can feel, touch, smell, even taste the statue with your mind.

The second type of meditation employs the use of sound (Mantras) to focus the mind. Mantras are particular words, phrases, or affirmations, whose repetition during meditation raises the consciousness to higher states. In Yoga, the act of repeating a Mantra with the use of Mala beads is called Japa, derived from the Sanskrit word "jap," meaning "to utter in a low voice, repeat internally."

Audibly reciting a prayer during meditation also constitutes a Mantra, which you should sound with purpose and deep feeling for optimal effects. Intent and mind-focus are crucial when repeating any Mantra, as is voice tonality. For example, chanting involves rhythm and pitch, which puts the mind and body into a trance-like state when performed correctly. Religious chants and hymns are Mantras that inspire and transport us to an expanded state of awareness, facilitating a Spiritual awakening. I will discuss Mantras in more detail in the next chapter of this section.

The third type of meditation method involves visualization. Visualization meditations are very popular and effective while being easy to practise. To employ this type of meditation, all you have to do is choose an object to meditate on and visualize it with closed eyes. Visualization meditation stimulates the Mind's Eye since it involves Astral Light, which is the foundation of all visual images.

A powerful adaptation of this exercise is to visualize a Deity, such as a God or Goddess, from a pantheon of your choice (Figure 142). Not only will you receive the expected effects of a visualization meditation, but you may imbue into your Aura the energetic characteristics of the Deity you imagined.

For optimal effects, it is best to have the actual object on hand, such as the statue of the chosen Deity. You may hold the object to feel its energy or place it at eye level before you as you examine all of its intricate details and take note of them mentally. Then, you are to close your eyes and imagine what you just saw, as you focus and concentrate on holding that image in your Mind's Eye without interruption.

Figure 142: Visualization Meditation

When starting the visualization meditation practice, you can focus on a point, line, square, or circle and then reproduce the image in your Mind's Eye through imagination. However, focusing your attention on a Three-Dimensional object has specific effects that you cannot achieve with a two-dimensional plane, such as fully awakening your Astral senses.

To begin meditating on a Three-Dimensional object, start with something simple such as a piece of fruit, and then progress to a more complicated shape, like a Deity statue. Also, be mindful that all colours have different vibrations, and by visualizing a colour, you invoke its corresponding energy into your Aura at a subtle level. Therefore, pay attention to how a visualization meditation makes you feel when colours are involved.

MEDITATION STEPS

When planning a meditation, make sure that you do it in a quiet and pleasant place when you know you will be undisturbed. Many people like to use incense to clear their space of negative energy, thus making it sacred. Incense also contains specific properties that elevate the mind and prepare it for meditation. Make sure to burn incense before preparing the space, rather than during meditation, as it can interfere with breathing and be a distraction.

Sage, Frankincense, and Sandalwood are the most popular incenses because of their healing properties and calming effects. They also are known to activate Ajna Chakra, which is a prerequisite in meditation. However, my personal favourite is the Indian incense Nag Champa, which has a pleasant aroma and high-vibrational quality.

Mornings are usually the best time for meditation, especially on an empty stomach. Once you bring food into the body, wait for at least four to six hours before meditating since the body will be working hard to digest food which transforms into Pranic energy that powers up the system. Meditating at night is also advised since we are more relaxed naturally—meditating before sleep facilitates a calm and balanced mental state, promoting healthy sleep.

If you make meditation a part of your Yogic practice, you may find that allotting five to ten minutes to it is enough, which should be performed at the very end. However, when meditating independently from your Yogic practice, a fifteen to twenty-minute time frame is optimal and will yield the best results. Be mindful that the more time you devote to it, the better your results will be.

Meditations are usually performed while sitting, although you can meditate while standing, walking, or laying down as well. Although, beginners should avoid lying down while attempting to meditate since drifting off into sleep is common with inexperienced people.

Sukhasana, Siddhasana, and Padmasana are the recommended meditative poses that range depending on your flexibility. When practising these meditative Asanas, you should place your hands on the knees in either the Jnana or Chin Mudras.

Sitting in a chair works as well and is no less effective when attempting to meditate. Beginners may find it the best option since chairs provide the necessary support for the back and spine to focus more on the meditation process itself. You can kneel on the floor as well, with or without a cushion for your knees, whatever you find most comfortable.

Whatever posture you choose, the key is for the back and spine to be held straight during the meditation while keeping your hands on the sides, enabling the optimal channelling of Pranic and Chakric energies. Also, when you are upright, the body is most relaxed and steady, which heightens your ability to concentrate and go inwards.

After choosing the meditation posture and your concentration point, the next step to focus on is breathing. The Pranayama Yogic Breathing technique is optimal, where attention is placed on Diaphragmatic and Thoracic breathing since expanding the abdomen will maximize oxygen intake while grounding your inner energies. This type of breathing activates the entire Chakric system, including the lowest two Chakras, Muladhara and Swadhisthana. People that naturally breathe only through the chest involve the higher and middle Chakras while leaving the crucial Earth and Water Chakras mostly unused, resulting in an unbalanced mental state that gives rise to stress and anxiety.

Breathing allows you to control the process of meditation; hence be mindful of your inhale and exhale the entire time. Your breath should be slow, deep, and rhythmic. Make sure to keep a relaxed and calm composure. If you lose control over your breath, don't panic; instead, bring it back into control and resume your rhythm.

While meditating, you will find that your thoughts wander frequently. Do not be alarmed; it is a natural part of the process. In fact, the harder you focus on your chosen object, especially with the eyes closed, your Ego will do everything in its power to sabotage your attempts. Meditating is not about quieting the Ego's thoughts but about learning not to listen to them by maintaining focus on the task at hand.

Mantra meditations are helpful for beginners since they allow you to redirect your thoughts instead of emptying your mind by silencing them. When you find yourself distracted by your thoughts, return to your chosen point of focus or divert your mind by placing your attention back on your Mantra. You can also use your breath to gain back control over the mind by redirecting your attention to it when the mind wanders.

In the beginning, you may feel uncomfortable while meditating. Your body will twitch, cramp up, your legs will fall asleep, or you will develop impatience and even agitation. Do not be alarmed when this happens since it is a sign that your meditation is working. I have found that while learning to meditate, the first hump to get over is learning how to relax your body since it is the Ego that uses the body to distract you and deter you from your goal. You will find that the more times you repeat the meditation process, the easier it will get.

When your meditation begins to work, the Ego will lose grasp over the mind, for the time being, resulting in an elevated state of consciousness. The effect will be a silent and calm mind with pure thoughts in the background devoid of personal meaning. When you have reached this critical point, maintain it as long as you can. The more times you can get yourself to this point during meditation, the easier it will become to tune out of your Ego and raise the vibration of your consciousness. After some time, you may develop the natural ability to do this even without meditation, which will enable you to contact your Higher Self instantaneously to receive its guidance and wisdom.

Finally, work on purifying your mind in daily life. The more you develop a strong character and a moral and ethical nature, the meditation process becomes more accessible. Be persistent and determined to push through in your meditations, even if it seems you are not getting anywhere. If you give up too early, you forfeit the incredible benefits of meditation, which are endless. As the day follows the night, know that you will reach the goal of your meditations if you keep at it regularly and follow the prescribed steps.

CANDLE FLAME MEDITATION (TRATAKA)

Trataka in Sanskrit means "look" or "gaze," since this practice involves gazing steadily at a small object such as a black dot, candle flame, a statue of a Deity, and a geometrical drawing such as a mandala or Yantra. A steady flame from a candle (Figure 143) is a natural magnet for the eyes and mind and is considered the most practical and safe. As such, it is most widely used by Yogis.

Trataka is a Hatha Yoga technique that comes under the category of Shatkarma (Sanskrit for "six actions"), which are six groups of purification practices of the body via Yogic means. The aim of Shatkarmas is to create harmony between the Ida and Pingala Nadis, thereby creating a balance between your mental, emotional, and physical states. Trataka is the Shatkarma science of vision.

The eyes are the "windows of the Soul," the medium through which our minds communicate with the external environment. They allow in Light, illuminating the inner Self. Trataka is a technique that lets us look within our minds and Souls through the eyes. Since our minds are constantly engaging with what our eyes look at, Trataka's single-pointed awareness allows us to calm the subconscious mind, powered by the Ego. As the Ego goes into neutral, its continual thought patterns slow down, which allows the consciousness to rise and enter higher states of mind.

Stilling the mind and its thought patterns is a prerequisite for meditation (Dhyana). By focusing your gaze on a candle flame, you are activating Ajna Chakra, which not only has a calming effect on the mind but is the doorway to higher states of consciousness. As such, with regular Trataka practice, one's psychic abilities heighten, as does intuition, enabling higher levels of understanding of the mysteries of Creation.

Figure 143: Candle Flame Meditation (Trataka)

With Trataka, the mind becomes purified and invigorated, enhancing one's concentration (Dharana) and eradicating all issues associated with the eyes and vision. In addition, heart and respiration rate and the activity of other organs slow down, promoting rejuvenation via one's Pranic energy.

Trataka balances the Sympathetic and Parasympathetic Nervous Systems, relieving nervous tension. Also, dormant areas of the brain get stimulated with regular Trataka practice, while activity-dominant areas get a chance to recharge themselves, promoting a healthy brain. Finally, regular Trataka practice improves sleep quality by calming the mind while treating depression and other mental and emotional issues.

Trataka should be practised at the end of your Yoga sequence, after Asanas, Pranayamas, Mudras, and Bandhas. When practised on its own, it is best performed in the morning, when the mind is quiet, and eyes are more active. It can also be performed at night, before sleep. Avoid Trataka on a full stomach, as is the case with all Yogic practices.

To begin the Trataka meditation, sit in a dark room where you will be undisturbed for the exercise duration. Then, light a candle and place it on a small table approximately two to three feet in front of you at eye level (Figure 144). Make sure there is no draft in the vicinity that can affect the movement of the candle flame.

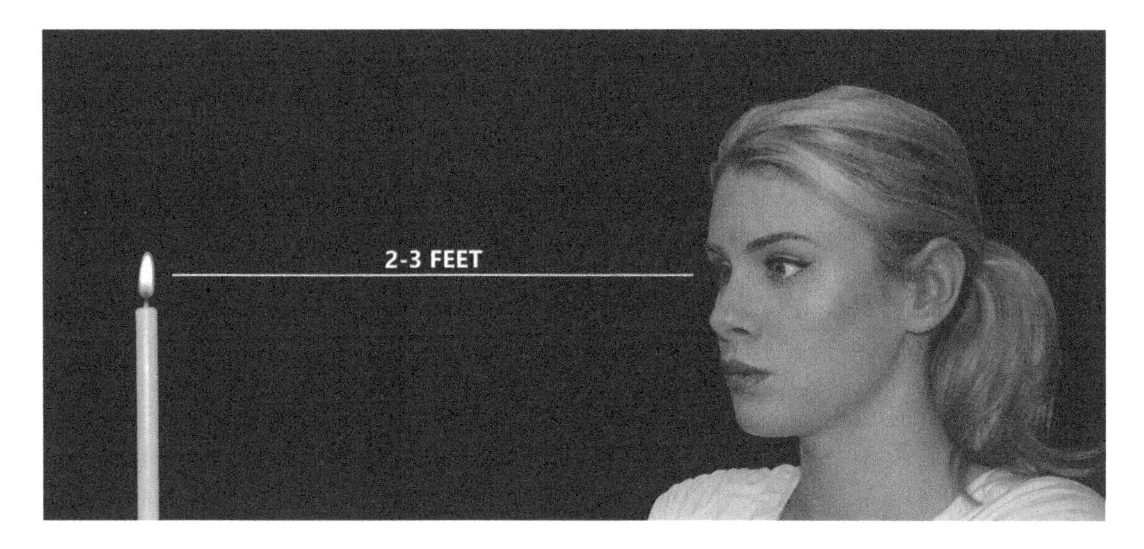

Figure 144: Candle Flame Placement

Sit in any comfortable meditation Asana with your hands on your knees in either Jnana or Chin Mudras. Your spine and head should be held straight. Close your eyes now while relaxing your body, especially the eyes. Ensure that the body is kept steady throughout the exercise.

Open your eyes now and start gazing at the candle flame. Your ideal gazing spot is the red tip of the wick. Maintain the gaze for as long as you can while avoiding blinking or moving the eyeballs in any way. Do not strain the eyes as the tension may cause them to flicker. Stop if the eyes start to water.

By becoming one with the flame, you should lose awareness of all bodily sensations. Your Being will become externalized, drawing you away from all distractive mind-chatter. If the mind begins to wander and your concentration lowers, bring the focus back on the candle flame.

After one to two minutes, close your eyes and gaze at the after-image of the flame in the space before you. If the after-image begins to move side to side or up and down, you can stabilize it by focusing on it harder. When the image starts to fade, bring it back through memory. When it is completely gone, open your eyes and begin gazing at the candle flame again.

Repeat this process three to four times if you are a beginner, taking no more than two minutes in total. When you are ready to end the exercise, rub your hands together for five seconds to generate Pranic energy and then place them on your eyes for ten seconds to absorb it. Always end the Trataka meditation in this way, which provides healing energy to your eyes.

As you get more experienced with the Trataka meditation, increase its duration up to ten minutes. People who have insomnia, depression, or other mental and emotional issues should devote up to twenty minutes to this exercise.

Note that people suffering from glaucoma, epilepsy, or severe eye ailments should not practice Trataka. Instead, they can substitute their point of focus with a black dot, performed in a well-lit room. Although meditating on a black dot will yield similar benefits as Trataka, it is less potent since it omits the focus on the after-image, which effectively opens the Mind's Eye with regular use.

YOGA AND THE FIVE ELEMENTS

Yoga helps us purify and balance the Five Elements of Earth, Water, Air, Fire, and Spirit (Space). Doing so restores these Elements to their optimal health within the body and unfolds our inner powers and abilities that correspond with each Element. However, since each of the Five Elements is responsible for different structures in the body, disease and psychological suffering may occur if any Element becomes impure or falls out of balance with another Element.

Since the Earth Element ("Bhumi" in Sanskrit) relates to all solids, it corresponds with the physical body, namely the skeletal and muscular systems. The Earth Element includes all tissues in the body, including the skin, teeth, nails, and hair. The physical body is the vehicle of our consciousness and our foundation that grounds us to Planet Earth.

The Water Element ("Jala" in Sanskrit) relates to all fluids; 60% of our physical body consists of water, which moves through us via our circulatory system. We can also find water in our brain, heart, lungs, muscles, kidneys, and even bones. In addition, our blood, sweat, saliva, urine, semen, and vaginal and uterine fluids also contain water. Our physical and mental health depends on our body's water flow since the Water Element regulates consciousness.

The Fire Element relates to digestion and metabolism and is concerned with hunger, thirst, and our need for sleep. Fire is called "Agni" in Sanskrit, the God of Fire in Hinduism. In the practice of Asanas, Agni refers to the internal warmth and heat that is generated in specific postures. The Fire Element relates to our Souls, our source of Light that has the power to create and destroy.

The Air Element ("Pavan" in Sanskrit) relates to our respiratory system and is concerned with expanding and contracting Pranic energy in the body. Prana is Light energy, the Life Force that all living organisms require for survival. The air around us carries Pranic energy; the mere act of breathing brings Prana into the body. Pranic energy is also needed to power the mind. For this reason, breath control (Pranayama) is essential in all Yogic practices since one of the aims of Yoga is to focus the mind and become Self-aware.

Spirit/Space Element ("Akasha" in Sanskrit) powers our inner cognitive functions. It is our source of love, truth, wisdom, inspiration, and faith. However, Spirit energy can become corrupted through the absence of reason and illogical thinking, which creates fear. Our greatest fear relates to survival on the Physical Plane, as our primal fear of death. We fear death because we cannot know with certainty what happens when we die since we have no memories beyond this life. As it is Eternal and Timeless, Spirit gives us faith in the afterlife—the continuation of our existence beyond death. The best way to experience Spirit energy is by silencing the mind and going deep within. Meditation is the most optimal way to tune into the Spirit within us to induce peace of mind and bliss while bringing inspiration into our daily life.

ACTIVATING AND BALANCING THE ELEMENTS

There is a natural order of the Elements in the body. While engaged in Asana, Pranayama, Mudra, Mantra, and meditation, practising conscious awareness of the Elements in the body allows us to channel Pranic energy into their corresponding Chakric centres. By activating our Elemental powers, we can achieve balance in mind, body, and Soul.

The Earth and Water Elements are below the navel. Whenever we focus our attention on our pelvic region, whether through movement, meditation, or breathing techniques, we stimulate these two Elements into action.

Stationary Asanas facilitate stability by deepening our connection with the Earth. As our physical body gets grounded, we establish our physical foundation, thereby connecting with the Earth Element. Our muscles become supple while the joints become steady. The body itself becomes strong and firm. Asanas connect us to our feet and become aware of our body language and movements. The mind becomes grounded and focused. Since stationary Asanas slow the metabolic fire, they cool down the body and stabilize the mind.

Transitioning from one Asana to the next takes on a flowing action as we attempt to move fluidly through our movements. Our ability to hold an Asana and then let it go allows our minds to become adaptable from one moment to the next. The grace and resilience accompanying Asana practice enable us to connect with the Water Element. Our consciousness becomes more open and aware of our surroundings, taking us out of our minds and attuning us to the present moment.

The Fire Element is placed in the middle of the torso, in the Solar Plexus area. Generally, the Fire Element gets activated through dynamic Asanas that involve movement and flow. However, there is a breaking point in stationary Asanas when the body begins generating heat, making the body tremble, inducing sweat. This breaking point is when the Ego and mind want to quit holding the Asana. Invoking the necessary energy and willpower to continue will facilitate an even more significant increase in the body's Fire Element energy, resulting in burning out the toxins from the other Elements. According to Yogis, some Asanas increase the digestive fire to such a degree that they can remove diseases in the body entirely.

The Air Element is in the middle of the chest and is our primary centre of Pranic energy. Our muscles, joints, and other supportive tissues expand when we breathe. As a result, our mind opens up through different Pranayama techniques while the body becomes light as a feather.

The mere act of breathing stimulates the Air Element into action, although with controlled breathing, we can focus Pranic energy into any area of our body to facilitate healing. Breath control allows the individual to focus their Pranic energy during the practice of Asanas. Prana is powerful in cleansing the body of toxins since it activates the purifying Fire Element. The Water Element gets stimulated if we focus the Pranic energy into our abdomen area, such as through Diaphragmatic Breathing.

The Element of Spirit, or Space, is in the head and is most accessible through meditation techniques, especially ones that utilize the Mind's Eye. When we perform Asanas and Pranayama techniques with grace, focus, and conscious awareness of our movements, thoughts, and emotions, we infuse love, care, and dedication into our practice which activates the Spirit Element.

Utilizing a balanced sequence of Asanas that include movement and stillness has tremendous benefits in balancing the Elements. It allows us to regulate the Fire Element and harmonize the Earth and Air Elements, which are natural enemies—as the body deals with grounding, the mind deals with thoughts. While one is solid (Earth), the other is Etheric (Air). Balancing the body and mind allows one to connect with the Soul, which seeks unity with the Spirit.

Asanas make the body and mind firm and grounded while making the limbs flexible. Flexible limbs allow a more significant movement of Pranic energy through the Nadis that run through them. When the Air Element is optimized in the body, we can add the necessary fuel to the Water and Fire Elements. A flexible body has great benefits for one's Chakric system, which is one reason why Asanas are so attractive to the general population.

***

An efficient and simple way to balance the Five Elements is with Hand Mudras (Figure 145). In addition to increasing or decreasing the Elements, each Hand Mudra has added mind-body benefits, as mentioned in their descriptions. To perform the Hand Mudras for the Five Elements, follow the instructions outlined on page 312.

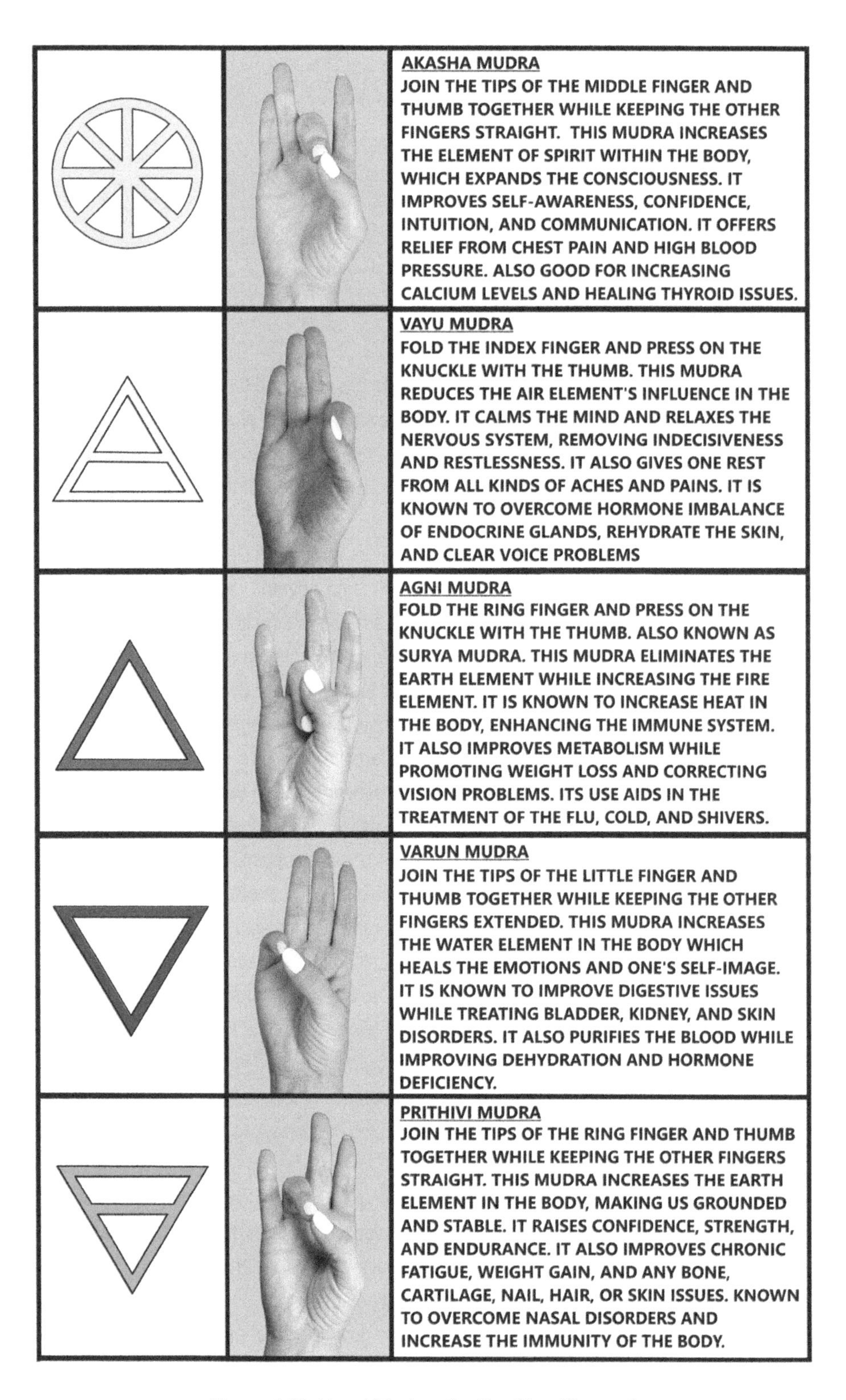

Figure 145: Hand Mudras for the Five Elements

AYURVEDA

The holistic medicine of Ayurveda dates back to the Vedic era at around the same time as Yoga was developed. Although seemingly unrelated, Yoga and Ayurveda share the same culture, philosophy, language, and methodology and are considered sister sciences by Hindus. While Yogic practices deal with harmonizing our mind, body, and Soul, Ayurveda provides an understanding of our physical and mental constitutions and how diet and lifestyle affect our bodies and minds.

Ayurveda's basis is the theory of the "Tridosha" (Sanskrit for the "Three Doshas), the three forces or "humours" in the body—Vata (wind), Pitta (bile), and Kapha (phlegm). Vata governs movement in the body, Pitta governs digestion and nutrition, and Kapha is the energy that forms the body's structure, mass, and fluids. While the Three Doshas primarily influence our physical body, they also have subtle counterparts that affect the mind and the Five Koshas: Prana, Tejas, and Ojas. The activities of our bodies and minds are dependent on the proper functioning of the Three Doshas. When they are out of balance, they contribute to disease processes.

The Tridosha are also responsible for the individual preferences in foods, including flavours and temperatures. They govern the creation, maintenance, and destruction of body tissue and the elimination of waste products from the body. They are also responsible for psychological processes, from negative fear-based emotions to loving ones.

Ayurveda also includes the science of the 108 Marmas or energy points in the body. Marma points are vital points in the body that are infused by Pranic energy and influenced by consciousness. There are many benefits to working with Marma points, including but not limited to: clearing psychological and emotional blocks, improving circulation and energy flow, alleviating muscle pain and joint stiffness, and relieving tension and anxiety.

The essences of the Three Doshas arise from the Five Great Elements, called the "Panchamahabhuta" in Ayurveda (Sanskrit). Each of the Three Doshas is a combination of two of the Five Elements: Vata is Air (Vayu) and Spirit (Akasha), Pitta is Fire (Agni) and Water (Jala), and Kapha is Earth (Prithivi) and Water (Jala), as shown in Figure 146. The Three Doshas depend on one another for balance and health of mind and body. For example, the air principle kindles bodily fire while water controls it, preventing bodily tissues from burning up. Air also moves the water; without Vata Dosha, Pitta and Kapha are immobile.

People can also be Bi-Doshic or even Tri-Doshic, meaning they share qualities with two or three Doshic types. Thus, there are a total of seven types of constitutions in Ayurveda: Vata, Pitta, Kapha, Vata-Pitta, Pitta-Kapha, Vata-Kapha, and Vata-Pitta-Kapha. Understanding the Doshas allows us to balance our inner energies and align our Koshas, improving our psychological, mental, and emotional health.

However, even as we are fated to live under the specific governance of particular Elements in this lifetime, we may still fluctuate in the Doshas when significant changes occur in our psyche, environment, diet, climate, etc. Thus, under certain circumstances and conditions, one Dosha will predominate, while in other situations, another will.

The most important principle to keep in mind when working with the Doshas is that like increases like, while opposites balance one another. Therefore, food, weather, and situations that have similar characteristics as the Doshas will increase their energies, while those with opposite characteristics will decrease them. The same concept applies to Yogic practices like Asanas, Pranayamas, and Hand Mudras, which can either balance a Dosha or aggravate it, depending on the nature and mechanics of the exercise performed.

Figure 146: The Five Elements and the Three Doshas

THE THREE DOSHAS

Vata Dosha

As the energy of movement in the mind and body, Vata Dosha is associated with the Air Element. Vata is dry, cold, light, mobile, active, hard, fine, rough, erratic, changeable, and clear. On a subtle level, Vata relates to Pranic energy responsible for all psycho-physical functions in the body. Prana is carried in the body by the Five Prana Vayus, each playing a specific role in harmonizing the mind and body. Vata is considered the most powerful of the Three Doshas since it carries both Pitta and Kapha.

Vata regulates all movement processes in the body at a microcellular and macroscopic level. Breathing, blinking of the eyelids, movements in the muscles and tissues, and heart pulsations are all governed by Vata Dosha. In addition, Vata governs catabolism, the process of breaking down large molecules into smaller ones to be used as energy. Air Element-related inner processes, like imagination and creativity, are influenced by Vata, including emotions such as inspiration and anxiety.

Vata types are governed by the second sheath of the material self, the vital body—Pranamaya Kosha. Vata's area of operation is the lower part of the trunk that includes the large intestine and the pelvic cavity (Figure 147). It also works through the bones, skin, ears and thighs. If the body develops an excess of Vata energy, it accumulates in these areas.

Autumn is known as the Vata season for its cool and crisp weather. People with Vata Dosha are usually physically undeveloped. They are thin and lean with prominent joints and visible veins and muscle tendons. Vata types tend to have an innate innocence and seek a Spiritual life. They enjoy meeting new people, doing creative activities, and experiencing new environments.

Vatas are highly mentally active, quick-witted, humorous, clever, and innovative. They are strongly influenced by Planetary and Moon cycles, the weather, the people they surround themselves with, and the foods they eat. Since they tend to have colder than average body temperature, Vatas enjoy hot, humid weather.

Vatas are proficient at multitasking, although they have issues with commitments and completing projects. They are generally ungrounded, which makes them forgetful, moody, stressed, and have trouble sleeping. They often eat heavy foods to ground and tranquillize their active minds and ingest stimulants like coffee and sugar not to burn out since they have low physical stamina. Vatas are prone to digestive issues and poor blood circulation while having naturally lower than average immunity.

According to Ayurveda, a Vata-dominant person should implement meditation, Yogic practices, and other calming and balancing activities in their daily schedule. They need to keep their bodies warm by avoiding cold weather and exercising, including performing cardiovascular activities. Vatas should spend time in nature regularly to ground themselves and go to sleep before 10 PM to ensure a good night's sleep. Like all Doshic types, a Vata-dominant person needs to implement a healthy diet and avoid foods that aggravate their condition. (Consult Table 5.) Finally, Vata types would benefit from drinking warm beverages often while avoiding stimulants, such as coffee, alcohol, chocolate, and other sugars.

Pitta Dosha

Pitta is the energy of transformation and is therefore aligned with the Fire Element. Pitta is hot, oily, light, mobile, fluid, sharp, and sour-smelling. It governs digestion, absorption, and nutrition assimilation while regulating body heat, skin colouration, and visual perception. Pitta's subtle form is Tejas or Agni, the Fire of the mind that is responsible for willpower, confidence, intelligence, understanding, reasoning, focus, and self-discipline.

Pitta relates to the principle of metabolism that deals with converting food into useable energy that runs cellular functions. Metabolism is broken down into two processes—catabolism and anabolism, which are governed by Vata and Kapha Doshas.

Pitta types are ruled by the mind-body, the third sheath of the material Self—Manomaya Kosha. Pitta's area of operation is the central area of the trunk that contains the stomach, liver, spleen, gall bladder, duodenum, and pancreas (Figure 147). Most Ayurvedic schools also attribute the small intestine to Pitta instead of Vata since it operates in conjunction with the digestive fire. In addition, Pitta works through the sweat glands, blood, fat, eyes, and skin. If there is pain anywhere near the Solar Plexus in any organs described above, Pitta energy may be imbalanced.

Summer is known as the season of Pitta because of its hot weather and sunny days. Pitta types are usually of average height and weight, with a toned body and moderate frame. They have good blood circulation and healthy skin and hair. Since Pittas are dominated by the Fire Element, they are inherently self-determined, motivated, competitive, goal-oriented, tenacious, intense, and irritable. Pittas are athletic and have an easy time putting on muscle. As natural-born leaders prone to aggression and conflict, they are often challenged by negative emotions such as doubt, anger, hate, and jealousy.

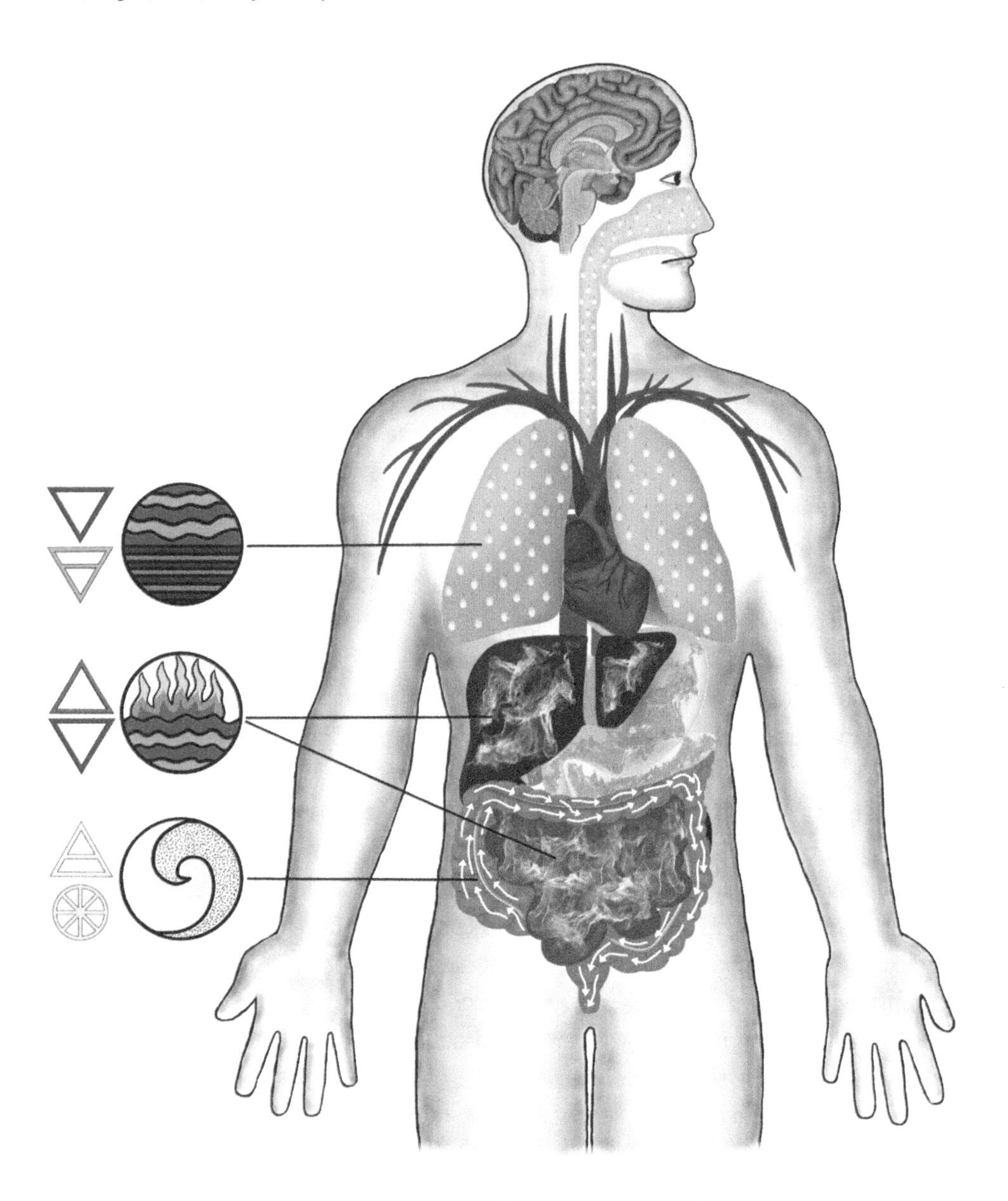

Figure 147: The Three Doshas and Body Zones

Pittas are generally always hungry with quick metabolisms and are predisposed to mood swings if they don't eat. They often ingest large quantities of food and liquid and enjoy cold drinks. Pittas are sensitive to hot temperatures and are susceptible to skin inflammations, acne, dermatitis, and eczema. Their body temperature is higher than average, and their hands and feet are usually hot. Pittas tend to work too much since they are smart and have a strong desire for success.

Ayurvedic medicine suggests that Pitta-dominant people need to cultivate moderation in all things and not take life too seriously. They need to make time for fun activities to balance their work-life, which often dominates. Pittas should avoid extreme heat while implementing a healthy diet. (Table 5). Daily meditation, Yogic practices, and other calming and balancing Spiritual activities are recommended for Pittas to tranquillize their irritable temperament.

Kapha Dosha

As the Archetypal Mother Earth energy, Kapha Dosha provides the material for physical existence, bringing solidity to the subtle Elements in the body. Kapha is cold, wet, oily, heavy, slow, dull, static, soft, dense, and cloudy. It relates to bodily water that gives our body resistance to the outside Elements to maintain longevity on a cellular level. Kapha provides skin moisture, joint lubrication, brain and nervous system protection, immunity to diseases, and wound healing.

Kapha's subtle form is called Ojas, which is Sanskrit for "vigour." Ojas links consciousness and Matter; it is the vital fluid-like energy of the Water Element that supports the mind's functions. Ojas is responsible for memory retention. It supplies us with mental strength, endurance, and powers of concentration.

Kapha types are ruled by the food body, the first layer of the material Self—Annamaya Kosha. Its area of operation is primarily the lungs, although Kapha is also present in the nostrils, throat, sinuses, and bronchi (Figure 147). Water Element-related emotions such as love, calmness, and forgiveness are associated with Kapha Dosha and negative feelings like greed and envy. Kapha has a direct influence on Ego attachments.

The season of Kapha is spring, when things are most fertile, and plant life begins to grow again. Kaphas usually have well-developed bodies with thick bones and strong body frames. They have low but regular appetites and slow-acting metabolisms and digestive systems. They tend to gain weight, so they need to exercise regularly. The influence of the passive Elements of Water and Earth makes them emotionally and mentally stable, loyal, and compassionate. They rarely get upset and think before they act. As such, they journey through life in a slow, deliberate manner.

Kapha types have a systematic approach to life; they generally like to plan things out instead of being whimsical like Vatas. They have powerful empathic abilities and strong sexual energy. Kaphas are patient, trusting, calm, wise, romantic, and have healthy immune systems. However, they are prone to breathing issues like allergies and asthma and have a higher risk of heart disease and mucous build-up than other Doshic types. In addition, since the Water Element predominates, Kaphas retain information well and are thoughtful in word and deed. They emotionally relate to the world, making them susceptible to depression and lack of motivation.

In Ayurveda, a Kapha-dominant person is advised to focus on regular, daily exercise, a healthy diet (Table 5), and maintaining a warm body temperature. In addition, they should fill their time with activities that inspire and motivate them while establishing a regular sleep routine since Kapha types are known to oversleep.

TABLE 4: Ayurvedic Constitution Chart (Three Doshas)

Aspect of Constitution	Vata Type (Air and Spirit)	Pitta Type (Fire and Water)	Kapha Type (Water and Earth)
Height & Weight	Tall or Very Short, Low Weight	Constant Weight, Medium Height	Short but Sometimes Tall, Heavy, Gains Weight Easily
Frame	Thin, Lean, Slim	Medium, Toned	Large, Stocky, Well-Built
Skin	Rough, Dull, Dark, Easily Cracks, Dry, Cool	Soft, Fair, Rosy, Oily, Warm, Freckles and Moles	Smooth, Pale, Light, Moist, Oily, Cool, Thick
Eyes	Sunken, Small, Dry, Brown, Raises Eyebrows	Sharp, Piercing, Green, Gray, Light Brown	Big, Attractive, Blue, Thick Eyelashes, Gentle Look
Lips	Small, Thin Lips, Cracking	Thick, Medium, Soft, Red	Large, Smooth, Rosy
Hair	Dry, Thin, Dark, Frizzy	Fine, Straight, Oily, Smooth, Blonde or Red	Thick, Curly, Wavy, Dark or Light
Teeth	Very Small or Big, Irregular, Protruding, Gaps	Medium Sized, Soft, Bleeding Gums	Full, Strong, White, Well-Formed
Nails	Dry, Rough, Brittle	Thin, Smooth, Reddish	Big, Soft, White, Glossy
Body Temperature	Less than Normal; Palms and Feet Cold	More than Normal; Palms, Feet, and Face Hot	Normal; Palms and Feet Slightly Cold
Joints	Visible, Stiff, Unsteady, Crack Easily	Loose, Moderately Hidden	Firm, Strong, Large, Well-Hidden
Sweat	Normal	Very Easily, Strong Smell	Slow to Start but Profuse
Stool	Hard, Dry, Twice a Day	Soft, Loose, 1-2 Times/Day	Well-Formed, Once a Day
Urination	Sparse	Profuse, Yellow	Moderate, Clear
Immune System	Low, Variable	Moderate, Sensitive to Heat	Good, High
Endurance	Poor, Easily Exhausted	Moderate but Focused	Steady, High
Appetite & Thirst	Variable, Fast Intake of Food and Drink	High, Excessive, Must Eat Every 3-4 Hours	Moderate, Constant, Can Tolerate Hunger and Thirst
Taste Preference	Sweet, Sour, Salty	Sweet, Bitter, Astringent	Pungent, Bitter, Astringent
Physical Activity	Very Active, Gets Tired Easily	Moderate, Gets Tired Easily	Lethargic, Moves Slowly, Does Not Tire Easily
Temperament/ Emotions	Fearful, Changeable, Adaptable, Uncertain	Courageous, Motivated, Confident, Irritable	Calm, Loving, Greedy, Attached, Self-Conscious
Sensitivities	Cold, Dryness, Wind	Heat, Sunlight, Fire	Cold, Dampness
Speech	Fast, Frequent, Unfocused, Misses Point Easily	Focused, Direct, Good at Arguments, Goal-Oriented	Slow, Steady, Soft, Firm Speech, Not Big Talker
Mind State	Hyperactive, Restless	Aggressive, Intelligent	Peaceful, Slow, Steady
Personality	Creative, Imaginative	Intelligent, Willful, Efficient	Caring, Patient, Thoughtful
Social	Make and Changes Often	Friends are Work Related	Long-Lasting Friendships
Memory	Low, Forgets Things Easily	Moderate, Average Memory	High, Remembers Well
Schedule	Irregular Schedule	Long Workday	Good at Keeping Routine
Dreams	Skies, Winds, Flying, Jumping, Running	Fire, Lightning, Violence, War, Colourful Views	Water, River, Ocean, Lake Swimming, Colourful Views
Sleep	Sparse, Interrupted, Disturbed, Less than 6hrs	Variable, Sound, 6-8hrs	Excess, Heavy, Prolonged, 8hrs or More
Finances	Extravagant Spender, Spends Money Frivolously	Average Spender, Focus on Luxuries	Frugal, Saves Money, Only Spends When Needed
Total	=	=	=

HOW TO DETERMINE YOUR DOSHIC RATIO

Each human being has a unique ratio of the Three Doshas, depending on which one of the three Elements of Air, Water, and Fire is dominant in us. In Sanskrit, the personal blueprint of energies that rule us in life is called "Prakriti," meaning "the original or natural form of condition of something—its primary substance." The current state of the Three Doshas, after the moment of conception, is the "Vikruti," meaning "after Creation." It refers to our constitution after being exposed to and altered by the environment. The Vikruti defines our Doshic imbalance.

There are three ways to determine your Doshic ratio, two of which you can do on your own using this book and access to the internet. The other method is to see an Ayurvedic practitioner who will use pulse and tongue reading as diagnostic tools. If you want the most accurate diagnosis, I recommend all three.

The first method is to use the chart in Table 4 and diagnose yourself. Starting at the top of the chart with "Height & Weight," choose which one of the Three Doshas descriptions best describes you. Once you have selected it, put a checkmark at the bottom of one of the Vata, Pitta, or Kapha columns in the final row where it says "Total." Then, continue with the second aspect, "Frame." and do the same. And so on, until you have finished going over the entire chart. Finally, add up the totals for each of the Three Doshas and put a number after the equals sign in the last row.

The Dosha with the highest number will generally indicate your primary constitution, while the Dosha with the second-highest number will indicate your second dominant Dosha. If you have two Doshas that are relatively equal, you are Bi-Doshic or even Tri-Doshic if you have a similar ratio between all Three Doshas. If one of the Doshas has a significantly higher number than the other two, as is often the case, then that is your dominant Dosha.

The second "do it yourself" method uses Vedic Astrology to determine your Doshic ratio, which you can compare with your results from the chart in Table 4. Since the science of Ayurveda aligns with Vedic Astrology, you need to obtain a Vedic Astrology Birth Chart, which you can find online. Keep in mind that you will get an entirely different readout from a Vedic Astrology Birth Chart than one through Western Astrology. However, don't let that confuse nor alarm you because you will be focusing primarily on the Ascendant and the Houses.

Vedic Astrology is more accurate at evaluating the Macrocosmic energy influences associated with your time of birth since it is aligned with the actual positions of the Star Constellations. So, to get this right, you need your exact time of birth. In Western Astrology, your time of birth is second in importance to your day of birth since Western Astrology prioritizes the Sun Sign. Using Vedic Astrology to determine your Doshic ratio is an age-old, proven method used by Hindus and other Ayurveda practitioners since its inception.

Before explaining how to gauge your Vedic Astrology Birth Chart, you need to know the Doshic nature of the Planets and Zodiac Signs. Vata Dosha is represented by Gemini, Capricorn, Aquarius, and Virgo because these four signs are ruled by Mercury (Gemini and Virgo) and Saturn (Capricorn and Aquarius). Mercury and Saturn are Vata Planets since they correspond with the Air Element.

Pitta is represented by Aries, Leo, and Scorpio as these three Signs are ruled by Mars (Aries and Scorpio) and the Sun (Leo). Mars and the Sun are Pitta Planets since they correspond with the Fire Element. And lastly, Kapha is represented by Taurus, Cancer, Libra, Sagittarius, and Pisces since these five signs are ruled by Venus (Taurus and Libra), Jupiter (Sagittarius and Pisces) and the Moon (Cancer). These three are Kapha Planets since they correspond with the Water Element.

As for the last two Navagrahas, Rahu's energy influence is akin to Saturn, only more subtle. Therefore, it relates to the Vata Dosha. On the other hand, Ketu's energy influence resembles Mars, although subtler, making it correspond with Pitta Dosha.

I will be using my Vedic Astrology Birth Chart (Figure 148) as an example to show you how you can determine your Dosha. I am using a South Indian Birth Chart whose presentation is slightly different than a North Indian one, although the results are the same. Keep in mind that I am showing you a basic method of doing this using a Vedic Astrology Birth Chart (Rishi Chart), which provides general information regarding the location of Planets. However, I am omitting the Navamsa Chart, which shows the active quality and strength of the Planets.

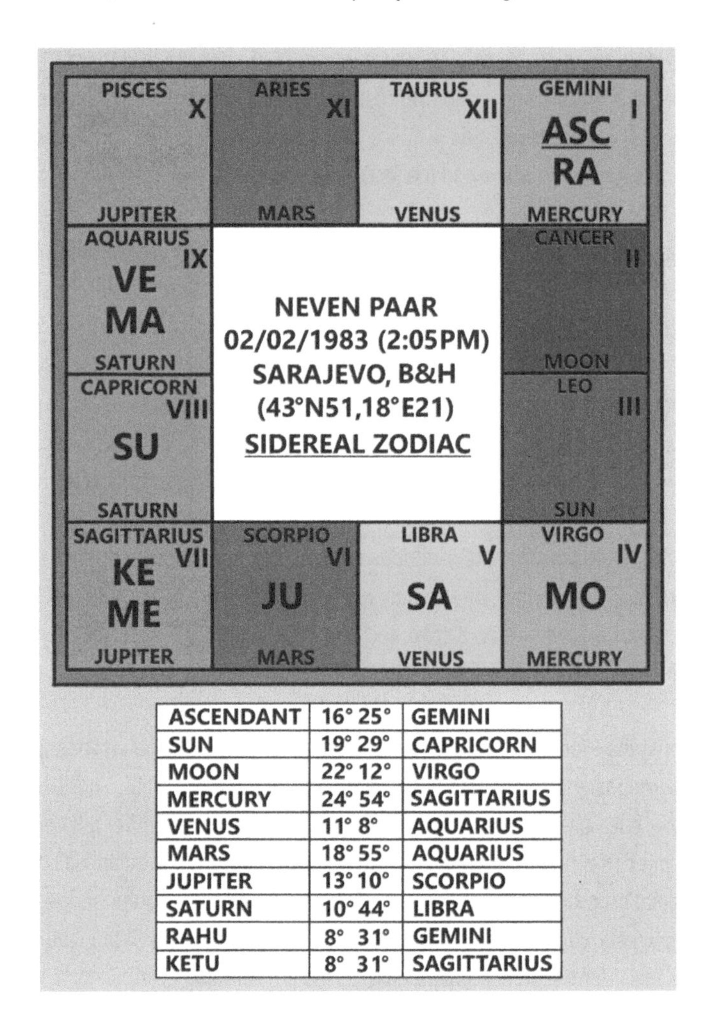

ASCENDANT	16° 25°	GEMINI
SUN	19° 29°	CAPRICORN
MOON	22° 12°	VIRGO
MERCURY	24° 54°	SAGITTARIUS
VENUS	11° 8°	AQUARIUS
MARS	18° 55°	AQUARIUS
JUPITER	13° 10°	SCORPIO
SATURN	10° 44°	LIBRA
RAHU	8° 31°	GEMINI
KETU	8° 31°	SAGITTARIUS

Figure 148: The Author's Vedic Astrology Birth Chart

A full Vedic Astrology Birth Chart generally includes both Charts and the Nakshatra (Lunar Houses). It is a rather complex yet thorough science that requires serious study to be able to interpret an entire Birth Chart. For this reason, I also recommend seeing a trained and skilled Vedic Astrologer to help you read your full Birth Chart so you can get the most optimal results.

Once you have obtained your Birth Chart, first take a look at your Ascendant and determine its Lord or ruling Planet. According to Vedic Astrology, your Ascendant is the most significant influence on you since it is your body. In Sanskrit, the Ascendant is called "Tanur Bhava," meaning "the house of the body." Whatever Zodiac Sign your Ascendant falls into usually represents your dominant Dosha.

Next, look at your Ascendant ruling Planet and what Zodiac Sign it falls into. For example, my Ascendent is Gemini, a Vata Sign whose Lord is Mercury. However, my Mercury is in Sagittarius, a Kapha Sign ruled by Jupiter. So far, my Chart analysis points to a Vata constitution with an influence of Kapha.

Next, look at your First House, see which Planet or Planets are placed there, and determine their Dosha(s). For example, I have Rahu in the First House, a Vata Planet. So now we have another strong indicator that I am a Vata personality, with some influence from Kapha. However, our analysis doesn't end there.

Take a look now at your Moon Sign, which represents your psychological nature, including your thoughts and emotions. Keep in mind that the Moon has a more significant impact on females than males because of the connection between one's feminine nature and the Moon. As you can see, my Moon is in Virgo, which is a Vata Sign whose ruling Planet is Mercury.

Next, take a look at your Sun Sign, which is indicative of your essential vitality and character expression. Males tend to express their Sun Sign more than females because of the connection of one's masculine nature and the Sun. My Sun Sign is in Capricorn, ruled by Saturn, another Vata Planet.

Now you need to look at your Birth Chart as a whole to determine which Planets are dominant overall. While the Ascendant, Moon, and Sun Signs carry the most weight in determining your Doshic ratio, Rahu and Ketu are considered least important. The other Planets are all equal in importance. If a particular Planet is prominent, it will affect all aspects of one's life, including their constitution. Also, you need to pay specific attention to Planets placed in their own Sign.

In my Birth Chart, from the nine Planetary attributions plus the Ascendent, I have an equal balance of Mercury and Saturn (three each), with two Jupiter, one Venus, and one Mars. Therefore, as predicted, my Birth Chart has an abundance of Vata Planets (six), with three Kapha and one Pitta. Also, and most importantly, my Ascendant, Moon, and Sun Signs are all Vata. This indicates that I am a Vata personality with an influence of Kapha and a touch of Pitta.

Finally, take a look at the Planet or Planets in your Sixth House (health and wellness) and Eighth House (death and longevity) to get some insight into Doshic imbalances and disease potential. The Sixth House rules all aspects of one's healthy lifestyle, such as diet, nutrition, exercise, and the pursuit of self-empowerment. For example, in my Birth Chart, I have Jupiter (Kapha) in my Sixth House, which indicates a predisposition to over-indulgence, liver issues, and blood circulation problems. And my Sun (Pitta) in the Eighth House suggests weight gain and blood pressure issues. This points to my Doshic imbalance coming from Kapha and Pitta influences.

So now, how does this information compare with my Western Astrology Birth Chart? Well, since my Sun Sign is an Aquarius, my Moon Sign is Libra, and my Ascendant is Cancer, and Western Astrology prioritizes the Sun Sign, I am of the Air Element constitution, with an influence of Water. Keep in mind that I am using the traditional Zodiacal correspondences with the Four Elements. So, my results match my outcome with Vedic Astrology. However, this is not to say it will coincide for everyone. And remember, the main reason I am prioritizing Vedic Astrology in this case, even though I've studied Western Astrology my whole life, is because it is the sister science of Ayurveda. Thus, we are following the traditional way of determining your Dosha.

As far as the Ayurvedic Constitution Chart in Table 4, one-half of my checkmarks went to Vata Dosha while the other half went to Pitta. Even though my Birth Chart does not reflect a Pitta constitution, since I have constant Kundalini activity in my Body of Light, my physical body feels like it is on fire a lot of the time, which affects me at a cellular level. So now you see why it is crucial to analyze your Birth Chart and the Ayurvedic Constitution Chart—you might not get the same results.

Remember what I said earlier: the Doshas are not fixed. Even if you may be predisposed to one Dosha or several, you may still fluctuate depending on the changes in your psychology, environment, climate, etc. Ayurvedic science is not permanent and unchanging, but it keeps evolving along with you. Therefore, I advise you to connect with your Higher Self and let it be your teacher and guide to be aware of inner changes and adjust accordingly.

AYURVEDIC DIET

The three primary sources of Pranic energy are the Sun (Fire Element), the wind (Air Element), and the Earth below our feet (Water and Earth Elements). The Sun is our main source of Prana, which energises us through its Light rays. The air around us also contains Prana, which we absorb through the lungs and the Chakras. We take in Pranic energy from the Earth as well via our Foot Soles. The Earth also nourishes us through the foods it produces, which contain Pranic energy at varying degrees of vibration. As such, what we eat directly affects us at all levels of consciousness.

The quality of our minds, bodies, and Souls is highly dependent on the essence of the food we bring into the body. Once the food is converted into useable Pranic energy by the digestive system, the Body of Light's thousands of Nadis carry it into every body cell. Herein is the essence of the popular saying, "You are what you eat." As such, finding the proper diet can make the difference between a healthy mind, body, and Soul, or one that is diseased. Although dis-ease can manifest physically, it can be of a mental, emotional, and Spiritual nature as well.

In Ayurveda, our physical and psychological processes are dependent on the proper functioning of the Three Doshas. If they become out of balance, disease processes can manifest on physical and subtle levels. As such, Ayurveda is primarily concerned with the energies of different foods to balance the Doshas. It is not worried about nutritional requirements but that the food is in harmony with our nature. For example, food can either enhance mental processes and peace of mind or disturb them.

Liquid intake is also crucial in Ayurveda since what we drink nourishes our Life Force. For example, stale water, or contaminated water, can disturb our Prana and unsettle our emotions and thoughts. The same goes for alcohol, coffee, and other stimulants. Essentially, everything we take into the body affects us at all levels of consciousness.

The first step to adjusting your diet to optimise your energy system and physical body is to find your Doshic ratio using your Vedic Astrology Birth Chart and Table 4. Other than eating foods that align with the nature of your Doshic ratio or your dominant Dosha(s), there are other factors of food intake to consider. These include the correct preparation of foods and the right combination, the proper amount and frequency of meals and the correct time of day to eat your meals. Another factor is the right attitude of the person preparing the meal. For example, if the meal is made with love, it will resonate with that frequency, which will have a healing effect when ingested. Conversely, food prepared with a negative attitude will contain toxic energy that can harm the system. And you always wondered why eating your mother's or grandmother's cooking always made you feel so good.

Another essential point is to be in a calm mental state while eating the food since food taken in a negative mood can have adverse effects. Think of food as fuel while your digestive and energy systems are the engine and your physical body is the main supporting structure, the vehicle's body. Therefore, harbouring negative energy while bringing fuel into the system can poison the fuel, exacerbating and heightening your negativity, and even imbuing it into body cells and tissue. As such, cellular degeneration and deterioration can occur over time, contributing to disease processes, including cancer.

It would help if you also were mindful of seasons and climate so you can adjust your diet accordingly. For example, an anti-Kapha diet should be followed in the winter and early spring, while an anti-Pitta diet is more appropriate for the summer and late spring. Finally, you should give an anti-Vata diet priority in the fall.

The Bi-Doshic types that have an equal ratio of two Doshas should modify their diet by season. For example, Pitta-Kapha types should follow an anti-Pitta diet in the summer and fall and an anti-Kapha diet in the winter and spring. Conversely, Vata-Kapha's should implement an anti-Vata diet in the summer and fall and an anti-Kapha diet in the winter and spring. Furthermore, the Vata-Pitta types should follow an anti-Vata diet in the fall and winter and an anti-Pitta diet in the spring and summer. Lastly, the Tri-Doshic types who share relatively equal qualities in all three Doshas should follow an anti-Kapha diet in the winter and early spring, an anti-Pitta diet in the summer and late spring, and an anti-Vata diet in the fall.

Depending on the climate of where you live, certain diets will be more appropriate for you, while you should avoid others. For example, damp, cold regions should emphasise an anti-Kapha diet, while hot climates should implement an anti-Pitta diet. Conversely, an anti-Vata diet is most appropriate for cold, dry, windy climates.

Table 5 represents foods you should emphasise in your diet and ones you need to stay away from. Foods that are not listed can be judged by comparing them to related foods in each category. The rule of thumb to follow is that favoured foods reduce the influence of a Dosha, while foods you should avoid increase it. By following your prescribed diet, you are trying to balance your Dosha(s), positively impacting the mind, body, and Soul and preventing disease processes from occurring. Therefore, apply these diets along with other considerations just mentioned.

TABLE 5: Food Guidelines for the Three Doshas

Food Type	Vata Dosha		Pitta Dosha		Kapha Dosha	
	Favour	Avoid	Favour	Avoid	Favour	Avoid
Fruits	_*Most Sweet Fruit_ _*Most Moist Sweet Fruit_ Apricots Avocado Bananas Berries Cherries Dates (fresh) Figs (fresh) Grapefruit Grapes Kiwi Lemons Limes Mango Melons (sweet) Oranges Papaya Peaches Pineapple Plums Raisins (soaked) Prunes (soaked)	_*Most Dried Fruit_ Apples Cranberries Pears Dates (dry) Figs (dry) Persimmon Pomegranates Raisins (dry) Prunes (dry) Watermelon	_*Most Sweet Fruit_ Apples Avocado Berries (sweet) Dates Figs Grapes (red and purple) Limes Mango Melons Oranges (sweet) Pears Pineapple (sweet) Plums (sweet) Pomegranates Prunes Raisins Raspberries	_*Most Sour Fruit_ Apricots Bananas Berries (sour) Cherries (sour) Cranberries Grapefruit Grapes (green) Kiwi Lemons Oranges (sour) Peaches Papaya Persimmon Pineapple (sour) Plums (sour) Strawberries	_*Most Astringent Fruit_ Apples Apricots Berries Cherries Cranberries Figs (dry) Mango Peaches Pears Persimmons Pomegranates Prunes Raisins	_*Most Sweet & Sour Fruit_ Avocado Bananas Dates Figs (fresh) Grapefruit Grapes Lemons Kiwi Mangoes Melons Oranges Papaya Pineapple Plums Watermelon
Vegetables	_*Vegetables Should be Cooked_ Asparagus Beets Cabbage (cooked) Carrots Cauliflower Chillies Cilantro Corn (fresh) Garlic Green Beans Mustard Greens Okra Olives, Black Onions (cooked) Peas (cooked) Potatoes (sweet) Pumpkin Radish (cooked) Seaweed Squash Spinach (cooked) Sprouts Squash Turnips Watercress Yams Zucchini	_*Frozen, Raw, or Dried Vegetables_ Alfalfa Sprouts Artichoke Beet Greens Broccoli Brussel Sprouts Cabbage Cauliflower Celery Eggplant Leafy Greens Lettuce Kale Mushrooms Olives (Green) Onions (raw) Parsley Peas (raw) Peppers (sweet & hot) Potatoes (White) Radish (raw) Spinach (raw) Tomatoes	_*Sweet & Bitter Vegetables_ Artichoke Asparagus Beets (cooked) Broccoli Brussel Sprouts Cabbage Cauliflower Celery Cilantro Corn (fresh) Cucumber Green Beans Jerusalem Kale Leafy Greens Lettuce Mushrooms Okra Olives (Black) Onions (cooked) Parsley Peas (fresh) Peppers (green) Pumpkin Potatoes (white) Sprouts Squash Zucchini	_*Pungent Vegetables_ Beets (raw) Carrots Eggplant Chillies Garlic Horseradish Mustard Greens Olives (Green) Onions (raw) Potatoes (sweet) Radishes Seaweed Spinach Tomatoes Turnips Watercress Yams	_*Most Pungent & Bitter Vegetables_ Artichoke Asparagus Beets Bitter Melon Broccoli Brussel Sprouts Cabbage Carrots Cauliflower Celery Cilantro Chillies Eggplant Garlic Green Beans Kale Leafy Greens Lettuce Mushrooms Mustard Greens Onions Parsley Peas Peppers Radishes Spinach Sprouts Turnips Watercress	_*Sweet & Juicy Vegetables_ Corn (fresh) Cucumber Olives Okra Parsnips Potatoes (sweet) Pumpkin Seaweeds Squash Tomatoes Yams Zucchini

*continued on next page

Food Type	Vata Dosha		Pitta Dosha		Kapha Dosha	
	Favour	Avoid	Favour	Avoid	Favour	Avoid
Grains	Basmati Rice Brown Rice Couscous Durham Flour Oats (cooked) Quinoa Wheat	Barley Buckwheat Corn Crackers Granola Millet Muesli Oats (dry) Pasta Polenta Rye Spelt Wheat Bran	Barley Basmati Rice Blue Corn Brown Rice (long grain) Couscous Crackers Granola Oats (cooked) Pancakes Pasta Quinoa Spelt Wheat Wheat Bran	Bread (with yeast) Brown Rice (short grain) Buckwheat Corn Millet Muesli Oats (dry) Polenta Rye	Barley Buckwheat Corn Crackers Granola Millet Muesli Oats (dry) Polenta Quinoa Rye Spelt Wheat Bran	Basmati Rice Brown Rice Bread (with yeast) Couscous Oats (cooked) Pasta Wheat White Rice
Animal Foods	Beef Chicken (white) Duck Eggs (fried or scrambled) Seafood Turkey (white)	Lamb Pork Rabbit Venison	Chicken (white) Eggs (white) Rabbit Turkey (white) Shrimp (small amount) Venison	Beef Duck Eggs (yolk) Lamb Pork Seafood	Chicken (white) Eggs (scrambled) Rabbit Shrimp Turkey (white) Venison	Beef Chicken (dark) Duck Lamb Pork Seafood Turkey (dark)
Dairy	Butter Buttermilk Cheese Cottage Cheese Cream Cow's Milk Ghee Goat's Cheese Goat's Milk Kefir Milk Sour Cream Rice Milk Yoghurt	Milk (powdered) Goat's Milk (powdered) Ice Cream	Butter (unsalted) Cheese (unsalted) Cottage Cheese Cream Milk Ghee Goat's Milk Goat's Cheese (unsalted) Rice Milk	Butter (salted) Buttermilk Cheese (salted) Ice Cream Kefir Sour Cream Yoghurt	Buttermilk Cottage Cheese Ghee Goat's cheese (unsalted) Goat's Milk Soy Milk	Butter Cheese Milk Cream Ice Cream Kefir Rice Milk Sour Cream Yoghurt
Legumes	Mung Beans Tofu Lentils Urad Dal	Aduki Beans Black-Eyed Peas Chick Peas Fava Beans Kidney Beans Lima Beans Peanuts Pinto Beans Soy Beans Split Peas Tempeh	Aduki Beans Chick Peas Kidney Beans Lima Beans Mung Beans Pinto Beans Soy Beans Split Peas Tempeh Tofu	Lentils Peanuts Tur Dal Urad Dal	Aduki Beans Black-Eyed Peas Kidney Beans Lima Beans Peanuts Mung Beans Pinto Beans Split Peas Soy Beans Tempeh Tofu Tur Dal	Chick Peas Urad Dal
Nuts	Almonds Brazil Nuts Cashews Coconuts Filberts Hazelnuts Macadamia Pecans Pine Nuts Pistachios Walnuts	None	Coconuts	Almonds Brazil Nuts Cashews Filberts Hazelnuts Macadamia Pecans Pine Nuts Pistachios Walnuts	None	Almonds Brazil Nuts Cashews Coconuts Filberts Hazelnuts Macadamia Pecans Pine Nut Pistachios Walnuts

*continued on next page

Food Type	Vata Dosha		Pitta Dosha		Kapha Dosha	
	Favour	Avoid	Favour	Avoid	Favour	Avoid
Seeds	Chia Flax Halva Pumpkin Sesame Sunflower Tahini	Popcorn	Chia Sunflower Tahini	Flax Halva Popcorn Pumpkin Sesame	Chia Flax Popcorn Pumpkin Sunflower	Halva Sesame Tahini
Spices/ Condiments	Basil Bay Leaves Black Pepper Cardamom Cayenne Cloves Chutney Chilli Peppers Coriander Cumin Cinnamon Dill Dulse Fennel Garlic Ginger Ketchup Oregano Mayonnaise Mint Mustard Nutmeg Paprika Rosemary Saffron Sage Sea Salt Soy Sauce Tamarind Turmeric Vinegar	Horseradish	Cardamom Cilantro Chutney (sweet) Cloves Coriander Cumin Dill Dulse Fennel Kombu Mint Rosemary Saffron Tamarind Turmeric	Basil Bay Leaves Black Pepper Cayenne Chili Pepper Cinnamon Chutney (spicy) Garlic Ginger Horseradish Kelp Ketchup Mustard Mayonnaise Nutmeg Oregano Paprika Pickles Sage Sea Salt (in excess) Soy Sauce Tamarind Vinegar	Basil Bay Leaves Black Pepper Cardamom Cayenne Cilantro Cinnamon Cloves Chilli Peppers Chutney (spicy) Coriander Cumin Dill Fennel Garlic Ginger Horseradish Mint Mustard Nutmeg Oregano Paprika Parsley Rosemary Saffron Sage Soy Sauce Turmeric	Chutney (sweet) Kelp Ketchup Mayonnaise Sea Salt Tamarind Vinegar
Sweeteners	Fruit Sugar Honey Cane Sugar Maple Syrup Molasses Raw Sugar	White Sugar	Fruit Sugar Cane Sugar Maple Sugar Raw Sugar White Suger	Honey Molasses	Honey (raw)	Brown Sugar Fruit Sugar Cane Sugar Molasses Maple Syrup White Sugar
Oils	Almond Avocado Canola Coconut Corn Flaxseed Olive Safflower Sesame	None	Coconut Olive Sunflower Almond Canola	Corn Flaxseed Safflower Sesame	Almond Corn Sunflower	Avocado Canola Flaxseed Olive Safflower Sesame

YOGIC PRACTICES TO BALANCE THE DOSHAS

Once you have determined your constitution (Prakriti) using your Vedic Astrology Birth Chart and Table 4, you can use this knowledge to modify your Yogic practice to best fit your needs. As mentioned, most people align with one Doshic type, although it is not uncommon to have traits of several. Regardless, once you have worked out your Vata-Pitta-Kapha ratio or simply your dominant Dosha, you can use that information to determine which Yogic practices are best for you to balance your mind and body.

Asanas can either increase or decrease your Dosha. Some have a grounding and calming effect, while others are energizing. Some Asanas stimulate the digestive system and heat up the body while others cool it down. The same goes for Pranayamas and Hand Mudras. However, some of the more basic Pranayama exercises, including the Four-Fold-Breath (Sama Vritti), can be used by all Doshic types.

Use the following information as general guidelines for working with the Asanas, Pranayamas, and Hand Mudras from this book to get optimal results. (For various Beginner, Intermediate, and Advanced Asanas, refer to pages 312-318.) Also, keep in mind that the guidelines below are not fixed and should be adjusted according to changes in weather, climate, diet, and one's psychology.

Also, not every Yogic exercise is included in the guidelines, which generally means all Doshic types can use it. Before starting any Yogic practice, though, make sure to read its description and precautions thoroughly. Allow your Higher Self to guide you in this process while following the instructions as they are given.

Head Mudras, Postural Mudras, Lock Mudras, and Perineal Mudras are generally concerned with specific Spiritual aims. These include awakening the Chakras, activating the Bindu, utilizing the Ambrosia nectar (Amrita) dripping from the Bindu, stimulating the Kundalini into activity, and ensuring that the Kundalini pierces the Three Granthis on its upwards rise (as in the case of Bandhas). Therefore, all Doshic types should implement their use to obtain their particular goals. In addition, Mantras and meditation techniques also have specific aims that are beneficial for you, irrespective of your Dosha.

Yogic Practices for Vata Dosha

Vata types will significantly benefit from a grounding, calm, and contemplative Asana practice, which will counter their tendency to feel spaced out and agitated. For example, Vrksasana (Tree Pose) and Tadasana (Mountain Pose) plant your feet into the ground, which reduces anxiety and nervousness that Vatas are prone to. Virabhadrasana I and Virabhadrasana II (Warrior I and II) accomplish the same thing while building strength. Utkatasana (Chair Pose) is good to ground the Vata while building heat in the body.

Fast-paced flow sequences (Vinyasas) build heat in the body and aggravate Vata types, who are naturally prone to fatigue and burn-out. Instead, Vatas should move slowly and deliberately using the Hatha Yoga approach that extends the length of time poses are held. In addition, Vatas should approach transitions between poses with conscious awareness instead of being rushed, ensuring that the mind remains balanced and calm. For example, Virabhadrasana III (Warrior III) is a powerful balancing Pose that forces the Vata to focus and concentrate on one point instead of being all over the place with their thoughts.

Poses that work on the colon, intestines, lower back, and pelvis balance Vata types since they bring energy back into the torso base, Vata's area of operation. Since Vatas are prone to constipation, twists and forward bends have a healing effect since they compress the pelvis. Also, hip openers and face-down backbends are beneficial for them.

These include Balasana (Child's Pose), Bhujangasana (Cobra Pose), Paschimottanasana (Seated Forward Bend), Baddha Konasana (Cobbler's Pose), and Malasana (Squat/Garland Pose). Dhanurasana (Bow Pose) also extends the lower back and puts pressure on the pelvis.

Since Vatas naturally have weaker bones, looser ligaments, less fatty padding, and are susceptible to pain, they should avoid some of the more Advanced Asanas like the Salamba Sarvangasana (Shoulderstand), Halasana (Plow Pose), Sirsasana (Headstand), Vasistha-sana (Side Plank), Pincha Mayurasana (Forearm Stand), and Urdhva Danurasana (Wheel Pose).

Because of their unpredictable nature, Vatas should make Asana practise a routine and perform it at certain times on specific days of the week. In addition, they should implement a longer than usual Shavasana (Corpse Pose) when starting and ending a practice because of its grounding effect.

Pranayamas that cool down the body like Sheetali (Cooling Breath), Sheetkari (Hissing Breath), and the Lunar Breath should be avoided. Instead, Vatas can implement Pranayamas that increase heat in the body, like the Solar Breath, Kapalbhati (Skull Shining Breath), and Bhastrika (Bellows Breath) Pranayama. However, they need to be careful with the latter two since they increase energy in the body, which can overstimulate the mind. In addition, Vatas generally suffer from overthinking, anxiety, and stress, which is why they should use specific Pranayamas to soothe and pacify the mind. These include Anulom Vilom (Alternate Nostril Breathing Method#1), Nadi Shodhana (Alternate Nostril Breathing Method#2), Bhramari (Humming Bee Breath), and Ujjayi (Ocean Breath) Pranayama techniques.

Finally, Hand Mudras that increase Vata Dosha are Jnana Mudra, Chin Mudra, and Akasha Mudra. These should be practised if one has a deficiency in Vata Dosha. In contrast, Hand Mudras that decrease Vata are Vayu Mudra and Shunya Mudra.

Yogic Practices for Pitta Dosha

Since Pitta types tend to overheat, they should avoid Yoga poses that cause excessive sweating. In addition, they need to cultivate a calm and relaxed attitude towards their Yoga practice instead of looking at it as a contest since Pittas are drawn to physically demanding postures.

Pitta types will benefit from a cooling, heart-opening Yoga practice performed in a non-competitive way. The Hatha Yoga approach is more appropriate for Pittas over Vinyasa, focusing on more prolonged duration of poses and slow, deliberate transitions. Beginner Poses like Bitilasana (Cow Pose) and Bidalasana (Cat Pose) are good to balance Pitta and should be practised in unison. Standing forward bends and heart-opening poses like Ustrasana (Camel Pose), Sarvangasana (Bridge Pose), and Urdhva Mukha Svanasana (Upward-Facing Dog) help reduce Pitta. Also, Trikonasana (Triangle Pose) and Bhujangasana (Cobra Pose).

The seat of Pitta is the stomach and small intestine, which is why they are susceptible to increased heat in the digestive tract. Forward-folds, twists, and backbends like Balasana (Child's Pose), Dhanurasana (Bow Pose) and Urdhva Dhanurasana (Wheel Pose) help regulate Pitta and extract excess bile. Conversely, side bends like Ardha Matsyendrasana (Seated Spinal Twist) and Parsvottanasana (Intense Side Stretch) aid in relieving excess heat from the internal organs.

Pittas should avoid Hot Yoga (Bikram and Vinyasa) and practise in a cooled down, air-conditioned environment. In addition, they should avoid holding long inverted poses that create a lot of heat in the head. For standing poses, the best ones for Pitta open the hips, including Vrksasana (Tree Pose), Virabhadrasana I and Virabhadrasana II (Warrior I and II), and Ardha Chandrasana (Half Moon). Other beneficial poses that open the hips are Baddha

Konasana (Cobbler's Pose), Uthan Pristhasana (Dragon/Lizard Pose), and Parivrtta Uthan Prissthasana (Reverse Dragon/Lizard Pose).

Pittas should quietly focus on the breath when entering Shavasana (Corpse Pose), which will calm the mind and centre them in the body and heart. Likewise, they need to avoid Sirsasana (Headstand) since it heats up the head too much. For inverted poses, they should practise Salamba Sarvangasana (Shoulderstand) instead.

Since Pittas are naturally hot, they should engage in Pranayamas that can cool them down, including Sheetali (Cooling Breath), Sheetkari (Hissing Breath), and the Lunar Breath. On the other hand, Pittas should avoid Pranayamas that raise more heat in the body like the Solar Breath, Kapalbhati (Skull Shining Breath), and Bhastrika (Bellows Breath). Mind balancing and calming Pranayamas are recommended, like those suggested for Vata types.

Lastly, Hand Mudras for Pitta Dosha excess are Prana Mudra, Varun Mudra, and Prithivi Mudra. If you have a deficiency in Pitta, perform Agni Mudra to increase it.

Yogic Practice for Kapha Dosha

For Kapha Dosha types, warming and energizing Yoga practice like Vinyasa is ideal since they need to counter their natural tendency to feel cold, heavy, slow and sedated by creating heat and movement in the body. However, they need to gradually build their capacity instead of pushing themselves into advanced postures. Although Kaphas have the most strength of all the Doshes, they can suffer from lethargy and excess weight when they are out of balance.

Since Kapha's area of operation is the chest (lung region), Asanas designed to open up the thoracic cavity (ribcage area) will prevent the accumulation of mucous. However, most standing poses are invigorating for Kaphas, primarily when held for a more extended period. Backbends like Ustrasana (Camel Pose), Dhanurasana (Bow Pose) and Urdhva Dhanurasana (Wheel Pose) heat up the body and unlock the chest, allowing for better circulation of Prana. Also, Setu Bandha Sarvangasana (Bridge Pose) and Ardha Purvottanasana (Reverse Table Top) are beneficial. Unlike Pitta, Kapha types can hold their backbends for a longer time.

Kaphas should be mindful to move through flow sequences quickly to avoid being cooled down while practising conscious awareness. Twists and stretches are good because they detoxify and strengthen the body and boost the metabolism. These include Trikonasana (Triangle), Parivrtta Trikonasana (Revolved Triangle), Ardha Matsyendrasana (Seated Spinal Twist), and Pravottanasana (Intense Side Stretch). Poses like Salamba Sarvangasana (Shoulderstand), Adho Mukha Vrksasana (Handstand), and Sirsasana (Headstand) are the primary reducers of Kapha because of their tremendous power to heat up the body. Navasana (Boat Pose) is excellent to ignite and warm up the core and is recommended for Kapha types.

Kaphas should try to do their Yoga practice early in the morning to get their metabolism going and keep them energized and motivated throughout the day. The duration of Shavasana (Corpse Pose) should be kept a bit shorter for Kapha types. Instead of practising Tadasana (Mountain Pose) for grounding, Kaphas should perform Utkatasana (Chair Pose), Vrksasana (Tree Pose), or Virabhadrasana I and Virabhadrasana II (Warrior I and II) instead since they are more physically demanding.

Pranayama exercises that heat up the body and calm the mind should be implemented. These include the Solar Breath, Kapalbhati (Skull Shining Breath), Bhastrika (Bellows Breath) and Ujjayi (Ocean Breath) Pranayamas. In addition, opening the lungs through vigorous breathing is beneficial. Kaphas should avoid all Pranayamas that cool down the body like Sheetali (Cooling Breath), Sheetkari (Hissing Breath), and the Lunar Breath. Instead, they can use the mind soothing Pranayamas suggested for the Vata types if they feel mentally unbalanced.

In conclusion, Hand Mudras for Kapha Dosha excess are Agni Mudra and Varun Mudra. Prithivi Mudra can be used to increase Kapha if one has a deficiency.

Yogic Practices for Bi-Doshic and Tri-Doshic Types

If the individual constitutes two dominant or three dominant Doshas, they need to implement a practice that is a mix of each. Use the guidelines above for each of the Doshas you are a combination of. A person can generally tell which dominant Dosha seems out of balance. For example, if someone is a Vata-Pitta, if they find themselves irritable and angry and digest their food too quickly, they know to follow the Pitta guidelines to get this Dosha into balance. Conversely, if they exhibit too much mental activity and general anxiety, they should implement a Vata pacifying Yoga practice. Also, be mindful of the seasons and weather. A Vata-Pitta type will need to balance Vata during the colder, fall and winter months, while in the spring and summer, when the weather is hotter, they will need to balance Pitta.

SIDDHIS-PSYCHIC POWERS

The subject of Siddhis, or supernatural powers and abilities, is largely misunderstood in Spiritual circles and requires clarification. In Sanskrit, Siddhi means "fulfilment" or "accomplishment," implying the gifts one receives after completing the different stages or degrees of advancement through Spiritual practices such as meditation and Yoga. Since the aim of all Spiritual practices is Spiritual Evolution, Siddhis are psychic powers that become unveiled as the individual integrates the Spiritual energy and raises the vibration of their consciousness.

In the *Yoga Sutras*, Patanjali writes that Siddhis are attained when the Yogi has achieved mastery over their mind, body, and Soul and can sustain concentration, meditation, and Samadhi at will. Mastery over the Self is an integral part of one's journey towards Enlightenment, including governance over the Elements. By obtaining control over our inner reality, we can exert a mental force that affects the outer reality—As Above, So Below.

Although Siddhis can be achieved through Yogic practices and living an ascetic lifestyle, a more accelerated way to their attainment is through a full Kundalini awakening. I have already talked about the various Spiritual gifts that unveil to the Kundalini awakened initiate during their transformation process. Some of these gifts are attained initially, while others are unlocked in the years that follow. Regardless of the stage of attainment, all Siddhis are a by-product of the Spiritual transformation.

As the individual aligns themselves with Cosmic Consciousness and integrates the high vibrational energy of the Spirit, they begin to experience Oneness with all of existence. Since the Spirit connects us all, there is no separation between us and the objects and people around us—we are all One. Thus, the integrated Spiritual energy becomes the medium through which we can experience extrasensory perception.

By optimizing our Spiritual Chakras (Sahasrara, Ajna, and Vishuddhi), we can attune to the essence of the Spiritual energy, whose vastness stretches out infinitely in all directions. As such, psychic abilities will begin to unveil to us, including Clairvoyance, Clairaudience, Clairsentience, empathy, telepathy, and other gifts resulting from a heightened perception of reality.

The process of consciousness expansion involves optimising the Chakras via the White Light of the Spirit. We receive the Spirit through Sahasrara while Ajna Chakra (Mind's Eye) serves as our psychic centre and Vishuddhi as our connecting link with the four Elemental Chakras below. It is the interplay of Sahasrara and Ajna Chakra that yields most if not all the Siddhis since Sahasrara is our connecting link with Cosmic Consciousness. As you will see in the description of the Siddhis, many psychic gifts or powers that one attains result from expanding one's consciousness and taking on the properties of Cosmic Consciousness.

Although Siddhis are gifts from the Divine, they can also hinder us on our Spiritual journey if we focus on their attainment too much. Siddhis should be experienced, examined, and let go of to allow the consciousness to continue to expand to even greater heights. If the Ego gets involved and tries to control the process or even benefit from the development of Siddhis, the vibration of one's consciousness will lower, blocking the way to further advancement. In that sense, Siddhis are a "double-edged sword" that needs to be approached with a proper understanding and the Ego in check.

As part of sacred texts, the subject of Siddhis and their description is presented in a cryptic manner which is done purposefully to confuse and divide the masses. On the one hand, we have the profane who only seek these supernatural gifts to satisfy their Ego's desire for power. These people interpret the sacred texts literally, knocking on the door of the Cosmic mysteries in vain. On the other hand, the sincere seekers of truth, who are pure of heart and worthy of these Divine mysteries, possess the master key to unlocking the hidden meanings in these sacred texts.

Ancient people veiled Universal mysteries and truths in metaphors and allegories, including symbols and numbers that held Archetypal value. The traditional method of passing down sacred knowledge was abstract and subtle, bypassing the Ego and communicating directly with the Higher Self. The Siddhis are also presented in such a fashion. On the surface, they seem like incredible supernatural feats that defy the laws of physics. However, when you apply the master key, you understand that their description is metaphoric for inner powers unveiled through the evolution of consciousness.

THE EIGHT MAJOR SIDDHIS

In Tantra, Hatha, and Raja Yogas, there are eight primary "classical" Siddhis that the Yogi attains on their path to Enlightenment. They are called Maha Siddhis (Sanskrit for "great perfection" or "great accomplishment") or Ashta Siddhis, which means "eight Siddhis." The Ashta Siddhis are also known as Brahma Pradana Siddhis (Divine attainments). As you will see in the following descriptions of the eight major Siddhis, they directly result from fully awakening the Kundalini and the Spiritual transformation that follows in the years to come.

Ganesha, also known as Ganapati or Ganesh, is the son of Lord Shiva and Goddess Parvati. He is known as the remover of obstacles, which is why he is pictured with an elephant head. According to Hindu tradition, Ganesha brings blessings, prosperity, and success to anyone who invokes him.

Ganesha is the representative of Muladhara Chakra, the abode of the Kundalini. For this reason, he is often represented with the serpent Vasuki wrapped around his neck or belly. However, an atypical depiction is with him sitting, standing, or dancing on the five or seven-hooded serpent Sheshnaag. Both Vasuki and Sheshnaag represent the Kundalini energy—the ultimate remover of obstacles whose purpose is to maximize one's potential as a Spiritual human being.

Ganesha is also known as Siddhi Data—the Lord of the Siddhis (Figure 149). He is the one who bestows the Ashta Siddhis to the eligible individuals through the Kundalini awakening process. In the Tantra tradition, the Ashta Siddhis are considered as eight Goddesses who are consorts of Ganesha and personifications of his creative energy (Shakti).

Figure 149: Lord Ganesha and the Ashta Siddhis

Anima and Mahima Siddhis

The first two classical Siddhis are polar opposites which I will discuss together for better understanding. Anima Siddhi (Sanskrit for "ability to become infinitely small like an atom") is the power to become incredibly small in size instantly, even to the extent of an atom. On the other hand, Mahima Siddhi (Sanskrit for "ability to become huge") is the power to become infinitely large in an instant, even to the size of a Galaxy or the Universe itself.

These two Siddhis arise from the individual consciousness expanding to the Cosmic level after a full Kundalini awakening, allowing them to wilfully expand or contract their Being so that they can become infinitely small or infinitely large. Both of these Siddhis are also influenced by the heightened imaginative abilities that develop during the Kundalini transformation. It is the coupling of imagination and expanded consciousness that activates Anima and Mahima Siddhis within us.

Anima Siddhi requires that the individual imagine something in their heads, such as an atom. By holding its vision, the Astral sense becomes activated, enabling the individual to feel the Atom's essence, thereby knowing its purpose and function in the Universe.

Conversely, if the individual visualizes something grand in size, such as our Solar System or even the Milky Way Galaxy, their Being can stretch out to its size to feel its essence (Mahima Siddhi). These abilities are possible because the foundational substance of the Cosmic Consciousness, the Spirit, is elastic and malleable, allowing those who have attained its level to assume its form and fluctuate in size to any degree they desire through imagination directed by willpower.

The second interpretation of Anima Siddhi deals with the legendary "Cloak of Invisibility" mentioned in many Ancient traditions—the ability to become energetically undetectable to other people (including animals) at will. As the full spectrum of the inner Cosmic Planes becomes activated after a full Kundalini awakening, the individual can raise their consciousness willfully to a Higher Plane (Spiritual or Divine). Doing so allows them to neutralize (still) their vibration to appear invisible in the Lower Planes (Mental and Astral) that the average person vibrates on, rendering the person "small as an atom."

If we follow the same logic, Mahima Siddhi allows the individual to willfully heighten their vibration to appear grand in size to other people, even Godlike. Remember, both Anima and Mahima Siddhis result from Spiritual Evolution, whose purpose is to bring us closer and closer to the Mind of God and assume its vibration. In both interpretations of the Anima and Mahima Siddhis, the prerequisite of their development is for the individual to master the Elements, namely the Fire Element.

Anima and Mahima Siddhis' more general interpretation is as metaphors for the Spiritual power the individual achieves when they have expanded their consciousness to the Cosmic Level and have achieved Oneness. With Anima Siddhi, one can enter into anything they desire, such as an object or a person, when they become "the size of an atom." In contrast, by becoming infinitely large (Mahima Siddhi), the individual can feel the essence of the entire Universe since they infinitely stretch out their consciousness. We see in both cases the inner power that gets awakened when an individual has integrated the Spiritual consciousness and can step out of their physical body at will.

Garima and Laghima Siddhis

The third and fourth classical Siddhis are also polar opposites as the first two. Garima Siddhi (Sanskrit for "ability to become very heavy") is the power to become infinitely heavy in an instant by using your willpower. Conversely, Laghima Siddhi (Sanskrit for "ability to become very light") is the power to become infinitely light, therefore almost weightless. As Anima and Mahima Siddhis dealt with size, Garima and Laghima deal with weight, which is the force of gravity that acts upon an object's mass.

By becoming as heavy as one desires through Garima Siddhi, the individual cannot be moved by anyone or anything—other people's vibrations bounce off their Aura as they remain firm in their poise. Garima utilizes the power of virtues, morals, and having an "Iron Will." People who allow their Inner Light to guide them consciously choose Spiritual Evolution over satisfying their Ego's desires and bringing unnecessary Karma into their life. Moral values give people a purposeful existence and unshaken willpower. They allow people to vibrate at a higher frequency by aligning them with the higher Cosmic Planes. These righteous people avoid the Lower Planes' energetic effects, rendering them unmoved emotionally and mentally, especially when other people's vibrations bombard them with their lower vibrations.

To fully maximize Garima Siddhi's potential, the individual needs to optimise their Spiritual Chakras and attune their willpower with their True Will that only their Higher Self can bestow upon them. The True Will's vibration is so high that if one becomes receptive to it and allows it to guide their consciousness, they will neutralise their own lower vibrations and all vibrations being directed towards them from the environment. By maximising your willpower, you become a Master Manifester, a Self-sustaining, All-expressing, conscious Creator of your inner reality that is like a God-human to all people who haven't developed the same power.

Laghima Siddhi, on the other hand, makes one almost weightless, enabling levitation and even flying. On the surface, Laghima Siddhi defies the law of gravity and laws of physics. It greatly appeals to the uninitiated who seek these Siddhis for personal, monetary gain. By achieving levitation in the physical realm, many people desire to benefit financially by displaying this phenomenon to the masses.

Like many people in my position, I have been fascinated with levitation since I had the Kundalini awakening seventeen years ago. I desired this gift not because I sought to gain from it financially but because I saw it as tangible proof of the Kundalini transformation that I could show others to inspire them to achieve the same.

However, after years of extensive research, I have concluded that legends of levitation are nothing more than fanciful stories with no verifiable scientific proof. In other words, a human being cannot lift off the ground and defy the laws of physics by using psychic powers. The purported levitations people have seen with their own two eyes are merely illusions of which there are countless methods and techniques.

Instead, the concept of levitation is a veil to confuse the profane. It reveals to the worthy initiates the powers that awaken within oneself when the Body of Light is activated. The Body of Light, our second body, is elastic and mouldable and does not adhere to gravity and physics laws since it is weightless and transparent. Using our Body of Light, we can travel within the inner Cosmic Planes and perform many miraculous feats such as flying, walking on water and through walls, etc.

Our Body of Light is utilised during Lucid Dreams (which happen involuntarily) and Astral Projection (which is consciously induced). Both phenomenons are a type of Out of Body, Soul travel experiences that I will discuss in more detail later when I devote myself wholly to the subject.

Another type of Out of Body travel is called Remote Viewing, which is the ability to bilocate to a remote area on our Planet using the mind's power. Remote Viewing is Astral Projection on the Physical Plane that uses the Body of Light to travel somewhere on Earth and see what our two physical eyes can't see by using the Third Eye. In early occult and Spiritual literature, Remote Viewing was referred to as "Telesthesia," which is the perception of distant events, objects, and people by extrasensory means. Secret government programs reportedly used gifted individuals to seek impressions about distant or unseen targets through Remote Viewing.

Prapti Siddhi

The fifth classical Siddhi, Prapti (Sanskrit word implying "stretching of the body" or "power of reaching"), allows the individual to travel anywhere instantaneously with the application of their willpower. Prapti Siddhi perfectly follows Laghima Siddhi as the Body of Light's ability to travel via consciousness, using the Merkaba.

As discussed in a previous chapter, the Body of Light allows us to travel inter-dimensionally within the various inner Cosmic Planes, which is an expression of Prapti Siddhi. However, if we desire to travel to remote places on Planet Earth, we can do so through the Physical Plane. On the surface, this manifestation of Prapti sounds a lot like

Astral Projection, but it is not. Although the two are related, since they both use the Body of Light for execution, Astral Projection is a technique that requires preparation and is therefore not instantaneous like Prapti.

I have already discussed Kundalini awakening's optimisation of the imagination and willpower, but I have merely touched upon the ability that develops of experiencing thoughts in "real-time." A full Kundalini awakening localises the Inner Light inside the brain, bridging the conscious and subconscious minds. As the two parts of the mind become One, the left and right brain hemispheres are unified, allowing for a pure, uninterrupted stream of consciousness. This experience has a peculiar effect on one's thoughts which become as real as you and me to the experiencer.

It takes a long time to tame the consciousness and gain control over one's visualisation power, which involves optimising the willpower. Once achieved, though, you will have the ability to consciously travel (bilocate) anywhere you want and experience it as real the very moment you think it. If you wish to travel to Egypt, for example, and see the Great Pyramid, you merely have to visualise it, and your Soul will be projected there instantly via the Merkaba. Or, if you need a break from your everyday life and want to spend a few minutes on a beach in Mexico, you can visualise being on a beach and experience it as real.

To get the most from this experience, when visualising something, it helps to have a photograph or image of where you want to go to form the most accurate vision of that place. You are then to hold the image in your mind, which you will experience as real through your Astral senses.

I want to point out that Prapti Siddhi is only achievable after the individual has completed the Kundalini awakening process, thus localising the Inner Light within the brain. Other components necessary for this Siddhi's execution are optimising Ajna Chakra, activating the Body of Light, and maximising the spin of the Merkaba by unlocking the full potential of the toroidal energy field. (Note that the Body of Light and the Merkaba are used for any kind of Out-of-Body travel.) I will describe this phenomenon's science in greater detail later on as I unravel more of the extraordinary abilities that unveil themselves to the Kundalini awakened individuals.

Prakamya Siddhi

The sixth classical Siddhi, Prakamya (Sanskrit word implying "willfulness" or "freedom of will"), gives one the power to achieve and experience anything they desire. This Siddhi allows the individual to materialize anything they want out of thin air seemingly and realize any dream. If they wish to be somewhere or even be with someone sexually, their desire is satisfied the moment they have this thought. Prakamya Siddhi is characterized by the instantaneous fulfilment of one's deepest desires through the application of willpower.

This Siddhi may seem like something out of a superhero movie on the surface. The ability to manifest anything we desire instantaneously transcends the limitations of the laws of the Universe and the laws of physics. However, if we apply this Siddhi to the Lucid Dream world, then we begin to understand the true potential of our experiences through the Body of Light. The Lucid Dream world is as real to our consciousness as the Physical World as far as experience is concerned.

During my seventeen years of living with awakened Kundalini, I have experienced these types of gifts and much, much more. The Lucid Dream world fulfilled all of my Soul's desires, which I began rapidly experiencing three to four months after my initial awakening in 2004. I have found that Prakamya Siddhi serves not only to fulfil your Soul's desires but to extinguish them over time.

My life experiences have taught me that one of the most efficient ways to overcome any desire within yourself is to engage in it until its energy is drained out of you. Of course, I am referring to temporal Ego desires that fall within the realm of normalcy and not unnatural desires such as physically hurting other living Beings. One of the functions of the Lucid Dream world is to extinguish the desires of the Kundalini awakened initiates whose ultimate goal is Spiritual Evolution and union with the Godhead.

I would often project out of my body into wherever my Soul wanted to go in the Lucid Dream world. I visited distant Stars and Galaxies and Inter-dimensional places on our Planet with strange Beings that I saw for the first time. Often, I would "download" information from these Beings concerning Creation's mysteries and the future of the human race in the same fashion as Neo downloads new abilities and skills as computer programs in "The Matrix" movie. In the span of one hour of dreaming, I could download the equivalent of twenty books worth of information from intelligent Beings in our Universe.

A handful of times, I became aware that I was downloading information outside of me and could recall a sentence or two of what I was receiving. For the most part, the information was cryptic, imparted to me through numbers, symbols, metaphors, and Archetypes in either the English language or other Earth languages.

When I was in the presence of what looked like Extraterrestrial Beings, they spoke to me telepathically in their tongues, which somehow, I understood. I could usually tell Extraterrestrials from other Beings such as Ascended Masters, Angels, or other Deities because their appearance was humanoid but clearly not human since some features were different.

I felt blessed and privileged to have made contact with other intelligent Beings in the Universe through consciousness. After all, I had no other way of obtaining the unique knowledge they imparted to me but through direct experience, and my thirst for knowledge after awakening Kundalini grew daily.

Over time, I naturally developed a technique of un-focusing my Mind's Eye in a Lucid Dream to step into a reality which I term "hyper-consciousness," a state beyond the realm of human consciousness. As a result, I often found myself somewhere I have already been in the real world, only a futuristic version of the same place with never-before-seen objects and technological devices. The scenery resembles an LSD or Peyote trip, although different since it has a futuristic component.

For a while, when I projected into this futuristic world, I would hear techno music inside my head that matched what I saw as if I was in a movie. My jaws would clench as an ecstatic rapture filled my heart, trying to integrate my visual. This hyper-reality taught me about parallel Universes that our consciousness can experience through the Body of Light and the Lucid Dream world.

I remember wanting to spend a month skiing and being unable to do so in real life due to time constraints. That very night I found myself in a high-class resort in what looked like the Alps. The scenery was everything I desired and more. I spent what seemed like a full month there, in terms of the number of experiences, all within the eight hours of sleep that I was out. When I woke up, I no longer felt the need to go skiing since that desire was satisfied in my Lucid Dream.

I have travelled to other places in the world in the same fashion. If I was somehow limited to travel in real life, I often found myself visiting that place at night. The main difference was that time was transcended in the Lucid Dream world. You could spend months and even years in a place in the Lucid Dream world, equivalent to eight hours of sleep in real life.

After visiting many countries and cities in my dreams, I have found that there are resorts and hot spots in the Lucid Dream world where other people travel to if they need a "power" vacation. In addition, many individuals I met on my Lucid Dream travels seemed too unique to be a projection of my consciousness. Often, we would exchange personal information concerning who we are in real life, although I could never verify someone in the real world.

Over the years, my "command centre" or base of operations became New York and Los Angeles, although they were different versions of those same cities. Since I visited both cities in real life, I found that the feel was the same in the Lucid Dream world, but they looked radically different with different architecture and landscapes.

When I revisited either city in a Lucid Dream, it seemed almost identical to the last time I was there in a previous dream. I even had an apartment I owned in New York that I would come back to, and it was the same as the last time I was there with objects where I left them. Interestingly, a stream of memories would flood back from the previous time I was there in a dream which meant that my consciousness was able to have different life experiences in various places simultaneously as the real world.

Every time I entered the Lucid Dream world, I was aware of my potential. I was light as a feather and could fly, levitate objects and project my consciousness in a split-second from one place to another. I could also manifest any partner I wanted to have sexual relations with, experience what it is like to be ultra-rich and famous, fly a plane or drive a Ferrari, and much more. When I would imagine something I desired, it usually would appear right in front of me. The sky is the limit as far as what your Soul can experience in the Lucid Dream world, and the fulfilment of your desires is personal to you and you only.

Keep in mind that there is no concept of distance in a Lucid Dream. When you think of an experience you want to have, you are immediately in the act of having that experience, in a location which your Soul chooses for you. The Body of Light contains the five senses of sight, hearing, touch, smell, and taste, allowing for a completely realistic experience. We may be experiencing the real world via the Body of Light as well, only through the physical body's interface. The few times I tried virtual reality, I felt similar sensations to what I have experienced in the Lucid Dream world.

One of the main differences between satisfying your desires in the Lucid Dream world and the World of Matter is that there is no mind chatter or guilt in the Lucid Dream world since it is a pure desire being fulfilled. The mind chatter results from the Ego, which is directly linked to the physical body and the material world. Since the Lucid Dream transcends the physical realm, it is void of Ego; hence the mind is empty, allowing for a most optimal Soul experience.

Vashitva and Ishitva Siddhis

The seventh and eighth classical Siddhis, Vashitva and Ishitva, blend into one another, and as such, I will discuss them together as expressions of the same power. Vashitva Siddhi (Sanskrit word implying "powers of control") allows the individual to command their own and other people's mental states via willpower. The individual can entirely influence the actions of any person on Earth with Vashitva Siddhi.

Conversely, Ishitva Siddhi (Sanskrit for "superiority" and "greatness") is the ability to control nature, biological organisms, people, etc. This particular Siddhi gives the individual absolute Lordship over all of Creation and makes them a God-human in other people's eyes. Ishitva Siddhi makes one a Master of the Five Elements—a living Magus.

According to *The Kybalion's* Principle of Vibration, all things vibrate at a particular frequency. Quantum physics corroborates this claim and adds that every time we look at something in the outer world, we influence its vibratory state. Ancient Hermeticists have known the power of the mind for thousands of years. After all, the foundational Principle of *The Kybalion* is "The All is Mind, the Universe is Mental."

If the Universe is a mental projection that is moulded by our minds, then our thoughts and emotions are also a mental construct that we can alter. Hermeticists have taught their initiates that willpower can be used as a Tuning Fork to transmute our mental conditions and those of other living Beings, even changing the states of Matter. They believed that if we can maximise the power of the mind, we can obtain governance over other people, the environment, and reality in general.

Vashitva and Ishitva Siddhis are expressions of mind-powers that can be realised when the individual raises the vibration of their willpower and thus their consciousness. Even though we can achieve Vashitva Siddhi by applying Mental Laws, the only way to truly realise Ishitva Siddhi is through Spiritual Evolution. Becoming Enlightened not only maximises the willpower's potential, thereby optimising Vashitva Siddhi, but it also allows us to surrender our will to the Godhead completely and align with its high vibrational frequency. In doing so, we become Self-energised Tuning Forks that induct everything around us with our high vibrations, changing the mental and emotional states of all living beings and even altering the vibrational state of immaterial objects in our immediate environment.

Since we constantly communicate telepathically, maximising our willpower gives us the power of mind over mind, allowing us to completely dominate other people. According to *The Kybalion's* Principle of Mental Gender, "Gender is in everything; everything has its masculine and feminine principles; gender manifests on all Planes." This Principle states that we each have a masculine and feminine component of the Self—the "I" and "Me."

The "I" is the masculine, objective, conscious, voluntary Force that projects—the willpower. The "Me" is the feminine, subjective, subconscious, involuntary and passive part of the Self that receives—the imagination. The will, which is the Fire Element of the Soul, projects into the imagination, thereby creating a visual image, an expression of the Water Element. The Air Element is the thought, the medium of expression of willpower and imagination.

The "Me" is like a mental womb that gets impregnated by the "I" to create a mental offspring—the visual image." The "I" always projects, while the "Me" receives. These dual cognitive components are a sacred gift given to us by our Creator to be conscious Co-Creators of our reality. However, the only way we can manifest our own desired reality is to use our willpower to generate mental images to guide our lives. If we become mentally lazy, thus rendering our willpower inactive, our existence will be guided by other people's willpower, either directly or through environmental stimuli. Such is the Law. The "Me" component must always be fueled by an "I," whether our own or someone else's.

People who are conscious of these Mental Laws can raise the vibration of their willpower to control their reality and affect the "Me" component of other people, thereby making them think whatever they desire. By influencing someone's thoughts, we invariably affect how they feel and what actions they perform. Since these Mental Laws work on a subconscious level, the person who is being influenced hardly ever realises they are being mentally inducted. Instead, they believe that the inducted thoughts are their own when, in reality, they are seeds planted by someone else. The psychic phenomena of thought transference, suggestion, and hypnotism are examples of using the Principle of Gender to affect other people's minds.

As I have discussed at great length in *The Magus*, any reality being shared by multiple people is controlled by the individual who vibrates their willpower at the highest frequency. The people who share this individual's reality look up to them naturally and consider them their leader and guide. These evolved people are charismatic, personable, and sexually attractive, which has less to do with physical appearance and more to do with personal magnetism. They usually communicate directly to the Soul, thereby bypassing the personality and the Ego. These special people engage and inspire others in ways that seem magical to those individuals who don't understand the science behind the Universal Laws that are being employed.

The most efficient way to achieve Ishitva Siddhi and achieve Lordship over Creation is to awaken the Kundalini and raise it to the Crown. When a highly Spiritually evolved individual has raised the vibration of their consciousness to the Spiritual Plane, they naturally dominate the Planes below it that most people vibrate on. They also dominate the animal and vegetable kingdoms which are sub-divisions of the Physical Plane.

It is not uncommon to see an Enlightened person walk among tigers, lions, bears, crocodiles, poisonous snakes, and other potentially deadly animals. We have all heard of this phenomenon before, but most people don't know its science. By channelling the high-vibrational Spirit energy, which is Light and love, these Spiritually evolved individuals have overcome their own fear that triggers dangerous animals and makes them attack humans. Thus, the awakened individual bypasses the animal's survival mechanism and connects with their love energy, resulting in being embraced instead of attacked.

A person whose willpower is resonating at the frequency of the Spirit dominates all those who have not achieved the same state of consciousness. These Spiritually evolved individuals appear as God-humans to the common folk who swarm them to bathe in their intoxicating Light.

As a final note, it is possible to alter states of Matter with the application of willpower and even make Matter appear and re-appear. *The Kybalion* clarifies that if we raise the vibration of Matter, we alter its frequency and thus its density and even state. However, since it requires a great deal of energy to accomplish this feat with the mind alone, very few Adepts in history have achieved this, some of which found themselves central figures of religions. We have all heard the miracles of Jesus Christ, where he turned water into wine and used five loaves and two fish to multiply these items and feed 5000 people.

A more common and provable example of altering Matter with the power of the mind is to turn ice into water, water into steam, and vice versa, by heating and cooling the body. Another example is levitating a light object such as a piece of paper or controlling the movement of a candle's flame. To accomplish any of these mental feats, the individual needs to contact or be close to the item to infuse it with their Pranic energy, whose flow and state they can control with their minds.

Perhaps in the future, when humanity has collectively Spiritually evolved, we will have more remarkable examples of controlling Matter with our minds, since the Universal Laws operate on all Cosmic Planes and the Higher Planes always dominate the Lower Planes. Interestingly, the Ancients never spent too much time trying to influence Matter with their minds. They knew that the true gift of these Mental Laws was to apply them to their own mental and emotional states to aid in their Spiritual Evolution. Reaching the mind of the Godhead was their only true goal since by doing so, one becomes a part of the Universal Laws, thus optimising the Ashta Siddhis.

PART VII: POST-KUNDALINI AWAKENING

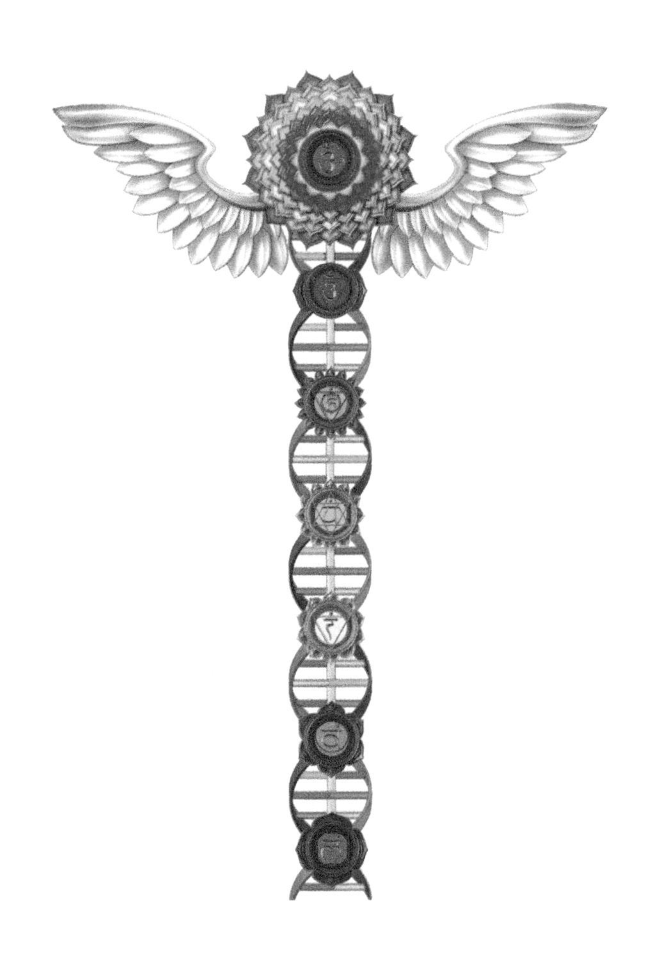

SYMPTOMS AND PHENOMENA AFTER AWAKENING KUNDALINI

Most Kundalini awakened individuals are concerned about how the transformation will unfold over time and the general timeline of when they will unlock particular gifts (Siddhis). This is one of their main questions and interests. After talking with dozens of awakened individuals who completed the process by raising the Kundalini to the Crown, I have found that the manifestations are almost the same for everyone and usually happen systematically. One experience gives rise to the next one, and in this way, the Kundalini energy transforms the mind, body, and Soul over time, unlocking many psychic gifts along the way.

As I discussed in the introductory chapter on the Kundalini, once the activation of the Body of Light has taken place and the energy becomes localized in the brain, a permanent awakening has taken place. Some symptoms and phenomena manifest within the first week, while others take a bit longer than that. In this section, I will break down these experiences one by one, in sequential order for the most part, from the initial stages, into the following months and years. Keep in mind, however, that I am only covering full awakenings, not partial ones. With partial awakenings, the manifestations and gifts are specific to whatever Chakra(s) the Kundalini has activated, varying from one Chakra to the next.

In fully awakened individuals, the first two initial manifestations are the Light in the head and the constant vibratory sound heard on the inside akin to a low hum. If the person has no prior knowledge of the Kundalini, they may mistake the latter phenomena as the onset of tinnitus, a physical ailment where you hear a constant ringing in your ears. However, they will notice that the sound greatly amplifies when they focus on it, sometimes keeping them up at night as it did for me.

The Light in the head is tricky because it comes in waves at first and may even cause pressure in the head, causing a headache or migraine. So, you might think several factors could be causing this phenomenon at the beginning. After a few weeks, however, it will become apparent that once you close your eyes, energy is present inside your head that flashes Light frequently. It often pulses like a living, breathing organism, especially when you are in an inspired state. You might even experience Light flashes of other colours, especially purple, although I have found that the presence of the White Light is relatively consistent. Of course, it is not as bright as looking at the Sun but dim yet very noticeable with eyes closed.

You may also see orbs of Light within your peripheral vision that may appear when you have an epiphany about something or are in an inspired state. They are generally electric blue and small but quite noticeable. It is usually a single orb of Light, although there can be several. People have suggested that these orbs may be Guardian Angels.

As you begin bringing food into your body, your digestive system will transform it into Light energy, feeding the newly awakened energy system. Since the Kundalini is amplified by Pranic energy from food and sexual energy, it will gradually change you on all levels, physical, mental, emotional, and Spiritual. Some of the more immediate effects are body twitches and a feeling of ants crawling on your skin. It is important not to panic when this occurs, as it is a normal part of the process. It means that the energy is sublimating and reaching the nerve centres, literally infusing them with Light, fueling them.

You might also feel muscle jerks or occasional spasms come seemingly out of nowhere, usually when your body is still and in a relaxed state. As your nervous system adjusts to this new energy present within you, your temperature can fluctuate, making you feel hot one moment and cold the next. I recommend wearing extra clothing not to make yourself susceptible to getting a cold or flu when you are cooling off.

The rate and power of your heartbeat will also be affected as your body adjusts to changes in your energy system. The heart can beat so fast sometimes that it feels like you are about to have a heart attack, especially if you are unaware of this common Kundalini symptom. Because the mind is processing emotions from the subconscious, the accelerated heartbeat is usually the result of a fearful emotion present, which may appear out of nowhere and be gone the next second. As a result, the heart will often skip a beat; then, it will speed up until you calm yourself down.

The heart will also react when intense emotions are present, especially ones that channel raw Fire energy. The power of the heartbeat can sometimes be so strong that it feels like it is trying to come out of your chest. Your respiration rate is directly affected by changes in your heart rate, often resulting in mild hyperventilation when your heart rate goes up. Since your Sympathetic Nervous System activates in this case, I recommend implementing a calming breathing technique to take back control over your body. Keep in mind that however alarming these heart palpitations may seem, there is nothing to fear. The mind makes matters worse by creating panic, so try to remain calm, and it will pass.

Since the Kundalini is now active within you permanently, you may also feel pulsations in your sacrum as it is pumping the Kundalini current through your Light Body. If there are energy blockages, there might be uncomfortable pressure in the sacrum, which may cause mild pain. However, I have found that the Kundalini system compensates for energy blockages by reducing the magnitude of the Light it is channelling.

Another notable phenomenon, albeit a rare one, is psychokinetic interference with electrical equipment. For example, the day after I had the Kundalini awakening, my bioelectricity was so high that when I focused my mind on a nearby TV, I caused a disturbance in the channel stream on command. I had also heard of cases where individuals blew out the needle on their record player when they touched it or made CDs skip. The phenomenon always entails either making contact with an electrical device or using the power of the mind to alter its function in some way while exhibiting higher than normal bioelectricity.

Sometimes, pain is present in different organs, or there is a general sense of discomfort in areas where organs are present. The pain is usually mild, although the mind might exaggerate these effects, as it does when it experiences fear of the unknown. The mild pain or discomfort is normal, and it means that the energy is entering into and cleansing different Spiritual counterparts of the organs and parts of the body. The most important thing to remember is to remain calm as all of these processes occur because they usually don't last long. However, if you fixate on them and blow them out of proportion, they will persist longer.

Let me reinstate what I said in an earlier chapter—the Kundalini energy works on a subtle, non-physical level, although it often may feel like the effects are physical. Keep in mind that another part of you is awakening to your consciousness, the Body of Light. The Body of Light has subtle counterparts to the physical organs, which serve a Spiritual purpose on a higher level.

I hope this explanation clears up any misunderstandings on this topic because I often hear Kundalini awakened people say that the energy is working in the physical body and shaping and "hammering" the organs, which is simply not true. It feels like it, yes, but that is only because now there is another part of the Self awakened, a non-physical component—the Body of Light, which contains the various Subtle Bodies that correspond with the Five Elements.

Another symptom that occurs early on is massive fluctuations in vitality. For example, you may be hyperactive and feel a need to move around or exercise, followed by complete energy depletion and lethargy. These energy swings result from Kundalini's effects on the mind. When it takes over, the Kundalini gives you access to an abundance of energy, followed by a crash the moment the Ego takes back its control over the mind. When you learn to overcome the Ego's effect on the mind, however, you will tap into the source of the Kundalini energy and have incredible vitality 24/7.

As your consciousness purifies over time, its vibration rises, enabling it to localize within the Spiritual Body, the highest aspect of the Body of Light. It is almost like a transplant process is occurring inside, which may be worrying at times. As such, it may require some time to adapt to what feels like a foreign entity inside of you.

The Body of Light is the vehicle of the Soul. The physical body, on the other hand, is the vehicle of the Ego. The Soul uses imagination and intuition, which are received through the heart. The Ego uses logic and reason, and it operates through the mind. The sibling of imagination is the inspiration that fuels the Higher Self, the Soul. The Kundalini energy inspires because its purpose is to bring you in-Spirit. The Kundalini Fire changes states over time to bring about a mystical, transcendental perception of the new reality you are in—the Fourth Dimension of Energy or Vibration.

HOLY GUARDIAN ANGEL (THE HIGHER SELF)

Every human being has a Higher Genius, otherwise known as the Holy Guardian Angel, or Higher Self. This is the Spiritual part of you that is of God-the Creator. Although beyond duality, your Higher Self aligns with the polarity of your Soul. As such, you can refer to it as a he or she, whatever gender your Soul is. The primary purpose of the Kundalini awakening is to create a link between your consciousness and your Holy Guardian Angel. Then you will become a channel for their wisdom for the duration of your life here on Earth. And quite possibly beyond.

Your Holy Guardian Angel resides in Sahasrara Chakra (Figure 150). Whenever you raise your consciousness to its level, your Higher Self is present. By connecting with it, your consciousness feels as if it has grown wings, transforming you into an Angelic presence while this link is maintained. You are still yourself, but a higher part of you that resonates with the vibration of the Divine Light of the Creator.

Most people have moments throughout the day when they connect with their Holy Guardian Angel, usually when in an inspired or creative state of mind. Then there are those moments when the Holy Guardian Angel briefly touches us with its energy, giving us Divine insight into a subject in the form of an epiphany. However, these moments are usually short-lived since the Ego always begins to question the experience, severing the connection with the Higher Self. As a result, the individual drops down from Sahasrara into a lower Chakra of one of the Four Elements.

Figure 150: Holy Guardian Angel (The Higher Self)

To establish a permanent connection with your Holy Guardian Angel, an exaltation of consciousness must take place first. Then, once the Soul has assumed complete dominance over the Ego, the Spirit Element can descend and transform you entirely. After this transfiguration process is complete, you will permanently establish contact with the Holy Guardian Angel. You may still operate from any Chakra when you require its powers of expression, although your consciousness will mainly work from the three Spirit Chakras of Vishuddhi, Ajna, and Sahasrara.

Much of the Kundalini content in in this book is not something I learned from other books or heard from someone else, which is why you will find that a lot of this information is original. Some knowledge has been built up from books during the first number of years after awakening Kundalini. Once the foundation had been laid, and I aligned with the Higher Genius, he took over as my inner teacher and guide. Afterwards, most of my knowledge was imparted to me directly by my Holy Guardian Angel through Gnosis. However, to reach that pinnacle in my Spiritual Evolution where I can become a channel to something greater than me, I had to spend many years developing myself into a beacon and channel of Light.

Every human being can become a channel for their Higher Self if they dedicate themselves to their Spiritual journey and follow some road map of achieving Enlightenment. We must all become Resurrected in the Spirit Element and become our own saviours. The work in *The Magus* is geared towards achieving that goal. Once you have gained permanent contact with your Holy Guardian Angel, they will become your teacher and guide for the rest of your life. You will not need any more teachers, nor guides in physical form as you will become the teacher and student in one.

Your Holy Guardian Angel will begin to communicate with you every time there is a continuation in consciousness, and your Ego is silent. It will teach you about the mysteries of the Universe and Creation regularly as you go about your daily life. It will give you further insight into everything you learned in the past and everything you think you know now. Whatever you take in from the outside world will now be filtered by the wisdom of your Holy Guardian Angel.

You may continue learning from books, although you will find that you will get more from your Holy Guardian Angel about life than you can from any written texts. Books are good to build up your knowledge concerning specific subjects, but your life philosophy you will learn directly from your Holy Guardian Angel.

Since you cannot control this ongoing communication and learning process, you will begin to feel like you are two people in one. I often find myself talking to my Higher Self like two entities are living inside of me. The cool, calm, collected, and all-wise one is the Higher Self, while the Ego is the one that messes up and needs guidance. And the way I see it, I am neither of them and both of them at the same time.

My Ego used to feel like the consciousness that it once ruled over was hijacked by something else, although nowadays, it has accepted this dual reality of the Self. It still has its reactions like any Ego does, but the Higher Genius stands aside, watches how I express myself and checks me when I get out of line. He is the Silent Witness of the perpetual present moment that lives in Eternity. He is there to calm me down when I need it and give me the right advice on what to do or how to behave when I am in a dilemma. His overall purpose is to teach me how to improve my character and personality to become more Spiritual. So, I leave myself in his hands and try to let him lead the way for the most part.

Your Holy Guardian Angel is essentially self-serving; it is constantly teaching you how to become a better channel for its Light, even if the Ego must suffer. As you learn to serve your Higher Genius, however, you are invariably learning how to serve God-the Creator, which means you are Spiritually Evolving. Since your Higher Genius is your God-Self, its impetus for action comes directly from the Source of all Creation.

What is fascinating about Kundalini science and philosophy is that it is a new and growing field whose foundation and framework haven't been established yet. Therefore, it is up to all Kundalini awakened individuals to contribute their knowledge and experience for the generations ahead of us to continue building upon. If I can assist in helping you gain contact with your Holy Guardian Angel, then I have done my job. The rest I leave in their hands. As such, I urge all of you to take what you have learned from me and continue to develop my theories and practices further.

No book or body of knowledge on the Kundalini has the ultimate answers. There are always gaps to be filled. As such, I invite all Kundalini awakened individuals to be courageous and step outside their comfort zones to help develop this Kundalini science further. We are all scientists and laboratories in one package, learning, experiencing, and sharing our findings with the world.

STATE OF BEING AFTER THE AWAKENING

After a full Kundalini awakening, once the Body of Light has been activated, it may take some time to develop it sufficiently with food intake. The next step is to allow the Spirit energy to permeate the consciousness so that you can align fully with the Spiritual Body, an aspect of the Body of Light. To accomplish this, however, you must first overcome the Karmic energy in your lowest four Chakras and sufficiently develop the top three that are of the Spirit Element.

The Spiritual Body is shaping itself as the Body of Light is being integrated. How long this process takes depends on many factors, which are personal to everyone. It is a rather lengthy process, and if I had to take an average guess, I would say seven to ten years. If you have a method to work on the Chakras, such as the Spiritual Practices in this book or Ceremonial Magick ritual exercises as presented in *The Magus*, then it will take substantially less time. On the other hand, if you allow the Kundalini to purify the Chakras over time naturally, it will take much longer.

Overcoming fear is the key to Spiritual Resurrection, which includes purging and purifying the Chakras. It took many years for negative energy to develop within the Chakras; it will invariably take many years to cleanse. How long exactly? It all depends on how much fear you have in your system.

I know people who, after a dozen years of living with awakened Kundalini, are still at the mercy of their fear and anxiety, which has been a foreign concept to me for almost a decade now. I often get fearful thoughts, as we all do, but for me, it is a momentary experience that is washed away in the realm of Non-Duality of the Bindu Chakra within seconds. No fearful thought or emotion can debilitate me or take over my consciousness long enough for me to be overly bothered by it.

A few weeks to a few months after the initial Kundalini awakening, you will feel a sense of energy moving inside the body and the head, and you may feel like your brain is "broken." This state of mind will result in scattered thoughts and the complete inability to focus on anything for too long. Also, most people report feeling complete apathy for everything that they used to care about.

Feelings of love for others will be overtaken by an emotional numbness that will be long lasting and seemingly permanent. There will be no continuity of thought, and a general sense of confusion will be present. You can't turn to the Ego for answers anymore since it will have minimal control over you. The Ego realizes it is slowly dying as this inner Fire is released through the Kundalini. You have to surrender to this process right away instead of trying to fight it or rationalize it too much.

Unfounded fears and anxiety will surface at different times, without any reason other than to be released from the system. It may be scary at first, but once you understand that it is all part of the process, it will be much easier to relax and allow it to unfold.

Once the Kundalini reaches the head, a connection to different parts of the subconscious form and a bridge is built between the conscious and subconscious minds. Memories of the past might come to the forefront of consciousness. This process is normal, and it doesn't need to be examined too much. It would be best if you let these memories go as they come up. Hanging onto some memory of pain or fear will only amplify it within the mind. Instead, use the power of love in the Heart Chakra to purify and exalt the memory through tears if needs be.

At first, because this is all such a new experience, it will be somewhat uncomfortable, and the Ego will be trying in every way to figure out what is happening. Having books such as this one on hand is crucial to knowing where things are headed so you can relax. Strange manifestations such as rushes of energy, muscle jerks, and feeling energies moving inside of you in snake-like patterns are just a few of the possible experiences you may have.

There will be pressure felt in different areas of the body, especially the head and the heart. You will also feel energy openings in the feet and palms over time, bringing on a feeling of a cool, calm wind rushing into them. This is the Spirit energy entering you to bring about the feeling of general weightlessness, which may manifest shortly after.

Remember that even though the Spirit energy will seemingly permeate your body early on in your transformation process, the actual integration of your consciousness with the Spiritual Body can only occur once you have cleansed your Chakras. And that process is entirely dependent on how much Karmic energy you have stored in each Chakra. So if you are someone who has very little Karmic energy, as you have been working through it through many lifetimes, then you may be destined to have an easy-going and quick transformation.

Another critical point is that once the conscious and subconscious minds have been bridged, your thoughts will take on a degree of realness like never before. Your thoughts will appear real to you, like whatever you are thinking of is present right in front of you, which adds to the general feeling of fear and anxiety. If you do not have complete control over your thoughts, which most of us do not after the initial Kundalini awakening, fear and anxiety are the defence mechanism against whatever comes up from the subconscious mind.

This "realness of thoughts" occurs because the inside and outside are now One. There is no break in consciousness unless you choose wilfully to listen to the thoughts of the Ego. As all the Chakras are open, their powers are streaming into your consciousness all at once. Your Sacral Chakra, Swadhisthana, powers the subconscious, while the Heart Chakra, Anahata, fuels the conscious mind. The Sun represents the conscious mind, while the Moon represents the subconscious. For this reason, you see visual depictions of the Sun and Moon in conjunction within many Spiritual pantheons and traditions, primarily Hermetic Alchemy.

CHAKRAS, SUBTLE BODIES, AND DREAMS

Within a few weeks after the initial Kundalini awakening, dreams start to take on a different quality as the inner energies sublimate/transform further. This noticeable change is seen in the dream world as the Astral Light gradually builds up inside you. At first, your dreams will take on different meanings, meant to teach you a lesson or inform you about something Archetypal occurring in your subconscious. As you are progressing through the Chakras, however, your dreams will be affected by the nature of their energy. Your experiences begin in the lowest two Chakras, Muladhara and Swadhisthana, as these two correspond to the Astral World. All inner experiences start in the Astral World, through the Astral Body, otherwise called the Emotional Body.

Once a scene takes place in your dream, you will have to figure out what it means and what that scene is trying to communicate to you. Different occult symbols, power animals, and numbers may be present as part of metaphoric events that will impregnate upon your consciousness some life lesson that you need to learn to move ahead on your journey of Spiritual Evolution. These lessons also exist to help your Soul evolve and attune your mind to changes in your Aura as they are happening. As you are progressing through the lower three Chakras, the types of events occurring in your dreams are meant to elicit an emotional or logical response in you that you must examine afterwards. There will be different outside presences felt and seen in your dreams, including Angels, Demons, and Deities, often clothed in everyday garb and presenting themselves as people.

Once you have entered into the Heart Chakra, you can project out of your body through Sahasrara, the Crown Chakra and experience the world of Lucid Dreams. However, it is hard to precisely determine which Subtle Plane a dream is taking place in and from which Chakra it is being projected. Unless you are in a Lucid Dream, these dreams are happening subconsciously where your consciousness is so engulfed in the experience it is unaware it is dreaming. Therefore, the only real way to determine what Cosmic Plane you are in is to examine the dream's content.

Keep in mind that in one given night, you may experience multiple dreams in various Subtle Planes as your consciousness oscillates in rate or frequency of vibration. You can sometimes hear the vibrational pitch inside your head change as you enter different realms of the Inner World, the same way as the radio frequency changes when you switch from one radio channel to another.

Emotionally charged dreams are happening in the Earth and Water Elements, Muladhara and Swadhisthana Chakras. Especially Swadhisthana, since it corresponds to the Higher Astral or Emotional Body, although as mentioned, the Muladhara Chakra also touches upon the Astral Plane. If the content is more logical, where you have to figure out something in your dreams like a detective, then it most likely is being projected through the Fire Element, Manipura Chakra. In this case, your consciousness needs to use your willpower and intellect in your dream to figure things out.

The Kundalini energy is trying to lay the foundation so you can start Lucid Dreaming, otherwise called Astral Travelling. Lucid Dreaming only occurs in sleep, while Astral Projection is an Astral Travelling technique that you can induce in the waking state. It is essentially the same idea; you use your Body of Light respective to the Subtle Plane you are trying to enter, to consciously or unconsciously experience that Cosmic Plane.

The Subtle Bodies range in feeling the same sensations as the physical body. The lowest Subtle Body, the Astral Body, is densest in the level of the realness of experiencing that Plane, as it is primarily concerned with your lower emotions. When you enter into the Mental Plane, though, things begin to feel more real. In the Spiritual Plane, the realness of the experience is greatly enhanced as the vibration of the Spiritual Body is substantially higher than the Subtle Bodies of the Lower Planes. Experiencing the Divine Planes is marked by intense ecstasy, which is the nature of those Planes.

LUCID DREAMING

About three to four months into the Kundalini transformation process, you begin to Lucid Dream. Considering the awe and wonder of the Lucid Dream world, this is one of the first Spiritual gifts that manifest for the Kundalini awakened individual and a big step in their Spiritual Evolution process. Lucid Dreaming results from the Kundalini energy entering the Heart Chakra, Anahata, since this Chakra is the contact point with the Spirit Element Chakras that lie above it.

In Lucid Dreams, the consciousness is completely liberated from the physical body and aware that it is experiencing a dream. Pure consciousness is the Law that guides Lucid Dreams. This awareness enables the individual consciousness to be like a "kid in a candy store" and experience whatever adventures your Soul desires. It is exhilarating to realise that you are in a dream and can do whatever you wish by merely thinking it into existence.

Interestingly, the first thing people seem to want to experience in the Lucid Dream world is flying through the air with the power of their minds. Since your Body of Light is weightless, gravity is not a factor anymore, which allows for this phenomenon.

Lucid Dreaming is a full Out-of-Body Experience that is quite a thrill for the first time. It happens after enough Light/Pranic energy has been built up through food intake, allowing you to vault out of your physical body during sleep through Sahasrara, the Crown Chakra. Furthermore, this experience has a liberating effect on consciousness. By entering these Higher Planes of reality, no more fear or pain plagues you, which allows you to relax for a change and enjoy this gift.

The Lucid Dream world is filled with beautiful environments and scenes, all stemming from your enhanced imagination coupled with the infinite potentiality of Cosmic Consciousness. By projecting out of your body through Sahasrara Chakra, you enter the field of Cosmic Consciousness, which is boundless. All Lucid Dreams feel like you are fully present in whatever magical place you projected into, as your Soul feels every sensation like it is happening to the physical body. However, everything that is happening is a result of the imaginative capabilities of Anahata, fueled by Sahasrara, whose source energy is Cosmic Consciousness.

The Soul uses the Body of Light as the vehicle of travel in the inner Cosmic Planes, enabling the consciousness to experience them as real. The Body of Light is tied to the physical body by the Silver Cord (Figure 151), also known as the "Sutratman" in Sanskrit, composed of the two words "sutra" (thread) and "Atman" (Self). The Sutratman is essentially the life thread of the Soul. This metaphysical cord ensures that our Body of Light can make its way back to the body after Astral travelling. Upon death, when the Soul leaves the physical body permanently, the Silver Cord becomes severed.

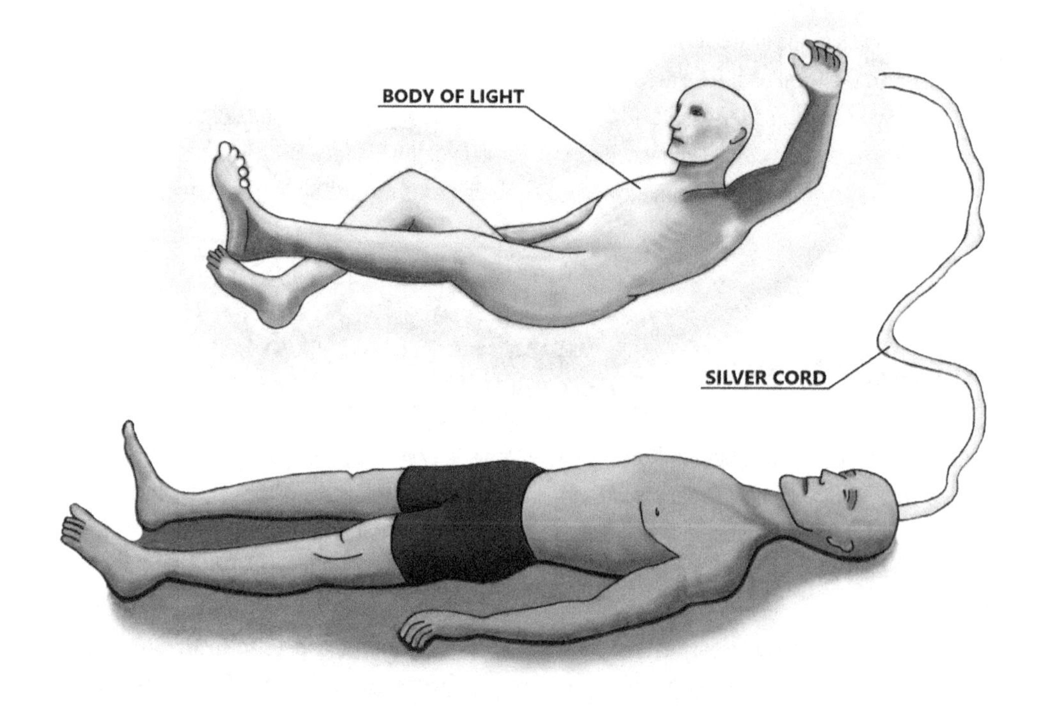

Figure 151: Lucid Dream Projection

ASTRAL LIGHT BUILDING UP AND EXPANDING

As you begin to Lucid Dream regularly, you may start to experience occasional dream paralysis where your consciousness is so engulfed in your dream that you can't wake up for up to a dozen hours or more. This phenomenon occurs due to the Astral Light building up inside your system even more over time. At its peak, the Light energy can be so potent that it involves your senses in such a way that the mind is experiencing everything so completely real that it can't separate itself from the dream.

When I say the word "Astral," I am not relating to the Astral Plane of the Earth and Water Chakras but how this term is commonly used in Spiritual circles. "Astral" represents the inner Cosmic Planes, realms, and worlds that are beyond the Physical Plane yet are inextricably tied to it. So when you are trying to describe this invisible science to other people, you may use the term "Astral" to encapsulate all the non-physical Planes of consciousness. And "Astral Light" refers to the inner Light that manifests these Cosmic Planes into existence.

It is crucial to understand that many of the different phenomena and manifestations after the initial Kundalini awakening result from the Astral/Inner Light growing and expanding over time within the energy system. As it expands, it infuses the Chakras with Light energy, systematically permeating and acting through the various Subtle Bodies. Once it is finished infusing the Chakras of the Four Elements, it begins to work on the Spiritual Chakras and the corresponding Spiritual Body, injecting it with Light energy. Afterwards, the Astral Light of the Kundalini transforms into liquid Spirit energy (Amrita), which then powers the Ida and Pingala Nadis, or channels. As it does so, the Kundalini circuit will be complete and continue sustaining itself through food intake. The Bindu will become activated, serving as a valve that regulates the entire Kundalini system, resulting in a metaphysical and mystical state of consciousness.

Approximately five months after my Kundalini awakening, as the Astral Light continued to build up inside me, it changed my perception of the Physical World. It transformed my physical sense of sight as Astral Light started to permeate all objects around me, resulting in a shimmering, silvery glow transposed on everything I was looking at. As discussed earlier, this was the most wondrous manifestation and one that I continue to revel in to this day. This gift gives me the illusion that the outside world is entirely contained within my head, in my mind. When I focus my gaze outward, there is a strange sensation like I am looking at the inside of my forehead.

During the Kundalini transformation process, the Astral Light building up begins to awaken the different brain centres as well. It starts to channel and circulate this Light in various parts of the head area as it does so. Once my physical sight was transformed and the brain centres opened up, it marked the beginning of a new life for me—the complete experience of the Fourth dimension, the Dimension of Vibration. Every time I looked at the world in front of me, I was reminded of the illusion of the material world of Matter since I could now see the World of Energy underneath it.

As it transformed my visual sight, I also gained the ability to see everything before me from a higher perspective, as if I am standing in the clouds. Only now, what I was looking at also had this digital makeover and Light beaming out from behind objects, completely remodelling what I was seeing. Sometimes I could be so absorbed in what I saw that it would dematerialize right in front of me, and I could see it as pure energy. And if I continued my meditation further and got more absorbed in what I was seeing, I could see everything before me as if it is projected onto a 2D background, like a movie screen. The only difference is that the movie screen is made of pure Light energy, projected from the Sun. This vision attests to the theory that we are living in a Holographic Universe.

THE HOLOGRAPHIC UNIVERSE

During the first year after awakening the Kundalini in 2004, I had a second Holographic Universe experience that furthered my understanding of the nature of reality. This experience was like the first one that happened during my Kundalini awakening although self-induced. It began as a dream, with me standing alone in a field, surrounded by a wooden fence. Everywhere I turned, I saw this fence. On the other side of the fence were my Ancestors, all talking simultaneously in a chaotic manner in my native tongue, Serbo-Croatian. Then, out of nowhere, a complete silence permeated the atmosphere.

A voice appeared and said, "Do you want to know the truth of things?" I responded with an affirmation, not verbally, but with curiosity in my heart. The second I accepted this offer, the vibrational pitch inside my head began to change. I found myself slipping into the vibration, losing consciousness within my dream like I was being transported into another dimension of space/time.

All my Astral senses became suspended as I went further and further within myself. It felt like I was going through a wormhole via my consciousness. Instead of fearing this experience, however, I had faith. Finally, I emerged on the other side and opened my eyes. As I looked around me, I saw the Holographic world. The walls and floor in front of me were transparent, with objects seemingly suspended in space. The walls and objects glowed with an almost velvet-like appearance. I didn't look at my body during this time since I was so mesmerized by this concrete-less reality. Complete silence was present everywhere. I felt like pure consciousness, without limits, swimming in the darkness of space. However, what was unique, and the first and only time this happened in my life, was that the usual vibration pitch inside my head now sounded like a Mustang engine, a low growling sound.

Although I was unsure whether I was on Earth or another Planet, the objects started to look familiar as I looked around further. Finally, my memories began to come back, and I realized that instead of being somewhere new, I was sitting on my bed, in my room where I was sleeping a minute before. This entire vision lasted for about ten seconds, although in slow-motion. Once the memories started to come back, which began my questioning of this extraordinary experience, the vibration in my head began to shift until it came back to its usual frequency. As this was happening, I saw the Holographic Universe turn to concrete Matter before my very eyes.

This experience was never to repeat itself in my life again. However, it didn't have to. I got the answer I was seeking and never looked back. I learned that not only are we living in a Holographic Universe, but the vibration of our consciousness may hold the key to Interdimensional and possibly even Interplanetary travel. This theory is supported by an ancient text called *The Emerald Tablets of Thoth the Atlantean*, written by the Atlantean Priest-King Thoth, of whom the Egyptian God Thoth is a descendent. He mentioned that humans could travel throughout the Universe by changing the vibration of their consciousness at one point in time, thus validating my claim.

After my second direct experience with the Holographic reality, I was left with new questions to be answered. For one, where is the Hologram projected from in our Universe? One theory is that each Solar System has its own Hologram that is projected from its Sun. However, some astrophysicists support another hypothesis that the Hologram is projected from the nearest black hole.

You see, a black hole has more mass than all the nearby Solar Systems combined, meaning it carries massive amounts of data in a compact space. This data is sent outwards to form distinct parts of the Universe, and everything contained within that Three-Dimensional space, which is reflected in the black hole's Two-Dimensional Plane, like a mirror. Now, if one were to pass through the black hole, they would enter a higher dimension, theoretically, exemplified in the movie "Interstellar" as the Fifth Dimension of love that transcends space and time. Of course, these theories are speculation only and will remain as such, but I have always felt privileged to be one of the few people on this Planet that had not one but two direct experiences with the Holographic reality.

FURTHER GIFTS UNVEILING

Having the inner, Astral world open to me at all times was causing it to be transposed onto what I saw with my physical eyes. As a result, I started to see things that were not of this world as this Light energy was building up inside me. I saw shadowy Beings in forests, Angelic presences, and even Demonic ones, the most common of which growled and had red eyes. I saw many of them in my dreams, while others were present in my environment, and I could glance at them for a split-second before they were gone from my sight.

My connection to everything around me grew daily. Through the Mind's Eye, I developed another sense, the ability to feel objects I was looking at intuitively. I could weigh their energy with my thoughts and feel their Astral form, their Spiritual blueprint with this ability. These phenomena were possible because the Kundalini completely awakened my Astral senses, and I could see, touch, taste, smell, and hear within the Inner Cosmic Planes.

Since my Mind's Eye was exponentially expanded, I began exploring regular meditations to see how far down the rabbit hole I could go and if I could unlock further gifts within me. Thus, I began meditating everywhere I went, whether on subways or busses, in class, or at work. I liked meditating by focusing on people and allowing myself to get absorbed in their energy. If I concentrated on a person long enough, I would slip out of myself and start to see their energy emanating from their physical body. It looked directly behind them, although it was a part of their consciousness. The experience usually began with seeing their Etheric double, which looks like an imprint of their energy field coming out a few inches from their physical body. However, as I went in deeper and continued to un-focus my eyes as I viewed their energy body, I would start to see the full spectrum of their Auric colours.

If I remained in meditation for over ten minutes, though, I began to change states of consciousness and could see the person from the perspective of an ant, or sometimes a greater and even larger being. The rule of thumb was that the longer I kept focusing on them, giving them my undivided attention, the more I was able to scry into what I was seeing and see energy fields that are typically undetected by physical sight.

If somebody was near me and I focused on their face instead of their whole body, I could see their features change right before my eyes. Sometimes they morphed into animal faces or became very old or young as I focused on them. Other times their faces morphed into what looked like Extraterrestrial Beings because they were simply out of this world. These experiences affirmed for me that we are all Light Beings of pure consciousness who have lived on many different Planets in other Solar Systems and Galaxies in a continuous chain of lives that never ends.

At this point, as I could feel the world around me, I was starting to become an antenna (Figure 152), receiving vibrations from outside of myself. The Kundalini was now beginning to operate from the Spiritual Body. However, even though this happened relatively quickly in my life, it did not mean that the Kundalini transformation process was complete. It may start to work through the Spiritual Body, but as long as latent energies need to be worked through in the Chakras, the Kundalini energy will stagnate, and there will be a clear division in mind, body, and Soul. This dispersion of Kundalini energy will result in a perplexed and lost state of mind for a long time. Confusion and the inability to concentrate or make decisions are just a few of the negative side-effects of being in this state.

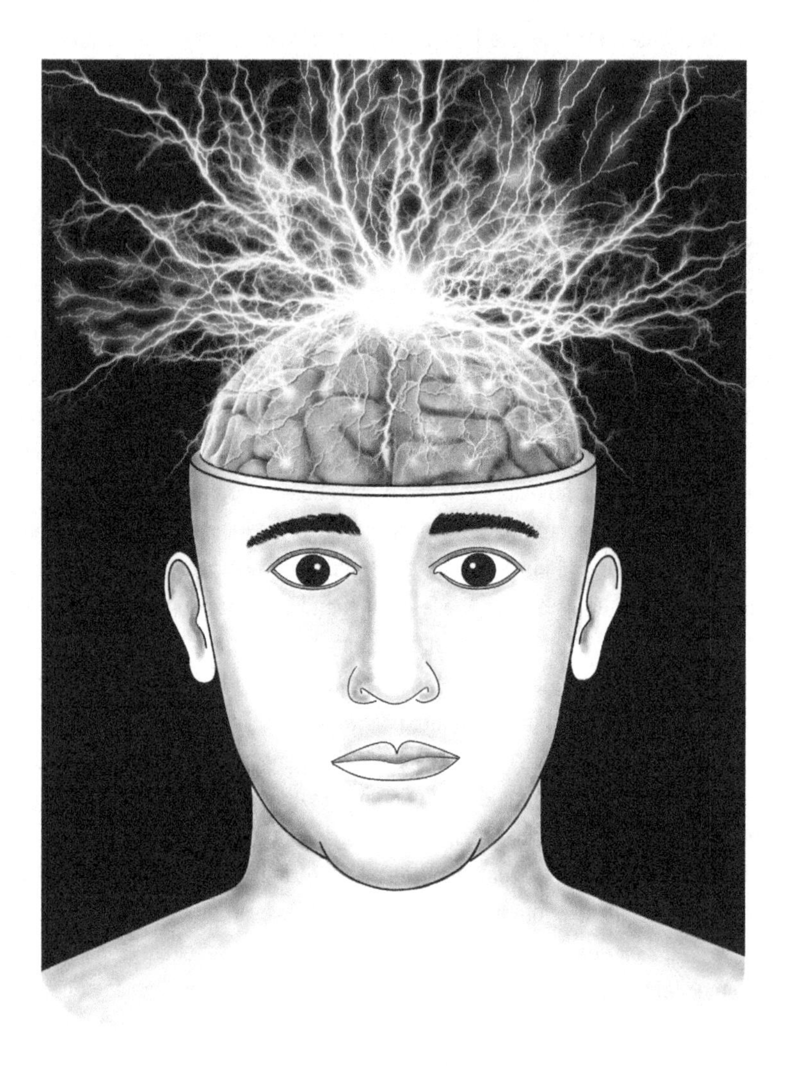

Figure 152: The Human Brain Antenna

I have never come across anyone who has purged the negativities of the lower Chakras in a short period after a full Kundalini awakening. In reality, it is possible, but this means the Soul has been purging and clearing the Chakras well before the Kundalini awakening took place. To integrate fully into this new level of consciousness in a small time-frame, you would have to be a rather Saintly figure who has worked on their Karma from this life and previous lives. Otherwise, there will still be many manifestations in your mundane life where the Kundalini is working on your lower Chakras. However, there have to be many lessons learned in those areas before the Kundalini can completely localize in the Spiritual Body and operate without blockages or stagnations in energy.

KRIYAS AND SYNCHRONISTIC EVENTS

Some awakened individuals report performing spontaneous Kriyas—Kundalini Yoga and Hatha Yoga movements. This phenomenon occurs from the Kundalini Light animating the physical body to perform these movements while the conscious self is on autopilot. Interestingly, knowledge of the Kriyas surfaces somewhere deep from the subconscious since they are usually consciously unknown to the person performing them. The body performs these Kriyas for a little while the Kundalini acts on the body, energising it. The key behind this phenomenon is the individual being in a state of inspiration, which neutralises the Ego. The moment that the Kundalini Light dissipates, the Ego takes over the consciousness again, and the Kriyas stop.

Another manifestation while in this Kundalini inspired state is automatic writing. The individual may feel compelled to write, again seemingly on autopilot while the Kundalini energy channels through them. The produced content is often not recognizable to the Ego when examined afterwards, begging the question of where it came from. The individual may even express themselves in other languages, some not of this Earth. For example, I have a Kundalini awakened friend who has been channelling cryptic letters and symbols while in this inspired state that resembles some dead Ancient language or even an Extraterrestrial one. Whatever he is channelling, he feels compelled to do it and has no conscious control over the process.

Many more manifestations will occur as the consciousness is learning to live in this new world of pure energy, and the Ego is loosening its hold over you. You will start to have many synchronicities and begin noticing patterns in your daily life. For example, number patterns are common, which often occur as you get some inner urge to look at the time or view some technological device that displays numbers. For myself, the number 1111 came up very often. Other Kundalini awakened individuals report synchronicities with the same number.

The purpose of 1111 is to let you know that you are now functioning on a different Spiritual level and that awakening has taken place. The 1111 Angels, or Divine energies, want to let you know that you are being guided and protected by higher forces. You may also see other strings or series of numbers such as 222 or 333. This phenomenon occurs as the external, material reality becomes interconnected with the inner Astral world—the two are becoming One.

Your imaginative powers are blending into the Cosmic Consciousness and its power of imagination which is vast and boundless. You are no longer a separate entity but are now operating within the Cosmic Mind framework. Your mind is gradually becoming absorbed into the Cosmic Consciousness.

As your consciousness slowly evolves, it is learning to operate according to the framework of the Universal Principles. These Principles are the Principles of Creation— the Seven Principles (fundamental Truths) that outline Universal Laws which govern all of Creation. These Laws form the basis of *The Kybalion*—the occult Hermetic book written at the beginning of the 20th century that profoundly impacted me personally and was a precursor to my Kundalini awakening, as mentioned in the introduction to this work. You are learning to become a part of the Principles of Creation and operate within their context consciously, as you form a part of the Universal Laws.

THE NEED FOR SPIRITUAL ALCHEMY

There will be immense changes on the mental and emotional level after experiencing a full and sustained Kundalini awakening. For many people, a flood of negativity streaming forth into the consciousness may occur, stemming from the Kundalini blowing open all the Chakras as it rises from its abode in the sacrum through the hollow tube of the spinal column.

As fear and anxiety permeate your system, these dark energies will need to be dealt with before you can experience the more positive aspects of the awakening. The negative emotions are felt in the Water Chakra, Swadhisthana, related to the subconscious mind. Negative thoughts, however, are a result of a corrupted Air Chakra, Anahata. Keep in mind that until you clear your negative thoughts and emotions, you cannot function solely through intuition, which is one of the goals of the Kundalini awakening process. Instead, you will feel weighed down by these dark energies as they seemingly run your life.

The negative thoughts and emotions may appear foreign at first. However, upon closer examination, you will realize they are your own. You will also become attracted to other people's negative energies since like attracts like. Often, you won't distinguish between the two since you will be so open to other people's energies that they will feel like they are your own. And to some extent, they are, since by being around others, we take on their energy.

Generally speaking, communication is 93% telepathic for all of humanity, which we express subconsciously, mainly through our body language and voice tonality. After awakening the Kundalini, though, you will consciously experience this higher form of communication since you will have control over your vibrations. And since we are all constantly inducing each other through the vibration of our thoughts and emotions, when you gain control over your inner state, you can control the mind-state of other people as well. But to achieve this, you will need to cleanse your thoughts and emotions so that your willpower can dominate your consciousness.

Early on in your transformation journey, you will notice it has become challenging to be around some people in your life. These people are often friends or even family members you used to spend a lot of time with before. After the awakening, though, you may find that being around these same people will make you anxious and stressed out. This phenomenon occurs because of the negativity inside you since your own Demons will feed off the fear energy projected by the Demons of other people.

Very negative-minded people, who are easily angered or overly pessimistic about life, will become highly draining. As you are feeding your Demons with the fear energy of other people, they will invariably rob you of your

Prana, your Life Force. Therefore, I advise you to reform your life and limit contact with people who negatively affect you. You may be able to go back to spending time with these people once you evolve Spiritually past this negative state. Still, while you are overcoming your issues, it is best that you only spend your time with positive-minded individuals.

You are no longer an average person, and you need to come to terms with this. The faster that you accept that you need to help yourself, the quicker you will evolve. If you choose not to deal with these types of issues, you will suffer. It is crucial to adopt a confident attitude from the beginning of your transformation because overcoming these challenges imposed on by the Kundalini energy will make the difference between winning and losing the battle inside of you. You can either be inspired about your new journey or so down that you will hate yourself, your life, and curse God for putting this Kundalini "burden" on you. It is common to feel this way often at the beginning, especially if you had an unplanned, spontaneous awakening.

It would be best if you started developing the mindset of a Spiritual warrior right from the start. You must invoke courage and strength so that you can face your Demons, and if they try to scare you, which they will, you will remain unshaken in your poise. Fear-based beliefs, negative thinking, and traumatic memories all have to be released and overcome in this process.

Your Ego is slowly dying, and it knows it. You have to surrender to the Kundalini energy and choose faith and love over fear. The concept of fear and its effect on your energy system will challenge you for many years, but in the end, if you remain positive and strong, you will prevail. Remember that this transformation process is Universal; if you realize that you are not alone in experiencing these challenges, you can draw inspiration from those who came before you and overcame these trials and tribulations.

CHALLENGES IN YOUR PERSONAL LIFE

As you are being remodelled in mind, body, and Soul and have been given many consciousness upgrades, it means that you are now functioning at a different level than other people. The faster you can accept this and realise that concerning your family and friends, you will be unique and different now, the quicker you can learn to adapt to your new reality correctly. This adaptation comes with a certain sense of loneliness because nobody you know will understand what you are going through. Let me reiterate this critical point. You are different now, and unless someone has gone through what you are going through, they will not understand, plain and simple.

It took me many years and many attempts at an understanding from my family and friends to realise that I am alone in this and will not get the support I need from people I know. And the faster you can recognise that you should not blame other people for not understanding you, the better you will re-integrate with them. After all, if you have chosen to stay in society and continue being a part of it, it does not matter what your truth is if others do not understand you. You will need to learn to blend in, to "fake it until you make it."

It is okay to lie sometimes in this regard if the truth is complicated for others to comprehend, and you know it will not make a difference if you attempt to explain your new reality. It is essential not to despair, though. We are programmed to seek counsel from other people when we are in a difficult situation, but in reality, we have all the answers within us if we know where to look. You can overcome all the obstacles and challenges if you have faith in yourself, the Universe, and the Kundalini transformation process. Keep in mind that since this Kundalini science is still relatively unknown to the public, most people presently won't understand you. If and when knowledge of the Kundalini becomes a part of the mainstream, you will be able to get more support from the outside world.

You will have many sleepless nights for the first few years after a full and sustained Kundalini awakening. Therefore, whatever you have planned for the morning will often have to wait or be postponed. If it cannot be delayed, you will need to learn to make good excuses for not being 100% after a sleepless night. Kundalini is often most active at nighttime, especially when you are in REM sleep. Here is when your consciousness is on autopilot, allowing the Kundalini to do what it intends.

Because of its intensity, you will not be able to induce sleep often, especially since this entire process will be relatively foreign to you. Most often, the fear of what is going to happen next prevents you from relaxing so you can fall asleep. The faster that you accept these challenges as a new part of your life, the better off you will be in the long run. I wish I could tell you that these challenges will not confront you, but I would be lying.

In a spontaneous awakening, it is almost certain that you will fear the process to some extent, which will affect your sleep. In my case, I was diagnosed with insomnia a year after the Kundalini awakening. Sometimes getting a professional diagnosis helps in having the proper excuse for missing obligations in the morning, such as classes in school or work. Of course, my condition was a temporary one, and I knew this, but I felt some sense of comfort in having a valid excuse for my symptoms.

Over time, I found ways to get optimal rest without inducing sleep, which helped me much while dealing with this sleeplessness issue. I have discovered that if you lie on your back and consciously observe the processes of the Kundalini energy moving through your body, you can rest your physical body enough to be less sluggish the next day. This method helped me rest my body, although I could not find a solution to resting my mind.

It will be almost impossible to avoid mental and emotional exhaustion by not inducing sleep, so you will have to learn to function while you are in that Lucid mind-state. Sadly, there is no choice in the matter. I will say, though, that if there is a will, there is a way. If you choose to remain inspired, even in the face of adversity, you will prevail. And if you decide not to, it doesn't matter how strenuous your challenge is, you will fail. Hence, adopt a winner's attitude right from the start, and you will benefit greatly on this journey.

My first book contains the Spiritual practice of Ceremonial Magick and the various exercises that I used on my journey to help me deal with the initial negative state of mind brought on by the awakened Kundalini energy. These ritual exercises are presented as part of Spiritual Alchemy programs, the same ones that I underwent many years ago when I was faced with these same challenges. They are meant to shed the Karmic energy of the lower Chakras so that you can eradicate all fear and anxiety in your system and ascend higher in consciousness. I have found that while the ritual techniques worked to cleanse the Chakras, they also allowed me to get better sleep and overcome my insomnia.

Right from the beginning of my Ceremonial Magick journey, I began to feel calmer and more balanced while achieving some level of control over mental states. And this effect was cumulative, I found; as I kept working with this Spiritual practice daily, I became more centred and grounded, which positively affected my sleep. The banishing ritual exercises that one is given right at the beginning of their Ceremonial Magick journey aid in clearing the Aura of unbalanced energy, which allows for more peace of mind. And when the mind is at peace, you can fall asleep easier.

Other than helping me sleep, these ritual techniques gave me a tool to combat the many mental and emotional challenges I was undergoing. They cleansed my Chakras over time and allowed me to stay inspired while this Kundalini transformation process was unfolding. Before I found Ceremonial Magick, I was feeling very helpless.

Once I discovered Ceremonial Magick, though, there was no turning back. Finally, I had the tool I was seeking to develop myself into a Spiritual Warrior and succeed on this journey.

I practised this sacred art of energy invocation for five years, every day. These Magickal exercises grounded me, expanded my imagination and intuition, and most importantly, removed fear and anxiety from my Aura. They enhanced my willpower and compassion while strengthening my intellect and purifying my emotions. I was amazed by how well these ritual techniques worked and how they complemented what the Kundalini energy was trying to achieve. For this reason, I chose to share these ritual techniques and more in my first book to give other people in the same position that I was in the tools they need to help themselves and advance further on their Spiritual journey.

ALIGNING WITH THE BODY OF LIGHT

Once you have cleansed and tuned your lower four Chakras and mastered the Elements of Earth, Water, Fire, and Air, your consciousness can elevate and localise in the higher three Chakras of the Spirit Element, from where it will operate onwards. This shift in consciousness indicates a new experience of living in the world, unhampered by fear and anxiety.

Your new vehicle of consciousness, the Spiritual Body, is your gift and reward for all the Spiritual Alchemy work you have put in up to this point. In most cases, many years will have to pass before the Karmic energy in the lower Chakras is overcome, especially if you had a spontaneous Kundalini awakening. For me, it was precisely seven years after my awakening that I fully aligned my consciousness with the Spiritual Body. Once this occurred, further Spiritual transformations ensued.

Since all the petals of the Thousand Petalled Lotus of Sahasrara were finally open for me, the entirety of my primary brain centres also became awakened. My Pineal and Pituitary Glands, the Thalamus, and the Hypothalamus were optimised to synchronise my body with the expanded consciousness, now in overdrive. I finally established the correct flow of Spirit energy upwards and back down again through the Crown.

The next step in the transformation process was consciousness fully aligning with the Spiritual Body. Once it was complete, further developments in my Mind's Eye occurred, awakening the ability to leave my body and see myself in the third-person.

In the past, I had random moments where I could step outside of my body, but these experiences were generally short-lived. I could not sustain this Out-of-Body Experience since my Ego was too active, keeping my consciousness confined to my physical body. Now, I could focus on any external object, and if I concentrated on it for more than a minute or so, my consciousness left my body as I became One with it. Sahasrara Chakra was involved in this phenomenon but also my Palm and Foot Chakras. It felt like the Spirit energy just got sucked out of my body through my head and limbs.

This new development in my Mind's Eye strengthened my connection to the outside world in a new way. Different sounds started to take shape in my head as animated images. Each sound had an associated visual component that came and went in waves, energised before me by some higher power of imagination.

A deep silence pervaded my mind as if I walked on clouds with my feet on the ground. Some of these manifestations began developing years before, but I could not fully attune to these higher powers because I was still at the mercy of my fear and anxiety. I had to clear all fear and anxiety to give the Kundalini energy a clear pathway for these higher faculties to awaken.

I believe this process of unlocking particular abilities is Universal for everyone. There is a systematic way in which the Kundalini transformation unfolds over time. As God-the Creator gave all humans a five-star physical body pattern with the same facial features, I believe we were also given the same energy components and potential. Jesus Christ referred to this when he said we are all the same and we are all One. It might take some time for Kundalini awakened individuals to unlock the same abilities as I did, but eventually, they will all get there. Everyone is on different timelines concerning their Spiritual Evolution process, but the endgame is the same.

Once you align your consciousness with the Spiritual Body, you will bypass your mind, allowing your Being to partake in the Spiritual Realm, the realm of Non-Duality. This realm is highly mystical and transcendental, as you will experience. For example, the mere act of listening to music will create rapture in your heart, unlike anything you have ever felt before. It will feel like the song is playing just for you, and you are the star of an epic Hollywood movie, which is your life. Even if your life is ordinary at this point, you will feel like you can become anything as you are in this state of perpetual inspiration.

The physical body will start to become partially numb to sensations as well. This phenomenon results from the Kundalini transforming into fine Spirit energy, which expands the system while circulating inside you. As a result, the primary energy channels of Ida, Pingala and Sushumna become fully open and work in synchronicity with one another. The Spiritual Body is established as the primary carrier and regulator of consciousness, although you might still need to do more work on the lower Subtle Bodies. Ultimately, consciousness needs to rise entirely above the lower Subtle Bodies, which requires complete purification of Karmic energy present in those areas. Once this is accomplished, the individual will altogether rise above their Wheel of Karma.

As you are going through the different transformations in mind, body, and Soul, I advise you to trust the process instead of fearing it. Although many years are needed to observe this transformation process taking place within you before you can finally let go and have faith that you are in good hands, knowing ahead of time that you are safe is half the battle. In any event, you don't have a choice but to surrender to this process, so the faster you can do so, you will only benefit yourself.

To fear is to fail since fear is the fuel of the Ego, which it uses to bind you to itself and prevent you from moving ahead on your journey. The Ego wants you to fear the process as it knows it can use this fear against you, allowing it to hold onto its identity a bit longer. It knows that for you to transform into a Spiritual Being of Light fully, it will have to be eradicated, which it tries to avoid at all cost. As mentioned, you can never destroy the Ego while living in the physical body, but you can reduce it to a small fragment of consciousness, one that is under the complete control of the Higher Self.

Instead of spending time worrying and over-analysing the Kundalini transformation process; instead, you should spend time grounding yourself and learning how to relax. The Kundalini energy wants to help you Spiritually evolve, not to hurt you in any way. The internal pain you are experiencing is generated by the Ego; to overcome it, you must learn to negate its thoughts. You must relax and have faith that you will be okay as the Kundalini is working through you.

Some of the manifestations I am talking about here occur in the later stages of the Kundalini transformation process. It is essential to recognise that the Kundalini process continues to unfold for the rest of your life after the initial awakening. Though the first few years can be challenging while the purification is taking place, once it is complete, other gifts and phenomena can and will continue to manifest since the journey is ongoing.

BODILY CHANGES AND DIET

Once you have fully awakened the Kundalini and risen it to the Crown, it will remain permanently in your brain now, which is an exciting time indeed. For the rest of your life, the food and water you bring into your body will be the primary factors that sustain the newly expanded energy system, ensuring that everything is running smoothly.

Food transforms/sublimates into Pranic/Light energy, while water supports and moderates the consciousness. This Light energy will increase inside of you and power the Kundalini circuit, which funnels out of the Bindu Chakra. Although you may not presently understand how these components come together, you will in due time when this part of the process unveils to you.

You will experience fluctuations in your appetite also during the Kundalini transformation process. For example, you might feel a need to eat more for a little while, followed by a need to eat less. Many periods in my journey prompted me to eat a lot, so I ate substantial meals multiple times per day. Once I felt this natural desire to eat more, it signalled me that my system was in overdrive to sublimate food into Light energy. I generally welcomed this change, although the people in my life would wonder why I was putting on weight rapidly and not caring about how much I was eating.

My friends and family always found it strange that I fluctuated in weight as I would often lose or gain up to ten pounds per week. I usually lied concerning this situation since when I told the truth, many people thought I was making excuses for not caring about how I looked, while others thought I was simply crazy. People thinking I was crazy throughout my life was a challenge I had to overcome and find my way around.

Also, be mindful of new desires to eat things you have never eaten before. For example, you may be a vegetarian or vegan your whole life and suddenly develop an interest in eating meat. Or perhaps the converse occurs, and if you have been a meat-eater your entire life, you may develop the desire to be a vegetarian or vegan. Listen to what your body is communicating to you in this regard since it may know something that you are consciously unaware of.

The meat gives your body the necessary protein that the body needs to repair muscles and make hormones and enzymes. Protein is a significant energy source for the body that is crucial in advancing your Kundalini transformation. Sometimes, however, if the animal was pre-killed in a gruesome fashion, as is the case with many slaughterhouses, the fear energy of the dying animal gets embedded in the meat, further aggravating your already fragile system. Again, respect your body's desires because your Soul communicates to you through the body at a deeper level.

Keep in mind that these desires to try new things often don't last long since their larger purpose is to expand your mind to other possibilities in life. I highly recommend eating organic food as much as possible since it will filter better through your body as it contains more Pranic/Light energy that your body needs to continue your transformation. I believe that genetically modified foods expose you to DNA degradation, which causes cancer and other bodily ailments plaguing much of the modern world. And when you are shopping for meat, try to eat kosher or halal meat where the animal was killed respectfully, and the meat should be free of negative energy.

When it comes to water, it is time to stop drinking tap water altogether unless it comes from a clean water source such as a stream. Most tap water, especially in big cities, contains many contaminates that are harmful to your mind, body, and Soul. Either begin drinking quality bottled water or, better yet, invest in a water filtration system that filters harmful metals such as fluoride, which is known to calcify your Pineal Gland.

Keep in mind that as the Kundalini is working through you, especially in the early stages, your kidneys will be working overtime, making them hotter than usual. The kidneys work with the Adrenal Glands, which will also be in overdrive since their function is to produce and release hormones in response to stress. As a result, the Adrenals are often the first to experience exhaustion in the initial stages. Getting filtered water without contaminants into your body will soothe your kidneys and Adrenals and help overcome this exhaustion phase of the Kundalini transformation.

DEVELOPING ALLERGIES

As you go through this transformation process and your appetite changes almost daily, you may also develop new food sensitivities and allergies, so be mindful of this. For example, I never had an allergy in my life. But then, nine years into the awakening, I developed an allergy to almonds, bananas, and rapini, all within two years. And I'm not talking about mild sensitivities. I'm talking about full-blown allergic reactions which hospitalized me every time.

I have eaten and loved bananas my entire life. It was my favourite fruit which I ate almost daily. In fact, it was one of the only fruits I ate. Then one day, out of the blue, I had an allergic reaction to it which sent me to the hospital. Since then, if I have a trace of banana in anything, I react immediately. So clearly, this developed over time, and I believe it is linked to the Kundalini transformation process.

For some reason, the body rejects particular energies from certain foods, resulting in an allergic reaction. As a result, my face swelled up with hives and welts, and my eyes became watery as my body began shutting down. I was unable to breathe at one point, and I had to call an ambulance which gave me a high dose of an anti-histamine medication through an IV. Regular over-the-counter anti-histamines will not work in these instances, I tried. At the very least, you will need an Epipen or an emergency visit to the hospital.

Perhaps the allergic reaction happens because of this correlation between Kundalini awakening and histamine release in the body. This higher level of histamine gets released once the Light Body is integrated and fully awakened, which gives one the sensation that there is a shot of novocaine in the body. The entire physical body feels partially numb, which becomes a permanent part of everyday existence afterwards. I do not know precisely why allergic reactions occur. Still, I can only imagine that the Kundalini energy cannot integrate whatever energy is released from the ingested food, which acts on the physical body, making it go into disarray. Whatever it is, I am mentioning it here so that if and when it does happen to you, you will know why and what it is and that you must get help immediately.

THE ESSENTIAL NUTRIENTS FOR TRANSFORMATION

As I have been going through the transformation process, I noticed that sweets have a particular effect on the Kundalini energy. Every time I eat something with sugar in it, I find that my Ego gets amplified, and my thoughts speed up and become uncontrollable, negatively affecting my composure. Therefore, when I am going through a difficult time mentally and emotionally, it becomes a hindrance to ingest sweets, so I try to stay away from them as much as possible.

Protein is essential as you are transforming from the inside, therefore eat meats and plenty of fish. Your body requires zinc while undergoing this process, and fish has plenty of zinc. The Kundalini works like a battery. It has a positive and negative current expressed through the Pingala and Ida channels, the masculine and feminine energies. They carry bioelectric current, which is regulated by your sexual energy. These channels need a medium to work through; otherwise, they burn out the system. This something is the fluid of the Kundalini system, which is regulated by zinc.

Your body also needs zinc to make proteins and DNA, especially when undergoing a genetic transfiguration like in the beginning phases of the Kundalini transformation. Zinc is also required for histamine storage. The body produces high levels of histamine when your consciousness is being localized in the Spiritual Body.

Zinc is directly related to your sexual energy, which I will discuss later on. Therefore, bringing zinc into the body is of paramount importance. Since your body doesn't store excess zinc, you must obtain it from your diet. I recommend doing so without over-the-counter supplements since they do not synthesize zinc in the body as food does. Fish, as well as pumpkin seeds, contain a lot of zinc. If you start using supplements, you create too much of this liquid-like energy unnaturally, which impedes your ability to focus, thus bringing your mind out of balance.

Your willpower component, which the Pingala Nadi regulates, will be drowned in this liquid energy which contains zinc. Compared to a battery, the battery acid, which is regulated by zinc, will drown out the opposing charges from the electrical current, and the battery will not work correctly. If you get your zinc from food, it synthesizes most optimally, which you will be able to feel. Zinc works with the water in the system to regulate your consciousness. Remember, the Ida Nadi adds the Water Element to your system, which governs your emotions.

PHYSICAL EXERCISE AND ILLNESS

While undergoing the Kundalini transformation, it is advisable to implement regular physical exercise into your life like Yoga (Asanas), jogging, weightlifting, competitive sports, swimming, biking, dancing, etc. As your heart rate increases during exercise, more blood flows into the brain, bringing oxygen and necessary nutrients. Exercise also helps release beneficial proteins in the brain that keep the neurons healthy, promoting the growth of new neurons. Remember, while the awakened Kundalini energy is transforming your nervous system, your brain works overtime to build new neural pathways to accommodate these inner changes. Therefore, regular exercise expedites this process.

On an energetic level, physical exercise is essential because it helps you synthesize the inner changes, grounding them into the Physical Plane so that your mind and body can function as one unit. Conversely, if you only work on healing your inner energies while negating your body, you will be sluggish physically, adversely affecting your mental state.

Physical exercise for at least one hour per day has also been shown to lower and reduce the stress hormone cortisol while releasing dopamine, serotonin, and endorphins in your brain. Thus, exercising cleanses your brain of unwanted chemicals while elevating your mood and motivation level, which can be highly beneficial in the early stages after awakening Kundalini. And with an increase in serotonin levels, which converts to melatonin at night, you will have an easier time falling asleep. In addition, competitive sports are an excellent outlet to blow off steam and regulate the effect of the Fire energy on your mind, especially in males in whom the Fire Element is more dominant.

An awakened Kundalini strengthens your immune system, allowing you to overcome illnesses quicker than the average person. However, if you are ill from the cold, flu, or other common ailments, be mindful not to overdo it with over-the-counter medication. Since your psychic sensitivity will be higher than average after an awakening, even the smallest changes in your body's chemistry can have a powerful effect mentally and emotionally.

Finally, if you suffer from headaches, which is common in the initial phase of adjusting to the new energy inside you, take Advil or Ibuprofen. I find that Advil stimulates the Ida Nadi, soothing the consciousness and relieving the headache much better than Tylenol, for example. In fact, to this day, I am not against taking an occasional Advil when needed, while I try to stay away from absolutely all other over-the-counter medications.

THE NEED FOR DISCRETION

As you may have figured out by now, a Kundalini awakening is a mysterious, elusive phenomenon that is not a part of the mainstream. Many people recognize the word "Kundalini" from Kundalini Yoga, thinking it is a type of Yoga, nothing more. And ones who know about its power to transform a human Spiritually are often in the dark about some of its more fantastic manifestations that rare individuals like myself have been privileged to experience. And as you are reading about these Spiritual gifts that unfold in the later stages, I realize how difficult it must be to grasp these relatively abstract concepts because you have to have these experiences yourself to understand me truly.

Although the process of Kundalini awakening is Universal, people's accounts are varied, as you understand by now. In this day and age, most people had partial awakenings, limiting them in the scope of side effects and Spiritual gifts. The people who had the full awakening, though, are generally challenged by the same issues. But in the sea of people's accounts, full awakenings are scarce. Typically, when someone has a full awakening, they write a book or set of books describing their experiences, enabling advanced individuals like myself to ascertain where we are in this limited but growing field of Kundalini science.

On a collective level, society is not up to par with the Kundalini experience since not enough people have had it for it to be included as part of general knowledge. Sadly, this means that medical personnel trained to help us heal mentally, emotionally, or physically will be of no use to us when undergoing a Kundalini transformation. Therefore, as you go on with your journey, the rule of thumb you will learn to be true is that unless someone has had the awakening themselves, and at the level that you did, they will not understand what you are going through. Thus, the faster you can accept this fact, the smoother your journey will be.

That being said, I advise you to learn to keep the truth to yourself about what you are going through. I know this isn't easy because other than needing advice at times from other people you usually rely on, you also want the world to understand what you are going through. So my advice seems counter-intuitive to some extent since we are all there to help each other, but you will realize there is no choice in the matter. Most people in your situation, myself included, have had to learn this eventually, or they deal with a lifetime of being ostracized, being called crazy, having unsuccessful romantic relationships, losing friends, and even becoming distant from family members.

This is a solitary journey for the most part, and since it is such a rare experience, you might meet a few people in person in the city or town that you are in who will understand you. You will find many people over social media if you know where to look, but not in person.

You need to learn to hide the truth about what you are going through from your family, friends and even strangers if you choose to blend in and continue being a regular part of society. I am not someone who will ever propagate lying, being an Aquarius hell-bent on always speaking the truth, but in this particular case, you will learn you don't have much choice in the matter. If you don't take my advice and tell people about your experience, you will soon experience everything I am warning you about, which may make you feel generally alienated from others, resulting in further loneliness and depression. People are afraid of what they don't understand, and they shun it from their existence if they have a choice. And in this respect, they do have a choice, and even the best of people, the most compassionate ones, will end up judging you because they very simply don't understand you. Please don't blame them; accept this fact.

Also, and this part is essential: you don't have to explain yourself to people. It is not your duty to do so. There is nothing shameful about your reality, and you need to protect yourself and others from what is happening to you. People who have not gone through what you are going through now cannot assist you. Putting your life into their hands will be catastrophic for your Spiritual journey as these people will unknowingly lead you astray every time. Also, a big part of the Kundalini awakening process is becoming your teacher and guide. I have said this before, and I meant it: all the answers to your problems are within you if you ask the right questions and have faith in yourself. Instead of turning to someone else for solutions, including someone like me with a lot of knowledge and experience, you need to learn to get in touch with your Higher Self and turn to them instead. No one can compensate for your Higher Self; they are the only intelligence that can give you the right advice every time.

I chose to blend in with others and keep trying to lead a normal life as I was going through the Kundalini transformation process. As such, I had to learn to tell lies when others inquired about the issues I was undergoing. It does not hurt anyone not to know the truth concerning this matter, especially when you know ahead of time that these people can't help you. Telling them the truth and making them sceptical about your sanity will only harm you since now you will have to deal with setting them straight on top of helping yourself.

Many strange symptoms will surface in your life as you are undergoing the Kundalini transformation process. In almost all cases, these symptoms will be temporary, although they may last for many years. Sleepless nights, emotional ups and downs, erratic behaviour, inability to focus, fluctuation in weight, and excessive and uncontrollable sex drive are just a few examples that may come about on your journey. If you decide you don't want to be judged by other people, you must mask these issues. Telling others that your symptoms result from undergoing a Kundalini awakening will undoubtedly make people think you are losing a grip on reality, making them lose faith in you as a person. They often believe that you are trying to make up an excuse they can't understand to confuse them, typical for someone at the onset of mental disease.

Your best way to navigate around circumstances is to lie in this matter. Permit yourself to do so since nobody will accept your excuses for not meeting expectations, such as getting to work or school on time, being there for someone mentally or emotionally, or fulfilling your daily tasks. Your situation falls outside the societal norm; therefore, it is critical to tell a lie to protect yourself. Even if you are not comfortable with the idea, you will find that lying about what is happening will make this process easier on you, and you may still be granted second chances to prove your worth to others. If you do not, you will keep hitting a brick wall with people and situations in your life.

The idea of lying is to take something too fantastic to believe and replace it with something an average person would understand. For sleepless nights, you can say you have bouts of insomnia, which is why you are not 100% in the morning. For emotional ups and downs, you can blame it on something going on in your life. Get creative but make your excuse something that an average person will understand and can sympathize with.

Remember, you have to be your therapist and doctor and find solutions to your problems. If you want to share with people who will understand you, get their perspective, and ask for advice, find them on social media instead. Hundreds of groups and pages have gathered Kundalini awakened individuals that have gone through what you are going through and can assist you. Many of them are on there for that reason, and they are thrilled to help you in any way they can. I have met some fantastic individuals on social media groups in this way.

I advise you to be critical minded when talking to strangers on social media, though. Some claim they have had a Kundalini awakening, but in reality, they might not have even if they genuinely believe their claims. Many Spiritual phenomena nowadays are being classified as Kundalini awakenings. And then there are hundreds of people who had a partial awakening and think they have all the answers. These people are the most difficult ones to spot and potentially the most harmful. So it helps to have some level of discernment in this matter and inquire about other people's experiences before taking their advice since there is no faster way to be led astray than to put your faith in the wrong person.

I see all kinds of good and wrong advice in social media groups, and I could spend an entire day addressing and clarifying each post. And I did this many years ago and have aided over two dozen people by giving them the right advice at the right time and helping them along their journey of awakening. Some contact me to this day to thank me for being there for them when they needed me. Through social media groups, I realized that my knowledge and experience in this matter could be of great assistance, crystallizing my purpose over time. So I went from writing articles and making videos on the Kundalini to eventually reaching out to the broader public with books such as the one you are reading.

THE FOLLY OF PRESCRIPTION MEDICATION

As you are undergoing the Kundalini transformation process and your mind is in disarray, you may often exhibit strange behaviour to which other people around you will react. Naturally, the people I am referring to are the ones closest to you, including family, friends, and colleagues. After witnessing your erratic behaviour, they may call you crazy or insane, which will confuse you even more about your state. After all, you will be undergoing tremendous emotional and mental pain, which you don't understand and which you seemingly won't have any control over.

At your weakest moments, your family or friends may suggest that you see a psychiatrist or therapist of some kind and talk to them about your problems. After all, these licensed personnel are trained to help people who are undergoing similar symptoms.

However, the problem is that these therapists have usually never even heard of the Kundalini, let alone have had an awakening themselves. And how can a doctor diagnose you about something that the medical field doesn't even recognize? You are not crazy, and you do not have any real reasons to be depressed. Also, if all of your emotional and mental problems began after awakening Kundalini, isn't it clear that the Kundalini is the cause behind the effect and not something external?

Regardless, many awakened individuals do follow that route, and they see a psychiatrist or therapist. After all, we are conditioned to listen to one another and accept advice on life issues, especially when we are desperate for answers to our problems. And, as you understand by now, undergoing a Kundalini transformation after a full and sustained awakening will bring on some of the most significant challenges yet. From talking to many people in the same position as me many years ago, seeing a psychiatrist always yields the same results. The psychiatrist listens to your problems, but since they don't know what you are talking about when you mention the Kundalini, they usually do the first thing when coming across a person with mental or emotional problems—they prescribe medication.

For the symptoms that a Kundalini awakening brings on, these medications are either anti-psychotics or anti-depressants. The nature of anti-psychotics is to block neural impulses that carry information from the subconscious to the conscious mind. They shut down what is happening on the inside so that it may appear that you are feeling better on the surface since you are will not hear negative thoughts anymore. On the other hand, the anti-depressants usually boost your serotonin and dopamine levels to create a fabricated feeling of being happy and joyful. Sadly, being prescribed any type of prescription medication by a medical doctor is the wrong approach to managing a Kundalini awakening.

Even though you may be exhibiting symptoms akin to chronic depression, bipolar, or schizophrenia, these states are temporary and need to be worked through by the Soul. They result from the influx of Light brought on by the Kundalini, whose purpose is to eradicate any negative energy present in your Chakras. Therefore, overcoming these emotional and mental challenges is the necessary step in advancing Spiritually.

Having awakened the entire Tree of Life, you will have access to parts of Self that have been hidden from you until your awakening. The Kundalini Light bridges your conscious and subconscious minds allowing many of your traumas and neurosis to emerge.

If you block out subconscious activity from the consciousness, these emotional and mental issues will be left at bay, unprocessed. Over time, this harmful unconscious content will build up, creating even more psychological problems, which will persist until the individual gets off the medication. If the individual chooses to continue being on medication, they may develop a lifetime dependency on the drug since getting off may prove more challenging. Sadly, the moment they began taking prescription medication, they inadvertently put their Spiritual Evolution on pause, and it will remain as such until they stop taking it.

While on medication, the Kundalini energy cannot do what it intends to, which is to continue the process of inner transformation. "Out of sight, out of mind" may temporarily diffuse problems, but it will not solve them. In fact, it will create even more future issues. Mainly, prescription medication is designed to develop a dependence on the drug itself since the individual never learns to deal with their problems naturally. They do not create neural pathways that enable them to find solutions to problems and cure their negative states; instead, they rely on the drug as a crutch that does it for them.

Kundalini energy is biological, and it needs the human faculties to work through. If some external drug shuts down the channels of information transmission, then you will put on the Kundalini process of cleansing hold. Once the individual gets off the drug, the Kundalini energy will be stirred into activity again. The same process will occur, this time coming on even stronger and more uncontrollably.

You have to understand that the Kundalini process will not give you more challenges than your Soul can handle. Your Soul is the one that chose to have this experience in the first place and the one that put it into motion. The Ego experiences pain, fear, and anxiety since it is the Ego that has to be transformed in this process. Instead of turning to prescription medication, which is the Ego's way out so that it can protect its identity, you will be doing a service to your Soul to find another way to deal with your mental and emotional problems. Your Spiritual Evolution is the only thing that matters in this lifetime. No terrible thought or emotion, no matter how scary it may appear, will harm you physically.

The Kundalini awakening process needs to be approached with the fortitude of mind, strength, and courage. Fear and anxiety are temporary, and if you persist through the process, you will inevitably emerge on the other side as a transformed person. It may take many years, but dawn always follows the night. All one has to do is get through the night.

CREATIVITY AND MENTAL HEALTH

Spiritual reality is an invisible science measured and quantified by intuition, emotions, and intellect. But most of what comprises the Spiritual reality cannot ever be proven, which is why we have a division in our society between believers and non-believers. The non-believers are primarily people who only rely on science, which relies on proof. But to take away faith into something greater than yourself and put your hands in science alone is just robbing yourself of the juice, the nectar of tasting the Spiritual life. Seeing is believing, but conversely, believing is also seeing. If you can believe in something that other people believe in, then it will manifest in your life in due time. Such is the Law.

We know much about the science of tangible reality, the world of Matter, but understand very little about invisible realities. So instead of pondering the age-old question of who or what God is, let's focus on humanity and the Spiritual gifts some of us are given that make us seem God-like in the eyes of other people. And the most precious gift our Creator gave us is the ability to create. But where does creativity come from, and why do some people have more of it at their disposal than others?

Gopi Krishna and other awakened individuals have said that all human creativity is a by-product of Kundalini activity in the body, implying that everyone's Kundalini is active to some degree. This may sound like a radical statement to some people, but I believe this to be true as well. I also think that the Kundalini influences unawakened people subliminally. These people are consciously unaware of their creative process and cannot tap into the source of their creativity like the awakened can.

One of the purposes of the full Kundalini awakening is to raise and evolve the consciousness to a higher degree so that you can become consciously attuned to your energy system's functioning, including the creative process, instead of it being something happening in the background affecting only your subconscious.

Also, this part is essential; the Kundalini has not pierced the Three Granthis in most unawakened people, which means that their creative energy is limited, as are the Chakras through which this energy can express. The average person has active Kundalini, but since they have not overcome Brahma Granthi, they can only express their creative energy through Muladhara Chakra. As such, they are bound to their Ego, primarily seeking physical pleasures, which causes unhealthy attachments and fears. A person in this position will never reach their optimal creative potential, nor will they significantly impact society. Sadly, with humanity's low level of evolution in today's day and age, most people are in this state.

The more willful and ambitious types have generally overcome this first Granthi and have enabled the expression of their creative energy through Swadhisthana and Manipura Chakras. Still, they are bound by the Vishnu Granthi, which lies directly above, preventing the Kundalini from reaching the Heart Chakra, Anahata, which will awaken the unconditional love energy within them. Therefore, they may use their creative energy to satisfy their ambitions, but they may lack a higher vision to truly make them stand out from the rest of the people.

And then we have the savants of our society, the prodigies and visionaries who have pierced Vishnu Granthi, allowing them to use even more of their creative potential. Their Kundalini may be operating from the higher Chakras enabling them to perform incredible feats and access information and abilities that other humans don't have. However, even they are limited by dualistic thinking resulting from an untied Rudra Granthi between Ajna and Sahasrara Chakras. As such, we cannot compare their creative potential with someone who has pierced all Three Granthis and has fully awakened their Kundalini, unleashing unlimited creative potential.

The genius of scientists such as Newton, Tesla, and Einstein, and philosophers like Pythagoras, Aristotle, and Plato may well be attributed to the workings of the Kundalini in their Light Bodies. Similarly, the talent of musicians like Mozart, Beethoven, Michael Jackson, and artists like Michelangelo, da Vinci, and Van Gogh could be the working of the Kundalini energy at a subconscious level. And let us not forget the athletic abilities, skills, and will to win of athletes like Muhammad Ali and Michael Jordan. These people were so legendary that we still revere them as God-like figures, and their tales of greatness will live on forever.

A few of these great men and women describe having the means and methods of tapping into the source of their creativity, and they were well aware that they were channelling some higher form of intelligence when they were in these inspired states. However, they were not aware of the existence of Kundalini, nor did they report something like it working through them. So all we can do is speculate based on what we saw in these people and the work they left behind.

These influential figures had something special: a connection with the Divine that gave them particular insights, powers, and skills that people around them didn't have. Many of them were so ahead of their time that they changed the course of human history. But we will never know whether it was the Kundalini that was directly responsible for their greatness or it was something else.

KUNDALINI AND MENTAL HEALTH

If Kundalini is active in everyone to a greater or lesser degree, significantly impacting the psyche, it is no wonder that no major progress has been made in mental health. The Kundalini is not even recognized as a real thing in the medical field. Apart from developing medication that can turn on and off certain parts of the brain which receive impulses from invisible forces in the energy system, the current scientific understanding of mental health is rudimentary at best. To truly understand how the mind works, the mental health field needs to have a proper foundation laid in the invisible science of the human energy system to develop cures that treat more than just symptoms.

I have always been fascinated as I watched the inner workings of my mind while undergoing the Kundalini awakening process. Some days I would have such an emotional high, which was often followed by a profound low, all in a matter of minutes. These emotional ups and downs did not happen to me before the awakening. My emotions became so highly charged by the Kundalini energy that if my mind was working in a positive direction and thinking happy thoughts, those emotions became enhanced, and I was more content than ever. If my mind was thinking in a negative direction, though, and I was thinking sad or unhappy thoughts, then my emotions would get so low that I would feel downright depressed. And it made no sense why my depression was so intense when just a minute before I was incredibly happy, and there was no apparent change in my state other than what I was thinking about.

This incredible shifting between happy and sad states I attributed to the workings of my mind and the quality of my thoughts. For this reason, at the beginning of my Kundalini awakening process, when I had very little control over my mind and what I thought about, I was having these emotional episodes. These episodes can be compared to someone diagnosed with bipolar mental disease, although I found it was to a lesser degree than the episodes I heard some bipolar people have.

What separates the two cases is that I have always known the difference between right and wrong and would not act on my emotional impulses. At the same time, some people allow these inner psychological workings to run their life and take over their mind, body, and Soul. The key is to recognize the situation for what it is and not blow it out of proportion. One must understand emotions as something tangible, something which can be moulded and changed with the application of the mind. Knowing this difference, you must work on controlling your thoughts since it is the "chicken that came before the egg" scenario and not the other way around. You must be a cause instead of an effect and readily shape and mould your mental reality with willpower.

What is a disease in this respect but a dis-ease—something which is making you feel uncomfortable and uneasy? Physical illness is usually a result of some foreign material entering your physical body and causing a change or deterioration at a cellular level. Does this idea of a foreign body coming into you also apply to mental health, or is it something within you that causes mental and emotional issues? To answer this correctly, we need to look at what thoughts are and if they are inside of us only or can they be something outside of us, which makes its way into our Aura, to experience them.

The Kybalion, which elucidates the Seven Principles of Creation, says that we are all communicating telepathically and that our inner "Me", the creative component that generates images impressed by our "I" component, is always working and cannot be turned off. Therefore, the challenge is using your willpower, your "I," to continually give impressions to your "Me" component. If you get mentally lazy and do not use your willpower like God-the Creator intended you to, then other people's "I's" will give your "Me" component its impressions. However, and this is the pitfall: you will believe they are your thoughts and will react as such.

These thought senders are all around us, and some of them are the thoughts of other people, and some are Spiritual entities outside the physical realm, which take part in our Inner World and can impact our minds. These Angelic and Demonic Beings influence our thoughts, especially if we don't use our willpower to its fullest capacity. In the case of Demonic Beings, their influence can result in full-body possessions if you listen to them and do their bidding.

These complete takeovers of your mind by hostile foreign forces are very real indeed. Conversely, receiving communication from Angelic Beings may result in complete Spiritual rapture and bliss. In the case of empaths or telepaths, they are open to the influence of Spiritual entities more so than the average human as they are continually receiving vibratory impulses from the outside world. Someone with an awakened Kundalini falls into this category; it is very challenging to differentiate between your own thoughts and thoughts of someone or something outside of you.

The key, in any case, is to understand the Inner World of the Mental Plane of thoughts as something that is not particular to only you and that throughout the day, many thought vibrations will enter your Aura from the outside world. We are all a part of this hub, this "thought world," and we are continually inducing the invisible world with our thoughts, affecting other people subconsciously. Thoughts have energy; they have mass and are quantifiable.

Loving, positive thoughts are higher in degree in the vibratory scale than are negative, fearful thoughts. Loving, positive thoughts keep the Universe in motion, while negative, fearful thoughts contribute to keeping humanity at a low level of Spiritual evolution.

A war between the Angelic and Demonic Beings has been waged for as long as humanity has existed. It is an invisible war on the Astral Plane and Mental Planes, where human beings serve as the conduits of these invisible forces. Currently, given our low level of Spiritual evolution, it is safe to say that Demonic Beings are winning the war. However, according to religious scriptures from all over the world, it is the destiny of humanity to eventually usher into the Golden Age, meaning that Angelic Beings will win this war for good.

Schizophrenic patients are those people who have higher than average receptivity to the invisible world, but what separates them from psychics (who are either telepaths, empaths, or both) is that people with schizophrenia cannot tell the difference between their thoughts and thoughts outside of them. In many cases, they are under the control of Demonic entities who have established a foothold in their Aura by feeding off their fear energy.

Demonic entities, which are intelligent Beings, the source of which is unknown, look for weak-minded people that they can feed on. Once they find a person susceptible to their influence, they will take over their minds and bodies, which over time extinguishes the Light from their Souls so that they become vehicles for these Demonic forces, nothing more. They become husks or shells of their former selves. Although the Soul can never truly be extinguished, once the separation happens in the mind, it becomes almost foreign to the individual who lost their connection with it. It is still there to be tapped into again, but it takes a lot of mental effort and Spiritual work to regain that connection.

STRENGTHENING THE WILLPOWER

In the first few years after awakening Kundalini, my willpower was tested often concerning my decision-making process. Whenever I became convinced of an idea, I could, within seconds, be persuaded that the opposite is true. For a long time, it was challenging to make decisions because I was aware that I was negating the validity of its counterpart by following any course of action. I knew and understood that any idea could be a good idea given enough proof in the direction of that idea. But for most ideas, there is also enough proof that their opposition is correct as well.

This process went on for many years until I had attained a stronger connection to my willpower. To achieve that, though, required an immense amount of mental work and effort on my part. By gaining a correct link with my willpower, I also aligned with my Soul unprecedentedly. Working with the Fire Element and Manipura Chakra via Ceremonial Magick ritual exercises helped me achieve this.

If you do not have a firm connection to your willpower, which is your Soul's expression, then you will fall prey to the duality of the mind and impulses of the Ego. I have seen this time and time again in Kundalini awakened individuals, and it is one of the most significant challenges they face.

The awakening activates all the Chakras so that they are all functioning simultaneously. As the conscious and subconscious minds become bridged, the result is a high level of emotional charge since the activity in the Mental Plane is amplified. For this reason, many Kundalini awakened individuals are so emotionally sensitive and changeable with their decision making. Since their receptivity to outside vibrations heightens, they need to learn to differentiate between their thoughts and those entering their Aura from the environment. One of the ways to mitigate this occurrence is to connect with the Soul and strengthen the willpower, enabling discernment and discretion.

Once you learn to make a decision, the other challenge is to commit yourself to it and follow through. Doing so transforms you into a person whose word can be trusted and not someone who allows their changeable emotions to lead the way. Building up your Soul by developing virtues and overcoming vices will make you a person of honour that others will respect.

Although there are various Spiritual Alchemy practices you can use to optimise your inner functions, many of which are included in this book, Ceremonial Magick was the answer for me. Its ritual exercises enabled me to boost my intuition, willpower, memory, imagination, emotions, logic and reason, etc. By invoking the Elements through Magickal means, I could optimise my inner functions by attuning the Chakras. These internal components of Self are weak in the first place because of Karmic energy stored in the Chakras pertaining to each function. For example, if your intuition is weak, then you may need to work on Ajna Chakra. Conversely, if your willpower is weak, so is Manipura Chakra since the Fire Element is responsible for its expression. And so on.

KUNDALINI AND CREATIVITY

There is a definite correlation between being happy and inspired and exhibiting high creative abilities. When one is experiencing positive emotions, the inner drive to create becomes amplified. It manifests as an inner longing, a passion or desire to create something beautiful. This relationship between creativity and inspiration is symbiotic. You cannot be creative without being inspired, and to get inspired, you need to be creative in finding a new and exciting way to look at life.

If you get stuck in your old way of thinking, relating to the Ego instead of the Soul and Spirit, both your inspiration and creativity will suffer. There needs to be a constant renewal of your mental and emotional reality that can be achieved once you live in the present moment, the Now. As you draw energy from this infinite field of potentiality, your state of Being will be inspired, opening up your creative abilities.

My creativity became infinitely expanded in the seventh year after awakening the Kundalini in 2004. I experienced a complete opening of the Lotus Petals of Sahasrara Chakra, which allowed me to enter the Now and function through intuition. I noticed a strong correlation between overcoming the duality of my mind, strengthening my Willpower, and enhancing my creative abilities. Once I obtained a permanent link with my Soul, I became perpetually inspired, overcoming my fear and anxiety and tapping into my creative source. In this incredibly high state of inspiration, I felt a need, a yearning, to express this newfound creativity somehow. As such, my journey of creative expression through multiple mediums began.

My first expression was through visual art since it was something I was good at my entire life. I found that this high inspired state just flowed through my hands as I painted, and I was developing techniques that I seemingly pulled down from the Aethyrs. I started painting in the abstract style and would channel colours, shapes and images that vibrated and danced in my Mind's Eye as this process was unfolding. I realized that the true source of creativity is from the Soul, but it is channelled through Ajna Chakra via Sahasrara.

When I was expressing creativity in this enhanced way, all of my higher components were turned on and functioning simultaneously. I readily received impulses from the Higher Self and the Crown Chakra, which combined with the Fires of my Soul to channel through the Mind's Eye. The creative process seemed to take over my mind and body like I was possessed. I found that while in this state, time would fly in an unprecedented fashion as many hours would pass in the blink of an eye.

What I noticed is that my inner creativity was able to recognize and replicate beauty. Here is the key, I believe, because when I am in an inspired state, which is now a permanent state of Being for me, I see beauty all around me and recognize it in everything. The energy of unconditional love, which is the foundation of inspiration, creativity, and beauty, transposes everything I see with my eyes. Therefore, if I engage in a creative act, I can channel something beautiful by using my body as a vehicle.

Beauty has a form that I believe can be quantified. It is well balanced and harmonious. It is colourful if it wants to be experienced as joy. There is texture to it and often a mixture of Archetypes that convey vital ideas to the Soul. We can express emotions through beautiful works, and naturally, all creative expressions are meant to move you emotionally in some way.

If beauty wants to be seen as sorrowful, there may be a lack of colour and more serene shapes used to express it. If it wants to be seen as melancholy, colours respective to this feeling are used, such as shades of blue. This process of channelling beauty is not limited by visual arts alone but can be seen everywhere. For example, we can express sorrow through song and melody. This correlation implies that colours, as well as musical notes, express states of consciousness. It accounts for the feeling behind the music as well as visual art and sculpture.

All the colours we find in nature come from the visible spectrum of Light. The visible spectrum is the part of the electromagnetic field that is visible to the human eyes. Electromagnetic radiation in this wavelength range is called visible Light or merely, Light. This fact implies that all musical notes on the music scale also relate to Light energy. Now you can see why your creative potential becomes infinitely expanded once you awaken the Kundalini and receive an influx of Light into your Aura.

I experimented with creative expressions for many years and found myself able to channel new ones with ease. I explored singing and music and expressed my creativity through the written word in poetry and inspired writing. However, I have learned the importance of balancing creativity with logic and reason. You cannot just create haphazardly, but it has to have a structure, an intellectual foundation somehow. I learned that beauty has form and function, and it is this marriage between the two that needs to be followed when creating; otherwise, your creative expressions will miss the mark.

SAHASRARA AND THE DUALITY OF THE MIND

For maximum alignment with the willpower and the Fire Element of the Soul after a full Kundalini awakening, the Thousand Petalled Lotus of Sahasrara needs to be fully opened. However, in the scenario where it is a partial opening of Sahasrara, as a result of not allowing the Kundalini to complete its mission upon the initial rising, it can result in energy blockages in the head. In this case, Ida and Pingala Nadis will continue being influenced by Karmic energy in the Chakras below Vishuddhi, the Throat Chakra, instead of being liberated and free-flowing in the Body of Light as is the case when the Lotus unfolds entirely.

When Rudra Granthi is pierced, the Kundalini has to rise with full force to Sahasrara, allowing the top part of the Sushumna channel that connects the middle of the brain to the Crown to widen and transmit enough energy to open Sahasrara's Petals. Sahasrara's flower head is closed in unawakened people; when Kundalini rises, it begins to open in the same fashion as watching a time-lapse of a flower in bloom. Each petal opens to receive the Light coming in from the Soul Star and Stellar Gateway Chakras above (Figure 153). If some of Sahasrara's Petals remain closed, the Crown will not be fully activated, resulting in blockages accumulating in the head area over time.

Once the Kundalini rises from Muladhara, it seeks to leave out of the body through the Crown, resulting in Sahasrara's Petals unfolding like a flower, ready to receive the Light. Sahasrara is named the "Thousand Petalled Lotus" because there are theoretically a thousand Petals, each connected with countless minor Nadis or energy channels that carry Pranic energy from different areas of the Body of Light that terminate in the head area. There are hundreds, potentially even thousands, of these nerve endings in the brain. Each one is like the branch of a tree that carries Pranic energy in, through, and around the brain. As you open the Crown fully, it allows many of these Nadis to reach outward to the surface of the top part of the head. It often feels like bugs crawling on your scalp or energy zaps or twitches as these brain Nadis are being infused with Light.

As discussed, once you awaken the primary six Chakras below the Crown, different parts of the brain unlock, as do the Minor Chakras in the head that correspond with the primary Chakras. The entire psychic energy system serves to channel Light energy throughout your Body of Light, which allows your consciousness to experience transcendence while embodying the physical body. Once the Crown Lotus fully opens, the Soul exits out of the body, allowing the consciousness to reach the Transpersonal Self in the Chakras above the Crown.

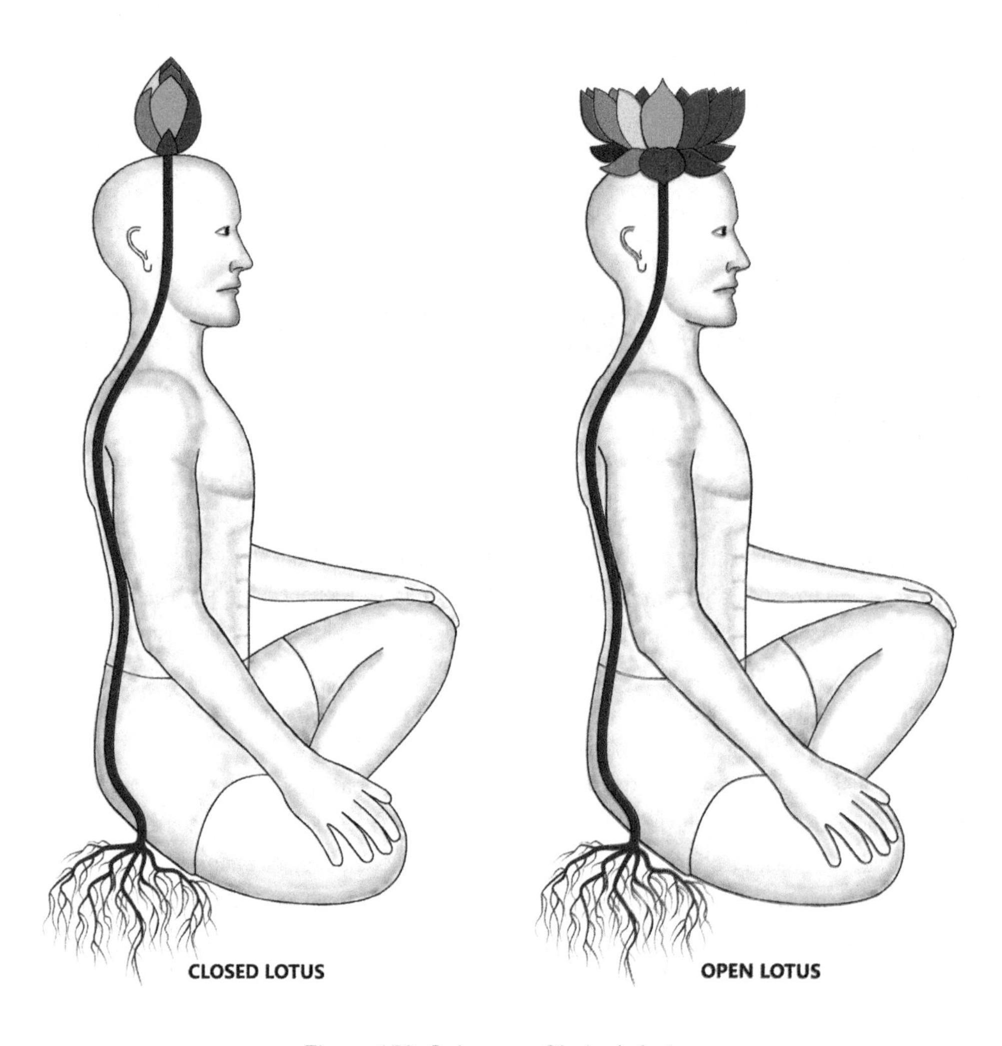

Figure 153: Sahasrara Chakra's Lotus

The minor Nadis serve as psychic receptors powered by the Light inside the body, which is built up through food intake. This Light in the body works with the Light brought in from Sahasrara Chakra. As mentioned before, the Body of Light is like a tree whose roots are in the ground while the torso serves as the tree's trunk. The trunk carries the primary Chakras while the body's limbs serve as major branches of the tree. These branches carry Light energy through their Seventy-Two Thousand Nadis, which extend out to the skin's surface, although on a subtle level. The Thousand-Petalled Lotus releases the individual consciousness from the body, connecting it with the Cosmic Consciousness in Sahasrara.

Sahasrara is at the top, centre of the head and acts as a portal through which White Light is brought into the energy system. This Light is filtered through the Chakras below. However, if some of the Lotus petals remain unopened due to blockages in the primary Chakras and Nadis, the flow of the Kundalini becomes obstructed, resulting in mental and emotional problems (Figure 154). Therefore, the Kundalini needs an unobstructed flow from Muladhara, through Sahasrara, and beyond to the Transpersonal Chakras above.

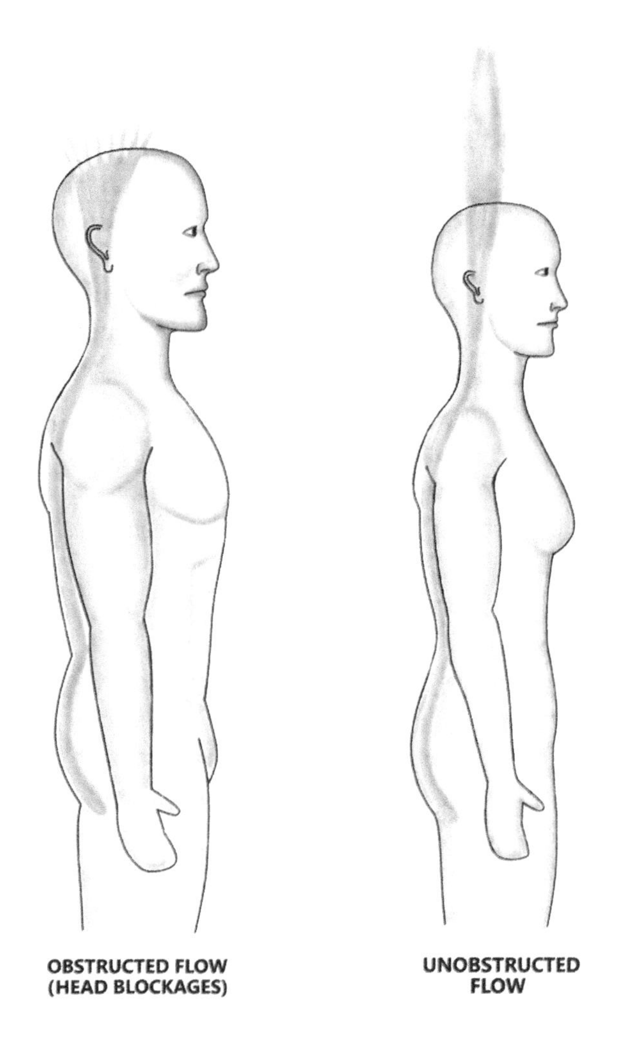

Figure 154: Kundalini Flow through Sushumna

You can alleviate psychological issues with the use of Spiritual practices, like Ceremonial Magick, which cleanse and remove blockages in the Chakras and Nadis. The reason why Ceremonial Magick is the most potent Spiritual practice that I have come across is that it most effectively allows you to invoke the energies of each of the Five Elements to tune their corresponding Chakras. In turn, the Nadis that connect with the Chakras are purified, including Ida, Pingala, and Sushumna, whose flow is optimised. If any blockages at the initial Kundalini rising hampered the energy reaching and opening the Sahasrara Lotus completely, you would also eliminate these blockages. Once out of the system, the Kundalini will naturally rise again to finish the job by unifying Shiva and Shakti at the Crown Chakra, Sahasrara.

INTROVERT VS. EXTROVERT

If some of the Lotus Petals are closed, it is a sign that energy is stagnating and moving improperly in the head. This issue can cause pressure in the head and even headaches. Too much Light in the head causes a person to become inverted, focusing on their inner thoughts, especially at the back of the head where the subconscious mind operates from. Remember, your mind-state is dependent on where you focus your attention in the many levels or layers of consciousness.

Introverts use logic and reason via the Lower Mental Plane when cerebral or the Astral Plane when experiencing emotions. Introverts are affected by the Light of the Moon, which gives many illusions. This Lunar Light is the source of duality since it is only a reflection of the Light of the Sun, which is a singularity.

Extroverts use the Light of the Sun and are action-oriented, unlike introverts who are more known for their thinking and feeling. Extroverts don't spend much time in their heads; instead, they operate from their hearts which is more instinctual. They express themselves through verbal communication, allowing their actions to lead the way. Most extroverts draw their energy from their environment and the people around them. As such, they like big crowds and being the centre of attention.

Conversely, introverts like being alone or with a few friends they trust. They draw their energy from within themselves, so their thoughts and emotions are so crucial to them. They are methodical in their approach to life and don't use words as anchors like extroverts do but express themselves through their body language instead.

On the surface, it may seem that extroverts are more confident, but this isn't always the case. Because introverts use their mind more, they are more careful in their decision-making process, making more logical conclusions that provide fruitful results. Extroverts generally bypass the mind and make decisions with their gut. If their intuition guides them, their choices can be beneficial, while when their instincts lead them, they often suffer. When willpower is dominant, extroverts operate from the Higher Mental Plane, while when they are channelling their intuition, they are influenced by the Spiritual Plane. Extroverts are generally led by their Soul, while introverts are more prone to being led by their Egos.

The Kundalini awakening is meant to make you more of an extrovert, although you will invariably fluctuate between both states throughout your Spiritual journey. For example, you will spend more time being an introvert in the beginning stages when the Ego is more active, while in the later stages, when you fully attune to your Soul and Higher Self, you will become an extrovert. This is because the Spiritual path always begins in the mind but ends in the heart.

Your alternation between introverted and extroverted states during your Kundalini awakening process depends on what Elements you are working with naturally via the Kundalini fire or through ritual invocation techniques. The Water Element relates to your emotions, which can be voluntary or involuntary, like instinctual emotions—as such, working with this Element will make you introverted. The Fire Element relates to your willpower which motions your body to act, thus making you an extrovert. The Fire Element is expressive of Archetypes and truth, being tempered by the Light of the Sun. Conversely, the Water Element demonstrates the duality of the mind, acted on by the Lunar Light.

The Air Element (thoughts) vibrates between them, fueling them both and giving them their dynamism. Thoughts can be conscious, motioning the willpower, or subconscious, acting on the feelings. And finally, the Earth Element, related to physical activity and being in the present moment, makes one an extrovert. The density of the Earth

Element prevents too much thinking or feeling, which only leaves us with action. The Earth Element is directly related to the Soul and being led by one's inner impulses, whether intuition or instincts.

EMOTIONS VS. REASON

A powerful dichotomy that presents itself in the fully Kundalini awakened individual is the constant battle between the emotions and the intellect, expressing itself through logic and reason. Emotions (feelings) are a result of our past conditioning as well as our inner desires. Some feelings are instinctual and involuntary, while others we have control over.

Logic is the systematic study of arguments, whereas reason applies logic to understand or judge something. These two inner components are two sides of the same coin. They represent the part of us that can perceive the truth of the matter and make judgements concerning our decision-making. Reason can predict outcomes; it acts like a super-computer that reads the reality around us. It then gives us informed calculations enabling us to perform the most optimal action possible, which will yield the best results.

Emotions are impulses that drive us to take action at the moment. They are influenced either by self-love or unconditional love for all humanity. When controlled by self-love, emotions are not concerned with results but with feeling good and getting what the Ego wants when they want it. Emotions are thus linked with personal desires. When influenced by unconditional love, the Soul is exalted, and the focus is on building virtues and the pleasure one gets from being a good person.

Lower emotions are expressed through the Water Element along the Astral Plane of reality. The higher emotions rise as high as the Spiritual Plane, however. Logic and reason are always influenced by the Fire Element acting on the Air Element, along the Mental Plane. It cannot project higher than the Mental Plane.

The Ego and the Soul can take over both emotions and reason. However, the Soul always operates via the energy of unconditional love acted on by the Spirit and Fire Elements. The Soul understands that we are Eternal and our spark will continue past physical death, so it seeks unity and recognition of oneness with other human beings. It does not act out of self-love; only the Ego does since the Ego lives out of the mind where it recognizes the duality of Self and other Selves. It guards and protects the body, fearing its eventual death. This fear energy is what drives much of the emotions that the Ego influences.

Sometimes our emotions can tell us something so firmly, which goes entirely against what our reason tells us, and vice versa. This process will go on for many years in the Kundalini awakened individuals. However, at the higher points of the Kundalini awakening, you will overcome personal, lower emotions, and your reason and logic will align with the Soul and Higher Self, the Spirit. It is impossible to succeed in life while only following your feelings since they can be so volatile, and acting on them often yields very negative results. Emotions that are an expression of some inner desire have no logical basis for the most part. By acting on them, we often get ourselves into trouble.

But even though we like to do what feels good, as is our natural impulse, through the Kundalini awakening process, you learn to curb the lower emotions since your Ego is in the process of dying. As a result, you can look ahead and perform actions that align with higher emotions that project through the lens of unconditional love. Often you will find that these higher emotions are also aligned with the logical part of you, and this balance between the two will yield the most favourable results in your life.

The balance between higher emotions and reason is, in fact, the proper foundation necessary to live a happy, successful life. Over time, you will build up your character and a degree of fortitude, which was unfathomable at the beginning of your Kundalini awakening journey. You will learn to live with an emphasis on proper conduct and action coming from a place of morals and ethics. This mode of living is the natural expression of the Fire of the Kundalini and the feeling of the Glory of God, which permeates your Heart Chakra, Anahata.

KUNDALINI AND FOOD TRANSFORMATION

Gopi Krishna became renowned in the late 1960s as one of the foremost authorities on the Kundalini awakening phenomenon in the Western world. Although Arthur Avalon's *The Serpent Power*, published in 1919, was the first book to introduce the concept of the Kundalini to the West, Gopi wrote a series of books focusing entirely on the Kundalini, which got translated into English for the Western world. This happened around the same time as Yogi Bhajan introduced his brand of Kundalini Yoga into the United States. Between the work of these two men, the entire world became familiarized with the word "Kundalini."

Gopi wrote many books on the Kundalini for the next twenty years. While his work was more philosophical, Yogi Bhajan taught the practical methods through Yoga to activate this elusive and mysterious energy within his students. However, the Kundalini science has not advanced much beyond the work of these two men. The one notable figure that came along and had a significant contribution in this field is Swami Satyananda Saraswati, who wrote many books on Tantra and Yoga and elucidated the practices to follow their paths while providing the means and methods of how to awaken your Kundalini. The work of Swami Satyananda has significantly influenced my contribution to Tantra and Yoga in this book. And I would be remiss if I didn't mention David Frawley's extensive work on Yoga and Ayurveda, which has been of tremendous service to the Western world and me personally.

I have already talked about Gopi's initial Kundalini awakening and his peril after having an incomplete rising. This situation tormented him until he found a solution. His despair resulted from the Ida channel remaining dormant while Sushumna and Pingala activated when his Kundalini awakened. It manifested as debilitating anxiety that made life impossible for Gopi, some days wishing he was dead. However, this situation requires further examination since it is a common occurrence that could happen to anyone. For example, I have dealt with the same problem, although in a different context and have found solutions to fix it. Having a clearer picture of the mechanics of what happened to Gopi will enable you to use my solutions to fix this issue if it happens to you too.

After Gopi's Kundalini awakening, since Ida's cooling, passive, Water energy was not present, the hot, active, Fire energy of Pingala was working overtime. However, this situation only made matters worse for him. The Ida channel activates the Parasympathetic Nervous System, which calms down the body and mind. In contrast, the Pingala channel starts up the Sympathetic Nervous System, putting the body and mind into "fight or flight" mode. Imagine having the SNS system on permanently and being unable to turn it off. Consequently, I've been in this exact situation, so I know what that is like and how to fix it. The only difference is that I already had the tools to overcome it by the time that happened to me, which Gopi did not have.

If this happens to you, and it can happen even during later stages of the Kundalini transformation, every moment of your life becomes a state of crisis. The worst part, I have found, is bringing food into the body, which creates the most agonizing fire that feels like it is burning you alive from the inside. I lost ten pounds in the first week when dealing with this situation, and Gopi also mentioned rapid weight loss. You see, the hot, intense Pingala channel needs to be balanced by the cooling energy of Ida; otherwise, the system goes into disarray, negatively affecting the mind. Every morsel of food you take in manifests as debilitating stress and anxiety, which exerts and exhausts your Adrenals Glands. This state of mind can take a toll on your life, feeling like it is a life-or-death situation that no one around you can help you with. Imagine the despair you go through and the state of emergency while being the only one that can help yourself. I have been there.

The moment you ingest food, it begins to transform into Pranic energy, which powers the Pingala channel and kicks it into high gear since the high quantity of Prana is not being evenly distributed through both primary Nadis. Gopi knew from Tantric and Yogic teachings that he most likely didn't awaken Ida, so he knew what to focus on to try and help himself. He knew that only Ida contained the cooling power he needed to balance his energy system. And me, well, my help was Gopi, who went through the same thing and wrote about it in his books that I had read up to that point.

Gopi made every effort to activate Ida through meditation. The meditation he used was the visualization of a Lotus flower in his Mind's Eye. By holding its image over time, the Ida channel finally activated at the base of his spine and rose upwards into his brain. He felt its cooling, soothing energy, which balanced out his energy system. His mind became well regulated now. He found solace in food intake and even began to eat in excess, focusing mainly on oranges, probably to replenish his worn-out Adrenal Glands.

Visual thoughts, which are pictures in the mind, are the effect of the Ida channel, not Pingala. So it is not a coincidence that Gopi Krishna activated Ida by forcing himself to form a visual picture in his Mind's Eye and hold that image with a mighty concentration.

It is essential to understand that if a Kundalini activation and rising is to be successful, all three channels of Ida, Pingala, and Sushumna must rise into the brain simultaneously. To create a well-balanced psychic system and complete the Kundalini circuit in the newly developed Body of Light, Ida and Pingala must rise into the centre of the head at the Thalamus and blow open Ajna Chakra. Then, they continue moving towards the point between the eyebrows, the Mind's Eye centre. If you have awakened Ida and Pingala channels, but they have become blocked, or one or both has a short-circuit sometime in the future, you can correct the flow of these Nadis again by focusing on the Third Eye.

If Ida and Pingala drop below the Seventh Eye Chakra or the Bindu point at the back of the head, the Kundalini circuit will cease to function. To restart it, you have to meditate on the Mind's Eye and hold an image using your imagination and Willpower. This practice will re-stimulate Ida and Pingala and reopen the Seventh Eye and the Bindu Chakra. As such, the Nadis will realign and reconnect the entire Kundalini circuit in the Body of Light. Another meditation that may work if there are blockages in the Bindu is to hold your attention one centimetre away from the Bindu point until the energy is realigned and flowing correctly. Likewise, by focusing one centimetre away from the Seventh Eye Chakra, you can also align that point.

I will get into these exercises and meditations in more detail in the chapter titled "Kundalini Troubleshooting" towards the back of the book. These meditations are paramount to stabilizing your Kundalini system. I have discovered all of these meditations myself in the past seventeen years, and as such, you will be seeing them for the first time in this book. If there were mass Kundalini awakenings and the whole world needed guidance and quickly, my meditations would be the answer to many energy-related issues that people could experience. So how did I think of them?

When I underwent problems with the Kundalini circuit, I would lay on my bed for hours, days, even weeks, looking for different energy "trigger" points in the head area to meditate on that could remove energy blockages and realign the Nadis. Sometimes you even need an Ajna or Sahasrara Chakra re-activation, although it is impossible for these centres to close once the Kundalini energy has awakened them fully. During this discovery process, I was determined to find solutions at all costs that allowed me to prevail. "If there is a will, there is a way," I always said, and "any problem has a solution," even if it's a problem of an energetic nature. I never accepted failure in this regard so that through my discovery process, I would find solutions that I could one day share with the world as I am now.

My discoveries have been tried and tested many times in my life when Kundalini system issues challenged me. And all of them work. Understand that the Kundalini is very delicate but also very volatile. Many things we do as humans which are readily accepted as the norm in society can and will short-circuit the Kundalini system. For example, how we treat each other as people, traumatic moments, and even the use of drugs and alcohol can be very detrimental to your Kundalini system. Once you finish this book, you will have the keys to overcoming any issues with the Kundalini system and not be at its mercy when it malfunctions.

FOOD SUBLIMATION/TRANSFORMATION

The process of food sublimation/transformation yields many different experiences as time goes on. For example, after activating the Body of Light upon the initial Kundalini awakening, you will feel a sense of inertia and lethargy for some time afterwards since the body uses all of the Pranic energy it gets from food to build up the Kundalini circuit. As a result, you may feel uninspired and unmotivated to perform your daily tasks. You may also want to isolate yourself from other people and be alone. Keep in mind that these rather uncomfortable manifestations are not permanent. As you evolve, they will pass.

After the initial awakening, you will most likely find yourself in a negative mindset mentally and emotionally as you are nourishing your Body of Light through food intake. Your dopamine and serotonin levels will drop since the body is in overdrive to synthesize food into Pranic Light energy. It takes a few months for the energy to stabilize and for you to feel some sense of life purpose again. During this transformation process, your motivation and drive, as well as your willpower, will enter hibernation mode. You will have to give yourself a break and take some time off from whatever you plan to work on and accomplish during this period. However, I can guarantee that you will re-emerge from this experience stronger and more invigorated than ever.

During the initial parts of the build-up process, the Kundalini Fire gets sublimated into Spirit or Light energy. At first, it is in a state of potential as latent heat. However, as you bring food into the system, it feeds the fire and makes it grow. As it grows, it intensifies, which begins to feel like you are burning up from the inside. Finally, at the peak point of the heat's intensity, as the heart races and anxiety is at an all-time high, the fire starts sublimating and becomes Spirit energy.

The most important thing to understand from this process is that the Kundalini Fire will be in a continuous state of transformation and transmutation. It changes form as you keep eating and drinking water to regulate and cool off its effects. I would often find myself running to the kitchen to get a glass of water to cool off. My parents would watch in disbelief, trying to figure out if their son had turned into a drug addict because my behaviour was alarming. At other times, I would need a glass of milk if the heat was too intense and my body lacked nutrients. So, I suggest that you be ready with that glass of water or milk whenever you need it and have a good excuse for your strange behaviour if you don't live alone.

This process is very intense for a few weeks to a few months at most. Afterwards, it stabilizes and become smoother. The beginning part of the awakening is genuinely the most challenging since the fire inside you feels like it is burning you alive, and due to its intensity, your stress and anxiety go through the roof. Part of the fear you experience is the Ego trying to figure out what is happening but cannot since it normally functions by predicting things based on what it has already seen, and it has never seen something like this before.

This sublimated Kundalini Fire, which I can only describe as a cooling, Mercurial Spirit, is meant to fuel the Kundalini circuit. While the Kundalini begins as a raging fire, remember that this state is only one of its temporary forms. Knowing this ahead of time can save you a lot of heartaches, so don't forget what I said. Over time, and with food intake, the Kundalini Fire transforms into a peaceful, ethereal, liquid Spirit energy that soothes you and washes away the negativity the system encountered previously.

Being patient as this process occurs inside of you is half the battle. Remember, nothing remains static while the Kundalini is transforming you; metamorphosis is a process of constant change. Therefore, you must learn to welcome the inner changes instead of fighting them. For this reason, many awakened individuals advocate surrendering to the Kundalini energy at all costs. Now you can see why it is easier said than done. However, you will see that you have no choice in the end.

Although the raging fire can be very uncomfortable at its peak stages, it will inevitably become a cooling Spirit energy. Whether you choose to be an active or passive participant in the process is totally up to you. I cannot tell you how long it will take to transform since the timing varies from person to person, but I advise eating nutritious food and being calm, patient, and relaxed as much as possible.

Invoking negative thoughts and doubt will only stimulate fear in the system, which will cause an adverse effect. Being calm while the raging fire of the Kundalini is acting will release serotonin and oxytocin, allowing the sublimation into fine Spirit energy to occur. Dopamine and adrenaline hinder this process; the body must activate the Parasympathetic Nervous System instead of the Sympathetic one.

It helps to place the tongue on the palette of the mouth while this process is occurring. This act will connect the Ida and Pingala Nadis and make it easier to keep the mind calm and sublimate the energy. As the raging fire transforms into Spirit, new pockets of energy open up in the central abdomen area and on its right side. Here is where this new Spirit energy seems to begin its ascent upward along the Ida and Pingala channels in the front of the body. These pockets of energy, located in front of the kidneys, create the feeling of Oneness, Eternity, and complete absorption into the Spirit.

THOUGHTS IN "REAL-TIME"

After a full and sustained Kundalini awakening, Light energy will continuously be present inside the brain. Since the Light serves to bridge the conscious and subconscious minds, it has a particular effect on your thoughts. While in this unusual state of Being, your thoughts will begin to appear very real to you. Like whatever you think of is present there with you in real life. This phenomenon is partly a result of the Kundalini piercing Anahata, the Heart Chakra, on its upward rise, awakening the Silent Observer aspect of the Self.

This part of the Self, combined with the tenuous Light inside your head, will give you the feeling that all thoughts in your mind are real and not merely just ideas. As you think, the Silent Observer part of the Self watches this process take place in the Heart Chakra like an innocent bystander. But, conversely, once this part of the Self is awakened, so is its opposite—True Will. It is the generator of all reality, the Higher or God-Self.

Experiencing your thoughts as real is, in fact, the catalyst behind the fear and anxiety that presents itself right after a complete and permanent Kundalini awakening. As deep, subconscious thoughts are united with conscious thoughts, everything interior appears more real than ever. It can be a terrifying and confusing experience at first, as it was for me and many others going through the same thing. It becomes difficult to tell the difference between your conscious thoughts and the projected fears from your subconscious.

This new "realness" of thought is the source of the elated feelings of happiness from inspired thinking, including the intense depression resulting from negative, fear-based thoughts or ideas. Both Angelic and Demonic forces can now permeate your mind, and the challenge becomes being able to tell the difference between the two. Adverse thought senders can either be your hidden skeletons in the closet, thoughts being projected from other people's minds or even outside entities that live in the Astral and Mental Planes.

After awakening Kundalini, your next step in the process of Spiritual evolution is to master these two Planes, especially the Mental Plane, since what you think about will determine the quality of your reality. In New Thought Philosophy, this is expounded upon by the Law of Attraction, which states that you bring positive or negative experiences into your life by focusing on positive or negative thoughts. *The Kybalion* supports this theory, as the Law of Attraction is based on the core Hermetic Principle of Creation which states that "The All is Mind, the Universe is Mental." This implies that your thoughts are directly responsible for your experience of life since the difference between the World of Matter and your own Mental reality is just a matter of degree. Therefore, Matter is not as real and concrete as we perceive it to be but is the Thought of God, which works with your thoughts to manifest your reality. Hence, we are Co-Creators with our Creator through the mind, through thoughts.

The Hermetic Principle of Correspondence, "As Above, So Below," tells us that the higher Planes affect the lower ones, explaining why the Mental Plane affects the Physical Plane. This axiom is also regarded as the basis of practising Magick. Aleister Crowley defined Magick as "the science and art of causing change to occur in conformity with Will." Even though our thoughts determine reality, we need to get in touch with and tune into the willpower that powers our thoughts. The process of manifestation into the physical reality has at its source the impulse of the True Will from the Spiritual Plane, which becomes a thought in the Mental Plane, triggering an emotional response in the Astral or Emotional Plane, and finally manifesting in the Physical Plane of Matter.

For this reason, working with the Elements and purifying each Chakra is of paramount importance on the Spiritual journey. The subconscious mind is no longer something deep and hidden inside the Self; it becomes something right there in front of you every waking moment of the day, whose function you can observe. The reason for this is because Ajna Chakra is now awakened and operating at optimum capacity after receiving an influx of Light energy through the awakened Kundalini. The Mind's Eye is the "tool" we use for introspection and seeing into the workings of the subconscious mind.

Remember, Karmic energy (in the sense of referring to negative energy stored within the Chakras) results from an opposing viewpoint, belief, or memory that in the case of individual Chakras relates to a particular part of the Self. The old Self, the Ego, is what we need to purify and consecrate so that the new Higher Self can take its place. The

Self uses different powers activated by the energies in the Chakras as they are the source of these powers. At the beginning point of the awakening, the Self will have more reference to the Ego than ever, but as we purify our concept of the Self, we are shedding the Ego.

It becomes necessary to cleanse the subconscious mind because, as stated earlier, you must first master your Demons, the negative aspects of your psyche, before you can reside in the higher Chakras and be one with the Spirit Element. By aligning your consciousness with the higher three Chakras of Vishuddhi, Ajna, and Sahasrara, you are aligning with the True Will and the Higher Self.

Because you cannot turn off this process, as it has been triggered by the awakened Kundalini, having the tools to purify the Chakras and master the Elements will become more relevant to you than anything else at this time in your life. Otherwise, you will be at the mercy of the psychic forces within the Cosmic Planes. Therefore, you must develop yourself into a Spiritual warrior at this point as your mind, body, and Soul are being remodelled daily by the newly awakened Kundalini energy.

EMPATHY AND TELEPATHY

Once the Kundalini circuit is open, and the Spirit energy is circulating in the Body of Light, your consciousness gains the ability to leave the physical body at will. As you funnel out of your physical body through the Crown Chakra, you experience your Spirit energy pervading everything you perceive with your physical eyes in the material world. This experience adds to the real-time perception of reality; only now you can feel and embody the energy of every object in your environment. Through your Heart Chakra, you start to feel the essence of whatever you put your attention on as your Spirit energy transposes onto that which you look at or hear.

When watching a violent movie, for example, you can feel and experience the energy of a violent act by transposing your body into the body of the person you are watching. This process occurs automatically and instantaneously, without conscious effort. All that is required to make this phenomenon happen is giving the movie your undivided attention. It is quite a magical experience at first and one of Kundalini's greatest gifts. It starts to develop when enough Spirit energy has been sublimated through the Kundalini Fire and food intake. It can happen by the end of the first year of the awakening, maybe even earlier.

This transformation and manifestation enables you to attune to other people's feelings when focusing your attention on them. This process is how you grow in empathy. You literally step into their body with your Spirit and can feel what they feel. If you are not giving them attention by looking at them, all you must do is listen to them as they are talking, and you tune into their energy through sound. This manifestation occurs through your connection with sound. It is a form of telepathy—reading people's minds and the quality of their thoughts.

Empathy is reading people's feelings and the emotional energy of their hearts. Sufficient Spirit energy needs to pour into your newly developing Body of Light through food transformation/sublimation to create both manifestations. It is like a wave that is created, and your attention is the surfboard. With your attention, you can now surf the wave by focusing on things external from you.

It would help if you learned to separate yourself from whatever emotions or thoughts you are experiencing by understanding that it is not projected from inside but from outside. The Ego can get confused, thinking it is the Ego from whom these emotions or thoughts are projected, which can cause fear and anxiety. Once you have gone beyond your Ego and can separate yourself from what you are experiencing, you can do so without any negativity. However, this might only occur in the later stages of the Kundalini transformation, once the Ego is purged and fear and anxiety have lessened their energetic charge or have left the system entirely.

When you first start to experience this phenomenon, it might be unclear to differentiate who you are and who other people are. It is one of the biggest challenges in the first few years of the awakening since so many emotions and thoughts will be running through your mind and heart that you will be swayed backwards and forward like a boat in stormy ocean waters. The key is to stabilize your interior and learn to navigate the turbulent waters. In this way, you are learning to gain control over your life, maybe for the first time. The Greek aphorism "Know Thyself" is essential to implement at this stage in your life. You will need to take hold of your thoughts and emotions by understanding your energy projections and other people's.

An important note on both telepathy and empathy—once you develop a stronger connection with your Spiritual Body, these psychic gifts will become permanent, meaning you can't turn them off anymore. You cannot decide that it is just too much to bear and that you simply don't want to take part in it anymore. Sometimes it can be quite overwhelming since you are at the same time dealing with your anxiety and fear while also taking on others'.

It would help if you had introspection at this time. You should take some time to yourself if you are not used to doing that because you will need it. If you have been a social butterfly your whole life, you cannot be around other people all the time anymore. It's time to change these habits and take time to yourself as well. Alone time is the only way for proper introspection because some of these thoughts and feelings of other people will stay with you for days, weeks even. You have to learn to let them go and not make them a part of who you are.

Over time, once you can differentiate between the two and have cleansed and purified your Ego, you will be able to spend more time with others and less time alone. In addition, you will be able to tune into other people's love energy, which now feeds your energy. Not in a way that you are a psychic vampire that steals other people's energy but in a way where you accept love and give it back so you can maintain selfless love energy exchange with people you interact with. Love energy is nourishment for the Soul for all of us, and this is why we need each other. To learn to channel pure love without attachment, you will first need to overcome your negativity.

ETHICS AND MORALS

Once the Kundalini is active, there comes a significant shift in consciousness, and you notice that your concept of ethics and morals through proper behaviour and conduct is developing. In other words, you begin to act with moral principles in all life situations, naturally. Unity of the Self and the rest of the world grows, causing you to feel connected to all things from a moral standpoint. There comes absolute respect towards humankind as this Kundalini awakening process is occurring.

Over time, the Kundalini begins to eradicate personal memories of the past, thereby exalting the Higher Self over the Ego. This process allows you to live in the Now, the present moment, most optimally. It can be a very confusing state at first because, as explained, the Ego functions by referring to memories about itself. As memory is fleeting, though, the Ego begins to drop away through the Kundalini purging process since it can no longer associate with past events. As such, the Spirit and Soul become exalted. Naturally, you will start to develop a high ethical standpoint since, in the present moment, you realize that the right way to conduct yourself is with respect and honour toward all living things.

This moral upgrade is a natural development for any person undergoing the Kundalini awakening. It is a gift. All people with awakened Kundalini are humanitarians and give selflessly in one way or another. They are seemingly on autopilot in most cases once they have surrendered themselves to the Kundalini energy. A complete surrender must occur to achieve this state, and this surrender is inevitable for everyone going through the transformation process.

No matter how much the Ego holds on, it ultimately knows it will take a backseat to the Soul and Spirit. Eventually, its hold is lessened. A solid ethical and moral foundation is the birthright of all Kundalini awakened people. Our overall destiny as human beings is to love and respect one another instead of taking advantage. Once you have developed yourself ethically, you will recognize that we are all brothers and sisters since you will be nearer to the Mind of the Creator than ever before.

Ethics and morals are connected with unconditional love energy building up in the Heart Chakra. You begin to feel the whole world in your heart as One essence (Figure 155), coupled with the desire to channel this newfound love energy to others. And as you project love energy towards other people, your character begins to build virtues whose foundation are ethics and morals.

You begin to feel a sense of honour since we are all brothers and sisters born of the same Creator. When you are in the present moment, in the Now, you can attune to that part of yourself that is Eternal—the Holy Guardian Angel. Your Higher Genius begins to teach and guide you on your Spiritual journey. They teach you how to be a better human being every day of your life. The Holy Guardian Angel teaches you about the Universe and imparts knowledge and wisdom daily. It is all-wise and all-good and has the highest moral compass because it is part of God-the Creator.

Figure 155: The Heart Chakra and Oneness

Being kind towards others makes it easy to separate the good people from the bad ones or ones without a moral compass. I find that for the most part, though, people are good, and when you treat them with love, they reciprocate. By honouring and respecting them, you channel love towards them that feels like a Light beam that shoots out of your chest. Once this beam of Light energy enters the Aura of another human being, they absorb it and send it back to you through their Heart Chakra. This perpetual love energy circuit only severs when one of you begins to think with their Ego, asking what's in it for them. If people of the world didn't have massive Egos, we would naturally be exchanging love in this fashion, eradicating evil on a global scale.

I have also found that learning to act through an ethical lens has made me love and respect myself more. As you recognize the goodness inside you and choose to share it with others, you invariably learn to love yourself. After all, other people are just reflections, mirrors of ourselves. We are all the Creator, and the Creator is One. It is crucial to learn to love yourself because you overcome your insecurities by doing so. One method of learning to love yourself is to be comfortable in the Now, which overcomes your insecurities.

In most cases, some external factor triggers them, making you go inwards inside your mind. Once you are introverted, and inside yourself, you lose touch with the Now and the realm of pure potentiality where anything is possible. By staying in the Now, though, you become extroverted instead, and as long as you remain present, you won't go inside yourself where you can access your insecurities.

The Kundalini awakening is meant to make you into a Being of Light, and as such, this upgrade enables you to live life to your fullest, perhaps for the first time. To get the most out of life, you need to be in a state where you can recognize the opportunity in everything you are experiencing to take that opportunity to experience something new and grow Spiritually. Morals and ethics go hand in hand with being in the Now. Conversely, being in the Now relates to the concept talked about by Jesus Christ—the Glory of God.

The Glory of God relates to attuning your consciousness to the realm of Eternity—the Kingdom of Heaven. You can reach this realm through the Now, but you must completely surrender yourself through faith to enter it. Only your intuition can contact the Eternal Kingdom as it requires your Ego to be silenced to experience it. The Glory of God is an emotional rapture that comes from experiencing Oneness with all things. It is the Realm of pure potential and Non-Duality. It may seem far-fetched to think you can resonate with this concept but believe me; it is attainable. One of the purposes of the Kundalini transformation is to take you into the Kingdom of Heaven eventually. Note that although the experience of the Glory of God is usually momentary for the average person, highly evolved Kundalini awakened individuals can stay in that state indefinitely.

It is essential to understand that these concepts and ideas mentioned above are connected. One gives rise to the other, which then awakens something else. These are natural expressions of becoming a Being of Light through the Kundalini awakening. It truly is an upgrade and a new way of living on this Planet. Others may never know what you are experiencing, but they will see the changes you are undergoing through your actions.

The key is to stay inspired during this transformation process. You must avoid allowing the occasional negativity inside the mind to bring you down and make you lose hope. Instead, see it as something temporary that you will overcome with time. The entire Kundalini transformation process unfolds as the years go by. One experience leads into the next as everything about you is continually changing and evolving. It takes many years before you truly can reap the benefits of being transformed into a Being of Light, but it will all make sense when you do.

PART VIII: KUNDALINI AND LUCID DREAMS

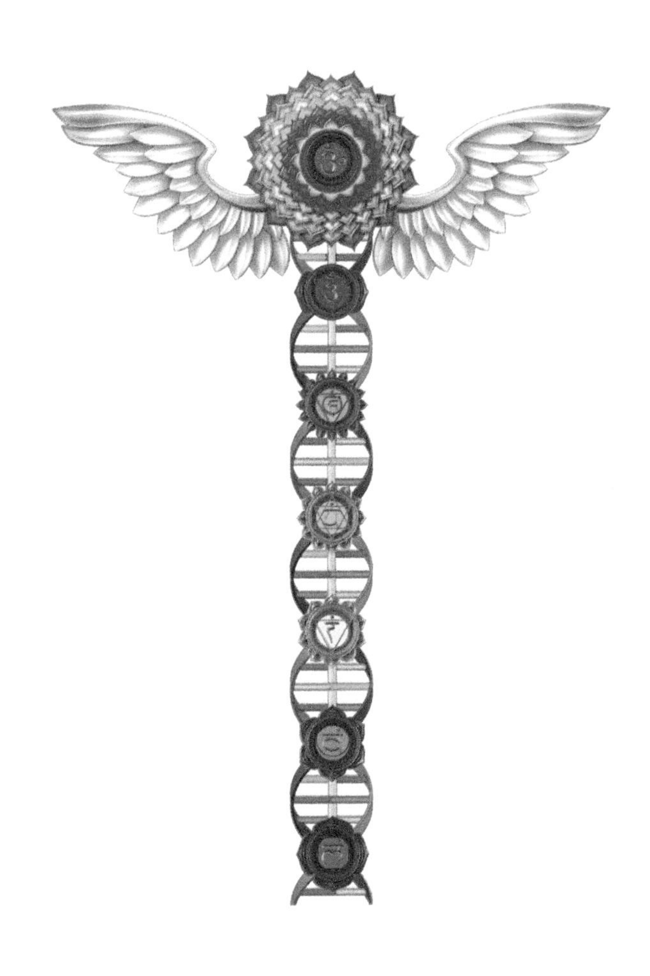

THE WORLD OF LUCID DREAMS

Lucid Dreaming in the Inner Worlds is a critical topic of conversation within Kundalini circles. Kundalini awakenings guarantee the experience of Lucid Dreaming, which takes place on the Inner, Cosmic Planes. Lucid Dreaming is a form of Out-of-Body Experience (OBE) which occurs during sleep while your consciousness is in the Alpha State. The Alpha State is a dream state where the body is resting, but consciousness is still awake. It is a state between normal waking consciousness and sleep.

This state is most commonly triggered when you wake up briefly in the early morning at around six or seven and then go back to sleep after having already slept for at least five hours so that your physical body is rested. But when you are undergoing an intense buildup of Astral Light, such as right after the initial Kundalini awakening, if you have fully activated your Body of Light, you will find yourself Lucid Dreaming almost every night. This experience occurs because there is a surplus of Light energy present, which funnels your consciousness out of Sahasrara Chakra, through the Bindu, to have this experience.

You can also induce Astral travel while awake, but it is more challenging to achieve since you have to transcend the physical body somehow. For this reason, it is usually best to explore Lucid Dreaming during sleep when you are in an Alpha State and the physical body is already rested.

A Kundalini awakened person will experience a myriad of Lucid Dreams, almost nightly, after a permanent awakening. This phenomenon can go on for many years. During a Lucid Dream, the Kundalini circuit is active, and the body is fed Astral Light/Spirit energy through food sublimation/transformation. The terms Astral Light, Spirit, Prana and Kundalini energy are all interchangeable. The difference is their state, which is dependent on the level of Spiritual evolution you are at, though they all originate from the same substance. In essence, Kundalini energy is Light energy, which transmutes into different states during the Kundalini process of transformation.

Once you have built up a sufficient amount of Light energy and are in an Alpha state, your consciousness vaults out of the physical body through the Crown Chakra, and you enter into one of the Cosmic Planes. As mentioned so far, these Planes exist in a dimension apart from the Third Dimension of Space and Time. Now, suppose the experience is an Out of Body one, and you vaulted out of the Crown Chakra. In that case, you are most likely entering one of the Spirit Chakras or Transpersonal Chakras above the Crown and "surfing" their corresponding Plane. Since these Planes are beyond Space and Time, your consciousness can experience a lifetime of events in one hour. You will sometimes wake up like you physically underwent these experiences and will find yourself mentally drained.

As discussed, we each have a body-double made of Light; an elastic substance called the Body of Light. Lucid Dreaming is a type of "Astral projection," a term coined by Theosophists in the 19th century. Although Lucid Dreams happen almost involuntarily, Astral Projection is a fully consciously induced experience—a Soul projection into one of the Astral/Inner Planes. In the case of Lucid Dreaming, this projection occurs spontaneously as the Body of Light vaults out of the physical body during the Alpha sleep state. It merely leaves the physical body, having you wake up somewhere else, in some strange and usually never-before-seen land.

In a Lucid Dream, there is no break in consciousness. Your subconscious and conscious are now working in unison, so the content of your dreams changes to include things that you often think about consciously. Your imagination is perpetually active in a Lucid Dream as you are the experiencer and the experience in one. Very often, you are projected somewhere that you have never been before with content that you consciously never thought about. It is most common, though, that when you have a Lucid Dream, to see elements familiar to the consciousness so that it would not be too much of a shock to the Self as you are undergoing this experience.

For this reason, Lucid Dreaming involves your imaginative abilities, although infinitely expanded. In a Lucid Dream, your Higher Self, your Soul, is the conductor of the experience. It always chooses where to go and what to experience. However, you cannot consciously choose your experience like in an Astral projection. Since we are connected with both our Ego and our Soul in our waking state, the Lucid Dream experience will seem foreign to the consciousness to a great extent. The Ego is entirely inactive in a Lucid Dream since it belongs to the physical body, which is transcended.

WAKING UP IN A DREAM

The most fantastic thing about Lucid Dreams is that the consciousness experiences a reality outside of the physical one, though it feels authentic. The first step of every Lucid Dream is your consciousness becoming aware that it is dreaming. It happens instantly as the consciousness realizes that the setting is "different" from the Physical World, but its experience is very much the same.

A popular method of realizing you are dreaming is to train yourself to look at your hands as soon as you find yourself in a dream. There are no fixed shapes in dreams, and everything appears fluid and elastic like it is moving ever so gently. Therefore, the fingers on your hands would be all shapes and sizes, so when you look at them, you can see them move up and down ever so slightly. This recognition signals to the brain that you are in a dream, thereby awakening your consciousness fully.

There is usually a sense of excitement when this happens since a part of you realizes that you are a conscious creator of your reality now, and you can experience whatever you desire with the help of your imagination. Since your Ego is transcended, the Soul takes over the experience, and you find yourself in a state where you are creating your reality and experiencing it simultaneously. You have full access to your willpower and can control the content of your dream. You cannot control the setting, but your Soul can choose where it wants to go and can use your Body of Light as a vehicle to get there.

Your experience will be similar to how you experience the physical reality, the World of Matter. However, the main difference is that you are limited by Time and Space in the Physical World. For example, you cannot be in Paris by merely thinking it, but you have the choice to get on a plane and fly over there. The entire experience, though, will take some time to complete until you can get to Paris. In a Lucid Dream, you can think of somewhere you want to be, and you will be there in an instant. There is no break in consciousness from when you think of where you want to be and you being projected there the moment you have this thought—it is all one fluid experience.

The Soul has full knowledge of all the places it can venture to in this vast Universe of ours, which are as Infinite as God-the Creator. Thus, in a Lucid Dream, your Soul will automatically project somewhere for you to experience its environment. However, the following morning, when you wake up from your experience, your Ego will not be able to figure out how and why you went there or what it was. After all, the Ego is limited to what it has seen, and it has only experienced things of the Earth. All the Ego will know is that the experience was incredible, and you will feel grateful for it.

DEVELOPING ABILITIES IN YOUR DREAMS

Once you are projected into a Lucid Dream, you will have complete control over your Body of Light wherever its setting may take place. Neither space nor time nor gravity can limit this second vehicle of consciousness. However, since you are not bound by gravity, one of the first gifts to develop is flying through the air like Superman (Figure 156). This ability is the most fun and usually the first one to manifest for everyone. Flying in a Lucid Dream is the only way to genuinely experience flight without the use of machines which is exhilarating, to say the least.

Figure 156: Flying Like Superman in a Lucid Dream

The consciousness soon finds itself able to perform other feats which would be impossible to achieve in physical reality. For example, since the Body of Light is weightless and is not bound by Matter and gravity, and since everything in the Astral plane is Holographic without any fixed form, you will develop the ability to walk or fly through objects. Another ability that emerges is Astral telekinesis—the ability to levitate objects in the Inner, Astral Planes and move them with the power of the mind.

To perform telekinesis and move objects in the Physical World with the mind, you must first learn to use this skill in the Astral world since the two work on the same principles. I have seen documented video footage of people who claim they have psychic powers where they move light objects in a vacuum, although minimally. However, to displace heavier things than a small piece of paper, let's say, would require an immense amount of mental energy, which is a feat seemingly impossible and something that we never documented. I believe that it can be done, though, using the same mental principles and mind over Matter. However, the person doing it would have to be such a Spiritually evolved person that they would appear God-like to others and not merely psychic. Jesus Christ performing miracles in *The Holy Bible* is one example of how evolved you would have to be to affect the state of Matter with your mind.

Other gifts that develop in the Lucid Dream world is the ability to read people's minds, make yourself as big or small as you want, and generally fulfil any desire you have in your daily waking life, such as sleeping with a person of your choice. The Lucid Dream world is a Wonderland for the Soul and satisfying on all levels of existence. In addition, it does not carry the Karmic consequences of fulfilling your Soul's desires, no matter what they are.

After having had these Lucid Dream experiences for many years in my life, I am left with many doubts concerning the development of Siddhis, the supernatural abilities mentioned in Hindu scriptures. However, Siddhis are not exclusive to Hindu sacred texts since psychic powers are displayed in all religious books, irrespective of their culture or tradition, which leaves us with the following predicament: perhaps the Prophets, Saints, Yogis, and other Holy figures from these books were talking about the Lucid Dream world when they mentioned humanity's ability to gain these extraordinary powers.

We may never know the answer to this, but in my experience, there is more proof that what I am proposing is accurate than these powers being something that we can attain physically. For example, every levitation claim has been debunked, from the East to the West, and what we think are displays of psychic powers always end up being some kind of magical illusion or trickery.

Therefore, it cannot be a coincidence that as I continued to Lucid Dream in my early years after a Kundalini awakening, I was slowly developing every one of these psychic abilities that scriptures talk about. However, no matter how hard I tried to exhibit these powers in physical reality, they remained exclusive to my dreams, although my Soul experienced them as real.

KARMIC ENERGY IN DREAM STATES

While in the Lucid Dream state, you can also consciously try to find solutions to problems you might be facing in your life. This experience will only happen when you have accessed the Spiritual Plane. Its purpose is to help you master this Plane by accessing Karmic energy particular to one of the corresponding three Spirit Chakras. The Divine Planes are without Karma and, as such, are pure joy. Keep in mind that it is your Soul, not your Ego, that is being trained here; hence, it will seem automatic that you are projecting into whatever Chakra needs work.

You may not always have the ability to fly in your dream, but you will still be able to control its content to a large extent and be consciously aware that you are dreaming. Every experience is fundamentally different in a Lucid

Dream. Once you have begun to have these experiences, your consciousness becomes trained to awaken in the dream.

For the most part, the heavy Karmic energy in the lower Cosmic Planes keeps the consciousness asleep and unaware that it is dreaming. Therefore, it needs to have a few moments when it is not engulfed mentally and emotionally to realize it is experiencing a dream which prompts the Soul to take over its content.

Although much of what you will experience is your imagination in hyperdrive, some of the places you will visit in the Lucid Dream world are real and not a by-product of your enhanced imagination. Suppose your consciousness does not wake up while in the dream, which is the first step to the dream becoming a Lucid one. In that case, everything will continue on autopilot, and you will continue having a regular dream experience.

BINAH AND THE ASTRAL BLUEPRINT

The Lucid Dream world is very different from the Physical World, yet similar in how the consciousness experiences it. The Ancients believed that every city or place on Earth has an Astral-double that can be visited during sleep while Lucid Dreaming. Where you go depends on where your Soul wants to take you and is not something that you can control consciously through the lens of the Ego.

This Astral-double reality goes hand in hand with the Qabalistic teachings, which state that Malkuth, the Earth, has a Holographic blueprint, which is in another dimension of reality. This dimension occupies the same space and time, although it is in a different vibratory state. In the Qabalah, that reality is represented by the Sephirah Binah. Binah is associated with the Holy Ghost of Christianity, the Spirit Element, awakened through the Kundalini. It is the foundation of all that is.

A full Kundalini awakening is an awakening of the Body of Light so that we can intuitively read the energy of Binah while living a physical existence. This concept goes hand-in-hand with what we have been examining so far and all the different components that make up the totality of the Kundalini awakening experience.

Since the Kundalini awakening releases the Soul from the physical body, it transforms the Self on all levels through the influx of Light energy in the Aura. Light energy filters into each of the Seven Chakras since each Chakra is one of the colours of the rainbow, as part of the White Light spectrum.

As each Chakra is expressive of a Cosmic Plane, the awakening of the Kundalini allows the individual to exist on all Planes of existence simultaneously. Their Tree of Life becomes fully open, and each of its respective Sephiroth (states of consciousness) fully accessible. The individual consciousness expands, resulting in unification with the Cosmic Consciousness above.

Since Binah is one of the Supernal Sephiroth on the Tree of Life, it belongs to the Spirit Element. Binah is also the Sphere of faith and the mental faculty of intuition. As awakened individuals become Beings of Light, they connect with the Solar Light energy from the Sun, which is expressive of the truth of all things. The Solar Light conveys Archetypes, coupled with the Lunar Light of the Moon that reflects thoughts. In this way, the intuition can perceive beyond the physical senses through the sixth's sense of Ajna Chakra.

The Soul leaves the physical body during sleep and enters one of the Cosmic Planes external to the Self, although reflected in the Aura. In other words, the idea of distance does not pertain to the Soul's journey in the Cosmic Planes, as it can be projected wherever it wants to go in an instant. The Aura is the Microcosm of the

Macrocosm, meaning that everything in the outer Universe is also within the Aura. Through this Principle or Law, the Soul can Astral travel during dream states, especially Lucid Dreams.

After a full Kundalini awakening and transformation, once the individual attunes to the workings of the higher Chakras, the mind becomes bypassed, and illusions vanish. The individual begins to fully function on intuition as the Lunar Chakra, Ajna, reads the Archetypal energy from the Solar Chakra, Sahasrara, enabling one to live in truth and Light.

As we gain an intimate relationship with Binah, we can understand the unreality of the Physical World at a deep level, which allows us to transcend the World of Matter and see life as something not to be taken too seriously. We realize that our Souls are sparks of consciousness from the Sun that will live on past this life. This understanding brings much joy, happiness, and inspiration into our lives, allowing us to reach our full potential and manifest our dreams and goals in life.

SLEEP PARALYSIS

Lucid Dreaming can be such a powerful experience where the force of your dreams engulfs you so that you undergo sleep "paralysis," meaning that the consciousness is so involved in the Lucid Dream reality that it does not want to pull itself out of it. Sleep paralysis can go on for over a dozen hours at a time. However, you can experience a lifetime of joy and happiness beyond Time and Space in the Lucid Dream world within that same amount of time.

Sleep paralysis can be an issue if you have things to do in the morning the next day. You will need to learn to deal with this because if you are experiencing it, it won't be straightforward to snap out of it until you naturally awaken. I had this issue, especially during the first two to three years after the awakening. Some nights I would sleep in for up to sixteen hours, completely unable to get up until the experience finished. Sleep paralysis is more common in the earlier years of the Kundalini awakening than in the later years as your consciousness is becoming adjusted to the Inner Worlds that open up within you to explore.

Once you try to wake up from sleep paralysis while in a Lucid Dream, you will be putting an incredible strain on your brain since your brain's cycles will still be resonating with this Inner reality. In addition, the brain's activity is heightened during sleep paralysis since the brain is under the impression that what it is experiencing is real.

While undergoing sleep paralysis, you will have overcome your physical body since a Lucid Dream is an Out-of-Body Experience. During this time, your physical body will feel numb to your consciousness, and your Mind's Eye will be undergoing extreme hyperactivity. The Lucid Dream is experienced entirely through the Mind's Eye, as you vault through it and out of the Crown into the higher Cosmic Planes. As your consciousness becomes adjusted to the Lucid Dream reality over time, it will learn to differentiate between the Inner reality and the Outer reality. As such, you will be able to switch in and out of these two states on command. This learnable skill will develop with experience.

I have never heard of sleep paralysis being detrimental to you or your health. As mentioned, the main challenge is waking up from it when it is required of you to do so. If you find yourself Lucid Dreaming almost nightly, you may encounter this issue, so be ready when it happens. It will help if you have excuses prepared on hand if you cannot make your morning plans. Simply saying "I can't wake up" is not going to cut it in the modern world.

Also, keep in mind that while you are undergoing sleep paralysis, you will look possessed to other people who view you while in this state, so be careful who has access to your room while you are sleeping. I recommend that you tell whoever you live with about this issue, so they will leave you alone if they find you in this state.

I remember many times trying to wake up from sleep paralysis, and the moment that I would force myself to open my eyes and sit up, the Inner reality grabbed hold of me and pushed me back down on the bed. It does not help that when you are Lucid Dreaming, your physical body feels so heavy like it is made of lead. You may sometimes feel like the Outer and Inner realities are fighting for supremacy over the consciousness. However, as your consciousness becomes more aware of these different Inner Worlds and experiences them, it will be able to shift in and out of other realities on command.

It is not dangerous to be in sleep paralysis. Apart from being spacey and tired afterwards, I have never experienced any other after-effects, nor have I heard of any from other Kundalini awakened individuals. The tiredness comes from all of your inner functions being involved in a Lucid Dream, which puts further strain on your physical body instead of resting it.

I will also add that you may be having such a great time in this Lucid Dream reality that you may not want to snap out of it no matter what you need to do the next day. Also, be mindful that your body may heat up more than usual during this time, resulting in profuse sweating. Undergoing sleep paralysis enables the Kundalini energy to transform you from the inside, so there is heightened Kundalini activity while in this state.

HOW TO INDUCE A LUCID DREAM

During the first two years of the awakening, I used to Lucid Dream almost nightly. However, the second year after awakening Kundalini, I got involved with the Golden Dawn, where I began the Five Elements Spiritual Alchemy process through Ceremonial Magick, altering how I dream. While I was working on each of the lower four Chakras, from the bottom up, the Elemental energies would often put me in a dreamless state.

This process put lucid Dreaming on hold during this period since I would allow outside energies to permeate my Aura and take hold of my consciousness, which lessened the power of my Kundalini. As I described in the introduction, I needed to do this so I could learn to function better in my waking life since my mental and emotional Self was in complete disarray. After tuning my Chakras and sufficiently Spiritually evolving, I stopped working with Ceremonial Magick, which removed these foreign energies from my Aura. As such, my Kundalini became more potent than ever, and the Astral Light began building back up through food intake, enabling me to start Lucid Dreaming again in a more balanced manner.

Over the years, I have discovered the most optimal methods to get myself to slip out of my body during sleep and into a Lucid Dream. For example, I have found that if I am lying on my back, with palms outstretched, this will induce the Lucid Dream experience. If I am on my side, the body is resting, and consciousness cannot leave it since it is too engrained in physicality. However, if I wanted to induce a Lucid Dream consciously, I would set the alarm for six to seven in the morning, which gave my physical body enough time to rest (five hours at least) if I went to bed between midnight and one in the morning. Then, before going back to sleep, I would sometimes tell myself to wake up in the dream, which I found worked. Other times I didn't need to trick my mind in any way, but the buildup of Astral Light was so intense that it pulled me into a Lucid Dream.

It is essential to allow yourself to exit from the physical body and into a Lucid Dream without consciously fighting this experience. If you induce fear or anxiety as you try to achieve this, you will most likely fail. Also, keep in mind that the physical body needs to be fully rested to accomplish this. If the physical body is still tired, consciousness cannot vault out of it. And if the body is rested but the brain is not, you may not go into a Lucid Dream but may even go into a deep sleep. The brain needs to be rested so that it can resonate with Alpha brain waves necessary to induce this experience.

For a few years after the initial Kundalini awakening, my body was so built up with Light energy that I would slip into a Lucid Dream right when I went to bed. As I lay on my back with palms outstretched, I would feel myself exiting from my body while still being conscious. While my eyes were closed, they would roll upwards naturally, trying to look at the back of my head. Doing so tuned my consciousness with my Mind's Eye, enabling me to vault through its doughnut-shaped portal. Consciousness has to pass through the Mind's Eye portal to exit out of Sahasrara, the Crown Chakra, fully. The Bindu Chakra also plays a part in this experience, and it needs to be unobstructed and unblocked to achieve this.

OFF-WORLD EXPERIENCES IN LUCID DREAMS

When I was experiencing Chakras above the Crown, I visited vast and majestic, never-before-seen lands and experienced emotional rapture that is the stuff of legends. My boundless consciousness vaulted me across Time and Space to the furthest reaches of our Galaxy, where I could expand my Being to the size of a Solar System and beyond and witness Cosmic events akin to supernovas. Other times I was transported to different Planets in and out of our Solar System to communicate with the Beings that live there (Figure 157) and experience their environments. I will never forget the transcendental feeling that these off-world experiences brought on. It is as if my Soul touched infinity and could go anywhere it wanted. And the best part is that I was fully conscious while it was happening.

The beauty and mysticism of the foreign lands I visited are unprecedented, affirming that I left our Planet through consciousness. Just being able to reach and experience the energy of these other worlds has been a true gift of the Kundalini awakening. It confirmed something that I had always known even without definitive proof: we are not alone in the Universe.

What I found most interesting about these Planetary visitations is that they all had atmospheres that could harbour life, with plants, animals, and humanoids that lived there. I say humanoid because most non-human intelligent Beings I have contacted in the past seventeen years looked like us for the most part. They were often taller or had bigger eyes or fairer skin. Some had pointy ears or different shaped heads, while others had longer limbs and other variations of our body parts. I even encountered pure Light Beings on our Planet that presented themselves to me as Gods. In my many experiences, some Beings spoke to me in different languages, which I could somehow comprehend, while others directly communicated to me telepathically.

In one of my more recent off-world Lucid Dream experiences, I visited a Planet where plants, animals, and humanoids lived in complete harmony with one another, sharing their Planet's resources. Plant life was incorporated as part of the infrastructure in this world, and animals were roaming the streets interacting with the humanoids. The experience began with my consciousness projecting into their atmosphere, flying, and looking down on the terrain from above. Although I can get around the Cosmos with intent alone, my consciousness needs a vehicle to get around during Lucid Dreams, which is the Kundalini activated Body of Light.

Once I descended, I could not walk fifty steps without encountering a body of water, which was integrated with the vegetation and buildings as part of a whole. The entire scene looked like some futuristic theme park with animals walking around everywhere. Most of their animals were quadrupeds, comparable in size to the humanoids.

When I paid no attention to the animals, they usually ignored me back. At the same time, if I got scared by seeing an animal's unusual appearance, my fear of it would cause it to get defensive and sometimes even try to attack me. The animal matched my energy for the most part, which explains why so many of our Planet's animals are in enmity with humans since we generally don't treat them with love and respect.

Figure 157: Close Encounters of the Fifth Kind

I have found that every off-world experience is different. Sometimes the plants and animals were much greater in size than ones on Earth, while at other times, they were smaller. The plants' shapes, textures, and colours were always striking and unusually different. The animals also had strange features and characteristics.

Hollywood movies do an excellent job of depicting what other worlds would look like if we could make our way there physically. However, most people are unaware that we don't need rockets to go to outer space and experience Extraterrestrial life; we can accomplish this through consciousness. Through the Body of Light and the Lucid Dream world, we can trek vast distances of space in a split second and come back with life-changing experiences that alter our view of ourselves and our place in the Universe.

How much intelligent life exactly is there in the Universe? All one needs to do is follow the logic. If Earth is the only Planet that can harbour life in our Solar System, and there are billions of other Solar Systems in the Milky Way Galaxy alone, then imagine the potential. And don't forget that the Milky Way Galaxy is just one of the billions of Galaxies in the Universe. The number is astronomical, unlimited, and infinite even. And since we are all sharing our existence in this beautiful and vast Cosmos, our paths frequently may cross while roaming these other dimensions. When we touch each other and transmit energy to one another, whether intentional or not, it is always a very blissful and beautiful experience.

As a final note, I want to mention that I never felt any hostility from other off-world Beings since they constantly communicated to me with pure love. And I always reciprocated and shared with them as I would with a family member. Sometimes these communications would occur in deep dream states as part of one continuous stream of consciousness. However, as I would consciously become aware of the experience and my Ego turned on, the contact would often abruptly end. Therefore, I tried to keep my Ego in neutral without getting too excited when these contacts were happening to prolong the experience as long as possible.

Not only did these experiences touch my Soul and leave a lasting impact on me for the rest of my life, but often I would walk away with incredible knowledge and understanding about the nature of the Cosmos, humanity, and the purpose of life in general. Furthermore, it made me realize that all living things in the Universe, no matter what Planet or Galaxy they are from, have one primary goal in life that they pursue at all costs: Spiritual Evolution.

PART IX: KUNDALINI-LOVE, SEXUALITY, AND WILLPOWER

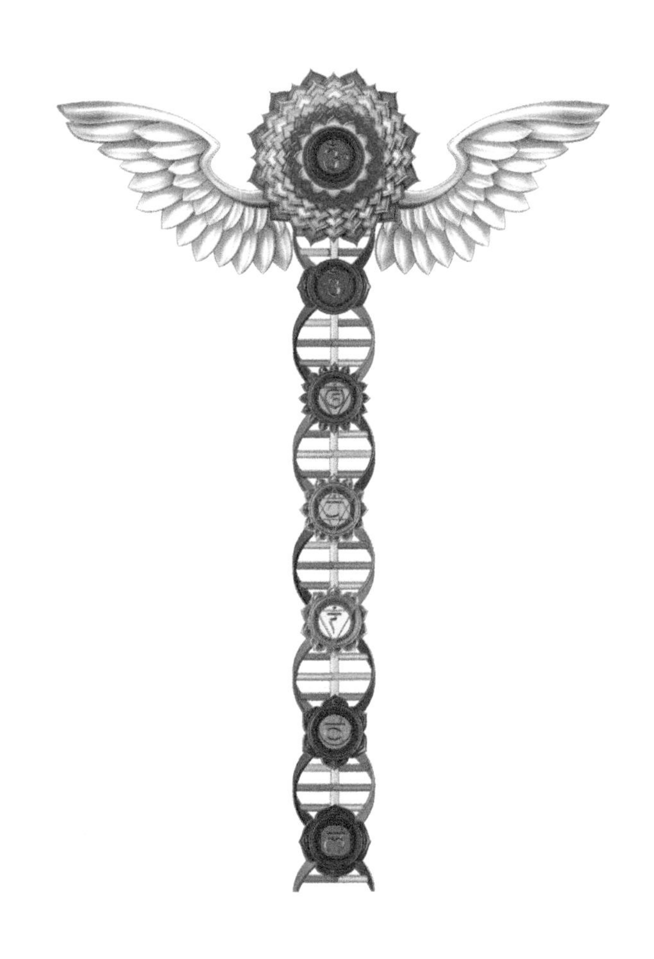

LOVE AND RELATIONSHIPS

A Kundalini awakening is the first step of a complete transformation in your mind, body and Soul. As this experience will evolve into such a radical shift from who you used to be, one of your main challenges will be to integrate into society and to try to blend in with others. Although you will be a different person now, to people who have known you your whole life, you will still be the same no matter what you share with them.

Interestingly, once someone has gotten to know you, especially a family member or a close friend, it becomes almost impossible to change their mind about you. The only way they can start to view you differently is when they see a change in your behaviour over a longer period of time. One of the distinct ways in which your behaviour will be altered is in your expressions of love towards other people. As such, this topic requires in-depth examination.

Firstly, love has many expressions and is the foundation of many things. It is the source of inspiration, creativity, faith, joy, romance, and other positive things in life. It is also the source of unity between people and the energy that binds us. It makes us laugh and cry together. It also inspires us to embrace one another and to procreate. The bonds which we have created over time with others we either inherited or we built over time. The inherited relationships are with family members, while friendships are something we earned during our lives. We also created bonds with romantic partners and may have chosen one partner with whom to build a family and spend the rest of our lives.

Understanding the source and fuel of the Kundalini energy will enable us to understand love better. In essence, Kundalini energy is part sublimated Pranic energy and part sublimated sexual energy. This Life energy gives us vitality and affects our inner being on every level. Kundalini awakenings result in Heart expansions, or the increase of Love energy, at the core of your being. A Heart expansion is the natural expression of your Heart Chakra as you integrate the energy of love in your mind, body, and Soul. Your Heart Chakra becomes expanded, which will feel like a complete release in the Astral (Emotional) and Mental Planes.

As love energy builds up in your Heart Chakra, Anahata, you will no longer feel at the mercy of negative thoughts since they will lose the ability to impact you like they used to. This release will also be felt in your emotions as the love energy permeates your heart, purifying and washing away your negative emotions. Remember always that love energy cleanses and clears all thoughts and emotions. It is the Universal reconciler and purifier of all negative energy, no matter on what Cosmic Plane it may be manifesting.

Once your Heart Chakra is filled with love energy, this energy will filter into your physical heart. You will now be carrying love energy with you on all levels of Being. With so much love present, your heart will be more powerful than ever, which will give you a noticeably stronger heartbeat and often elevated heart rate. Love energy is synonymous with Light energy since Light is the essence of love. And Kundalini energy is Astral Light, or sublimated sexual energy, which is love. Remember always that you cannot have the Kundalini without love and Light, and vice versa. In essence, all three terms mean the same thing.

THE FOUR FORMS OF LOVE

According to the Ancient Greeks, there are four different forms of love: Eros, Philia, Storge, and Agape. Eros is erotic, passionate, romantic love that involves sexual attraction. Romantic love is generally expressed between people of the opposite Soul genders since every human being is either an expression of Shiva or Shakti (Figure 158). Thus, romantic love transcends the expression of gender on the Physical Plane. Sexual expression involves the physical body because it is associated with sensation and pleasure from physical acts like kissing and sexual intercourse.

The second form of love, Philia, is the love of friends and equals. Philia is the love of short-term and long term friends, some of whom go back to our childhood. Friends are freely chosen and generally share common values, interests, and activities. Friends reflect who we are; we see ourselves in our friends and who we choose to give our time to. Philia is love that is expressed through the mind. Since it involves opening up to friends and exchanging our beliefs and imperfections, Philia can be very beneficial to our growth in many areas of life.

The third form of love, Storge, is the love of parents for children and vice versa. However, Storge goes beyond the immediate family to include all family members in your family tree that share the same DNA. Storge is essentially the bonds we inherited in this lifetime through chance. The difference between Philia and Storge is that we are obligated to express love to family and show gratitude, while friends we can pick and choose. The catalyst behind Storge is our memories since family members have been a part of us since birth.

And finally, the fourth form of love, Agape, is unconditional love and empathy for all humanity. This love for other people, regardless of circumstances, is called selfless love. Agape is the greatest of the four types of love; it is the Universal love we freely share with all human beings. The source of Agape is our love of God and a recognition that we are all brothers and sisters from the same Creator.

Agape is expressed through the Spirit. As mentioned, the purpose of a full Kundalini awakening is to undergo a complete Spiritual transformation to become a permanent embodiment of Agape. Since I have already discussed Agape to a large extent, I want to focus on how a Kundalini transformation affects our other love expressions, namely romantic love, love of friends, and familial love.

ROMANTIC LOVE

After awakening Kundalini, love energy will naturally manifest into your life and filter into your relationships with other humans. In terms of romantic love, you will find all barriers fall away in your ability to attract lovers. Also, you will find that as you progress further with your Kundalini transformation and get more and more in tune with love energy, your charisma will heighten.

You will become almost irresistible to the opposite sex. This happens because as we tune in to our centre, we realize that it is not what we do but how we do it that makes us attractive to the outside world. Our base energy attracts others, not the words we say. Through this process, you become genuine and operate with a magnetic purpose that people around you can detect energetically.

The personality is something that the Ego uses to relate to the outside world. In the case of romantic love, it stands in the way of communicating from the heart. The opposite sex can feel if you communicate with your Ego or with your Soul. If you try to use the Ego to attract a mate, the other person's Ego reacts, which immediately puts them on the defensive, and no love energy is created or channelled.

Figure 158: Shiva and Shakti in a Loving Embrace

For a genuine connection to be built, there has to be a two-way love energy circuit formed between both people. This circuit starts with communicating from the Heart Chakra, Anahata, which is then reciprocated naturally. Understanding this concept will shed light on why finding the right thing to say to attract a female does not work for most males. This effect occurs because it is not about what is said; it is about the energy that underlies the said things. Females are more emotional than males, and therefore males are successful in attracting females only when they have come up to their emotional level for their intentions to be understood. If the intentions are impure, the female will detect this and become defensive.

Most intentions from the Ego carry negative Karmic consequences since the Ego is always pondering, "What's in it for me?" Hence, there is a control or manipulation factor with the Ego to get what it wants, like having sexual relations with someone just because they look good. On the other hand, intentions projected from the Soul are generally pure. For example, the Soul will become attracted to someone in a romantic sense and want to get to know them, and then sexual relations will naturally occur without being the first thing in the person's mind. For this reason, you will hear both males and females say they have a "connection," implying that their Souls are in communication and not the Egos.

Two Souls of the opposite gender that share love energy can create an energetic "spark", activating the romantic love between them. However, for this spark to occur, other factors have to come into place as well, such as chemistry and compatibility. This energetic reaction results in a chemical reaction in the body, activating feel-good neurotransmitters (dopamine and norepinephrine) that generate romantic love feelings.

As human beings, our main desire is to love and be loved. People who have no wealth and have not accomplished any of the goals society imposes on them and have instead spent their lives loving from the heart will attract love back and be in a position to find true happiness. Then there are people who have obtained high levels of wealth and success but are terrible at attracting lovers because they come from the place of Ego rather than love. This energy works against them in attracting a mate. They wonder why they can't seem to make it happen, while the poor, less well-off person has ten times more success in this area. The secret is in channelling love energy, nothing more.

When it comes to romance, if you are attuned to the love in your heart, you will give off an energy that will attract others to you. This formula works for both males and females. This feeling, when genuine, generates pure magnetism in a magical way. Your charisma is increased tenfold, as is your ability to connect with every human being, whether a child or an older person. When you speak, you reach right into the Soul of another human being, and the personality barrier is broken through completely. Remember that the Ego uses the personality as its reference point while the Soul uses the character. Therefore, you must bypass the Ego when attracting a mate.

By speaking from the Soul, you immediately create rapport and a connection with all human beings, and with potential mates, an attraction is formed no matter how you may look physically. Sexual attraction is not about looks; it is about the energetic connection between two people. This connection is what people mean by "good vibes," that we all seek when meeting new people.

LOVE OF FRIENDS

In the case of friendships with other people, you will find yourself easily connecting to others once you build up the love energy in your Heart Chakra. You will become a confidant and best friend to many people in your life. As you cut through the lens of the personality, you can communicate to the Souls of other people directly, and they feel this in their core. By sensing your love energy, a person will feel they can trust you, which will create a stronger bond between you. Because of this feeling, friends naturally will want to respond with an equal amount of love energy or more.

We develop an attachment to one another through friendships which gives us feelings of calm, security, social comfort, and emotional union. Attachment is associated in the brain with neuropeptides oxytocin and vasopressin; while males experience more of a rise in vasopressin levels, females experience a rise in oxytocin. We find these chemicals also involved in expressions of familial love and romantic love between longer-term partners.

A Kundalini awakening makes you stop taking life so seriously since you realize that your essence belongs to Eternity and your Soul will live on past physical death. Moreover, by recognizing the unreality of the material world, more love energy will fill your heart, which will increase your capacity for humour. Spiritual people are very lighthearted, and their aptitude for joking and comedy is much higher than the average person.

Humour adds fun to a conversation, and it is a fantastic outlet for saying what is on your mind without being judged and scrutinized by others. It creates and maintains bonds between people since it creates irresistible positive emotions. Humour takes the edge off the seriousness of life because everything is impermanent at its core, except the Spiritual substance that underlies all things. As such, comedy gets us in touch with the Spirit by breaking the intellectual constructs of the mind. Humour is abstract; it is beyond logic. We laugh at something because it is so illogical that we can't wrap our minds around it, so we laugh to break the tension. Remember, the mind is linear, while the heart is not. For this reason, humour is the language of the Soul.

Spending time with friends is a joyous activity that involves plenty of good laughs in most cases. After all, we want to spend time with certain people because we feel good around them. They make us smile and laugh and bring insight and wisdom into our lives. In this sense, you will be an asset for friends and someone they want always to keep close to them.

The Law of Love states that by giving out or sending love, you will receive it threefold. This Law is an ancient mystery that many Adepts of Light are aware of. Love truly does make the world go round. It keeps things moving, progressing, and evolving. So, naturally, while you learn to channel love energy to other people, your friend base expands exponentially.

I have accumulated many, many friends throughout my journey and continue to do so. And it all comes very naturally to me since I talk directly to a person's Soul. People recognize my good intentions the instant I open my mouth, which dismantles their defences. To this day, everyone around me wonders how I can talk to a stranger like I have known them my whole life. The answer is very simple—I am being myself. And by being myself, my True Self, it attracts people to me.

Everyone wants to bond and connect; it is at the deepest level of our Being. As such, welcome new friends into your life and invest your energy with them. Take a chance to be yourself when meeting someone new and have faith in the process. You may be surprised at the outcome. We recognize ourselves in other people because we are all God at our deepest core. And, as you keep being yourself with strangers, you will develop the ability to make new friends, which is a skill you can use for the rest of your life.

The Kundalini naturally wants us to be in the moment, in the Now, as it allows us to channel love energy and be extroverted. If you were a more introverted person before the Kundalini awakening, you would experience this shift as time goes on. When we are extroverted, we seek to bond with other people and channel and share love energy. On the other hand, when we are introverted, we dwell inside our minds.

Since the mind is expressive of the subconscious, it is an area where fear manifests. As such, introverted people often get anxiety from the idea of interacting with others and making new friends. The concept of bonding with others requires them to share about themselves and be extroverted, which can be challenging when you are within yourself practising self-love. By only using yourself as your love energy source, you cut yourself off from other people that can help you recharge. Being introverted will not help you make new friends, although it won't affect the friendships you made before you became introverted.

Kundalini is creative, love energy which always seeks to express itself somehow. Comedy is an artistic expression since it requires you to think abstractly to make jokes and have fun with other people. Welcome comedy in your life and let it become a part of you. Be a beacon of love for yourself and others. Allow the experience of channelling love to friends to aid you in learning more about yourself and the Universe that you are a part of.

FAMILIAL LOVE

As the Kundalini sublimates more and more through the intake of food and water, Love energy accumulates in your heart and the Kundalini circuit. During this time, family ties become renewed, and you develop a stronger bond with all family members, especially your parents and siblings. Your family is special, especially your immediate family that has been with you for most of your life. You realise this as you are going through the Kundalini transformation journey, especially the later years, resulting in an ethical standpoint towards your family.

For me, after twelve years of living with awakened Kundalini, a strong desire developed to connect with my parents and try to understand them from a different perspective. Not in a way where it's always about me and my needs and how annoying they are with their nagging that most parents do. But in a way where I look beyond my instinctual defensive reaction to them and recognise the continual sacrifice they make for my sister and me. The level of love they must have for us to always put us first even when we are being bad.

Indeed, the love a parent has for a child is something special. And learning to appreciate your parents' love develops a sense of honour towards them, a duty to repay them with the same amount of patience and love even if it takes you your entire life. And if you have had issues with your parents in the past and feel that you didn't get the attention you deserved, now is the time to work out those issues and reconnect with them.

By becoming the change you wish to see in the world, people will naturally change to adjust to the new you. But it takes effort on your part to make that change, including not blaming others for things not being like you want them to be. It is on you to take responsibility for every relationship in your life and realise that you can make the change.

It is easy to get out of friendships, and romantic relationships you may find are not working anymore, but relations with your family members are for life. They are God-given and cannot be escaped in this lifetime, even if you want to run from them. Even in the worst situations and scenarios, you need to forgive your parents instead of harbouring negativity towards them, even when you feel it is deserved. You need to understand the amount of Karmic effect they have on your life that won't get neutralised until you take charge of the situation and apply unconditional love by forgiving their transgressions towards you. Forgiveness will go a long way in this regard; it will enable you to re-spark that energetic link between you, which is necessary for your continual Spiritual development.

And if you have siblings, it is time to bond with them more than ever. If they have wronged you, then forgive them and accept their love back in your life. I have been blessed to have had the most fantastic relationship with my parents and sister. For this, I am most grateful. But I recognise that not everyone has been blessed in such a way and that many people have challenging relationships with their family members. In any case, you need to forgive whatever wrongs were done to you, no matter how difficult it may be. Your goal, your mission, is to keep growing Spiritually.

Healing your relationship with your parents is most important because our parents influenced us the most, sometimes inadvertently, through DNA and conditioning. For example, the expression of your masculine energy and how you channel this energy, especially to male friends in your life, reflects your relationship with your father. Conversely, how you express your feminine energy, relating to how you channel that energy towards females in your life, reflects your relationship with your mother.

And in terms of romantic love, you will be attracting people who will help you overcome the Karmic energy between you and your parents. If you are a male, then you will be attracted to females that remind you of your mother and the Karma that needs to be overcome between you two. If you are a female, then vice versa. This Universal Principle manifests subconsciously, whether you like it or not. Its purpose is to help us learn to love one another and further our Spiritual Evolution.

Let us not be confused about the application of this Universal Principle as it pertained to the immoral and perverse theories of Sigmund Freud. Referred to as the Oedipus Complex, Freud concluded through faulty research that all young boys and girls have incestuous desires for their opposite-sex parents and see same-sex parents as rivals. Freud's error in judgement lay in transposing his troubled childhood and the unusual and strange relationship with his parents, especially his mother, to his psychology work.

In modern times, the Oedipus Complex is not recognised as a real thing in the psychology field since it has no basis in reality. Nevertheless, Freud must have realised that we attract partners that remind us of our parents but erred in judgment in applying this Universal principle. His conclusions were affected by his own life experience and unresolved issues in his subconscious, which must have been triggered when he realised that this Universal Principle exists.

The attraction between the sexes occurs subconsciously and relates to a behaviour that we recognise in another person that reminds us of our parents. In essence, this attraction develops so that we can heal mentally and emotionally. After all, our parents were the first Archetypal male and female that we identified in our lives. We grew up under their care and the guidelines they set for us. As a result, our Soul and Ego evolved, trying to appease our parents while also trying to break free from them and become independent.

Depending on the polarity of our Souls, we learned to imitate either our father or mother's behaviour and integrate it as our own. And as we accepted their love, we learned to love others as well. This expression of love then is most influenced by our relationship with our parents. However, understand that this Universal Principle of attraction only applies to the Mental and Emotional Planes. Physical attraction is something different entirely.

Depending on the quality of your relationship with your parents, it will affect the quality of your romantic relationships. You will notice that when your relationship with your parents changes for the better as you learn to communicate with them Soul to Soul, this will heal those parts of the Self, allowing you to attract different people in your life for romantic purposes.

In the case of abusive parents, it is most common to be attracted to abusive partners since you are programmed to relate to the opposite sex through mental and emotional abuse. However, as you overcome and forgive this abuse from your parents, you will invariably attract people in your life who treat you well and will learn to stay away from abusive people. This is the most common expression in our society of this Universal Principle since we all know people who were mistreated by their parents and, in return, attract abusive romantic partners.

KUNDALINI AND SEXUAL ENERGY

It is essential now to talk about the role of sexual energy in the Kundalini awakening process. The Kundalini energy is powered by sexual energy channelled inwards through the spinal column and into the brain. I say powered because once the Kundalini is awakened, the buildup of sexual energy coupled with Pranic energy from food intake causes the expansion of consciousness over time.

Sexual energy can also be an impetus or catalyst behind the Kundalini awakening. It is the sublimation of this sexual energy through Tantric sex practice or a form of meditation, which causes it to go inwards to activate the Kundalini at the base of the spine. Without this activation, the Kundalini lies dormant as latent energy potential in the Root Chakra, Muladhara.

What is sexual energy exactly? Sexual energy is creative energy within the Self fueled by Muladhara and Swadhisthana Chakras. It powers and sustains our minds while being a significant source of inspiration. While our carnal desires come from Muladhara, the Earth Chakra, Swadhisthana, the Water Chakra, is responsible for the tangible emotion of sexual desire.

When we focus our sexual energy on a person we are attracted to, we create a powerful desire to be with that person. Sexual desire is felt in Swadhisthana Chakra as a euphoric emotion akin to butterflies or tingling in your abdomen. This energy is then projected from our abdomen area into our brains through the nervous system.

Sexual energy relates to Apana Vayu since it involves the workings of Muladhara and Swadhisthana Chakras and the expulsion of sexual liquids from the body (semen in males and vaginal fluid in females). In contrast, Pranic energy is generated by Samana Vayu (the digestive fire) and Hara Chakra, the body's storehouse of Prana.

Sexual energy also powers our imagination when channelling it into the Heart Chakra, Anahata, thereby stimulating our minds and thoughts. Sexual energy also affects our Soul centre, the Solar Plexus Chakra, Manipura. It kindles the Fire of Manipura while energizing our willpower. It becomes dynamic energy that fuels our drive, motivation, and determination on the Mental Plane.

When sexual energy is projected into the Root Chakra, Muladhara, it becomes our impetus for action on the Physical Plane. Therefore, sexual energy is used by all our Chakras. Although Pranic energy is considered a blind force, sexual energy is intelligent. However, both energies are necessary to power our Chakras and bring them to life.

While Prana is Life or Light energy, sexual energy is the energy of creation. It is sometimes difficult to discern between sexual energy and Prana, and many Spiritual teachers confuse the two and even say they are the same thing. However, from examining my energy system over the years, I have found that they are two distinct energy types that work with each other and require each other to fulfil their functions.

Also, it is vital to distinguish between Kundalini energy and sexual energy. Along with Prana, sexual energy powers the Kundalini energy once awakened. However, Kundalini energy has its own components related to the expansion of consciousness and expressions of Self.

Once Kundalini is activated, sexual energy becomes essential since it animates the Kundalini, allowing you to tap into your new abilities. For example, you cannot use the enhanced creativity and imagination to their highest potential if you lack in sexual energy needed to tap into them. Sexual energy is a more subtle force than mere Prana as it allows us to access any part of ourselves when we focus our minds.

There is a direct correlation between sexual stimulation and the activity of the Kundalini, which lies in the Earth Chakra. As you get sexually excited, you create a static electric charge that can spark the Kundalini energy into motion the same way you would jump-start a car battery. Therefore, building up sexual excitement through Tantric practices and turning it inwards could result in a powerful Kundalini awakening.

Why is there a correlation between sexual arousal and the awakening of Kundalini? The answer may lie in our life's purpose here on Earth, which is a testing ground for Souls. For example, God-the Creator created human beings and gave us Free Will to choose how we want to express our sexual energy: look to gratify the Ego by desiring to have sex as a form of physical pleasure or use this same energy and draw it inwards through Tantric practices to awaken our latent Kundalini energy. In the case of a physical climax or orgasm, we expel this energy out of us and release it back into the Universe. When we draw this energy inwards through the brain via the nervous system, we seek to transform Spiritually. Every moment of the day is a test of our Free Will and whether we want to exalt our Soul or Ego who seek to do radically different things with this Divine energy.

Most people are entirely unaware that there is another reason they have sexual energy within them since they are so focused on using it merely for pleasure. The world's population is more driven by sexual impulse and the desire for sex than anything else in life. If people only knew another way to use this gift, it could completely transform how we perceive sexual energy. I believe that this is one of the essential roles Kundalini awakened individuals play in the world right now: not only to be emissaries of the Kundalini energy but also to enlighten people on the power and potential of their sexuality.

SEXUAL AROUSAL AND BEING "HORNY"

The masculine sexual energy relates to the Fire of the Earth Element. It is strongly driven by the Physical Plane, which acts on the Astral Plane of the Water Element. The Fire of Earth transforms into the emotion of sexual excitement through Swadhisthana Chakra.

While males are more motivated by their Earth Chakra regarding sexual arousal, females are influenced more by the Water Chakra. This explains why sexual arousal in males is strongly influenced by a female's physical appearance, while a female is more turned on by how a male makes her feel.

The masculine sexual energy is like a fire that comes on quickly, burns brightly and becomes extinguished promptly. Conversely, feminine sexual energy is like water: slow to heat up, but once it boils, it keeps going for a long time. A male's Fire energy is responsible for warming up a female's Water energy. Therefore, males spend their time and energy working on their Alpha qualities to attract females. On the other hand, females spend a lot of time and energy on improving their physical appearance to be more attractive to males.

While men generally have stronger libidos, women have an increased range and intensity of arousal. A male can get an erection seemingly with no stimulation and feel sexually excited or "horny." In contrast, it is rare for a woman to feel the same without being stimulated first. Part of the reason is that a male's body is driven by testosterone, which is faster-acting than the female sex hormone, estrogen.

The occult symbology and meaning of the word "horny" give us further insight into how sexual arousal works and its purpose. Horny suggests animal horns, symbolic of humanity's animalistic nature. After all, we share a desire for sexual relations and procreation with all Earth animals. However, horns are also associated with the Devil and his Demonic minions in Christianity and other religious and esoteric traditions. In fact, "Hornie" is an 18th-century Scottish term for the Devil.

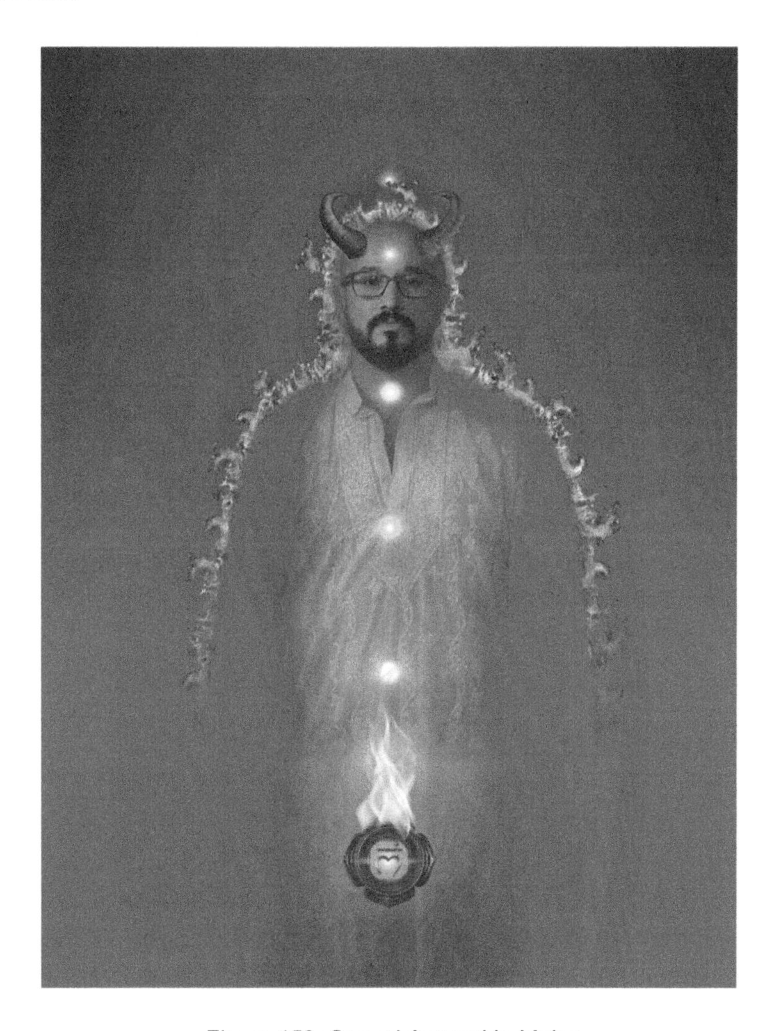

Figure 159: Sexual Arousal in Males

When a male becomes sexually aroused or horny, a Fire begins to burn in their loins which enflames their whole Being (Figure 159). This Fire is projected from their Earth Chakra, Muladhara, associated with the Physical Plane and the World of Matter. Consequently, in the Tarot, The Devil Card is referred to as the "Lord of the Gates of Matter."

This is because the Devil represents the Physical World, the antithesis of the Spiritual World of God. To further add to the symbology, Capricorn, the Mountain Goat (a horned beast), a Fire of Earth Zodiac Sign, is associated with the Devil Card in the Tarot.

In the Hermetic Tarot, the Devil Tarot Card features a giant beast with horns whose head is shaped like an inverted Pentagram, suggesting the connection between the Lower Self, the Ego, and the Devil. The Devil has large, bat wings and the lower body of an animal with a fire burning in his loins (in some depictions). He is holding a torch in his left hand that points downwards, towards the Earth, and has one hand pointing upwards, towards the Heavens (As Above, So Below). He stands atop an altar to which are chained two naked, male and female, humans, with horns. They are bound to the Devil because of their lust for one another.

Lust is defined as the overwhelming desire to have sexual relations with someone for the purpose of physical pleasure. Lust is the antithesis of love; it is considered one of the seven deadly sins because of its often unbalanced expression. The Devil and his minions are responsible for compelling humanity to engage in the seven deadly sins. It is no wonder that the word "Devilish" applies to someone being sinful, including engaging in a lot of sexual activity with multiple partners.

Therefore, as Sahasrara Chakra attunes us to our Holy Guardian Angel, our God-Self, the Earth Chakra connects us to its opposite—the Devil. Both are personifications of the Self, which we can connect with through the mind. However, the Devil is not wholly bad but is an expression of our animal nature that we must respect and keep under check. Consequently, the Earth Chakra is our doorway into the Devil's Kingdom, the Demonic Realm we call Hell. It is no coincidence that Hell or the Netherworld (Underworld) is depicted as a fiery pit deep within the Earth's crust.

One of the reasons Christianity and other religions have vilified sex is its transformative power. Time and again, abstinence has shown its potential in poisoning the mind and producing sick and perverted expressions that are out of synch with nature and God. Conversely, engaging in sexual activity in a balanced, respectful, and loving manner can lead to a Spiritual awakening. So instead of demonising sex and creating an aversion towards sexual relations as a way to get closer to God, we need to seek to understand it so we can tap into its tremendous power.

SEXUAL RELATIONS

Once you have had a full Kundalini awakening, you will understand the true purpose of sexual intercourse and its symbolic significance as unifying the masculine and feminine energies. This unification happens at the level of the Mental Plane, which allows us to transcend the duality of the mind so that we can reach the Spiritual Plane.

At birth, we were put into this world of duality and given either a male or female body. As humans, we naturally seek to balance out our sexual energies. One of the ways we do it is through sexual intercourse. We desire to be with a person that complements our sexuality to find unity at a Spiritual level. Sexual intercourse is a type of ritual that involves the integration of two physical bodies. When the penis enters the vagina during this process, the two bodies literally become one.

Between two people of opposite sexes both undergoing Kundalini awakenings, sexual relationships can be a truly magical experience. The Kundalini energy between them creates a kind of battery, thereby expanding its power twofold. This expansion of Kundalini energy results in heightened awareness and more profound transcendental experiences. It also allows the partners to attune themselves to their respective Spiritual bodies at a degree impossible to reach on their own.

One partner's energy fuels the other partner's energy. Since each partner's Tree of Life is activated, so are the energies that comprise the totality of their consciousness. When two Kundalini awakened partners connect sexually, they are each fed at the deepest levels of their being by the energy of one another, healing them simultaneously. The energy of one partner pushes out the negativity of the other just by being in their presence, as their Auras become intermingled. They don't even need to be touching for this to occur. They simply have to be in the same vicinity as each other to be on the same frequency or wavelength.

For Kundalini awakened individuals, the actual act of sexual intercourse becomes Tantric. As a result, both partners are enabled to experience internal orgasms due to the sexual energy being triggered at a deeper level by one another's Kundalini. Throughout my Kundalini journey, I have had the privilege of being with a few Kundalini awakened women, and the sexual connection we shared was unbelievable. As soon as we got near each other, it manifested as a heightened state of awareness, amplifying our sexual energy to such a degree that I would find myself often trembling just by being around them.

Sexual intercourse is a unification ritual, a type of bond or sublimation of the sexes on the Physical Plane that induces the same effects on the Astral and Mental Planes. Its purpose is to transcend the lower Cosmic Planes so that the vibration of consciousness can raise and enter the Spiritual Plane. As such, healing occurs on all levels, mind, body and Soul.

RETAINING YOUR SEXUAL ENERGY

Another critical question regarding sexuality that I am often asked is whether it is wise to ejaculate while the Kundalini process occurs. For example, when it might be okay to ejaculate and when should one save their seed? Keep in mind that males usually ask this question, although the same principle applies to females.

Kundalini uses your sexual energy and the Prana from food to power the Kundalini energy circuit. I have found that at peak points of this sublimation/transformation process, it is essential to save your seed by avoiding sex and masturbation altogether. Just one orgasm can rob you of your vitality for up to 24 hours or more. This significantly hinders the transformation process while allowing the Ego to have a stronger foothold in the consciousness, causing fear and anxiety to amplify within you.

Sexual energy grows in power over time, and the longer you save your seed, the more you are transforming the Kundalini on the inside. At its highest peak, when you are feeling most sexually pent up and excited, sexual energy is working with Prana to change the quality and state of the Kundalini energy within you. This process is the transmutation, or transformation of the raw fire of Kundalini into a more delicate, Spirit energy which takes over, powering the system.

Now, I am not saying to be celibate like a monk or priest and never to masturbate or have sex again. This would be unhealthy and counterproductive to your growth since you must tend to the physical body and its needs as well as your Spirituality. Instead, I am saying to abstain from sexual release for the first period after the initial Kundalini awakening and then re-integrate sex and masturbation back into your life in a balanced fashion. Remember that a successful life is about balance, not neglecting one thing for another.

However, once the Kundalini has been awakened, it is wise for a few months to restrain from ejaculating altogether. This rule applies to both men and women. Sexual energy is vital; if you ejaculate, you will feel lifeless and drained, needing to rebuild your sexual energy somehow.

I have discovered that the body requires Zinc while rebuilding the sexual energy within you after a release. Therefore, I suggest that instead of waiting for your body to rebuild it naturally, take a Zinc supplement or eat some fish or pumpkin seeds that contain high amounts of Zinc. Zinc is essential because it is the battery acid, while the Kundalini acts as the AC/DC electrical current. Without Zinc, the battery does not run at its optimum capacity and needs to recharge.

Once you have awakened the Kundalini, depending on where you are in your transformation process, you will develop the ability to embody other people and feel their energy, including people you watch on television and in movies. This "gift" may soon feel like a curse when you apply it to pornography since it will enable you to feel what you are watching like it is happening to you. There's no need for a virtual reality set after you awaken the Kundalini. However fun and exciting this can be at first, though, do not allow yourself to develop a porn addiction and go backwards in your Spiritual Evolution process.

You need to regulate masturbation and not engage in it more than once or twice a week and only before bed so that your body can rebuild the sexual energy by the morning. Since this process will go on for the rest of your life, you need to treat your sexual energy with respect. You are no longer functioning like an unawakened person who can masturbate and ejaculate multiple times in the day and remain unaffected. You will feel robbed of your vitality every time you ejaculate, so be mindful of this.

I have found that masturbation can be a great aid when you cannot induce sleep otherwise since it allows you to welcome rest and turn out like a light bulb once you drain your sexual energy. Pent up sexual energy can make the mind haywire and even induce anger and aggression, especially in males, which can keep one up at night. But again, try not to masturbate more than a few times a week and only after the initial Kundalini sublimation/transformation process is complete. How will you know it is complete? You will feel a new type of energy working inside of you that replaces the raw Kundalini Fire. This energy has a transcendental effect as it grows and expands the consciousness more and more as time goes on.

As a final note on this topic, since having loving, sexual relations with one partner can be beneficial for your Spiritual growth, I don't suggest that you cut out sex entirely at any point in time without consulting your partner first. If you callously abstain from sex with your partner without explaining yourself, they might feel like something is wrong with them, which will compromise the integrity of your relationship. This is unwise, especially if you have good chemistry with that person and see a future with them.

Instead, communicate your needs with your partner and maybe make a compromise to have sex once a week or every few weeks for a little while, and then increase the frequency when you are past the point when you have sublimated the Kundalini energy. Spilling your seed with a loved one can be draining on the body, but it can be beneficial to your Spiritual Alchemy since there is an exchange of positive, healing energy at a subtle level.

However, ejaculating through masturbation is absolute drainage of your sexual essence into the Aethyr, with nothing in return. People who develop porn addictions open themselves up to Demonic entities attaching themselves to their Aura so they can feed off their released sexual energy.

An Incubus is a Demon in a male form that feeds off the sexual energy of females. Conversely, a Succubus is a Demon in female form that feeds off the sexual energy of males. Incubi and Succubi are known to seduce people in dreams and have sexual relations with them so they can rob them of their sexual essence by making them climax. They are also personified in the mind by adult film actors when watching pornography.

People who feed these Demons often have a difficult time breaking free of them and stopping their porn addictions. Pornography is free for a reason; it is an empty void whose purpose is to steal people's sexual essence and take away their potential to Spiritually transform. There is a political reason for this, which is beyond the scope of this work, but I mention it here so that you are aware of it and don't fall for its trap.

SEXUAL CRAVINGS

Since Kundalini can be awakened by sexual energy turned inwards, it means that we can expand its capacity, which invariably affects our sexual urges. For example, when the Kundalini is at its peak transformation in the initial stages after the awakening, you may feel like an animal in heat. As a result, you may exhibit sexual cravings like you haven't experienced before. Once the initial period of sexual energy sublimation is complete, though, you will feel a release from this intense sexual excitement as your libido becomes balanced.

However, since the process of sexual energy sublimation is ongoing, and since you may experience short-circuits where you will need to rebuild your energy channels, your sexual urges may fluctuate significantly for the rest of your life. They often come in waves, where your sexual energy comes on very strongly for a short period, bringing with it an intense urge for a release, followed by an extended period when you are in balance.

However, when looking at the course of your entire life after awakening Kundalini, your sexual energy will be relatively balanced. These fluctuations I am talking about occur for about 20-30% of that time. Never forget that the Kundalini is an intelligent energy that never gives us more than we can handle.

When I recommended that you don't masturbate or have sex more than a few times a week, I referred to this need that may develop for a sexual release. There is no point in torturing yourself even when it is beneficial to save your seed. Doing so will cause havoc in your mind and be counterproductive to your growth.

Therefore, if you need a release, do it once or twice a week, but only at night before sleep if masturbating. Get used to not being haphazard with your sexual releases. You need to adopt a scientific approach to the inner changes happening in your body, which is your laboratory. Take control over this process instead of letting the process control you.

When your sexual energy is being generated, you will feel it build up in your abdomen in Swadhisthana Chakra. Sometimes, it may come on so strong that it makes you hyperventilate. Naturally, this period is when you need to permit yourself to have balanced sexual activity in your life. However, as powerful as these sexual urges may be, you need to be level-headed and not take it as a sign to turn into a nymphomaniac and be frivolous with your sexual activities.

It will be an incredible hindrance to your Spiritual path if you aren't careful with whom you engage in sexual activities. Other than exposing yourself to sexually transmitted diseases, you are putting yourself in a position where you take on people's energies, good and bad, by having sexual relations with them.

Instead, I advise you to find one consistent partner, someone with whom you have good chemistry, even if it's just physical at first. Be transparent about your intentions, and don't lead people on. If you put yourself in a position where you can accrue bad Karma from being with someone when all you need is a sexual release, you are better off masturbating to take the edge off.

I recommend having sex over masturbation since sex exchanges vital energy while masturbation does not. You will notice a difference in how you feel after a release with either activity. Masturbation will leave you highly drained after an orgasm, whereas sexual intercourse can make you feel fulfilled after, with the right partner. You will need some time to rebuild your sexual energy in either event. Masturbation will feel like it requires significantly more time to rebuild after.

I mentioned that you need to save your seed as much as possible after awakening Kundalini, but keep in mind that I primarily referred to the window period when you are building up your energy channels through sexual energy and Prana. I recognize that having a healthy sex life and sexual release through masturbation is as natural as our organic bodies. After all, your sexual energy can come on so strong that it makes you feel possessed if you don't do something about it. However, as with all things in life, being conscientious and controlling your actions is the key to success. Listen to what your body is communicating to you and release some pressure when needed. Balance in mind, body and Soul is the true path of the initiate of Light.

You may also have a period in your life when you will have a significantly lower sex drive, and your cravings for sex may seem non-existent. Do not be alarmed if this happens; it is a normal part of the process. Therefore, adjust to this period accordingly. It usually does not last very long. However, it signals a time for introspection and building up the energy through food intake when it does happen. Do not feel guilty if you cannot satisfy your partner like you used to but let them know what is happening and do what you can to get them to understand. If they do not and choose to make you feel guilty because of this occurring to you, you need to rethink your relationship with them.

SEXUAL ATTRACTION

All people want to be perceived as attractive to others to have an abundance of love and relationships. However, most people don't realize that they have complete control over this process. There are Laws that govern the process of attraction, especially sexual attraction, and those people that know these Laws consciously can spark attraction in others with the application of their willpower.

For example, a Kundalini awakened person, after many years of personal transformation, becomes very attractive to other people. This is because their changes in mind, body, and Soul alter how they think and their behaviour, making them naturally attractive to everyone they meet. As a result, these people have an easier time finding a romantic or sexual partner and finding new friends in their lives.

Many awakened people overlook these personal changes and attribute this newfound attraction to destiny or chance. In reality, there is an invisible science behind it. The Laws concerning sexual attraction between humans correspond with Universal Laws that govern all of Creation. Creation is, in a sense, perfect, and the energy of attraction is one of the ways it seeks to remain as such.

So what is sexual attraction then? The best way to explain sexual attraction is to say that it is nature's way of improving our gene pool. In other words, sexual attraction is how nature ensures that the most evolved humans will procreate and continue the existence of our race.

Nature is continually in the process of evolution, and those humans who are in line with this Law and are masters of their realities are the ones who have activated their latent DNA potential to become the best versions of themselves. As a result, these people have become attractive to others, which allows them to have an easier time finding a mate and procreating.

Even though sexual attraction is a natural expression, learning the traits of these evolved people who exert dominance in their lives allows you to "fake it until you make it." In other words, you don't have to start off being a sexually attractive person, but you can learn the behavioural traits of these types of people and use these traits in your own life to be attractive to others.

Understand that attraction applies to both men and women. You can attract a romantic or sexual partner, but also new friends since all humans naturally gravitate towards attractive people. We recognize something special in attractive people and want to be around them. In reality, what we perceive in these people is a better version of ourselves.

THE FIRST TWO MINUTES OF MEETING

Attractive people are charismatic, free, and uninhibited in every way we all want to be. They are leaders instead of followers and demand attention at all times, even when they are silent. They are never afraid of speaking their minds and are courageous and assertive. They are strong-willed and calm, even in the face of adversity.

Attractive people are often funny and entertaining but also relaxed, calm, and collected. They have certain beliefs about themselves, which they uphold at all times. These people do everything earnestly and with all of their hearts. They are passionate and live life to its fullest, with no regrets. They take what they want and make no excuses for their actions.

Even though you may not be exhibiting some of the qualities mentioned above, do not despair. Nature allows us to remake ourselves every moment in time, and you can use its Laws to start becoming an attractive person. The key is to focus your energy on becoming attractive to new people you meet since the first two minutes of meeting a new person are the most critical. This means that if you exhibit certain qualities during those first two minutes, you will have sparked attraction in the other person.

Attraction works in two ways. If a new person you meet is of the opposite sex (depending on the polarity of their Soul), they will feel sexual attraction towards you. If they are of the same sex, they will want to be your friend. In both cases, if you spark attraction, you will have the power to make that person a part of your life in some way.

Most people don't realize that who we think we are is only real to us and the people who know us. In other words, strangers have no idea who we are. Thus, first impressions are crucial. Attraction has much to do with the image of who you think you are and how you can manipulate that image to present yourself to someone new you meet. Once you have created a perception of yourself in those first two minutes, the other person will either feel attraction towards you or not.

The essential factor to understand is that we have the power to mould our image of ourselves through our willpower. Remember, we all have Free Will, and how you exercise your Free Will impacts the level of attraction you create in other people.

THE PSYCHOLOGY OF ATTRACTION

When you want to come off as attractive, understand that it is not about what you say to a person but how you say it. It is not the words but the body language and vocal tonality that count. However, to go even deeper, it is the inner energy with which you talk to a person that will cause attraction or not.

Your demeanour must always be cool, and your vocal tonality must be energetic and captivating, expressing power and dominance. These are the behavioural traits of an Alpha personality. Alpha people are masters of their realities. They are born leaders that take what they want. Being an Alpha is a state of mind that exemplifies fortitude and stillness in emotions. Alphas are not moved by things externally unless they choose to be. Their reality is never compromised because they simply do not allow it. They run the show, and others follow.

Alphas only talk to be heard by others. They do not seek approval, nor do they speak to listen to the sound of their voice. Therefore, when you talk to someone you desire to be attractive to, be mindful that what you are saying is captivating. There must be power in your voice tonality and intention present; otherwise, you will bore the other person. For example, if someone yawns while you are talking, you failed. Whatever you say, you must be talking directly to the other person's Soul.

You must learn to break through the barrier of other people's personalities and their Egos. To accomplish this, you should look the other person in the eyes the entire time while speaking with confidence. Your power of purpose must be so strong that it is mesmerizing and hypnotizing to others. The opposite sex should lose themselves in your energy.

Highly evolved Kundalini awakened people come from a higher place when they speak to others. Since their consciousness is operating from the Spiritual Plane, they are aligned with their True Will, which increases their personal power. As such, they are powerful communicators who speak with purpose and intent. People naturally gravitate towards them as their energy is inspiring and uplifting to be around.

To become a naturally attractive person, you have to build yourself up to be someone of solid values, ethics, and morals. You have to love yourself and love life in general. If you love yourself and are content and satisfied with your life when you are with a person of the opposite sex, you will never come from a place of neediness but a place of desire. Think about this for a second. When you need something, it means you lack something within yourself. This idea is already unattractive, putting the other person on the defensive.

A powerful method of sparking and maintaining sexual attraction is being cocky and funny. Cockiness is defined as "being boldly or brashly self-confident." Being cocky around others immediately puts you on a high pedestal since you will come off as someone of high value. However, being cocky can appear very arrogant, which is unattractive, so it helps to add a proper dose of humour. Humour is fantastic because you can say what is on your mind without being judged and scrutinized in the process.

Interestingly, using logic and reason to build attraction fails most times. Keep in mind that attraction is not logical in any way. Logic is, in fact, the antithesis to attraction. Being playful, speaking in metaphor, and being indirect under all circumstances is a far more powerful way to spark attraction. The conversation must be fun; otherwise, you will create no attraction.

Once you have sparked attraction, the key behind maintaining that attraction is to continually project that you are cool, funny, and confident. That time spent talking to you is a gift to the other person because you are a person of high value. You take what you want because you can, which subconsciously lets the other person know that you are an influential person who manifests their reality. So not only do they want to be with you, they want to be you.

THE IMPORTANCE OF INNER BELIEFS

You have to have high and firm inner beliefs about yourself, which means that inner work is essential to attract the opposite sex. Of course, it helps to look good, be in good shape, be clean, shaven, well dressed, and smell pleasant. However, even these things come very secondly to being confident and believing in yourself. The breakdown I learned from dating gurus in my early 20s is that looks are 30% of attraction, and the inner work I am talking about here is the other 70%.

It is we who must give ourselves value. If we do not love ourselves and find ourselves lacking, we will project our insecurities onto other people, and they will perceive us as such. If we believe that we are exceptional and unique, then subconsciously, other people will also believe it and spend the entire time around us trying to figure out why we are so great. This mystery will be very attractive to them.

In reality, attraction is about personal power. If you try to court a person and are going out of your way for them, supplicating yourself, you are communicating that you are not a person of high value, your time is not important, and you have low personal power. If you are willing to give a stranger your personal power willingly merely because they are attractive physically, then you are communicating to them that you are a person of low value, simple as that. As such, you are setting yourself up for failure right away. Maybe, by some stroke of luck, they will want to date you, but they will only be with you to take advantage of you in some way since you communicated to them from the beginning that you don't respect yourself.

Subconsciously, people have no respect for individuals who do not respect themselves. Respect is something earned, not given. Love is given always and equally, but respect is earned. Thus, you have to learn to love and respect yourself. If you feel that you do not love yourself as much as you should, then examine why that is. If you have past traumas that need healing, then focus your attention on overcoming those traumas instead of finding a mate. You need to be in a good place before having a healthy love relationship with someone. And that starts with loving yourself.

People who love themselves have some kind of purpose in their lives. Their purpose is often the most important thing to them. If you don't have a true purpose in your life right now, I suggest spending more time trying to find or discover it. Explore new creative activities and learn new things about yourself. Do not be afraid to change things up in your life and explore new avenues. Break out of your comfort zone and do the things you always wanted to do. Finding your purpose could give you everlasting joy and happiness. It will make you love yourself and your life, which is very attractive to other people. It will also make you know yourself better to master those parts of Self that need work.

You are unique in every way and are a rare find. If you have not discovered this about yourself yet, then it is time to do so. Time spent with you is special, and other people should be so lucky that you choose to give them your time. If you love yourself, then you will be indifferent to the outcome of meeting someone new. Finding a romantic partner or new friend will be a bonus in your life instead of a necessity. Indifference to the outcome of meeting someone new will create a kind of energetic void that the other person will feel compelled to fill. Doing so will only add to your level of attraction.

If you have a boring life and want to meet a romantic partner, you will have a challenging time. Being someone's entire life brings a lot of pressure to perform and make that person happy always. Eventually, most people give up and walk away from a relationship like that. You have to focus first on being at peace with yourself and loving yourself because if you do not love yourself, you will have difficulty finding someone to love you and fill that void within yourself.

To be an Alpha, you must believe in these Principles in the deepest corners of your Soul instead of seeing them as tactics or a form of manipulation. If you see it like that, then inevitably, the opposite sex will detect your behaviour as a form of manipulation, which is unattractive. After all, people hate when someone tries to manipulate them. Instead, they like transparency, even if it is something as direct as "I'd like to sleep with you."

If you desire to work on yourself but lack the method of approach, then my first book can aid you in that regard. *The Magus* is designed to help you reach your highest potential as a Spiritual human being, making you very attractive to other people. You have to learn your True Will in life and connect with your Higher Self. If your vibration of consciousness is high, your thoughts and emotions will be impacted, thereby affecting your behaviour with others.

Becoming the master of your reality will give you abundance in your life, including all the romantic relationships and friendships you desire.

Kundalini awakened people who have achieved a high level of consciousness are liberated from this World of Matter. Their capacity to have fun is much higher than those people who take life too seriously. We all want joy and fun in our lives. Therefore, the more you can see meeting new people as a fun activity, you will have more success.

The idea of having fun with the opposite sex and playing this game of sparking attraction is a manifestation of channelling your love energy. When you seek to attract someone instead of manipulating them, your actions won't carry Karmic consequences, so long as they don't have a romantic partner. Instead, you will create good Karma for yourself when you can create a fun conversation that someone you meet will want to partake in willingly. Doing so will enrich your life since by creating attraction and maintaining it, you will be bouncing love energy back and forth with the other person and building it. As such, filling your life with more love energy will take you further ahead on your Spiritual journey.

BECOMING A SPIRITUAL WARRIOR

Since the Spiritual journey brings a lot of Karmic shedding, you need to develop yourself into a Spiritual warrior. You have to learn to be tough and take on challenges head-on instead of running away from them. If you do not, you will be broken apart by the Five Elements of your Being. The parts of yourself which you need to conquer will overcome you instead.

As you have learned so far, Spiritual Evolution is not all fun and games; there are times when you will be very uncomfortable in your own skin. The concept of developing yourself into a Spiritual warrior is of such great importance, especially while undergoing a Kundalini transformation process. Remember, metamorphosis requires something old to die for the new to take its place. How you conduct yourself during painful periods will make all the difference in your life.

The Dark Night of the Soul is not a single night of mental and emotional anguish, but it may come on many times in your life and last for weeks, even months. Transformation requires you to be strong in the face of adversity. Though our society often emphasizes Enlightenment being an enjoyable experience, not very many people speak about the negative aspects of reaching that goal and the challenges along the way.

Kundalini awakening is an awakening to the Dimension of Vibration. This means that you can no longer hide from energies and partake only in the positive ones while discarding the negative, as most people do. Instead, you become a part of both, the positive and negative, concerning their effects on your thoughts and emotions.

Most unawakened people can choose to not deal with mental and emotional issues as they come up. They can choose to ignore negativity and lock it up in the subconscious, which is like a vault with all the mental "stuff" you decided not to deal with, like traumatic memories one chooses to ignore. But with a full Kundalini awakening, that vault opens permanently like Pandora's Box. Everything that was ever an issue in your life, including suppressed and repressed emotions and thoughts, need to be dealt with and overcome.

For example, traumatic memories that altered how you function in the world have taken the form of personal Demons, which are now embedded in your Chakras as Karmic energy that needs to be neutralized. Since each Chakra is synonymous with one of the Five Elements, this is what I meant when I said that you must overcome the Elements instead of allowing them to overwhelm you. Elemental energy has to be cleansed, purified and mastered for the vibration of your consciousness to freely rise to a higher frequency, unhampered by lower energies.

DEALING WITH POSITIVE AND NEGATIVE ENERGIES

As human beings, we naturally embrace positive energy. We can't seem to get enough of it. We take it in, experience it, enjoy it, and seek more. And so, we have structured our lives in such a way where we can receive positive energy while avoiding negative energy.

Positive energy comes in many forms. Love, joy, and happiness are just a few, but there are many more like excitement and inner peace. Conversely, negative energy comes in the form of conflict. It almost always includes nervousness, anxiety, and other expressions of fear energy.

Fear is an essential building block of life, and you need to learn to use it, not be used by it. We are programmed to run from fearful situations as much as possible since our body is on an alert, signalling that we are in danger. However, by running from fear, you are robbing yourself of your opportunity for growth. On the other hand, if you embrace fear, you can learn something new about yourself that will take you further on your Spiritual Evolution journey.

Figure 160: Becoming a Spiritual Warrior

As a Kundalini awakened initiate, you will soon learn that you have two choices in life. One, you can stay as a part of society and learn to live with the negativity and challenges that daily life can bring, or two, you can leave your community altogether. In the latter situation, you would discard your material possessions and relationship ties with people in your life and go off to live in a Temple or Ashram somewhere, entirely devoting your life to Spiritual growth.

However, in most cases, people choose to stay in society and be a part of the play of life. If you do this, as I have and countless others that came before me, you will need to develop yourself into a Spiritual warrior so that you can deal with the fear and anxiety that negative energy brings. You must learn to put on your Spiritual armour and take up your metaphoric shield and sword (Figure 160) to defend yourself while learning to attack. You will need both to win the fight.

Your shield is the unconditional love in your heart (Water Element) that can take on anything, while your sword is your willpower (Fire Element) that cuts through all illusions to get to the truth. Your willpower is not afraid of adversity; it welcomes it, knowing it is an opportunity for growth. Keep in mind that even though it is more challenging to make it work as part of regular society than to run away from it and evolve in isolation, it is far more rewarding.

In its passive state, the Kundalini works through the Element of Water, expressed through the feminine, Ida Nadi. Our consciousness receives energies from the outside world, which are felt through the Mind's Eye and experienced as emotions. As a Kundalini awakened individual, simply being around other people brings negativity since by being an empath, you intuitively feel the darkness of people's Souls. But if you work on developing yourself into a Spiritual warrior, you will embrace the challenge of fitting in and making it work in modern-day society.

In most instances, what bothers us about other people is what we carry in ourselves. So, by developing yourself into a Spiritual warrior and overcoming those things, you will find that you will no longer see those things in others, at least not in a way where you can't be around them. So, in this way, other people's negativity can be an asset to you and a catalyst for growth.

BUILDING UP YOUR WILLPOWER

You must build up your willpower using the Fire aspect of the Kundalini energy, which is channelled through the Pingala Nadi. Of course, it helps if you are already someone who deals with people and difficult situations with a certain degree of ease. However, when you can feel people's negativity in real-time, it is a much more challenging situation that has its own learning curve, especially at the beginning point of your transformation journey, when your emotions have precedence. In any event, all initiates must begin their journey of becoming a Spiritual Warrior by learning how to neutralize the negative energy that life's events and the people around them can bring.

Willpower is like a muscle, and you must treat it as such. If you work out this muscle daily, it becomes stronger and more powerful. The foundation of your willpower grows with time, and it becomes more difficult to get taken off course through negativity experienced by way of outside influence. Fire (willpower) always dominates over Water (emotions) once applied correctly. This concept is crucial to understand. Energy is a blind force, as is emotion.

Energy is passive and is experienced inside the Aura as a feeling. You can manipulate this feeling with the proper application of willpower. At first, you will find yourself moved around by your emotions like a passenger in a boat at sea. But with daily practice, you will overcome your anxiety and fear and be able to use your Demons constructively instead of allowing them to rule you. This is not easy to master within the Self and is perhaps the biggest challenge for any Kundalini awakened initiate. But it can be achieved. And it must if you are to maximize your Spiritual potential. You have incredible power inside of you now, but you must learn to tame it and use it productively in your life. You must overcome your fears and Demons by conquering your Lower Self, the Ego. Only then can you be Resurrected Spiritually and align your consciousness with your Higher Self.

TO CHANGE YOUR MOOD, CHANGE YOUR STATE

How you apply your mind and what type and quality of thoughts you choose to listen to you will determine your success in this endeavour. Your negative emotions will either overcome you or you will neutralize them; these are your two choices. Therefore, if you are experiencing a negative emotional state, it is crucial to treat it like blind energy that can be subdued with the application of your willpower. To achieve this, apply *The Kybalion's* Principle of Mental Gender and focus on the opposite pole of the emotion you are trying to change within yourself. This will allow you to alter its vibration and turn it from a negative pole into a positive one.

This method is called "Mental Transmutation," and it is a very powerful technique of taking control over your reality and not being a slave to your emotions. I have used this Principle my entire life, and it has been one of the primary keys in my success with mental mastery. The way it works is simple: if you are experiencing fear, concentrate on courage; if you are full of hate and want to induce love, then focus on it instead. And so on with different expressions of opposite emotions.

Learn to speak positively to yourself instead of being self-defeating. Don't say that you can't do something; instead, tell yourself that you can. Never allow yourself to get down and admit defeat. Instead, shift your mind to focus on the positive of a situation, like seeing it as a learning lesson that will help you grow as a person. Don't dwell on your negative emotions or mind-state but be proactive and willfully and willingly concentrate on cultivating its opposite. It helps to remember an instance in your life when you felt that positive emotion you are trying to induce in yourself. As you hold its memory in your mind, it will begin to affect the negative feeling and start transforming it into a positive one. To change your mood, you must change your state. Never forget this. Failure is a choice.

Another method of overcoming negative emotions is to shift your mind into an active state by engaging in an inspirational activity. Remember, to be inspired, you must be in-Spirit. An act of inspiration involves being in tune with the Spirit energy, which positively affects your consciousness. To become inspired, you can also engage in physical activity, transforming the negative emotion by increasing the Fire Element within the body.

Another method of being in-Spirit is to directly tune into the mind, bypassing the body, and engage in some creative activity which will involve the Fire Element as well as the imagination (Air Element), slowly shifting the energy from negative to positive. To create is to attune to positivity in oneself since you need love energy to create. Some physical activities that are essential in building up willpower are walking, running, doing Yoga (Asanas), playing sports, or dancing. Creative activities include painting, singing, and writing.

Building up the willpower is not an easy task, and it takes many years to overcome fear and anxiety after awakening Kundalini. But if you apply yourself and take baby steps daily to accomplish this task, you will develop yourself into a true Spiritual Warrior that can deal with all life situations in a relaxed and calm manner. By working towards this goal, the love energy which you carry in your heart will expand until it overcomes you and takes you over entirely. Love is the key to this process; the love of oneself and love of other people.

THE POWER OF LOVE

Love transmutes/transforms any negatively charged emotion or thought into a positive one. Creating and using your imagination is also an act of love. Love energy powers your creative process which is required to see alternate ways of perceiving your mind's content. Positive thoughts and emotions can only be induced by love. By applying the energy of love to a negative, fear-based emotion or thought, you are changing its form and substance. Love acts as the force of fusion between two opposing ideas, completely neutralizing and removing fear, the driving force behind all negative thoughts.

At the Crown Chakra, this process is voluntary and continuous. Hence, the Crown is considered the ultimate in consciousness and void of Ego. Fear exists only on the mental level where duality occurs. It can be likened to False Evidence Appearing Real (FEAR). In other words, fear results from a lack of understanding or an improper interpretation of events.

The only way to interpret an event is through love. Lack of love creates fear, which produces Karma since Karma exists as a safeguard for the Spiritual Plane. Karma is the result of memories of events improperly interpreted due to lack of understanding, creating division between the Self and the rest of the world. This division generates fear. However, if you take away the fear, you are left with unity, which breeds faith. Through faith, you will find love, which is the ultimate in human understanding.

By learning to operate through unconditional love, you Spiritualize the Heart Chakra, which allows your consciousness to elevate into the Spiritual Plane to experience the higher three Chakras of Vishuddhi, Ajna, and Sahasrara. This state creates a rapture in the heart, manifesting the Kingdom of Heaven spoken about by Jesus Christ. When achieved, you sit at the right hand of God and are a King or Queen in Heaven, metaphorically speaking.

This is the esoteric interpretation of Jesus Christ's teachings. It is no coincidence that he was always symbolically depicted with a burning heart and a halo around his head. Jesus completed the Kundalini awakening process and came to tell others of it, although he conveyed his teachings in cryptic parables so that only the worthy could understand. Jesus knew never to cast "pearls before swine," which was the traditional method of passing down Spiritual and esoteric teachings in the olden days. As *The Kybalion* says, "The lips of wisdom are closed, except to the ears of understanding."

In this Universe, all things evolve and resolve back to where they originated from. Since our Universe was created by love and everything is an aspect of it, love is also the unifying factor in all things and their end-product. By maintaining a loving attitude in your heart, you are silencing other parts of your mind that create chaos and imbalance. Love silences the Ego and centres you so that you are in touch with your Soul and Higher Self. Because of its power of transformation, love is portrayed as fire symbolically, since the Fire Element consecrates and purifies all things, bringing them back to their original, pure state.

In the same way, because of its Universal power, all things bow down to love. That means that once you apply love to any action, other people will respond in kind. Love demands respect. It speaks the truth, and it compels others to do the same. Love is the Law of the Universe, especially when it is consciously applied. As such, love needs to be under the governance of the will.

There would be no need for governments and policing if all people awakened their Kundalini energy. It would activate people's higher virtues, and since love would be the guiding force behind all their actions, problems between people would cease to exist. Fighting and division would end, and the world would balance itself. It is no wonder that all Spiritual people say that the highest manifestation of God on our Plane of existence is love.

Think about the many instances in the past where a famous poet, musician or artist had their heart "broken." In their hurt feelings, they turned towards expressing through the creative activity that they were masters at. And in doing so, they healed themselves. Love is the ultimate healer of all pain and suffering. And Fire is the absolute transformative Element used to transform the negative energy of fear and anxiety into pure love.

LOVE AND THE PRINCIPLE OF POLARITY

To understand how energy works psychologically, you must understand the concept of a dark room and what happens when you allow Light inside. You can spend an Eternity focusing on the dark and trying to expel it from the room, or you can simply open up a window to bring in the Light.

The idea behind this metaphor is to focus on the opposite of that which you are trying to overcome within yourself. To do so, you must use the Hermetic Principle of Polarity, which is present in all things. It states that everything in nature is dual and has two poles or extremes that are different in degree but made of the same substance. This Principle implies that all truths are half-truths and that all paradoxes can be reconciled.

You will find that love energy, in one of its various forms, is the opposite of any negative thought or idea you will ever encounter in life. For example, if one lies, they will have turned to Self-hate, and if they apply love to this equation, they will speak the truth. To speak the truth is to love yourself and others. Truth is an aspect of love. If one is angry and violent, they must use an aspect of love and apply temperance, which will give them humility, and in turn, they will overcome their anger. If one is greedy, they will need to use love energy and apply it to become charitable and give to others as they do to themselves.

The notion of the seven deadly sins of lust, gluttony, greed, sloth, wrath, envy and pride are at the basis of most of negative thoughts, emotions and beliefs. Applying love energy turns these negative states into positive ones, which are chastity, temperance, charity, diligence, patience, kindness, and humility.

Fear is the opposite of love, and the seven deadly sins are based on different aspects or manifestations of fear. In most cases, it is fear energy that is motivated by the survival instinct whereby the person disassociates themselves from the rest of the world and individualizes and isolates themselves psychologically. The concept here is to take care of yourself, but in the case of the seven deadly sins, this concept does so without due respect to other people.

Putting yourself before other people and with disregard to them creates a lack of equality and balance. Doing so is an act of Self-love, instead of Universal love that liberates us. By operating from Self-love, you act from the Ego.

Operating from the Ego isolates you from the rest of the world and takes away the channel of love, which is necessary to be truly happy, joyous, and content with yourself and your life.

THE EGO AND THE HIGHER SELF

It is challenging to distinguish between the Ego and the Higher Self, especially if you are in a conflict with someone and the heat of the moment. I always like to ask myself the following few questions before responding to a dispute, "How does what I am about to say or do affect the big picture? Positively or negatively? Will it help or harm the situation?" In other words, "Will the situation be resolved, or get complicated further? If what I am about to say or do only helps me while harming others, which is often an instinctual response, it comes from the Ego. On the other hand, if it positively affects a situation and potentially resolves it, even if it will harm my pride, then it is of the Higher Self, and I should proceed with it.

The Universe makes the formula very simple. If our actions or statements in life will cause a positive change in other people's lives, it will activate the love principle, and we will attain unity. Selfless actions are most favourable for our Spiritual Evolution as they create positive Karma while inducing bliss. However, selfish actions directed towards only tending to your needs and desires, with disregard for other people, attach negative Karmic energy to your Aura and bind the Ego further to your consciousness. Being selfish in word or deed always yields toxic fruits that make the illusion of Self greater. Remember, the greatest con the Ego pulled is making you believe it is you. So don't fall for it.

The more you help others, and the less you focus on yourself, the more love and unity you will feel with all things. However, doing so is not only confusing for the Ego, but it is counterintuitive. As such, the Ego will always try to sway you in the opposite direction. But if you proceed with an action or statement that triggers the love principle, even if it compromises the Ego, you will align with your Higher Self so you can experience bliss. In many instances, though, you will have to believe it before you see it because the Ego is faithless by nature, which is why it can't see the big picture.

To truly prioritize your Spiritual Evolution, you must start taking full responsibility for your actions, including conflicts in your life. Stop blaming others but understand that it takes "two to tango." Being the first to apologize doesn't make you weak, but it shows that you are taking accountability for your part in the conflict. Subconsciously, this lets the other person know they need to do the same.

Conversely, if you continue being defensive, they will return the favour, and nothing will get resolved. The conflict will continue to escalate, keeping your love energy with that person severed and even jeopardizing your relationship. People tend to mirror each other's behaviour, especially during conflict. Therefore, be careful with your actions and statements because what you put in, you get back.

By developing yourself into a Spiritual Warrior, an emissary of God-the Creator, you work on expanding your capacity to love unconditionally. First, you must learn to love and respect yourself, your Higher Self, and then apply that same amount of love to other people. Consequently, by showing love to other people, you show love to your Higher Self, and vice versa. You must remodel your character and personality by developing ethics and morals that seek unity instead of division. In doing this, you will distance yourself from your Ego, allowing a complete transfiguration of mind, body, and Soul to take place that can bring everlasting happiness to your life.

BEING A CO-CREATOR OF YOUR REALITY

Many people experience tremendous challenges on the mental and emotional level after a Kundalini awakening. After the influx of Light energy and becoming attuned to the Dimension of Vibration, one can no longer close themselves off from the outside world, but their consciousness is open to it 24/7. As this happens, the individual might perceive the Kundalini energy as something foreign that is not a part of them, yet it controls their life. For example, many awakened individuals say they feel possessed by this energy and that a complete surrender to it is the correct answer. However, the Kundalini energy is passive since it is the feminine energy of the Goddess Shakti. This Life energy requires us to be active participants in the process of Creation since all passive energies need a catalyst to set them into motion.

The heart is the motivating principle, the first impulse that receives its impetus from the willpower, the Fire of the Soul. If willpower is continuously being used, it energises the heart, moving the mind, and the body follows. After a full Kundalini awakening, the optimised energy system operates as a blind force until willpower controls it. Since willpower is masculine, it acts on the feminine energy of the Kundalini, animating it and making it move in the desired direction.

Indeed, the Kundalini is feminine energy, representing creativity, imagination and all parts of the Self, representing the negative, passive energy current. On this note, understand that negative and positive energy currents have nothing to do with good or bad but are concerned with projection and reception—masculine energy projects, while feminine energy receives. Since a Kundalini awakening is a complete process of transformation, it involves not just the feminine aspect of the Self but also the masculine. It challenges you to use your newfound expanded masculine energy by using your willpower, which allows you to be in charge of your reality at all times.

It is crucial for you to actively control the workings of the mind, which will, in turn, influence and control the body. The precursor of all action is thought, while the progenitor of thoughts is willpower. Willpower is at the core of all things. Thus, being a Co-creator with the Creator is the substantial challenge of the Kundalini transformation, one that you need to start overcoming daily.

We are on Planet Earth to manifest whatever reality we desire, and it is a gift from our Creator to have this ability. However, if we don't use this ability to our fullest potential, we will suffer emotionally and mentally. And more so, if we do not use our willpower to control our reality, we will invariably be influenced by others who will do our thinking for us. Therefore, there is no other way to live than to take full responsibility for your own life.

Also, if the body is unmoved by the mind, you will fall prey to the workings of the Ego, which is an intelligence apart from the Soul and Spirit that seemingly runs on automatic. The Ego is linked with the survival of the physical body, operating through the passive element of Water. If your willpower is not active, you will constantly be under the control of the body and the Ego. Willpower is a muscle that requires training, which can be challenging to work with but rewarding beyond measure. The blind energy of the Kundalini should not animate the body without the willpower being present and in use since that implies external factors are its catalyst. Instead, willpower should control the Kundalini energy, which then impacts the mind, setting the body in motion.

Mind over Matter is a false statement. It is heart over mind, impacting Matter. The heart comes first since willpower operates through it. The mind is merely a blind medium between the body and the heart. If it does not receive impressions from willpower, it will welcome ideas from the wills of others, and there will no longer be control of the Kundalini energy. Instead, the mind will be the one in control. People get this part wrong. They sometimes act like the Kundalini is something external to the Self that needs to be listened to and followed while forgetting the overall purpose of the Kundalini awakening.

Kundalini is an awakening of the Spiritual Self, the heart, and the willpower of the True Self, which now can pour into the body and control it through the mind. Before this can be achieved, though, much work has to be done on the interior. You have to train yourself to combat the outside world's negativity and overcome it. The outside world, including people and the environment, constantly creates negativity that projects into your Aura, detrimentally affecting your energy field.

The more significant challenge past awakening the Kundalini is daily learning to live with the energy. You must understand the ins and outs of living with this energy and control it instead of being controlled by it. *The Kybalion's* Principle of Mental Gender comes into play when undergoing a Kundalini transformation which states that the feminine and masculine components of the Universe are present within the mind as well. If you don't use your willpower, your energies will be driven by external factors like other people's willpower. This Principle or Law of the Universe cannot be overcome or destroyed. Instead, it needs to be respected and applied. Free Will is a gift and one that requires our utmost attention. After all, in the words of Voltaire, "With great power comes great responsibility." And if you want to wield great power and be a catalyst for change, hard inner work is required for success.

MANIFESTING YOUR DESTINY

To manifest the life you always dreamed for yourself, you will have no choice but to align with your willpower and learn to use it. But, on the other hand, laziness and failure to implement your willpower will result in stagnation or devolution in every case. Also, it will turn your life into chaos, where you become the Moon of other people's Suns, instead of being your own Sun, the centre of your Solar System. In other words, other people will be in charge of your reality since your attention will be on pleasing them instead of yourself.

You have to understand that you need to love yourself first before you can healthily love others. And showing yourself love means that you must make your own decisions in life and guide your path. You must put all of your trust and faith in yourself and know that you are a gift to this world. You are unique, even if you must believe this blindly before seeing it manifest. Other people can give you advice that you should weigh with critical thinking and discernment, but every decision you make has to be yours.

One of life's great mysteries is that we are meant to be Co-Creators with our Creator. We are not destined to be mere reflections of other people's realities. With God in our hearts, we can live our dreams, and by doing so, we will help the collective evolution of humanity. Human beings are intrinsically good, but belief in oneself is of prime importance if you are to overcome your Ego and align with your Higher Self. You see, most people are not seeking the meaning of life but feeling the raw excitement of being alive. We all want to live in the moment and taste the fruits of the Eternal Spirit, which is our birthright.

To start manifesting your destiny, you must let go of all limiting beliefs that have allowed you to be content with a mediocre life. You are not your past conditioning, and in every waking moment, you have the power of your will to remake yourself entirely. You have Free Will, but you have to learn to exercise it and use it productively. Then, you can be the hero of your own story if you choose to be. It is a lot of responsibility, but the level of power one has is counterbalanced by how much responsibility one must take on.

By learning not to fear change, you can fulfil your Soul's desires and be happy. However, first, you must embrace your God-given right to be a Co-Creator of your life. Lazy, unmotivated people sit idly by and let life pass them by, harbouring some false belief about what destiny is. They have forfeited their willpower and are under the pretence that whatever is meant to happen will happen. But in reality, if you don't make something happen, it will not happen. It is as simple as that.

If you continuously hope and pray to win the lottery, but you did not even buy a lottery ticket, how do you expect to win? Many people I have come across have this viewpoint. They want to believe that it is just a matter of time before the Universe rewards them for their "hardships," but they are doing absolutely nothing to be the catalyst for change in their lives. They believe that their position and conditions in their life result from external factors and that everything is "meant to be." These people take zero responsibility for their reality and act like victims to everything life throws their way. They have found solace in this victimization process, and instead of snapping out of it and taking control, they blame others and the Universe itself that they aren't happy with their lives.

The above viewpoint is erroneous at its core. Understand that the Universe is a vessel of blind energy that requires the use of our Free Will to enact change. Without using your willpower, things will remain as they are, allowing the Ego to have complete control over your life. And the Ego wants to pleasure the body at any given moment; it has no concern for the future. Remember always that the Universe wants to give you what you want. If you choose to be lazy, the Universe will provide you with the ramifications of that action. However, if you take accountability for your life and make changes, the Universe will reward you.

Expect that the Universe will complete whatever thoughts and desires you project into the Astral World, so be careful what you think about and wish for. This Universal Principle that forms the Law of Attraction needs to be used with precision and great responsibility. You will suffer if you use it haphazardly since nothing manifests by chance. Everything that manifested in your life is a result of you magnetizing the Astral World with your thoughts. You asked to be where you are in life, whether consciously or subconsciously. Until you realize this, you will not progress further. If you let other people do your thinking for you, they take control of your reality while you are simply a passenger on your journey, which is sorrowful to your Creator. God wants you to be a winner in life, not a loser to whom things simply happen without their conscious control.

Nobody, including your parents and loved ones, can tell you how to live your life. Only you can decide that for yourself. And it is your responsibility to allow yourself to figure that out. You can achieve any goals and dreams if you apply the right energy into manifesting them while being determined, persistent and downright stubborn to make them come true. If you listen to others tell you what you should be doing, then you have failed yourself and your Creator.

The path of the Kundalini initiate is the path of a Spiritual warrior. Spiritual advancement requires the active participation of the Self with the Universe, which involves playing the role of a Co-Creator in this reality. This Spiritual path is not about becoming just a King or Queen of Heaven. It requires that you become a King or Queen of Hell first. In other words, you must learn to deal with negativity and master it. You must master all parts of the Self that prevent you from being the best version of yourself. You must invoke courage and face your fears and overcome them while learning to listen to the voice in your head that inspires you to live in Light and truth.

Fully Kundalini awakened individuals in touch with the world of energy are constantly receiving positive and negative energy influences externally and internally. They are fully open to the forces of Light but also Darkness. Living with an awakened Kundalini is far more challenging than living without one because it requires you to embrace this new reality and make use of your new powers. It requires you to use your Free Will Principle at a higher level than before. You must motivate yourself and search for answers within instead of looking outwards for answers. You must be your own Saviour, instead of waiting for some Deity to come down from the Heavens to save you.

As a Kundalini awakening is a full activation of the Heart Chakra, it is essential to note that the heart becomes the guiding force in your life. The heart is the Ego's opposite. The Ego seeks to satisfy the physical body while the heart is expressive of the Soul and Spirit. Therefore, learning to live renewed from the heart centre and using your willpower at all times is one of the greatest challenges of all but one that yields the most incredible fruits if mastered.

WORK AND SCHOOL LIFE

One of the significant challenges of the Kundalini awakening and transformation process is performing at work or in school. I am targeting work and school here since I am talking about the nine to five obligations we put forth to maintain a healthy lifestyle. You need money to survive in modern-day society; therefore, I guess you will have had some daily job that sustains you financially. On the other hand, if you are at a young age and are just starting your life, then maybe you are not working full-time yet, and you are in school, as I was when I first had the Kundalini awakening. Or perhaps you are juggling both work and school, and you were graced with the Kundalini awakening, either a spontaneous one or a consciously induced one.

Whatever the case, if you have chosen to tough it out at work and (or) stay in school, life will meet you with particular challenges along the way. I have already talked about this briefly but feel the need to get into more detail on this topic. Firstly, you will have experiences nightly when the Kundalini energy is very active, and you cannot induce sleep to be fully rested in the morning. This situation is something you will have to adjust to early on. You cannot change it but can only adapt to it.

My advice is to learn to relax as much as possible. Find a sleeping position that works best for you. If you are sleeping on your side, then chances are you will go into a deeper sleep than if you lie on your back. If you lie on your back, your body is in a meditative state, and most often, this will result in an Out-of-Body Experience and a Lucid Dream. Lucid Dreams are fun and exciting, but they will not give you the deep sleep you need if the focus is to be as rested as possible in the morning so you can take on your nine to five. Remember, Lucid Dreams occur in the Alpha State when the consciousness is neither fully asleep nor fully awake. It is often accompanied by REM sleep which means "Rapid Eye Movement." In REM, your eyes are rolling to the back of your head while you are sleeping. It is not dangerous to be in REM mode, but it can be taxing and strenuous on your physical body.

While you are at work or in school, you may not be feeling the most balanced emotionally or mentally some days, which may result in you having an "episode" in front of co-workers or peers. It is best to get yourself into a different mindset while you are at work or in school if you want to remain incognito to others. Reserve your emotions for when you are alone or have a family member or a special friend you can confide in.

Having an emotional episode in front of people you can't trust will jeopardise your job. I remember many instances when I had to remain calm in front of my boss or professor at school to preserve my work or school integrity. It is challenging to deal with authority figures while undergoing a Kundalini transformation since they will not understand what you are going through, yet their job is to keep you in line. As I mentioned before, it helps to have acceptable excuses on hand, and often you will have no choice but to lie about your situation so that you can get a pass.

Feeling alienated due to the condition you are in will make your life far more complicated than if you tell a lie. It helps to make friends at work or school since you will sometimes need them to cover for you. Try extra hard with these people always, since they will be of great use to you in certain situations. I remember having close friends in school that would sign me into morning classes when I could not make it on time due to being unable to sleep the night before. This situation happened to me many times. It also happened that if I were feeling down and moody, my co-workers would cover for me with excuses for my boss, whose job is always to evaluate his employees' work performance.

Remember, most people will not understand what you are going through, but friends and family can accept that you need help sometimes with whatever you believe is happening to you. People that love you will show understanding and offer assistance even though they might not fully comprehend your situation. Therefore, don't write people off in your life entirely just because they can't relate to your situation. A true friend does not judge you but shows you love when you need it. Dealing with a Kundalini transformation, you will see who your real friends are.

INSPIRATION AND MUSIC

People often ask me to tell them how a Kundalini awakening improves their everyday lives. Although this is an evolutionary mechanism that can vault you into another state of reality, the practical change effect is that it makes you inspired. Being inspired implies that you are in-Spirit and not in the Ego. You are functioning at a higher state of reality where anything feels possible. By connecting to the ineffable, Eternal, unlimited Spirit energy, you can explore the true potential of life.

The Spiritual Realm is a place of pure power and infinite possibility. You can only access it through the Now, the present moment. A Kundalini awakening triggers this state within you. Once the Kundalini circuit is open and optimized, nourishing itself with every morsel of food, it activates a continuous process of inspiration.

Sure, you will oscillate between Ego and Spirit as you prioritize tasks in your life since you still have to deal with its mundane aspects. However, it will be accompanied by this perpetual movement of Kundalini energy within you that is the source of unlimited inspiration. It creates a sense of wonder and innocence, the same as you'd see in a child who has not developed an Ego yet. It is beautiful and breathtaking every moment of every day, especially once you have reached the point in evolution when you can see Light in all things, as I described previously.

You see, the Kundalini is our way back to the Source of all Creation. When we achieve this state of consciousness, life activities become effortless. The pain and anxiety of human life, including mental and emotional suffering, is replaced by inspiration, fulfilment, inner peace, and lasting happiness. The joy that one experiences in their heart and the rapture that comes with it is unbound. Indeed, to live fully as Spiritual human beings and get the most out of life, we need to be inspired. And a Kundalini awakening gives us this.

Many times in my life, I have found myself in such ecstatic states that I needed to clench my teeth to ground the feeling as the Kundalini energy coursed through me. I often experienced the most intense inspirational states simply by listening to music. Your taste in music determines the kind of emotion you will experience since all music seeks to create some feeling in you. My favourite type of music and the one I find my Kundalini energy most amplified is epic movie music. This includes movie music from composers like Hans Zimmer, who did the soundtracks for The Dark Knight Trilogy, The Last Samurai, Gladiator, The Rock, Thin Red Line, King Arthur, Dune, Man of Steel, Inception, Interstellar, and many more.

Inspiring movies that take your mind and heart on an emotional journey generally deal with higher consciousness themes. Themes of honour, loyalty, respect, and mystical wonder are among my favourites since they tap into the deeper parts of my Soul that the Kundalini transformation has awakened. These themes and epic movie music inspire me and keep me in very high states throughout the day, enabling me to write, draw, and otherwise tap into my expanded creativity.

I listen to music every single day, sometimes for hours on end. Doing so puts me in an inspirational state of mind where it feels like whatever I am listening to is the soundtrack to whatever task I'm doing. For example, driving and listening to epic movie music feels like whatever song I am playing is part of the soundtrack to my life. I have found music to be the most significant source of inspiration on my Kundalini journey, and I am so grateful for being part of a society with so many amazing musicians and composers present.

PART X: KUNDALINI DAMAGE-CONTROL

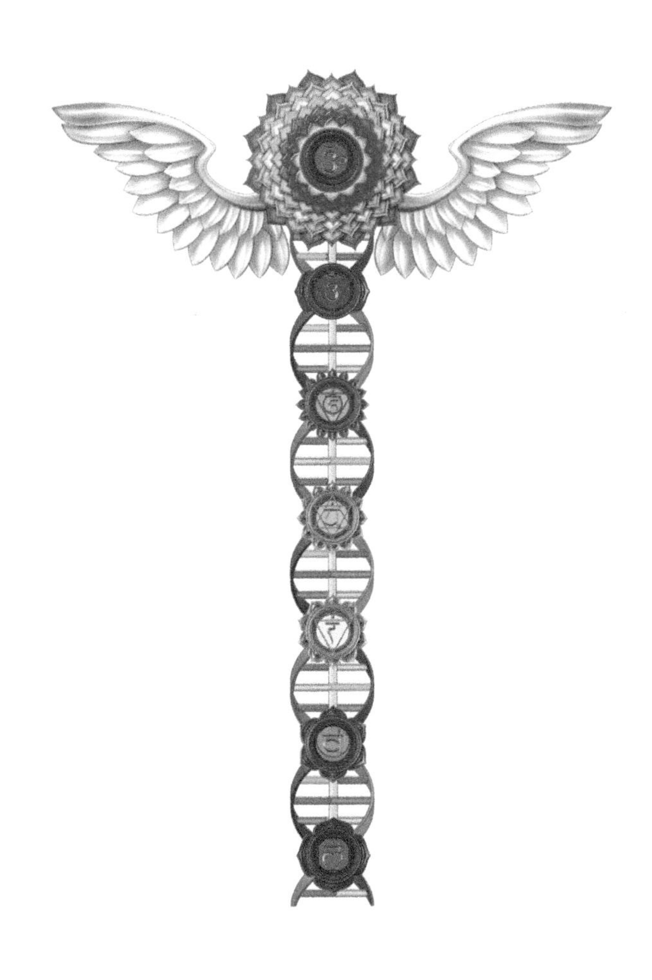

KUNDALINI AND SHORT-CIRCUITS

As you are going through the Kundalini awakening process and integrating the energy within yourself, you will likely encounter some pitfalls which can happen as a result of either Ida or Pingala short-circuiting. In speaking to many other Kundalini awakened individuals over social media and in person, I have discovered that these "short circuits" are a common issue. However, most people are unaware that they can reconnect the Ida and Pingala channels to create a proper energy flow in the head again. I call this process "Kundalini Manual Restart." You can restart the system manually with meditation exercises that I discovered instead of just waiting for the Universe to help you.

Sushumna can never short circuit as its energy flow is through the hollow tube of the spinal column, and it is connected to the centre of the brain, the Third Ventricle area containing the Thalamus, Hypothalamus, and the Pineal and Pituitary Glands. As Sushumna reaches the brain's centre, its energy spreads outwards like tentacles to the outer parts of the brain and the head. But Ida and Pingala, as they are ancillary channels or Nadis, regulate the mind, body and Soul and are affected by thoughts and emotions. To be exact, Ida governs the emotions, while Pingala controls the willpower. Ida is expressive of the Water Element, while Pingala is expressive of the Fire Element. It is common for them to short-circuit if the quality of thoughts and feelings within becomes intensely corrupted.

Over the years, I have found myself in this situation many times. Overbearing anxiety about the future, a fear-ridden mind, inability to think clearly, or obsession with past events are typical thoughts or emotions that can substantially hinder the Kundalini system. They go against the Spirit and take one out of the Now, the present moment, completely shutting down one's source of inspiration, the Crown.

Kundalini short-circuits usually occur due to a fear-based thought or emotion overtaking the mind for an extended period. Common examples include the end of a loving romantic relationship, loved ones passing away, intense pressure at work or school, etc. The less common events include being raped, kidnapped, witnessing a murder, or other traumatic situations where your life is in jeopardy. In all of these examples of potential life events, some less bad or gruesome than others, the common thread is triggering stress and anxiety that overtakes the mind, body, and Soul.

When events like this occur, your body is in "fight or flight" mode with the Sympathetic Nervous System in full gear. The Ego clings to negative thoughts with all its might, trying to work them out internally. As such, your consciousness is taken out of the Spirit Element and the higher Chakras, making you lose connection with the transcendence factor. Depending on the duration of stress and anxiety, the Ego can quickly overtake the Higher Self during this time, putting either Ida, Pingala or both of the channels in jeopardy. If you somehow can snap out of this state in time, you can avoid a short-circuit, but this is all dependent on what you focus your attention on for the next little while.

What is most common is a short circuit in Ida, the feminine channel, which occurs due to the emotions being overtaken with fear energy. Ida is passive, as are the feelings. Recall that if all three channels are working correctly, the Spirit energy becomes released within the Self, permeating the Body of Light and resulting in a Nirvanic rapture. While in this state, one does not think in terms of past or future. Instead, they exist in the Now, bringing about the mystical transcendence I mentioned.

When you are taken over by something emotionally challenging in the present moment that brings with it a high degree of fear energy, you are immediately taken out of this transcendental state. If the negative emotion is powerful enough, it can collapse the Ida channel. This would mean that you will lose touch with the transcendence in the emotions, making your natural state negatively charged. As such, your capacity to experience fear will be tremendously heightened.

Remember what I said many times before: the highest state of the Kundalini awakened consciousness is one where duality is transcended, including the experience of fear. A fully Kundalini awakened individual is meant to overcome fear altogether. However, unless you live in a Temple or Ashram somewhere and are away from the unpredictability and chaos of modern-day society, you will invariably encounter life events that get you back in touch with fear. How you deal with these events depends on whether you will preserve the integrity of the Kundalini system or things will fall out of balance.

Since Pingala is related to how you express your willpower, it can also collapse due to inactivity and not following your True Will. If this happens, you no longer receive an influx of the Fire Element. You may have transcendence in your emotions, but you will lack the inspiration. The necessary surge of masculine energy you need to strive in life will be gone for the time being. You will become stagnant in your life's journey and not accomplish much at all.

On the other hand, there is no goal too high and no task too difficult when Pingala is fully active. Pingala is less likely to short circuit as long as you follow your Spiritual path and act consistently with your willpower. Ida and Pingala are supposed to balance each other out when functioning correctly. The transcendence in the emotions, coupled with continual inspiration, should make you feel like a Demi-God who can accomplish anything you set your mind to. Every waking moment is a rapture, and you are the cause and effect, the question and answer in one—the Alpha and the Omega. The Spirit is continually feeding your Soul, and your Higher Self directly communicates with you.

A typical example of how Pingala can short-circuit is in an unhealthy or toxic situation, such as a co-dependent romantic or parental relationship where other people do your thinking for you. Anything that affects your Free Will and your God-given right to make your own decisions in life affects how the Pingala channel functions. Therefore, it is of crucial importance to continually generate your own reality through the use of your willpower. That being said, it usually takes a little while for Pingala to be put in jeopardy. It is more related to your beliefs in life, as is the nature of the Fire Element. Emotions are instantaneous, so Ida is more often in jeopardy.

Sushumna cannot ever short circuit since to do so would be to drop your Kundalini energy entirely and have it not function at all, and I have never heard of this happening. I believe once it is open, it is open for life and the hollow tube of the spinal column carries this energy from the coccyx, the tailbone, to the centre of the brain. Perhaps the only possible way it can ever stop working is with some serious spinal cord injury. Still, I have never heard of that happening to anyone, so I am merely speculating.

Since the Sushumna channel releases Kundalini energy into the brain, which then spreads outwards, the central connecting part from the brain's centre to the very top of the head right above it is the primary channel or current of

Sushumna. It is the thickest in terms of the Kundalini strands that come together to create this channel. Kundalini strands are likened to spaghetti, although even thinner. They are the Nadis that spread outwards from the energetic centres, the Chakras, and the three primary Nadis that terminate in the head. In this way, these strands of Kundalini energy reach the surface of the head, trunk, and limbs. They look like tree branches that carry Kundalini energy through the Body of Light on the inside.

There are more Kundalini strands in the head than anywhere else in the body. After all, the head and brain are the "command centre," the headquarters that regulate all of the mind's processes. The heart, though, governs the operations of the Soul. But the heart expresses through the mind. Therefore, the mind is the medium of expression for the Soul and Spirit. As mentioned, the Heart Chakra, Anahata, is another critical energy centre in the body where most of these Nadis converge and branch out from. So now you can see why the Hermetic Axiom of "All is Mind, the Universe is Mental" is the backbone of all Hermetic philosophy. Our minds are the connecting links between Spirit and Matter. And the mind expresses through the brain, which is the Central Nervous System of the body, along with the spine.

The Sushumna channel can never short circuit, but the connection from the brain to the top of the head can. It does not happen as often as short-circuiting Ida and Pingala, but it can and does happen. It usually happens if Ida, as well as Pingala, are collapsed at the same time. It can also occur if you focus your willpower on thinking internally too much. You put your attention on your subconscious by doing so, pulling the energy towards the back of the head instead of upwards.

We are meant to focus our energies to the front of the head, into Ajna Chakra, corresponding with our natural, waking state. And by focusing on the Third Eye, we create a link with Sahasrara above. Therefore, obsession and obsessive thoughts can be very detrimental to the energy flow within the brain and can create blockages. Proper alignment to the top centre of the head is necessary to attain the state of transcendence since the Crown represents Oneness. Any unbalanced thoughts then or improper use of willpower compromises the entire Kundalini system since its purpose is to keep you in the present, the Now, in a constant feeling of inspiration.

KUNDALINI AND RECREATIONAL DRUGS

Substance use and abuse is an essential topic within Kundalini circles that is often overlooked because of its taboo factor. Regardless, this topic needs to be brought to Light because many individuals turn to recreational drugs, including alcohol, at some point on their journey to help them cope with the mental and emotional issues that ensue following a Spiritual awakening. I was one of those people many years ago, so this topic is dear to me because of my own experiences and my desire to share them with others in an informative way.

After being predisposed to a wild, socially active lifestyle, I went through the crux of my Kundalini transformation in my mid-20s. Being someone who always believed in living life to its fullest and without regrets, I experimented with recreational drugs and alcohol even before awakening Kundalini. I was more of an enhancement user, though, who used substances to connect me to the Spiritual reality instead of someone who did it to numb the emotional pain of undesired events in life.

However, after the awakening, I started using cannabis to help alleviate the tremendous fear and anxiety that permanently became a part of me. And so, I experimented with different strains of cannabis for the next dozen years of my life. Through experience came the wisdom and knowledge of the science of recreational drugs and alcohol so that when I turned my back on both later on in my life, I knew exactly why I was doing it—I knew what I was losing and what I was gaining in the process.

I believe in full transparency on this topic so that you can understand the real repercussions of substance use and abuse. After all, Kundalini awakened individuals in a North American society live a much different lifestyle than awakened individuals in India or other parts of the world. We all want to "fit in" and be "cool" and accepted by our peers. And ones that don't have a much rougher ride than ones that do.

From speaking to many Kundalini awakened people over social media and in person, I concluded that most have experimented with drugs and alcohol at some point in their lives and that it's a common theme. Therefore, completely disregarding this topic is unrealistic and leaves you open to harm. Instead, understanding the science behind recreational drugs and alcohol when applied to the Kundalini system will enable you to make a conscious decision about their use on your awakening journey. You will also know what to do when you have gone too far with their use and have put the integrity of the Kundalini system in jeopardy.

CANNABIS AND ITS PROPERTIES

Cannabis is the most popular recreational drug globally and always has been. Consequently, Kundalini awakened individuals are prone to experimenting with it and even making it a part of their Spiritual journey. Most of you know what cannabis does and its effects, but many are unaware of the vast science behind it and its intricate properties.

Cannabis, also known as marijuana or "weed," is a psychoactive drug intended for medicinal and recreational use. It is used for its mental and physical effects, providing results such as a change in perception, heightened mood, and the numbing of the physical body. The cannabis plant is naturally grown on the Earth. Its use has become so widespread that many countries, including Canada, have legalized its use.

Cannabis contains all Five Elements within it, and it activates all of the Seven Chakras. The very leaf of the cannabis plant is symbolic, as it has seven points or parts that comprise it. Seven is a significant number in esotericism and religious traditions. Firstly, we have the seven colours of the rainbow (related to Seven Chakras) and the corresponding Seven Ancient Planets (Figure 161). Next, we have the seven days of the week (corresponding with the Seven Ancient Planets), seven keynotes in the musical scale, seven continents, seven seas, seven holes that lead into the human body, seven capital (deadly) sins, seven capital virtues, seven Hermetic Principles of Creation, seven Seals of the Apocalypse in *The Holy Bible*, Seven Archangels, seven levels of consciousness in Buddhism, seven gates of dreaming in Shamanism, and the seven Heavens of Islam, Judaism, and Hinduism. These associations allude to seven being a very Spiritual number, coinciding with marijuana being a highly Spiritual drug.

Cannabis is used in medicine to heal the mind, body, and Soul. It numbs physical pain for cancer patients and affects the emotional state of those people diagnosed with mental and emotional issues. For example, people diagnosed with clinical depression turn to cannabis because of its euphoric effects. It has been proven in clinical studies that cannabis re-grows cells and renews them. When applied correctly and in the proper doses, cannabis can be beneficial for you at a cellular level.

A few religions, such as the Rastafarians, even use it regularly as part of their religious practice. Some sects also use it as part of particular meditation techniques within their tradition or groups. Most of the world realizes cannabis's power to connect to the Spirit and heal the mind, body, and Soul. Other than alcohol, people generally turn to cannabis to get a glimpse of transcendence in the safest way possible.

Cannabis makes you feel happy and elated. It puts you in touch with the present moment, the Now, which elevates your consciousness past the negativities of the mind's content. Unlike alcohol and most other recreational drugs on the Planet, no one has ever overdosed on cannabis. Of course, one should act responsibly, such as not operating motor vehicles when under its influence.

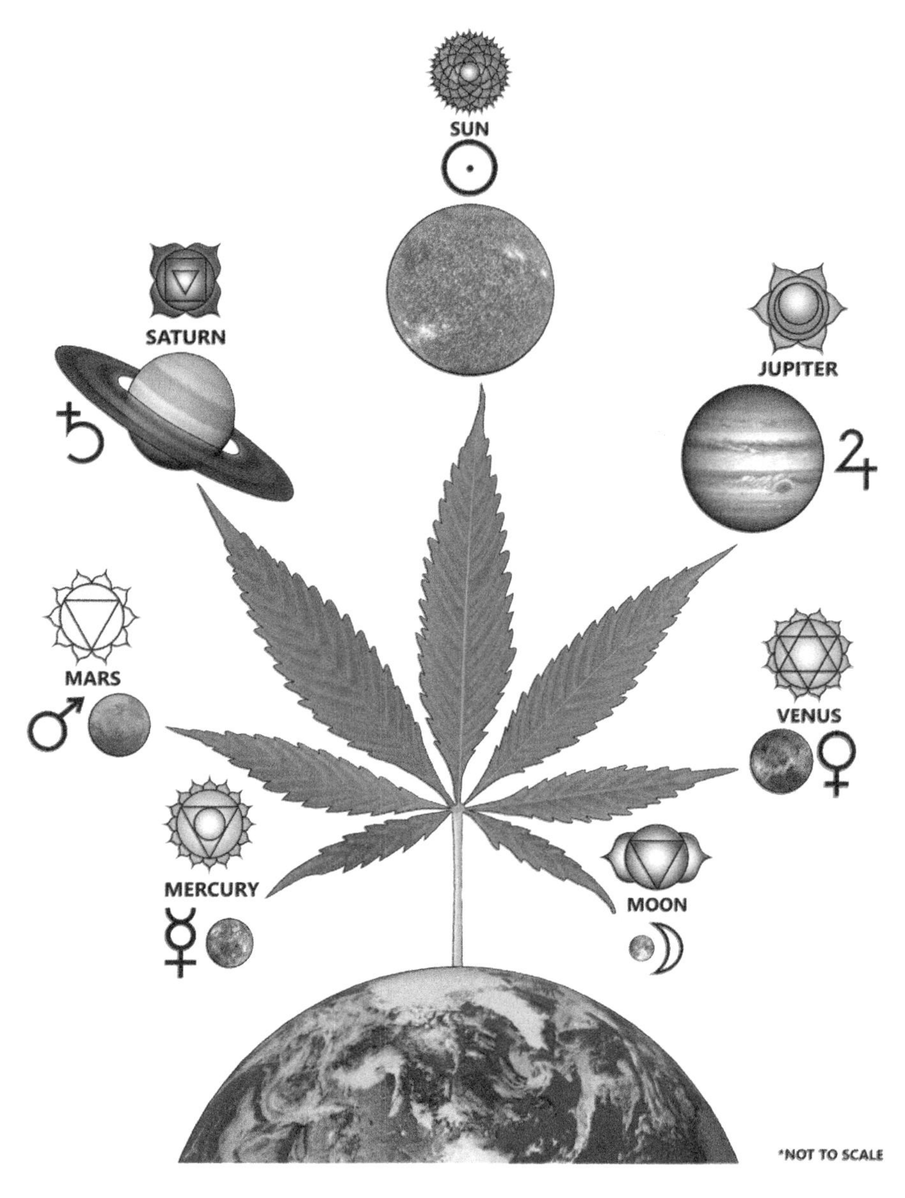

Figure 161: Cannabis Leaf and its Magickal Correspondences

KUNDALINI AND CANNABIS USE

Smoking cannabis on your Kundalini transformation journey can have positive effects. However, you must approach its application like a doctor and use the information from this section as a guideline for treatment. As mentioned, certain types and strains of cannabis work well to alleviate some of the potential adverse effects in the mind and body after a full Kundalini awakening. These include anxiety, stress, brain fog, moodiness, depression, sleeplessness, creative blockages, the inability to focus, etc.

Cannabis can give you temporary relief from these symptoms, which can be quite welcome when you are in a desperate situation, as many are. However, you should know right from the start that smoking cannabis is a means to an end and not the end in and of itself. If you view each smoking session as a learning experience, like a scientist of the mind, you can learn to reproduce most of its effects over time without its use.

Cannabis was my go-to method of alleviating stress in my 20s and the only recreational drug that I found beneficial on my Spiritual journey. I eventually quit smoking it altogether, and I will describe the positive effects since there are many. Still, when I was dealing with fear and anxiety or exploring heightened mystical or transcendental states, I used cannabis. For this reason, I will focus on cannabis more so than other recreational drugs in this section and give you the fundamental science behind it, as I learned it over the years. My knowledge and experience in this area can help many who are open to trying and using cannabis but lack guidance.

Cannabis can be very beneficial by helping to clear up blockages or improper movement of the Kundalini energy in the system. It moves the Kundalini inside the Light Body and accelerates its flow through the inner channels. Once it speeds it up, you are found in an Out-of-Body state with a whole range of Spiritual experiences. These experiences include heightened inspiration and creativity, Gnosis, and mystical visions.

Once you vault out of your body, you will remain there while the cannabis acts on the Kundalini. This process takes a minimum of half an hour and can last up to three, even four hours. Also, since the Pranic energy moves quicker through the Kundalini system, it pushes out any negative or fear-based thoughts or emotions for the time being. For this reason, cannabis is often prescribed medically to people with chronic anxiety or depression. And since Kundalini awakened individuals are prone to mental and emotional issues that stem from fear and anxiety, cannabis can be quite beneficial to you to help you overcome those states.

As such, I believe cannabis can have a positive role in your Spiritual journey. It can either serve as a powerful catalyst that can trigger a full Kundalini awakening or aid you in the transformation process if you are already awakened. Because it is easy to obtain and use, it is advantageous to individuals who feel stuck on their Spiritual journey and have nowhere to turn to for emotional or mental support or need that extra push or nudge to get them back on track. After all, while in those "high" states, the Ego becomes silent, enabling us to contact our Higher Self and ask for guidance.

However, there are pitfalls to smoking cannabis which need to be discussed and explored. For example, you should not smoke cannabis too often because doing so puts the Kundalini into overdrive, which can have harmful effects. In other words, you shouldn't solely use cannabis to help you overcome your negative emotional state but should find a powerful Spiritual practice like Ceremonial Magick, Yoga, or any of the Spiritual modalities from this book and then use cannabis as a spice. Cannabis is only a temporary fix or a medium to explore higher states of consciousness. That being said, I have never heard of someone living with an awakened Kundalini who smoked cannabis a few times a month and who harmed themselves Spiritually.

Since cannabis speeds up the Kundalini system, this can be either good or bad. It is a good thing because pushing out the mental and emotional energy blockages ensures that Ida and Pingala function correctly. However, it can be harmful when there isn't sufficient Prana in the Kundalini system that cannabis can act on. If it starts to move too fast, it can damage the overall energy system. For this reason, I said it is crucial not to smoke cannabis every day. Instead, give yourself time between days to rebuild your energy system with food intake. Otherwise, blockages or a full short-circuit can occur.

Cannabis is a drug that primarily works on emotions; hence, Ida's feminine channel is in jeopardy when smoking cannabis or ingesting it in edible form. Pingala short-circuits less often than Ida, and it is often the result of a gradual process of not using your masculine principle, your willpower, for some time. If you use cannabis haphazardly, you even run the risk of short-circuiting the Kundalini energy at the centre of the brain, where all three Nadis meet before rising to Sahasrara. This situation can only happen if you overuse cannabis and smoke every day, especially if you are smoking strains that are not conducive to the Kundalini system, like many Indicas.

Rebuilding the channel from the brain's centre to the top of the head is a lengthy procedure that can often be achieved with a type of meditation that I present following this chapter. But if this meditation does not work, more Pranic energy might be necessary to rebuild the channel received through food intake and the conservation of your sexual energy. Doing so can restore the Kundalini strands in the brain, and with the use of the meditation presented, you can realign the Kundalini and bring it back up to Sahasrara again.

Most Kundalini awakened individuals I have met on my journey have experience with cannabis. Many of them use it occasionally and find it beneficial on their Spiritual journeys. To be clear, I am not propagating the use of cannabis, but I cannot negate its positive effects either. With that in mind, cannabis is not for everyone, so tread carefully if you choose to experiment with it since its effects vary from person to person. However, there is a high level of consistency regarding particular types and strains that I will discuss.

Cannabis is volatile. This is its nature. If you smoke whatever you are offered in social circles, you can get yourself into trouble. It is common to anticipate a positive experience with street weed but get a negative one instead. Instead of relaxing your mind as you expect, it can make you paranoid and agitated instead.

A good knowledge base of cannabis strains will enable you to get a "controlled" high. It will allow you to control the high process and know what to expect. Different strains have different mental, emotional, and physical effects. If you are psychically too sensitive for its use, though, it won't matter what strain you smoke; you might still get paranoia and anxiety every time you use it. In my experience, it is more common for women to get paranoid when using marijuana than men. Regardless, it all depends on your psychological makeup.

Understand that it is impossible to naturally have the Kundalini energy expand your energy system if you are smoking cannabis daily. Cannabis needs the Prana from the food you eat, and it saps it every time you use it. Therefore, if you smoke daily, there will not be sufficient Pranic energy in your system for cannabis to act on. As a Kundalini awakened individual, you mustn't abuse any drugs. Non-awakened people can get away with abusing cannabis, while an awakened person cannot.

Suppose you are many years into your Kundalini transformation and have overcome the initial fear and anxiety. In that case, it might be wise to omit the use of cannabis on your Spiritual journey altogether. By inserting it into the equation, you will sap the Prana from your energy system, adversely affecting your goal of naturally reaching transcendental states of consciousness. Furthermore, you will pay for every positive transcendental experience when using cannabis since you will have to rebuild the Pranic system the next day. And if you overuse it, which is common, and tax the Prana more than you put in, you will be setting yourself back significantly on your Spiritual journey.

TYPES AND STRAINS OF CANNABIS

It is critical to exercise moderation and use cannabis with wisdom and respect to avoid damaging your energy system. I cannot overstate this enough. Instead of just wholly discouraging its use, which would be unrealistic considering the plant's popularity and Spiritual power, I can offer some insight into the different types and strains of cannabis and warn against the use of others.

In the past, cannabis was something that grew as a plant outside, which would be cut, dried, and then smoked to produce a "high." This high was always almost the same since cannabis retains specific characteristics outside and loses and gains other properties when grown inside. This type of cannabis is called Cess. It is natural, outdoor grown, and widely used on Caribbean islands and then imported to North America.

Cess is how most people over the age of forty know cannabis since this is what they were exposed to while growing up. In the past ten years, though, the field of cannabis study has evolved tenfold, and different types of cannabis have flooded the market. The main reason cannabis has evolved as a plant is its use in the medical field. As cannabis became accepted as alternative medicine, certain strains were developed, which I will discuss in detail. I have found some of these strains to be very beneficial to the Kundalini awakening process and some useless and even harmful.

The two main types of cannabis that evolved past the Cess era are Sativas and Indicas. Sativas have a high content of Tetrahydrocannabinol (THC) and less Cannabidiol (CBD), while Indicas have less THC and more CBD. CBD is what gives the body a sensation of numbness. It is the stuff that makes the body feel "high." The higher the CBD content, the more significant sedating effects on the physical body.

Indicas are often prescribed to cancer patients and people who have multiple sclerosis, arthritis, and epilepsy. The reason why Indicas are suitable for these people is because of their body-numbing and pain-alleviating properties. Most patients with diseases that create physical pain are prescribed Indicas as it is a body-numbing agent. Many of these patients also often have problems with eating, and Indicas are known to increase appetite more than Sativas. The typical effect of many Indicas is "couch-lock," meaning it tranquillizes your body and mind so much that you find yourself unable to get up off the couch.

Cancer patients are also often prescribed CBD oil because of the concentrated and high level of CBD, delivered in the form of liquid drops. When cannabis is ingested, it is delivered faster into the body and is usually much more potent. With CBD oil, you have complete control over how much CBD you want to bring into the body since the effects are cumulative to how many drops you take.

Sativas are more of a head or mind high since THC is psychoactive, meaning it profoundly affects one's psychology. Sativas helps alleviate mental and emotional issues as this type of cannabis increases creativity while inducing euphoria and calming down the mind. Sativas are often prescribed to people that undergo mental and emotional problems, including chronic anxiety, depression, neuroses, and other issues where the mind is overtaken by negativity while the physical body remains unaffected. Sativas work great to relax you but leave you relatively cognizant and functional. On the other hand, most Indicas, in my experience, seem to turn off all cognitive functions.

Hybrids are a mix of both Indicas and Sativas. I have found the use of some Hybrids to be quite beneficial, but they usually have much less CBD and more THC, which is the nature of Sativas.

In terms of the Kundalini transformation journey, cannabis can be very beneficial in treating bouts of anxiety, fear, and the overall emotional and mental negativity that a full Kundalini awakening brings about in most cases.

Also, if you are having difficulty with your appetite due to being overtaken by fear, smoking cannabis generally produces the "munchies", meaning you will desire and welcome food after you smoke it. Cannabis is also suitable for insomnia, which I had an issue with for a few years into the awakening. Although Indicas are often prescribed for insomnia by doctors, I always slept like a baby after a session of smoking Sativas.

In terms of my personal experience with cannabis, I have only used Sativas and learned to stay clear of Indicas early on in my journey. Sativas always relaxed my mind while taking me on a pleasant mental "trip." They removed all fear and anxiety by neutralizing my Ego. When I was under the influence of Sativas, I was enabled to positively reframe everything because of the heightened feeling of mental elation that I was experiencing. I also was more in touch with the moment, the Now, and very inspired. I always felt that my Higher Self was in command for the most part when I was under the influence of Sativas. Other Kundalini awakened individuals all reported the same effects. We all generally used Sativas and did not find much use in Indicas. This is because the Kundalini is a subtle energy that affects one's psychology instead of the physical body.

Many different types of strains are available on the market, with varied effects on the mind, body, and Soul. Some Sativas are better for inspiration and uplifting, while others are grounded but clear. Yet others are very imaginative and thought-active. When the mind is calm, as is the nature of what cannabis is known to induce, it naturally goes into a higher state and taps into the Cosmic Mind.

Sativa strains I enjoyed include Jean Guy (one of my favourites), Diesel, Sour Diesel, Ultra Sour, Cheese, Nukim, Jack Harer, Grapefruit, Strawberry, Champagne, Great White Shark, Candy Jack, G-13, Green Crack, Blue Dream, Maui Wowie, Chocolope, Romulan, Pina Colada, White Castle, Zeus, G-13 Haze, New Balance, and Moby Dick. Keep in mind that this list is current up to 2016, which is when I stopped using cannabis. Since then, I am sure there have been new Sativa strains developed that are useful but not on this list.

I found that I never really had a negative experience with any Sativa since they made me productive and creative instead of lethargic. On the other hand, Indicas would numb me entirely and turn off my mind. This state of mind may sound appealing to some of you, but understand that by turning off the mind, the inspiration turns off as well. So the best way to understand Sativas and Indicas is to say that Sativas inspire while Indicas numb.

Some Indicas are enjoyable, though, and they are the ones that numb you a little but still keep you relatively inspired. These Indicas are generally of the Kush and Pink variety, such as Purple Kush, Pink Kush, Kandy Cush, Cali Cush, Lemon Kush, Bubba Pink, Chemo, and OG Kush. Trainwreck is also another great Indica that I found was very inspiring. All of these Indica strains have a high content of CBD but also a proper level of THC. They calmed me down while removing all anxiety and fear from my system.

My favourite cannabis strain is a Hybrid called Blueberry, a grounding yet mind-expanding and inspiring strain. Other Hybrids that I found worked for me are Rockstar, White Widow, Pineapple Express, Girl Guide Cookies, Blueberry Durban, Hiroshima, Grape Ape, Chemdawg, AK-47, Tangerine Dream, Alien Cookies, White Russian, Lemon Haze, Jack Haze, and Purple Haze.

METHODS OF USING CANNABIS

There are four ways to smoke cannabis. You can either roll a joint, use a pipe, use a bong, or vaporize the cannabis. I always smoked joints, and the reason is that it was the most efficient way to get the desired effects from the Sativas. Pipes and bongs would concentrate the cannabis strain too much, which would lose the subtle effects I was going for. Using a pipe or a bong would give me more head pressure and "body buzz" I was going for. Both methods would suspend my cognitive faculties to a certain extent instead of expanding them, as smoking Sativas in joints would do.

Also, instead of clearing up blockages, I would often create new ones if I used a pipe or a bong. I only had positive effects when using an ice bong, which created the desired euphoria by filtering the smoke through ice cubes.

Vaping cannabis involves heating it without actually burning it. The vaporizer device uses heat to release the active ingredients in the form of a vapour that you inhale. Smoke is not created with this method since combustion does not occur. Vaping is safer and less harmful to health than smoking cannabis. It does not contain any harmful smoke toxins such as tar, ammonia, and carcinogens found in cannabis smoke.

I found vaping interesting because it was the cleanest way to get high, but it did not stimulate my Kundalini energy much. I got high, but it would usually not last long, and it would tire me out tremendously afterwards. Also, I needed to eat more food with vaping since it sapped more Prana from my system than smoking Sativas. Therefore, I was not a big fan of vaping overall.

CANNABIS CONCENTRATES AND EDIBLES

To give you the most comprehensive view of cannabis, I have to address concentrates and edibles. Concentrates are cannabis-derived extracts that contain concentrated amounts of the psychoactive compound Tetrahydrocannabinol (THC) and an assortment of other cannabinoids and terpenes. I will only address the two most popular concentrates—Hashish and Shatter.

Hashish is the oldest form of concentrate known to man, and although its use is not as widespread in North America, countries like Lebanon and India still produce black market Hashish for export. Shatter is a type of concentrate that is believed to be the purest and most potent type of cannabis product. It contains between 60-80% THC, compared to smoking cannabis which averages 10-25% THC. Both Hashish and Shatter are meant to be smoked, not ingested.

The main reason why people use concentrates instead of smoking cannabis is because they are more efficient in producing the desired high since they are higher in potency. In addition, they provide faster relief of mental, emotional and physical issues.

In terms of my own experience with concentrates, I have found Hashish to give me similar effects as smoking Indica strains of cannabis. I say similar, but not the same. The body buzz or body high is the collective effect, although Hashish is more potent than Indica strains and has more hallucinogenic properties. I found myself lacking mental functionality under its influence. In most cases, my cognitive faculties would be turned off entirely, whereas, with Indicas, I could still function to some extent. Regarding the Kundalini activity, I did not find Hashish helpful in removing blockages in the system as I did with smoking Sativas.

Shatter, on the other hand, is a whole different animal. Smoking Shatter, popularly known as doing "dabs," is a cumbersome procedure. It requires you to use a unique device for smoking called an "oil rig" and a torch lighter. The oil rig is similar to a bong, only specifically created for smoking Shatter. I found it rather inconvenient to smoke Shatter because of the specialised tools required. Joints and even pipes you can smoke just about anywhere, whereas bongs and Shatter are mainly smoked indoors. Vaping you can do outdoors in compact vaporiser devices or indoors in more elaborate ones.

I have found Shatter to give me the most prominent high I ever had off cannabis type products. I found its impact similar to the effects I got from Sativas, only far more considerable. I got very high, very quickly. It was inspiring, yes, but because of the high concentration of THC, it would wear me out very quickly. First, it stimulated my Kundalini into activity, but then as I stayed high for an extended period, it just turned it off entirely. Once this happened, it did not matter where I was; I needed to close my eyes and rest. I was burnt out very quickly with the use of Shatter, and because of this, I could not do dabs more than a few times a month.

This brings me to an important point: the necessity for sleep after smoking cannabis or concentrates. I found that other than with Sativas, I was always exhausted after the high wore off and needed to sleep right away in most cases. Vaping and Shatter got me the most tired and burnt out. In most cases, I was not functional afterwards. Hence why I primarily stuck with smoking Sativas in joints only.

Another popular cannabis product is edibles. These are cannabis-infused foods and drinks. When you eat activated cannabinoids, the metabolised THC becomes even more psychoactive than ever as it is absorbed through the digestive system rather than the bloodstream. As a result, the high produced has an entirely different sensation than that of smoking cannabis.

The most popular and widely used edibles are cannabis brownies and cookies. All edibles are made by incorporating cannabis oils and butters, which means that just about any food recipe can include cannabis. The most challenging part of edibles is the proper dosing. Since effects take time to set in, sometimes up to two hours, it is easy to take the process for granted and ingest more than you need, which can and does lead to an unpleasant experience. I have personally witnessed people have massive psychotic breaks from overdosing with edibles. Because of the tendency for people to take too many edibles since it takes a while for them to kick in, I am dumbfounded that their use is legal. It is highly irresponsible for governments to include edibles as part of legal cannabis products without informing people on proper dosage and potential side effects when not followed.

Edibles stimulate the Kundalini energy into activity, and a smaller dose can push out any mental or emotional blockages. On the other hand, if you take too much, the entire experience can be so intense that you will feel like you are on LSD, mushrooms, or another highly psychoactive drug.

CONTROLLED SUBSTANCES AND SHORT-CIRCUITS

When it comes to alcohol, I don't feel the need to describe what it does and how it works since I think it's common knowledge. Instead, I will mention alcohol's direct effect on the Kundalini system for those of you who have made it a part of your life. Alcohol can and does create energy blockages when used in excess. It can short-circuit Ida and Pingala, but this is rarer than compared to recreational drugs. However, copious amounts of alcohol, which work to affect your state of mind and shift it to a high degree, can harm your Kundalini system.

The rule of thumb is that any recreational drug or substance which affects and alters the state of mind can hurt the Kundalini awakened person. Coffee in significant quantities can also be detrimental. I have never experienced a short circuit due to drinking coffee, but then again, I have never had more than three cups of coffee in a day. I believe that the general rule of thumb of any substance which affects the thoughts and emotions can and will cause a short-circuit if overused.

Hard, illegal drugs such as cocaine, ecstasy, MDMA, mushrooms, LSD, and others can short-circuit either Ida or Pingala or both. Cocaine works to amplify willpower primarily, which then puts Pingala in jeopardy. Overuse of cocaine can most definitely cause a short-circuit. On the other hand, Ecstasy and MDMA work on emotions and feelings, which puts Ida in peril.

While cocaine increases dopamine levels, ecstasy and MDMA increase serotonin levels. The incredible high will be followed by a potentially devastating emotional low when either your dopamine or serotonin levels are depleted. For this reason, cocaine addicts generally have anger issues, while regular ecstasy or MDMA users suffer from depression—their nervous systems are completely out of balance.

Mushrooms and LSD are powerful psychoactive drugs with high hallucinogenic properties that affect Ida and Pingala. After all, hallucinating affects both willpower and emotions at the same time. The same goes for alcohol abuse, which puts Ida and Pingala at risk. Since it is grown in the Earth, the same as cannabis, mushrooms are the safest way for one to experience altered states of consciousness. However, one must be prepared for this experience mentally and emotionally since it lasts for many hours.

Cannabis, as mentioned, puts Ida in danger. Still, nowadays, with the varied and powerful cannabis strains available that impact both willpower and emotions, it can affect both Ida and Pingala. For example, I can imagine that smoking too much of an Indica strain can be detrimental to the integrity of one's willpower since this type of marijuana turns off the Fire Element's influence almost entirely. Conversely, smoking Sativa strains of cannabis, which affect the emotional state, the Water Element, can and does jeopardise the Ida channel when done in excess.

I don't agree with people saying that cannabis is a gateway drug to hard, illegal drugs like the ones I mentioned and injectable ones like heroin. If anything, cannabis is a gateway to the mind. If you have a propensity to try drugs and experiment with them, you will do so without necessarily trying cannabis first. As a final statement on this topic, I wish to emphasize that there is zero therapeutic value to using any of these recreational drugs other than cannabis, which is also used as a medicinal drug.

***

I hope that my experience with cannabis and cannabis-related products have been insightful, as intended. However, understand that cannabis is not for everyone. Therefore, make your own judgements and proceed at your discretion based on the information you have received. Regardless, the taboo in society needs to be removed concerning cannabis use, especially for the sake of Kundalini awakened initiates, because most awakened people I have come across drew positive experiences from using it.

Also, keep in mind that present-day strains are much more powerful than ones of the past and should be approached with caution. It is best to always start with a small dose and increase accordingly so that you can get familiar with the effects of a particular strain. Listen to your body and mind and approach cannabis like a scientist so you can figure out what strains work well for you.

Using cannabis in a meditative and ritualistic setting will have much different effects than smoking it recreationally with friends or at parties. I always advise to use cannabis with proper intention and Spiritual work in mind. As a Kundalini awakened individual, Sativas were a blessing in my life when I was in a time of need. If they did not exist, I probably would not have smoked the other types of cannabis at all.

However, it is easy to develop a dependency on cannabis if you smoke regularly. Anything can start off as a positive thing and then turn negative if you overdo it. I found myself in this situation for about a year and a half, right before I decided to quit altogether in 2016.

After quitting what became my addiction at the time, I experienced tremendous positive changes in mind, body, and Soul that are worth mentioning. Firstly, my drive and ambition have increased tenfold. Irrespective of some people saying otherwise, smoking cannabis affects productivity in your life. A lot. You may not see it if you are stuck inside the frame like I was, but it does. It also affects your desire to stand out from the crowd and seek greatness.

Cannabis makes you content with life, and when you are overly comfortable, you stop seeking change and trying to better yourself and your life. When you are high, you elevate above your emotions, but because you don't process them naturally, you rob yourself of learning from them and advancing in different areas of your life. After all, one of the reasons why we have such powerful feelings is because we are meant to learn from them and grow psychologically.

Cannabis neutralises fear, which is good when you are desperate, but remember, fear exists to make us strong. By becoming dependent on any substance to help us deal with fear energy, we prevent ourselves from further evolving naturally. Yes, life is more difficult without drugs and alcohol to help us take the edge off. But the more challenging something is, the reward is that much sweeter.

If you introduce drugs and alcohol into the equation, you prevent yourself from developing the necessary mental anchors that help when dealing with challenging times. As humans, we require life's resistance to become strong and learn to deal with difficult situations in life. We need fear as a building block so we can develop courage.

Keep in mind now that I am speaking to people who have developed a dependency on cannabis. If you smoke it a few times a month, I don't see how it can have any real adverse side effects. Just be mindful that you are dealing with something that can become addictive if you don't practice moderation.

PART XI: KUNDALINI MEDITATIONS

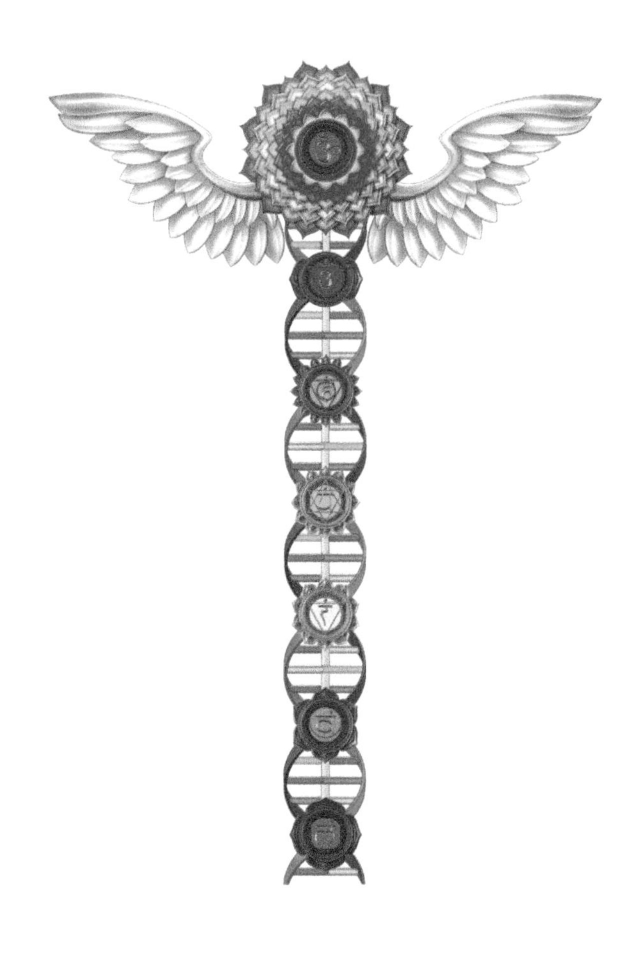

TROUBLESHOOTING THE SYSTEM

Having gone through many challenging situations during my Kundalini awakening, I was forced to troubleshoot my issues and discover ways to help myself. Most people will go through adverse experiences that shock the Kundalini system and then cope with the ramifications without viable methods of helping themselves. Most awakened people who experience a Kundalini short-circuit work on rebuilding the energy back through food intake, which could take at least a few months or more. However, I have found ways to reconnect the channels through different meditations in as little as half an hour at most, sometimes even a few minutes. I will discuss these meditations below, giving you proper guidance on applying each for various situations.

1. Tongue on Roof of Mouth (Jiva Bandha)

Place the tip of your tongue on the fleshy mound right behind your upper teeth. The middle of your tongue should lock in with the indented part in the roof of your mouth. This powerful exercise called Jiva Bandha in Yogic teachings is essential for Kundalini awakened individuals since it completes the Kundalini circuit by allowing the energy to move upwards. It first enters the frontal part of the Mind's Eye tunnel, slightly between the eyebrows, and then progressively passes through the Fourth, Fifth, Sixth, and finally, Seventh Eye, which is one of the exit points of the Kundalini that completes its circuit.

Performing this exercise directs your focus into the highest two Spirit Chakras, Ajna and Sahasrara, instead of the lower Chakras. It will enable your Higher Self to take over the consciousness through intuition received from Ajna Chakra, overcoming the impetus from the Lower Self, the Ego. Make this exercise a regular part of your day. Try to have your tongue on the roof of your mouth as often as possible to allow the energy to channel upwards into the frontal cortex of your brain. This area is where Ida and Pingala converge at the Mind's Eye centre right above the middle of your eyebrows, just inside the head.

This particular exercise is also used to rebuild the Kundalini system once you have experienced a short circuit. Remember, unless Ida and Pingala converge at Ajna Chakra, the Kundalini circuit will remain open, which will cause mental and(or) emotional problems. Placing the tongue on the roof of the mouth with continuity and diligence will allow Ida and Pingala to re-converge at Ajna and naturally move upwards into the Seventh Eye Center as one stream of energy. As such, the Kundalini circuit will close, which will allow you to experience the ecstatic realm of Non-Duality, the Spiritual Realm, through the Bindu Chakra at the top, back of the head.

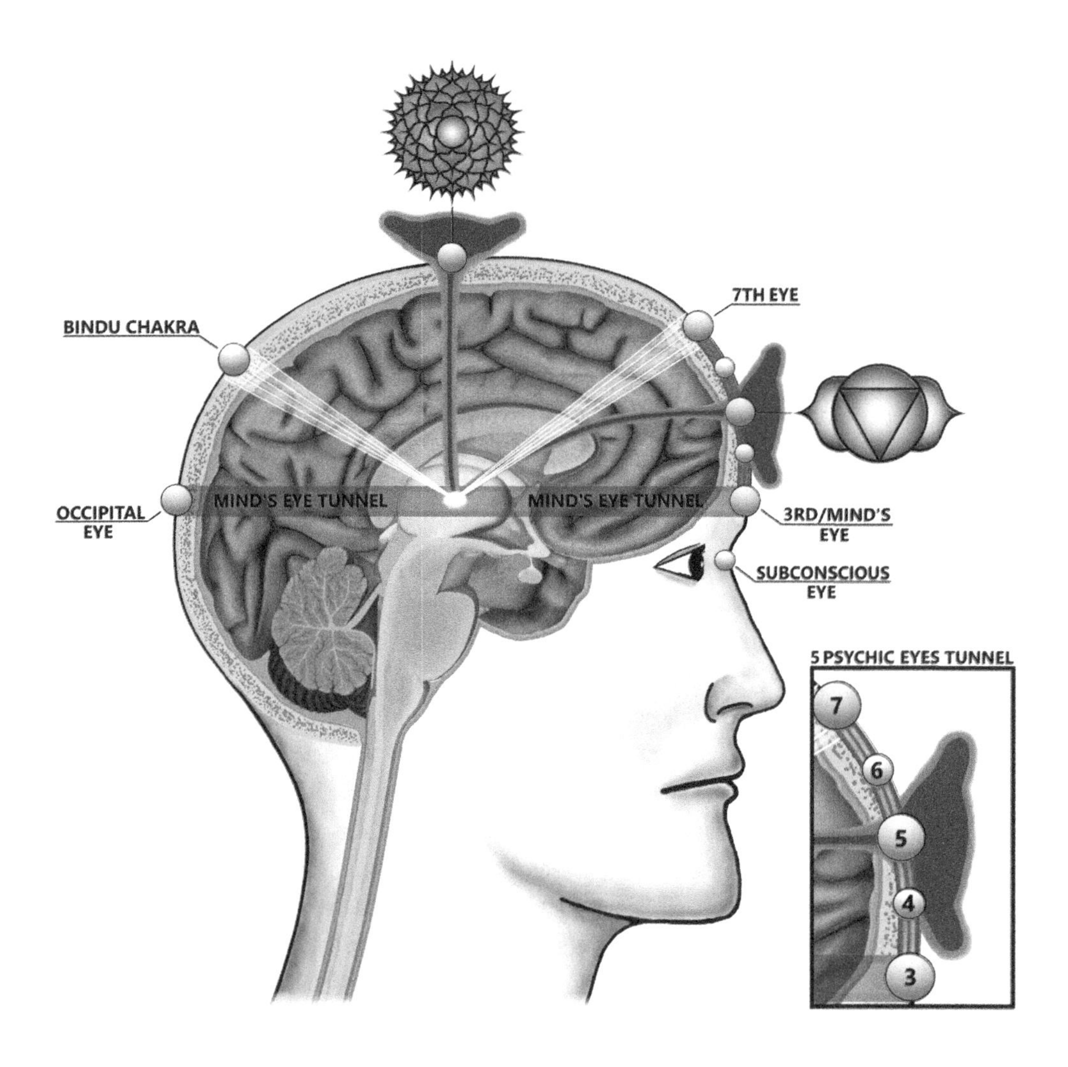

Figure 162: The Major Head Energy Centres

2. Mind's Eye Meditation

The first and most critical meditation is on the Mind's Eye, Ajna Chakra's energy portal, a centre of consciousness that is a window into the Cosmic Realms. This portal's frontal entrance is located between the eyebrows, just above eye level, on your forehead. However, the location of its meditation point is one centimetre from the skin's surface, inside the head. (Use Figure 162 as a reference for locating the Major Head Energy Centres, while Figure 163 refers to the actual meditation points related to those centres.)

You can look up at this point with your eyes closed by slightly projecting your eyes upwards. Ida and Pingala converge at this point, which is necessary to complete the Kundalini circuit. If you fall short of this convergence of Ida and Pingala, the circuit will not be fully active within the Body of Light.

Focusing your attention on this point during meditation stimulates the Pineal Gland, which has an intimate connection with the Soul. You will feel a magnetic pull towards the Mind's Eye if you focus on it correctly. Attention should always be placed at the Mind's Eye, which, when appropriately applied, stimulates the Bindu at the back of the head, affecting the flow of energy in the Kundalini circuit and making it funnel outwards from the Bindu.

To perform this meditation correctly, lie on your back with your hands outstretched and gently place your attention on the Mind's Eye. You can control your breathing with the Four-Fold Breath, which will also aid in allowing you to attain a meditative state. Attention needs to be held on the Mind's Eye even while any thoughts or visuals run through your mind. If you keep your attention at this spot successfully for approximately two to three minutes, sometimes less, the re-convergence will occur, and the energy system will reactivate.

Now, during the day, you will have clarity of mind and thoughts, including equilibrium in your emotions. You may not feel like you made a big difference at first, but once you take in some food and get some good sleep, you will feel a sense of renewal and will start to generate inspiration again. Without this convergence of Ida and Pingala, it is impossible to create momentum and remain inspired for any significant length of time.

3. Seventh Eye Meditation

The Seventh Eye is located where your hairline meets your forehead, in the centre. This location point is approximately one centimetre outside your head, right above that point. The Kundalini energy needs to exit from this point since the Seventh Eye is the counterpart of the Bindu point at the top back of the head. They work together to circulate Kundalini energy throughout the body.

If the Kundalini circuit is stagnant or inactive, this is one of the meditations you can do to kick-start it back up again. If there is a blockage at this point or the Kundalini circuit has ceased functioning, it is necessary to re-open this channel and get it to funnel the energy correctly. If this point is not active, you will notice no visual component associated with your thought processes and that your inspiration is low. Your imaginative powers will be affected, and you will lose your connection to the Now, the present moment, making you introverted and fall prey to the Ego.

The Third Eye centre is the access point for the energy to move to the Seventh Eye and the Bindu at the back of the head. Therefore, I recommend doing the Mind's Eye meditation first to help move the energy upwards into the higher centres of the head. Then, focusing on the Seventh Eye will complete the final step of moving the energy out of the head to complete the circuit.

For this meditation, lie on your back with your palms outstretched and focus the energy at the Seventh Eye centre. Perform the Four-Fold Breath to calm your mind. If you hold your attention on the Seventh Eye for two to three minutes uninterrupted, the Kundalini energy will rise and pass through this point. As such, the Bindu will become reactivated, allowing the Kundalini circuit to flow correctly in the Body of Light.

For the rest of the day, I recommend spending time in solitude. In my experience, once I do the Seventh Eye meditation, my energy gets quite affected for the day, which throws me off when I interact with others. This exercise saps Prana from the system, making you come off lifeless, unbalanced, and emotionally down when talking to other people. After a good night's sleep, though, the circuit should regenerate with Pranic energy and become optimised, getting you back to 100%.

Also, food intake is essential to power the system back up after this meditation. You may need a day or two of food intake to fully regenerate your inner energies since working with the Seventh Eye and Bindu puts more strain on the Kundalini circuit than just working with the Mind's Eye. These two points are the exit points of the Kundalini energy; thus, working with them can highly affect your psychological state.

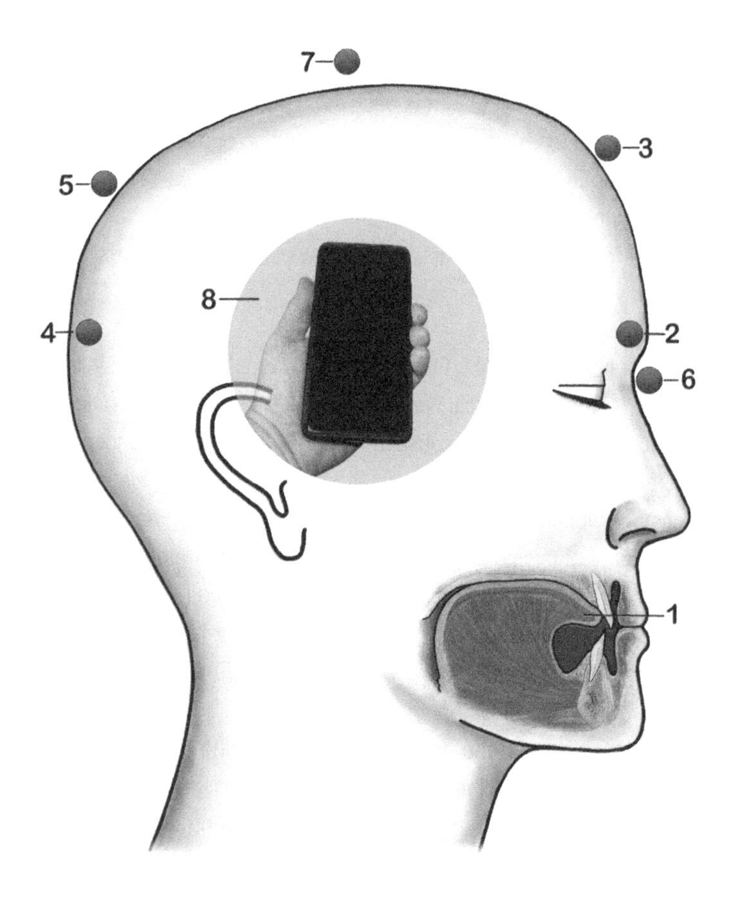

Figure 163: The Kundalini Meditations

4. Occipital Eye Meditation

This meditation is for more advanced initiates because you have to have built up the Spirit energy inside your system (which only occurs when the Kundalini circuit is active for some time) so that it starts to transform from the Fire energy into a cooling liquid, Spirit energy. This Spirit energy will make you feel like you are made of liquid Mercury, which brings about a cooling feeling in your Body of Light and complete transcendence in consciousness.

This liquid Spirit pours into the back of the head naturally. Some people have even reported a feeling of it dropping to the back of their throat. In my opinion, these claims are misunderstandings that relate to perception. As I discussed in an earlier chapter, it is easy to mistake something happening in the Body of Light as happening to the physical body after a Kundalini awakening. After all, both are experienced as real to the consciousness, and since the Body of Light is a new thing, the consciousness needs some time to learn to differentiate between the two. This is my opinion, at least, but one that I am willing to debate with anyone, having witnessed this phenomenon for over seventeen years.

The Occipital Eye is located directly opposite the Mind's Eye. Therefore, you should focus on a meditation point one centimetre on the inside of the head to pull the energy to the back of the head. However, if you find that this is not working for you, you can focus one centimetre on the outside of the head in the same area. Since you are trying to pull the energy back in your head, you might need to work with both meditation points since energy can get trapped there and will require some creativity on your part to push through and create a proper flow.

To aid in this meditation, I like to imagine my Astral Self standing one foot outside of me, looking directly at the back of my head. By holding this vision or by keeping my attention at one of the two meditation points for the Occipital Eye, an alignment will occur where the liquid Spirit energy gets pulled towards the back of the head, which pushes out any stagnations or blockages of energy, optimising the flow of the Kundalini circuit.

5. Bindu Chakra Meditation

The Bindu Chakra is essential because it is the exit point that completes the Kundalini circuit. When the Kundalini is allowed to funnel out of this point, consciousness experiences Oneness with all things, a state of perpetual meditation and pure transcendence. This is because the Bindu is the doorway to the Causal Chakra, where duality meets Non-Duality. Therefore, meditating on this point is vital to maintaining the integrity of the Kundalini circuit. There needs to be a constant subtle pulling of the energy outwards to the top back of the head.

An adequate flow of energy at this point causes you to see yourself in the third-person. It creates a feeling of your consciousness being elevated above your physical body where you can see your face from a third-person perspective. This way, you continually perceive your physical Self, your facial expressions and the energy you put out into the Universe, along with your inner thoughts, simultaneously. This state of Being indicates a high state of Spiritual evolution with the Kundalini energy.

The Bindu point is at the top back of the head, directly opposite the Seventh Eye. Its meditation point is one centimetre outside the head, just like the Seventh Eye. This meditation is more common than the Seventh Eye and will alleviate more problems, mentally and emotionally. When there is too much stagnant energy in the head, the Ego will use this situation for its agenda by introducing negative thoughts that create fear to hijack the consciousness. This will cause the Kundalini to drop down from the Bindu Chakra. There doesn't have to be a short-circuiting of any channel for this to occur; it can happen from increased stress or the harbouring of negative thoughts for an extended period.

To perform this meditation, lie on your back with your hands outstretched while focusing on the Bindu Chakra's meditation point, which is one centimetre outside of the top, back of the head. Perform the Four-Fold Breath to calm the mind and enter a meditative state. Focusing on this point affects the Bindu and the Causal Chakra, which is intimately linked with the Bindu.

The key to these head meditations is to focus your attention on a particular point inside or outside the head for two to three minutes with total concentration. I like to imagine myself tapping the meditation point continually with my index finger. Keep in mind that I am talking about imagining my Astral finger doing this with the power of my mind. This way, I incorporate imagination and willpower, thus utilizing both the Ida and Pingala channels. Doing so stimulates the energy and pushes it outwards, thereby completing the circuit. This meditation can also be performed while sitting down, while the other meditations mentioned so far work best lying down, in my experience.

6. Subconscious Eye Meditation

The Subconscious Eye allows all fully Kundalini awakened individuals to see the content in their subconscious mind to gain mastery over their thoughts and reality. This psychic centre lies at the point where the middle of the eyes meets the bridge of the nose. However, suppose there is an increase of negative energy and fearful thoughts within the mind. In that case, this release point gets blocked up, and the individual cannot view the subconscious content.

Ida may collapse simultaneously, or it is Ida collapsing that often causes this psychic centre to close. Remember, all stress, anxiety, and negative, fearful thoughts put Ida in jeopardy when focused on for too long. If Ida does collapse, or if it happens on its own, this point will need to reopen before it can function well again. The location you need to focus on is just above the bridge of the nose, one centimetre outside of the head.

When you are breathing, this psychic centre breathes with you. Pranic energy is being fed into the Subconscious Eye that enables you to have healthy thoughts and emotions. Every waking breath should renew your mind when these psychic centres work correctly. If any energy at this point stagnates, you will have an unhealthy, fear-ridden mind. You will have a hard time looking forward to the future and will cling to the past, continually thinking about it obsessively.

Obsessive thoughts or emotions often cause this psychic centre to get blocked up since by thinking obsessively about something, you are focusing your attention on the back of your head too much, which can pull energy away from the Five Psychic Eyes and the Subconscious Eye, causing some of them to get blocked up. Remember, the actual location of the subconscious mind is at the back of the head, while the Subconscious Eye is a window or portal that enables us to view its content.

This meditation is to be performed while lying down with palms outstretched. It would help if you utilized the Four-Fold Breath to keep yourself in the right mind state while you perform this meditation. Attention is to be held at the point described for at least two to three minutes, uninterrupted. If successful, there will be a cooling feeling on the bridge of the nose, and you will feel the pressure there as energy exits out of it into the atmosphere before you. You will feel an immediate release from past thoughts and an ability to think about and be excited about the future.

7. Sahasrara Chakra Meditation

Sahasrara Chakra is the most critical Chakra in the context of a Kundalini awakening since it is our connection with the Spiritual Source, the White Light. Sahasrara is the highest on the body at the top, centre of the head, and its function regulates the complete Kundalini circuit when opened and active. Therefore, there always needs to be a flow of energy into it; otherwise, the Kundalini circuit will cease functioning. In the rare event that the Kundalini energy drops down from Sahasrara, this simple meditation can raise it back up again, causing the central flow of energy through Sushumna to function correctly. Remember, Ida, Pingala, and Sushumna unite at Ajna as one stream of energy that rises to Sahasrara. So if this stream of energy drops below Sahasrara, this is the meditation you need to use to bring it back up.

To perform this meditation, lie on your back with palms outstretched. First, utilise the Four-Fold Breath to get yourself in a meditative state. Next, close your physical eyes and roll them back, trying to look up at the top of your head, approximately two centimetres above the centre of your skull. Although Sahasrara is at the top, centre of the head, I have found that focusing two centimetres above it instead of one, or directly on it, facilitates a necessary push for the Kundalini energy channel to rise into Sahasrara.

Hold your attention on this point for two to three minutes, uninterrupted. If successful, you will feel a flow of energy move through your brain, reaching Sahasrara. If this does not work and you feel a definite drop from Sahasrara, then you will need to rebuild the Kundalini strands in your head through food intake, transforming food into Light energy or Prana. You may need a few weeks to a month. You can perform this meditation every few days as you rebuild your Body of Light fuel to take care of this situation.

8. Holding an Image in the Mind Meditation

Another fundamental meditation that can help alleviate mental and emotional problems is to imagine a simple object in your mind and hold its visual image with total concentration. It helps if the thing you are imagining is something that you have in your hand often, like your cellphone, so that you can reimagine how it looks and feels in your hand, using your Astral senses and the power of your mind.

This meditation is helpful if there is a blockage at the Bindu Chakra and when no other head points meditations work. It is a powerful meditation because it incorporates both the Ida and Pingala channels during its performance. When you do any mental activity that requires your willpower, you are using your Pingala channel. Conversely, when using your imagination and are thinking up an image in your mind, you are using your Ida channel. By holding a picture in your mind for an extended period, you are reopening and realigning both Ida and Pingala and allowing them to funnel out the Bindu Chakra, as is natural for them to do in fully Kundalini awakened individuals.

You will notice that if you perform this meditation, the visual component of holding the image in your mind will enhance and become more defined. You may even feel movements of energy in your body, along the front of your torso, on either side, where Ida and Pingala channels are. You may also feel streaks of energy moving through the front of your face.

For example, an alignment may occur in an energy channel that centrally moves across your chin to your bottom lip. You may also feel energy moving within your brain, as the Kundalini strands are being infused with liquid Spirit. If you feel any of these movements, it is a good sign that your meditation is working and Ida and Pingala are aligning. When your meditation is successful, you should finally feel pressure at the top back of your head as your Bindu Chakra gets infused, signalling that the Kundalini circuit has fully reactivated.

9. Becoming One with an Object Meditation

Another powerful meditation to optimise the Ida and Pingala channels and realign the Kundalini circuit is to focus on an object in front of you for an extended period. This meditation aims to exit outside of yourself and become one with the object, feeling its essence. You become externalised when you do this, allowing the Nadis to realign and assume their natural flow. It is generally our mind's content and the misuse of our willpower that blocks or stagnates the flow of the Nadis.

The key is to keep an empty mind and intense focus on whatever object you are meditating on. Feel its texture and use your Astral senses on it. Clear your mind, and don't listen to the thoughts of your Ego as it tries to deter you from the task at hand.

You can also meditate on a fixed point of your choice or a picture. However, I find that meditating on a Three-Dimensional object works better since you can use all of your Astral senses on it, enabling your mind to keep busy, which induces silence. Using the Astral senses in meditation is a good distraction for the mind since it cannot focus on that and thinking simultaneously.

Absorb yourself entirely in the object or fixed point, or picture, without losing focus. You can blink, although your eyes should water slightly when done correctly, signalling a powerful concentration. As you perform this meditation, be mindful of the Bindu point at the top back of the head. After about five to ten minutes of this exercise, you should feel your Nadis realign as your Bindu point becomes infused with energy. This is a sign that the Kundalini circuit has become optimised.

10. Meditating on the Earth Star Chakra

Since the Earth Star Chakra provides the feminine and masculine currents for the Ida and Pingala Nadis, if there is a lack of energy streaming through either of them, you might need to meditate on their source to power them back up again. You can do so by placing your attention on the soles of your feet and holding it there, uninterrupted, while focusing on the Earth Star six inches below the feet.

Remember, the Pingala channel runs through the right leg and heel, while the Ida channel runs through the left. Both connect with the Earth Star Chakra. So if you did your meditation correctly, you would feel an energy alignment at the lower part of the heel corresponding with Muladhara Chakra, signalling that Ida or Pingala have reactivated. At the same time, meditating on the Earth Star provides the most optimal grounding necessary to keep the other Chakras and Subtle Bodies in balance. So, practice this meditation often, even if you aren't experiencing issues with the Ida or Pingala channels.

***

A final note on Kundalini short-circuits and the meditations presented in this chapter. First, understand that short-circuits, in general, are not dangerous in a physical sense but a psychological one. Therefore, doing these meditations cannot harm you but can significantly benefit you Spiritually and allow you to control your reality experience instead of being at the mercy of the Kundalini energy.

However, even though these meditations have worked for me in almost all instances, I cannot guarantee that they will work for you every time. Having developed them, I have obtained an intuitional connection with each meditation where, after diagnosing the problem, I can implement the right one to a 90% accuracy. This I cannot impart on you but hope that you can learn to do the same with practice and experience.

I believe that the manual for our Kundalini systems is the same and that the Creator would not make my Kundalini system different from yours because we are all made of the same physical, emotional, mental and Spiritual components. Hence, I believe that Kundalini issues are Universal, meaning that these meditations should work for you also.

In closing, I hope that by using these meditations, you will look for ways to advance them and find discoveries of your own. We must collectively keep the Kundalini Science continually evolving and reaching new heights so that those who come after us will build on our mistakes and findings. In doing so, we are not only developing ourselves, but the Kundalini Science as a field of study.

PART XII: KUNDALINI COUNSELLING

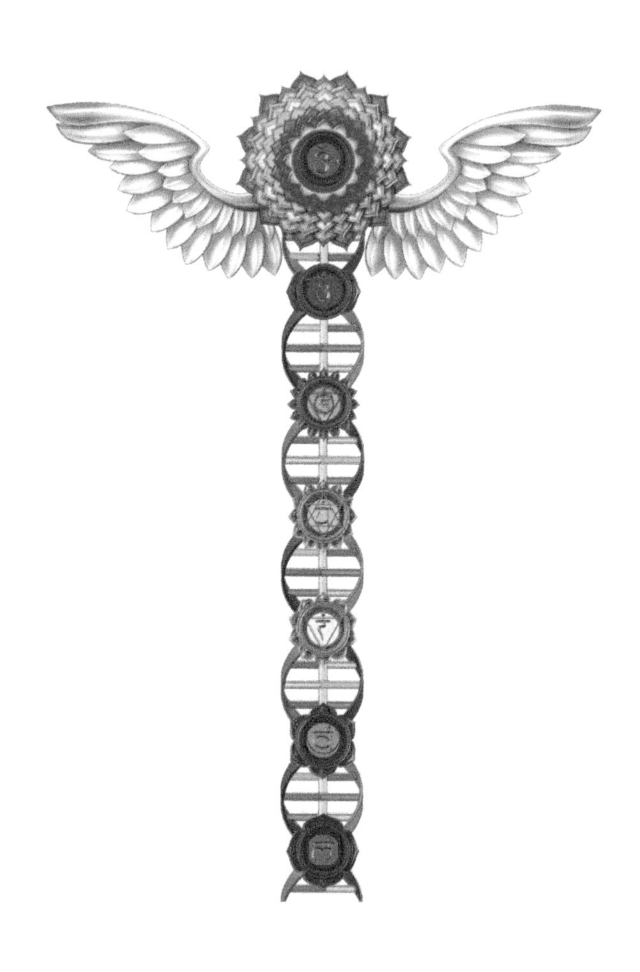

GENERAL TIPS

Over the past seventeen years, I have had many Kundalini awakened people contact me over social media asking for advice on what to expect and how to deal with potential issues that arise in their transformation process. I found that many of their questions and concerns were the same, and their inquiries shared a common thread since the transformation process is Universal. This chapter will discuss these commonalities and share some general tips for those of you amid a Kundalini transformation.

The Kundalini is not a physical manifestation, although it often feels like it is. As the Body of Light is perfecting itself over time, consciousness oscillates between the physical body and the Body of Light, trying to make sense of things. Before the awakening, consciousness used to only operate from the physical body. Therefore, the different manifestations of the Kundalini may feel physical at first, but they are not.

People often tell me that they feel pressure in different parts of their body, usually in their head or heart area, and ask why this is happening. They want to know when it will stop and whether these issues will progress to bodily diseases. Understand that the Kundalini is working through an area with psychic centres it needs to awaken to localise the energy there. Sometimes, this requires pushing against energetic blockages formed over time by negative thoughts and beliefs about oneself and life in general. Although it feels like physical pressure, it manifests on the Astral Plane. However, since the mind is the connecting link, it misinterprets this information. After all, the mind has never experienced anything like this before, and it gets confused easily in this situation. So, it is not uncommon for the person experiencing these sensations to begin to feel fear and anxiety from thinking that something harmful is happening to their physical body.

The Chakras and the surrounding nerves that innervate the organs need to be infused fully with the Light of the Kundalini to allow it to circulate unimpeded in the Body of Light. Due to Karmic energy accumulating in the Chakras throughout someone's life, these areas can become blocked. The Kundalini needs to apply pressure in this area through mild and steady heat to eradicate and remove these blockages.

The Kundalini is raw Fire energy that transforms into liquid Sprit through the sublimation of Prana via food intake coupled with the transmutation of one's sexual energy. This Spirit energy can pierce through any blockages, but it first needs to be converted into its subtle form by the Kundalini Fire. From observing this process in my own Body of Light, I have found that this transformation happens in the area where the Kundalini is clearing blockages.

The most common areas for blockages to be cleared are the head and the heart. People will feel pressure in their head for months, maybe even years, while the Kundalini is transforming into this finer liquid Spirit and opening the brain centres. And as you have learned so far, there are many critical brain centres to be opened, like the Thalamus, Hypothalamus, and Pituitary and Pineal Glands. The brain is the hub that contains these important energy centres. The Chakras and the Nadis are connected to the brain via the nervous system. The brain is the motherboard;

proper wiring needs to be created in the Body of Light for it to operate most efficiently. Otherwise, the Kundalini circuit will not work correctly.

Anahata, the Heart Chakra, is another critical area where the Kundalini Fire must work through energetic obstacles to create the necessary wiring. After Hara Chakra, Anahata is the second-largest convergence of Nadis in the body. On the left side of it is the Ida channel which needs to open correctly to optimise its energy flow. On the right side is the Pingala channel. Both require a sufficient flow of this Spirit energy working through them not to feel strange pressure, which creates fearful and worrisome thoughts.

After the Kundalini energy awakens, palpitations in the physical heart are frequent as high levels of adrenaline, dopamine, and serotonin are released in the body, causing an accelerated heart rate. The occasional skipping of heartbeats happens as well, which I have found to be caused by fear-based memories that surface from the subconscious to be reexperienced to remove their emotional charge.

These situations are nothing to worry about since they are Universal in their expression and will continue to manifest for years to come, especially in the early stages. With different hormones being pumped into the heart, incredible feelings of heightened elation are experienced. The rush of energy in the heart is ecstatic and impossible to describe to someone who hasn't experienced it. The adrenals can become exhausted throughout this process, which you can replenish with Vitamin C.

The Kundalini energy may also encounter blockages in other body areas, usually in the torso. The energy may work through different organs, and it can feel like an organ is in danger. I have never found this to be the case, though, nor have I heard of anyone having real organ failures in this situation. So, again, it may feel physical to you, but it will not negatively impact the organ. However, it should be noted that there can be psychosomatic effects if you are too focused on thinking that the pressure is physical. In other words, you may develop physical pain, but only because you are so concentrated on the idea that it manifests. Still, however, it does not manifest in a way that can harm you.

Overall, my advice is always the same, and this advice applies to all things concerning the awakening at any stage—if you feel fear, go through it. Please don't focus on the fear since it is the fear that affects you negatively and not the Kundalini itself. Fear creates anxiety, which works against the Kundalini. It battles the Kundalini process as it is occurring inside of you. The physical, emotional and mental Subtle Bodies need to be relaxed and at peace for the Kundalini to do its work. If there is anxiety present in any one area, it will prevent the flow of the Kundalini in one of its many different states. These blockages will only seem to get stronger and worsen if you invoke anxiety. Instead, you need to practice being relaxed in mind, body and Soul even when the experience may seem intense.

Once the Kundalini is wholly awakened and working through you, it is best if you stop meditating for a little while. At this point, all that does is focus the energy inside the head, which is no longer necessary. If you have awakened the Kundalini, you have already reached the goal of all meditation anyways. Therefore, spending as much time away from your thoughts and more time in nature or with people will benefit you. When I say people, I mean positive-minded people, not negative ones. Relaxing in all parts of the Self and focusing on bringing in nutritious food will be all that is required of you.

Do not despair if you are having difficulty sleeping, as will often happen during the first few years after the awakening. There is no use in trying to induce sleep at all costs, only to get frustrated when it doesn't happen. Instead, go and do something productive to work off the energy preventing you from sleeping. Doing creative activities will help transform the energy and put you in touch with the imagination and willpower, which will help inspire you and aid you in reaching a calm state, inducing sleep naturally. Always remember, creativity also uses love energy, so any activity that is a creative one is productive since it uses love. This rule applies as you are going through the awakening at any point in your life. We are always trying to align with love as much as we can as we go through this.

I had insomnia for years after my awakening and would oscillate between intense Lucid Dreams and complete lack of sleep and the inability to induce dreams at all. Over time, I learned not to worry or stress out when this happens, although this can be difficult to do if you have something important the next day that you need to be well-rested. You have to learn to go with it and not fight it. There is no choice. As soon as you accept this, you will be better off. Living the regular nine to five lifestyle can be a challenge, but it is one that you need to accept and work through. The more you fight it, the more you are hindering the Kundalini transformation process.

If you cannot induce sleep during the night, the body is signalling to you that it does not need rest. Maybe the mind does, and you can rest the mind by simply relaxing on your back while awake. It sometimes helps to take a melatonin pill right before bed that you can find at your local drug store. But if you cannot induce sleep, it merely means that there is too much activity in the Body of Light, and you need to accept this. You will be a little more lucid the following day, but you should be able to tackle everything you need. Not being able to sleep means the Kundalini is in overdrive, transforming your mind, body, and Soul at a deep level. Put yourself in autopilot mode as much as possible and let it do what it needs to do.

One aspect of the Kundalini transformation is that the amount of sleep needed to function 100% the next day is substantially less than a person without active Kundalini. Six hours of sleep should suffice most days, I have found. A full eight hours of sleep is optimal, while anything more than eight is excessive and not needed. However, in the beginning stages, you may need more than eight hours of sleep, especially if your Kundalini is very active during the night.

As the years went by, I have found that more than eight hours of sleep left me less focused and sluggish the next day. Optimally, between six to eight hours of sleep has been proven to be the best for me. I had also had many sleepless nights when the Kundalini was very active. But I overcame this by relaxing my mind during the night instead, which allowed me to still function at 95% the next day with my usual laser-like sharpness and focus. However, this was after at least five years of the Kundalini transformation process and once I tuned my consciousness with the Higher Self. If you find yourself aligned more with your Ego, you will need more sleep.

COMMON QUESTIONS

After assuming the role of Kundalini teacher and guide over many years, I have responded to countless questions from many different Kundalini initiates about their awakening and transformation process. I have compiled the most common inquiries into a series of Q and As from our correspondences.

I had a spontaneous Kundalini awakening almost one year ago. Now, the emotional turmoil and fear that I am faced with are unbearable. I have lost my job, my relationships have fallen apart, and I am ready to give up. I have no more energy left to continue forward. What words of wisdom do you have for me?

Don't despair, my friend. Many people have been in your shoes, and many more will be in the future. As bad as things may seem now, always remember that dawn always follows the night. Success is not determined by how fast you fall but by how quickly you get up and try again. You have to develop resistance to these challenges that you are faced with, and you will find the solutions you seek. Don't let fear cripple you, but instead, face your fears, and you will gain courage. All successful people shine when they have nothing left, when all their energy is gone, and their tank is on empty. They use these moments to prove who they are by finding energy from within themselves to conquer their fears and find success.

Remember, FEAR is False Evidence Appearing Real; it lives in the realm of duality. The True Self, though, is in the realm of Non-Duality. It is a Fire that no one but yourself can put out. And time is ticking away for all of us. Therefore, we must all look at life's challenges and see them as tests of our willpower. We must have faith in ourselves and the Universe and meet these challenges with determination and persistence to succeed.

Find your solace in the company of like-minded individuals going through the same Kundalini awakening process and make brothers and sisters of them. You are not alone in this. We are all destined to transform into Beings of Light. It is not an easy process, though. The harder the journey, the sweeter the reward. Many roads lead to the same goal. If one does not work, try another. Never give up and be down on yourself because if you are willing to quit, the Divine has no place for you in the Kingdom of Heaven.

Whenever my Kundalini energy becomes very active, I become incredibly paranoid, anxious and afraid. I wonder if I should see a therapist even though I'm not sure if they will understand what I'm going through. But, before doing that, what else can I do to overcome these difficult emotions?

The paranoia and anxiety you are experiencing are typical of what you are going through. Your condition, though, is not one that can be described as clinical. You are best off keeping the experience to yourself to save yourself the disappointment of not being understood by medical personnel. More importantly, to protect yourself from being put on prescription medication that will substantially hinder your transformation process. Spend time outside, connect with nature, and do things external to you instead of overthinking what you are going through. The Ego doesn't like that it is undergoing a death process, so it wants to scare you and make you feel negative about this.

Most importantly, think positively about the whole experience. You are among the elite in the world, and you have been chosen for whatever reason. Frankly, years of living in a bad mental state, as is the case in many newly awakened Kundalini initiates, are well worth the precious jewels that await you in the future. Besides, your mentality is only a facet of who you really are. Remember that and be brave. Focusing on fear will prevent you from living with courage. Instead, be courageous, and the fear will vanish.

There are times when I feel as if my Ego is finally out of the way, but then it returns with a vengeance, bringing on great fear and emotional pain. Often, it feels like I am dying a slow and painful death. Why can't this be over with? What is happening to me?

Pain and pleasure are both aspects of the same thing. They are linked to how one reads the reality around them through the mind. By bridging the conscious with the subconscious, the speed of the pendulum that swings between pleasure and pain is increased exponentially, giving rise to many mental issues. The difference is that with a Kundalini activated person, this process is only temporary and serves to eradicate negative memories, acting as a wall between the world of pure potential and the limits created by the mind in its quest for survival.

The Self that has survived thus far is the Ego. The Ego is dying! It doesn't want to die, much like any other intelligent force in this Universe. So the eternal witness of the Now, your real Self, stands aside as the Ego feels the pain knowing that in its death lies true life. Remember, it took many years for the Ego to develop. As every action has an equal and opposite reaction, know that it will take many years for it to die as well. It is a normal part of the transformation process, as is the pain accompanying it.

Once the sufferings of the Ego are cleared, consciousness is free to experience the pure emotion of the Void, which is a Nirvanic rapture. So take your time, don't hurry, and after some time, the mind will settle, and you will become who you are meant to be—a Being of Light!

For the past few months, I have been plagued with debilitating headaches that sometimes last throughout the night and even into the next day. I also feel mysterious pains that come and go in different areas of my body, mainly the torso. What can be done? Is this a normal part of the Kundalini process?

If you have headaches as a result of an awakened Kundalini, you will notice that if you take a step back, your headaches are not caused by the Kundalini but instead by how the mind is interpreting what is happening. This is because the Kundalini operates within the Astral Plane, but we can feel it like it is in our physical body. It operates through a different dimension from the material one that the physical body is a part of.

Maintain relaxation at all times, drink plenty of water, and the headaches will vanish. Avoid stressful situations and when a headache occurs, try to figure out its cause and then avoid creating that same cause the next time or being around it.

Physical pains are attributed to negative energy and Karmic memories stored in the physical body and organs. Therefore, when the Kundalini has, on an Astral level (because it only operates Astrally), permeated the areas that hold the Spiritual counterparts to the body's physical components, there will be feelings of physical pain felt as it is cleansing through the negativity in those Spiritual counterparts.

This process is normal and will subside over time. Try a different diet, Yoga, or grounding techniques to alleviate the pain. Remember, by focusing your attention on the pain, you make it stronger. So, turn your attention elsewhere, and the Kundalini will move to where your awareness is. A fearless mind has no barriers in the Kundalini process!

I have been having different visions involving cats. Sometimes they are big, and sometimes they are small. They have been silver, black, yellow and reddish-orange. However, the most prominent vision was a cat with a broken tail. I'm struggling to make sense of it. Is something broken inside me?

Interpret visions like this from the point of view of the mind. If the mind is relaxed and enjoying these images, they are fleeting experiences, and they don't matter. However, if the mind tangles up with these symbols and tries to interpret everything happening, you create a maze for yourself that is hard to get out of without attaching fear to the outcome.

Visions in dreams are usually a result of what the mind is preoccupied with in the waking state. Since you just had the awakening and are experiencing a lot of Kundalini activity daily, these visions in your dreams are trying to let you know something about that.

Cats, regardless of their colour, are symbols of the Kundalini. In Ancient traditions, cats represented the Great Feminine aspect of Divinity. These dreams are letting you know that you are undergoing Kundalini activity. The broken tail might mean an energy blockage, but then again, it might not. It might mean the mind interpreted a crackling of energy inside you.

Don't get caught up in all of these dream interpretations. The end-result of a Kundalini awakening is a total detachment from the mind's entanglement. You must bypass the mind to be in the Now, the present moment, and draw energy from the field of pure potentiality. One day, these things will mean absolutely nothing to you from the big picture point of view.

After my initial Kundalini awakening, I remember seeing many mystical visions with all kinds of symbols. Now they are gone, but so is most visual, involuntary thought altogether. I sense things intuitively, as my consciousness has elevated above fear. Remember this when it comes to the awakening, "All things dissolve and resolve into all other things." What you see now, you won't even remember years from now.

I feel fragile, vulnerable and my emotional state is constantly up and down. I have anxiety and paranoia, and I need help. I'm not sure if doctors can help me with anything related to Kundalini, but I don't know who else to turn to. What should I do?

No mental health professionals can help you with mental and emotional problems that you're facing from an awakened Kundalini. They will be eager to treat you medically, which you do not want. I went to see a psychiatrist who apparently "knew" about the Kundalini at one point in time. During the visit, I learned that she didn't know anything since one can only truly know about the Kundalini if they have some personal experience. It was a waste of my time and money, and most of all, it resulted in disappointment. False hope can have very adverse effects in this process since it can make you give up even faster than you usually would be inclined to do.

If you are in a fragile state, be your own doctor and your personal Saviour. With the Kundalini, please don't put your faith in other people's hands unless those people have had the awakening themselves. If you need comforting, listen to some Self-help talks. A Kundalini awakening will also awaken the guru within, the Higher Self. Now is the time to learn to trust yourself and be your own guide and teacher.

Mental issues, anxiety, and paranoia are common for people in your situation. We've all been through it. Find something that calms you down and makes you happy, which gives you an escape from the mental turmoil. Find a hobby that occupies your body, mind and Soul. Write, paint, go for walks, do something inspiring. If you focus on negativity, you will get negativity in return. It will help if you don't focus on the mental issues as they are temporary.

If you see a medical professional about this, you might feel worse afterwards since they will throw around words like chronic anxiety, bipolar, and schizophrenic. The symptoms exhibited by an active Kundalini might be similar, but that doesn't mean that you have the ailment itself. Unlike unawakened people diagnosed with these diseases, we go through these challenges and emerge on the other side, stronger and more refined. It is just a matter of time and patience.

One thing I always learned is to follow my own drumbeat. Listen to the voice inside, and don't let others tell you what's happening. You guide your narrative. Disregard what others are saying about what you are going through. You know the truth deep inside of you, so start listening. You are fine! It is just the Ego scaring you since it knows it is losing its power over the consciousness. Your True Self lives in silence, a place of no thought!

I feel immense pressure from my forehead up to the top of my head, and my thoughts are uncontrollable. I feel like I'm going crazy like my brain is broken. What can I do to find balance?

If you have a buildup of energy at Sahasarara and Ajna Chakras, you need to ground yourself. If you are overthinking and feel in touch with anxiety and fear, grounding your energies will help you. Grounding will silence your mind, allowing the fear to vanish. From personal experience, if you have a lot of energy in your head, you will become introverted and overthink. So try to focus on the emotional aspect of the Self by getting in touch with your feelings, and the energy will balance itself out.

It helps to focus on your Foot Chakras and especially on your abdomen. By focusing on your abdomen, you neutralise the Air Element (thoughts) and connect to the Water Element (emotions). Doing so will put you in touch with your feelings and bring the energy down from your head. As you send the energy into your belly, you will create a comfortable and steady Fire in that area through breathing and meditation. Practice silent meditation, and you should be able to feel the energy in different places other than your head. Meditation is necessary to bring the energy down into the abdomen and reconnect the Kundalini circuit.

I've been trying to rationalize and intellectualize my process, which has gotten me nowhere. I understand that it's time that I go beyond the mind and my thoughts, but I don't know how or where to start. Can you offer any insight?

Instead of focusing on your thoughts, silence the mind to step outside of yourself through meditation and controlled breathing. See yourself in the third-person as you observe your physical body and facial gestures, and become the Silent Witness in the Now, the present moment. By stepping outside of yourself, you bypass the Ego to connect with the True Self, the Holy Guardian Angel, through whom you can experience the Glory of God and countless other Spiritual riches.

To help you get there, meditate on your Mind's Eye by focusing on your eyebrow centre. Then, with open eyes, see the world outside and inside simultaneously. At this point, you will see yourself as other people see you. You can attain this experience through practice. It will slowly shift your perception from being entangled in the illusion of the Ego and falling prey to fear to becoming external and objective and taking part in God's Kingdom of the Light that gives us love, truth, and wisdom.

This is what is meant when Adepts and Sages mention they have attained the Unity of all things. Remember, you are merely a thought image in the Mind of God. This World of Matter that our senses partake of is but the Eternal Dream of God, and our power to think and dream allows us to be Co-Creator with our Creator. Let those with ears hear this great Universal truth.

Ever since my Kundalini awakened, it's the only thing I want to talk to others about. I want others to know and experience what I have. But whenever I've opened up to anyone about my experiences, they either didn't understand or made me feel as if I was crazy. Should I just keep this experience to myself from now on?

In terms of who you tell you had a Kundalini awakening, I will say to share with 10% of the people in your life and don't share with the other 90%. Sharing by itself has expectations of being understood. The fact is that not even 10% will understand, but they will at least believe you through compassion and faith that you are telling them the truth. So if you want to save yourself from a lot of disappointment, I recommend you keep the experience to yourself in most instances.

If someone mentions Kundalini and knows about it, share your experience with them. Even then, unless the person has had an awakening, they will have varied opinions about the topic and will be unable to follow everything you are saying.

We relate to one another through past experience and common ground as human beings. But, unfortunately, on the topic of Kundalini, most people cannot connect. And if you want to avoid negativity and ignorance from others, feel content with yourself and your own experience and lead by example instead of telling them that you are in training to be the example.

When the Kundalini has finished its work with you, however many years it takes, you will not have to say anything; others will know you are unique and special. They may not understand everything you tell them since a person often has to see something to believe it, but when you become the Light source and lead the way, people will be intrigued and inspired by you. Then, they will follow. After all, people are drawn to those that allow their inner Light to shine because they subconsciously give them permission to be themselves and do the same.

My experiences with the Kundalini have been like being in Heaven at times while at other times, in Hell. However, I was taught to fear Hell and long for Heaven in the afterlife with my religious upbringing. But now, having had these experiences in my daily life, I feel that it's all meaningless. Though I have had incredibly beautiful experiences, my nihilism holds me back from wanting to share them with others. I'm lost and confused. Any insight?

A human is a dual being partaking both of Heaven and Hell. Since we have Free Will, how we exercise it aligns our consciousness with either of them. The Kundalini is an energy that connects Heaven and Hell so that humanity can partake of both in our frail state. Focusing on the Hell aspect, we become participants in it. Conversely, when we focus on Heaven, Hell dissolves into nothingness as our consciousness becomes elevated.

Hell is produced by the Lunar Light, which reflects the Light of the Sun; hence it is illusory. However, Heaven is the Light of the Sun itself. It is Immortal, ineffable, and infinite. It speaks the truth and lives in righteousness. On the other hand, Hell exists only as a fragment of the imagination. It is not the imagination in totality since that belongs to Heaven, but a mere reflection of it. Fear is only a reflection of the Light of the Sun but is not the Light in and of itself. Only when humans choose to be in Hell do they partake of it, according to how much fear energy binds them to it.

By sharing theories, experiences and explanations with others, we are on a quest for knowledge. Knowledge is power, or more importantly, the power of truth, which is an antithesis to fear and Hell. Truth is Light and love. It is Heaven. Beings that speak the truth according to their level of evolution are Beings of Light. Sharing through loving-kindness makes them partakers of the Heaven that is their birthright.

Nihilism is created by baseless theories that life is meaningless because one has drawn themselves away from the Light through pessimism and selfishness. Once the fruits of Heaven escape a person, many turn to despair as they try to make sense of things while choosing to remain ignorant of the truth and take accountability for their thoughts and actions.

Nihilism requires one to take a good look at themselves with an open heart and mind and curb their pride long enough to see that a change in needed to get back on track. It requires us to take responsibility for our reality so that we can continue to grow and Spiritually evolve. Nihilism is often a step in the journey when the darkness becomes stronger than the Light. However, it should never be a final destination.

We are all here to learn from one another. There is ever-present the duality of Heaven and Hell since both exist as relative concepts. However, only one of them is Eternal and Infinite, and that one is the higher truth between the two. Focusing on Hell keeps one within the Mental Body sheath where this duality is apparent.

Learning the Principles of Light and love, including Self-love, will enable you to recognize the truth of the Unity of all things and induce silence of mind. Through silence, you can remove yourself from the clutches of the Mental Body so that your consciousness can enter the Spiritual Body. Since the Spiritual Body partakes of Archetypes, you will be enabled to recognise the truth without duality, which is that we are all sparks of the one source of Light, the Sun. Love is what binds us; truth keeps us going, while justice brings us Eternal glory. Wisdom feeds the Soul, and any intellectual mumbo-jumbo becomes like leaves in the wind.

I keep having dreams of giant dragons. Sometimes they appear snake-like in their movements, and they hiss and attack me. They are so powerful that I don't even fight back. Is there any meaning to this?

Dragons are the symbol of the Kundalini in the Chinese tradition. As the Kundalini is in movement while you sleep, two things are apparent that are impacting your imagination: first is the sound of the energy flowing within you as a mild buzzing or hissing sound heard inside your body. The second is the symbol of this energy from the collective unconscious, like a snake or Dragon, projected into your imagination.

The Dragon attacking you is a good thing since it means that the Kundalini is in overdrive, infusing your Body of Light with often intense jolts of energy. It also means that your Ego is being worked on, which is a sign of transformation. Going with the vision in your dream and not fighting it means your Ego accepts the Kundalini transformation process. Be neutral as this is happening and accept the images, irrespective of how scary they may seem in retrospect. Induce courage to continue surrendering yourself to this process, and you will emerge on the other side as a more refined Spiritual Being.

It is not uncommon also to see different symbolic elements in your dreams as the Kundalini is working through your Chakras. For example, when working on optimising your Water Chakra, Swadhisthana, you may see different bodies of water, like oceans, seas, and lakes present. Conversely, when Manipura is being targeted, an influx of the Fire Element will be present, colouring your dreams with scenes of fire and flame. So you see, what you dream about is symbolic of the energy changes happening within your Aura and its impact on your imagination.

What can I do to awaken my Kundalini? Is there a method I can use to facilitate this experience?

Although there is no sure-fire method to awaken the Kundalini, engaging in Yogic practices like the ones presented in this book can prepare the mind, body, and Soul for a Kundalini awakening to occur. The same applies to the practice of Ceremonial Magick and following a regimen like the Spiritual Alchemy Programs presented in *The Magus*. Also, the use of Spiritual Healing modalities like Crystals, Tuning Forks, Aromatherapy, and Tattvas work on cleansing and tuning the Chakras, which can cause a Kundalini awakening. So, you see, prioritizing your Spiritual Evolution and being proactive by implementing a regular Spiritual practice in your life is the only thing you can do to bring yourself closer to this goal.

A Kundalini awakening usually happens unexpectedly, so you cannot know when it will happen, but you can control what you do to make it happen. Since it is such a monumental experience, the Soul must be ready for it, which generally requires preparation over many lifetimes. It would be impossible for me to ascertain exactly where you are in your Soul progression; only your Higher Self knows that. But by focusing on being a good person with strong morals and values ensures that you are on the right path. Practice loving-kindness with yourself and others and be honest at all times. Once you walk in the Light, you allow the Light to infuse into your consciousness and awaken the Kundalini. A Kundalini awakening is just the next step for your Soul to take to evolve and the most important one since it liberates it from the body, completing its mission here on Earth.

EPILOGUE

In the beginning, was the White Light. All-Encompassing. Infinite. Without beginning and end. The Mind of the All. Pure Spiritual Consciousness. Then, this First Mind, which is energy and Force, created the Second Mind to generate Forms. The All, being One, divided itself into Two since all Creation requires the separation or division of its original substance. The All could not experience its power and potential until it created a polar opposite. Hence, the White Light generated the darkness of space.

The White Light also created Stars, whose groupings formed Constellations and Galaxies that make up the whole of the Universe. Now the All can manifest different worlds and living things—Souls that contain the characteristics of the All. Souls contain the Light since they are of the Light. However, they also contain the darkness since they partake of the Universe—the World of Matter floating in the darkness of space.

All Forms and living things in existence are made of the thought-stuff of the All. They are not inseparable from the All but are a part of it, only they are in the act of the All's experience, embedded in Time and Space. The experience and the experiencer are One; however, their separation is but an illusion. While Matter is on one end of the spectrum, as the densest manifestation of the All, the effect, the cause is the White Light that vibrates so high that it is invisible to the senses, yet it interpenetrates all of existence.

The primary function of the Stars is to generate Light into the darkness of space. The iris of the Sun is a portal into the other side of reality, the White Light of the First Mind. The Stars birthed all living things in the Universe since every organic being has Soul and consciousness. And the Soul is nothing more than a spark of Light from its respective Sun. The Ancients called the Sun "Sol," which is the origin of the word Soul as the essence of a living thing.

The Suns of the Universe attracted nearby Planets to create Solar Systems. There are billions of Solar Systems with trillions of Planets in the Universe. The Suns made livable environments on certain Planets that orbit them so they could cultivate Souls. However, only some Planets were chosen for this task.

In our Solar System, the only Planet that can harbour life is Earth. Our Sun then, through its Light, created all life on Earth. It nourishes it with its heat and Pranic energy. So you see, the ultimate purpose of all the Stars in the Universe is to harbour Souls. A Soul was never born, and it will never die. Once the Soul has learned the lessons of the Solar System it incarnated on, it transfers its spark from one Sun to another at the time of physical death, continuing its evolutionary journey through the Universe.

As the human Soul becomes implanted in the physical body at birth, it becomes locked to it. The Soul keeps reincarnating on Planet Earth until its evolution reaches critical mass, resulting in its release from the body in a given lifetime. The lessons of this Solar System relate to the full activation of the Seven Chakras, which can only be achieved by awakening the Kundalini and raising it to the Crown. When the human energy system becomes optimized, the Soul will no longer need to reincarnate on Planet Earth, but its next life will be on a new Planet in a different Solar System somewhere in the Universe.

Our ultimate purpose on Planet Earth is to fully awaken the Kundalini and liberate the Soul from the body. In doing so, we become the Sun of our Solar System, fully activating the higher powers of the Light within us. These higher powers are expressed through the Planets that orbit the Sun, corresponding with the Seven Chakras in their fully activated state. Thus, as you can see, a full Kundalini awakening enables us to experience the totality of our energy potential here on Earth in the present incarnation.

Once we raise the Kundalini to the Crown, we unite our consciousness with the Cosmic Consciousness of the White Light and the First Mind. We then begin to participate in Infinity that stretches out to the furthest reaches of the Universe, unlocking psychic gifts that enable us to transcend Time and Space. We can see, feel, hear, touch, smell, and taste things at a distance since the Three-Dimensional World no longer limits our consciousness. Instead, we become elevated to the Fourth Dimension, the Dimension of Vibration, or energy.

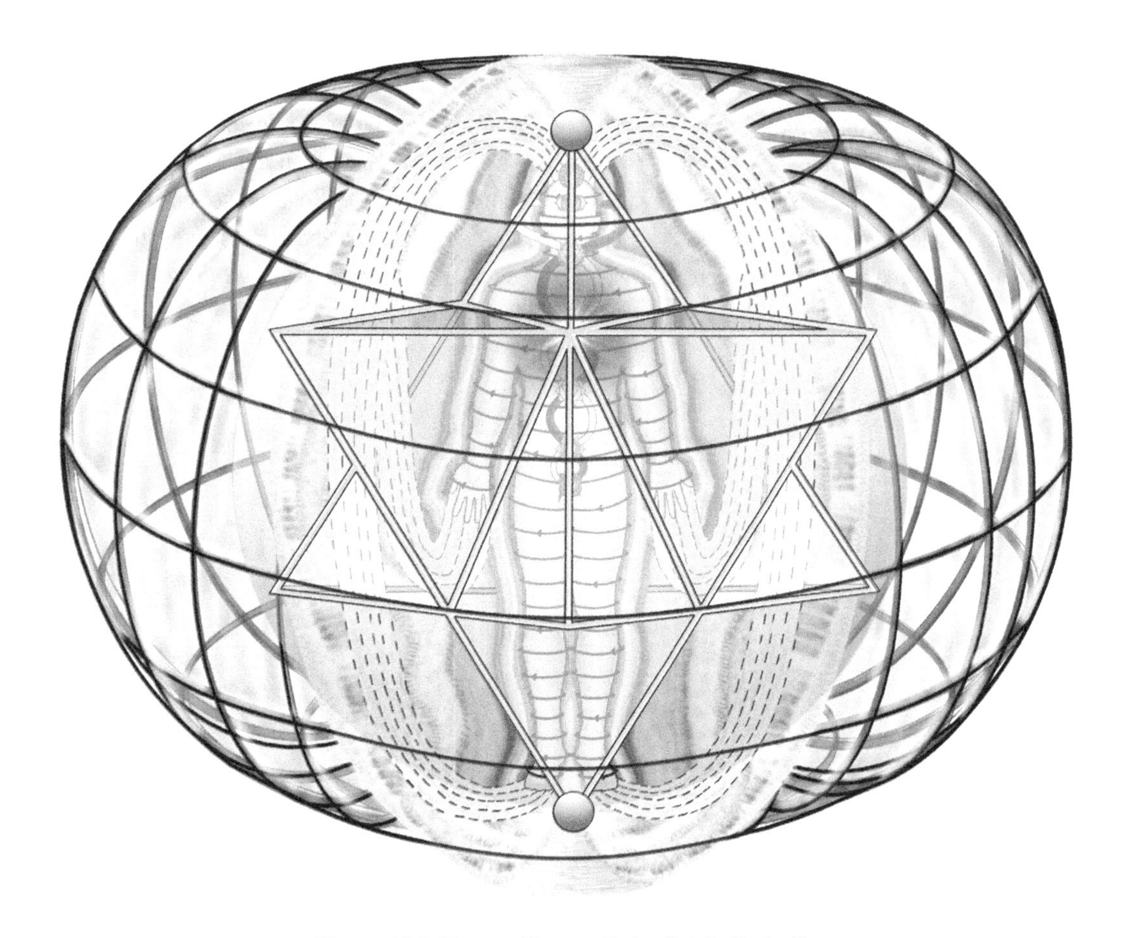

Figure 164: Human Energy Potential Optimisation

One of the essential gifts of a full Kundalini awakening is activating the Body of Light and optimising one's toroidal energy field—the Merkaba. This geometric structure becomes the Soul's vehicle of consciousness that enables Interdimensional and Interplanetary travel. The Soul can leave the body at will through the Body of Light and the Merkaba. It can now travel via our Sun into other Suns in the Universe because the individual is now One with the First Mind. This is the origin of Astral Projection which is the conscious projection of the Soul into different realms and Planes of consciousness. However, when this experience happens during sleep, unconsciously, it is called Lucid Dreaming.

Although the full Kundalini awakening and the activation of the Body of Light is a one-time event, the Spiritual transformation process that ensues can take a few dozen years or more. We must overcome the individual Karma before reaching the final frontier in human consciousness, the Fifth Dimension of Love and Light. Never forget, to become pure and worthy vessels for the Light, the Chakras must be optimized and tuned to perfection.

With that in mind, I hope that I have given you the keys in this book to achieve this task. Whether you have already awakened the Kundalini or are still in the process of learning and preparing for this experience, you now know every element and facet of the Kundalini awakening process and the Spiritual transfiguration that follows. Therefore, use *Serpent Rising* as a manual for the different Spiritual practices presented herein, and continue to work on your Chakras, preparing your Soul for Ascension.

In closing, it has been my pleasure sharing everything I have learned on my seventeen-year journey of living with awakened Kundalini. *Serpent Rising: The Kundalini Compendium* has been an incredible journey of discovery for me as well, connecting the dots and building on the framework of the evolving Kundalini science. My final advice for you is to take to heart everything you read about in this book and get excited about your future. The Kundalini is your gift from the Creator; don't squander it by wasting time on distractions that don't serve you anymore. Instead, focus your energy on fulfilling your ultimate mission on this Planet, and ill see you on the other side.

APPENDIX

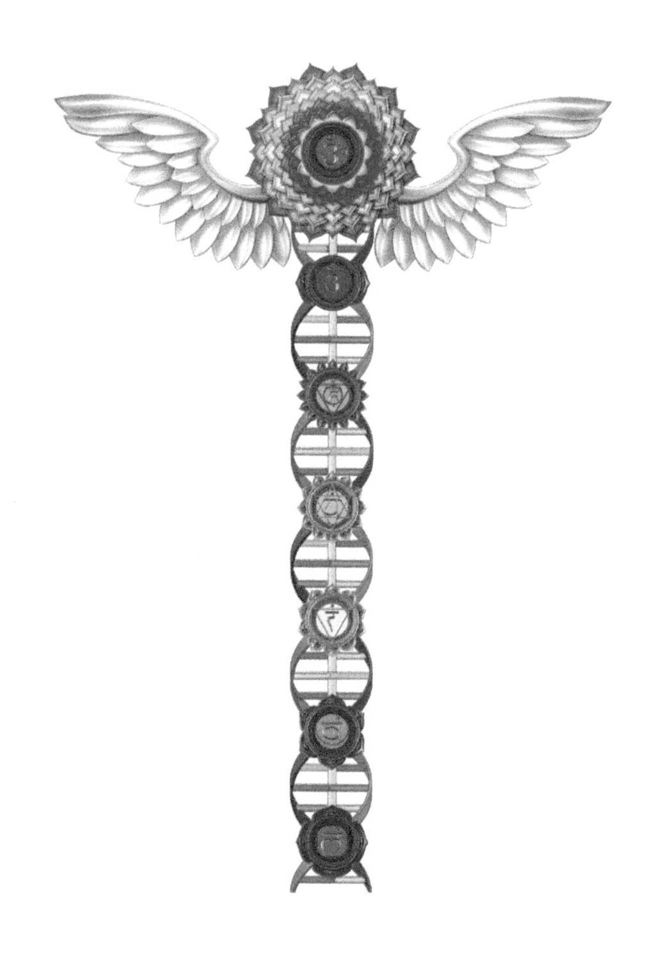

SUPPLEMENTARY TABLES

TABLE 6: The Seven Ancient Planets and their Correspondences

Planets	Elemental Affinity	Expressions/Powers	Gemstones	Tuning Fork Hz	Essential Oils (Advanced List)
Saturn	Earth; Feels like Earth of Air	Karma, Truth, Wisdom, Structure, Discipline, Intuition	Jet Black Onyx, Diamonds, Smoky Quartz	295.7	Myrrh, Patchouli, Cassia, Cypress, Spikenard, Mimosa
Jupiter	Water; Feels like Water of Fire	Mercy, Abundance, Unconditional Love, Morals, Ethics	Sapphire, Lapis Lazuli, Turquoise, Aquamarine	367.16	Anise, Clove, Hyssop, Nutmeg, Clary Sage, Dandelion, Cedarwood, Sarsaparilla, Cumin, Opoponax
Mars	Fire; Feels like Earth of Fire	Ambition, Drive, Renewal, Action, Survival, Competition, Passion, Willpower	Ruby, Garnet, Red Agate, Bloodstone, Red Coral	289.44	Ginger, Basil, Black Pepper, Peppermint, Tobacco, Dragon's Blood, Wormwood, Pine
Sun (Sol)	Air; Feels like Air of Fire	Self-Identity, Healing, Vitality, Courage, Creativity, Inspiration, Imagination	Amber, Tiger's Eye, Gold Topaz, Goldstone, Carnelian, Zircon, Sunstone	252.44	Chamomile, Juniper, Frankincense, Marigold, Rosemary, Cinnamon, Saffron, Cedar, Orange, Lime
Venus	Fire; Feels like Water of Earth	Desire, Creative Expressions, Romantic Love, Friendship, Sensuality	Emerald, Jade, Aventurine, Malachite, Rose Quartz, Green Agate, Peridot	442.46	Rose, Red Sandalwood, Ylang-Ylang, Cardamom, Geranium, Lilac, Vetiver, Spearmint, Violet, Vanilla Bean, Plumeria, Valerian
Mercury	Water; Feels like Water of Air	Logic, Reason, Communication, Intellect, Learning	Orange Sapphire, Orange Spinel, Tourmaline, Imperial Topaz, Citrine, Fire Opal, Amazonite	282.54	Lavender, Lemongrass, Lemon Verbena, Yellow Sandalwood, Orange, Mace, Peppermint, Orange Bergamot
Moon (Luna)	Air; Feels like Earth of Water	Feelings, Emotions, Illusions, Caprice, Fertility, Clairvoyance	Moonstone, Pearl, Beryl	420.88	Jasmine, Camphor, Eucalyptus, White Sandalwood, Willow, Lemon, Myrrh, Lily
Earth	Earth	Stability, Grounding, Practicality	Black Tourmaline, Obsidian, Hematite	272.2	Cypress, Mugwort, Oleander, Patchouli, Vervain, Vetiver

TABLE 7: The Twelve Zodiac and their Correspondences

Zodiac	Ruling Planet, Sub-Element	Expressions/Powers	Gemstones	Tuning Fork Hz	Essential Oils (Basic List)
Aries	Mars (Fire), Fire of Fire	Creative Energy, Drive, Initiative, Enthusiasm, Competition, Courage, Dynamism, Confidence	Bloodstone, Carnelian, Diamond, Garnet, Red Jasper, Ruby	144.72	Black Pepper, Rosemary, Ginger, Basil, Peppermint, Mandarin, Orange
Taurus	Venus (Earth), Air of Earth	Patience, Sensuality, Persistence, Determination, Sensitivity, Practicality, Conventionality	Amber, Rose Quartz, Blood Coral, Golden Topaz, Emerald, Sapphire, Turquoise	221.23	Ylang Ylang, Rose Vetiver, Geranium, Sandalwood, Melissa, Marjoram
Gemini	Mercury (Air), Water of Air	Intellect, Learning, Communication, Humour Analyzing, Adaptability, Versatility, Nonconformism	Aquamarine, Agate, Chrysoprase, Pearl, Moonstone, Citrine, White Sapphire	141.27	Bergamot, Fennel, Lavender, Chamomile, Peppermint
Cancer	Moon (Water), Fire of Water	Tenacity, Sensitivity, Emotionality, Intuition, Sympathy, Protective Instinct, Empathy	Moonstone, Ruby, Emerald, Pearl	210.42	Fennel, Juniper, Lavender, Jasmine, Clary Sage, Eucalyptus
Leo	Sun (Fire), Air of Fire	Charisma, Ambition, Creativity, Authority, Vitality, Generosity, Affection	Amber, Tourmaline, Carnelian, Ruby, Sardonyx, Onyx, Golden Topaz	126.22	Rosemary, Frankincense, Myrrh, Lemon, Lime, Cinnamon
Virgo	Mercury (Earth), Water of Earth	Discrimination, Analyzing, Reliability, Diligence, Practicality, Adaptability, Independence, Teaching	Blue Sapphire, Pink Jasper, Carnelian, Jade, Moss Agate, Turquoise, Zircon	141.27	Melissa, Myrtle, Patchouli, Sandalwood, Lavender
Libra	Venus (Air), Fire of Air	Harmony, Justice, Self-Expression, Diplomacy, Romance, Sensuality, Sociability, Shrewdness	Lapis Lazuli, Opal, Diamond, Emerald, Rose Quartz, Peridot	221.23	Geranium, Fennel, Tea Tree, Rose, Cardamom, Melissa
Scorpio	Mars (Water), Air of Water	Regeneration, Sexuality, Transformation, Justice, Passion, Loyalty, Power, Independence, Magnetism	Aquamarine, Black Obsidian, Garnet, Agate, Topaz, Beryl, Apache Tears, Coral	140.25 (Pluto)	Patchouli, Rose, Geranium, Ginger, Jasmine, Clary Sage
Sagittarius	Jupiter (Fire), Water of Fire	Optimism, Love of Freedom, Cheer, Honesty, Philosophy, Charity, Inspiration, Exploration	Turquoise, Topaz, Sapphire, Amethyst, Ruby	183.58	Clary Sage, Clove, Hyssop, Bergamot, Cedarwood, Eucalyptus, Cardamom
Capricorn	Saturn (Earth), Fire of Earth	Organization, Conscientiousness, Pragmatism, Ambition, Conservatism, Discipline	Ruby, Black Onyx, Smoky Quartz, Garnet, Agate	147.85	Myrrh, Vetiver, Eucalyptus, Geranium, Sandalwood
Aquarius	Saturn (Air), Air of Air	Intuition, Creativity, Spirituality, Independence, Innovation, Originality, Meditation, Humanitarian	Garnet, Sugilite, Amethyst, Blue Sapphire, Moss Agate, Opal	207.36 (Uranus)	Neroli, Myrrh, Sandalwood, Violet Leaf, Lavender, Lemon
Pisces	Jupiter (Water), Water of Water	Deep Emotions, Intuition, Imagination, Compassion, Empathy, Ethics, Sympathy, Humour	Amethyst, Jade, Aquamarine, Rock Crystal, Bloodstone, Diamond, Sapphire	211.44 (Neptune)	Bergamot, Clove, Geranium, Myrrh, Cypress, Tea Tree, Clary Sage

GLOSSARY OF SELECTED TERMS

Note: The following is a selection of terms that are either undefined in the original body of text or require further definition. Use this section to help further your knowledge of the given subjects. Since this book generally deals with Eastern Spirituality, most of the terms presented here are from the Western Mysteries.

Adam Kadmon: An abstract concept referring to the Yechidah, the Kether Sephira that filters into the Chiah (Chokmah) and Lesser Neschamah (Binah) to form the Greater Neschamah, the True Self and part of us that belongs to the Supernals. In *The Zohar*, Adam Kadmon is the "Heavenly Man," the large organic Spiritual body in which each human being is considered a single cell, maybe less. In terms of the Four Worlds of the Qabalah, Adam Kadmon represents the First World of Archetypes, Atziluth, the World of Primal Fire. Thus, Adam Kadmon essentially refers to the Divine Light, the Freudian Super-Ego, or the Higher Self from the Supernals.

Ain Soph Aur: The Three Veils of Negative Existence. This term is used in the Qabalah to describe the Source of Creation. In the literal sense, Ain translates as "Nothing," while Ain Soph is "Infinity". And finally, Ain Soph Aur is "Limitless or Eternal Light". Thus, in the Qabalah, the term Ain Soph Aur is often used in reference to the Infinite White Light.

Aleister Crowley: A British occultist, poet, novelist, and Ceremonial Magi, who was one of the original members of the Hermetic Order of the Golden Dawn. After leaving the Order, Crowley founded the religion of Thelema in the early 20th century, identifying himself as the prophet of the Aeon of Horus, which coincided with that period in time. Crowley publicly referred to himself as the "Great Beast 666," as he sought to challenge the taboos in the Christian-driven, restrictive Elizabethan society he lived in, which is why he got a bad reputation over the years. However, his contribution to the occult world is indispensable, and he opened many doors for future seekers everywhere.

Alpha State: Otherwise called the "Hypnagogic State" or "Trance State." The Alpha State of brain activity occurs between being awake with mental activity (Beta State) and sleep (Theta State). This state is reached when your brain waves slow down to between 8 and 12 Hz, which is common when you daydream or dream (at night). We can consciously induce the Alpha State through meditation, hypnosis, or the use of Spiritual healing modalities. Being in this state will heighten your memory recall and intuition while reducing anxiety. People who can operate from the Alpha State during ordinary waking consciousness can control their reality since their connection with their Higher Self is greater. Therefore, they can use the Universal Laws consciously and with intent.

Angels: Positive thought senders that exist inside and outside one's energy field, the Aura. Angels are objective entities or Intelligences that exist outside the Self and become contracted within the Aura when we choose by Free Will to listen to them and do their bidding. Angels feed on love energy, like their counterparts, the Demons, feed on fear energy. Angels are subservient to God- the Creator. Angelic energy is the source of human virtues, as Demonic energy is the source of human vices.

Archetypes: Primordial structural elements of the human psyche. Archetypes are original models after which other similar things are patterned. They are Universal, meaning that all humans partake in them. Archetypes give us the mental foundation on which to build our realities. They are found in the highest world, Atziluth, the World of Primal Fire in the Qabalah.

Binah: The third Sephira on the Tree of Life, atop the Pillar of Severity. Binah is the Great Mother and the Sea of Consciousness that contains all Forms in existence. It represents the feminine aspect of the Self, the highest expression of the Water Element. Through Binah, the Spirit energy impregnates ideas into our minds. Thus, it represents the state of consciousness that governs inner faculties like intuition and clairvoyance. Binah corresponds with Ajna Chakra, our psychic centre that provides empathy and telepathy. Binah is the receptive, passive aspect of the Self, the Understanding (Binah's title) that can comprehend the wisdom of Chokmah. Its colour is black, corresponding with the Planet Saturn on the Tree of Life; the Planet of faith, Karma, and time, all aspects of Binah.

Ceremonial Magick: Synonymous with Western Ritual Magick. A series of rites involving the incantation (vibration) of Divine names of power, usually combined with symbolic tracings of geometric symbols, like the Pentagram or Hexagram, within the practitioner's Magickal circle. The purpose of Ceremonial Magick, like with other Spiritual Healing practices, is the attunement of Chakras for Spiritual Evolution. Popularized by the Hermetic Order of the Golden Dawn, Ceremonial Magick forms a branch of Hermeticism. The end-goal of using Ceremonial Magick is achieving Enlightenment.

Chesed: The fourth Sephira on the Tree of Life, situated below Chesed on the Pillar of Mercy. It represents a state of consciousness that governs the inner faculties or expressions like unconditional love, compassion, and memory. For this reason, Chesed's title is "Mercy." Chesed allows us to build morals and ethics as it cultivates wisdom. Chesed has an affinity with the Water Element, and it corresponds with the Planet Jupiter. Chesed is the Spiritualized Sacral Chakra, Swadhisthana, because of its connection to the Supernals through the Tarot Path of The Hierophant on the Tree of Life.

Chokmah: The second Sephira on Tree of Life, atop the Pillar of Mercy. As the active Spirit energy, Chokmah represents the state of consciousness where we can discover our True Will. It is the Great Father energy and the masculine aspect of the Self, the highest expression of the Fire Element. Thus, it is the Sephira through which our Higher Self, or Holy Guardian Angel, communicates to us through Wisdom (Chokmah's title). The colour of Chokmah is grey. The Zodiac is the physical manifestation of Chokmah since the Stars serve to channel the unmanifested White Light of Kether. Chokmah functions through the Mind's Eye Chakra, along with Binah.

Dark Night of the Soul, the: A period of desolation that an individual undergoes when rapidly evolving Spiritually. All sense of consolation is removed during this time, creating a type of existential crisis. Before transforming Spiritually, the individual must face the dark side full-on and embrace the mental and emotional turmoil. It is not uncommon for the individual to isolate themselves from other people during this time and shed many tears as they purge old emotions. However, after this tumultuous period is complete, the clutches of the Lower Self will have lessened, aligning the consciousness more with the vibration of the Higher Self. The Dark Night of the Soul is a necessary phase of suffering on the path towards Enlightenment that is not a one-time process but is generally encountered many times on one's Spiritual Evolution journey.

Daath: As the hidden, eleventh Sephira on the Tree of Life, Daath is the "Great Chasm," or the "Abyss" that divides the Supernals from all manifested Creation. Fittingly, it corresponds with the Throat Chakra, Vishuddhi, which separates the Spirit from the lower Four Elements. Through Daath, we enter into Hell or the Underworld, the opposite pole in the mind that gave rise to the Ego, the negative part of the Self. As such, Daath represents the "death" of the Ego that is necessary for our consciousness to rise to the Supernals. Daath is known as the "Sphere of Knowledge" since knowledge allows us to transcend our bodies and attune our consciousness to Higher Realms.

Deity, a: A supernatural Being of Divine origin. This word is often used in polytheistic religions instead of God or Goddess. In Ancient traditions, a Deity is a Being with greater powers than those of ordinary humans but who interacts with them, most often to enlighten them somehow and further their evolution. Monotheistic religions have only one Deity, whom they accept as God-the Creator, while polytheistic religions accept multiple Deities.

Enochian Magick: The crowning jewel of the Hermetic Order of the Golden Dawn's system of Magick. This Inner Order practice should only be undertaken when Spiritual Alchemy with the Elements has been completed. In *The Magus*, Enochian Magick refers to "Spiritual Alchemy Program III," which implements the use of the Nineteen Enochian Keys or Calls that pertain to the Five Elements. Enochian Magick is a complete system of Magick that stands apart from other Ceremonial Magick ritual exercises in *The Magus* but is part of the whole as well.

Freemasonry: Freemasonry, or Masonry, refers to the oldest fraternal organisation in the world. Contrary to popular belief inspired by conspiracy theories, the true purpose of being a Freemason is improving your moral nature and building character through a course of self-development. The three degrees of Freemasonry in the Blue Lodge are Entered Apprentice, Fellowcraft, and Master Mason, which the initiate enters into ceremonially. Afterwards, the initiate is taught the meaning of the symbols pertaining to their degree ceremony, which is the traditional method of passing down sacred teachings.

Geburah: The fifth Sephira on the Tree of Life situated below Binah on the Pillar of Severity. Titled "Severity" or "Justice," Geburah corresponds with the Fire Element and the individual willpower that gives us motivation, determination, and drive. As the source of our competitiveness, Geburah can also make us aggressive and angry when unbalanced by its opposite, Chesed. Geburah is the Spiritualized Solar Plexus Chakra, Manipura, because of its connection to the Supernals through the Tarot Path of the Chariot on the Tree of Life.

Golden Dawn, the: Ancient Western Mysteries School that teaches its students the Qabalah, Hermeticism, Tarot, Astrology, Geomancy, Egyptian and Christian Mysteries, and Ceremonial Magick (including Enochian Magick). There are many Golden Dawn Orders globally, most of which teach the same course material. The Golden Dawn course material was made public by Israel Regardie in "The Golden Dawn", first published in 1937. The original Golden Dawn Order was called the Hermetic Order of the Golden Dawn, established in 1888 by a group of Freemasons, the most notable being Samuel Liddell MacGregor Mathers. Today, most of the Hermetic Order of the Golden Dawn offshoots are called by variations of that same name.

Hod: The eighth Sephira on the Tree of Life, at the bottom of the Pillar of Severity, whose title is "Splendour." Hod's state of consciousness pertains to the inner faculties of intelligence, particularly logic and reason. This Sphere has an affinity with the Water Element, although the Fire Element is involved as well in its function as is the Air Element. As such, Hod expresses through the three Chakras of Swadhisthana, Manipura, and Anahata. It corresponds with the Planet Mercury and is the colour orange. Hod represents a lesser form of the energy of Chesed, mediated through Tiphareth. The Ego often uses Hod to deduce reality and make future decisions. In the Golden Dawn system, Hod corresponds with the Practicus grade.

Hebrew Letters, the: Twenty-Two Letters that are part of the Qabalistic philosophy but stand apart as their own Spiritual system. Each letter is a symbol and a number with many ideas associated with it. These ideas bring forth certain Archetypes that are resonant with the energy of the Major Arcana of the Tarot. The three Mother Letters (primary) correspond with the three Elements of Air, Water, and Fire, while the seven Double Letters (secondary) correspond with the Seven Ancient Planets. Finally, the twelve Simple Letters (tertiary) correspond with the Twelve Zodiac.

Hermes Trismegistus: A historical figure who lived during the oldest dynasties of Egypt. Known as the "Scribe of the Gods," or the "Master of Masters," Hermes was the founder of Hermeticism and is considered the father of occult wisdom. All the fundamental teachings in all esoteric and religious sects can be traced back to Hermes. His wisdom and knowledge about the mysteries of the Universe and life were so great that the Egyptians deified him as one of their Gods, calling him Thoth-the God of Wisdom. Greeks revered him also and made him one of their twelve Olympian Gods, also calling him Hermes. As the Romans syncretized their religion with the Greek religion, they referred to Hermes as Mercury. Hermes was considered the greatest World Teacher, and a few Adepts that came after him, including Jesus Christ, are considered by many scholars to be his reincarnation. It is believed that the Spirit of Hermes incarnates approximately every 2000 years as the World Teacher to enlighten the world in Spiritual, religious, philosophical, and psychological areas by introducing a modern language to teach about the Spirit and God, reconciling all divergent viewpoints.

Hermeticism: A philosophical, religious, and esoteric tradition based primarily on the teachings of Hermes Trismegistus, which includes Astrology, Alchemy, and the Principles of Creation as described in *The Kybalion*. The philosophical aspects of Hermeticism are contained in the "Hermetica," comprised of the *Corpus Hermeticum* (also known as *The Divine Pymander*) and *The Emerald Tablet of Hermes*, the key of Alchemy. Hermeticism is an invisible science that encompasses the energies of our Solar System concerning human beings. Hermetic writings have greatly influenced the Western esoteric tradition, namely the Golden Dawn Order.

Kether: The first and highest Sephira on Tree of Life, atop the Middle Pillar. Relates to the White Light Principle (Ain Soph Aur) since it acts as a channel of it into the lower Chakras. Its colour is white, representing the Light that contains the seven colours of the rainbow—the Major Chakras. Kether corresponds with Sahasrara Chakra and shares the same title—the Crown. It represents the transcendental state of consciousness that is beyond the duality of the mind. Kether is also our gateway to the Transpersonal Chakras above the Crown. As the Divine Spirit, Kether is the highest expression of the Air Element. It represents the Monad, the singularity, and the highest conception of the Godhead.

Kingdom of Heaven, the: Synonymous with the Kingdom of God. The Kingdom of Heaven is one of the essential elements in the teachings of Jesus Christ that refers to the fulfilment of God's Will on Earth. It is a state of mind akin to Christ Consciousness, where there has been a descent of Spirit into Matter, and they are now One. In Christian teachings, one must be Resurrected, metaphorically speaking, to enter into the Kingdom of Heaven. As every human's destiny, this lofty state of higher consciousness can be attained once the Kundalini energy rises to the Crown, fully activating the Body of Light and optimizing one's toroidal energy field (Merkaba). Following the Spiritual transformation, the individual will have their head in Heaven and their feet upon the Earth, as a God-human.

Major Arcana, the: Twenty-Two Trumps of the Tarot Cards. Corresponds with the Twenty-Two paths on the Tree of Life and the Twenty-Two Hebrew Letters. The Major Arcana represent the Archetypal energies in transit between the ten Sephiroth on the Tree of Life. They correspond with the three main Elements of Air, Fire, Water, the Twelve Zodiac, and the Seven Ancient Planets, comprising the entirety of our Solar System.

Malkuth: The tenth and lowest Sephira on the Tree of Life whose title is "the Kingdom." As such, Malkuth relates to Gaia, the Planet Earth, and the Physical World of Matter. It corresponds with Muladhara Chakra and has an affinity with the Earth Element. Malkuth's colors are citrine, olive, russet, and black, representing the three Elements of Air, Water, and Fire in a denser form. In the Golden Dawn system, Malkuth corresponds with the Zelator grade.

Mercury (Alchemical Principle): Within the Alchemical process, Mercury is the transforming substance. Its role is to bring balance and harmony between the other two Alchemical Principles—Sulfur and Salt. Mercury is the Life Force, the Spirit energy. In the first stage, when it is opposite to Sulfur, it takes on the fluidic, feminine Principle of consciousness as the Great Mother—the Water Element. In the second stage, once Sulfur has been extracted and returned yet again, it becomes known as Philosophic Mercury, or the Secret Fire—the Spirit Element. Philosophic Mercury is the substance that gives rise to the Philosopher's Stone, the goal of the Alchemist.

Middle Pillar, the: Otherwise called the Pillar of Balance or Pillar of Mildness on the Tree of Life. It is self-balancing while bringing equilibrium to the other two Pillars—the Pillar of Mercy and Pillar of Severity. The Middle Pillar brings unity to the many dualistic, contending forces in life. It comprises the Sephiroth Kether, Daath, Tiphareth, Yesod, and Malkuth. This term also relates to the Middle Pillar ritual exercise (from *The Magus*), which is an invocation of Light meant to balance the psyche and aid in Spiritual Evolution. The Middle Pillar represents the Air Element and is grey in colour. It corresponds with the Sushumna Nadi in the Kundalini system.

Netzach: Seventh Sephira on the Tree of Life along the Pillar of Mercy. Titled "Victory," Netzach represents a state of consciousness dealing with emotions, particularly desire and romantic love. Netzach has an affinity with the Fire Element, although the Water Element is involved in its expression and the Air Element. It expresses through the three Chakras of Swadhisthana, Manipura, and Anahata, the same as Hod. Netzach, Hod and Yesod, the Astral Triangle, are the three most commonly accessed Spheres used by the average person. Netzach corresponds with the Planet Venus, and its colour is green. In the Golden Dawn system, Netzach corresponds with the Philosophus grade.

Nirvana: An Eastern term commonly associated with Jainism and Buddhism. Represents a transcendental state of Being in which there is no suffering nor desire, as the Self experiences Unity with the rest of the world. In Indian religions, Nirvana is synonymous with Moksha or Mukti, the release from the cycle of rebirth as pertains to the Law of Karma. Nirvana signifies the alignment of individual consciousness with Cosmic Consciousness as the final goal of all Spiritual traditions, religions, and practices. A precursor to achieving Nirvana is awakening the Kundalini to the Crown and attaining full Light Body activation. Nirvana implies that one has reached Enlightenment. It is comparable with the other two Eastern terms, Satori and Samadhi.

Philosopher's Stone, the: A legendary Alchemical substance capable of turning base metals (such as mercury) into gold or silver. Veiled to the profane who only desired financial profit, this term has a hidden meaning related to the most sought-after goal of Alchemy— Spiritual transformation. Therefore, when you hear that someone has found the Philosopher's Stone, it means they have completed the Great Work (Spiritual Alchemy) and have become Enlightened.

Pillar of Mercy, the: The right Pillar on the Tree of Life comprising the Sephiroth Chokmah, Chesed, and Netzach. The Pillar of Mercy is the masculine, active, and positive Pillar otherwise called the Pillar of Force. It represents the Water Element and is white in colour. In the Kundalini system, the Pillar of Mercy corresponds with the Pingala Nadi.

Pillar of Severity, the: The left Pillar on the Tree of Life comprising the Sephiroth Binah, Geburah, and Hod. It is the feminine, passive, and negative Pillar otherwise called the Pillar of Form. It represents the Fire Element and is black in colour. In the Kundalini system, the Pillar of Severity represents the Ida Nadi.

Prima Materia: Otherwise called the "First Matter", it is the primaeval substance regarded as the original material of the known Universe. Synonymous with the Spirit as the first substance and the Source of everything in existence. In Alchemy, the Prima Materia is the starting material required for creating the Philosopher's Stone. It is the "Anima Mundi"- the World Soul, the only vital force in the Universe.

Salt: The physical body that grounds and fixes the other two Alchemical Principles, Mercury and Sulfur. It represents the crystallization and hardening of all three Principles together. Salt is the vehicle of physical manifestation and the Third Dimension of Time and Space expressed through the Earth Element. Salt, Mercury, and Sulfur form the Trinity in Alchemy.

Sex Magick: Any type of sexual activity used in a ceremonial or ritualistic setting with clear underlying intent. The idea behind Sex Magick is that sexual energy is a potent force that can be harnessed to magnetize the Astral Realm and attract whatever one desires or to call in Deities from various pantheons. One form of Sex Magick ritual is to use sexual arousal or orgasm to visualise something you are trying to achieve or obtain. As such, Sex Magick is like a battery for your willpower when performed with an open heart and mind. However, if Sex Magick is practised with an impure mind, it will only attract lower entities to feed on the sexual energy being invoked. These lower entities can then attach themselves to you and continue to feed on your sexual energy until cleared.

Spiritual Alchemy: In the same way as Alchemy deals with turning base metals into gold, Spiritual Alchemy deals with transforming the practitioner's energy and Enlightening them (infusing them with Light). This can be achieved through Spiritual Healing modalities and practices, including Yoga and Ceremonial Magick. Spiritual Alchemy requires working with the Five Elements, which correspond with the Seven Chakras. The goal of Spiritual Evolution is Illumination, as the individual consciousness is exalted and united with Cosmic Consciousness. Through this process, the individual establishes a link with the Higher Self or Holy Guardian Angel, their God-Self. The Spirit Element must be integrated within the Aura, which marks the completion of the Great Work and the restoration of the Garden of Eden.

Sulfur: It is the Soul present in all living things in the Universe. It comes from the Sun as the Light of God and is the masculine Principle, the Great Father—the Fire Element. Alchemical transmutation's whole process depends on the Principle of Sulfur and its proper application. Sulfur is the vibrant, acidic, active, dynamic Principle. It serves to stabilize Mercury, out of which it is extracted and into which it returns.

Tarot, the: A sacred art mainly used in Divination. The Tarot comprises seventy-eight playing cards, divided into four suits of fourteen cards each, plus Twenty-Two Trumps (Major Arcana). Tarot cards feature incredible imagery containing timeless, esoteric wisdom. They have an inextricable connection with the Qabalah and the Tree of Life, and they serve as the key to the occult sciences and a road-map of the different components of the human psyche. Thus, the Tarot is a complete and intricate system used to describe the unseen, invisible forces that influence the Universe.

Thirty Aethyrs: Concentric circles that interpenetrate and overlap one another, thereby comprising the Aura layers. The Aethyrs are the Spiritual components of the Cosmic Planes in the Enochian System. Each of the Thirty Aethyrs carries a masculine and/or feminine sexual current which can be invoked using the Nineteenth Enochian Key. The Thirty Aethyrs work directly with the Ida and Pingala Nadis in the Kundalini system.

Tiphareth: The sixth Sephira on the Tree of Life along the Middle Pillar, whose title is "Harmony" and "Beauty." It represents a state of consciousness of inner faculties dealing with imagination and the processing of thoughts and emotions. As the central Sephira on the Tree of Life, Tiphareth is concerned with processing the energies of all the Sephiroth, except Malkuth. Within occult knowledge, Tiphareth is known as the Sphere of Spiritual Rebirth and Christ or Krishna Consciousness, where Spirit and Matter become united as one. Tiphareth has an affinity with the Air Element, although, since it corresponds with the Sun, it also has aspects of Fire. Thus, the placement of Tiphareth is somewhere between Anahata and Manipura Chakras, through which it expresses. Tiphareth's colour is golden-yellow. In the Golden Dawn system, Tiphareth corresponds with Adeptus Minor, the First Grade of the Second Order.

Yesod: The ninth Sephira on the Tree of Life along the Middle Pillar, whose title is "Foundation," concerning the Astral blueprint of all things in existence. Yesod represents the Astral Plane, the contact point for the Inner Cosmic Planes. It represents a state of consciousness of the inner faculties dealing with the Ego and its thoughts and impulses. Sexuality and the fears of the subconscious mind are also expressed through Yesod. Its placement is somewhere between Swadhisthana and Manipura Chakras, which it works through. Yesod has an affinity with the Air Element, with aspects of the Water Element. Its colour is violet-purple, and it corresponds with the Moon Planet. In the Golden Dawn system, Yesod represents the Theoricus Grade.

BIBLIOGRAPHY

Note: The following are a list of books from my personal library that served as resources and inspiration behind the present work. Every effort has been made to trace all copyright holders of any material included in this edition, whether companies or individuals. Any omission is unintentional, and I will be pleased to correct any errors in future versions of this book.

KUNDALINI

Arundale, G.S. (1997). *Kundalini: An Occult Experience.* Adyar, Madras, India: The Theosophical Publishing House

Bynum, Bruce Edward (2012). *Dark Light Consciousness.* Rochester, Vermont: Inner Traditions

Dixon, Jana (2008). *Biology of Kundalini: Exploring the Fire of Life.* Lulu Online Publishing

Goswami, Shyam Sundar (1999). *Layayoga: The Definitive Guide to the Chakras and Kundalini.* Rochester, Vermont: Inner Traditions

Khalsa, Gurmukh Kaur, with Ken Wilber, Swami Radha, Gopi Krishna, and John White (2009). *Kundalini Rising: Exploring the Energy of Awakening.* Boulder, Colorado: Sounds True, Inc.

Krishna, Gopi (1993). *Living with Kundalini: The Autobiography of Gopi Krishna.* Boston, Massachusetts: Shambhala Publications Inc.

Krishna, Gopi (1988). *Kundalini for the New Age: Selected Writings of Gopi Krishna.* Edited by Gene Kiefer. New York, New York: Bantam Books

Krishna, Gopi (1997). *Kundalini: The Evolutionary Energy in Man.* Boston, Massachusetts: Shambhala Publications Inc.

Krishna, Gopi (1975). *The Awakening of Kundalini.* New York, New York: E. P. Dutton

Krishna, Gopi (1972). *The Biological Basis of Religion and Genius.* New York, New York: Harper & Row Publishers

Mahajan, Yogi (1997). *The Ascent.* Delhi, India: Motilal Banarsidass Publishers

Melchizedek, Drunvalo (2008). *Serpent of Light: Beyond 2012.* San Francisco, California: Weiser Books

Mumford, Jonn (2014). *A Chakra & Kundalini Workbook.* Woodbury, Minnesota: Llewellyn Publications

Paulson, Genevieve Lewis (2003). *Kundalini and the Chakras.* St. Paul, Minnesota: Llewellyn Publications

Perring, Michael "Omdevaji" (2015). *What on Earth is Kundalini?-Book III.* Varanasi, India: Pilgrims Publishing

Semple, J. J. (2007). *Deciphering the Golden Flower: One Secret at a Time.* Bayside, California: Life Force Books

Swami, Om (2016). *Kundalini: An Untold Story.* Mumbai, India: Jaico Publication House

Weor, Samael Aun (2020). *Christ's Will: Kundalini, Tarot, and the Christification of the Human Soul.* www.gnosticteachings.org: Glorian Publishing

Weor, Samael Aun (2018). *The Yellow Book: The Divine Mother, Kundalini, and Spiritual Powers.* www.gnosticteachings.org: Glorian Publishing

White, John (1990). *Kundalini: Evolution and Enlightenment.* St. Paul, Minnesota: Paragon House

ENERGY HEALING AND CHAKRAS

Bernoth, Bettina (2012). *Auric Lights: Light is the Medicine of our Future.* CreateSpace Independent Publishing Platform

Bettina, Bernoth (1995). *Magical Auras.* CreateSpace Independent Publishing Platform

Burger, Bruce (1998). *Esoteric Anatomy: The Body as Consciousness.* Berkeley, California: North Atlantic Books

Butler, W.E. (1987). *How to Read the Aura, Practice Psychometry, Telepathy and Clairvoyance.* Rochester, Vermont: Destiny Books

Chia, Mantak (2008). *Healing Light of the Tao: Foundational Practices to Awaken Chi Energy.* Rochester, Vermont: Destiny Books

Chia, Mantak (2009). *The Alchemy of Sexual Energy: Connecting to the Universe From Within.* Rochester, Vermont: Destiny Books

Dale, Cyndi (2018). *The Complete Book of Chakras: Your Definitive Source of Energy Center Knowledge for Health, Happiness, and Spiritual Evolution.* Woodbury, Minnesota: Llewellyn Publications

Dale, Cyndi (2009). *The Subtle Body: An Encyclopedia of Your Energetic Anatomy.* Boulder, Colorado: Sounds True, Inc.

Dale, Cyndi (2013). *The Subtle Body Practice Manual: A Comprehensive Guide to Energy Healing.* Boulder, Colorado: Sounds True, Inc.

Gerber, Richard, M.D. (2001). *Vibrational Medicine: The 1# Handbook of Subtle-Energy Therapies.* Rochester, Vermont: Bear & Company

Grey, Alex (2012). *Net of Being.* With Alyson Grey. Rochester, Vermont: Inner Traditions International

Grey, Alex (1990). *Sacred Mirrors: The Visionary Art of Alex Grey.* Rochester, Vermont: Inner Traditions International

Judith, Anodea (2006). *Wheels of Life: A User's Guide to the Chakra System.* Woodbury, Minnesota: Llewellyn Publications

Leadbeater, C.W. (1987). *The Chakras.* Wheaton, Illinois: The Theosophical Publishing House

Lockhart, Maureen (2010). *The Subtle Energy Body: The Complete Guide.* Rochester, Vermont: Inner Traditions

Ostrom, Joseph (2000). *Auras: What they are and How to Read Them.* Hammersmith, London: Thorsons

Zink, Robert (2014). *Magical Energy Healing: The Ruach Healing Method.* Rachel Haas co-author. Portland, Oregon: Law of Attraction Solutions, LLC.

BRAIN AND BODY ANATOMY

Carter, Rita (2019). *The Human Brain Book.* New York, New York: DK Publishing

Childre, Doc and Martin, Howard (2000). *The Heartmath Solution.* New York, New York: HarperCollins Publishers

McCraty, Rollin (2015). *Science of the Heart: Exploring the Role of the Heart in Human Performance (Volume 2)*. Boulder Creek, California: HeartMath Institute

Power, Katrina (2020) *How to Hack Your Vagus Nerve*. Independently Published

Splittgerber, Ryan (2019). *Snell's Clinical Neuroanatomy: Eight Edition.* Philadelphia, Pennsylvania: Wolters Kluwer

Wineski, Lawrenece E. (2019). *Snell's Clinical Anatomy by Regions: Tenth Edition.* Philadelphia, Pennsylvania: Wolters Kluwer

YOGA AND TANTRA

Ashley-Farrand, Thomas (1999). *Healing Mantras: Using Sound Affirmations for Personal Power, Creativity, and Healing.* New York, New York: Ballantine Wellspring

Aun Weor, Samael (2012). *Kundalini Yoga: Unlock the Divine Spiritual Power Within You.* Glorian Publishing

Avalon, Arthur (1974). *The Serpent Power.* New York, New York: Dover Publications, Inc.

Bhajan, Yogi (2013). *Kriya: Yoga Sets, Meditations & Classic Kriyas.* Santa Cruz, California: Kundalini Research Instititute

Buddhananda, Swami (2012). *Moola Bandha: The Master Key.* Munger, Bihar, India: Yoga Publications Trust

Feuerstein, Georg (1998). *Tantra: The Path of Ecstasy.* Boulder, Colorado: Shambhala Publications, Inc.

Frawley, Dr. David (2010). *Mantra Yoga and Primal Sound: Secrets of Seed (Bija) Mantras.* Twin Lakes, Wisconsin: Lotus Press

Frawley, David (2004). *Yoga and the Sacred Fire: Self-Realization and Planetary Transformation.* Twin Lakes, Wisconsin: Lotus Press

Hulse, David Allen (2004). *The Eastern Mysteries: The Key of it All, Book I.* St. Paul, Minnesota: Llewellyn Publications

Japananda Das, Srila (2019). *Yantra: Power and Magic.* Independently Published

Kaminoff, Leslie and Matthews, Amy (2012). *Yoga Anatomy.* Champaign, Illinois: Human Kinetics

Maehle, Gregor (2012). *Pranayama: The Breath of Yoga.* Innaloo City, Australia: Kaivalya Publications

Prasad, Rama (2015). *Nature's Finer Forces and Their Influence Upon Human Life and Destiny.* CreateSpace Independent Publishing Platform

Saraswati, Swami Satyananda (2013). *Asana Pranayama Mudra Bandha.* Munger, Bihar, India: Yogi Publications Trust

Saraswati, Swami Satyananda (2013). *A Systematic Course in the Ancient Tantric Techniques of Yoga and Kriya.* Munger, Bihar, India: Yoga Publications Trust

Saraswati, Swami Satyananda (2012). *Hatha Yoga Pradipika.* Munger, Bihar, India: Yogi Publications Trust

Saraswati, Swami Satyananda (2007). *Kundalini Tantra.* Munger, Bihar, India: Yoga Publications Trust

Saraswati, Swami Satyananda (2012). *Meditations From the Tantras.* Munger, Bihar, India: Yoga Publications Trust

Saraswati, Swami Satyadharma (2019). *Yoga Kundali Upanishad: Theory and Practices for Awakening Kundalini.* Independently Published, United States

Satyasangananda, Swami (2013). *Tattwa Shuddhi.* Munger, Bihar, India: Yogi Publications Trust

Swami, Om (2017). *The Ancient Science of Mantras: Wisdom of the Sages.* Amazon.com: Black Lotus Publishing

Vivekananda, Swami (2019). *Raja Yoga: Conquering the Internal Nature*. Kolkata, India: Advaita Ashrama

Weor, Samael Aun (2018). *Sacred Rites for Rejuvenation: As Simple, Powerful Technique for Healing and Spiritual Strength.* www.gnosticteachings.org: Glorian Publishing

Woodroffe, Sir John (2018). *Introduction to Tantra Sastra.* T. Nagar, Madras, India: Ganesh & Company

Yogananda, Paramahamsa (2019). *Autobiography of a Yogi.* Los Angeles, California: Self Realization Fellowship

Yogananda, Paramahamsa (2019). *The Second Coming of Christ: The Resurrection of the Christ Within You.* Volumes I-II. Los Angeles, California: Self Realization Fellowship

AYURVEDA

Lad, Vasant (2019). *Ayurveda: The Science of Self-Healing.* Twin Lakes, Wisconsin: Lotus Press

Frawley, Dr. David, (2003). *Ayurveda and Marma Therapy: Energy Points in Yogic Healing.* Co-Authors Dr. Subhash Ranade and Dr. Avinash Lele. Twin Lakes, Wisconsin: Lotus Press

Frawley, Dr. David, and Lad, Vasant (2008). *The Yoga of Herbs.* Twin Lakes, Wisconsin: Lotus Press

The Ayurvedic Institute. *Food Guidelines for Basic Constitutional Types* (PDF)

Frawley, Dr. David (1999). *Yoga & Ayurveda: Self-Healing and Self-Realization.* Twin Lakes, Wisconsin: Lotus Press

Frawley, Dr. David and Summerfield Kozak, Sandra (2012). *Yoga for Your Type: An Ayurvedic Approach to Your Asana Practice.* Twin Lakes, Wisconsin: Lotus Press

Frawley, Dr. David (2013). *Ayurvedic Healing: A Comprehensive Guide.* Twin Lakes, Wisconsin: Lotus Press

Frawley, Dr. David, and Ranada, Dr. Sabhash (2012). *Ayurveda: Nature's Medicine.* Twin Lakes, Wisconsin: Lotus Press

VEDIC ASTROLOGY

Frawley, Dr. David (2005). *Ayurvedic Astrology: Self-Healing Through the Stars.* Twin Lakes, Wisconsin: Lotus Press

Frawley, Dr. David (2000). *Astrology of the Seers. A Guide to Vedic/Hindu Astrology.* Twin Lakes, Wisconsin: Lotus Press

Sutton, Komilla (2014). *The Nakshatras: The Stars Beyond the Zodiac.* Bournemouth, England: The Wessex Astrologer Ltd.

Kurczak, Ryan, and Fish, Richard (2012). *The Art and Science of Vedic Astrology.* CreateSpace Independent Publishing Platform

HAND MUDRAS

Menen, Rajendar (2013). *The Healing Power of Mudras: The Yoga in Your Hands.* New Delhi, India: V&S Publishers

Saradananda, Swami (2015). *Mudras for Modern Life: Boost Your Health, Re-Energize Your Life, Enhance Your Yoga and Deepen Your Meditation.* London, Great Britain: Watkins

Hirschi, Gertrud (2016). *Mudras: Yoga in Your Hands.* Newburyport, Massachusetts: Weiser Books

Le Page, Joseph and Lilian (2014). *Mudras For Healing and Transformation.* Ft. Lauderdale, Florida: Integrative Yoga Therapy

Carroll, Cain and Revital (2013). *Mudras of India: A Comprehensive Guide to the Hand Gestures of Yoga and Indian Dance*. Philadelphia, Pennsylvania: Singing Dragon

Advait (2015). *Mudras: 25 Ultimate Techniques for Self-Healing*. CreateSpace Independent Publishing Platform

GEMSTONES AND TUNING FORKS

McGeough, Marion (2013). *Crystal Healing & the Human Energy Field*. CreateSpace Independent Publishing Platform

Lembo, Margaret Ann (2017). *The Essential Guide to Crystals, Minerals and Stones*. Woodbury, Minnesota: Llewellyn Publications

Permutt, Philip (2016). *The Crystal Healer: Crystal Prescriptions That Will Change Your Life Forever*. London, England: Cico Books

McKusick, Eileen Day (2014). *Tuning the Human Biofield: Healing with Vibrational Sound Therapy*. Rochester, Vermont: Healing Arts Press

Hall, Judy (2003). *The Crystal Bible: A Definitive Guide to Crystals*. Iola, Wisconsin: Krause Publications.

Hall, Judy (2009). *The Crystal Bible 2*. Iola, Wisconsin: Krause Publications.

Beaulieu, John (2010). *Human Tuning: Sound Healing With Tuning Forks*. High Falls, New York: BioSonic Enterprises

AROMATHERAPY

Lembo, Margaret Ann (2016). *The Essential Guide to Aromatherapy and Vibrational Healing*. Woodbury, Minnesota: Llewellyn Worldwide

Cunningham, Scott (2020). *Encyclopedia of Magical Herbs*. Woodbury, Minnesota: Llewellyn Worldwide

Kennedy, Anne (2018) *Aromatherapy for Beginners: The Complete Guide to Getting Started With Essential Oils*. Berkeley, California: Althea Press

Wormwood, Valerie Ann (2016). *The Complete Book of Essential Oils and Aromatherapy*. Novato, California: New World Library

Davis, Patricia (2000). *Subtle Aromatherapy*. Essex, United Kingdom: Saffron Walden

Covington, Candice (2017). *Essential Oils in Spiritual Practice: Working With the Chakras, Divine Archetypes, and the Five Great Elements*. Rochester, Vermont: Healing Arts Press

SACRED GEOMETRY

Melchizedek, Drunvalo (1990). *The Ancient Secret of the Flower of Life: Volume 1*. Flagstaff, Arizona: Light Technology Publishing

Melchizedek, Drunvalo (2000). *The Ancient Secret of the Flower of Life: Volume 2*. Flagstaff, Arizona: Light Technology Publishing

WESTERN MYSTERIES

Agrippa, Henry Cornelius (1992). *Three Books of Occult Philosophy*. St. Paul, Minnesota: Llewellyn Publications

Anonymous (2005) *The Emerald Tablet of Hermes*. With Multiple Translations. Whitefish, Montana: Kessinger Publishing

Copenhaver, Brian P. (2000) *Hermetica: The Greek Corpus Hermeticum and the Latin Asclepius in a New English Translation, with Notes and Introduction*. New York, New York: Cambridge University Press

Doreal, M. (Unknown). *The Emerald Tablets of Thoth the Antlantean*. Nashville, Tennessee: Source Books

Everard, John (2019). *The Divine Pymander*. Whithorn, Scotland: Anodos Books

Mumford, John Dr. (1997). *Magical Tattwas: A Complete System for Self-Development*. St. Paul, Minnesota: Llewellyn Publications

Paar, Neven (2019). *The Magus: Kundalini and the Golden Dawn*. Toronto, Ontario: Winged Shoes Publishing

Regardie, Israel (1971). *The Golden Dawn*. St. Paul, Minnesota: Llewellyn Publications

Three Initiates (1940). *The Kybalion: Hermetic Philosophy*. Chicago, Illinois: Yogi Publication Society

Unknown (2003). *Esoteric Order of the Golden Dawn: Theoricus 2=9 Grade Manual*. Added to by G.H. Frater P.D.R. Los Angeles, California: H.O.M.S.I.

Woolfolk, Joanna Martine (2006). *The Only Astrology Book You'll Ever Need*. Lanham, Maryland: Taylor Trade Publishing

RELIGIOUS TEXTS

Ashlag, Rav Yehuda (2007). *The Zohar*. Commentary by Rav Michael Laitman PhD. Toronto, Ontario: Laitman Kabbalah Publishers

EasWaran Aknath (2007). *The Dhammapada*. Tomales, California: Nilgiri Press

EasWaran Aknath (2007). *The Upanishads*. Tomales, California: Nilgiri Press

Griffith, Ralph T.H. and Keith, Arthur Berriedale (2017). *The Vedas: The Samhitas of the Rig, Yajur (White and Black), Sama, and Atharva Vedas*. CreateSpace Independent Publishing Platform

Moses (1967). *The Torah: The Five Books of Moses* (Otherwise known as the Old Testament). Philadelphia, Pennsylvania: The Jewish Publication Society of America

Muhammad (2006). *The Koran*. Translated with Notes by N.J. Dawood. London, England: Penguin Books

Saraswati, Swami Satyananda (1997). *Bhagavad Gita*. Napa, California: Devi Mandir Publications and Motilal Banarsidass Publishers Private Limited

Stiles, Mukunda (2002). *Yoga Sutras of Patanjali*. San Francisco, California : Weiser Books

Various (2002). *The Holy Bible: King James Version* (Includes the Old and the New Testament). Grand Rapids, Michigan: Zondervan

ONLINE RESOURCES

3 Sanskrit Mantras to Boost Your Meditation Practice - Reference page for Mantras (www.yogiapproved.com/om/3-sanskrit-mantras-boost-meditation-practice/)

7 Mantras to Create the Life You Want - Reference page for Mantras (www.chopra.com/articles/7-mantras-for-creating-the-life-you-want)

7Pranayama-Breath of Life - Reference page for Yogic philosophy and practices (www.7pranayama.com)

71 Yoga Mudras: Get Surprising Benefits in 29 Days, Supported by Science – Reference page for Yoga Mudras (www.fitsri.com/yoga-mudras)

9 Powerful Mantras in Sanskrit and Gurmukhi - Reference page for Mantras (www.chopra.com/articles/9-powerful-mantras-in-sanskrit-and-gurmukhi)

Anatomy of the Aura - Reference page for the Aura and its parts (www.auraology.net/anatomy-of-the-aura)

An Intro to the Vagus Nerve & the Connection to Kundalini - Reference page for the connection between the Vagus Nerve and Kundalini (www.basmati.com/2017/05/02/intro-vagus-nerve-connection-kundalini)

Astrological Aromatherapy-Blends for Your Star Sign - Reference page for Aromatherapy (www.baseformula.com/blog/astrological-aromatherapy)

Astrology and Ayurveda - Reference page for Astrology and Ayurveda (www.astrobix.com/astrosight/208-astrology-and-ayurveda.html)

Astrology and the Chakras: Two Sides of the Same Coin - Reference page for Astrology and the Chakras (www.innerself.com/content/personal/intuition-awareness/astrology/4410-astrology-a-the-chakras.html)

Aura Colour Guide - Reference page for the Aura and its parts (www.auraaura.co/aura-colors)

AuraFit: Mobile Biofeedback System - Official page for the Aura reading technology invented by Bettina Bernoth Ph.D. (www.aurafitsystem.org/)

Aura Shapes - Reference page for energy problems in the Aura (www.the-auras-expert.com/aura-shapes.html)

Ayurveda and Asana: Yoga Poses for Your Health - Reference page for Yoga for the Doshas (www.yogajournal.com/lifestyle/health/ayurveda-and-asana/)

Best Ayurveda: Body constitution Type Chart - Reference page for Ayurveda (www.bestayurveda.ca/pages/body-constitution-type-chart)

Bija Mantra - Reference page for Bija Mantras (www.hinduscriptures.com/vedic-culture/bija-mantra/24330/)

Charms of Light: Energy, Healing, and Love - Reference page for Crystals (www.charmsoflight.com/gemstone-crystal-healing-properties)

Descartes and the Pineal Gland - Reference page for the Pineal Gland and its historical research (https://plato.stanford.edu/entries/pineal-gland/)

Designing a Yoga Routine for Your Dosha - Reference page for Yoga and the Doshas (www.chopra.com/articles/designing-a-yoga-routine-for-your-dosha)

Encyclopedia Britannica - Reference page for all branches of knowledge (www.britannica.com)

Esoteric Other Worlds: Tattva Vision - Reference page for working with Tattvas (www.esotericotherworlds.blogspot.com/2013/06/tattva-vision.html)

Ethan Lazzerini-Crystal Healing Blog, Guides & Tips - Reference page for Crystals (www.ethanlazzerini.com/crystal-shapes-meanings/)

Freedom Vidya-Meditation on the Chakra Petal Bijas - Reference page for Chakra Petal Bijas (www.shrifreedom.org/yoga/chakra-petal-sounds/)

Greek Medicine.Net - Reference page for the brain and nervous system (www.greekmedicine.net/physiology/Brain_and_Nervous_System.html)

Hatha or Vinyasa Yoga: Which One is Right for You? - Reference page for Hatha and Vinyasa Yogas (www.healthline.com/health/exercise-fitness/hatha-vs-vinyasa)

How to Balance Your Vital Energy & Chakras With Essential Oils - Reference page for Chakras and Essential Oils (www.motherhoodcommunity.com/chakra-essential-oils/)

How Does Exercise Affect the Brain? - Reference page for the effects of exercise on your brain (www.dana.org/article/how-does-exercise-affect-the-brain/)

Institute for Consciousness Research - Reference page for Kundalini research and human energy potential (www.icrcanada.org)

Intro to Ayurveda: Understanding the Three Doshas - Reference page for Ayurveda (www.yogajournal.com/lifestyle/health/ayurveda/intro-ayurveda/)

Male and Female Chakras - Reference page for gender in Chakras (www.rootshunt.com/maleandfemalechakras.htm)

Natural Chakra Healing-Seed Mantras for Each Chakra - Reference page for Bija Mantras (www.naturalchakrahealing.com/chakra-seed-mantras.html)

Neural Correlates of Personalized Spiritual Experiences - Reference page for the connection between brain anatomy and Spiritual experiences (www.academic.oup.com/cercor/article/29/6/2331/5017785)

Relationship Between Chakras in Human Body, Planets & Medical Astrology - Reference page for the association between Chakras, Planets, and Endocrine Glands (www.anilsripathi.wordpress.com/relationship-between-human-body-chakras-planetsmedical-astrology/)

Rocks with Sass - Reference page for Crystals and their shapes (www.rockswithsass.com/blog/2020/4/13/crystal-shapes-their-meaning-and-uses)

Science of the Heart - Reference page for the HeartMath Institute and their research (www.heartmath.org/research/science-of-the-heart/energetic-communication)

Scrying in the Spirit Vision. Part I: Tattva Vision - Reference page for working with Tattvas (www.fraterooe.livejournal.com/4366.html)

Six Typical Energy Problems and How to Heal Them - Reference page for energy problems in the Aura (www.nataliemarquis.com/six-typical-energy-problems-and-how-to-heal-them/)

SlimYogi: An Illustrated Step-By-Step Guide to 90 Slimming Yoga Postures - Reference PDF for practicing Yoga (www.mymission.lamission.edu/userdata/ruyssc/docs/Stretch-An-Ullustrated-Step-By-Step-Guide-To-Yoga-Postures.pdf)

Spiritual Ayurveda: Our Five Subtle Bodies and Three Subtle Essences - Reference page for Ayurveda (www.maharishi.co.uk/blog/spiritual-ayurveda-our-five-subtle-bodies-and-three-subtle-essences/)

Tattwas and Antahkarana Instructions - Reference page for the Tattvas (www.manas-vidya.blogspot.com/2011/09/practice-antahkarana.html)

The Chakras and Gender-Masculine/Feminine Energies - Reference page for gender in Chakras (www.naturalchakrahealing.com/chakras-and-gender-masculine-feminine-energy.html)

The Crystal Compendium EBook - Reference page for Crystals (www.crystalgemstones.net/crystalcompendium.php)

The Disengagement of the Reticular Activating System (RAS) - Reference page for the Reticular Activating System's role in Spiritual awakening (www.spiritrisingyoga.org/kundalini-info/the-disengagement-of-the-reticular-activating-system)

The Kundalini Consortium (www.kundaliniconsortium.org)- Reference page for Kundalini research and human energy potential

Vedic Astrology & the Chakras - Reference page for the association between Chakras and Planets (www.alchemicalbody.wordpress.com/2013/06/01/vedic-astrology-the-chakras/)

Vibrational Energy Medicine - Reference page for the Chakras (www.energyandvibration.com/chakras.htm)

What are Bija Mantras - Reference page for Bija Mantras (www.satyaloka.net/what-are-bija-mantras/)

What are the Ayurveda Doshas? Vata, Kapha, and Pitta Explained - Reference page for Ayurveda (www.healthline.com/nutrition/vata-dosha-pitta-dosha-kapha-dosha)

What are the Benefits of Yoga & Meditation - Reference page for Yoga and meditation (www.poweryoga.com/blog/benefits-and-differences-yoga-meditation/)

What is Aromatherapy? - Reference page for Aromatherapy (www.webmd.com/balance/stress-management/aromatherapy-overview)

What is Yoga Meditation? - Reference page for meditation (www.sivanandayogafarm.org/what-is-yoga-meditation/)

What to Know About Your Brain's Frontal Lobe - Reference page for brain anatomy (www.healthline.com/health/frontal-lobe)

Yoga For Balancing the Doshas - Reference page for Yoga for the Doshas (www.ekhartyoga.com/articles/wellbeing/yoga-for-balancing-the-doshas)

Yoga Journal: A Beginner's Guide to Meditation - Reference page for meditation (www.yogajournal.com/meditation/how-to-meditate/let-s-meditate/)

Yogapedia - Reference page for Yogic philosophy and practices (www.yogapedia.com)

Yogapoint-India - Reference page for Yogic philosophy and practices (www.yogapoint.com/index.htm)

Wikipedia-The Free Encyclopedia - Reference page for all branches of knowledge (www.wikipedia.org)

IMAGES RESOURCES

Figure 2: The Three Nadis Post-Kundalini Awakening - Yogi Mahajan's *The Ascent.* (Page 6.)

Figure 5: The Complete Kundalini Circuit - Swami Satyananda Saraswati's *Kundalini Tantra.* (Page 288.)

Figure 6: The Brain Filled with Light - Christopher & Dana Reeve Foundation's *How the Spinal Cord Works* (Online Page.)

Figure 10: The Pentagram – Henry Cornelius Agrippa's *Three Books of Occult Philosophy.* (Page 180.)

Figure 15: Ida and Pingala Nadis and Ajna Chakra - Genevieve Lewis Paulson's *Kundalini and the Chakras.* (Page 184.)

Figure 16: The Electromagnetic Field of the Earth – Peter Reid's *The Earth's Magnetic Field* (Online Image.)

Figure 20: Aura Anatomy – Bettina Bernoth's *AuraFit Training Manuscript* (Page 11.)

Figure 22: The Kundalini Toroidal Field – Bruce Burger's *Esoteric Anatomy: The Body as Consciousness.* (Page 54.)

Figure 23: The Seven Chakras and Nerve Plexuses – Anodea Judith's *Wheels of Life: A User's Guide to the Chakra System.* (Page 12.)

Figure 24: Brain Expansion and Chakric Correspondences - Swami Satyananda Saraswati's *Kundalini Tantra.* (Page 35.)

Figure 26: The Minor Head Chakras (Crown) - Genevieve Lewis Paulson's *Kundalini and the Chakras.* (Page 150.)

Figure 31: Location of the Psychic Eyes - Genevieve Lewis Paulson's *Kundalini and the Chakras.* (Page 140.)

Figure 37: Orientation of Tetrahedrons in Males and Females - Drunvalo Melchizedek's *The Ancient Secret of the Flower of Life: Volume 1.* (Page 49.)

Figure 42: The Limbic System – Paul Wissmann's *Basic Ganglia and Limbic System* (Online Image.)

Figure 51: Conus Medullaris and Filum Terminale – Cyndi Dale's *The Complete Book of Chakras: Your Definitive Source of Energy Center Knowledge for Health, Happiness, and Spiritual Evolution*. (Page 78.)

Figure 57: The Electromagnetic Field of the Heart - Doc Childre and Howard Martin's *The Heartmath Solution*. (Page 34.)

Figure 59: The Heart Chakra Center– Anodea Judith's *Wheels of Life: A User's Guide to the Chakra System*. (Page 197.)

Figure 123: Mula Bandha Contraction Point - Swami Satyananda Saraswati's *Asana Pranayama Mudra Bandha*. (Page 476.)

Figure 128: Vajroli, Sahajoli, and Ashwini Mudras Contraction Points - Swami Buddhananda's *Moola Bandha: The Master Key*. (Page 81.)

Figure 134: Sushumna Nadi Layers and the Cosmic Egg - Cyndi Dale's *The Subtle Body: An Encyclopedia of Your Energetic Anatomy*. (Page 276.)

Figure 147: The Three Doshas and Body Zones - Vasant Lad's *Ayurveda: The Science of Self-Healing*. (Page 27.)

Figure 151: Lucid Dream Projection - Veenu Sandal's Online Article *Spirit 'Walk-Ins' and Matters of the Soul* (Online Article.)

Figure 153: Sahasrara Chakra Lotus - Swami Satyananda Saraswati's *Kundalini Tantra*. (Page 307.)

Figure 154: Kundalini Flow through Sushumna - Genevieve Lewis Paulson's *Kundalini and the Chakras.* (Page 16.)

Made in the USA
Las Vegas, NV
22 April 2024

88992636R00326